What's New in This

This edition of *Using Visual FoxPro 6, Special Edit* entirely new, with coverage of the exciting features of Visual FoxPro 6! Here are some highlights of the new material:

Chapter 8—Accessing Remote Data

- How to create views that access SQL Server and other remote back ends
- Upsizing your data

Part IV—Object-Oriented Programming

- An entire section now covers object orientation!
- Learn about the essence of object orientation in clear, easy-to-understand English! (Chapter 13)
- See how Visual FoxPro incorporates OOP into the most powerful database for PCs (Chapter 14)
- Build your own classes and energize your applications into the 21st century (Chapters 15 through 17)
- Leverage the power of Visual FoxPro's Foundation Classes and Component Gallery to make development easier than ever before! (Chapters 18 and 19)

Part V—COM

- Understand COM, Microsoft's centerpiece technology for developing enterprise-wide and Internet-wide applications (Chapter 20)
- Harness the power of COM in your Visual FoxPro applications (Chapter 21)
- Use applications like Microsoft Word and Excel to add functionality to your applications (Chapter 21)
- Turn your applications into enterprise-wide COM servers (Chapter 22)
- Learn how Visual FoxPro and COM make your Visual FoxPro skills marketable for a whole new generation of Internet-wide and enterprisewide applications in the n-tiered client/server model (Chapter 22)

Chapter 24—Visual FoxPro and Year 2000 Compliance

- See how Visual FoxPro protects your investment for the Year 2000

Special Edition Using

Visual FoxPro 6

que®

Special Edition Using

Visual FoxPro 6

Menachem Bazian, Jim Booth, Jeb Long,
Vin Miller, Celia Silver, Robert A. Byers

201 West 103rd Street, Indianapolis, Indiana 46290

Special Edition Using Visual FoxPro 6

International Standard Book Number: 0-7897-1808-1

Library of Congress Catalog Card Number: 98-86968

Printed in the United States of America

First Printing: *December 1998*

00 99 98   4 3 2 1

Trademarks

Warning and Disclaimer

EXECUTIVE EDITOR
Bryan Gambrel

ACQUISITIONS EDITOR
Angela Kozlowski

DEVELOPMENT EDITOR
Christopher Kazim Haidri

MANAGING EDITOR
Patrick Kanouse

PROJECT EDITOR
Heather Kaufman Urschel

COPY EDITORS
Charles Hutchinson
Tonya Maddox
Sean Medlock

INDEXER
Diane Brenner

PROOFREADERS
Kim Cofer
Wendy Ott

TECHNICAL EDITOR
Dallas Releford

SOFTWARE DEVELOPMENT SPECIALIST
Michael Hunter

INTERIOR DESIGN
Ruth Lewis

COVER DESIGN
Maureen McCarty

LAYOUT TECHNICIAN
Ayanna Lacey

Contents at a Glance

VI | Other Visual FoxPro Topics

Contents

About the Authors

Menachem Bazian, CPA, is director of Client Services for LNW Consulting Services, LLC, a Business and Technology Consulting Firm based in New York City. Menachem has been a developer and consultant for 13 years. He is an internationally known expert on object-oriented analysis, design, and development and has lectured extensively on the subject. He also possesses expertise in business process analysis and redesign, which he uses regularly in the service of his clients. Menachem has spoken frequently at conferences, including the FoxPro and Visual FoxPro Developer's Conferences from 1990–1998, various regional FoxPro conferences across the U.S. and Canada, the Foundation for Accounting Education, The N.Y. State Society of CPAs' annual accounting and computer shows, and others. He has written for many magazines, including *Databased Advisor* (now *e-Biz Advisor*), *FoxPro Advisor*, *New Accountant*, and more.

Jim Booth is a Visual FoxPro developer and trainer. He has written articles for the major FoxPro journals and has spoken at conferences in North America and Europe. He has been the recipient of the Microsoft Most Valuable Professional Award every year since its inception in 1993. He is married and the father of three boys, and wishes he could program them as easily as Visual FoxPro. His house is also populated with two dogs, a cat, a fish, and a bird.

Jeb Long has 35 years experience in software design and engineering at some of the most prestigious technical organizations in the country. Since leaving Ashton-Tate Corporation in 1990, he has worked as an independent consultant and author, and has written technical documents, several books, and articles for technical journals. While at Ashton-Tate, he was the dBASE language architect and was responsible for the dBASE language components for all versions of dBASE III and IV, except for the initial version. During 14 years at the California Institute of Technology's Jet Propulsion Laboratory, he was responsible for software tasks in support of our nation's planetary exploration program. Among these tasks were programs to calculate interplanetary trajectories, to process telemetry from space vehicles, to simulate spacecraft propulsion subsystems, and to support spacecraft tests and operations. He was actively involved in the Mariner and Viking Missions to Mars. He and his wife Elizabeth, a technical writer who works closely with Jeb in writing all of his books, now live on a hill overlooking Los Angeles.

Vin Miller is a Senior Analyst at InvestLink Technologies, a New York City-based software development firm providing database, Internet, and telephony solutions for the defined contribution industry. He has programmed in FoxPro since 1990. He is the co-author of *Family Planning and Population: A Compendium of International Statistics*, as well as several scholarly articles on international demographics and research methods.

Ceil Silver has been in the computer industry since 1967, first as a COBOL and RPG programmer, and from there filling many corporate positions involving applications software development, systems software support, and software project management. She has been an independent consultant in the NYC metropolitan area since 1989, specializing in database applications and systems analysis for a variety of industries. Her current development tool of choice is Visual FoxPro. She is also founder of the Westchester FoxPro Chapter of PADD (Professional Association of Database Developers), in Westchester County, NY.

Robert A. Byers is a nationally recognized authority on database management systems for microcomputers. He is currently a partner in Balleisen-Byers, a developer of client/server database products for desktop computers. A former manager of the Mission Control and Computing Center at the Jet Propulsion Laboratory in Pasadena, California, Mr. Byers has held numerous positions of responsibility in the computer and communications industries over the past 32 years. He has served on several government advisory panels for Communications and Data Handling, including the select panel on Data Handling and Avionics for the Space Shuttle and NASA's Planetary Data Systems Working Group. He was actively involved with the development of dBASE, and often acted as a spokesman for Ashton-Tate prior to their purchase by Borland. He has served as an independent consultant on microcomputer software to several major corporations, and has developed vertical market applications software for the medical and retail business communities. The author of numerous technical papers and several best-selling computer books, he also holds a U.S. patent on Distributed Signal Processing. His *Everyman's Database Primer* became a standard and was translated into several languages. An engineer by training, he has a B.S.E.E. from California State Polytechnic University at San Luis Obispo, M.S.E.E. from Georgia Institute of Technology, and has done additional post-graduate work in Communications Theory at U.S.C. He has been employed by Ampex Corporation, Bell and Howell, the Georgia Tech Research Institute, and JPL.

Dedication

With love to the most brilliant woman I have ever known: Shirley Bazian (1932–1982). I hope I made you proud, mom.

- Menachem Bazian

To my wife, Carole, and my three boys—Vincent, Louis, and Edward—and also to my wife's friend Judy Rado. Without their encouragement, my work on this book could not have been completed.

- Jim Booth

To my loving wife, Charlene.

- Robert A. Byers

To my wonderful wife and friend, Elizabeth.

- Jeb Long

To Renée, for enduring the click and rattle of late-night coding, and the boos and grunts of extra-inning baseball. Summer 1998.

- Vin Miller

To my daughters, Rachel and Carla: anything is possible!

- Ceil Silver

Acknowledgments

Writing a book is a bear of an undertaking, not only for the author but for those around him. Mere words cannot do justice to the effect these people have had on me, either through technical assistance or moral support. Still, words are all I have.

First of all, to the incredibly talented team of people at my new firm, Levine Mandelbaum Neider Wohl, LLP. To the partners, Mark Levine, Jay Neider, and Lester Wohl; to Glenn Davis, Michael Giller, Tery Gingold, Valerie Jaraique, Carol Lechner, Katherine McCoy, Renee Neil, and Joe Vecchio. Thank you for welcoming me into your firm and showing trust in me. I enjoy working with you all.

To David Lazar, Robert Green, Jim Saunders, Susan Graham, Randy Brown, Calvin Hcia, and so many people on the Microsoft Fox team. You guys created another super winner here. Thanks.

To my incredible editors at Que. To Angela Kozlowski and her merry crew, thanks for being so understanding and for working with me.

To David Blumenthal, Yair Alan Griver, Lior Hod and everyone at Flash Creative Management. Thank you for 6 1/2 fascinating years. Oh, and to Chushie (What's the count now, Alan?).

To the people in the Fox community I have had the pleasure of knowing and working with: Pat Adams, Steven Black, Jim Booth, Chaim Caron, Barry Cunningham, Sue Cunningham, Doug Dodge, Mike Feltman, Tamar Granor, Doug Hennig, Nancy Jacobsen, Jim Korenthal, John Koziol, Barry Lee, Ken Levy, Patrick Logan, Valid Matisons, Paul Maskens, Michael Meer, Andy Neil, John Petersen, Rod Paddock, Alan Schwartz, Ceil Silver, Drew Speedie, Toni Taylor-Feltman, and many more. There are so many of you that I cannot mention you all, but you all have had a special place in helping make my work possible and fun.

Once again to my friend and mentor, Martin Star. I can never say thank you enough for all you have taught me. How'm I doing, Marty?

To Chaim Wasserman. For once words fail me. I have no idea what I could say that would be appropriate for all the times you have been there throughout the years. "Thank you" seems pitifully inadequate, but it's all I have.

To Mark and Meryl Berow and Marc and Judith Stoll. Together we have shared much happiness and adversity. I couldn't imagine having better friends. Thanks.

To Mordecai and Charlotte Glicksman, and their twins, Chana Tova and Elisheva. Thanks for sticking with me over the years. We've come a long way together and I look forward to sharing with you for a long time to come.

I leave for last the people who mean the most to me. To my father, Murray Bazian, and my brothers, Ben and Sol. Thanks for all your advice and help. Even if I don't say it enough, I appreciate it.

To my beloved wife, Anna: Once again you had to put up with a book and you did it with remarkable aplomb. I know that this is never easy on you and I appreciate your support.

To my incredible twins, Barry and Sam. Somewhere along the line, when God was handing out blessings, he looked at your mother and me and decided that we should have you. I don't know what I did to earn it, but I thank him every day for both of you. Over the years I have laughed with you and cried with you. But, above all, I have watched with neverending awe and amazement, as you have grown into two strapping young men from the little infants I worried over in the neonatal intensive care unit. Your wit, charm, and intelligence are a constant source of joy to me. Now, if only I can get you guys to do your homework and go to bed on time, life would be almost perfect :).

Finally, to Isaac. You are much too young to read this now. Still, in a few years when you have grown a little and learned to read, perhaps these words will have some meaning. You entered our lives and have turned life into a neverending series of new experiences. Neither your mother nor I ever really imagined that a baby could change our lives quite as much as you did but I can tell you that all of us, your big brothers included, bless the day you decided to join us. You have taught us a lot, believe it or not. I look forward to each and every day with you.

- Menachem Bazian

I would like to thank all of the people who frequent the electronic forums for Visual FoxPro. Their questions have motivated me to investigate aspects of Visual FoxPro that I may never have looked into on my own. Special thanks go to John Petersen for his insights and assistance. Additional thanks go to Menachem Bazian for his guidance and inspiration during the writing of this book.

- Jim Booth

Grateful acknowledgment is extended to all the people who made this book possible with their enthusiastic support and encouragement, including the MCP Editorial and Publishing staff, with special gratitude to Angela Kozlowski, Bryan Gambrel, Chris Haidri, and Dallas Releford. To Elizabeth Long—thanks for all your editorial assistance and encouragement in developing and preparing the chapters for this book.

- Jeb Long

My thanks go out to the members of the far-flung electronic FoxPro community who have made up my virtual office for the past ten years. The online associations, made primarily through CompuServe's FoxForums, have provided a major source of continuing education and professional feedback, leading to ongoing real-world friendships.

- Ceil Silver

Tell Us What You Think!

As the reader of this book, *you* are our most important critic and commentator. We value your opinion and want to know what we're doing right, what we could do better, what areas you'd like to see us publish in, and any other words of wisdom you're willing to pass our way.

As the Executive Editor for the Database team at Macmillan Computer Publishing, I welcome your comments. You can fax, email, or write me directly to let me know what you did or didn't like about this book—as well as what we can do to make our books stronger.

Please note that I cannot help you with technical problems related to the topic of this book, and that due to the high volume of mail I receive, I might not be able to reply to every message.

When you write, please be sure to include this book's title and author as well as your name and phone or fax number. I will carefully review your comments and share them with the author and editors who worked on the book.

Fax: 317-817-7070

Email: cs_db@mcp.com

Mail: Bryan Gambrel
        Executive Editor
        Macmillan Computer Publishing
        201 West 103rd Street
        Indianapolis, IN 46290 USA

Introduction

In this chapter

Welcome to *Using Visual FoxPro 6, Special Edition*! This book is your guide to the exciting world of working with the latest release of Microsoft's award-winning database product, Visual FoxPro.

Visual FoxPro has a long and illustrious history as the most flexible and powerful database application on the market. Starting from its origination as Fox Software's FoxBASE product, "Fox" (as it's known among its international community of developers) has always been known for its reliability, speed, and effectiveness as a programmer's database product.

This book is designed to take you into the world of Visual FoxPro. Whether you're a beginner, intermediate, or advanced user, this book has what you need to strengthen and improve your development efforts.

What *Is* Visual FoxPro?

Don't laugh, it's not that silly a question. FoxPro has changed radically over the years. It's not a bad idea to take a little time and review how it has gotten where it is. This will give you additional perspective on the product you're now reading about.

The History

Back in the "old days" (the late 1980s), FoxBASE was intended to be a dBASE clone. If dBASE did it, FoxBASE would do it better and faster (or at least that was the idea). Although FoxBASE had some revolutionary features in it, it was not really intended to be revolutionary; it was designed to be better and faster and, above all, *compatible* with dBASE III.

FoxPro 1.0 was the first departure from the compatibility dance with dBASE. It began to introduce some new concepts in GUI design and ways of developing software that put it ahead of the by-then floundering dBASE.

FoxPro really came into its own with version 2.0. When FoxPro 2.0 was introduced, several key technologies were included that revolutionized the PC database development market:

- The addition of *Rushmore* did the unthinkable. All of a sudden, tables with millions of records were not only possible but feasible in a PC database system without moving to other, more expensive, technologies. I distinctly recall Dr. David Fulton, the founder of Fox Software, demonstrating searches on a table with over a million records that completed in a fraction of a second. The crowd went wild, and a new era was born.

- *SQL statements* were another revolution introduced in version 2.0. For the first time, Fox developers were using single statements that replaced entire procedures. SQL was, and still is, *the* language of data.

- FoxPro 2.0 also introduced a somewhat WYSIWYG means of developing reports and screens with the addition of the Screen and Report Designers. The Screen Designer generated code, but definitely enabled a new and exciting way of developing GUIs in a text-based environment.

I could go on and on, but you get the idea. FoxPro 2.0 was the real advent of the exciting capabilities you have today in Visual FoxPro. GUI design services, SQL, and lightning-fast data access were its hallmarks.

Windows support was added in FoxPro 2.5. Support for Dynamic Data Exchange came along for the ride, but as anyone who was around in those days will testify, the Windows version of 2.5 had the look and feel of a DOS app made to look "windowsy."

The next major revolution had to wait until the release of Visual FoxPro 3.0. Once again, FoxPro, now in the hands of Microsoft (which bought out Fox Software during the development of FoxPro for Windows), revolutionized the database development world. Version 3.0 added a host of long-awaited features and took the PC database development world by storm. Here are just a few of the features added in 3.0:

- The *Database Container*, also known as the *DBC*, added support for stored procedures, data rules bound to tables, and a host of additional data functions that Fox developers had been anticipating for years.

- *Views*, which are updatable SQL cursors, added a whole new method of accessing data for processing, GUI representation, and reporting. Two types of views were supported, local and remote views. A *local view* is a view based on Visual FoxPro tables. A *remote view* is a view based on any ODBC data source, including SQL Server, Oracle, Access—you name it. This revolutionary addition made Visual FoxPro the premier tool for accessing remote and local data. For all intents and purposes, creating enterprisewide applications and using data stored in remote data sources became almost as easy as using Visual FoxPro tables themselves.

- A full, robust implementation of *object orientation* turned the development paradigm on its ear. A robust object model and the capability to create your own classes and subclasses created an entirely new way of developing software.

Version 5.0 was an upgrade of 3.0 and contained a lot of bug fixes and some interesting new features. The capability to use and create COM servers (a topic covered in-depth in Part V of this book) was introduced. Some additional commands and functions were added and you saw the beginning of support for publishing Visual FoxPro on the Internet. But 5.0 was not a radical departure from 3.0.

Getting to Know 6

Version 6 is not a radical change either, but some of the changes to the product are momentous. Access and Assign methods (covered in Part IV of this book) introduce a new dimension to controlling data placed into your objects. The new Component Gallery and Foundation Classes ease your transition into creating object-oriented applications. Better COM support is probably one of the more significant changes, enabling easier and better creation and implementation of COM servers. Finally, as the clock continues to tick toward the end of the millennium, improved Year 2000 support is a welcome addition, as well.

The Bottom Line

Okay, here's the bottom line. Visual FoxPro is the premier development product for creating mission-critical, enterprisewide, object-oriented, client/server applications designed for local or global deployment.

But Isn't Visual FoxPro Dead?

Frankly, I'm getting really tired of hearing that question. I have been hearing it for years now. Visual FoxPro is *not* dead, it is very much alive and thriving. Despite what you might hear from some rumormongers, Visual FoxPro is the best product, even in the Microsoft suite, for developing database applications. Let's face it: Visual FoxPro was *designed*, from its inception, to handle data. It is fast, powerful, and flexible.

This doesn't mean that Visual FoxPro's role in application development is not ever going to change. Some change is already in motion. The world is beginning to move away from monolithic, single-tiered applications to multi-tiered (*n*-tiered) applications, as explained in the COM section of this book. Visual FoxPro is a natural for the middle (business rules) tier in a multitiered application.

As part of the Visual Studio product suite, Visual FoxPro is now part of a technology team for creating enterprise-wide solutions. The days of an application written only in Visual FoxPro (or Visual Basic for that matter) are numbered. As browsers such as Internet Explorer gain more intelligence, GUI front ends are going to be ported to browsers for a host of reasons. The back-end datasource will be whatever it is (Visual FoxPro, SQL Server, Oracle, or whatever). Sitting right in the middle will be our old friend, Visual FoxPro.

So, here's the deal. If you want to develop a premier application and maintain your investment for the future, Visual FoxPro is a great way to go.

What If I Have Old FoxPro Applications?

Your old applications should run unmodified under Visual FoxPro. Of course, you'll need to test this out, but that's the party line. In terms of upgrading an older FoxPro application to Visual FoxPro, you have three options:

■ *Continue coding the old way.* You can do this, to be sure, although once you modify a screen, Visual FoxPro automatically converts it to a form. If you do this, though, why bother upgrading to Visual FoxPro? You might as well stay with 2.5 or 2.6.

■ *Upgrade piece by piece.* This is a fairly popular method. As pieces of old systems need modification, you have an opportunity to upgrade each piece to the new technology of Visual FoxPro—even if that just means redoing the forms. This method has the benefit of incurring the least one-time cost (that is, the cost is spread out over multiple modification passes). The downside is that you do not gain as great a benefit from the object orientation offered by the latest version of VFP and you end up with a hybrid system for a while (part FoxPro 2.5/6 and part Visual FoxPro).

■ *Rewrite the whole thing.* Not a bad idea, if you can afford it. In fact, taking an existing system and rewriting it in Visual FoxPro is a wonderful learning opportunity. Presumably, you have most of the requirements worked out already. You can just start with the object-oriented analysis and design and work it through to development. When you're finished, you'll have worked out many of the bugs in your development process, developed a host of reusable objects, and have a definite measure of success to work with. You'll be ready to take on the world with Visual FoxPro.

The downside to totally rewriting, of course, is that it's the costliest approach. A great deal of time is spent doing tasks that have already been done.

Who Should Read This Book?

So, now that you know where Visual FoxPro fits in with the development world, it's time to examine what you can do to bring yourself quickly up the learning curve, and what you can do about upgrading your existing systems to Visual FoxPro (if you have a mind to).

Will *Using Visual FoxPro 6, Special Edition* help you in this process? The answer is a resounding *yes!* (Did you expect any other answer from the introduction to the book?) Seriously, *Using Visual FoxPro 6, Special Edition* is the book for you if you are:

■ A power user

■ An intermediate Xbase developer

■ An ambitious newcomer to the Visual FoxPro world who wants a comprehensive reference you can count on for excellent coverage of all aspects of the product

The book is also chock-full of practical routines and tips and tricks on using Visual FoxPro to its fullest as a development tool for mission-critical, object-oriented, client/server applications.

Are you ready to journey into the exciting world of Visual FoxPro? Then sit back, strap yourself in, and read on.

Conventions Used in This Book

This book uses various stylistic and typographic conventions to make it easier to use.

N O T E When you see a note in this book, it indicates additional information that may help you avoid problems or that should be considered in using the described features. ■

T I P Tip paragraphs suggest easier or alternative methods of executing a procedure. Tips can help you see that little extra concept or idea that can make your life so much easier.

CAUTION
Cautions warn you of hazardous procedures (for example, activities that delete files).

Introduction

Quick Review of the Visual FoxPro Interface

In this chapter

Over the past several years, an increasing number of complex applications have been built with microcomputer database systems such as FoxPro. But even with the tools that these systems provide—such as screen and report generators, libraries, and project managers—the total time needed to complete many applications has increased. Furthermore, users want to access data stored in other formats, and not only on their own machines but also on central database servers. FoxPro has grown from a DOS-based Xbase language to a Visual GUI (Graphical User Interface) application development tool in just a few short years. With the arrival of Visual Studio, FoxPro became a member of the Microsoft family of products and a vital part of the application development community. The focus of Visual Studio is to provide the programming and database tools to develop software that is capable of all of the things mentioned previously.

Previous releases of FoxPro began to address these problems. Although progress was made, something was still missing until the introduction of object programming. Many products have experimented with various degrees of object programming. Some products provide fixed definition objects, and the programmer has to use them as they are or not at all; they have no mechanism to start from a base object definition and build on it. Many people refer to this type of programming as object-based, not object-oriented. In fact, object-oriented developers look for features such as inheritance, polymorphism, subclassing, and event programming. Within the past couple of years, several products that have many of those features have been released. The authors feel, however, that Visual FoxPro presents the best implementation of an object-oriented, Xbase-compatible, database programming language to date.

This chapter introduces many basic concepts to ensure that all readers start from the same level.

Getting FoxPro Up and Running

Assuming that you have Visual FoxPro 6 (VFP) installed on your machine, how do you start it? When VFP installs, it creates a new Windows group called Microsoft Visual FoxPro and/or installs Visual FoxPro in the Start menu. In Windows NT, this group appears in the Project Manager. Double-clicking the group icon opens the group window, revealing an icon named Microsoft Visual FoxPro 6. This icon represents the main program. In Windows 95, VFP installs a group (now called a folder) in the Programs menu of the Start button. By default, the program folder gets the name Microsoft Visual FoxPro. Clicking this option opens another menu level that shows the available programs installed with Visual FoxPro. These programs correspond to the programs shown in the Visual FoxPro group window of the Project Manager. Figure 1.1 shows the Windows 95 version of this screen. Click the menu item Microsoft Visual FoxPro 6 to start FoxPro.

When you install Visual Studio, you have the option of installing several programs such as Visual Basic and Visual C++ as well as Visual FoxPro 6. Just as Office 97 is a suite of tools that perform certain functions such as word processing and creating and maintaining databases and spreadsheets, Visual Studio can be thought of as being a suite of programming tools. Most people install all the programs during the installation process or just a few, and you can elect to install whatever you want depending on your needs and interests. If you have the disk space, it is recommended that you install the complete package because you might need the other programs later. You can also purchase FoxPro 6 as a standalone product. This means that you can install the program without having to buy the entire Visual Studio package, which is expensive. The installation process as described above is pretty much the same in Windows 95 and Windows 98. The easiest way to install any software from Windows 95 and Windows 98 is to choose Start, Run and then give the location of the files you want to install.

FIGURE 1.1

Open Visual FoxPro 6 by using the Microsoft Visual FoxPro menu in the Programs menu of the Start menu.

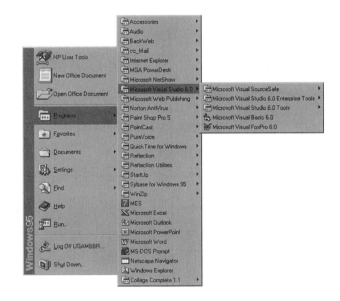

The Windows 95 Explorer provides another common way to start FoxPro. Use the Explorer to open the directory that contains Visual FoxPro and choose VFP.EXE from the file list, as shown in Figure 1.2.

If you use Visual FoxPro frequently, as I do, you might want to create a shortcut for it on your desktop. To do so, open Explorer as shown in Figure 1.2, but rather than double-click to start VFP, right-click and drag VFP.EXE from the Explorer onto the desktop. When you release the mouse button, a shortcut menu appears with the following options: Move Here, Copy Here, Create Shortcut(s) Here, and Cancel.

Choose Create Shortcut(s) Here to place an icon on your desktop that executes Visual FoxPro when it is clicked. Figure 1.3 shows the VFP shortcut in the process of being created.

N O T E There is another way to create a shortcut in Windows 95 and Windows 98. Move the mouse cursor over a blank area of the Windows screen (not on any icon) and click the right mouse button. A screen will pop up and from this choose New and then Shortcut. After you select Shortcut, you will be presented with a Create Shortcut dialog box with which you can tell the program where to find the .EXE file of the program you want to create a shortcut for. If you do not know that location, you can search for it using the Browse button. ▪

FIGURE 1.2

Open Visual FoxPro 6 by selecting it from the file list in the Explorer.

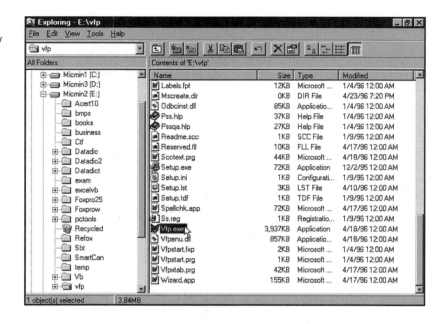

FIGURE 1.3

Create a shortcut on your desktop for Visual FoxPro 6.

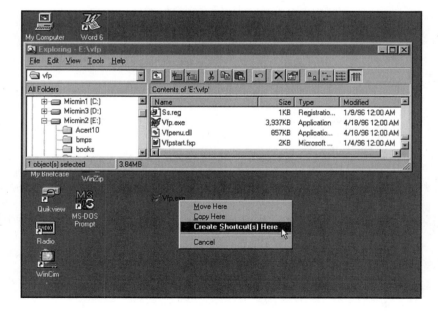

Finally, you can also run FoxPro by choosing the Run option in the Start menu of Windows 95 or Windows 98. Simply enter the program's fully qualified name and click OK. (You also can use the Browse button to find the file if you do not know its fully qualified name.) Figure 1.4 shows the Run dialog box.

FIGURE 1.4
Start Visual FoxPro 6 by
using the Run dialog
box from the Start
menu of Windows 95.

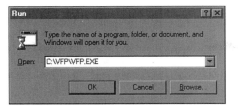

You can even start Visual FoxPro by double-clicking any program file (.PRG) from within the
Explorer, as long as you have associated the .PRG extension with the file VFP.EXE.

No matter how you start Visual FoxPro, it opens in its own main window as shown in Figure
1.5; it also automatically opens the Command window inside the main window. (You might see
an introductory splash screen that includes options to create a new project; explore the sample
applications; explore the online documentation; open an existing project; close the splash
screen; and to never display the splash screen again. Because this feature adds just one more
step before getting into VFP, most developers turn it off, so you might not see it.) FoxPro refers to the main window as the FoxPro desktop or the screen. Later, as you write code that
sends output to the screen (such as a report), FoxPro writes it in this window. FoxPro cannot
write directly to the Windows desktop.

FIGURE 1.5
Visual FoxPro 6's
desktop, or main
screen, opens with the
Command window
active.

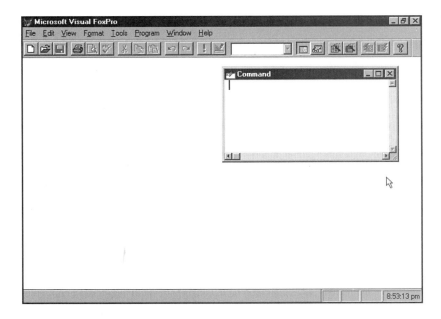

The Title Bar

The title bar across the top of the main window contains five objects. The first object from the
left is the application icon. Clicking it with either mouse button displays the Control menu,

which has commands that move and resize the screen. You can even close FoxPro from this menu.

Table 1.1 lists the options that are available from the Control menu.

Table 1.1	Control Menu Options
Option	**Definition**
Restore	Restores window to preceding size after minimization or maximization.
Move	Selects the main FoxPro window and enables you to move it by using the keyboard cursor controls.
Size	Selects the main FoxPro window and enables you to resize it by using the keyboard cursor controls.
Minimize	Reduces FoxPro to an icon.
Maximize	Maximizes the size of the main FoxPro window. When maximized, a window has no border.
Close	Closes FoxPro.

The title `Microsoft Visual FoxPro` appears left-justified in the title bar in Windows 95. You can easily personalize this title, however, just as you can any other property. There are three ways to change it. The old way is as follows:

```
MODIFY WINDOW SCREEN TITLE 'Michael P. Antonovich'
```

And the new way is

```
_SCREEN.caption = 'Michael P. Antonovich'
```

or

```
_VFP.caption = 'Michael Antonovich'
```

You'll probably want to put your own name in these commands.

The colored portion of the title bar also has a few other functions. First, you can click and drag it to move the window. Double-clicking it alternately maximizes and restores the window to its original size.

Finally, in case you are wondering, FoxPro gets the default color scheme for this title bar and all other window elements from the Windows Control Panel. Windows 95 stores color selections in the Registry.

Several buttons appear at the right end of the title bar. In Windows 95, the first button shows a horizontal bar across the bottom of the icon. Pressing this button minimizes the application and docks it in the taskbar at the bottom of the screen. Visual FoxPro continues running when it is minimized. If you want to restore a minimized application, click its name in the taskbar. (Minimizing individual windows within Visual FoxPro docks the window title at the bottom of the Visual FoxPro desktop.)

In Windows 95, the second button in this group toggles between two buttons: Maximize and Restore. The button used to maximize the Visual FoxPro desktop or the current window looks like a single window; the Restore button looks like two cascaded windows.

Windows 95 also has a separate Close button on the right side of each window. Clicking this button, which contains an X, closes Visual FoxPro (or the current window when you are in application windows).

Be Careful Which Button You Click

Many objects that open in their own windows display a similar Close button. Clicking this button closes the object. The potential danger is that these controls often appear immediately below FoxPro's main Close button. Thus, you can easily click the wrong Close button. As a developer, you will find that restarting VFP after making this mistake several times during a session is a major annoyance.

One solution stores the following program in FoxPro's main directory:

```
* This program intercepts a double-click on FoxPro's main
* screen and prompts the user to confirm that they want
* to leave FoxPro.
* Store this program as \VFP\REALQUIT.PRG

  LOCAL lnMsgResult
  lnMsgResult = MESSAGEBOX('Do you really want to quit FoxPro?', ;
      20, 'Exit FoxPro')
  IF lnMsgResult = 6  && User selected YES button
    QUIT
  ENDIF
```

Then, at the beginning of each session, type the following command to activate the accidental exit protection:

```
ON SHUTDOWN DO \VFP\REALQUIT
```

This routine runs not only when the user attempts to close Visual FoxPro directly, but also when the user attempts to close Windows without first closing FoxPro, or if the user includes the QUIT command in his or her program or types it in the Command window.

Rather than needing to remember to enter this command, consider adding it to the CONFIG.FPW file as a startup command, as follows:

```
COMMAND = ON SHUTDOWN DO \VFP\REALQUIT.PRG
```

The Main Menu Bar

The main menu bar appears on the second screen line of FoxPro's desktop. In many ways, this menu bar is like the tip of an iceberg. Each option in the menu, called a menu pad, displays a menu pop-up when you click it. A menu pop-up usually contains two or more menu options. Although a pop-up can have a single option, a better practice associates single actions with the menu pad directly.

You can select menu pads and their options in several ways. The most obvious method employs the mouse to click them. Pressing F10 activates the menu and highlights the first pad, File.

You might have noticed that each menu pad has one underlined letter. You can open that menu's pop-up directly by pressing the Alt key along with the underlined letter. To open the File menu, for example, press Alt+F. With any menu pop-up open, use the left- or right-arrow key to move to other pads. The up- and down-arrow keys open the current pad's pop-up list and move through its options.

In any given pop-up, some menu options might appear dimmed, which means that you cannot execute that option now. Usually, common sense tells you why the option is inappropriate. If you open the File pop-up before opening a table, database, program, or other file, for example, you cannot choose Save because you have nothing to save yet. Therefore, FoxPro automatically dims the Save option text.

While a pop-up is open, pressing the up- or down-arrow key moves the highlight from one option to the next. Pressing the left- or right-arrow key moves to the next menu pad and opens its menu pop-up—unless the highlighted option contains a right arrow along its right border, in which case pressing the right-arrow key opens a submenu that lists additional options. To choose a menu item, highlight it and press Enter. A mouse click works just as well. You can even press the underlined letter in the option, if it has one. Notice that in the pop-up menus, you do not press the Alt key with the underlined letter.

Some menu options have special key combinations, called *shortcut keys,* that enable you to jump to that option directly without going through the menu pads. FoxPro displays these shortcut keys along the right side of the pop-up menus. The shortcut key for File, New, for example, is Ctrl+N. This means that you can press Ctrl+N any time while you are in Visual FoxPro with the System menu active to open a new file. Table 1.2 summarizes the available shortcut keys.

Table 1.2   Menu Option Shortcut Keys

Menu	Menu Option	Shortcut Key
File	New	Ctrl+N
Open		Ctrl+O
Save		Ctrl+S
Print		Ctrl+P
Edit	Undo	Ctrl+Z
Redo		Ctrl+R
Cut		Ctrl+X
Copy		Ctrl+C
Paste		Ctrl+V
Select All		Ctrl+A
Find		Ctrl+F
Find Again		Ctrl+G
Replace		Ctrl+L

Menu	Menu Option	Shortcut Key
Program	Do	Ctrl+D
Resume		Ctrl+M
Run current Program		Ctrl+E
Window	Cycle	Ctrl+F1
Command Window		Ctrl+F2

TROUBLESHOOTING

I'm in the middle of a Visual FoxPro application and when I enter one of the shortcut keys, nothing happens. Shortcut keys are defined through Visual FoxPro's system (or main) menu. You can override or even replace this menu with your own menu, however, when you create custom applications. If VFP's System menu or any individual menu pad is not active, these shortcut keys are not active, either.

A visual clue that has become a Windows-application standard is the use of an ellipsis (...) at the end of a menu option to indicate that selecting the option opens a dialog box with additional options. Choosing File, Open, for example, does not tell FoxPro what to open. Therefore, when you select this option, Visual FoxPro displays its standard Open dialog box. Menu options without ellipses (such as File, Close) execute immediately when they are selected.

A similar standard uses the right arrow to indicate that the option opens another menu level, as in Tools, Wizards.

The File Menu Options   The File menu pop-up list contains options related to accessing files (creating new files, opening existing ones, closing, saving, and printing). Table 1.3 describes these options.

Table 1.3   File Menu Options

Menu Option	Description
New	Opens the New dialog box. The options in this dialog box enable you to create new projects, databases, tables, queries, connections, views, remote views, forms, reports, labels, programs, classes, text files, and menus.
Open	Opens the Open dialog box, which opens any file type listed under New.
Close	Closes the active window. If you press Shift and open the File menu, this option becomes Close All, which closes all open windows.
Save	Saves the file in the active window with its current name. For a new file that has no name, the option prompts the user for a filename.

continues

Table 1.3   Continued

Menu Option	Description
Save As	Prompts the user for a new filename before saving the file.
Save As Class	Saves the current form or selected controls as a class definition (active only from within the Form Designer).
Revert	Cancels changes made in the current file during the current editing session.
Import	Imports a Visual FoxPro file or a file formatted by another application. You can also use this option to start the Import Wizard.
Export	Exports a Visual FoxPro file in another application's file format.
Page Setup	Changes the page layout and printer settings for reports.
Page Preview	Displays pages in a window as they will appear when printed.
Print	Prints the contents of the current window, a file, or Visual FoxPro's Clipboard.
Send	Enables you to send email.
<project files if any>	Provides quick access to reopen any of the last four opened projects.
Exit	Exits Visual FoxPro. Choosing this option is the same as typing QUIT in the Command window.

The Edit Menu Options   The options in the Edit menu provide functions that are used for editing programs, forms, and reports. This menu also contains options that create object linking and embedding (OLE) objects. Table 1.4 lists the options that appear at various times in the Edit menu pad.

Table 1.4   Edit Menu Options

Menu Option	Description
Undo	Reverses an unlimited number of changes made in the current edit session. Changes made before the last save, even if made during the same session, are not reversible.
Redo	Performs a reversed change again.
Cut	Removes the selected text or object from current document and places it on the Clipboard.
Copy	Makes a copy of the selected text or object and places it on the Clipboard.
Paste	Copies the current contents of the Clipboard to the current insertion point.

Menu Option	Description
Paste Special	Used to insert OLE objects from other applications into a general field. You can embed objects or merely link them. Visual FoxPro stores a copy of embedded objects in the current object. When an object is linked, FoxPro stores a path and name reference to the original object only.
Clear	Removes selected text without copying it to the Clipboard.
Select All	Selects all objects in the current window. This option is used often in form and report design to move or format all objects at the same time.
Find	Displays the Find dialog box, which is used to locate text strings in files. Find options include the capability to ignore case, wrap around lines, match entire words, and search forward or backward.
Find Again	Repeats the last Find starting at the current insertion point position rather than the beginning of the document.
Replace	Displays the Replace dialog box, which is used to locate and replace text strings in files.
Go to Line	Used primarily during debugging to go to a specific line number in a program file. This option cannot be used when word wrap is on. (Of course, you don't have word wrap on when you edit your FoxPro programs—right?)
Insert Object	Similar to Paste Special, except that it does not assume that the object already exists and is stored on the Clipboard. The option embeds objects in general type fields. When chosen, Insert Object opens the other application without exiting Visual FoxPro. After creating the object in the other application, Insert Object returns to Visual FoxPro and inserts the linked or embedded object.
Object	Provides options for editing a selected OLE object.
Links	Opens linked files (OLE) and enables you to edit the link.
Properties	Displays the Edit Properties dialog box, which enables you to affect the behavior, appearance, and save options of the edit windows.

Several options from Table 1.4—Paste Special, Insert Object, Object, and Links—apply only to general fields and OLE. The rest of the options apply to editing programs and fields.

The Edit Properties dialog box, opened by choosing the last option in the Edit menu, gives you control over the editor's many properties. The behavior properties, for example, turn on and off drag-and-drop editing, word wrap, and automatic indent. (Unless you are using Visual FoxPro editor as a word processor, I do not recommend using word wrap.)

You can also specify the following:

- Alignment of text (usually left for programs)
- Number of spaces in a tab
- Editor font
- Use of syntax coloring (a helpful enhancement)
- Display of the column and row position of the insertion point

Finally, you can have VFP make a backup copy of the file when you edit it, compile the file when it is saved, save line feeds, and create an end-of-file marker. Figure 1.6 shows these features.

FIGURE 1.6

Use the Edit Properties dialog box to customize the editor properties of Visual FoxPro 6.

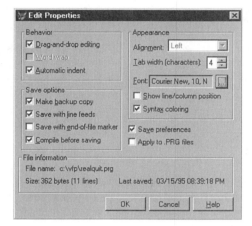

The View Menu Options   The View menu displays options that are appropriate for viewing the current table, if one is open. If you are not currently viewing a file, the menu displays a single option (Toolbar) that opens the Toolbar dialog box, which lists the available toolbars used by Visual FoxPro 6. On the other hand, if you already are browsing a table or editing a form, menu, or report, additional options appear as described in Table 1.5.

Table 1.5   View Menu Options

Menu Option	Description
Edit	Changes to an Edit layout style for viewing and changing records. The option displays fields vertically, and a horizontal line separates records (if grid lines are active).
Browse	Changes to a Browse layout style for viewing and changing records. The option displays fields horizontally; rows represent records and columns represent fields.

Menu Option	Description
Append Mode	Appends a blank record to the end of the table and moves the record pointer to the first field in it.
Design	Displays the Form, Label, or Report Designer.
Tab Order	Enables you to set the tab order in forms.
Preview	Shows a preview of labels or reports onscreen.
Data Environment	Defines tables and relations used in a form, form set, or report.
Properties	Displays the Properties dialog box for forms and controls.
Code	Opens the code windows when you are editing object methods.
Form Controls Toolbar	Opens the Form Controls toolbar while you are in the Form Designer.
Report Controls Toolbar	Displays the Report Controls toolbar, which enables you to add controls to a report.
Layout Toolbar	Opens the Layout toolbar, which helps you align controls.
Color Palette Toolbar	Opens the Color Palette toolbar, which enables you to select foreground and background colors for a control.
Report Preview Toolbar	Provides buttons that move between pages of the preview, change the zoom factor, print the report, and exit preview mode.
Database Designer	Opens the Database Designer, which maintains tables, views, and relationships stored in a database.
Table Designer	Opens the Table Designer, which enables you to make structure modifications to associated and free tables and to their indexes.
Grid Lines	Toggles the display of grid lines on and off.
Show Position	Displays the position, height, and width of the selected object or form in the status bar.
General Options	Adds code in a menu when you are using the Menu Designer.
Menu Options	Adds code to specific menu options.
Toolbars	Displays a dialog box that lists every toolbar used by FoxPro, enabling you to customize the buttons in toolbars and to create your own.

The Format Menu Options   The Format menu normally consists of options that control font characteristics, text indentation, and spacing. Additional options become available, however, when you are using the various Designers, and are described in Table 1.6.

Table 1.6 Format Menu Options

Menu Option	Description
Font	Selects a font and its characteristics.
Enlarge Font	Enlarges the font used in the current window.
Reduce Font	Reduces the font size used in the current window.
Single Space	Single-spaces the text in the current window.
1 1/2 Space	Uses 1 1/2-line spacing for the text in the current window.
Double Space	Double-spaces the text in the current window.
Indent	Indents the current or selected lines in the current window.
Unindent	Removes the indent of the current or selected lines in the current window.
Comment	Comments out the selected lines.
Uncomment	Removes comments from the selected lines.
Align	Opens options that align selected objects.
Size	Opens options that size selected objects.
Horizontal Spacing	Provides options that adjust horizontal spacing between selected objects.
Vertical Spacing	Provides options that adjust vertical spacing between selected objects.
Bring to Front	Moves the selected object to the top of the objects in a form.
Send to Back	Moves the selected object to the back of the objects in a form.
Group	Associates a selection of objects in reports and enables you to work with them as a group.
Ungroup	Breaks a group definition into individual objects again.
Snap to Grid	When you are moving objects, repositions the top-left corner to the nearest grid intersection when the mouse button is released.
Set Grid Scale	Determines how far apart the vertical and horizontal grids are.
Text Alignment	Aligns text in the selected object.
Fill	Defines a fill pattern for shapes.

Menu Option	Description
Pen	Defines a pen thickness and style for shapes.
Mode	Defines whether the background of an object is opaque or transparent.

Choosing the Font option opens a dialog box that displays a list of available fonts, their styles, and sizes. The option also displays a small sample of the font in a preview window. The font list contains all fonts that are defined in Windows. Fonts that have TT before their names are TrueType fonts, which can print over a large range of font sizes and still look good. If you are editing a program file, fonts preceded by a blank are either screen or printer fonts. These fonts look good onscreen, but they have to be sent to the printer as bitmap images (which print slowly) or they use a similar font for printing. I recommend the use of TrueType fonts. You can also control some additional effects in reports, such as Strikeout, Underline, and Color.

CAUTION

If you develop applications for other people, be careful which fonts you use. Unless you have shareware fonts that permit distribution, keep in mind that many fonts cannot be distributed freely. If your application uses a font that other computers do not have, formatted screens and reports may not come out as planned. Common fonts that currently ship with Windows 95 include Arial, Courier New, Marlett, Symbol, Times New Roman, and Wingdings. Check your current Windows manual to verify this list.

N O T E When you use the Enlarge Font or Reduce Font option, Visual FoxPro attempts to use font sizes stored in the font file, but it can calculate other font sizes based on multiples of existing font sizes or combinations of them. Visual FoxPro can create a 14-point font from information in the 6- and 8-point fonts, for example. ■

Unlike the Single Space, 1 1/2 Space, and Double Space options, Indent modifies only the current or selected lines in the current window. The option indents the line by the equivalent of one tab position each time you choose it. You can set the number of characters represented by a tab position through the Properties dialog box (Edit menu).

The Unindent option removes the equivalent of one tab from the current or selected lines each time you choose it. The Comment option precedes the selected lines with the characters *!*. Only if the selected lines begin with these characters will Uncomment remove the comment characters.

The Tools Menu Options The Tools menu provides a variety of programmer tools, ranging from wizards to the debugger. Table 1.7 defines the options in the Tools menu.

Table 1.7   Tools Menu Options

Menu Option	Description
Wizards	Lists and provides access to Visual FoxPro's wizards.
Spelling	Primarily spell-checks text fields and memos.
Macros	Defines and maintains keyboard macros.
Class Browser	Examines the contents of any class to view its properties and methods or even the actual code used to create the object.
Beautify	Reformats program files to add indenting and capitalization.
Debugger	Opens the Debugger window. This improved replacement for the Debug and Trace window adds windows for watch variables, locals, call stack, and the capability to track events and analyze coverage during testing.
Options	Provides access to Visual FoxPro configuration options.

FoxPro 2.6 introduced wizards, which are programs that guide the user through specific tasks such as creating a table. A wizard uses a series of windows that ask questions about the object that is being created.

Visual FoxPro also includes a spelling checker, which you can use to check the spelling of any object's text beginning at the current location of the insertion point. Although you can use this feature to spell-check program listings, that is not the intent. Instead, use the spelling checker to spell-check long text and memo fields.

The Macro dialog box enables you to create, edit, and view macro definitions. A macro definition consists of a series of Visual FoxPro commands that you can store and execute with a single keystroke. Previously FoxPro provided eight default macro definitions, which are assigned to function keys F2 through F9. Pressing F5, for example, executes the command DIS-PLAY STRUCTURE, which lists the structure of the current table. Table 1.8 shows the definitions of these default macros.

Table 1.8   Default Macro Definitions for Function Keys

Key	Command	Description
F2	SET	Opens the View window.
F3	LIST	Lists records from the current table; opens the GETFILE window if no table is being used.
F4	DIR	Lists all tables in the current directory.
F5	DISPLAY STRUCTURE	Shows the field definitions of the current table; opens the STRUCTURE GETFILE window if no database is being used.

Key	Command	Description
F6	DISPLAY STATUS	Shows the table open in each area. If an index is also open, F6 displays its expression. The key also shows the settings of SET commands and other system information.
F7	DISPLAY MEMORY	Displays the values stored in all memory variables, including system variables. F7 also shows the definitions of all menus, pads, pop-up lists, and windows.
F8	DISPLAY	Displays the current record; opens the GETFILE window if no table is being used.
F9		Enters append mode for the current table. Opens the GETFILE window if no database is being used.

In addition to these eight macros, you can define your own. In fact, because you can use a variety of key combinations to name macros, you can define more than 250 macros at one time.

The last option in the Tools menu is Options, which displays a multiple-page form that provides controls to customize the way you work with Visual FoxPro. VFP divides these controls into 12 distinct groups: Controls, Data, Debug, Field Mapping, File Locations, Forms, General, Projects, Regional, Remote Data, Syntax Coloring, and View. These groups are covered in more detail in the section "Setting Configuration Options" later in this chapter.

The Program Menu Options   The Program menu consists of six options that are related to compiling and running a program. Table 1.9 describes the Program options.

Table 1.9   Program Menu Options

Menu Option	Description
Do	Runs a program selected from a dialog box.
Cancel	Cancels the current program.
Resume	Resumes the current program from a suspended state.
Suspend	Stops the current program from executing but does not remove it from memory.
Compile	Translates a source file into object code.
Run	Runs the current program. (The option appears in the menu as Do, followed by the name of the PRG.)

The Do command opens a dialog box that enables you to select the program that you want to run. (You can also execute a program from the Command window; enter DO immediately followed by the name of the program that you want to run.) You do not have to compile a program before running it; you can run a PRG directly. VFP can compile the program automatically before running it.

N O T E   You can have VFP compile a program each time you save it. You can use the Edit Properties
dialog box to set this flag and save it for all PRG files. Subsequent new program files inherit
this property, but it does not affect existing PRG files. To change those files to automatically compile on
saving, you must set the property, open, and resave the files. ▦

Choose Program, Do, and select the program from the Do dialog box, which is similar to the
Open dialog box. The Do option differs from the Run option (which appears in the menu as Do,
followed by the name of the PRG), which executes the program in the current window.

VFP enables the Cancel option only when you are executing a program. To access this option,
you must suspend the program or be stepping through it in the Trace window.

N O T E   After suspending a program, you cannot edit the source code until you cancel the
program. ▦

Visual FoxPro enables Resume only while an executing program is suspended. The option
resumes a suspended program to normal execution mode.

To suspend a program, you first need to interrupt it. You can do this while you are using the
Trace window to step through the program. You can interrupt a program by inserting
breakpoints into the code, using the Trace window, or setting break conditions on variables or
expressions.

The Compile option opens a window similar to the Open dialog box, enabling you to select a
source file. The option takes the selected program source file (PRG) and compiles it. Click the
More>> button to display several additional options related to encryption and debugging, as
well as to create an error file (ERR), if desired.

The Window Menu Options   The Window menu contains options that manage open windows
onscreen. The menu provides options that enable you to Arrange All, Hide, Clear, and Cycle
through windows. In addition, the menu enables you to bring to the front any window that is
currently open. Table 1.10 lists the Window options.

Table 1.10   Window Menu Options

Menu Option	Description
Arrange All	Arranges open windows as non-overlapping tiles.
Hide	Hides the active window but does not remove it from memory.
Show All	Displays all defined windows.
Clear	Clears text from the application workspace or current output window.
Cycle	Moves from one open window to the next, making the next window the active one.

Menu Option	Description
Command Window	Makes the Command window active and brings it to the top, opening it if necessary.
Data Session	Makes the Data Session window active and brings it to the top, opening it if necessary. This window serves as a valuable tool for monitoring which tables are open in each of the 32,767 work areas.
<Window List>	Displays the first nine defined windows. If more than nine windows have been defined, a final option—More Windows— appears. To change focus to any window, simply click its name.

The Arrange All option resizes open windows to create non-overlapping tiles. Arrange All will not resize a maximized window. With two open windows, it splits the screen in half vertically and puts the active window on the left side. With three open windows, it also splits the screen in half vertically, putting the active window on the left side. The option then splits the right half horizontally, however, to display the other two open windows. If you have four open windows, each window receives one-quarter of the screen; the active window is placed in the upper-left corner. For more windows, you'll have to experiment.

The Hide option removes the active window from the screen. You cannot redisplay a system window (such as an edit window for a program) without reissuing the command that created it. If you hide a user-defined window, however, that window remains in memory; you can redisplay it with the SHOW WINDOW command. If you hide the current output window, it continues to receive output even while it is hidden, which means that you cannot see it. Upon redisplaying the window, you again see anything that has been written to it.

TIP Take advantage of the capability to write to a window while it is hidden to draw complex screens. Rather than amuse the user with a light show as your program paints a screen, hide the window, add the objects to it, and show the window fully developed.

The Clear option erases text from the current screen or active window. Notice that when you use the SHOW WINDOW command after hiding a window, that window does not automatically become the active window; its status depends on whether it was the active window when it was hidden and whether you activated another window in the meantime. (To ensure that a window is active, use the ACTIVATE WINDOW command.) Therefore, be careful about what you clear.

CAUTION
The CLEAR command and the Clear option in the Window menu are not the same as CLEAR WINDOW, which removes the window from both the screen and memory. The CLEAR command and the Clear option only remove the text from the window.

The Data Session option opens the Data Session dialog box, which displays a list of all tables that are open in the current session. The option also displays any relations defined among these tables, as shown in Figure 1.7.

FIGURE 1.7

The Data Session dialog box shows three work areas with defined tables and the relation set between two of them.

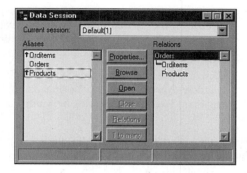

In the middle of the Data Session dialog box is a set of six buttons. The Properties button opens a window that displays the current table properties, indicating the data-buffering options that are in effect and any data filter or index order. The window also enables you to determine whether to allow access to all fields in the work area or only to fields selected with a field filter. Figure 1.8 shows the Work Area Properties window.

FIGURE 1.8

The Work Area Properties window is opened by choosing Properties in the Data Session window.

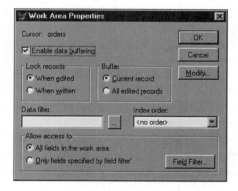

If you can open the table exclusively, you can change the structure by clicking the Modify button. This button opens the Table Designer shown in Figure 1.9.

This option enables you to change not only the fields for the selected table, but also the properties of those fields (captions, validations, defaults, and so on). You can also add, delete, or modify index expressions from the Indexes page of the Table Designer. The indexes defined here are part of the structural compound index for the current table. Finally, you can select the Table page to set record validations and triggers.

FIGURE 1.9

The Table Designer enables you to define not only the fields in a table, but also indexes, field properties, and table properties.

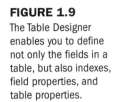

N O T E Visual FoxPro does not create indexes with .NDX extensions. The program can read .NDX indexes from earlier database systems, but it immediately converts them to its own internal index format, even though it may retain the .NDX extension. If you need to create a standalone index (.IDX) or a nonstructural compound index, you must do so from the Command window or from within a program by using the INDEX command. ▣

To open a table in a new work area, click the Open button in the Data Session dialog box. The Open dialog box appears to help you select a table. With a table assigned to a work area, you can browse through its records by clicking the Browse button.

The Close button closes the table in the currently selected work area (the highlighted one).

The Relations button enables you to define relations between files. If you already defined persistent relations through the Database Designer, however (or if you plan to), do not repeat those relations here.

The Help Menu Options   Help is the final menu pad of the System menu. Table 1.11 lists the options available in this menu. The first two options present different ways to access the help file to get information on commands, functions, or features. The third option lists support options that are available from Microsoft. The last option opens the typical copyright screen for the product; it adds additional functionality by providing system information and allowing the user to run other applications from within FoxPro.

Table 1.11 Format Menu Options

Menu Option	Description
Contents	Displays help information via an outline format.
Documentation	Opens the FoxPro online documentation.
Sample Applications	Describes the sample applications provided with Visual FoxPro.
Microsoft on the Web	Opens a second menu with options to use your Web browser to go to a variety of Visual FoxPro pages on the Web, the Microsoft home page, and several other locations.
Technical Support	Provides a list of available resources from Microsoft that offer additional help. The list includes a section that answers common questions.
About Microsoft Visual FoxPro	Displays the copyright screen for the product, along with whom it is licensed to, version date, resource filename, default directory, and product ID. Additional features include the capability to list system information and to run other programs.

The About Microsoft Visual FoxPro option displays an initial screen that contains the standard copyright and license information. The screen includes a special bonus: the System Info button. Click this button to display information about your system, as shown in Figure 1.10.

FIGURE 1.10
System Information is one of several categories of information for documenting your computer system that you can access from the About screen.

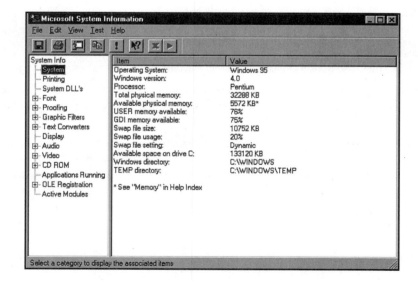

If you have problems with FoxPro and call Microsoft for assistance, print this screen first. In addition, you can display more than a dozen additional categories of available information by clicking the category name in the left window.

A bonus feature of the Microsoft System Info screen is the Run option in the File menu. Click this option to display a default list of applications that you can run. This list does not include every program on your system, but by clicking the Browse button, you can open a window from which you can select any application that is available to your system. Your capability to run other programs, of course, might depend on the amount of available memory on your machine. Figure 1.11 shows the Run Application window.

FIGURE 1.11

The About screen has an option that permits you to run external programs from within Visual FoxPro.

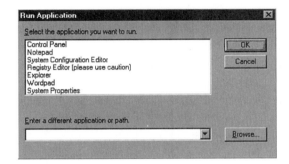

The Visual FoxPro System menu is dynamic; it changes as you perform different functions and use different VFP tools. Sometimes, the changes add or remove menu pads directly; at other times, the changes occur in the drop-down menus themselves.

The Toolbar

FoxPro has several toolbars, each of which is customized for the current task. This arrangement eliminates the confusion (and space problems) of having all buttons available at all times. This section briefly examines the main system toolbar, also called the Standard toolbar. You can experiment with the toolbars in FoxPro 6 by selecting View, which opens the Toolbar dialog box. From this dialog you can select specific toolbars or customize your own selection. You should only keep open the toolbars that you will need because the screen and workspace can become quite cluttered with a lot of toolbars on the screen.

The main system toolbar contains 20 buttons and one drop-down list. As you slowly pass your mouse over any button, a small box appears below it displaying the button's name. This box is called a ToolTip. ToolTips remind you of the buttons' actions, just in case you forget. Figure 1.12 shows the buttons on the Standard toolbar along with their names.

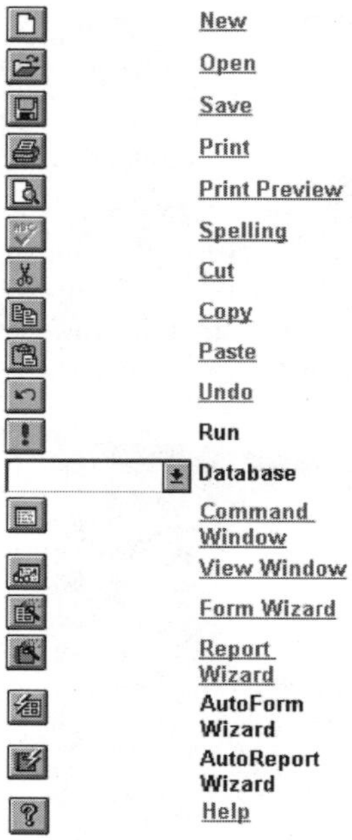

FIGURE 1.12

This figure shows the definitions of the buttons in the Standard toolbar.

New
Open
Save
Print
Print Preview
Spelling
Cut
Copy
Paste
Undo
Run
Database
Command Window
View Window
Form Wizard
Report Wizard
AutoForm Wizard
AutoReport Wizard
Help

Table 1.12 briefly describes the purpose of each button.

Table 1.12   Buttons on the Standard Toolbar

Button Name	Description
New	Opens the New File dialog box to create a new file.
Open	Opens the Open File dialog box to open an existing file.
Save	Saves changes made to the current file. By default, the button uses the file's original filename, except for a new file that has no name, in which case it prompts for a filename.
Print	Prints the active file, Command window contents, or Clipboard contents.
Print Preview	Uses a preview window to show what Print would output.
Spelling	Activates the spell checker.
Cut	Cuts the current selected text or object and places it on the Clipboard.
Copy	Copies the current selected text or object and places it on the Clipboard.

Button Name	Description
Paste	Copies the current contents of the Clipboard and pastes it at the current insertion point location.
Undo	Undoes the last action or command, with some limitations. The Undo button cannot undo a PACK command, for example.
Redo	Repeats the last command or action.
Run	Appears enabled if Visual FoxPro has an executable file open, such as a screen or program.
Modify Form	Switches the currently executing form back into designer mode.
Database	Lists the names of all open databases in a drop-down list. The current database appears in the text box. You can switch to a different database by selecting it from the list.
Command Window	Opens or pops the Command window back into view and makes it the active window.
View Window	Opens or pops the View window back into view and makes it the active window.
Form Wizard	Launches the Form Wizard.
Report Wizard	Launches the Report Wizard.
AutoForm Wizard	Creates a form from the current table.
AutoReport Wizard	Creates a report from the current table.
Help	Displays Visual FoxPro's Help Contents screen.

The Status Bar

The status bar appears at the bottom of Visual FoxPro's main screen if SET STATUS is ON. The status bar itself has two main areas: the message area on the left and indicator boxes on the right.

The message area is blank when no table is open in the current work area. When a table is open, the message area displays the following:

- The table's name
- The table's database name (enclosed in parentheses, if appropriate)
- The current record number
- The total number of records in the table

The Designers use this area to display the position and size of objects.

Finally, the message area displays the current sharable status of the file or current record using one of the following designations:

- Exclusive
- Record Unlocked
- Record Locked
- File Locked

Visual FoxPro also uses this portion of the status bar to display system messages that concern issues such as its progress during reindexing. Forms also use this area to display text messages associated with fields and controls, as well as position and size information while you are in the Designers.

The right end of the status bar contains either three or four indicator boxes. The first box on the left indicates the status of the Insert key. This box is blank when VFP's editor is in Insert mode; otherwise, the letters OVR appear, indicating overwrite mode. The next box displays NUM when the Num Lock key is on. The third box indicates the status of the Caps Lock key, displaying CAPS when the key is on. Finally, a fourth box may appear displaying the current time.

N O T E The View page of the Options dialog box (choose Tools, Options to display this dialog box) controls whether to display time in the status bar. Alternatively, you can enter SET CLOCK STATUS to turn on the clock in the status bar. ■

Controlling Windows

All windows, whether they are system windows or user-defined ones, have common features, although for any single window, one or more of the features may not be active. The following sections examine the Command window to help you become familiar with these features.

Zooming Windows

As mentioned earlier in this chapter, the title bar of a window has several buttons on the right side. The button with the lower horizontal line minimizes the window, representing it with an icon or docking it in the taskbar. (For windows within FoxPro, however, this button docks the icon on FoxPro's main screen, not the Windows desktop.) The button with the single window image maximizes the window. For a maximized window, the Restore button replaces the Maximize button; it has the image of two cascaded windows.

If you do not have a mouse, or if you just prefer not to take your hands off of the keyboard long enough to pick up the mouse, you can zoom the window by using shortcut keys. You can open the Windows 95 Window menu by pressing Alt+–. This shortcut key displays the options and their shortcut keys. Table 1.13 lists the shortcut keys, which work consistently across all Windows applications.

Table 1.13   Commands in the Window Menu with Their Shortcut Keys

Command	Shortcut Key	Description
Restore	Ctrl+F5	Returns the window to its original size.
Move	Ctrl+F7	Enables you to move the window with the arrow keys.
Size	Ctrl+F8	Enables you to size the window with the arrow keys.
Minimize	Ctrl+F9	Minimizes the window and displays it as an icon.
Maximize	Ctrl+F10	Maximizes the window.
Close	Ctrl+F4	Closes the window.
Next Window	Ctrl+F6	Activates the next window.

N O T E   The Next Window command in the Control menu duplicates the functionality of the Cycle option in the Window menu. Thus, you can use either Ctrl+F6 or Ctrl+F1 to cycle through open windows. ■

Resizing Windows

Maximizing and minimizing a window are not your only resizing choices; you can also "grab" any portion of the border to stretch the window. In fact, as you move the cursor around the border, you can see that Visual FoxPro divides the border into eight segments, one for each side and corner. Placing the mouse on any edge changes the cursor to show the direction in which the border stretches. Side segments stretch the window horizontally or vertically. Corners stretch the window in two directions at the same time.

If you don't have a mouse (but you really should get one before going much further with any Windows product; mice are relatively cheap and don't eat much), you can follow these steps to resize a window:

1. Press Ctrl+F1 to cycle through the open windows and activate the window you want to resize.
2. Open the control box by pressing Alt+– (Alt plus the hyphen/minus-sign key).
3. Choose Size by pressing S or by selecting the option and pressing Enter.
4. Now use the arrow keys to stretch the window. Notice that as you press the first arrow key, the cursor moves to the border in that same direction. If you continue to press the same arrow key, or the one for the opposite direction, the window expands or shrinks, respectively. If you press either of the two other arrow keys, the cursor moves to the corresponding corner first. Now you can use any arrow key to stretch or shrink the window from the current corner while the opposite corner remains fixed.
5. When you have the window sized the way that you want it, press Enter.

Later, when you create your own windows, you learn how to control which, if any, of these features remain active. Indeed, for some applications, you do not want the user to change the window's size.

Moving Windows

The easiest way to move a window is with the mouse. Simply click the title bar and drag the entire window anywhere on the screen. If you try to drag the window off the screen, VFP stops the movement when the mouse reaches a screen edge. Therefore, you cannot drag the window completely off the screen by using the mouse.

You also can move the window by using the keyboard. Follow these steps:

1. Press Ctrl+F1 to cycle through the open windows and activate the window you want to move.
2. Open the control box by pressing Alt+– (Alt plus the hyphen/minus sign).
3. Choose Move by pressing M or by selecting the option and then pressing Enter.
4. Now use the arrow keys to move the window.
5. When you have the window where you want it, press Enter.

Understanding Common Window Objects

Many common components appear in Visual FoxPro's dialog boxes, as well as in custom-designed forms. Figure 1.13 shows the most common components used in the Visual FoxPro interface.

FIGURE. 1.13

Examples of common screen elements used in Visual FoxPro.

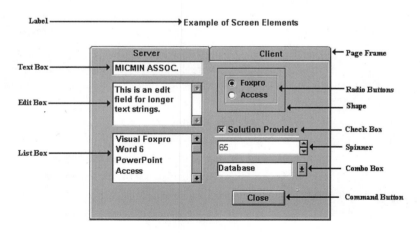

Labels A label is a fixed text string displayed in a form. VFP uses labels for titles and to identify other objects in forms.

Text Boxes　Text boxes contain character variables. These boxes can obtain their values from tables or they can represent memory variables. In either case, when text boxes appear in a form, you can edit them by selecting the text and making any changes.

Although a text box has a physical length onscreen, this physical length does not limit the length of the data that it contains. You control data length by using PICTURE clauses or by automatically truncating data to the length of table fields. You can also set the maximum length property of the text-box control. For longer values, text boxes can be more than one line high.

Edit Boxes　Edit boxes also enable you to edit character strings. The main advantage of an edit box is the scrollbar, which enables you to edit long strings and even memos.

List Boxes　The purpose of a list box is to display a series of options. Table 1.14 displays possible list sources.

Table 1.14　List-Source Values for List Boxes

Source ID	Source
0	None
1	Value
2	Alias
3	SQL statement
4	Query (.QPR)
5	Array
6	Fields
7	Files
8	Structure
9	Pop-up

Option Groups　Option groups (previously called radio buttons) limit the user to selecting one option from the group. Within a group of option buttons, you can select only one button at a time. In fact, the order of the option buttons in the group defines the value of a single variable. If you click a second button, the preceding selection is released. The setup is just like the preset buttons on a car radio.

Remember that a variable can have only one value.

A selected button displays a black dot inside the circle. A deselected button is just an empty circle.

A box automatically surrounds the option group on creation. This box is especially important visually if you have more than one option group in a form, because each group can have one—and only one—selected button.

Check Boxes   Visual FoxPro uses check boxes to represent binary states. Binary states are either on or off like a switch, thus the name: binary switch. Because many configuration options used by VFP are either on or off, forms that display them usually use check boxes. A selected check box, which represents the true state, contains a bold check mark. Otherwise, the box is blank. Although a form can have more than one check box, each one represents a unique variable or field. Therefore, you can select as many check boxes as you want.

Check boxes now support a third value, null, which means neither true nor false; its value is unknown. To use this capability, you must represent the check box value as a number ranging from 0 to 2. In this case, 0 represents false, 1 represents true, and 2 represents unknown. When a check box is set to null, its background is dimmed.

Spinners   Spinners provide an interesting way to select integer values. These elements use a text area to display the current value. To the right of this text area are two buttons, one on top of the other. The top button has an up arrow; the bottom one has a down arrow. Clicking the top button increments the spinner value; clicking the bottom button decrements the value. You also can change the value directly by selecting in the text area and entering a new value.

In most cases, spinners have minimum and maximum values. A good use for a spinner is to obtain the number of copies when you route a report to a printer. In this case, a minimum value might be 0 (no report) to 10 (10 copies).

Spinners can directly use only numeric variables, but you might reference the variable in this control to display and control other data types, such as dates or strings.

Combo Boxes   A combo box combines the best features of a text box with those of a list. Visual FoxPro uses two variations on combo boxes. The one shown in Figure 1.13 is a drop-down combo box, which enables the user to enter a new item in the box next to the button. The user can also click the arrow to the right of the box to display a list of predefined choices. The second type of combo box is called a drop-down list. The primary visual difference is that the arrow is connected to the text area in a drop-down list. Functionally, however, drop-down lists enable you only to select values that are in the list.

Command Buttons   Command buttons (or push buttons) appear as three-dimensional shaded rectangles. A command button usually displays a text caption or bitmap image that identifies its purpose. To execute the action associated with a button, simply click it.

Most Visual FoxPro dialog boxes have one command button that has a slightly darker border than the other buttons. This button executes as the default if you press Enter.

Some command buttons have ellipses (…) after their captions to indicate that they open another dialog box. Another common button convention uses the label MORE>>. When you click such a button, the current window expands to reveal additional options.

Page Frames   Finally, all of these controls (except for the initial label field) appear in a page frame. Each page in the page frame has a tab along the top. Sometimes multiple rows of tabs are necessary. Clicking a tab displays a new page of options within the same window.

Effectively, page frames provide a mechanism to display more controls in a single window by dividing them into multiple pages. Another way to think of page frames is to think of them as layers.

Visual FoxPro supports other elements for creating forms. In addition, a large number of OCX controls are provided with Visual FoxPro. Also, many of the OCX controls provided by third-party tool suppliers work with Visual FoxPro, as well as with Access and Visual Basic. The controls described in this chapter are the basic controls included with Visual FoxPro; they provide the basis for interacting with VFP dialog boxes, builders, and designers.

Introducing the Project Manager

The Project Manager has two primary purposes:

- It helps organize files for a project based on file type.
- It provides a container for gathering components of an application in preparation for compiling them to an application (.APP) or executable (.EXE) file.

Consider the fully developed project file that comes with FoxPro: the Tastrade project. To open a project, enter the following command in the Command window:

```
MODIFY PROJECT \VFP\SAMPLES\TASTRADE\TASTRADE.PJX
```

(Alternatively, you can choose File, Open.)

In the dialog box that appears, change the contents of List Files of Type to Project, if necessary. Next, use the Drives and Directories options to switch to the drive and directory in which the Tastrade example is stored. You should see the project name TASTRADE.PJX in the selection box. To select it, simply double-click.

N O T E   You can also enter the full pathname of the project file in the box immediately below the
label Filename. ■

The Visual FoxPro Project Manager should open, as shown in Figure 1.14.

FIGURE 1.14
Project Manager initially
displays all file types
for Tastrade.

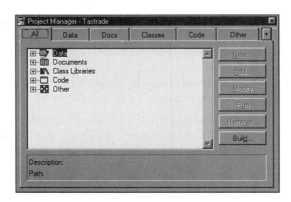

You should be aware of several features of the Project Manager. First, if you previously used FoxPro 2.x, the Project Manager no longer lists all files of all types in a single list; rather, it divides the files by type. Page tabs that identify the first group level appear across the top of the window. Each page further divides each major file group into specific file types. Using an outline structure, the following list shows the organization of files in a project:

Data
> Databases
>
> Free Tables
>
> Queries

Documents
> Forms
>
> Reports
>
> Labels

Class Libraries

Code
> Programs
>
> API Libraries
>
> Applications

Other
> Menus
>
> Text Files
>
> Other Files

N O T E Actually, you can get a single list by choosing Project, Project Info and then selecting the Files page of the resulting dialog box to see an alphabetical list of all files in the project. The list indicates the last modified date and code page for each file, as well as whether it is included in the project. ▪

In fact, you can see each of these groups by clicking each of the tabs successively. In Visual FoxPro, this form structure is called a *page frame*. By using tabs across the top of the page frame, you can select different groups of data. This structure makes more information fit on a single screen by creating page overlays; it also helps users organize information. In this case, you can more easily find the names of programs when they are grouped by type than you can when all types appear in a single mixed-type list, as in earlier versions of FoxPro.

If you click the Data page (and if no one else has been working with the project), you should see three subgroup titles below Data: Databases, Free Tables, and Queries. Notice the plus sign before Databases. In this outline-like structure, a plus sign indicates that additional details are hidden in this item. To view these details, click the plus sign (an action that is also called drilling down).

In this case, only one item drops out of Databases: Tastrade. This fact means that the project has only a single database named Tastrade.

Tastrade has a plus sign before it. Clicking the plus sign displays another set of categories:

Tables
Local Views
Remote Views
Connections
Stored Procedures

Later chapters define tables, queries, views, and remote data access, and further explain what these groups mean. For now, concentrate on the Tables line, which is preceded by a plus sign. Click this plus sign to list the tables stored in database Tastrade.

At this point, I should clarify the terms database and table. In the past, FoxPro developers used these terms interchangeably, but the terms were never meant to be interchangeable. The misuse of the term database started in the early days of Ashton-Tate's dominance in the database market. Because of the company's dominance for many years, the term database, as used to refer to a single table, persisted.

In 1995, Visual FoxPro corrected the misuse of these terms by creating a separate object called a database container, which holds and/or organizes one or more tables. Most FoxPro programmers can associate a table with a single file that has a .DBF extension and that contains records and rows of data. The introduction of the database container, however, goes beyond the mere collection of tables. The database container also provides a platform to expand the traditional definition of a table by providing the following:

- Support for long tables and field names
- Record validation clauses
- Field validation clauses
- Default values
- Stored captions
- Triggers for inserting, deleting, and updating records
- Persistent relations among tables in the database
- Referential integrity

Finally, the project displays another level beyond the list that contains the table's fields. Figure 1.15 shows the first portion of a fully opened outline for Databases.

You may want to take a few moments to explore the contents of various levels of the Project Manager. Not every group contains the files in this example, but you get the idea of the way that the Project Manager organizes files.

FIGURE 1.15
You can open successive levels of details about databases until you reach the list of table fields and indexes.

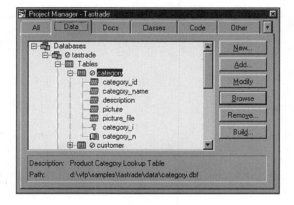

Adding and Removing Files

Adding a file is a simple process. First, select the group to which you want to add a file, and then click either New or Add. Project Manager knows what type of file you want to add by the group that you selected. If you choose New, VFP first prompts you for a filename; it then opens an appropriate builder or designer to create that file. If you select the Tables group in the Data category, for example, the Project Manager first prompts you to determine whether you want to use a wizard or a designer. If you choose the designer, you must assign a name to the created table. Then the Project Manager opens the Table Designer or wizard so that you can define the table's structure.

If the file already exists, click the Add button. Project Manager responds by prompting for the filename, using the Open dialog box, and then adding the file to the appropriate project group.

To remove a file, such as a table, highlight it and then click the Remove button. If the file is a database table, VFP displays a window asking `Do you want to remove the table from the database or delete it from the disk?` For other files, VFP asks a similar question: `Do you want to remove the file from the project or delete it from the disk?` In either case, deleting a file from the disk also removes it from the project.

 You can also see these options, like Remove, by right-clicking on the desired object.

Viewing Files

When you are viewing a file, the Project Manager treats tables differently from most other file types. To view a table, highlight it and then click Browse. This action opens the table in a Browse window, where you can view the table's records (represented as rows) and fields (represented as columns). Think of this action as "running" the table. Clicking the Modify button opens the Table Designer.

If, instead, you want to view a program's code, highlight it and click Modify. This action opens an edit window that lists the program code.

Similarly, click Modify to open and view a form, report, or label design. Each time you click Modify for one of these file types, VFP opens the appropriate designer tool.

You have just learned an important concept of object-oriented programming, called *polymorphism*. In each case in which you used Modify, the Project Manager opened the file with a different tool. Project Manager knew which tool to use because of the selected file type.

> **CAUTION**
>
> Using Modify to view a file can be dangerous because you can inadvertently save changes to the file. If you know that you did not make any changes, but VFP asks you to save your changes when you exit a file, just click No.

Modifying Files

To return to tables for just a moment, you may ask why you would click Modify in the Project Manager. Actually, the preceding section stretched the terms a little by using Modify to view program code, forms, reports, or labels. The Modify button actually told Project Manager to modify those items, even though you only intended to view them. Therefore, as you may guess, the Modify button for tables takes you to the Table Designer, which enables you to modify the table's fields and indexes, not just view them.

Think of the Browse button as being the action button for a table. You cannot run a table, but you can look at it. On the other hand, you certainly can run a program, screen, report, or label. In this case, Run is the action button. Therefore, Project Manager renames the Run button Browse for tables.

Does this fact mean that you can store your PRG files in the Code-Programs group and then click the Run button to test them? Absolutely! It does not matter whether you intend to build an application from all the files in the project or whether you merely want to run individual programs, reports, or labels—use the Project Manager as your standard tool for file organization and testing. Also consider keeping a separate VFP project for each physical project that you work on. You can include the same file—whether it is a table, program, form, or whatever—in more than one project file.

Furthermore, you do not have to save all individual files in a project in the same directory. Therefore, you might want to organize your files by type. Consider storing order-entry files in one directory, inventory files in another, invoices in a third, and so on.

Remember that any one application can call on tables or other files from several areas. Merely add the file to each project that requires it.

You probably have been wondering about another symbol in the group listings. This symbol—a circle with a slash through it—tells the compiler not to include this file in the compiled application or executable file.

Similarly, you may have noticed that one of the programs in the Code-Programs group is displayed in bold text. This formatting identifies the main program of an application to the compiler.

Setting Configuration Options

As mentioned earlier, Visual FoxPro enables the user to set a large number of parameters that determine how it works. In fact, VFP has so many options that they would never fit on a single screen page. But with a page-frame–style form, FoxPro can overlay several pages of options in a single window.

That is exactly what the Tools, Options command does. The resulting dialog box includes 12 tabs that divide the set options into the following logical sets:

- Controls
- Data
- Debug
- Field Mapping
- File Locations
- Forms
- General
- Projects
- Regional
- Remote Data
- Syntax Coloring
- View

Controls Options

The Controls page enables you to select class libraries and OLE controls. A class library contains one or more custom visual classes that you define from FoxPro's base classes. An OLE control is a link to other OLE-supporting applications (insertable objects) and ActiveX controls. Class libraries and OLE controls selected in this page appear in the Form Controls toolbar of the Form Designer when you click the View Classes button. Figure 1.16 shows the options in this page frame.

Data Options

The Data page includes options related to the following:

- Accessing data (including sorting-sequence methods)
- Search-string comparison
- Locking and buffering parameters for shared access

- Memo-block size
- Refresh rates

FIGURE 1.16

The Controls page of the Options dialog box defines connections to visual class libraries and OLE (ActiveX) controls when you are creating forms.

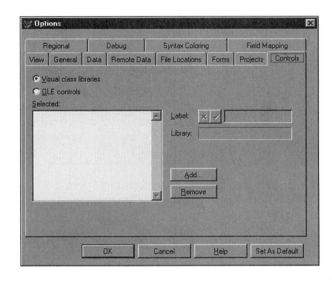

Figure 1.17 shows these settings.

FIGURE 1.17

The Data page of the Options dialog box defines features related to data access, retrieval, and display.

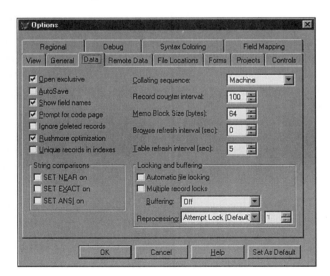

The Open Exclusive option determines how VFP opens a table in a shared environment. When this option is selected, VFP attempts to open the table exclusively, which means that no one else can have the table open. If you or someone else has the table open in another session or machine, VFP will not open it again. After VFP opens the table, no one else can open it.

Some commands require exclusive access to tables. These commands include the following:

- INDEX
- INSERT [BLANK]
- MODIFY STRUCTURE
- PACK
- REINDEX
- ZAP

 TIP If you work in a standalone environment, use SET EXCLUSIVE ON. Performance will improve because VFP does not have to check or maintain record lock tables (internal information that identifies which records or files are locked by a user editing them).

Autosave corresponds to the SET AUTOSAVE command. When this option is set, Visual FoxPro flushes file buffers back to disk when you exit a READ command or return to the Command window.

Show Field Names corresponds to SET HEADINGS and determines whether field names appear above columns during commands such as AVERAGE, DISPLAY, LIST, and SUM.

The Prompt for Code Page option determines whether to prompt users for a code page. Code pages perform character translations for international users when they are turned on. VFP displays the Code Page dialog box when you open a table exclusively and the table does not already have an associated code page. (See SET CPDIALOG in the VFP Online Help.)

Ignore Deleted Records determines how Visual FoxPro processes records that are marked for deletion when it performs a record-level function. First, you must understand that when you mark a record for deletion with the DELETE command, VFP does not physically delete the record; it merely marks the record in the table. Only the PACK command can physically delete marked records. Therefore, you need to decide whether you want to see or process records that are marked for deletion. In most cases, you probably don't want to process deleted records (unless you have a program option to recall deleted records). Therefore, you would check this option. When Ignore Deleted Records is not checked, VFP processes a record marked for deletion just as it does any other record in the table. This option corresponds to the SET DE-LETED command.

Since version 2.0, FoxPro has included a search-optimization technique called *Rushmore*, which uses existing indexes to perform data searches more rapidly. Under most conditions, you want to take advantage of Rushmore. At times, however, Rushmore might actually impede performance. You can globally control Rushmore with the Rushmore Optimization option. Most commands that use Rushmore also contain a clause that turns it off. Thus, you should turn on Rushmore in this page and turn it off only as needed in individual commands. (See SET OPTI-MIZE in the VFP Online Help.)

The Unique Records in Indexes option controls the default that FoxPro uses in creating indexes. If this option is not selected, indexes can contain duplicate key values. In other words, if you index on last name, the index file can contain pointers to two or more Smiths, for example. When the option is selected, indexes maintain pointers only to unique key values, even if multiple records with the same key value exist. In the case of the multiple Smiths, the index maintains a pointer to only the first one. If you do not select Unique Records in Indexes, you can selectively create unique indexes by using the UNIQUE clause of the INDEX command. While this option is set, you cannot create nonunique indexes programmatically. Unique Records in Indexes corresponds to SET UNIQUE.

Collating Sequence enables changes to the collating sequence during sorts to accommodate different character sets for users in other countries. The default, machine sequence, uses the ASCII equivalents of each character. This option corresponds to the SET COLLATE command. If you SET COLLATE to GENERAL, the indexes that you create will be case insensitive.

Record-Counter Interval determines how frequently VFP reports its progress during commands such as REINDEX and PACK. This value can range from 1 to 32,787 records processed. Increasing the frequency can affect performance, however, because of the need for more frequent screen updates. (See SET ODOMETER in the VFP Online Help.)

Memo Block Size defines the number of bytes that VFP assigns to a memo at a time, from 33 bytes on up. Values of 1 to 32 allocate blocks of 512 bytes (1 = 512, 2 = 1,024, and so on). The smaller the number of allocated bytes, the less space you waste in the memo file. New to VFP is the capability to set the block size to 0, which actually allocates space in single bytes, resulting in no wasted space. You pay a performance penalty, however, if you make the block size too small. When VFP creates a memo file, the block size for it remains fixed. (See SET BLOCKSIZE in the VFP Online Help.)

The Browse-Refresh Interval option determines how frequently VFP resynchronizes data displayed in a Browse screen with the actual table source. Numbers between 1 and 3,600 refer to the number of seconds between each refresh. A value of 0 causes a refresh as soon as another user updates the table with a new value and unlocks the record. This option also corresponds to SET REFRESH.

Table-Refresh Interval determines how frequently VFP resynchronizes data displayed from a table with the actual table source. Numbers between 1 and 3,600 refer to the number of seconds between each refresh. A value of 0 does not cause a refresh when another user updates the table. (See SET REFRESH in the VFP Online Help.)

The next three options control how string comparisons are made.

SET NEAR controls what FoxPro does when a search fails. If this option is not selected, FoxPro leaves the record pointer at the end of the file. When this option is set, FoxPro leaves the record pointer at the next record alphabetically from the position where it expected to find the search value. This option corresponds to the SET NEAR command.

The SET EXACT option also controls how FoxPro performs a search. When this option is set, the search field must match the search criteria exactly, character for character and in total length. When this option is not set, the search must match character for character, up to the length of the value on the right side of the search expression. This option corresponds to the SET EXACT command.

SET ANSI controls how SQL performs string comparisons. When this option is selected, Visual FoxPro pads the shorter of the two strings with blanks to make both strings equal in length. Then VFP compares each string, character for character, to see whether the strings match. When this option is not set, it compares the strings character for character, up to the length of the shorter string (on either side of the expression). This option corresponds to SET ANSI.

The last set of options affects how Visual FoxPro handles file and record locks in a multiuser environment.

FoxPro automatically sets and releases file and record locks for file-related commands when it shares tables. Normally, you want to have the Automatic File Locking option turned on unless you intend to handle all locks manually through your code. This option corresponds to SET LOCK.

Normally, FoxPro releases the current record lock if you set a lock on a new record. You may want to lock several records at the same time, however, to update them simultaneously. In these cases, you want to select the Multiple Record Locks option. You can also set this option programmatically with the SET MULTILOCKS command. Only by setting multiple record locks can you activate buffering.

Buffering determines how to maintain data in a multiuser environment. Visual FoxPro has five buffering methods. For more information on buffering, see CURSORSETPROP() in the VFP help system.

The Reprocessing options determine how frequently or how long Visual FoxPro attempts to establish a lock when the lock fails. When you are working in a shared environment, you typically want FoxPro to retry setting locks if the first attempt fails. This option controls the number of retries up to 32,000. In addition, values of –2, –1, and 0 have special meanings. For details on these options, see the command SET REPROCESS in the VFP Online Help.

Debug Options

The Debug options customize the way that the Debugger works. Figure 1.18 shows the options in the Debug page.

The first option enables you to select the environment for the Debugger. The environment option enables you to select either the Debug frame or the FoxPro frame. The Debug frame keeps all the debugger windows in one large frame called the Visual FoxPro Debugger. The FoxPro frame enables individual debugger windows to appear in the VFP main window. You can also display timer events during debugging. Be aware, however, that this option may result in a substantial increase in the debugger output.

FIGURE 1.18
The Debug page of the Options dialog box controls FoxPro's default Debugger features.

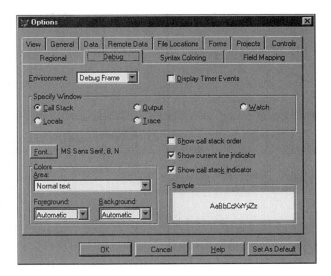

Next, you can specify which window in the debugger you want to define properties for. Properties that you can set include the font and colors.

Field Mapping Options

This feature, new to VFP 5.0, is one of the most useful for customizing the way that the form builders work. Previously, the type of object associated with each field type was fixed, and in most cases, that object was a text box. When you add a numeric field, you may not want to use a text box; you may want a spinner instead. Similarly, you probably want to use a check box as the default control for a logical field and an edit box as the default for a memo field. With the Field Mapping page, you can now set the default control associated with each field type, as shown in Figure 1.19.

You can even associate a field type with a custom class in a class library. You could associate a logical or integer field with a group of option buttons, for example, as shown in Figure 1.20.

This page also enables you to determine whether to implement drag-and-drop field captions. When checked, this option gets the field caption from the table-structure property, Caption, and includes it on the form when adding a field. Similarly, you can copy the field comments, input masks, and formats from comparable table-structure properties. These database options use the power of the data dictionary and help provide consistency across applications.

FIGURE 1.19
The Field Mapping page of the Options dialog box controls which base-class object is associated with each field type when you are using the Form Designer.

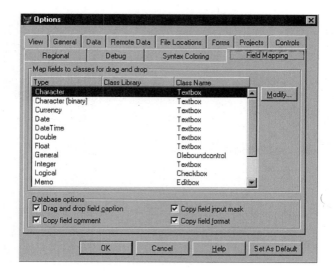

FIGURE 1.20
The Field Mapping page of the Options dialog box controls which base-class or custom object is associated with each field type by selecting Modify to display the Modify Field Mapping dialog box.

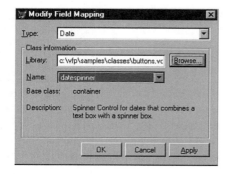

File Locations Options

FoxPro uses many files, and it should not come as a surprise that those files do not all reside in the same directory. VFP uses the File Locations page to define the locations for 10 classes of files. Figure 1.21 shows this page, and the following paragraphs describe some of the auxiliary files and tools that require their file locations to be specified.

FoxPro first attempts to locate tables and program files in the default directory if you do not supply a full pathname at the Default Directory prompt. The current directory can be any directory, not just the Visual FoxPro root directory. In fact, you can change the directory programmatically at any time with the SET DEFAULT TO command.

Use Search Path to tell VFP where to search for files that are not in the default directory. You can include multiple directories if you separate them with commas or semicolons. This option corresponds to the SET PATH command.

FIGURE 1.21

The File Locations page of the Options dialog box defines the paths of various auxiliary files and tools used by Visual FoxPro.

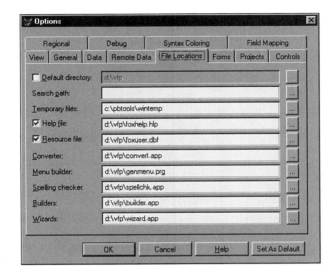

Although VFP attempts to keep as much data in memory as possible to improve performance, sometimes it must create temporary files in response to commands. Visual FoxPro writes these files to a common directory specified in the Temporary Files text area. In a networked environment, keep temporary files on a local drive to improve performance.

Help File identifies the name and location of the help file. Usually, this is the FoxPro help file. If you create a custom help file for your users, however, you can identify it here. You can change the current file at any time, of course, by using the SET HELP TO command.

The resource file—which stores information about the way you work, edit preferences, window size and position values, color schemes, printer information, and much more—is designated in the Resource File text area and check box. Usually, VFP stores the resource file as FOXUSER.DBF in the VFP root directory. In a networked environment, however, you can either have individual resource files or a shared resource file. To be shared, a resource file must be read only, which defeats some of its purpose. But would you want someone to change your color scheme to something like Hot Dog Stand in the middle of running a series of applications? In shared environments, you might need to write programs that work with two resource files: one private with read-write rights and one shared.

The converter application, in the Converter text area, takes objects such as screens and reports written for earlier versions of FoxPro and converts them to Visual FoxPro 6. This conversion consists primarily of a file restructuring. If you begin with a DOS version of a screen, the converter creates a Windows screen, but it cannot add features that are unique to VFP; you must, alas, do that yourself.

Most larger applications use a main menu to tie together various parts of the system. Rather than write menu code manually, you can save time by using the menu builder. The Menu Builder locates this tool using both the path and name.

To use the spell checker, you must identify its directory and name in the Spell Checker box, if it is not in the FoxPro root directory.

FoxPro includes builders for several objects, such as ComboBox and ListBox. *Builders* are tabbed dialog boxes used to create and modify the objects. Builders help set the properties for these objects.

Visual FoxPro comes with wizards that help develop various features of your application. All wizards must reside in the same directory and application file. The Wizards option identifies that directory.

Forms Options

Almost every application requires at least one form. Using the Form Designer requires a few special options, including grids, screen resolution, tab order, and template classes. Figure 1.22 shows the Form options.

FIGURE 1.22
The Forms page of the Options dialog box controls features used in the Form Designer.

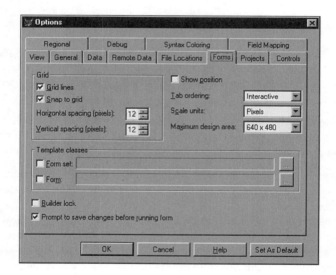

With Grid Lines, you can elect to show a grid. Dotted horizontal and vertical lines appear onscreen based on the spacing parameters defined later in the form page. You don't need to display the grid to use it; you can position objects in the grid's spaces by setting Snap to grid, regardless of whether the grid is actually displayed.

When turned on, Snap to Grid automatically moves objects to the nearest grid intersection when you change their position or add new objects. The option does not affect the positions of objects that you placed previously unless you try to move them.

The Horizontal Spacing option defines the number of pixels between horizontal grid lines.

The Vertical Spacing option defines the number of pixels between vertical grid lines.

When selected, Show Position displays the position of the upper-left corner and the size of the current object in the status bar.

Tab Ordering determines how to sequence fields that receive focus as you press the Tab key when running the program. Tab Ordering has two options: Interactive and By List. When Interactive is set, the user must press Shift while clicking the mouse to select the object order. At the same time, each object displays a small box with a number showing its current tab-sequence number. Alternatively, the tab order can be displayed as a list. You can reposition fields in the list by dragging them to a different position, thus changing the tab order.

In Windows, positioning of objects cannot be based on characters and rows because characters can vary in width and height from object to object. Instead, you position all objects based on pixels or foxels, which you can choose with the Scale Units option. Pixels are individual dots of color onscreen. Most VGA monitors use a standard 640-by-480 pixel display. Visual FoxPro, however, defines a foxel as being equivalent to the average height and width of a character in the current window font.

TIP Use foxels rather than pixels when you are transporting a screen from a character-based platform, such as DOS, to a graphical-based platform.

Use the Maximum Design Area option to match the resolution of the user's monitor and monitor driver. You can still develop using a higher resolution supported by your own display. The Maximum Design Area then limits the size of forms you can create so that they fit on the user's reduced-resolution screen.

CAUTION

If you develop applications for other people, beware of developing screens with a resolution largerthan those people use. Doing so will cause display problems when you attempt to install the application. Always use the lowest screen resolution of all your expected users.

You can define two template classes, which identify default templates for forms and form sets.

The button to the right of the Form Set text box opens the Registered Library drop-down list of available class libraries selected in the Controls page. Simply select the form-set class that you want to use as a default in designing your application.

The button to the right of the Form text box also opens the Registered Library drop-down list of available class libraries selected in the Controls page. Simply select the form class that you want to use as a default in designing your application.

Choose the Builder Lock option to automatically display the builders when you add controls to a form.

Finally, you can ask VFP to prompt you to save changes after you edit a form before running the form. If you don't do this, VFP automatically saves the changes before running the form.

General Options

The next page defines general options, including those that deal with compatibility, color, confirmation, and sound issues. The page also includes options that affect programming and data entry. Figure 1.23 shows this page.

FIGURE 1.23

The General page of the Options dialog box sets miscellaneous options that do not fit in any of the other tabs.

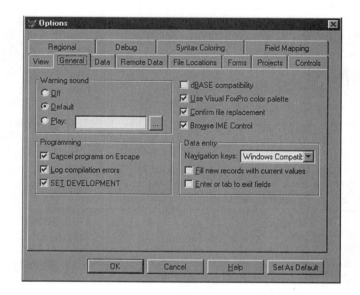

The Off option in the Warning Sound group determines whether to sound the bell when the user reaches the end of a field or enters invalid data. The corresponding command is SET BELL.

The Default option sets the bell frequency and duration to their default values. SET BELL TO [nFrequency, nDuration] supports frequencies from 19 through 10,000 Hz, with a default of 512. Duration ranges from 1 to 19 seconds, with a default of 2 seconds.

With Play, you also can choose a .WAV file to use instead of the impersonal beep. Click the button that has the ellipsis to display a dialog box from which you can pick a .WAV file.

N O T E   If VFP cannot locate the specified waveform, it uses a default defined in the Registry. If VFP finds no waveform there, it plays no sound. For you real techheads, the location of the default sound in the Registry is

`<C1>HKEY_USERS/.DEFAULT/APP EVENTS/SCHEMES/APPS/.DEFAULT/.DEFAULT/.CURRENT`

and

`<C1>HKEY_USERS/.DEFAULT/APP EVENTS/SCHEMES/APPS/.DEFAULT/.DEFAULT/.DEFAULT`

I do not recommend, however, that you make changes in the Registry without first making a backup of the Registry. ■

The dBASE Compatibility option controls the compatibility of Visual FoxPro with other Xbase languages. By default, this option is not selected, thereby enabling Visual FoxPro to run programs written in earlier versions of FoxPro and FoxBase. When the option is selected, Visual FoxPro interprets the commands shown in Table 1.15 differently.

Table 1.15 Commands Affected by the Set Compatible Command

Command	Compatible On	Compatible Off
@...GET...RANGE	Always checks	Checks range only if range data changes
@...SAY	Output to the FoxPro desktop scrolls as necessary	Output to the FoxPro desktop truncates after reaching the lower-right corner
@...SAY	Rounds the right-most digit in the PICTURE clause	Truncates the right-most digit in the PICTURE clause
ACTIVATE SCREEN	When activating the screen or a window, the cursor position is 0,0	When activating the screen or a window, the cursor position is unchanged
APPEND MEMO	The default extension is TXT	No default extension
GO/GOTO (with SET TALK ON)	Outputs a message with the current work area and record number	No message
INKEY()	Home and Shift+Home returns 26; Ctrl+ Left returns 1	Home and Shift+Home returns 1; Ctrl+L returns 26
LIKE()	Trailing blanks in both expressions are trimmed before comparison	Trailing blanks are retained and are significant
MENU and POPUP	Pop-up lists are placed in the active output window with the cursor positioned on an option	Pop-up lists are placed in their own window while the cursor remains in the active window
Nested Reads	Performs an implicit CLEAR GETS when returning to a higher level	Pending GETS remain when returning to a higher level
Passed Parameters	Parameters passed by reference remain available in the called procedure	Parameters passed by reference are hidden in the called procedure
PLAY MACRO	Adds an implicit Alt+F10 before macros that begin with A–Z; adds an implicit Alt before macros F1–F9	No implicit keystrokes are added

continues

Table 1.15   Continued

Command	Compatible On	Compatible Off
READ	Performs the VALID clause when you press Esc	Does not perform the VALID clause when you press Esc
RUN	Cursor moves to the first column in row 24 before beginning output; when done, scrolls output up three lines	Output begins at the cursor's current position; when done, scrolls output up two lines
SELECT()	Returns number of highest unused work area	Returns number of currently selected work area
SET MESSAGE	Displays the character expression in the last line of the screen	Displays the character expression only if SET STATUS is ON
SET PRINT TO	Output file has a default extension of .PRT	No default extension for output file
STORE	Cannot initialize all elements of an array	Can initialize all elements of an array
SUM	Uses the number of decimal places specified by SET DECIMALS	Uses the number of decimal places specified by the field being summed
SYS(2001,'COLOR') COLOR USE	Returns value of current SET COLOR. If a VFP path is set and USE includes a drive, VFP searches only that drive	Returns value of SET TO Color color pair. If a VFP path is set and USE includes a drive, VFP searches that drive first; then it searches the path

When selected, the Use Visual FoxPro Color Palette option tells Visual FoxPro to use its own default color palette when displaying .BMP (bitmap) images. Otherwise, VFP uses the color palette used to create the .BMP. This option corresponds to the SET PALETTE command.

The Confirm File Replacement option determines whether VFP shows a warning message before overwriting an existing file. This option corresponds to the SET SAFETY command.

The Browse IME Control is only enabled when using a double-byte character system. It displays an Input Method Editor when you navigate to a text box in the Browse window. It corresponds to the IMESTATUS function.

The General page includes three programming options, which primarily affect developers.

Selecting Cancel Program On Escape enables the user to press the Esc key to terminate a program's execution. Although this capability is essential during development, you might not want to enable users to press Esc while they are running a production version of the application. The program code provides a better, more secure place to control this option by means of the SET ESCAPE command.

Log Compilation Errors, when you compile a PRG file to create an FXP, APP, or EXE, causes VFP displays errors to the screen. You might prefer to log compilation errors to an error file rather than interrupt the compilation for each one. Then you can go back to the log file and deal with each error individually. The error file has the same root name as the PRG (when you are compiling standalone PRGs) or the project file (when you are compiling projects), but it uses the extension .ERR.

If you select the SET DEVELOPMENT option, VFP checks to see whether any changes have been made in the source file before running a compiled FXP. Similarly, if you work with projects that contain groups of files, the option checks the source of each component with the last compile date of the APP or application file. If any of the source files have more recent time and date stamps, the option recompiles the project.

Finally, this page contains three data-entry options, which affect the way that users interact with the applications.

The Navigation Keys option has two navigation options: Windows-Compatible and DOS-Compatible. This command corresponds to SET KEYCOMP. Some examples of differences between Windows and DOS navigation appear in Table 1.16.

Table 1.16 Differences Between DOS and Windows Compatible Modes

Windows	DOS	Function/Action
Enter	Ctrl+Enter	Selects the default button in a dialog box
Alt+letter	Single letter	Accesses keys for controls
Spacebar, Alt+Up Arrow, Alt+Down Arrow	Enter or spacebar	Opens a combo box that has focus
Up, Down Arrow	Tab	Moves between a group of option buttons
Selected	Not Selected	Status of browse field upon entry into cell

The Fill New Records With Current Values option tells Visual FoxPro to carry forward all fields from the current record to a new record. This feature has value if only a few fields change from one record to the next. This option corresponds to the SET CARRY command.

TIP SET CARRY includes a TO option that specifies which field values to carry forward. Often, this option is a better choice than carrying forward all fields.

When the user enters data in a field, Visual FoxPro automatically moves to the next field when it reaches the maximum number of characters for the current field. If SET BELL is ON, VFP beeps as it moves to the next field. If SET BELL is OFF, users have no warning that they are now in another field unless they are very observant. If you choose Enter or Tab to Exit Fields, you have the option to force users to press the Enter or Tab key to move from one field to the next

(SET CONFIRM). Although this option slows some data-entry people, it prevents them from accidentally writing data in the next field.

Projects Options

The Projects options pertain to features associated with using the Project Manager to maintain and compile applications. The page also includes options that affect the user of Visual Source Safe with VFP. The only two project-specific options are Project Double-click Action and Prompt for Wizards. Figure 1.24 displays this page of options.

FIGURE 1.24

The Projects page of the Options dialog box defines both Project Manager and Visual SourceSafe options.

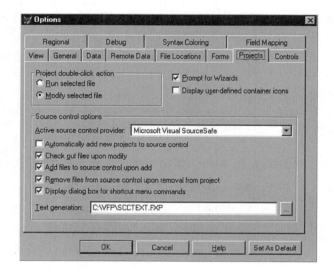

The first option determines the effect of double-clicking a filename in the Project Manager. Choose the Run Selected File option if you want to run a file when you double-click it in the Project Manager. Choose the Modify Selected File option to merely select the file for editing.

When checked, the second option—Prompt for Wizards—automatically asks whether you want to use a wizard when you are starting a new file from the Program Manager.

Display User-Defined Container Icons tells VFP to display the icons of user-defined containers in the Project Manager.

This page also contains the source-control options. If you have Microsoft Visual SourceSafe (VSS) installed, it appears in the combo box next to the Active source control provider text. Otherwise, <None> appears and all source-control options are inactive.

Visual SourceSafe provides the following advantages:

- Keeps developer teams in sync and tracks changes
- Prevents developers from overwriting one another's work
- Enables older versions of code to be reviewed and restored
- Maintains multiple branching versions of an application

Next are five check boxes that control a few of the features of Visual SourceSafe. The first check box, Automatically Add New Projects to Source Control, does exactly that. Usually, you want to make a conscious decision about when to add a project to VSS. (Simply open the project and choose Add Project to Source Control from the Project drop-down menu.)

The second option, Check Out Files Upon Modification, automatically calls up VSS when you click the Modify button in the Project Manager. Yes, Source Safe still prompts you to check out the file, but the menu comes up automatically and you need only click OK. Otherwise, you must manually check out the file before you attempt to open it; if you don't, the file will be opened as read-only. In either case, you will have to manually check the file back in after editing it.

The third option, Add Files to Source Control Upon Add, automatically puts new project files into VSS. Similarly, the fourth option, Remove Files From Source Control Upon Removal From Project, removes references to the file in VSS when you remove the file from the project. Notice that removing a file from a project does not delete it from disk; neither does it remove all references to the file from the VSS database.

The forth check box, Display Dialog Box for Shortcut Menu Commands, enables you to perform a VSS command from the project shortcut menu on multiple files.

The last option, Text Generation, identifies a file that stores integration information between VFP and VSS. Specifically, the file creates text representations of screen, menu, report, and label files. Currently, you might not have any other alternatives for this utility. Because the source code is provided, however, you can make modifications to the version supplied with VFP. In this case, you probably want to save your revision with a different name and, therefore, need to change the reference here.

Regional Options

Regional options your applications for local date, time, currency, and number conventions for international applications. If you click the first check box, Use System Settings, you cannot make any changes to the settings. Even if you need to make only one change, you must first deselect this box. Figure 1.25 shows the options available for Regional customization.

FIGURE 1.25

The Regional page of the Options dialog box defines formatting for dates and numbers.

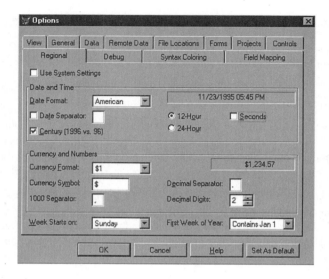

The first customization option, Date Format, controls the format that VFP uses to display the date and time. The default is American, but options exist for many other nations. There is even a difference between American and USA! (Hint: Watch the character between the month, day, and year.) You can even create and save your own custom format by following these steps:

1. Select the closest Date Format from the drop-down list.

2. To change the Date Separator, click the check box, and enter a new character.

3. To turn the display of the century on or off, click the Century check box appropriately. This being only a few short years from the turn of the century, however, you may want to begin writing applications with Century turned on.

4. To select either a 12-Hour or 24-Hour clock, click the appropriate button. Remember that the suffix AM or PM appears only when you are using the 12-hour clock.

5. To display seconds, make sure to check the Seconds check box.

For each of these changes, you should see the corresponding result on a sample date and time string in the upper-right corner of this area.

The Currency Format option places the currency symbol either before or after the number. You can set this option programmatically with SET CURRENCY LEFT¦RIGHT.

The Currency Symbol field defines the currency symbol. You can use any valid symbol in the current character set, including combinations of up to nine characters. You can set this option with SET CURRENCY TO.

The 1000 Separator symbol appears at every third digit on the left side of the decimal separator when this option is selected. The command SET SEPARATOR performs the same function in programs.

The Decimal Separator symbol separates the whole portion from the fractional portion of a number.

The Decimal Digits value defines the minimum number of decimal places used to show expression results. This value can range from 0 to 18. This option's function is equivalent to SET DECIMALS TO.

Additional options related to date determine the default week start day and the definition of what constitutes the first week of the year.

You can select any day of the week for the Week Starts On option.

The First Week of Year feature has three possible values:

- Contains Jan 1
- First 4-Day Week
- First Full Week

This information determines the value returned by WEEK(). WEEK() can override these default values.

Remote Data Options

The Remote Data options determine how Visual FoxPro establishes connections to remote data and works with remote data views. Figure 1.26 shows the available options.

FIGURE 1.26

The Remote Data page of the Options dialog box defines how Visual FoxPro establishes connections to remote data.

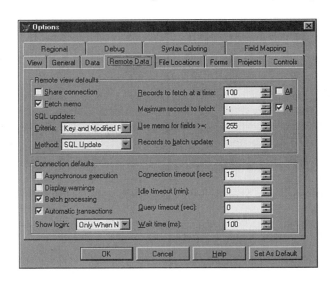

The first group of options establishes remote view defaults. A remote view is any data file that is not a Visual FoxPro table or database.

In many cases, a single remote ODBC connection enables you to open only a single view. By selecting Share Connection, however, you can open additional views.

Fetching memos across a remote connection can greatly increase network traffic. Therefore, VFP recommends selecting the option Fetch Memo, which retrieves the memo data only if the user activates the field.

Visual FoxPro provides several options for SQL updates. First are four Criteria options that determine whether VFP can update records in the source:

- Key Fields Only
- Key and Updatable Fields
- Key and Modified Fields
- Key and TimeStamp

These options determine conditions that enable SQL to succeed. This first one, for example, determines whether any of the key fields have changed in the source table since the data was retrieved. If so, the update fails.

The second SQL update option defines how to update the remote data. Visual FoxPro can perform a SQL Update on the selected records, or it can delete the old records and insert the modified ones by using the Method option.

The Records to Fetch at a Time option also limits traffic across a remote connection: It determines how many records to return from a query at one time. As you move through the records, the connection returns additional blocks of records until all records have been returned or you leave the view.

The Maximum Records to Fetch option places an upper limit on the total number of records returned by a query. You might want to consider using this option during testing, just in case your query incorrectly creates a Cartesian product view.

Some remote tables may support long character fields. The Use Memo for Fields >= option enables VFP to convert these long fields to memos automatically. Remember that a VFP character field supports a maximum 254 characters; therefore, 255 is a good default value for this option.

The Records to Batch Update option defines the number of records sent to the server in a single update statement. You can optimize network traffic if you batch multiple records in each update statement.

The Connection Defaults define how your application communicates with the remote data.

The Asynchronous Execution option determines whether control returns to your application immediately after it sends a SQL pass-through statement. In synchronous operation, control does not return until the entire result set is returned. In asynchronous execution, your application can do other things while it waits for the SQL to complete.

The Display Warnings option determines whether to display error messages during the processing of a remote SQL pass-through.

Batch Processing determines how to retrieve multiple result sets.

The Automatic Transactions option determines whether SQL transactions are handled automatically by Visual FoxPro or whether the application must include its own SQLCOMMIT() and SQLROLLBACK() functions.

Some servers require that the user log in before accessing the data. The Show Login option enables you to determine whether to show the login dialog box: always, never, or only when needed.

Connection Timeout specifies the number of seconds to wait for a connection to be recognized by the server.

Idle Timeout specifies the number of minutes that Visual FoxPro maintains the connection without activity. The default value, 0, requires that the application break the connection.

Query Timeout specifies how long (in seconds) Visual FoxPro waits for a result set to complete from a query before generating an error.

The Wait Time option specifies the number of milliseconds before Visual FoxPro checks to see whether the SQL statement has completed.

Syntax Coloring Options

The Syntax Coloring options enable you to change the colors used to display different types of text while you are working in the Visual FoxPro editor. The use of color makes your programs easier to read. You can to emphasize keywords, variables, or even comments in a different color to help them stand out. Figure 1.27 shows the options for syntax coloring.

FIGURE 1.27
Make your programs easier to read with syntax coloring.

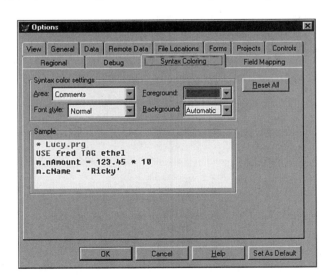

The types of text or Area that you can color include:

- Comments
- Keywords
- Literals
- Normal
- Operators
- Strings
- Variables

For each type of text, you can select a Font Style from the following:

- Automatic
- Normal
- Bold
- Italic
- Bold Italic

Finally, you can change the Foreground and Background colors of each text type. The drop-down list displays 16 possible colors, along with Automatic. To make your comments really stand out, for example, make them bold white text on a black or dark-blue background.

View Options

The View options determine how Visual FoxPro uses the status bar, if at all. These options also determine whether to display the recently used file list and whether VFP opens the last project automatically on startup. Figure 1.28 shows these options.

FIGURE 1.28

The View page of the Options dialog box defines several features of the status bar, as well as whether to track project use.

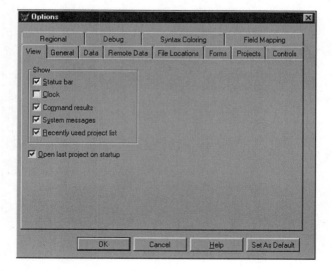

The Status Bar option controls whether to display the status bar, which appears at the bottom of the screen. When the status bar is not shown, FoxPro displays messages in Wait windows in the upper-right corner of the screen.

To continuously display a clock in the status bar, select the Clock option, which places the current system time in a fourth box at the right end of the status bar.

To display command results in the status bar, click the Command Results option. To see an example of a command result, open and pack a table. The messages in the status bar tell you how many records it has processed and the total number of records are command results. Indexing and reindexing also display messages as part of command results.

The System Messages option enables or disables the display of selected system messages. One example of a system message is Expression is Valid displayed by the Expression Builder when you validate an expression. Another example is the Attempting to lock... message that appears when VFP attempts to obtain a record or file lock in a shared environment. These messages appear in the status bar (when it is present) or in a wait window. This command corresponds to the SET NOTIFY command.

The Recently Used Project List option determines whether to display up to four recently used projects in the File menu.

The last option in this page—Open Last Project on Startup—tells Visual FoxPro to automatically open the last project used before exiting Visual FoxPro on startup the next time.

 T I P If you exit Options by clicking OK, the changes that you made affect only the current session. To make changes permanent, click the Set As Default option before you click OK.

If you hold down the Shift key while clicking OK, VFP writes the equivalent SET commands to the Command window. Copy the commands from this window and place them in your code to customize a program's properties.

Getting Help from Visual FoxPro

The last menu pad in the main menu is Help. You can active Help in four primary ways, two of which use this menu directly.

Microsoft Visual FoxPro Help Topics, which appears first in the Help menu, opens the main Help window. VFP uses a page frame type format to display three ways to select help topics. The first tab, Contents, provides an outline-like approach to navigating help by successively drilling down through more detailed levels.

N O T E Any time you press F1 with no text highlighted, VFP takes you to the Help Topics window.

The second page of the Help Topics page frame is labeled Index. This option requires a word or phrase that might appear in a help topic title. VFP uses this text string to search the available help topic titles, looking for a match. If VFP finds a match, it displays those topics.

The Find page of the Help Topics page frame lets you search by any keyword or phrase that might appear in the text of the help topics itself. This search requires more time, but it enables you to locate all topics that might use a specific word.

Direct commands provide another way to access help. If you need help on a specific command or function, enter the keyword HELP in the Command window, followed by the command or function, as in this example:

```
HELP AINSTANCE()
```

Finally, you can highlight a word in any text-edit window and press F1. VFP copies the word to the Search dialog box. If it matches a topic exactly, VFP immediately displays the topic. Otherwise, VFP pastes the word in the Search dialog-box string area and enables you to select an appropriate topic manually.

The following sections take a closer look at each of the methods.

Searching Help Via Contents

If you choose the Contents page from the Help Topics window, Visual FoxPro displays the top level of Visual FoxPro Help Contents. Figure 1.29 shows the initial screen.

FIGURE 1.29

The initial screen of the Visual FoxPro Help Contents shows four help categories.

This screen divides help into four topics:

- Glossary
- Language Reference
- Technical Reference
- Interface Reference

To open one of these topics, click the icon before the category name. Each topic can include additional topic levels. You can continue to drill down through the topics to find more specific information. Figure 1.30 shows the next help level that appears after you click the Language Reference icon.

FIGURE. 1.30

This figure shows the Language Reference topic open along with the Language Content topic showing the Language Reference A-Z topic.

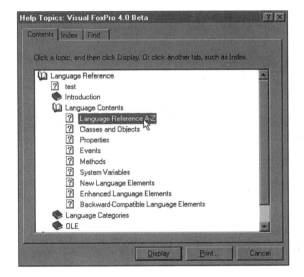

Language Reference consists of four subcategories, beginning with an introduction. Each subcategory is preceded by the icon of a closed book. To open the topic, double-click the book. There can also be books within books. When you reach the level of a document, the icon displays a page with a question mark on it. Double-clicking a page icon opens that specific help topic in a separate window.

Figure 1.31 shows that the Language Reference A-Z option displays a scrollable list of all commands, events, functions, and properties in Visual FoxPro. You can scroll through the list to find the command or function you want.

Notice the letter buttons at the top of the dialog box. Click one of these buttons to quickly move to the first command or function that begins with that letter. Suppose that you want to get more information on the command WEEK(). First, click the letter W to skip directly to commands and functions that begin with W. Next, scroll to WEEK() and click the function to display its help text. Figure 1.32 shows the help text for WEEK().

FIGURE 1.31

The Language Reference A-Z topic combines a scrolling list with command buttons to help you find a help topic.

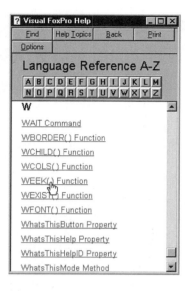

FIGURE 1.32

Help topics contain a brief description, syntax, return types, arguments, and remarks such as those shown for function WEEK( ).

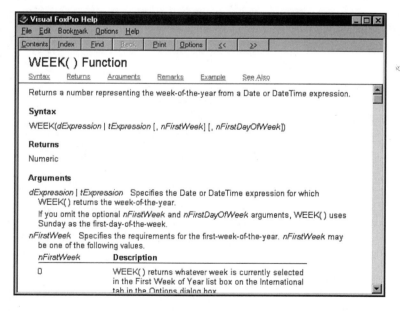

In any help dialog box, when you click green text with a solid underline, you jump to that topic immediately. Therefore, this type of text is called a *jump*. Green text with a dotted underline displays a pop-up window that defines the underlined term. A pop-up window can itself have green text with either solid or dotted underlines. To close a pop-up window, click anywhere outside it or press Esc.

Many help topics contain an option called See Also, which appears directly below the topic title. Click this option to display cross-referenced topics. Sometimes, you might not be sure exactly what command you need to look for. But by starting at a command or function that is closely related to the one that you want, you might find it by surfing through these cross-references.

Another common feature of most topics in the Language Reference is examples. If the current help topic contains examples, the word Example also appears in green immediately below the topic title. Click the green Example text string to see sample command lines or even a small program segment that illustrates the command's use. Figure 1.33 shows the examples provided for WEEK( ).

FIGURE 1.33

Most commands and functions include examples, like this one for function WEEK( ).

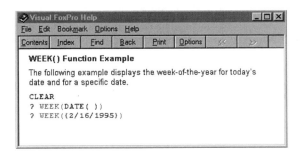

Notice that this window has both a menu with five options and a button bar with eight buttons. You can reach all the functions listed in the menu by using the buttons. Therefore, the following text reviews only the button options.

The button bar begins with the Contents button, which returns you to the Contents page of the Help Topics window. Similarly, the Index button corresponds to the second page of the page frame, and returns you to the alphabetical listing of all help topics, enabling you to jump to another topic easily. The Find button, corresponding to the third page of the page frame, enables you to refine your help search by entering one or more words related to the help topic that you want to find.

The Back option takes you back to help topics that you looked at previously; it does not make side trips to the Contents, Index, or Find page. To return to these pages, click their buttons directly. The Print option sends the text of the current help topic to your default printer. The << and >> buttons move you backward and forward alphabetically through the help topics.

The Options button opens another menu that contains a series of options. These options include one that enables you to Annotate the current help topic, which means that you can add your own notes to this help topic. Your annotations become associated with the topic, and any user who accesses this help file sees them as well. You can use this feature to further clarify the help text, provide your own examples, or even add references to your favorite FoxPro book.

The Copy option places a complete copy of the current help-topic text in the Clipboard; from there, you can paste it into another document. The Print Topic option provides another way to print the current topic text. Font enables you to change the font. If the current help font is too small to read, you can enlarge it. You can even make the font smaller if you want to see more of the text at one time and don't mind squinting.

N O T E   If you open an Example window, you must use the Options button in the button bar and choose Copy to place the example code into the Clipboard. From there, you can paste the code into a program file and test it. ▪

The Keep Help on Top option is useful if you want to keep an example (or perhaps the syntax) of a command on the screen while you return to the program and make your changes. Finally, you can set the colors to the help system or revert to the system colors with the Use System Colors option.

Searching for Help Via the Index

If you choose the Index from the Help Topics pageframe VFP displays a dialog that lets you enter the first few letters of the term for which you want to search. You can also use the list to select topics directly. Suppose that you want help on Create Classlib. Just enter **create classlib** in the first text box. (The search string is not case sensitive.) As you enter each letter, the list below the text box incrementally searches the help topics. The first letter, C, moves down the list to C. The second letter, R, moves further to CREATE. For the balance of the letters in the word create, the list does not change. But when you enter the c in classlib, the list moves again, this time to the topic CREATE CLASS. Only after you type the second L will the highlight move to the desired topic. For any search, you have to enter only enough characters to uniquely identify the topic; you do not have to complete the rest of the search string. You can also use the arrow keys or mouse to highlight the desired topic directly. Finally, click Display to show help on the highlighted topic. Figure 1.34 shows the screen just before it displays the topic.

The Index option only searches the help topic names. Sometimes, however, you might need to search for help but you don't know the topic name. In such a case, you want to search based on the help contents rather than the topic name. To do so, choose the Find page of the Help Topics window. Figure 1.35 shows how to search for help based on words contained in the help text rather than in the topic.

In this dialog box, you can enter a series of words in the first text box (numbered 1) to search for (trigger, in this example), or you can select words from a scrollable list (numbered 2). Notice that after you enter one or more words in the first text box, the second text box shows selected related words to narrow your search. The next list (numbered 3), at the bottom of the dialog box, shows the topics that contain the selected word or words. You can select these topics for display or fine-tune your search with additional words. A text field near the bottom of the dialog box shows the number of topics that currently match the search criteria.

FIGURE 1.34
Obtain help by performing a keyword search with Help's Index page, shown here finding the topic CREATE CLASSLIB.

FIGURE 1.35
Conduct a context search of help by using the Find options to locate all topics that contain selected words.

The Options button in this dialog box displays options that enable you to define how to conduct the search. Figure 1.36 shows these options.

FIGURE 1.36

Customize your context search by telling Help how to use the words and characters that you enter.

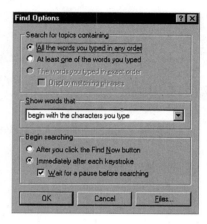

You can search for the following:

- Topics Containing All the Words You Typed in Any Order
- Topics Containing At Least One of the Words You Typed
- Topics Containing the Words You Typed in Exact Order

You also can search for topics that:

- Begin with the Characters You Type
- Contain the Characters You Type
- End with the Characters You Type
- Match the Characters You Type

Finally, you can have the search begin Immediately After Each Keystroke (incremental search) or After You Click the Find Now Button.

That is all you need to know to use Help effectively. After a little practice, you might find that you can get information from VFP's Help faster than you can from the manuals. ●

Introduction to Programming Concepts

What Is Programming?

Many years ago, when I encountered my first computer, the term "programming" had a very limited connotation. In fact, the word "computer" itself invariably evoked an image of a roomful of equipment set off in its own climate-controlled domain, surrounded by whirring tape drives and ablaze with flashing lights. Programming one of those iron workhorses meant setting out line after line of cryptic coded symbols in the mysterious act of communicating with the machine.

There was no GUI. The tools at that time were mainly of the hardware variety, such as keypunch machines to transform handwritten programs into machine-readable format and console dials to display and alter problematic memory locations. Debugging relied heavily on the primitive art of "desk-checking," a time-consuming but necessary evil in the days of 24-hour turnaround time. Programmers visually traced line by line through every branch of a program in order to exercise its logic and head off failures.

In the most general terms, *programming* means getting a machine to do what you want it to do. But the current computer scene is many magnitudes different from the early days of mainframes, having grown up in a variety of directions. Today's seemingly infinite combinations of hardware and software have produced correspondingly complex environments. As the selection of hard and soft components has broadened, so has the number of ways to accomplish that communication, and programming has come to mean many things to many people.

Some of the most casual computer users refer to using their employers' custom applications as "programming." Others use the term when they undertake a mail-merge operation through their word-processing program, or enter formulas into a spreadsheet, or design a building renovation using CAD. Macros and other scripting tools in some sophisticated programs enable the more adventuresome user to string together an intricate series of keystrokes and visual commands to perform a complicated task. In some cases, such as the Microsoft Office suite of applications, the system generates code from the user's macro entries. This Visual Basic for Applications (VBA) code can be displayed, saved as a program file, modified by the user, and rerun in its customized form. Examining code generated by tools is an excellent way to learn programming syntax.

In the world of Visual FoxPro, with its rich cache of development tools and apparently overwhelming choices of how to perform any particular task, there are also many different activities that can be classified as programming, a situation compounded by FoxPro's own evolution.

A Brief History of Visual FoxPro

In 1984, Fox Software introduced FoxBase to compete with the desktop database product it was modeled after, Ashton-Tate's dBASE II. At that time FoxBase was little more than a programming language and a data-handling engine. FoxPro acquired a GUI in 1989, and in 1991 took off solidly in its own innovative territory with the release of FoxPro 2.0. That product contained a fully integrated version of SQL, unequalled performance capabilities, open architecture in its development tools, and several design surfaces that actually generated code and applications from a user's onscreen manipulations.

FoxPro evolved into Visual FoxPro in 1995. It retained its procedural capabilities, primarily to maintain backward-compatibility, but added tremendously to its professional stature by becoming a fully realized object-oriented language as well. And, of course, there were still more development tools to work with! VFP is now in its third major release, version 6. Its outlook is very much expanded to encompass interaction with other major desktop and client/server products, and to build Web-based applications.

At the heart of all such activities, both in and out of the VFP environment, there is a type of interaction that goes back to the earliest days of computing. In the remainder of this chapter, you will explore what it means to produce your own programs using VFP elements and stylistic conventions.

Why Write Code?

Over the years, FoxPro has grown into Visual FoxPro, and each evolutionary step has enabled programmers to do more by simply and directly manipulating the tools supplied with the product. When you used FoxBase, you were responsible for coding everything, including your application's user interface. With FoxPro 2.0, you were given Power Tools that generated interface programs for you. Now there are wizards, builders, and design surfaces that mostly bypass code generation, but create a sophisticated interface for your applications nonetheless. You don't need to write much code at all.

So, before you get to the specifics of "how," let's address the issue of "why" you should learn to write programs:

- Generic interface components don't know your business rules. You need to add code at strategic points to customize an application to your requirements. You can make better use of the object model by understanding how and when to extend it with code.

- Code construction concepts apply to all forms of code packaging, whether a program of several printed pages or an object method of few lines.

- The tools themselves are written in code. Understand programming concepts, and you will better understand what is going on behind the scenes. As well, some of those tools are available as programs for you to examine, study, emulate, or even modify. For example, take a look at GenDBC.prg, found in the Tools\GenDBC\ subdirectory below your VFP home directory.

- Invariably you will reach the point where even the most powerful tools don't accomplish what you want. You can get around such weaknesses or holes with code. A good example of this is the View Designer, which shows you the SQL code generated from your selections. The View Designer covers a lot of bases, but sometimes you just can't get what you want without resorting to hand coding.

Learning to Program

One of the best ways to learn good programming practices is to find examples and study them. Well-commented, clearly laid out code will show you the possibilities.

The FoxPro line of development products has historically maintained an open architecture. Many of the tools that come with it are written in VFP's own language. When you use the design surfaces to build forms, classes, projects, reports, and database containers, the details of the entities you create are stored in VFP tables. Many developers use these programs and components as guidelines for their own programming efforts.

VFP 6 comes with a host of new tools beyond what was supplied in previous versions. Look for some of them in the subdirectories below the one in which VFP is installed, also known as HOME(). You can switch to it by simply typing **CD HOME()** in the Command window, or use the Windows Explorer to browse through the offerings. You should see subdirectories named Tools and Wizards, which contain many source items used to build the various applications.

N O T E   Visual FoxPro versions 3 and 5 came with wizards that generated application components to accomplish typical tasks. You could work with what the wizards created, but the wizards themselves were supplied in the form of compiled applications. In other words, you had no way of knowing *how* they worked their wizardry. In response to considerable outcry from the development community, Microsoft has supplied an even larger number of wizards with VFP 6 and a full set of source code for these and other tools. Look for a file named Xsource.zip in the subdirectory \Tools\Xsource\ under the VFP home directory. Unzip this file and use your software's option to maintain the directory structure in the zip file. This will enable you to view all of these programs, libraries, project files, and other components. ▪

As if this weren't enough, VFP 6 comes with a variety of samples that are enhanced to take advantage of this version's new features. The samples have been moved, along with the help files, into subdirectories of the MSDN Library that comes with Visual FoxPro. You can access information about the samples and utilities through the Help interface, as shown in Figure 2.1, or by typing **?HOME(2)** in the Command window to locate the path where you can find the files directly.

N O T E   The term "online help" takes on a whole new meaning with this release of VFP. Whether you purchase the standard, standalone development product or the entire Visual Studio suite, you receive a single-edition MSDN CD containing all the help files, samples, source, and additional support documentation for all the development tools. For a nominal yearly fee, you can become an MSDN Library subscriber and receive periodic updates. For free, you can access the MSDN Library contents by visiting Microsoft's new documentation Web site at msdn.microsoft.com (or go directly to the Visual FoxPro section at msdn.microsoft.com/vfoxpro). The Web site contains current technical and marketing product information for all the tools in Visual Studio, including samples, demos, and a considerable amount of downloadable resources. You will also find links to other sites relating to Visual FoxPro, third-party marketing sites, and independent support locations. ▪

Code Elements

Just as every spoken language contains nouns, verbs, adjectives, and syntax rules for putting them all together, so every computer programming language contains certain basic features. Visual FoxPro's language is no exception, and contains the following:

- Native commands and built-in functions to perform pre-defined actions.
- Literals and named constants that are used as-is in program operations.
- Memory variables and arrays to hold transient values of various types.
- Permanent data stored in tables, and the capability to perform I/O manipulations on these structures.
- Arithmetic operators to use with numbers, and string operators to manipulate character data.
- Logical evaluators to compare entities and select an appropriate response path.
- Looping constructs that specify conditions for repetitively running portions of code.
- Comments.
- Syntax, packaging rules, and construction principles that define how all the elements fit together.

Part
I
Ch
2

FIGURE 2.1
You can use the Help file to obtain information about the samples and utilities supplied with VFP. Click on the appropriate hyperlinks to either run or view source for the various applications.

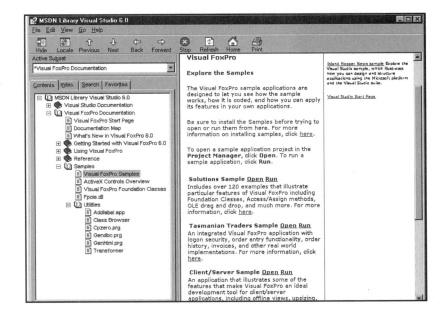

Commands and Functions

Visual FoxPro provides a rich supply of instructions to accomplish individual tasks. Each subsequent release of FoxPro since the earliest days of Xbase has aimed to maintain backward compatibility with previous versions. Consequently, the language has become "bloated" with commands that are infrequently used but require continued support only because their removal would break legacy code. And, of course, each new release adds exciting new features to the language.

Syntax   Documentation for all native VFP commands and functions is available in the Language Reference portion of the online Help file. Figure 2.2 shows the broad range of activities handled by the language components. To get to this view, select Help, Microsoft Visual FoxPro Help Topics from the system menu (or press F1) to bring up the new help file supplied on a separate CD, MSDN Library Visual Studio 6.0. In the left pane, drill down through Visual FoxPro Documentation, Reference, Language Overview, Language Categories, and through the list of command groups. Click on any category to display a list of instructions in the right-hand pane related by their intended use. Click on an individual command's hyperlink to reveal more detailed information about its syntax and use.

FIGURE 2.2

The numerous categories of commands appear on the left. Click individual instructions that appear on the right in order to view more detailed documentation about each command.

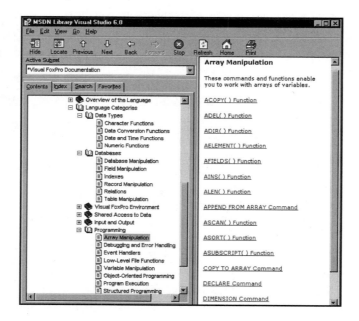

NOTE   The lists within each category are not exhaustive. The lists are a start, but check the alphabetical listing of the entire set if you don't find what you want in this breakdown.

If you know what instruction you want to use, you can go directly to its detailed description in various ways:

1. Look for the alphabetical list in the Help file's Language Reference.
2. Press F1, click Index, and type in the name you are looking for.
3. Simply type the name of the command you want to know about in the Command Window or any editing window, highlight it, and press F1.

TIP   The VFP color-coded program editor can provide unexpected visual cues to more information. For example, suppose you think you need to write a function to accomplish a task you don't know is covered in the native language. If you type a name for it and notice it change from standard black to the color of a keyword, you've stumbled over a resource you might not have to re-create! Highlight it and press F1 for more information.

However you arrive at it, you must follow the syntax exactly. VFP provides many options for issuing and using instructions, but it expects precision in terms of spelling, arrangement of parameters, and punctuation between clauses and lists.

N O T E   Since its earliest days, FoxPro has followed the Xbase convention that enables you to reduce keywords to their initial four letters. This feature was easier to count on with the limited command set of older versions, but it continues to be a handy convenience, especially when typing in the Command window. You can type your programs this way too, but be forewarned that programs in this format can be hard to follow. Not only must you unravel the logic of a routine, but you might first have to translate each four-letter root into its expanded keyword.

Moreover, Visual FoxPro now includes so many more built-in language components than in earlier versions that it has become impossible to ensure uniqueness of those first four letters in all cases. Obviously, VFP must recognize a command before it can run it, which means you might have to type more than four letters to achieve significance. ■

VFP is not case sensitive. Typically, developers adhere to their own standards, or those of their employers, to differentiate between VFP keywords and user-supplied options. While some developers type everything in lowercase so that they don't have to be bothered with the Shift key at all, many follow the practice of coding keywords in all uppercase, using mixed case for user-defined functions, filenames, variables, and so on. This is strictly a readability convention, as there are no restrictions within the language itself that dictate such rules. The same is true of blank lines and spaces. Within a program, one space is the same as several spaces between words, and many blank lines are no different from one blank line. The best practice is to use plenty of blank space and indentations to produce source code that is easy to read and therefore easy to maintain.

Behavior   *Commands*, like direct orders, are words grouped together to instruct the computer to take an action. Visually, they differ from functions, which are also computer instructions, in that functions end in a pair of parentheses. The parentheses can be empty or they can contain any parameters recognized by that function. Traditionally, a function returns a result, and that result is available at the point where the function call is made, as shown in this example:

```
ldDate = DATE()
```

In this line of code, the variable `ldDate` contains today's date after the function executes.

There are various ways to issue a function call:

■ Include a function call in an assignment, which is then available for further use by your program.
```
lnStart = SECONDS()              && Number of seconds since midnight
     < Other program commands >
lnDuration = SECONDS() - lnStart    && Calculate elapsed time
```

- Embed it in a logical test.

```
IF TABLEUPDATE()
    < Some processing if function was successful >
ENDIF
```

- Make it the object of a command of some sort.

```
?SEEK(lcRecord, lcTable, lcIndex)     && Display results of search
```

- Nest it within another function call.

```
lnCurentMonth = MONTH( DATE() )
```

- Precede it with an equal sign.

```
=ASORT(laArray)     && Sort an array
```

- Make an unadorned function call.

```
ADIR(laFiles, '*.PRG')     && Create array, one entry per program file
```

NOTE Sometimes you don't care what the return value is. You want a function to perform simply as a command, and you're willing to accept its default behavior. Unadorned function calls, which didn't exist prior to VFP 5.0, can apply to native functions, user-defined functions, and object methods. ■

Literals and Constants

The simplest form of information you can use in your code is unvarying data that you supply directly to your routines. A value that is coded into the routine that uses it is taken literally and thus is called a *literal*. For example:

```
lnWeeks = lnDays / 7                    && The number of days in a week is always 7
MessageBox('Processing Complete')       && The message is always the same
lnElapsed = DATE() - {06/01/1998}       && The start date remains the same
DIMENSION aArray[15,3]                  && The size of this array is fixed
```

If you assign a name to a literal, it becomes a *constant*. All references to that name in your code will be replaced by the value you supply. If you need to change the value, you only have to change it in one place, where the assignment is made, as shown in this example:

```
lnEmployeeCount = 53
    <Some processing>

FOR lnI = 1 TO lnEmployeeCount
    <Print invitations to the company picnic>
ENDFOR
```

TIP It's not a good idea to embed literals throughout your programs, particularly if there's the slightest chance that these values can change. Name them descriptively as constants and place them prominently in your code, usually in the beginning, for easier maintenance. Better yet, find a central place to store constants that pertain to your application. You can read such constants out of a data table or locate them in object properties.

Runtime Versus Compile Time   Constants can be assigned at runtime, as shown in the previous example, or at compile time with #DEFINE directives, such as the following:

```
#DEFINE ZERO 0.
```

Groups of #DEFINE statements can be maintained in a separate #INCLUDE file that you add to the beginning of your programs. Memory usage is reduced somewhat because the substitution is made during compilation, and resources are immediately released. This can, arguably, increase performance because the named constants don't need to stay in memory and references have already been resolved by the time they are encountered.

Part
I
Ch
2

Memory Variables

It's not always reasonable to expect to know ahead of time all the values that you want your code to use. Just as in an algebraic expression, you can assign a name to a value and then use that name as a stand-in for the actual value anywhere in your program code.

The simplest way to assign a value to a name is with the equal sign (=). You can also use STORE SomeValue TO SomeName. This syntax is convenient when you want to assign a single value to many variables at once:

```
STORE 0 TO lnOne, lnTwo, lnThree, lnFour, lnFive
```

Data Types   Visual FoxPro enables you to manage a rich assortment of data types in memory.

In VFP, a variable takes on the characteristics of the data it contains. If x = 5, x is a numeric variable. If the value of x is changed so that x = 'ABC', the variable's type is also changed to character. Furthermore, a variable that hasn't been established in any formal way is simply created the first time you refer to it by assigning it a value.

This chameleon-like quality of VFP variables is known as *weak-typing*, a distinguishing characteristic of the language that is not universally shared. Other languages, such as C++, require that you declare variables before you use them and that you identify and stick to their assigned data type.

> **CAUTION**
>
> Weak-typing can get you in trouble in your programs. Commands and functions expect to find data in a particular form. If you refer to a variable of the wrong type, as shown in Figure 2.3, your code will generate an error.

FIGURE 2.3
Even though the value of x is 4, it's in character form, not numeric as the square root function expects it to be.

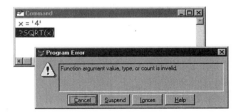

N O T E   Prior to VFP 6, the only sure way to determine a variable's current type was to test it with the TYPE() function. Unfortunately, the syntax for this function causes untold confusion.

The argument you pass to TYPE() within the parentheses must be a character expression. This means that you pass the *name* of the variable surrounded by quotes, not the variable itself. If you are passing an expression or a literal, it must also be in quotes. It is very easy to get "U" (for undefined) or an error message returned from the TYPE() function.

VFP 6 has a new and very welcome VARTYPE() function that is much more straightforward. You simply pass the variable, data, or expression you are interested in, and the return value is its current type. ▨

Scope   *Scope* refers to the life span and visibility of a variable. Variables can be

- Public
- Private
- Local

Public variables, also known as *global variables*, can be seen and used in any routine during the current VFP session. They remain in memory until they are released or until VFP terminates.

N O T E   Traditionally one program passed information to others via global variables. These might include logical flags indicating that certain processes had finished, so it was okay for something else to start. Now that VFP provides an object-oriented environment, many developers prefer to pass object references instead of memory variables because an object can contain a whole range of related data and behavior in its packaging. See Part IV, "Object-Oriented Programming," for more information on how this is accomplished. ▨

Private variables existin the current program. They are automatically released when the current program terminates if they haven't been specifically released before then. Private variables are also visible to any routines called by this one, which can lead to confusion in the called routine if it has its own variables with the same name. If no other declaration is made about a variable's type, VFP assumes that it is private.

Local variables have been around since VFP 3, and they only exist in the current routine. If a variable is local to an object method or other subroutine, it is released when the routine finishes.

TIP   Subroutines should declare all their variables as local in order to guard against using an unintended variable from a higher level program. This is done with a statement like this:

```
LOCAL lcName, lnNumber, ldDate
```

CAUTION

Explicit declarations of scope do not create variables or guarantee data type. PUBLIC gcPubVar, PRIVATE pnNumVar, and LOCAL ldDateVar only establish the intended life span of those variables once they are created. Until values are assigned, the variable type remains undefined, regardless of scope.

Arrays An *array* is a group of memory variables maintained as a unit. It can be visualized as a spreadsheet, where horizontal rows intersect with vertical columns at individual points called *cells*, and each cell can hold a piece of information. In fact, each cell can hold information of a different type from that of its neighboring cells.

Arrays are akin to data tables, with which they share terminology. Table records are sometimes called *rows*, table fields are referred to as *columns*, and the many fields in a given record can be of mixed types.

Of course, tables are permanent representations of data that can be used from session to session, whereas arrays are more like variables in that they remain in memory for the duration of their processing life, and then they are released. While an array is in scope, you can access any single cell of data by its row and column numbers, like this:

```
laPayment[1,5] = laPayment[1,3] * lnRate     && Multiply hours x Rate for this
entry
```

N O T E Notice in the preceding line of code that the array coordinates are set off between square brackets ([ ]). This is not a requirement, as parentheses could just as easily be used for the same purpose. Many developers use brackets, however, to distinguish array cell references from function calls. ▪

Arrays are very handy constructs for preparing intermediate results in the course of a routine. Because they remain entirely in memory, access is very fast. VFP has many native array-handling functions that are very efficient at filling, searching, sorting, and arranging data in arrays.

Naming Conventions Because of the confusion that can arise when a routine uses data of the wrong type or references a variable that has gone out of scope, many developers have adopted the recommended practice of embedding scope and type information into variable names. Typically a two-letter, lowercase prefix is concatenated to a descriptive name, such as lcStudentID, pdToday, or glOkToContinue. The prefix letters and their meanings are listed in Table 2.1.

Table 2.1 Typical Prefixes for Variable Naming Conventions

Scope (First Letter)

Letter	Meaning
l	Local

continues

Table 2.1   Continued

Scope (First Letter)

Letter	Meaning
p	Private
g	Public (global)
t	Parameter

Type (Second Letter)

Letter	Meaning
a	Array
c	Character
y	Currency
d	Date
t	Datetime
b	Double
f	Float
l	Logical
n	Numeric
o	Object
U	Unknown

Indirect Referencing and Macro Expansion   So far, you've looked at instructions and memory resident data. You've learned that commands and functions pose direct instructions to the computer and pass arguments that are actual pieces of information or named variables that stand in for data.

Some commands, particularly those that work with data in tables, expect names as arguments: names of tables, names of fields, names of reports. Names aren't subject to assignment in the same way that data can be assigned to a variable name. Yes, you can populate a variable with a name, but then it is simply a character string that has lost its inherent meaning.

Indirect referencing enables you to issue commands using names that vary. For example, you might read the name of the current backup file out of a field in a system table. In your program, you then surround that name with parentheses to indicate that the character string actually represents a name of another entity, and it's that other entity you want to reference:

```
lcFileName = System.Backup
USE (lcFileName) IN 0 ALIAS Backfile
```

You can take the issue of indirection a step further. Sometimes you are not even sure what *instructions* you want to run. In that case, you can extend the power of the VFP language by building strings of commands, clauses, and other reserved keywords, and then use them as if they were written into your program.

To accomplish this feat, you use a technique called *macro expansion*. Simply add an ampersand (&) to the front of a variable name, which signals to VFP that the literal contents of the variable should become part of the current execution string. The following is a simple example that shows how this feature works. Type it in the Command window and press F9:

```
x = "ON KEY LABEL F9 WAIT WINDOW 'I pressed F9' "
&x
```

Macro expansion is often used to restore environment settings at the end of a routine in which they have been changed. For example:

```
lcTalk = SET( 'TALK' )        && Capture the setting of TALK
SET TALK ON
SELECT * FROM MyDBF ;
    WHERE < criteria >
SET TALK &lcTalk              && Restore TALK the way it was before
```

Data Fields

Data that is kept in a table is subject to more rigorous identification than data in memory variables. Each field in the table has a fixed size and data type. Further, if the table is part of a database, there can be rules set up in database stored procedures that monitor values, conditions of uniqueness, and relationships with other tables.

Because data fields are limited to some predefined presentation, it is not as important to impose naming conventions on them. A data field of numeric type will not accept characters, for example. A logical field can only accept values of .T. (True) or .F. (False), no matter what you might try to enter instead. Field characteristics are stored in the table header and are available to the application on request.

See Part II, "Working with Data," for more information about data in tables and databases.

Comments

A comment line is one that starts with an asterisk (*) or the word NOTE. You can also add comments to any line of code by skipping at least one space and typing two ampersands (&&). Everything from the ampersands to the end of the line is considered a comment and is ignored by VFP.

Even though they are not compiled or run, comments serve a very important purpose in programming. Code can be very complex. Once it is written and in use, a program might not be looked at for months. Frequently the only reason to go back through a working program is that some new set of circumstances has caused it to fail. Code that is difficult to read is even more difficult to fix and maintain. Liberal additions of comments that spell out a routine's intended behavior make the task much easier for whoever has to pick up the logical threads. You will appreciate the effort even if it is your own code you are reviewing.

It is also a very good idea to place a heading of comment lines at the beginning of your coded routines. You might include such things as program author, creation date, purpose, expected output, parameter identification, and calling syntax. Many development shops set a standard look for such headers, which then serve as part of the overall project documentation.

Operators

VFP supplies a full set of symbol *operators* that manipulate data according to its type. The operations can be strung together to form complex expressions, but all data within such an expression must be of the same type. Some of the symbols produce different behaviors for different data types, as shown in Tables 2.2 through 2.5.

> **N O T E** Each table's set of symbols is presented in the priority order in which they are evaluated within an expression. It is the same concept that you learned in high school math: My Dear Aunt Sally stood for Multiplication, Division, Addition, Subtraction. ■

Table 2.2 Character String Operators

Operator	Action
+	Concatenates two character values.
-	Concatenates, while removing trailing blanks from the first value.
$	Searches for one character string within a second.

Table 2.3 Arithmetic Operators

Operator	Action
( )	Groups values to increase execution priority
**, ^	Exponentiation
*	Multiplication
/	Division
%	Modulus (remainder from division)
+	Addition
-	Subtraction

Table 2.4 Logical Operators

Operator	Action
()	Groups values to increase execution priority

Operator	Action
NOT, !	Logical negative; reverses an item's value
AND	Logical AND
OR	Logical inclusive OR

Table 2.5 Date Math Operators

Operator	Action
+	Addition (produces a date in the future)
-	Subtraction (calculates duration)

Evaluators

VFP uses a set of symbols, listed in Table 2.6, to evaluate the logical truth of an expression. These symbols, also known as *relational operators*, compare two values of the same type, resulting in a value of .T. if true or .F. if false.

Table 2.6 Logical Evaluators

Symbol	Comparison
<	Less than
>	Greater than
=	Equal to
<>, #, !=	Not equal to
<=	Less than or equal to
>=	Greater than or equal to
==	Exact string comparison

Conditional Execution

You won't always want your code to run every line for every condition. The power of programming languages comes from the capability to decide whether a particular action is appropriate to each and every different type of data or some other environmental circumstance. In VFP, you use these constructs to determine whether to proceed with one or another set of options:

- Use IF...ENDIF for one or two options. You can nest IF statements, but this can result in unwieldy levels of complexity.

```
IF lnAge > 10
```

```
            IF lnAge > 15
                IF llAllRequirementsFilled
                    < Schedule graduation >
                ELSE
                    < Schedule counseling >
                ENDIF
            ELSE
                < Schedule a particular test >
            ENDIF
    ELSE
        < Schedule a practice session >
    ENDIF
```

■ A single IIF() (Immediate IF) function is permissible in place of the IF...ENDIF construct, and is particularly useful when you are restricted to one line, such as in a report, label, or SQL statement. You supply three parameters to IIF(): a logical expression to test, an action to take if the expression evaluates to true, and an action to follow if the expression is false. As with IF...ENDIF, you can nest IIF() statements. Be forewarned that such complexity can be *very* difficult to debug.

```
lcGrade = IIF(lnGPA > 2.0, 'Passed', 'Failed')
lcMaritalStatus = IIF(UPPER(lcCode) = 'M', 'Married', ;
IIF(UPPER(lcCode) = 'D', 'Divorced', ;
IIF(UPPER(lcCode) = 'S', 'Single', 'Unknown') ) )
```

■ To evaluate a series of mutually exclusive conditions and specify different actions for each, use DO CASE...ENDCASE.

```
DO CASE
    CASE lnGroupSize < 10
        lnRate = lnFullRate
    CASE lnGroupSize < 25
        lnRate = lnFullRate * ln1stDiscount
    OTHERWISE
        lnRate = lnFullRate * ln2ndDiscount
ENDCASE
```

Loops

Looping constructs are special types of commands that divert program execution from its straight-line path. Loops enable you to specify some logical condition that determines whether to repeat a selected set of instructions or continue with the processing stream beyond the loop.

A loop consists of a pair of commands that bracket a coded routine. A condition is tested at the beginning of the loop, and if it evaluates to true, the subsequent instructions are run; otherwise, control continues after the END statement. VFP offers the following ways to execute loops:

■ DO WHILE...ENDDO   The condition included on the first line is evaluated. If it is true, VFP runs through the subsequent code. Whenever execution reaches ENDDO, VFP reevaluates the initial expression. As long as the condition remains true, the same set of instructions will be run over and over again.

```
DO WHILE lnNumEnrolled < lnMaxSize
    < Continue enrolling students until the class is full >
ENDDO
```

- SCAN…ENDSCAN   This command construct is used to process an entire data file. When VFP encounters ENDSCAN, control returns to the top of the loop, where it tests for an end-of-file condition. As long as the implied !EOF() condition remains true, each record in turn is subjected to the code that follows. Additional conditions can be applied by including FOR and/or WHILE clauses:

```
SCAN FOR Employee.Status = 'Active'
    < Processing applies only to current employees >
ENDSCAN
```

- FOR…ENDFOR   VFP can be instructed to run through a loop a certain number of times. Use fixed values, variables, or expressions to determine the number of iterations of the loop:

```
For lnI = 1 TO ALEN(aVendors, 1)
    < Write checks for each of the vendors in the array >
ENDFOR
```

- A VFP variant: FOR EACH…ENDFOR   This loop can be applied to every item in an array or in a VFP collection, without having to know how many items meet the existence test. This example looks at each column in turn, regardless of how many there are in the grid, and increases its size:

```
FOR EACH oColumn IN THIS.oGrid.Columns
    oColumn.Width = oColumn.Width * 1.25
    oColumn.Text1.Width = oColumn.Width
ENDFOR
```

All of these looping mechanisms enable you to use a LOOP or an EXIT command to escape processing before reaching the END statement. LOOP sends you back to the top to reevaluate the continuation condition. EXIT takes program control beyond the end of the loop to the remainder of the program. See Chapter 23, "Error Detection and Handling," for more information about loops.

Code Packaging

You can enter and run lines of code in the VFP Command window. In earlier versions of FoxPro, you could only enter a single line of code at a time followed by a press of the Enter key. Certain coding constructs that require multiple lines, such as IF…ENDIF or DO…ENDDO, could not be run in the Command window because the Enter key also acted as a signal to run whatever was typed.

In VFP, this limitation has been lifted. You can enter as many lines of code as you want and use the mouse or keyboard arrow keys to reposition the cursor. When you're done, highlight all the lines you typed and press Enter, or right-click the mouse and choose Execute Selection. The entire block runs as if it were a single line of code.

Running code in the Command window is a good way to test that it performs as you expect it to and to work out any kinks. If you want to be able to run it again without typing it every time, you must save the code block in a file as a program, procedure, function, or method.

Program Files

A VFP *program* is simply a text file with a .PRG extension. You create such a file when you type **MODIFY COMMAND** in the Command window. VFP opens an editing window with the default name Program1.prg. You have the option of changing that name when you save the file for the first time, or you can choose File, Save As from the system menu. If you type **MODIFY COMMAND MyProg**, VFP will first look for a program named MyProg.prg in its path. If it finds the file, VFP opens it for editing. If it doesn't find a match, it opens a new empty window with that name.

TIP Remember that because you can abbreviate most VFP instructions to four characters, you can type **MODI COMM** to accomplish the same thing as **MODIFY COMMAND**.

Now that you have an open window, enter your program, one instruction per line. It improves program readability to keep lines of code to a length that is viewable on a computer screen or a printed page. If one line isn't enough to complete an instruction, VFP enables you to continue onto the next line by typing a semicolon (;) at the end of the current line. Program readability is more than a stylistic concern. You will find that your programs are easier for you and others to maintain if you format them simply and clearly and keep a minimal amount of information on each line.

After you enter all required lines of source code into your program, you can direct VFP to convert it into object code by selecting Program, Compile from the menu. This step is not required, however, because VFP will compile it when it needs to—for example, when you type **DO MyProg** in the Command window. Regardless of when the program is compiled, VFP creates an .FXP file of the same name (MyProg.fxp) in the same directory where it finds the .PRG file (MyProg.prg).

TIP VFP bases its decision to compile on DOS file dates. Unless you issue a specific directive to compile, VFP will not recompile if it finds an .FXP file that is newer than the .PRG file of the same name in the same directory. This can lead to confusion over which version of code you are running. It is always safe to delete any questionable .FXP files and let VFP recompile what it needs.

For purposes of compiling or running code, VFP assumes that anything it finds in a program file is program code, with the exception of comments.

CAUTION

If a comment line ends in a semicolon, VFP treats the following line as a continuation of the comment, even if the next line doesn't begin with an asterisk. VFP continues to concatenate lines as long as it encounters semicolons, excluding more code than you might intend, as shown in the following code sample:

```
SET PATH TO
* I've changed the first line of the SET PATH statement,
* but I want to save it so I can change it back.
* SET PATH TO \olddata, \oldlibs, ;
```

```
SET PATH TO data, libs, ;
     progs, include, ;
     graphics, menus, ;
     metadata, reports
DO MyProg      && VFP will not be able to find progs\MyProg.prg
```

Procedures and Functions

By definition, a program file is a standalone .PRG file. There are no other special directives to identify it as such. A program file, however, can contain subroutines known as *procedures* and *functions* that you can run from within or outside your program. Functions are also known as *UDFs*, or *user-defined functions*. Subroutines can be packaged with other commonly used routines into a procedure file that makes no pretense of being anything more than a container. Such a file can be identified by a .PRC or .PRG extension.

A procedure is a routine in which the first and last lines are defined as follows:

```
PROCEDURE ProcedureName
     <your code lines>
ENDPROC
```

Likewise, a function is a coded routine bracketed by FUNCTION...ENDFUNC commands.

> **N O T E** ENDPROC and ENDFUNC can be replaced with RETURN, but any of the three are strictly for
> readability. You actually don't need to enter any type of terminating command, because VFP
> will recognize the end of the routine when it encounters an end of file or the start of another PROCE-
> DURE or FUNCTION. ▪

Typically, you execute a procedure the same way you would a program: via DO ProcedureName or DO ProcedureName IN ProgramName. A function call looks different. You simply type the function name followed by a set of parentheses:

FunctionName ( )

Program Flow At runtime, program instructions are executed line by line, one after another, except in the case of subroutines. When your program encounters an instruction to run a procedure or a function, it's as if all the lines of code in that routine were inserted immediately after your call. This is true whether the subroutine is in the same or a different file. At the completion of the subroutine code, execution continues at the line following the call, as shown in this example:

```
* This is the main program.
ACTIVATE SCREEN
?'Executing main program code.'
DO Proc1
?'Back in the main program after Proc 1'
x = Func1()
?'x = ' + x
?'Remaining program statements go here.'
RETURN
```

```
PROCEDURE Proc1
    ?'Executing 1st line of subroutine: Proc1'
    ?'Executing 2nd line of subroutine: Proc1'
ENDPROC

FUNCTION Func1
    LOCAL lcReturnVal
    ?'Executing subroutine code: Func1'
    lcReturnVal = 'Character string prepared in Func1'
RETURN lcReturnVal
```

You can place as many procedures and/or functions as you want within a single file, but they must all appear after the last line of your main program. Don't type any lines of main program code following the subroutines, as they will never be reached at runtime.

What's the Point?   You might be asking: If a subroutine is executed as if it were an inline part of the main program, why bother with moving it off to another location?

Subroutines add power and flexibility to a program. Name them descriptively, pass them parameters, and you can do any of the following:

- Rerun the same routine many times without recoding.
- Run the same routine from different parts of the program, or even from different programs.
- Expect different results based on variable information passed in to the routines in the form of parameters.
- Maintain an uncluttered, readable main program that clearly outlines the major steps without getting bogged down in detail.

What's the Difference?   Up to now I've talked about procedures, functions, and subroutines as if they were all the same. So, what is the difference? The simple answer is that conceptually there is no difference! They are all just routines subordinate to a program with many variations in how you can interact with them.

By convention, a function returns a value (but it doesn't have to) and a procedure probably does not return anything (but it can). After the first line, the differences are so easily overridden as to be academic. The major difference is that procedures and functions make different default assumptions about the nature of parameters passed to them. But again, these default assumptions are easily changed to suit your needs.

Even the different calling styles for procedures and functions are not hard-and-fast rules. You can run a function as if it were a procedure:

```
DO FunctionName
```

And you can call a procedure as you would a function, via assignment to a variable:

```
lcVar = ProcedureName()
```

Passing Parameters   Much of a subroutine's power comes from being able to perform actions on a variety of data. If you want the calling program to supply information for use in the subroutine, the first non-comment line of code after PROCEDURE or FUNCTION must be

PARAMETERS or LPARAMETERS. LPARAMETERS, like the LOCAL declaration itself, specifies that the scope is local to the subroutine. Parameters can be any type of data or expressions, up to 27 in a single routine.

By default, parameters are passed to a procedure by reference and to a function by value. *By reference* means that the subroutine receives a pointer to the actual variable. Any changes the subroutine makes are applied directly to the original. *By value* means that the subroutine sees a copy of the original variable. Its value at the time it is passed can be used in the subroutine, but the original remains intact in the calling program.

It's easy to override default parameter-passing behavior:

- SET UDFPARMS TO VALUE or SET UDFPARMS TO REFERENCE
- Surround a variable with parentheses (by value)
- Preface a variable with an at sign (@) (by reference)

Object Methods

Methods are simply a form of object-oriented packaging for subroutines. Methods use the same code construction principles as always, but the execution of that code is timed to coincide with an event that a particular object senses and responds to. You can find out more about the object model and adding method code to objects in Chapter 9, "Creating Forms," Chapter 15, "Creating Classes with Visual FoxPro," and Chapter 17, "Advanced Object-Oriented Programming."

The principal distinguishing characteristic of method code is the means by which it is fired. You run a method by entering its name as a command any place that you can enter program instructions. The name of the method must be fully qualified by the entire object hierarchy that defines its location. For example:

```
THISFORM.pgfPageFrame.Page1.cntPageObj.cntMover.cmdMoveButton.Click()
```

Although parentheses are not required, many developers usually follow a method name with a set of parentheses to identify it as a routine rather than object property.

Methods are not as universally available within an application as programs and subroutines tend to be. Access to a method is restricted by runtime conditions: Has the object been instantiated? Is there an available object reference? Is the method hidden or protected? The chapters in Part IV, "Object-Oriented Programming," explain how to gain access to method code.

As with other types of subroutines, you can pass parameters to a method, and you can expect it to pass back its results.

SQL Versus Procedural Code

SQL is not new to VFP. One of FoxPro's major strengths, early on and all along, has been its subset of SQL code fully integrated into the language. You can find out more about the commands and their syntax from the VFP help system and from the chapters of this book that deal with the Query and View Designers: Chapter 6, "Creating Basic Queries," Chapter 7, "Advanced Queries and Views," and Chapter 8, "Accessing Remote Data." After you start using the actual builders, you will continue to learn the nuances of SQL because the design surfaces generate and display code in response to your entries.

Anything you can imagine doing to data in tables can be accomplished via procedural code. Procedural code works on data one record at a time, and requires that your programs handle all the necessary I/O.

SQL, on the other hand, delivers a set of data that meets conditions you specify in a single command. Admittedly, that command can potentially contain a very complex arrangement of clauses. Given the right set of conditions, however, VFP is free to optimize its access to the data. All I/O is handled behind the scenes. The process can be lightening fast.

New in VFP 6

This section is not intended to be an exhaustive list of new features in Visual FoxPro 6. Look for information on new Access and Assign methods in Chapter 9, "Creating Forms," and Chapters 15–17 on class creation and management. See also Chapter 19, "The Visual FoxPro Component Gallery," and Chapter 18, "The Visual FoxPro Foundation Classes." Chapter 23, "Error Detection and Handling," talks about the enhanced Coverage Profiler application. And Part V, "COM," deals with many of the new interoperability features.

In terms of the VFP programming language, there are minor enhancements throughout that support the other new features. This mainly amounts to new clauses for existing commands and new properties, events, and methods in support of such features as OLE Drag and Drop, Active Document Applications, Coverage.app, and the new ProjectHook class.

There are some new and enhanced functions as well:

- AGETCLASS(), AVCXCLASSES(), and COMCLASSINFO() create arrays of class information.
- ALINES() parses lines from character and memo fields into an array; FILETOSTR() and STRTOFILE() convert files into character strings, and vice versa.
- AMOUSEOBJ() creates an array of mouse pointer information.
- GETHOST() and ISHOSTED() return information about the host of an Active Document.
- INDEXSEEK() performs a SEEK into an indexed table without moving the record pointer.
- NEWOBJECT() creates an object directly from the class library (.VCX file) in which it resides. Prior to this version, the only available function for object instantiation was CREATEOBJECT(). CREATEOBJECT() is still available, but it requires that the class library already be loaded in memory via a command such as SET CLASSLIB TO MyLib.vcx ADDITIVE.
- VARTYPE() identifies an expression's data type directly.
- HOME(2) points to the directory where VFP samples are loaded.
- TRANSFORM() now enables you to omit a format code and use a default supplied by the function.
- COMPILE DATABASE now automatically packs memo fields.

- CREATE FORM now enables you to specify a form or formset other than the default base class.
- Several handy functions from the separate Foxtools.fll library are now supported as native functions, as described in Table 2.7.

Table 2.7   Foxtools.fll Functions Added to VFP 6

Function	Description
ADDBS()	Adds a backslash to a path.
DEFAULTEXT()	Adds an extension if there is none.
DRIVETYPE()	Identifies drive type.
FORCEEXT()	Changes filename to include new extension.
FORCEPATH()	Changes filename to use new path.
JUSTDRIVE()	Returns the drive letter from a filename.
JUSTEXT()	Returns only the extension from a filename.
JUSTFNAME()	Returns only the filename, without extension.
JUSTPATH()	Returns only the path from a filename.
JUSTSTEM()	Reduces filename to first eight characters.

Part

I

Ch

2

PART

II

Working with Data

Defining Databases, Tables, and Indexes

Creating Tables for an Application

Suppose that you want to track orders for a small business. After thinking about what information you collect when taking an order, you might create the following initial information list:

- Order date
- Customer name
- Customer address
- List of items purchased
- Quantity of each item purchased
- Unit price of each item purchased
- Tax on each item purchased
- Extended order amount
- Method of payment

This list uses at least four obvious data categories to store information about an order. The first category pertains to customer information. The second category tracks information common to orders but not specific to individual items ordered, such as the order date, the total order amount, the method of payment, and so on. The third category contains the order details. In this category, you can envision one record for each item purchased in each order. Finally, the fourth category stores details on each product, such as product identification, description, and price.

Determining the Data Categories Needed

A logical question to ask at this point is exactly what information about the customer you need. Could you use more than a name and address? What happens if you need to back-order an item? Can you telephone the customer to pick up the order when you receive it? Does the customer have multiple shipping addresses but a central billing location? If so, which address do you enter? What are the customer's sales to date? Do you want to offer discounts to frequent customers? Have all the customer's outstanding bills been paid? Should you mail new orders to customers who have not paid their bills?

There might be even more questions, but the point is that now—during system and table design—is the time to ask these questions, not after the program has been created.

Suppose that after asking these questions (and for the sake of keeping this example fairly simple), you decide to track the following customer information:

- Company name
- Contact name
- Address
- Telephone number
- Fax number
- Outstanding bills total

- Purchases YTD (year to date)
- Standard payment method
- Credit card number
- Credit card expiration date
- Preferred shipper
- Date of last purchase

A review of the customer information, using the preceding list, could reveal several problems.

You have several orders from large corporate customers that have different shipping and billing locations. You further realize that simply storing the customer contact name might not be the easiest way to search the file if you know only a last name. Therefore, you need to break the name into first- and last-name fields. Similarly, an address consists of several components, including one or more street address lines, city, state or province, and postal code. Each of these components needs a separate field. Even a telephone number might not be sufficient detail for customers that have extension numbers.

What you are accomplishing with this task is *atomizing* the customer's information. Each atom defines a single element that further defines the customer. The following list shows the results:

- ID (a unique identifier for a customer)
- Company name
- Contact first name
- Contact last name
- Billing street address
- Billing city
- Billing state/province
- Billing postal code
- Shipping street address
- Shipping city
- Shipping state/province
- Shipping postal code
- Telephone number
- Telephone extension number
- Fax number
- Outstanding bills total
- Purchases YTD
- Standard payment method
- Credit card number
- Credit card expiration date

■ Preferred shipper

■ Date of last purchase

In your customer system, you might require even more fields. However, the preceding fields serve to show you how to create a table.

Naming Each Data Fact

Now you need to define a field name for each data element. Traditionally, FoxPro limited field names to 10 characters. The first character was restricted to an alphabetic character; thereafter, FoxPro accepted any characters with the exception of a space. With Visual FoxPro, however, you can define field names with up to 128 characters, but only if the field is in a table defined in a database. If you initially define a standalone table, called a free table, you must follow the 10-character limit.

Many field-naming conventions have been devised in previous versions of FoxPro to help make programs more readable. The conventions differentiate variables by type, by scope, and by whether they are memory or table variables. One common method defines fields in a table beginning with a two-character prefix followed by an underscore. This prefix identifies the table and is unique in the application. Using table identifiers, however, can become unacceptable in a couple of cases:

■ If you plan to implement your own data dictionary, you will have fields that have common data descriptions and definitions between tables. In this case, you want to keep the same field name in each table.

■ If you plan to transfer data between tables using memory variables created with SCATTER, you cannot have table identifier prefixes in the field names for GATHER to successfully replace the proper values. In the examples for this chapter, you will not use the table identifiers for these reasons.

Today, the generally recommended convention is to start each field name with a single character that identifies its field type.

In this naming convention, memory variables also begin with two characters: the first represents its scope and the second represents its type. The third character could be an underscore; however, the use of underscores is no longer encouraged. Table 3.1 shows possible character prefixes.

Table 3.1 Memory Variable Naming Convention Prefix Parameters

First Character	Second Character
G (Global)	C (Character)
L (Local)	D (Date)
P (Private)	L (Logical)
	N (Numeric)

Assigning Data Types

Deciding what information to save in a table is only half the battle in planning a new table structure. Next, you need to examine each data item and determine whether you should store it as `Character`, `Numeric`, `Date`, or some other data type. Furthermore, for `Character` and `Numeric` fields, you need to determine the number of required characters.

You can begin by looking at the available data types provided by Visual FoxPro.

Character   `Character` is the most common data type in most tables. Character fields store 1 to 254 characters, consisting of printable characters such as letters, numbers, spaces, and punctuation marks. Certain characters, such as `CHR(0)`, cannot appear in a regular `Character` field. You must define fields that require more characters as memos.

`Character` fields have a fixed size. If you define a field such as `Address` with 35 characters, it consumes 35 characters in every record, even if `Address` equals 15 Main Street. Although this might sound trivial, the difference of 5 characters in a 300,000-record file is more than 1.4MB. On the other hand, if `Address` requires more than 35 characters, Visual FoxPro stores only the first 35 and truncates the rest.

You can even use `Character` fields that consist entirely of numbers. For example, you should store ZIP codes, telephone numbers, and even customer IDs as character fields, for several reasons. First, numeric fields truncate leading zeros. Therefore, if you save a ZIP code such as 01995, Visual FoxPro would store it as 1995. Second, you might want to format a telephone number field as (215)084-1988. Finally, you might need to combine a field such as a customer ID with another field to form an index. Usually, you can combine fields into a single index expression only by concatenating character strings.

Perhaps a better way to determine whether to make a field `Character` or `Numeric` is to ask, "Will I ever perform calculations on this field?" If you answer yes, you might want to store it as `Numeric`; otherwise, store it as a `Character`. An exception is a numeric ID field. Even though you might need to increase the size of the ID field incrementally for new records, it works best as a right-justified character field with blank or zero padding to the left to fill the field. For example, you would zero-pad ZIP codes in a five-character field. You might also zero-pad customer ID numbers. Listing 3.1 shows one method of enlarging a zero-padded character customer ID.

Listing 3.1   `03CODE01.PRG`—Enlarging a Zero-Padded Character Customer ID

```
SELECT CUSTOMER
APPEND BLANK
REPLACE cCustomerId WITH INCR_ID()

FUNCTION INCR_ID
*************************************************************
*
* FUNCTION INCR_ID Increments a character ID that contains
*                  only digits
*
```

continues

Part

II

Ch

3

Listing 3.1 Continued

```
* Designed specifically for CUSTOMER..cCustomerId
*
**************************************************************
LOCAL pnCurDec, pnCurRec, pcCurTag, pcNewId
* Capture current position in file, # of decimals, and tag
  pnCurDec = SYS(2001, 'DECIMAL')
  pnCurRec = RECNO()
  pcCurTag = TAG()
  SET DECIMALS TO 0

* Get last customer id used
  SET ORDER TO TAG CUSTID
  GOTO BOTTOM

* Calculate the next available ID
  pcNewId = PADL(VAL(cCustomerId)+1, 6, '0')

* Reset file position and tag, return next available id
  SET ORDER TO TAG (m.pcCurTag)
  SET DECIMAL TO EVAL(m.pnCurDec)
  GOTO pnCurRec
RETURN m.pcNewId
```

Enlarging an alphanumeric ID is more difficult, but Listing 3.2 finds the numeric portion of a field and expands it incrementally.

Listing 3.2 03CODE02.PRG—This File Locates the Numeric Portion of a Field and Expands It Incrementally

```
USE CUSTOMER
APPEND BLANK
REPLACE cCustomerId WITH INCR_ID2()

FUNCTION INCR_ID2
**************************************************************
*
* FUNCTION INCR_ID2 finds the numeric portion of an id
*                   embedded in an alphanumeric field
*
* Designed specifically for CUSTOMER.cCustomerId
*
**************************************************************
LOCAL pnCurDec, pnCurRec, pnStartNum, pnEndNum, ;
      pnIdNum,  pcCurTag, pcNewId
* Capture current position in file and current tag
  pnCurDec = SYS(2001, 'DECIMAL')
  pnCurRec = RECNO()
  pcCurTag = TAG()
  SET DECIMALS TO 0
  STORE 0 TO pnStartNum, pnEndNum
```

```
* Get last customer id used
  SET ORDER TO TAG custid
  GOTO BOTTOM

* Find start and end of numeric portion of field
  FOR i = 1 TO LEN(cCustomerId)
     IF ISDIGIT(SUBSTR(cCustomerId, i, 1)) AND ;
                pnStartNum = 0
pnStartNum = i
     ENDIF
     IF NOT ISDIGIT(SUBSTR(cust_id, i, 1)) AND ;
        pnStartNum>0 AND ;
        pnEndNum = 0
        pnEndNum = i
     ENDIF
  ENDFOR

* Check if there is a numeric portion
  IF m.pnStartNum = 0
     = MESSAGEBOX('There is no numeric portion to this id')
     RETURN cCustId
  ELSE
  * If no alpha suffix, fix end of number position
     IF m.pnEndNum = 0
        pnEndNum = LEN(cCustomerId) + 1
     ENDIF
  ENDIF

* Extract numeric portion of last id
  pnIdNum = SUBSTR(cCustomerId, m.pnStartNum, ;
              m.pnEndNum - m.pnStartNum)

* Calculate the next available customer id
  pcNewId = PADL(VAL(m.pnIdNum) + 1, ;
              m.pnEndNum - m.pnStartNum, '0')

* Reconstruct entire id
* Add alpha prefix
  IF m.pnStartNum = 1
     pcNewId = m.pcNewId
  ELSE
     pcNewId = SUBSTR(cCustomerId, 1, m.pnStartNum - 1) + ;
              m.pcNewId
  ENDIF
* Add alpha suffix
  IF m.pn_endnum <= LEN(cCustomerId)
     pcNewId = m.pcNewId + SUBSTR(cCustomerId, m.pnEndNum, ;
              LEN(cCustomerId) - m.pnEndNum + 1)
  ENDIF

* Reset file position and tag, return next available id
  SET ORDER TO TAG (m.pcCurTag)
  SET DECIMALS TO EVAL(m.pnCurDec)
  GOTO m.pnCurRec
RETURN m.pcNewId
```

Part

II

Ch

3

Currency   To store dollar amounts, consider using a special numeric type called Currency. As a maximum amount, Currency can store a little more than $922 trillion. Currency defaults to a maximum of four decimal places and requires a fixed eight bytes of storage in a table.

N O T E   For those who love details, currency values range from –922,337,203,685,477.5807 to 922,337,203,685,477.5807. ▪

Date and DateTime   These two field types are similar in that they both store dates. Both types require eight bytes to store a date in the form YYYYMMDD, regardless of whether SET CENTURY is ON or OFF. DateTime uses a compressed format to store time stored as HHMMSS, with HH recorded by a 24-hour clock. If you convert a Date field to a DateTime field, the time defaults to 12:00:00AM.

There has been a lot of publicity in the media about the so-called year 2000 bug. Supposedly, when the clock turns over to the year 2000, some or all computers in the world that are not prepared will resort back to the year 1900 or other strange happenings will occur, causing chaos all over the world. Most of the problems associated with this factor will be rectified by the fact that most computers being built at present will work when we reach that spectacular date. Other companies and developers have been working on the problem and by the time the problem occurs, all should be solved. If you own an older personal computer, the safest solution is to upgrade or purchase a new one before that year. Most developers will already have the solution and most normal users will not have to worry about it.

N O T E   Dates range from 01/01/100 to 12/31/9999, and times range from 12:00:00AM to 11:59:59PM. ▪

T I P   You can stamp a record that has a DateTime field with the current date and time by using the DATETIME() function.

N O T E   Just as you can add 1 to a Date field to increase it incrementally by one day, you can increase a DateTime field by seconds. Because there are 86,400 seconds in a day, you need to add 86,400 to a DateTime field to increase it by one day. ▪

Double   Double fields are floating-point fields that store up to 18 digits in a compressed format that uses exactly eight bytes. In fact, no matter how many digits you use, the number of bytes remains fixed at eight. The only decision that you make is the number of decimal places.

N O T E   Double values range from –4.94065648541247E-324 to 1.79769313486232E ▪

Float and Numeric   Both of these field types support up to 20 digits with a maximum of 19 decimal places, but each digit requires one storage byte. FoxPro treats both types identically, which results in the same degree of accuracy. However, providing both fields maintains compatibility with dBASE IV, which differentiates between them.

Unlike `Double` fields, `Float` and `Numeric` fields enable you to specify the number of bytes required, because FoxPro stores the ASCII code for each digit in a separate byte. Therefore, if a field value always uses integer values less than 100,000, a field width of 6 with zero decimal places will suffice. To optimally size a `Numeric` field, try to determine the largest and smallest values possible. Sizing a field too small for the values that are being stored forces FoxPro to store asterisks in the field.

N O T E   Float values range from –.9999999999E–19 to .9999999999E+20. ▧

   When sizing fields, remember that negative values need a character position to store the minus sign.

CAUTION

If you store a calculation result in a field that has a fixed number of decimal places, FoxPro truncates the value to match the field definition, which can adversely affect the precision of the value. Subsequent calculations that use this truncated field might lead to apparent rounding errors.

General   The most common use for `General` fields is to store graphics. A `General` field is a specialized `Memo` field. FoxPro stores a `General` field in the same `.FPT` file used by other `Memo` fields in the table, but you cannot use it the same way. It is primarily used to store references to bound OLE objects.

Logical   `Logical` fields store binary information in the form of `.T.` or `.F.`. `Logical` fields store information with only two states, such as taxable versus nontaxable, male versus female, and shipped versus back-ordered. Forms often use `Logical` fields as the source for check boxes.

Memo   `Memo` fields not only store large character strings (greater than 254 characters), but they also provide a variable amount of storage per record based on block size. A *block* is a fixed number of characters that FoxPro reserves for a `Memo`. By default, FoxPro uses 64 bytes per block. This means that each group of 64 characters in a text string requires an additional block. If you have a string of 72 bytes, the extra eight bytes require a second block of 64 characters.

   From its 64 bytes, each block in a `Memo` allocates eight bytes to two 4-byte pointers. (These pointers tell Visual FoxPro how to find the preceding or following block.) Strictly speaking, the memo block has only 56 bytes.

You can change the block size by using the `SET BLOCKSIZE` command, which sets the number of bytes from 33 to 511 bytes. For larger blocks, use an integer from 1 to 32 to allocate blocks in multiples of 512 bytes. With the introduction of Visual FoxPro, you can also set block size to 0, which causes VFP to allocate space one byte at a time, resulting in no wasted space. However, performance will not be as good as when you use larger block sizes.

ıst use SET BLOCKSIZE before adding the first record with a memo. When you add the
.. memo, FoxPro embeds the current block size in the memo file. To change the block size
of an existing memo file, you must rewrite each Memo field. However, regardless of the block
size, remember that the first block reserves eight bytes for the pointers.

Why should you worry about the block size? The larger the block size, the more wasted space
memos consume if they vary greatly in length. On the other hand, the more blocks FoxPro
needs to store a memo, the less efficiently it retrieves the memo. The practice sounds more
like art than science, but in general, you want to define the block size as the most likely memo
length.

FoxPro stores memos in a file, separate from the .DBF, that has the extension .FPT. Whether
you have one Memo field or several in a table, FoxPro stores all memos in this one .FPT file. In
fact, if you have General fields, FoxPro stores them in the same file as memos. Pointers from
the .DBF file keep track of what information belongs to each record and field.

Because memo pointers point only one way—from the .DBF to the .FPT—you need to ensure
that .DBF and .FPT files never get separated. How can this happen? Perhaps you have a table
that contains a Memo field on two or more machines. If you copy (by accident, it is assumed) the
.DBF from one machine to another without also copying the .FPT file, the copy could be out of
synchronization with the current .FPT. If this happens and you add records before realizing the
problem, you might find that the memo text no longer corresponds with the proper records. It
is almost impossible to fix this problem without manually resetting the pointers from the .DBF
to the .FPT. Third-party tools are available to perform this very complex task.

N O T E   One solution stores the record key with the memo just in case the unthinkable happens. If
you have more than one Memo field per record, also store the field name with the key. ■

Don't worry about records without memos; FoxPro does not reserve additional storage space
in the memo file for them. However, every memo in every record requires a four-byte pointer
in the .DBF file, even if it is blank.

The following are typical uses for Memo fields:

- Character fields that only occasionally contain text
- Character fields that vary greatly in length or whose length cannot be predicted
- Text files, such as resumés, letters, and historical archiving of program versions

Using the Table Designer

Suppose that today is the start of a new project and you want to use the Project Manager to
organize your files. You need to create a project first. As is true of most functions, FoxPro
provides several methods of performing this task, such as using VFP commands, menu-driven
options, or the Project Wizard.

To start, choose File, New from the main system menu. The New dialog box appears (see
Figure 3.1).

FIGURE 3.1

Create a new project using the New dialog box.

Choose Project as the file type, and click New File. Because FoxPro requires a name to identify any file, it first opens the Create dialog box to request a project filename (see Figure 3.2). FoxPro uses the same dialog box for all filename requests.

FIGURE 3.2

Name a new project file using the Create dialog box.

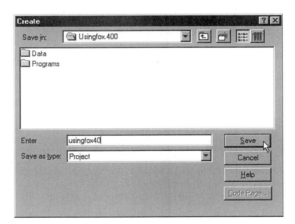

The Create dialog box displays the current or default directory. If you already have projects defined in this directory, they appear dimmed in the list box so that you cannot select them. They serve as a reminder not to use the same project name twice. You can switch to another directory or drive to store the project, but after you select a directory, you must enter the new project filename manually.

If you prefer a more direct method when creating tables and don't mind typing, enter the filename in the Command window as follows:

```
CREATE PROJECT PTOFSALE
```

Part

II

Ch

3

Using a command is quicker, but you must learn basic command syntax and you must already have a valid name and directory under which to store the project.

N O T E If you open a project and close it immediately, Visual FoxPro prompts you to delete the project file or retain it without adding any files. ■

Having created a project, FoxPro automatically opens it. Projects have page frames. Each page represents a different file type, identified by a tab across the top of the page. To select a page, click its tab. To create a table, click the Data page. Currently, this project has no defined tables (see Figure 3.3). Create a free table by selecting Free Tables and clicking New. VFP will then give you the option of using a wizard or the Table Designer to create the table.

FIGURE 3.3

Create a new free table by selecting the Data page in Project Manager and clicking New.

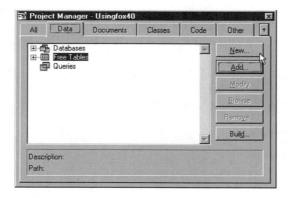

VFP next prompts you for a filename, this time for the table. For this example, call the table CUST.DBF.

Finally, FoxPro displays the Table Designer dialog box. This form has a page-frame object with three pages. The first page defines the table structure, the second one defines the indexes, and the third shows the status of the table. The table structure page should appear by default. If not, you need only click the Table page, as shown in Figure 3.4.

FIGURE 3.4

The Table Designer displays completed field definitions for CUST.DBF.

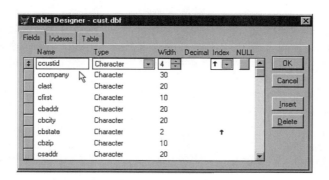

To define the table structure, enter the field information shown in Table 3.2, which includes field types, widths, and decimals. Notice that each customer is identified by a unique customer ID. Type the customer ID in the first field.

Table 3.2   Suggested File Structure for Fields in CUST.DBF

10-Character Field Names	Field Type	Field Width	Decimals
cCUSTID	Character	4	
cCOMPANY	Character	30	
cFIRST	Character	10	
cLAST	Character	20	
cBADDR	Character	20	
cBCITY	Character	20	
cBSTATE	Character	2	
cBZIP	Character	10	
cSADDR	Character	20	
cSCITY	Character	20	
cSSTATE	Character	2	
cSZIP	Character	10	
cPHONE	Character	13	
cEXTENSN	Character	4	
cFAXPHON	Character	13	
nBILLDUE	Numeric	9	2
nYTDORDR	Numeric	9	2
cPAYMETH	Character	2	
cCRDCARD	Character	16	
dCCEXPIR	Date	8	
cPRFSHIP	Character	10	
dLASTPUR	Date	8	

NOTE FoxPro does not require a file's unique field to appear first. However, some people prefer to list index fields—especially unique fields—first because that practice makes browsing and listing the table easier. Also, if you use the file in a list box to select customers, you can define it more easily if the unique fields appear first in the file. ■

When you enter field names in a free table, FoxPro prevents you from entering more than 10 characters. If you attempt to enter a duplicate field name, FoxPro generates an error message. For now, use the structured 10-character field names listed in Table 3.2.

Pressing Tab moves you to the Type field, which defaults to Character. This field uses a drop-down list. If you click the down arrow to the right of the field, a drop-down list appears showing possible values. For this example, simply accept the default type: Character.

Specify how many characters to reserve for this field. Character fields default to 10, but you can use the spinner to change that setting to any value from 1 to 254. Alternatively, you can edit the number directly. A nice feature of the spinner is that it starts slowly and picks up speed as you continue to click the arrow.

N O T E   If you are not familiar with them, spinners enable users to click either an up or down arrow to increase or decrease the displayed value. Spinners modify only numeric fields. However, you can combine a spinner control with other controls to simulate spinning any variable type, such as dates or index field values. Narrow the spinner control until just the arrows without space between are displayed. Then add code to the Click event of the spinner to modify the value property of the non-numeric control. ▩

Numeric fields use the decimal column to define the number of decimal places to reserve to the right of the decimal point. In fact, FoxPro activates this column only for Numeric fields. For a Numeric field such as nBillDue, you need two decimal places.

The next column displays the index direction, if an index exists, for the field.

The last column in the structure determines whether the current field allows null values. Null use is discussed later in this chapter, so you can skip this column for now.

After you enter the structure of the CUST file, the Table Designer dialog box should match the one shown in Figure 3.4. You can see only nine fields at a time, but by using the vertical scrollbar, you can move through all the table fields.

The buttons to the left of the field names enable you to rearrange the default field order when issuing a Browse or List command for the table. To make cFirst appear before cLast, click the button to the left of cFirst and drag the field up. While you hold down the mouse button, FoxPro displays a dotted box at the proposed new position of the field. When the field is in the desired position, simply release the mouse button; all subsequent fields adjust their positions.

When you have entered the complete table structure, click OK to exit the Table Designer and save the table. Because this table is new, FoxPro asks whether you want to input data records now. FoxPro assumes that because you created a table, you probably want to store data in it, but that is not always true. You might want to append data into a new table from an existing one, or you might want to add data by using a form. For now, click No and return to the Project Manager.

The name of the table that you just created now appears in Free Tables in Project Manager. To see it, click the plus sign to the left of the Free Tables line. The table has two symbols before it: a plus sign and a circle with a slash through it. In the Project Manager, the plus sign indicates additional levels that are currently hidden or rolled into the current line. If you click the plus sign next to a table name, Project Manager rolls out the table's fields. Notice that the plus sign changes to a minus sign. This change indicates that all levels are currently open. FoxPro uses the second symbol (the circle with the slash through it) during compilation to indicate that it should not include this file in the compilation. Project Manager should now look like Figure 3.5.

FIGURE 3.5
The Project Manager shows the fields in CUST listed below the table name.

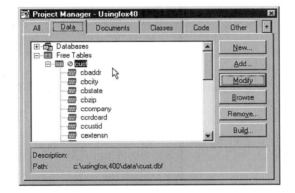

Using Nulls

In earlier versions of FoxPro, you could not determine whether a user intentionally left a field blank or merely forgot it. FoxPro interprets an empty field as being an empty character string, a numeric zero, or a logical False, depending on the field type. Any of these values could be legitimate entries for the field. If an employee file contains a field for the employee's middle initial, for example, does a blank mean that the employee did not enter his middle initial or that he does not have one? With numeric data, would a year-to-date field with a value of zero indicate that the customer had no transactions or that the sum of purchases and returns exactly canceled each other? Finally, with Logical fields, you cannot determine whether the user actually selected a false value or merely skipped the field. Suppose that John Smith missed the question "Are you married?" for which False represents NO? Mrs. Smith might have a question or two about that.

To use null tokens in a field (any field type), you must do two things. First, you must specify SET NULL ON in the Command window or in the program. Second, you must modify the structure and click the Null column button for each field that allows nulls. If you do not do this, FoxPro displays an error when you append a record with APPEND FROM or INSERT SQL and do not include a value for this field. FoxPro places the token .NULL. in fields that allow nulls and contain no values.

N O T E If you use SET NULL ON and do not select the Null check box for these fields, FoxPro will not allow nulls or blanks in primary or candidate key fields. (For more information, see the section "Using Primary and Candidate Keys" later in this chapter.) ■

CAUTION

FoxPro's default disallows nulls. If you enter SET NULL ON, you will not be able to skip a field without entering something in that field.

Remember the following rules when you use nulls:

- By default, APPEND BLANK does not trigger a null token in all fields of a new table record.
- When you are changing a Character field from a non-null field to allow nulls, blank fields remain blank.
- When you are changing a Numeric field from a non-null field to allow nulls, fields with values of zero remain zero.
- When you are changing a Character field from a null field to disallow nulls, a blank string is placed in the field.
- When you are changing a Numeric field from a null field to disallow nulls, a zero is placed in the field.

Modifying Table Structures

At some point in every project's life, you can expect to modify a table's structure. The severity of a modification can be classified by how much it changes the table and index files.

Adding a field, for example, is a small change because it has no impact on existing fields, although it does require rewriting the entire .DBF. Renaming a field also requires only a minimal change; in fact, it usually does nothing more than modify the .DBF header. However, if you rename a field that appears in an index, that index or tag must also be updated. Deleting fields, as long as they are not part of an index or tag, requires rewriting the entire .DBF but little else. On the other hand, modifying field sizes or the number of decimal places forces FoxPro to rewrite the entire .DBF, and can result in the loss of data. When you are changing the field type, FoxPro attempts to automatically convert the data to the new type, but it can also automatically trash the data if it does not know what to do or if the conversion does not make sense.

The following section examines various changes that you can make to table structures and explains the effects of those changes.

CAUTION

Before making any table structure changes, make a backup of the data file (.DBF) and all indexes.

Adding Fields

Adding new fields to an existing table is one of the safest changes you can make. In fact, problems occur only if you attempt to use the same field name twice. Even in that situation, FoxPro responds automatically.

FoxPro will not enable you to exit the name column if it is a duplicate of an existing field name. Rather, FoxPro displays an information box with the message `Invalid or duplicate field name` and enables you to edit it.

Deleting Fields

At some point, one or more fields in a table might become obsolete. Rather than waste space, you might decide to remove them from the table. To delete a field, simply display the table in the Table Designer dialog box (refer to Figure 3.4), highlight the obsolete field, and click the Delete button.

> **CAUTION**
>
> you delete a field and save the structure, it is gone forever, including any indexes that reference the deleted field. Make a backup copy of your .DBF before deleting a field.

Renaming Fields

Renaming fields might require only rewriting the .DBF header with the new field name. To change a field name, simply open the Table Designer dialog box, highlight the name, edit the name, and then save the structure.

As long as an open index does not reference the field, FoxPro renames the field when you save the structure. If the renamed field appears in an open index, FoxPro displays the warning shown in Figure 3.6.

FIGURE 3.6

This alert box appears when you are saving the modified structure and renaming a field used in an index.

When you click OK in this alert box, Visual FoxPro returns you to the Index page of the Table Designer to correct the index expression. You can redefine the expression by renaming the field name in the index expression. VFP does not automatically rename the field in the index expression when you rename a field used in it. Why isn't FoxPro smart enough to simply substitute the new field name for the old one in all the tags? FoxPro probably doesn't know whether you really mean to rename a field or to replace it with a new field.

TROUBLESHOOTING

I need to reverse the names of two fields in a single table, but issuing the `modify structure` command won't let me change the names. The Table Designer does prohibit you from renaming a table field with the name of another existing field in the table. However, you can accomplish this name switch by using an intermediate name, as described in the following steps:

1. Rename the first field to any name that is not currently being used.
2. Rename the second field to the first field's original name.
3. Rename the first field to the second field's original name.

Redefining Fields

Redefining field types, widths, or decimal places can be simple or complex depending on the change. For example, you can open the Table Designer dialog box, highlight a field, and increase the size of the field with no problem at all; FoxPro rewrites the .DBF to expand the field size. However, Character fields merely get blanks appended to them, and Numeric fields have more available digits to use. You can even change the size of an indexed field without any problems. Visual FoxPro regenerates the index when you close the Table Designer.

On the other hand, decreasing the size of the field or number of decimals can cause data loss. FoxPro accepts the change and asks whether you want to update the table structure when you leave the Table Designer dialog box. If you continue, FoxPro resizes the fields as requested. Character fields are shortened by truncating existing text to the new field size. Numeric data can lose decimal places or digits when it is shortened. Reducing the number of digits in the integer portion of the number can cause some values to be replaced by asterisks, thereby causing you to lose the entire number. On the other hand, VFP happily truncates decimal places.

Some changes in field types are more likely to cause disaster than others are. Changing a Numeric field to a Character field simply converts the number to a string, as though FoxPro used the STR function when it rewrote the table. Similarly, changing a String to a Numeric field appears to use the VAL function. Converting strings with leading numbers results in the numbers being saved to a Numeric field. FoxPro converts strings that begin with alpha characters (other than blanks) to zero when they are converted to numeric values.

Similarly, you can convert Date fields to Character strings by changing their type. FoxPro appears to transform the data by using the DTOC function. You can even change character-formatted dates back into true Date fields.

Most other conversions result in a loss of data. Again, the need to make a backup copy of a table before making any structural change cannot be emphasized enough.

Defining Order in a Table

No one would expect users to enter data in a sorted order (unless they key the entries in from a telephone book). Certainly, customers don't arrive at a business in alphabetical order or buy products sequentially by product ID. Wouldn't it be nice if they did? Because they don't, you must add records in random order, although you probably will want to view them sorted by one or more fields.

You can use the SORT command to reorder the records in a table. SORT takes an existing table and creates a new one sorted by a field or a combination of fields. The following command creates a new table called CUSTLIST that is sorted by the customer's last name:

```
SORT TO CUSTLIST ON Last
```

A more complex SORT creates a new table called CURCUST, which contains customers (sorted in descending customer ID order) who have made purchases this year. The following is the appropriate command to create the new table.

```
SORT TO CURCUST ON cCustId /D FOR Goods_Ytd>0
```

This method has two flaws. First, every new sort order duplicates the entire original table or filtered portion thereof. If you need several sort orders for a large table, you can quickly run out of disk space. Second (and more important), having more than one copy of a table inevitably leads to data inconsistencies. If you do not update all tables simultaneously, you soon will have several tables, each of which has some, but not all, of the recent updates.

Sorting does have its place. If you have a rarely changed table that has one preferred sort order, you might want to keep a sorted version of it. However, indexes provide a more effective way to enable users to view and retrieve data from a table in an orderly manner. Because a table can have more than one index, you can define different indexes for different views or reports.

 TIP Even with indexes, a table sorted by the same fields as the index performs just a bit faster.

Examining Standalone Versus Structural and Nonstructural Indexes

When indexes were first developed for database systems, they required a separate index for each index definition. To index the CUST table on both the customer number and their last name, for example, you would create two indexes, as shown in the following example:

```
USE CUST
INDEX ON cCustId TO CUSTID
INDEX ON cLast TO CUSTNAME
```

These statements would create two index files: CUSTID.IDX and CUSTNAME.IDX. These files are now referred to as *standalone indexes*, because each index file contains a single index entry and is independent of the others. You can have any number of standalone indexes defined for a given table, limited only by the FILES statement in CONFIG.SYS. When you open the table, you might open all indexes, as in the following example:

```
USE CUST INDEX CUSTID, CUSTNAME
```

Alternatively, you can open the table with only a single index:

```
USE CUST INDEX CUSTID
```

In both cases, the first index after the keyword INDEX controls the order in which FoxPro accesses the table records. In the first example, FoxPro updates and maintains both indexes if you add, delete, or modify records. In the second case, FoxPro maintains only CUSTID.IDX; in this case, FoxPro has no knowledge of CUSTNAME. If you make changes to CUST.DBF, CUSTNAME can lose synchronization with the table. In other words, the index might no longer point to the right records.

Finally, you can open each index separately by using the SET INDEX statement as follows:

```
USE CUST
SET INDEX TO CUSTID
SET INDEX TO CUSTNAME ADDITIVE
```

Now FoxPro opens both indexes, and CUSTID controls the access order. Notice the keyword ADDITIVE in the second SET INDEX statement. If you did not include that keyword, FoxPro would close CUSTID before opening CUSTNAME.

The problems with standalone indexes should be obvious. Because the names usually have no relation to their .DBF, you can easily forget which indexes belong to each table. In fact, your directories can soon become littered with obsolete and forgotten indexes that you no longer need, and no one remembers to which tables the indexes belong.

Furthermore, if you do not open all the indexes when you edit the table, FoxPro does not update the missing indexes. The indexes might point to the wrong records or even beyond the end of the table after you pack deleted records.

With the introduction of FoxPro, you now have structural and nonstructural indexes, also called *compound indexes*. These files are special index files that can contain several index definitions in one physical file. Now you can store all index definitions for one .DBF in a single file. You no longer need to worry about forgetting to open an index file or encountering nonsynchronized index pointers.

You define a compound index as shown in the following example:

```
USE CUST
INDEX ON cCustId TAG CUSTID OF CUSTSORT
INDEX ON cLast TAG CUSTNAME OF CUSTSORT
USE CUST INDEX CUSTSORT
```

The USE statement opens the CUST table, along with a nonstructural index called CUSTSORT. FoxPro calls a compound index *nonstructural* when its base name differs from the .DBF—in this case, CUSTSORT versus CUST. You can make the index *structural* by giving it the same base name as the .DBF, as in the following example:

```
USE CUST
INDEX ON cCustId TAG CUSTID OF CUST
INDEX ON cLast TAG CUSTNAME OF CUST
USE CUST
```

 TIP Omitting the OF clause in INDEX ON automatically creates or adds the index definition to a structural index.

In this case, you did not include the INDEX clause of the USE statement, but the index— CUST.CDX—opens anyway. When the structural index exists, FoxPro automatically opens it when you open the table. There is no way to forget to open the indexes if you store index expressions as tags in a structural index. Structural indexes should never get out of synchronization, although that is possible: one way would be to accidentally copy a different version of the .DBF or .CDX to the current directory.

Defining Normal and Unique Indexes

To create indexes for CUST.DBF, return to the Table Designer dialog box. Click the Indexes page to switch to the index definition page (see Figure 3.7).

FIGURE 3.7
The index definition screen displays four index definitions in the Table Designer.

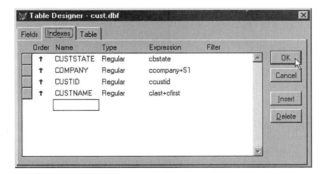

Four indexes are already defined. Index definitions begin with the tag name on the left, followed by the index type (accept the default, Regular), the tag expression, and a filter. Notice that FoxPro automatically assumes that you want to create a structural index. If you want to create a standalone index or a nonstructural index, you need to enter the syntax described in the preceding section into the Command window.

The arrows to the left of the names indicate whether the index is in ascending (up arrow) or descending (down arrow) order. To change the direction, select the row and click the button that appears with the arrow to toggle between ascending and descending.

Part
II

Ch

3

A regular index type means that FoxPro stores the value generated by the index expression for each table record in the index. If more than one record has the same expression, FoxPro stores the expression multiple times with separate pointers to each record.

In the CUST table, the last name might not uniquely identify every record in the table. You might have customers Bill Jones and Kevin Jones. Therefore, an index on the last name has repeated values, but you can use it as a regular index.

By clicking the down arrow next to Type, you can see another index type called Unique. Unique includes only unique expressions in the index. If more than one record generates the same index expression value, Unique stores only the first one encountered. If you define a unique index on Last in the CUST table, you cannot include every record in the index. Therefore, either Bill Jones or Kevin Jones would appear, but not both.

Defining Candidate and Primary Keys

The third index type, called candidate, creates a unique index, but the index includes every record in the table. Candidate indexes prohibit duplicate expression values for any two records in the table. What if you decide to change an existing regular index to candidate? After making the change, VFP prompts you to save the structure modification. Also appearing in the dialog box is a check box for checking data against the index. Whether you choose to or not, if you currently have duplicate data corresponding to the index definition, VFP warns you of this uniqueness error and changes the index back to regular. Your data will have to be modified before making this change.

> **CAUTION**
>
> Records marked for deletion are not ignored when a primary or candidate index tests for duplicate values. Therefore, when you try to add a new record that has the value in a field used in a primary or candidate index definition, a uniqueness error occurs and you will not be able to add the record until you pack the table.

A free table can have a candidate index, but only tables within a database container can have a primary index. CUSTOMER.DBF in the PTOFSALE database includes a field named cCustomerId; it's defined as a single field that uniquely identifies each record. Because indexing on this field generates a unique index that includes every record, it is a candidate index, but in this case, it is also the primary index. Occasionally, a single table can have more than one field that uniquely identifies each record. Each such index is a candidate index and qualifies as a potential primary key. However, any one table can only have one primary index. Primary keys often form relationships between multiple files and serve as lookup values in a referenced table.

Indexing on Complex Expressions

FoxPro does not restrict index expressions to single fields. In fact, any combination of fields can serve as an index expression. Beware of making an expression overly complex just to make it a candidate index. You might include Last_Name and First_Name to make a candidate index. But what if you have customers Jim T. Kirk and Jim C. Kirk? You might want to add another field to the index for the customer's middle initial. But such an index does not guarantee uniqueness. Some programs attempt to combine portions of a customer's last name with the last four digits of their phone number plus their ZIP code (maybe even age, sex, and title of their favorite *Star Trek* movie). It's easier to just assign a sequential customer ID to a new customer.

To build a complex expression, click the button to the right of the Expression text box in the Table Designer dialog box. FoxPro displays the Expression Builder dialog box (see Figure 3.8).

FIGURE 3.8

Use the Expression Builder dialog box to create complex index expressions.

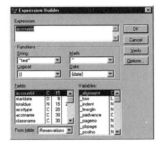

FoxPro uses the Expression Builder dialog box with many operations to help build complex expressions. The Functions section provides access to FoxPro's built-in functions, which are divided into four groups: Date, Logical, Math, and String. Click the arrow button to the right of a function field to display a drop-down list of functions. To select a function, highlight it and then press Enter or simply click it. FoxPro displays the selected function in the function list box and the expression text area. For a function, FoxPro automatically places the insert cursor inside the parentheses. Now you can enter the parameters.

Below the Expression list box, FoxPro lists the fields in the current table. You can choose a field to be added to the insert position of the expression; just highlight the field and press Enter. To select a field from a different table, click the arrow to the right of the From Table text box. Only open tables that appear in this list. If you need to reference a table that is not currently open, exit the Expression Builder dialog box, open the table in a new work area, and then reenter the Expression Builder dialog box. You can create indexes on fields from other tables, although that practice is not recommended. However, you do need the capability to access other tables in other situations that use the Expression Builder.

Finally, the Variables list box contains the current memory and system variables. This feature generally does not apply to defining indexes, but remember that FoxPro uses the Expression Builder dialog box in many places.

Figure 3.8 shows an index that alphabetically displays companies that have outstanding bills using cCompanyName and nOutstandingBillsTotal. Because cCompanyName is a Character field and nOutstandingBillsTotal is Numeric, you cannot simply combine them with a plus sign. To combine two or more fields of different data types, you must convert one or more of them to a common type—usually, `Character`. Use the `STR` function to convert `nOutstandingBillsTotal` to a string before concatenating it to `cCompanyName`.

Finally, before you click OK and accept an expression, FoxPro provides a utility that verifies the syntax. The Verify button checks the syntax and displays an error message if it cannot interpret the expression. Common reasons for invalid expressions include mismatched parentheses or a missing comma. For valid expressions, a message appears in the status bar telling you that the expression is valid.

Including User-Defined Functions Not only can you use FoxPro's predefined functions, you can also define your own. A *user-defined function* is any group of statements stored as a separate file or as a separate procedure or function in a program.

Suppose that you want to create an index based on sales regions. First, you need a separate table that relates ZIP codes to regions. Then you create a small function, similar to the one shown in Listing 3.3, to find the region.

Listing 3.3 `03CODE03.PRG`—**This Function Locates the Region of the Country that a ZIP Code Refers To**

```
FUNCTION GETREGION
LPARAMETER lcZipCode
************************************************
*
* This function uses file ZIPREGN with the
* following structure:
*
*     StartZip    C(10)
*     EndZip      C(10)
*     Region      C(10)
*
* All zip codes that fall in a zip code range
* defined by a record are assigned to that
* region. Otherwise, the region is left blank.
*
************************************************
LOCAL lcCurNear, lcCurArea, lcRtnRegion, lcA

* Use an inexact search
  lcCurNear = SYS(2001, 'NEAR')
  SET NEAR ON

* Store current work area - VFP supports 32767 work areas
  lcCurArea = SELECT()   &&Retrieves current work area number

* Check if ZIPREGN IS OPEN
  IF !USED('ZIPREGN.DBF')
     lcA = ('\VFP5BOOK\DATA\ZIPREGN.DBF')
     USE (lcA)
  ELSE
     SELECT ZIPREGN  &&selects work area where ZIPERGN is open
  ENDIF
```

```
* Check if controlling index is on STARTZIP
  IF !TAG() = 'STARTZIP'
     SET ORDER TO TAG STARTZIP
  ENDIF

  = SEEK(lcZipCode)
* Check if an exact match was found
  IF FOUND()
    lcRtnRegion = Region
  ELSE
  * Check if on last record
    IF EOF()
      GOTO BOTTOM
      lcRtnRegion = Region
    ELSE
      SKIP -1
      lcRtnRegion = Region
    ENDIF
  ENDIF.

* Check if beyond last zip code in range
  IF lc_ZipCode > ZIPREGN.EndZip
    lcRtnRegion = SPACE(10)
  ENDIF

* RESET  environment and area
  SELECT (lcCurArea)
  SET NEAR &lcCurNear

RETURN lcRtnRegion

* END OF FUNCTION GETREGION
```

N O T E   SELECT and SELECT() perform a variety of tasks. SELECT as a command requires as a parameter either a work-area number or a table alias name. SELECT 4, for example, opens work area 4. On the other hand, SELECT 0 opens the first unused work area beginning with 1. However, you usually do not know the work area number of a table. Instead, you can use the table alias to open its work area, as in SELECT CUSTOMER.

By itself, SELECT() returns the number of the current work area. You can also include a parameter of 0 to perform the same task. A parameter of 1 returns the highest numbered unused work area. Thus, ? SELECT(1) tells you that VFP supports 32,767 work areas. By supplying the table alias name as the parameter, as in SELECT('CUSTOMER'), you can get the work-area number for any open table. ■

To use the GETREGION function, simply place the following expression in the expression box of the index:

```
GETREGION(CUSTOMER.cBillingPostalCode)
```

Using Stored Procedures   The major disadvantage of using a user-defined function in an index expression is that FoxPro must be able to find the function to modify the index. Because you cannot store the function with the index, it can be easily misplaced, deleted, or forgotten when you transfer the table to another system. Thanks to the database container, you do have an alternative.

If the table is bound to a database, user-defined functions can be stored in the database, thus eliminating the search for a procedure or function.

N O T E FoxPro searches for procedures and functions in a specific order. It first looks in the current file. Next, it checks to see whether SET PROCEDURE TO defined a separate procedure library, and it looks there. Then it checks any previously executed procedure files as part of the same program. It searches the current directory for a file that has the same name as the procedure or function. Finally, it searches in another directory defined with FoxPro's SET PATH statement for a file with the same name. As you might expect, the farther down in the search sequence you go, the slower the application performs. ▪

Realizing Index Limitations   The limits of an index expression depend on the length of the index expression string, as well as its value. Index files reserve a limited amount of space for an index expression and its value.

For a standalone index, the index expression can consist of up to 220 characters. FoxPro limits the resulting index value to 100 characters. If you define the standalone index as a compact standalone index (a special case of standalone indexes that requires less total disk space), the index expression s hares space with the FOR expression. The combined length of both expression strings cannot be more than 512 characters. The individual index value cannot exceed 240 characters. A similar requirement applies to compound indexes. Compound indexes are nothing more than compact indexes with repeated tags; thus, they have the same limitations.

N O T E Short index expressions are more efficient than long ones. Also, choose fields that have short, meaningful values where possible. If complex long values appear to be the only way to define unique keys, create an "artificial" number, such as the customer ID field in CUSTOMER.DBF. ▪

Selecting an Active Index at Runtime

In applications that have standalone indexes, you can easily determine the active index. If a USE statement opens more than one index, FoxPro makes the first one in the list the active one by default. To change to a different index, use SET ORDER to change the controlling order. The following statements open CUSTOMER with two standalone indexes (CUSTID and CUSTNAME), the SET ORDER statement changes the controlling index from CUSTID to CUSTNAME:

```
USE CUSTOMER INDEX CUSTID, CUSTNAME
SET ORDER TO 2
```

To be clearer, you can also specify the index name rather than its position number in the list.

If the USE statement does not open the index files, issue the SET INDEX command to both define the index list and set the controlling index, as follows:

```
USE CUSTOMER
SET INDEX TO CUSTID, CUSTNAME ORDER 2
```

These options continue to work in Visual FoxPro. However, with the introduction of compound indexes, in which each index has a tag name, you need to add a TAG argument such as the following:

```
USE CUSTOMER
SET ORDER TO TAG CUSTNAME
```

In this example, assume that CUSTOMER has a structural index with tags named CUSTID and CUSTNAME. Although FoxPro automatically opens a structural index, it does not automatically set a controlling index. You need to use a command such as SET ORDER to select a tag.

 TIP You also can use USE CUSTOMER TAG CUSTNAME.

Part
II

Ch
3

The issue becomes more complex if you have both structural and standalone indexes. In the following statement, you again open CUSTOMER.DBF along with the structural index CUSTOMER.CDX, but FoxPro also opens a standalone index called CUSTZIP:

```
USE CUSTOMER INDEX CUSTZIP
```

Notice that you did not specify the structural index; FoxPro opens it automatically. Furthermore, CUSTZIP—not the structural index—has precedence in the index order over a standalone index. Therefore, CUSTZIP controls the record-viewing order in this case.

Appending Records

You create tables to add records to them. In fact, FoxPro is so sure that you want to populate a table with records as soon as possible that it prompts you to add records immediately on closing the table structure. Of course, this time might not always be the best time to add records. You might not even be the person to do the adding. But somewhere, sometime, someone (or some program) will add records to the table.

You can add records to a table in several ways. The following sections explore these options.

Adding Records Through BROWSE or EDIT Screens

Many casual FoxPro users begin by opening an Append window. To do so yourself, simply open the table and type APPEND in the Command window as shown in the following:

```
USE CUSTOMER
APPEND
```

These commands open an edit window, add a blank record, and place the cursor in the first field, as shown in Figure 3.9. After you enter data in the fields of the first record, FoxPro automatically adds another blank record and places the cursor in it. This process continues until you close the window.

FIGURE 3.9

APPEND opens this simple edit window when you add records.

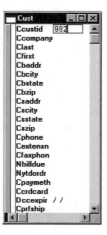

You also can open the Edit window directly with the EDIT command or open a Browse window with BROWSE. In these windows, FoxPro assumes that you want to edit or view existing records. You cannot simply move the cursor to a record beyond the last one to start entering a new record. Rather, you must press Ctrl+Y or open the Table pull-down menu and choose Append New Record.

Adding Records Programmatically

You can append records to a table from within a program in several ways depending on the source of the records. The code that follows enables users to add a new table record and update the fields directly.

```
* Code appends record to table and updates fields directly
  SELECT <table>
  APPEND BLANK

* Call a previously created form that allows the user
* to enter fields
  DO FillForm
```

However, you might not always want to modify the table directly. Many programmers prefer to modify memory variables that represent each of the table's fields (although buffering techniques in VFP are preferred). The sample code shown next creates a set of memory variables from a table and, after entering values for the memory variables, saves them to the table on request.

```
* Code creates a set of memory variables from table
  SELECT <table>
  SCATTER MEMVAR MEMO
```

```
* Call a previously created form that allows the user
* to enter fields
* Function returns .T. if user clicks the SAVE button to exit
  SaveIt = FillForm()

* If user clicks SAVE, append a blank record and
* gather the memory variable fields
  IF SaveIt
    APPEND BLANK
    GATHER MEMVAR MEMO
  ENDIF
```

The second example improves on the first because it does not add a new record to the table until the user decides to save the data.

Appending Data from Other Tables

Suppose that you want to append records to the current table from a second table. You could read through one record at a time, store the fields in memory variables, and then append these values to a record in the second table. The code in Listing 3.4 shows one implementation.

Listing 3.4   03CODE04.PRG—One Method of Appending Records to the Current Table from a Second Table

```
SELECT EMPLOYEE
SCAN
  SCATTER MEMVAR
  SELECT EMPL9
  APPEND BLANK
  GATHER MEMVAR
  SELECT EMPLOYEE
ENDSCAN
```

Rather than scatter values to memory variables, you can use an array to store the field values from a single record. The code in Listing 3.5 illustrates this method. (Remember that all the code listings are available on the Macmillan Web site at http://www.mcp.com/info.)

Listing 3.5   03CODE05.PRG—Another Method Using Arrays to Store Values from a Single Record

```
SELECT EMPLOYEE
SCAN
  SCATTER TO EMPLOYEE
  SELECT EMPL9
  APPEND BLANK
  GATHER FROM EMPLOYEE
  SELECT EMPLOYEE
ENDSCAN
```

Part

II

Ch

3

An alternative method enables you to copy all records from the first table into a two-dimensional array with a single command, thereby eliminating the loop. This method works only if the table does not have too many records. How many is too many records? The number of records times the number of fields per record cannot exceed 65,000. Listing 3.6 illustrates this method.

Listing 3.6   03CODE06.PRG—Yet a Third Method Using a Two-Dimensional Array

```
SELECT EMPLOYEE
IF RECCOUNT() * FCOUNT() < 65000
  COPY TO ARRAY aEmployee
  SELECT EMPL9
  APPEND FROM ARRAY aEmployee
ELSE
  SCAN
    SCATTER TO aEmployee
    SELECT EMPL9
    APPEND BLANK
    GATHER FROM aEmployee
    SELECT EMPLOYEE
  ENDSCAN
ENDIF
```

You might want to get even more sophisticated and copy blocks of 65,000 elements from one table to another, as shown in Listing 3.7.

Listing 3.7   03CODE07.PRG—A More Sophisticated Method—Copying Blocks of Data

```
SELECT EMPL10
GO TOP
IF RECCOUNT() * FCOUNT() < 65000

* Records can be copied in a single block
  COPY TO ARRAY aEmployee
  SELECT EMPL9
  APPEND FROM ARRAY aEmployee
ELSE

* Determine the maximum number of records to copy at a time
  nRecBlk = INT(RECCOUNT()/FCOUNT())
  nRemain = RECCOUNT()

* Loop until all records are copied
  DO WHILE nRemain > 0

  * Copy next block of records
    COPY TO ARRAY aEmployee NEXT nRecBlk
    SELECT EMPL9
```

```
      APPEND FROM ARRAY aEmployee
      SELECT EMPL10

   * Check if on last block
      nRemain = nRemain - nRecBlk
      nRecBlk = IIF(nRecBlk < nRemain, nRecBlk, nRemain)
   ENDDO
ENDIF
```

CAUTION

Any method that uses arrays works only if both tables have the same structure or if you use the `FIELDS` clause in the command to prearrange the order of the fields. Using an array eliminates the requirement that the fields have the same name in both files.

If you have the same table structure in both files, you can use a much simpler approach. The following command appends all records from `CURPROD` to `PRODHIST`:

```
SELECT PRODHIST
APPEND FROM CURPROD
```

If you want to append records from `CURPROD` only where field `lInProduction` equals `.F.`, use the following program lines:

```
SELECT PRODHIST
APPEND FROM CURPROD FOR NOT lInProduction
```

You can even specify, with the `FIELDS` clause, which fields to append.

CAUTION

The `FIELDS` clause identifies fields in the table that you are appending data to, not appending from. Furthermore, appended fields must have the same name and definition in both files.

Creating a Database

In Visual FoxPro, a database is a collection of tables. You can continue working with tables individually, as you would in the old FoxPro style. However, Visual FoxPro also provides several powerful enhancements for storing tables in databases. The balance of this chapter and the next chapter examine these enhanced properties.

First, create a database container to store the tables. The following command creates and names a new database in one step:

```
CREATE DATABASE SALES
```

You also can choose File, New, Database from the system menu, but like it does when you create tables, this method requires stepping through a series of dialog boxes.

One way to tell whether you have a database open is to look at the Database list box in the toolbar. Normally, this box is empty. If one or more databases are open, the current one is displayed in the box and the drop-down list enables you to change to another. In a program, you can return the name and path of the current database with DBC(), and you can change the current database with SET DATABASE. To determine the names and paths of all open databases, use the ADATABASES() function. The function creates a two-dimensional array with the database name as one element and its path as another.

To modify the contents of the current database interactively, use this command:

```
MODIFY DATABASE
```

This command opens the Database Designer. Figure 3.10 shows the Database Designer for the Tastrade application that comes with Visual FoxPro.

FIGURE 3.10

The Database Designer shows tables and relations for database TASTRADE.DBC.

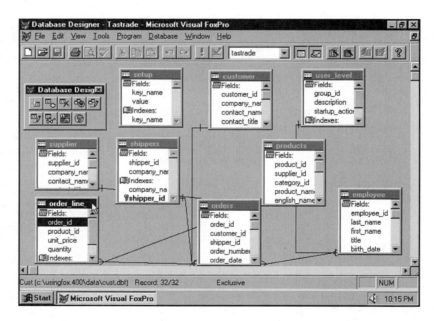

The Database Designer has its own toolbar. Figure 3.11 defines the buttons that it uses.

As you add tables to a database, they appear in the Database Designer window. Scrollbars appear as you add more tables. Each table lists the fields, followed by their indexes. A small key before an index name identifies the primary index. Relations between tables are shown with connecting lines. To browse a table, simply double-click it.

FIGURE 3.11
This figure shows the database toolbar buttons that are available from within Database Designer.

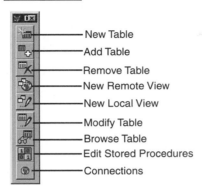

Database Toolbox

- New Table
- Add Table
- Remove Table
- New Remote View
- New Local View
- Modify Table
- Browse Table
- Edit Stored Procedures
- Connections

Part
II

Ch
3

Adding Existing Tables to the Database

To add an existing table (such as CUSTOMER.DBF) to the current database, click the Add Table button in the Database Designer toolbar or choose Database, Add Table. When the table appears in the design window, it can overlap or cover existing tables. You treat table definitions as you do any other window, and you can drag and resize them as you please.

N O T E You can add any table to only one database. Any attempt to add a table to a second database results in the following error message:

`File <filename> is part of a database` ▪

To modify the contents of a table, right-click any part of it and choose Modify from the shortcut menu. You also can left-click the table to select it and then click the Modify Table button in the Database Designer toolbar. This button opens the Table Designer dialog box, in which you can modify any of the table's characteristics.

Long Field Names One of the first changes you might want to make is to rename the fields that use long field names. In a database, you can have up to 128 characters per field name. To change a field name, simply highlight it and enter a new name. Spaces are not allowed in field names (FoxPro would not know when a field ended). One solution uses the underscore where a blank would be used to create clearer, more descriptive field names. However, the new recommended naming convention frowns on underscores. Rather, it recommends that you can make the first letter of each significant word in the field name uppercase and the rest lowercase. Unfortunately, the Table Designer in Visual FoxPro does not support case. In fact, Visual FoxPro displays field names in different case in different parts of the system. Browse window column headers, for example, are all initial capital letters.

N O T E Tables bound to databases can have 128-character table names. Use the Table Name text box in the Table Designer or a command like the following:

`CREATE TABLE orddetl NAME order_details` ▪

addition, the common naming convention for table fields includes a type prefix before the name. Figure 3.12 shows the first few fields of the CUSTOMER table with longer field names.

FIGURE 3.12

This figure shows the enhanced features that are available after you add tables to a database.

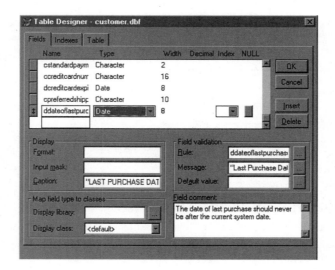

CAUTION

When you switch between long and short field names, you need to take a few steps. First, if you already have queries, reports, or programs that use 10-character field names, edit them before you use longer field names. Second, if you create queries, reports, or programs that have longer field names, they might not work if you remove the table from the database. (This action truncates the field names to 10 characters.) If the truncation does not affect the first 10 characters, you do not have a problem. But remember: FoxPro might automatically replace the last character or two with sequential numbers to ensure that each field name within a table is unique.

N O T E Many field lists used in Visual FoxPro—particularly those in wizards—display a limited number of characters. If you use table-identifying prefixes, or if you begin related fields with a common first word, you might not be able to distinguish the fields. You will not be able to distinguish the following two field names in many wizard field lists:

```
CUST_BillingAddressLine1
CUST_BillingAddressLine2
```

N O T E If you define long field names for a table, you must always use them. You cannot use either the shorter names stored in the .DBF or the truncated 10-character names described elsewhere in this section.

Field Format and Input Mask   You can store the field's preferred format and input mask for the field data in the database. The format and input mask options that you enter are the same as the available options in forms and reports. In fact, the purpose of storing them in the database comes into play when you are creating a field control in a form. When you create a field control in a form by dragging and dropping the field from the table to the form, the format that you specified in the Table Designer automatically sets the appropriate properties for the control.

Field-Level Validations   You also can add field-level validation rules in the Table Designer dialog box (refer to Figure 3.12). To add a rule, enter it directly in the Field Properties Validation Rule text box, or click the Expression Builder button (the button to the immediate right of the field, with the ellipsis on it). You have seen the Expression Builder before, so you already know how to use it. For the date-of-last-purchase field, you want to ensure that the date never exceeds the current system date. If it does, you want to display the error message Last Purchase Date Cannot Be a Future Date.

You can use any logical expression when you define a validation rule. You can even call a function for tests that are too complex to express as a single statement. The only restriction is that the function must return .T. or .F.. Field validation rules trigger when you attempt to move off the field or when the value changes due to an INSERT or REPLACE statement.

Field Default Values   Although the date-of-last-purchase field in Figure 3.12 does not contain a default value, you can add a default value for any table field. To default to the current system date, for example, place DATE() in the Default Value text box. The expression added for the default value must result in the same data type as the field itself; otherwise, FoxPro generates an error. FoxPro places the default value in the table field whenever you add a new record with a command such as APPEND or interactively in a Browse or Edit window.

Caption Values   FoxPro uses caption values as column headings when you browse or edit the table. By default, FoxPro uses the field name as the caption value. However, the field name might not always be the best choice. After all, if you use table prefixes or any other naming convention in the field names, you would not want to display them as field headings in Browse or Edit windows. You can define the caption based on the contents of another field or other variable, but the most common choice is to enter a simple text string in the Caption text box. This value is also used to create a label for a control when you are using the drag-and-drop method of creating field controls in a form or when you use the Form Wizard.

Field Comment   A field comment is a note to help document the meaning or purpose of a field. FoxPro stores this element as a Memo field; therefore, it can be as long you want. Figure 3.12 uses it as a reminder to use the current date to validate the input field. For other fields, a field comment could list possible values, tables used to validate an entry, and other information. You determine the use of a field comment; you can even ignore it. But the more information you store in the table definition, the easier it is to maintain it later.

This text appears after the label Description: when you highlight the field name in the Project Manager. This value is also used for the Comment property of a control when you are using the drag-and-drop method of creating field controls in a form.

Using Primary and Candidate Keys

Click the Index page of the Table Designer and open the Type drop-down list. From the earlier discussion about indexes, you remember that all four index types appear in this list. Remember that only an index that qualifies as a candidate index can be named primary. This means that the index expression references every record in the table with a unique value. You use the primary index to form relations with other tables. An Order table, for example, includes a customer ID with every order. FoxPro can relate the customer ID in that table to the customer ID in the CUSTOMER table to retrieve any or all of the customer's information.

Primary and candidate tests occur when VFP updates the record. Therefore, you might not get an immediate error if the key value is not unique until you move off the record.

Changing Table Properties Programmatically

In the past, changing table properties while you were in a program was difficult. The task basically required the program to re-create a new copy of the table with the changes and then copy the data from the old table to the new one. With Visual FoxPro, this task has become easier due to the addition of two commands: ALTER TABLE and ALTER COLUMN.

Suppose that you want to change the default value for a company name during data entry. You could use the following expression:

```
ALTER TABLE customer ALTER COLUMN company SET DEFAULT 'Documation'
```

In fact, you can do almost anything you want, as the ALTER TABLE syntax following this paragraph shows. Be aware, however, that this capability applies only to tables that are part of a database.

```
   [NULL¦NOT NULL]
      [CHECK Iexpression1 [ERROR cMessageText1]]
      [DEFAULT eExpression1]
      [PRIMARY KEY¦UNIQUE]
      [REFERENCES TableName2 [TAG TagName1]]
      [NOCPTRANS]
-Or-
ALTER TABLE TableName1
   ALTER [COLUMN] FieldName2
      [SET DEFAULT eExpression2]
      [SET CHECK Iexpression2 [ERROR cMessageText2]]
      [DROP DEFAULT]
      [DROP CHECK]
-Or-
ALTER TABLE TableName1
   [DROP [COLUMN] FieldName3]
   [SET CHECK Iexpression3 [ERROR cMessageText3]]
   [DROP CHECK]
   [ADD PRIMARY KEY eExpression3 TAG TagName2]
   [DROP PRIMARY KEY]
   [ADD UNIQUE eExpression4 [TAG TagName3]]
   [DROP UNIQUE TAG TagName4]
   [ADD FOREIGN KEY [eExpression5] TAG TagName4
      REFERENCES TableName2 [TAG TagName5]]
   [DROP FOREIGN KEY TAG TagName6 [SAVE]]
```

```
[RENAME COLUMN FieldName4 TO FieldName5]
[NOVALIDATE]
```

Examining Compatibility Issues

After the release of any major product upgrade, there is always a transition period in which some users are using the old version while others use the new one. You might need to share data between these versions. Eventually, you will need to convert the old system to the new version. This section describes some of the issues to consider during this transition.

Sharing Tables with FoxPro 2.x

In general, free tables can be shared between FoxPro 2.x and Visual FoxPro. However, FoxPro 2.x cannot share tables that have been included in a Visual FoxPro database. Attempting to use such a table in FoxPro 2.x results in the warning message Not a table/DBF. This behavior results from Visual FoxPro's changing the first byte of the .DBF file that identifies it.

Another problem occurs when you create a table in VFP that uses a Memo field. In VFP, the Memo field pointer is stored in four bytes rather than 10, as it was in previous versions of FoxPro.

If you remove a table from your system, a reference to it still exists in the database. You can remove such references by opening the database like a table and deleting the appropriate records. Similarly, if a database is accidentally deleted from disk, references to the database remain in the tables that were formerly contained in the database. The FREE TABLE command removes the database reference from a table. Thereafter, you can add the table to a different database or use it from FoxPro 2.x.

If you need to share tables with applications written in FoxPro 2.x, you cannot take advantage of the features provided by databases. In addition to being restricted to using free tables, you cannot define fields with the types Currency, DateTime, Double, Character (binary), or Memo (binary). These field types do not exist in FoxPro 2.x. If you can live with these limitations, you can share tables and their indexes with FoxPro 2.x. If you cannot, you might need to use a remote connection to the table using ODBC.

Conversion from Visual FoxPro 3.0

When you open a project file created in VFP 3 or 5, VFP 6 has a built-in converter that converts all your files in that project. Actually, what FoxPro does at this point is rebuild your project, so if files have been moved, FoxPro prompts you to locate them.

Also, when you try to open a database container created in VFP 3 or 5, VFP prompts you that the database container was compiled in a previous version if the database container has stored procedures. If you attempt to open a database created with Visual FoxPro 6, you will not need to be concerned. The only time you will get a prompt here is if the database was created with an earlier version. To solve this problem, type the following command in the Command window:

```
COMPILE DATABASE DatabaseName
```

Removing a Table from the Database

When it adds a table to a database, Visual FoxPro changes the first byte in the .DBF header and adds a relative reference to the .DBC, which prohibits you from using the table as a free table or from adding it to another database. However, you can run FREE TABLE as shown in the following example to reset the first byte in the .DBF file and clear the back link:

```
FREE TABLE CUSTOMER
```

Current values for this first byte in the .DBF include

0x02	FoxBASE0x03 FoxPro, FoxBASE+, dBASE III PLUS, dBASE IV (no memo)
0x30	Visual FoxPro
0x43	dBASE IV SQL table file, no memo
0x63	dBASE IV SQL system file, no memo
0x83	FoxBASE+, dBASE III PLUS (with memo)
0x8B	dBASE IV (with memo)
0xCB	dBASE IV ASQL table file, with memo
0xF5	FoxPro 2.x (or earlier) (with memo)
0xFB	FoxBASE

 TIP One way to hide data from other users and applications that read .DBF files is to change the first byte to something that other applications do not recognize.

Then you can add the table to another database (which, of course, sets the first byte again). But you don't need to move tables. You can open more than one database at a time within an application by including multiple OPEN DATABASE commands, as shown in the following example:

```
OPEN DATABASE databas1
OPEN DATABASE databas2 ADDITIVE
OPEN DATABASE databas3 ADDITIVE
```

Advanced Database Management Concepts

Database Design Techniques

No other single factor has a greater influence on the success of a database application than the design of the database itself. The way you organize individual data items in tables and then relate those tables with one another in a database forms the very foundation of the application. A poorly built foundation weakens the programs built on it by making them more difficult to write, more difficult to maintain, and more difficult to enhance as demands on the software grow. Furthermore, improper design might force the programmer to fall back on less efficient methods of coding, which thus require more time and are more susceptible to error.

Perhaps you learned programming from classroom courses that taught you good design methods right from the start. On the other hand, maybe you learned programming by doing it and learned good design methods by trial and error. In either case, this chapter should help you build on your existing skills to create better database designs. To do so, it examines several areas of database management.

Data Normalization

The most important thing you can do when you start a new application is design the structure of your tables carefully. A poorly structured database results in very inefficient code at best; at worst, it makes some features nearly impossible to implement. On the other hand, a well-designed set of tables will not only solve your current problem, but also provide the flexibility to answer questions that you don't yet anticipate. Perhaps even more important, you will write programs faster by taking advantage of queries and SQL SELECT statements to retrieve and maintain data. Finally, reports that might have required awkward manual coding under a denormalized structure almost write themselves when you use the report generator.

In general, the data structure of an application, more than any other factor, makes or breaks the application's success. Visual FoxPro is based on the relational database model proposed by E.F. Codd in 1970. Codd based his model on mathematical principles that govern relational set theory. By following only a few very specific rules defining the creation of sets, he proved that you can manipulate the data easily. His technique became known as *data normalization*.

All relational database theory revolves around the concept of using key fields to define relations between flat file tables. The more tables you have, the more relations FoxPro requires to connect them. Set theory does not demand, or even expect, that each table be connected directly to every other table. However, because each table is connected to at least one other, all tables in the database have direct or indirect relations with one another.

To examine the concepts of normalization, this section examines the Tasmanian Trader example provided with Visual FoxPro. However, it takes a view close to the beginning of the application-development process—just after establishing the data requirements.

Functional Dependencies

Assuming that you have decided what data fields you need, the next step is to divide them into tables. (Of course, you could put all the fields in a single table.) Even without normalization rules, it should be obvious that you do not want to repeat all the information about employees, customers, products, suppliers, and shippers for each item ordered. The only way to determine which fields belong together in each table is through functional dependency analysis. (It's not the same thing as taking away a computer terminal from a programmer; that's a functionally dependent analyst.)

Functional dependency defines the relationship between an attribute or a group of attributes in one table to another attribute or group of attributes in another table. In this discussion, the term *attributes* refers to fields. Therefore, you need to see which fields depend on other fields. A person's last name, for example, depends on his Social Security number (not originally, but at least according to the U.S. government). For any given Social Security number (person), there is only one corresponding name—not necessarily a unique name, but still only one name.

On the other hand, a Social Security number does not depend on a name. Given only a person's last name, there may be dozens, if not hundreds, of Social Security numbers. Even if you add a first name to the last, it still might not uniquely identify a single Social Security number. Imagine how many Bob Smiths there are, for example.

Thus, you can conclude that a last name is functionally dependent on a Social Security number, but not the other way around. You might even go the Orwellian route of referring to a person by his Social Security number.

Next, you might want to find other attributes that are functionally dependent on a Social Security number. Having gone through all the fields, you might have a list like the one shown in Table 4.1.

Table 4.1 Fields Functionally Dependent on a Social Security Number

Address	FirstName	Password	SalesRegion
BirthDate	GroupId	Photo	Ssn
Cty	HireDate	Position	StartSalary
Country	HomePhone	PostalCode	SystemUser
EmplId	LastName	Region	TaskDesc
Extension	LicenseNo	ReportsTo	Title

As a first pass at designing tables, you might group these fields into one table. Then, following similar logic, you might determine the functional dependencies in the remaining fields. Continue to group those attributes that have the same dependency in the same table. In effect, the number of functional dependencies determines the number of tables required.

Actually, if you follow this method of grouping fields, the resulting tables should be very close to a normalized form already. However, to guarantee that they are normalized, you should verify that they obey at least the first three rules of normalized data:

- First normal form: eliminates repeating fields and nonatomic values
- Second normal form: requires each column to be dependent on every part of the primary key
- Third normal form: requires that all nonprimary fields depend solely on the primary fields

First Normal Form

The first normal form eliminates repeating fields and nonatomic values. An *atomic value* means that the field represents a single thing, not a concatenation of values—just as an atom represents a single element.

In the early days of relational databases, there were some rather small limits on the number of fields allowed in a record. As a result, programmers concatenated fields to fit all the data into a single record. Thus, one field might contain something like the following:

12/03/9412/15/9401/05/95T

This value actually represents four fields: an order date, a start-production date, a completion date, and a flag to indicate whether the order was shipped.

Forming relations between fields, retrieving data, and performing other operations is not easy when a field contains multiple values. The need to perform substring searches and to parse the fields slows applications tremendously, not to mention adding extra complexity to the code. To bring this table into first normal form, you need to split this field into four separate fields: three Date fields and one Logical field.

Another common problem addressed by the first normal form is repeated fields. Again, it was not unusual for early database developers to hard-code the number of items that a customer could order. They did so by placing the ordered products' IDs in the same record as the general order information, as shown in the following table:

OrderId	OrderDate	ProdId1	ProdId2	ProdId3	ProdId4	Net
00006	08/04/94	A3426	B8483	C398		59.34

In this example, there is no problem as long as the customer never orders more than four items at a time. (Only three items were ordered in this example.) However, it would be difficult to search the database to determine how many units of each product have been sold because the program has to check each product column and then sum the results. Reports that display a list of customers who order specific products would be similarly difficult to produce. In fact, most reports need complex hand coding so that they can search each field. As a result, the reports tend to be more likely to generate errors and require more time to execute.

Of course, you could increase the number of possible products that a customer can buy, but how many is enough (5? 10? 20?)? If you select 20, what if most customers order only two or three items? The resulting database wastes a great deal of space. More important, depending on the way that the code reads these fields, it can spend a great deal of time processing empty fields.

One alternative is to define a database that has a variable number of fields. In fact, some database systems several years ago supported this feature; they even promoted it as the best solution, in their marketing department's opinion. Fortunately, FoxPro continued to support the true relational definition of tables and kept records fixed in length.

The first normal form replaces repeating fields with a single field. It then creates as many records as necessary (one per ordered item), as shown in the following table:

OrderId	OrderDate	ProductId	OrderNet
00006	08/04/94	A3426	59.34
00006	08/04/94	B8483	59.34
00006	08/04/94	C398	59.34

After performing this analysis on each table in the database, the preliminary relational model of the data is complete. This first normal form is called structural or syntactic normalization. However, it should never be your final goal. There can still be problems in the data that cause the code to be more complex than it needs to be.

Intuitively, you may not like the solution offered in the preceding example. For one thing, it repeats values—not within records, but across multiple records. And wherever repeated values occur, inconsistencies can occur. This problem is addressed in subsequent normal forms.

Second Normal Form

The second normal form requires that each column be dependent on every part of the primary key. Look again at the table that results from the first normal form:

ORDERS.DBF

OrderId	OrderDate	ProductId	OrderNet
00006	08/04/94	A3426	59.34
00006	08/04/94	B8483	59.34
00006	08/04/94	C398	59.34
00007	08/05/94	B8483	9.18

Because of the transformation performed by the first normal form, OrderId is no longer unique; neither is any other single field. However, the combination of OrderId and ProductId may be unique. Using this as a working assumption, you next need to examine the other fields to see whether they depend on the new primary key.

OrderDate depends only on OrderId, not on the combination of OrderId and ProductId. The same is true of OrderNet. Therefore, according to the second normal form, you need to remove these fields and place them in a separate table with a copy of the field on which they depend: OrderId. This results in two tables. Name the one that uses OrderId as the primary key, ORDERS.DBF; name the other, which contains a primary key on OrderId and ProductId, ORDITEMS.DBF. These new tables are as follows:

ORDERS.DBF

OrderId	OrderDate	OrderNet
00006	08/04/94	59.34
00007	08/05/94	9.18

ORDITEMS.DBF

OrderId	ProductId	LineNo
00006	A3426	0001
00006	B8483	0002
00006	C398	0003
00007	B8483	0001

Merely by following the rules of normalization, you have taken the original order data and derived a structure that consists of two tables: one table with information about the overall order and the other with details on each order. Notice that a new field has been added to ORDITEMS.DBF: LineNo. This additional field counts the number of items in the form. This field has a fixed size of four digits; thus, it enables up to 9,999 items to appear in the same order.

To associate the information in ORDERS.DBF with ORDITEMS.DBF, you form a relation between them based on OrderId. This relation is a one-to-many relation because, for every order in ORDERS.DBF, there can be more than one record in ORDITEMS.DBF. In fact, there is no limit to the number of items that the customer can order—one item or a million. (Well, actually, you set an arbitrary limit of 9,999 via the size of the field LineNo, but you can always increase the size of this field.) The program, when it is written to use related files, handles both situations equally well.

Third Normal Form

To reach the third normal form, the table must already be in first and second normal form. Then, you determine which field or combination of fields represents the primary key for the table. For the employee table, a logical choice would be either employees' Social Security numbers or their employee IDs. For the order table, OrderId makes a good choice.

For the order-items table, no single field uniquely defines a record. There can be more than one detail record for an order ID and `ProductId` can occur many times, both in the same order and across orders. `OrderId` also can occur many times within a single order. `LineNo` repeats the same sequence, beginning with 1 for each order. However, the combination of `OrderId` and `LineNo` is unique. Even if the same item appears more than once in a single order, its line-item value will be different. Thus, this file requires a composite primary key.

To illustrate third normal form, another field—`ProdName`—has been added. Suppose that the order-detail table includes the following fields:

ORDITEMS.DBF

OrderId	LineNo	ProductId	ProdName
00006	0001	A3426	Tape Drives
00006	0002	B8483	Modems
00006	0003	C398	Track Balls
00007	0001	B8483	Modems

To be in third normal form, all nonprimary fields must depend solely on the primary fields. First, determine whether `ProductId` depends solely on the key field combination `OrderId` and `LineNo`. The answer is yes, because there can be only one product ID for each combination of `OrderId` and `LineNo`.

Does product ID depend on the product name? This is a trick question. In some ways, it does, but product names may not be unique. Some products could have multiple sizes, colors, or other attributes. Each product has its own unique product ID but the same product name. Therefore, product ID does not depend solely on product name.

Does `ProdName` depend solely on the primary key fields? Not really. The product name is not a function of the order ID and line number; rather, it depends on the product ID. Remember that each product ID has one unique product name, although the product name might be assigned to more than one product ID. Therefore, this field fails the third normal form.

The solution in this case is to move the product name into a new file called PRODUCTS in which `ProductId` is the primary key. You might have reached this conclusion independently from your analysis of functional dependencies. Remember that normalization rules just reinforce functional analysis and common sense. The new table structure appears as follows:

ORDITEMS.DBF

OrderId	LineNo	ProductId
00006	0001	A3426
00006	0002	B8483
00006	0003	C398
00007	0001	B8483

Part II Ch 4

PRODUCTS.DBF

ProductId	ProdName
A3426	Tape Drives
B8483	Modems
C398	Track Balls
B8483	Modems

Of course, you need to perform this same analysis on every table in the application. When the analysis is complete, you can say that the application is normalized. Although there are additional levels of normalization, the need for them is rare. If you practice creating tables in third normal form, you can avoid most data structure problems. You usually do not want to include fields that can be derived from other fields in the same or related tables. For example, you might not want to include an order-total field in the order file if the detail file also contains the price of each item ordered—it is safer to sum the individual prices to arrive at the order total. Of course, the amount actually paid might go on the order to compare against the total due. Think of it this way: The customer typically pays against an order but is billed based on individual items.

Perhaps you feel overwhelmed by these rules. Actually, with practice, you will begin creating normalized files right from the start. Some wise person once said that true understanding comes only when you see it in your dreams. When you look at the data for a new application and immediately visualize multiple files in your head, you truly understand normalization.

When to Break the Rules

Normalization rules are not laws; they are merely guidelines to help you avoid creating data structures that limit the flexibility of the application or reduce its efficiency. However, no one will knock on your door and arrest you for breaking normalization rules (except maybe your boss). The following examples are situations in which breaking normalization rules might make sense:

- You need to write a library system that prevents any patron from checking out more than five books at one time. You could write the system by normalizing the file that tracks the books checked out; it would have to ensure that no more than five records exist for each patron. However, a single record with five fields—one for each book—might make this application easier to develop. (An alternative is to add to the main patron table a field that simply counts the number of books that the patron has currently borrowed.)

- An order ID actually consists of the concatenation of two digits that represent the year plus a five-digit sequential number. Because the order-date field also reflects the year, you could, in theory, extract it or use the date in combination with the sequence number. However, the ease of referencing a single field in this case probably outweighs the strict avoidance of repeating data that can be derived from other fields.

■ You have accepted a project to build a database for the National Association of Twins. Would you create a separate record for the name of each twin, or would you include twins in the same record? After all, you know by definition that there will always be exactly two names.

The intent here is to emphasize that normalization is a desired goal, but every once in a while, it makes sense to be a little abnormal.

Naming Conventions

Your first question might be, "Why do I need a naming convention? FoxPro does not require it." Although Visual FoxPro does not require a naming convention, using one makes code clearer. You will appreciate this benefit when you have to return to code that you wrote months or years earlier and try to remember what the variables mean. You might encounter similar problems when you try to work with code written by someone else. It can take considerable time just to determine the type, scope, and origin of variables. Using a naming convention solves these problems when you use the convention consistently and if you take into account the variable's type and scope. This practice can eliminate naming and scoping conflicts that are common in many large applications.

Attempts at implementing naming conventions in earlier versions of FoxPro met with limited success. FoxPro limited both table field and memory variable names to 10 characters. With so few characters available, using any of them detracted from a programmer's ability to assign meaningful names. Also, some proposed naming conventions limited users' abilities to transfer data between tables easily, especially when they were using commands such as SCATTER and GATHER. Thus, the issue became a trade-off; programmers felt that they had to choose between two conflicting goals. They could adopt a naming convention that identified a variable's source and type, or they could use all 10 characters to make meaningful names.

Now, with Visual FoxPro's support of long field and variable names, you can have both naming conventions and significant names. The following sections recommend naming conventions for different categories of variables. The sections also mention some possible variations that you might consider. Each section uses a slightly different method due to differences in the variables and objects that each variable attempts to name. However, implementing an overall naming convention for your applications will make supporting multiprogrammer development easier and result in fewer naming and scoping conflicts.

There is no one absolute naming convention. Rather, the one that you pick (or that your company standardizes on) becomes the right one. It is difficult, if not impossible, to switch to a new naming convention after you have worked with a product for some time. That is why the introduction of Visual FoxPro presents a rare opportunity to begin using a naming convention with your new applications, especially if you have never used one before.

Naming Issues Within an Application

Developers of independent applications do not often see the immediate advantages of implementing naming conventions. After all, they are the only ones who are working on the code and they know everything in it, right? Well, put aside an application for a few months and try to come back to it. How much do you really remember? The larger the application, the bigger the problem. It is easy to forget which variables each procedure uses. And what about the program that failed because Bill and Beth developed separate routines that use the same variables? Both situations lead to naming conflicts. If you reuse the same variable name, the program may accidentally overwrite values that are needed elsewhere. Suddenly, the application no longer works and users are on the phone, waiting patiently to politely inform you of a problem.

Visual FoxPro does not require that you adopt a naming convention. For many programmers, conforming to a convention might seem like wearing a straitjacket. Give it a try, though, and as you start developing Visual FoxPro projects, see whether things run more smoothly after you get used to the convention. Some working environments have a standard for programming, such as variable declarations and naming conventions. If you are a developer, you need to check with your client because it might have some requirements that you need to conform to. Otherwise, you should develop your own conventions because it is easier to use standards in your day-to-day operations.

The following sections describe some proposed naming convention rules for different variable types. Feel free to adopt what you like and discard the rest. Add additional rules if you need them. But when you have something that you like, stick with it for at least the duration of your current project. Also, keep an eye on the industry as naming conventions become more commonly used and more standardized.

Naming Memory Variables

You must follow some basic rules when naming a variable. A variable name:

- Must begin with a letter.
- Must contain only letters, numbers, and underscore characters. Spaces and special characters are not permitted, and underscores are frowned upon.
- Must not exceed 255 characters.
- Must not be a reserved word, or (if the variable is only four characters long) must not be the first four characters of a reserved word, that is, the first four characters of any Visual FoxPro command.

N O T E   You probably think that the third rule is a misprint. It's not. A memory variable can have up to 255 characters. Using that many characters means:

- You like to type.
- You have trouble coming up with significant, unique names.
- You don't want other people to be able to read your code.
- You have a good story to tell and you put it in each variable name.

Seriously, although 10 characters is too few, 255 characters is too many for most applications. ■

Microsoft's intent is to bring the object languages of its major products (such as Visual FoxPro, Access, Visual Basic, and C++) closer together. All these products support longer field names. Access currently supports up to 64 characters, and Visual Basic supports 40 characters. Other products that enable you to access their data via ODBC or OCX controls might have variable names of other lengths. If you intend to share data with one of these products, try to limit your variable-name sizes to match the smaller of them. In this way, you will eliminate potential name conflicts based on name size.

Variable Scope   The first attribute to consider when naming variables is scope identification. A variable's scope defines where and when it is known in a program. For example, a program can reference a *public variable* (global in other languages) from any line in the application when it is defined. The simple program shown in Listing 4.1 illustrates this concept.

Listing 4.1   `04CODE01.PRG`—**Public Variables Can Be Referenced Anywhere in Your Program**

```
* Main program
  DO SUB1
  ? abc

PROCEDURE SUB1
PUBLIC ABC
  ABC = 5
  DO SUB2
RETURN

PROCEDURE SUB2
  ? ABC
RETURN
```

Part
II

Ch
4

This example defines variable ABC as a public variable and initializes it in procedure SUB1. Any lower procedure or function called directly or indirectly by SUB1 after defining ABC can use it. Similarly, any higher routine that calls SUB1 can also use ABC after calling SUB1. The capability to reference a variable value in both higher and lower procedures is the key distinguishing feature of public variables.

Many programmers use public variables extensively, so they do not have to worry about where they define or use those variables. They can even initialize every variable in the main program. Although this practice actually gives them a scope of private (meaning that the variables are known only to the current procedure and any called procedure), the fact that the variables have been defined in the initial procedure makes them available to all subsequent procedures. However, this type of coding often results in problems. Primarily, it is difficult to locate errors caused when a "new" variable in a lower subroutine has the same name as the public variable. The program simply appears to inexplicably change the variable's value.

CAUTION

If you use a variable in a program without declaring its scope first, you cannot later declare it public without generating an error.

N O T E Declaring variables at the start of a PRG makes them available throughout the PRG, but private only to the PRG. If the PRG is called by another program, these variables will not be known in the calling program. On the other hand, a variable declared public will be known in all PRGs involved in the application after it is declared and defined. ▪

Private variables offer more limited scope. When initialized, these variables are known to the current procedure and all procedures that it calls. However, they are not known to the procedure that calls it, to any other higher procedures, or to procedures that follow a different calling sequence. In other words, the scope travels in one direction only: down one branch of the procedure call stack.

 T I P If you need a variable to be known across multiple branches of the procedure call stack, declare it public.

N O T E Declaring a variable private in the main routine has almost the same effect as declaring it public. The difference is that the private variable is known only within the current .PRG file. Of course, this makes a difference only when you have one .PRG call another. ▪

To see the scope of a private variable in action, change the line PUBLIC ABC to PRIVATE ABC in the preceding example. Although Visual FoxPro recognizes the variable ABC in routines SUB1 and SUB2, it is not known in the main program. In fact, FoxPro generates an error when it attempts to use that variable.

The manual states that declaring a variable private does not create a new variable; it merely hides any previous variable with the same name from the current module. When the program exits the current module, it reveals the hidden variables again.

A new scope introduced in Visual FoxPro is the *local variable*. A variable declared local is known only in the routine that declares and defines it; higher- or lower-level routines cannot use it. If you replace the PUBLIC ABC line in the example with LOCAL ABC, ABC exists only in SUB1; neither SUB2 nor the main program can reference it.

Although not specifically defined as a variable scope, variables defined in class definitions have unique status. First, like local variables, they exist only in the class that defines them. Second, they retain their values between references to the class. This is different from a local variable, which must be redefined and initialized each time the program executes the routine that uses it. Other languages refer to variables with similar scope as static variables. Unfortunately, you cannot define static variables outside a class definition.

As programs grow, it becomes easier to forget or confuse the scope of each variable. A common naming convention identifies a variable's scope by adding a scope-prefix character to each variable's name. Table 4.2 lists the available scope levels and suggests appropriate prefixes.

Table 4.2   Scope-Prefix Characters

Scope	Prefix	Example
Local	l	`llTaxableItem`
Private	p	`pnTotalDue`
Public/Global	g	`gcCurrentUser`
Static (Class Variable)	s	`snCounter`

N O T E   The need for a prefix in static variables that are used to define properties of a class or in event code is less obvious than for other variable scopes because these variables cannot be used anywhere else anyway. This convention does not apply to property or method names, just to other variables used with event method code.

In Chapter 13, "Introduction to Object-Oriented Programming," you learned how to store a reference to an object in a variable. Therefore, you might be tempted to use prefixes in these object reference variables. Strictly speaking, these variables might act like private variables in scope, but they are so different in use that they deserve their own naming convention. Those conventions are listed in Table 4.4 later in this chapter.

N O T E   Because naming conventions are optional, you might decide to use different prefix letters for scope. However, Visual FoxPro and Microsoft recommend these characters. Using them will help you read other programmers' code if those programmers follow the same recommended conventions.

Some developers include naming conventions for windows, procedures, functions, menu pads, and other objects. Because these names cannot be used outside their very restricted context, there is less likelihood of confusion. However, the "Naming Objects" section later in this chapter provides possible guidelines for these objects as well.

Variable Type   The next attribute of the variable that you can identify is its type. Knowing a variable's type can help prevent errors caused by using the wrong variable type in an expression. Suppose that you want to use a variable named START. By itself, the variable gives no indication whether it stores a date, character string, or number. Suppose that you want to use START in an expression such as the following:

```
? 'List records from ' + start + ' TO ' + end
```

Part

II

Ch

4

If START stores anything other than character-type data, Visual FoxPro quickly responds with the following error message:

```
Operator/operand type mismatch
```

On the other hand, using a prefix that identifies the variable type can immediately warn you of the need to convert the variable to a different type before you use it. The following line combines two variables that have the prefix gd with text strings. The prefix indicates that the variables are global variables of type Date. Notice that the variable type information provided by the second character of the prefix alerts you to a potential problem: You cannot directly combine text with dates. Therefore, you know to use DTOC() before concatenating the variables with text, as the following code illustrates.

```
? 'List records from ' + DTOC(gdstart) + ;
          ' to ' + DTOC(gdend)
```

Table 4.3 lists the variable types in Visual FoxPro, along with suggested prefixes. These prefixes represent Microsoft's recommendations, based on internal representations of these variable types.

Table 4.3 Type-Prefix Characters

Type	Prefix	Example
Array	a	gaMonthsInYear
Character	c	gcLastName
Currency	y	pyProductCost
Date	d	pdBirthDate
DateTime	t	ltRecordPackStamp
Double	b	lbAnnualRiceProduction
Float	f	lfMilesBetweenCities
General	g	lgSoundSample
Integer	i	liTries
Logical	l	llTaxable
Memo	m	lmProductDescription
Numeric	n	gnAge
Picture	p	lpProductPicture
Unknown	u	luSampleData

CAUTION

Using this naming convention requires that a variable have a two-character prefix. The first prefix character always denotes the scope and the second denotes the type. Although you could define these characters in reverse order, you should never switch the order of these characters after you start an application. If you do, the resulting confusion will make you wish that you never heard of naming conventions—and it will not make you popular with other programmers who need to read your code, if they follow the standard prefix order.

Using Case to Make Variables Readable   A variation on the preceding naming examples uses an underscore character between the prefix characters and the rest of the variable name. Often, underscores are included between individual words in the variable name. This personal preference of some developers is not part of the new Microsoft recommendation, but you might encounter it in the naming convention used by other applications. In fact, the recommended conventions proposed for Visual Basic, Access, and Visual FoxPro do not include the underscore anywhere in a variable name. The conventions rely on the fact that the first capitalized letter indicates the beginning of the unique portion of the variable name and the end of the prefix. Also, when the variable name consists of two or more words, the first letter of each word also begins with a capital letter. The rest of the characters are always lowercase.

The only time the recommended convention could conceivably pose a problem is if you use an external text editor that does not honor case. (That possibility is relatively remote these days.) On the other hand, Visual FoxPro does not yet completely honor the case of field names, which detracts from their readability. Most programmers define their variable names in many different ways. No matter how you do it, you should use the variable declarations and naming standards required by your client or customers. If these requirements do not exist, you should develop them for your own use. You should use names that mean something, such as `fileAccountJuly` or `FileAccountJuly`. However you choose to do it, you should have some organization and sensibility to your methods.

N O T E   Because naming conventions are optional, many variations exist. To some extent, this situation is good because experimentation sometimes leads to better methods. Many leading FoxPro developers have developed their own naming conventions over the years, some of which are better than others. At this writing, it is too early to determine whether these conventions will be abandoned for a common naming convention. Actually, global acceptance would be a surprise. Part of the problem is that the naming convention proposed for FoxPro is not completely consistent with other development languages yet. Another problem is that Visual FoxPro does not fully support cases in all the places where variables and field names appear. Finally, developers might use naming conventions for different purposes.

On the other hand, any naming convention probably is better than no naming convention, as long as it is strictly followed within the application. ▪

Part
II
Ch
4

Keep in mind that although you can enter variable names with the uppercase and lowercase rule as suggested earlier in this chapter, Visual FoxPro is case insensitive. FoxPro really doesn't care whether the variable is called `lsOrderEnter` or `lsorderenter`—both variables represent the same data memory location. This means that the burden of following such a naming convention is solely on your shoulders. Visual FoxPro's Documenting Wizard not only supports all uppercase or all lowercase, but also uses the case of the first occurrence of a variable and matches all subsequent occurrences. Thus, it even supports mixed-case variable names. Using initial caps for each word in a variable name, however, makes the variable easier to read.

Remember, FoxPro does not require that you use a naming convention. But following any naming convention (even one that you create yourself) generates the following benefits:

- It makes identifying the scope and type of a variable easier.
- It reduces syntax errors and undefined variable errors.
- It makes it easier for other programmers to identify the purpose of a variable when they look at your code.

Places where you might not want to use these prefixes in variable names include:

- Constants created with `#DEFINE`. (In fact, the recommended convention for these variable names is all uppercase.)
- Class names, properties, or methods.

Naming Fields in Tables

If you need to use free tables in an application, Visual FoxPro continues to limit field names to 10 characters. Even in such cases, some developers have proposed using character prefixes. One three-character prefix convention uses the first two characters of the prefix to uniquely identify the table. These characters can be the first two characters of the table name, but they don't have to be. The third character is an underscore to clearly separate the prefix from the rest of the field name.

If the same field appears in multiple tables, you can continue to use a table prefix. However, you should make the remaining seven characters exactly the same in each table in which the field appears. Suppose that you have a `Style` field in several databases. If style has the same meaning in each database, you might have:

`or_Style`	for the style in the order file
`pr_Style`	for the style in the product file
`in_Style`	for the style in the inventory file

However, if style means something different in each file, the seven characters should uniquely reflect this difference, as follows:

`or_CStyle`	for customer style
`pr_PStyle`	for product style
`in_ClStyle`	for cloth style

The recommended Visual FoxPro naming convention used with table fields uses only the first character of a field name to identify its type (refer to Table 4.2). The remaining nine characters uniquely identify the field. Because the same field name can appear in more than one table, you should always precede it with the file alias when you use it in code, as shown in the following example:

```
customer.cLastName
order.dOrderDate
```

> **CAUTION**
>
> Despite the recommendation that you use uppercase and lowercase, the Visual FoxPro Table Designer supports only lowercase. To make matters more confusing, commands such as DISPLAY STRUCTURE list field names in uppercase. The Browse and Edit commands label column headings by displaying field names with initial caps only. Thus, there is no way to differentiate case in a table name. This is another reason for some developers to use the underscore character after the prefix, or even between major words. Would the field C_RAP, for example, make more sense in a table that lists types of music, or would you prefer CRAP?

Never use just a letter to identify a work area, such as A.cLastName. Such a practice restricts programs to always opening tables in the same work area. When you write generalized code that more than one procedure can call, you cannot always guarantee a work area's availability for a table. Therefore, always reference fields by their table alias.

 TIP Even though Visual FoxPro may not honor case in field names, there is no reason not to use case when you are coding field names.

Applications rewritten with Visual FoxPro can take advantage of the enhanced table features of a database. (It is unlikely that anyone will modify existing FoxPro applications just to add long character names. As part of an application rewrite to take advantage of other VFP features, however, converting to longer character names makes sense.)

When you add a table to a database, you can define 128-character field names. As indicated earlier, 128 characters may be overkill. With this many available characters, there is no reason why you cannot adopt one of the naming conventions and still define significant names.

The trade-off in using a naming convention for table fields is the fact that some commands and procedures might not work with some conventions. Suppose that you include a table-prefix code in each field name. With 128 characters, you could include the entire table or alias name. But code that uses SCATTER and GATHER to transfer data between tables will not work because the prefix names would be different. Furthermore, Visual FoxPro will not automatically identify relations between tables. On the other hand, if you limit the prefix to a single field-type character in all tables, SCATTER, GATHER, and other table commands continue to work well.

Part
II

Ch
4

Finally, even if you adopt a naming convention for your table variables, using commands such as SCATTER can lead to unexpected problems. When you scatter table fields to memory variables, Visual FoxPro creates a memory variable with the exact name as the field. When you use that variable without an alias identifier, Visual FoxPro makes the following assumptions about whether you mean the table variable or the memory variable:

- Any variable used with STORE is assumed to be a memory variable.
- A variable that is assigned a value with a REPLACE statement is assumed to be a table variable.
- The variable on the left side of an equation is assumed to be a memory variable.
- Any variable on the right side of an equation is first assumed to be a table variable and then a memory variable.

 TIP You can override some of these assumptions by prefixing the variable with the table alias. If the variable is a memory variable, use m. as the prefix.

The following equation takes the table variable Quantity, adds sale quantity (SaleQty) to it, and then saves the sum in the memory variable Quantity:

```
Quantity = Quantity + SaleQty
```

If you have this statement in your code, you may wonder why Quantity never seems to increase. The following redefined statement, using the recommended naming convention, makes the assignment clearer:

```
m.nQuantity = m.nQuantity + m.lnSaleQty
```

This statement tells you that nQuantity is a numeric variable saved to a memory variable from a table (because the prefix has only a single character). It also clearly adds a local numeric memory variable, lnSaleQty, which represents the sales quantity.

Naming Objects

When you create an instance of a class, you store a pointer to it in a reference variable. You might want to include a special prefix to identify its class type. When you are looking at a property reference such as the following, it can be difficult to guess what class was used to create this object:

```
? Customer.City.Value
```

You may guess that Value represents the name of the city; therefore, the object probably is a text box within a form. The form is referenced by the object-reference name Customer, and the text box has the object-reference name City. But it could just as easily be a list or a combo box. The point is that you cannot be really sure to which class this object belongs. Why is this important? Knowing the class of an object tells you what properties, events, and methods to expect from it. Notice how much more information you know about the object when it includes an object prefix. Immediately, you know that it is a text box in a form such as the following:

```
? frmCustomer.txtCity.Value
```

This modified expression defines the object hierarchy. It says that a form named `Customer` contains a text box named `City` and that it returns the object's value. The recommended prefixes for naming object references are listed in Table 4.4.

Table 4.4   Object-Reference Name Prefixes

Object	Prefix	Example
Check box	chk	chkCurrentYrOnly
Combo box	cbo	cboShipMethod
Command button	cmd	cmdRecordMove
Command group	cmg	cgpReportOptions
Container	cnt	cntBitBucket
Control	ctl	ctlOrders
Custom	cst	cstDiscountCalculation
Edit box	edt	edbBugDescription
Form	frm	frmCustomerAddress
Form set	frs	fstCustomer
Grid	grd	grdProductMatrix
Grid column	grc	grcProductPrice
Grid column header	grh	grhProductFieldName
Image	img	imgProductPicture
Label	lbl	lblCustomerLabel
Line	lin	linSeparator
List box	lst	lstStatesList
Menu	mnu	mnuMainMenu
OLE bound control	olb	olbEmployeePicture
OLE	ole	oleExcelGraph
Option button	opt	optPaymentMethod
Option group	ogr	ogrPaymentDistribution
Page	pag	pagStoreConfiguration
Page frame	pfr	pfrPointOfSaleOptions
Separator	sep	sepFirstGapShape

continues

Part

II

Ch

4

Table 4.4 Continued		
Object	**Prefix**	**Example**
Shape	shp	shpTitleBox
Spinner	spn	spnReportCopies
Text box	txt	txtLastName
Timer	tmr	tmrStartProcess
Toolbar	tbr	btnFileSelect

This naming convention distinguishes object references by a three-character prefix.

Chapter 13, "Introduction to Object-Oriented Programming," describes ways to use a reference variable to shorten the full object reference. Because the complete reference can be rather lengthy to type, consider assigning aliases to recurring objects using the prefix for the lowest-level object, as follows:

```
txtCustCity = OrderForm.CustomerInfo.CityName
txtCustCity.Value = 'Redmond'
```

N O T E The recommended convention does not prefix characters to object names. However, you can use prefixes on object references. ■

Naming Issues Across Related Applications

All the conventions in the preceding section apply whether you develop a single application or multiple applications. However, it is more common for problems to occur when different teams develop different modules of larger applications. There are more possibilities for naming, scoping, and typing inconsistencies. The following paragraphs describe a few of these possibilities:

■ Suppose that two developers create two separate tables that share several common fields, but they name the fields differently and assign them different sizes. (In variations on this scenario, the developers name the fields consistently but assign them different sizes or assign the same sizes but different names.)

■ Now, suppose that you have the opposite situation: Two developers create fields in separate tables that have exactly the same name and definition. The problem is that the fields actually represent two different things.

■ Suppose that two developers create modules, each using his own data-naming conventions. If both developers use entirely different conventions, it may be possible to bring one module into alignment with the other by using a few replace statements. The real problem is when the naming conventions used by the two developers have common prefixes that do not mean the same thing. Suppose that one developer puts field type first and scope second and the other developer puts scope first and type second. In this case, does a variable labeled pl_thing represent a private Logical or a local Picture?

- Suppose that two developers create two separate applications and use the same variable name for different purposes. Each developer defines the variable as a different type, therefore causing confusion. However, a most difficult obstacle to resolve occurs when the same variables from the two separate applications have a different definition but are of the same data type. It takes longer to realize that the variables are actually different. If the applications are truly separate, this situation might not pose more than an academic question. But if the applications form two modules in a system, at some point a third developer might look at both applications and attempt to form a relation by using this field between the two tables.

Not many data dictionaries are products on the market yet, especially products that deal with cross-application development. But as Visual FoxPro begins to become more a corporate development tool than a department tool, the need for these tools will force their creation. In the meantime, you might want to consider assigning one person to be responsible for a list of field names and their definitions. Then, when anyone needs to create a new database, he must first consult this list to see whether the names that he wants are already in use, with the same or different meanings.

Another option is to create your own data dictionary. Our experience in developing and working with a data dictionary proved that it can quickly become an essential tool to your project.

Using Enterprise-Wide Naming Conventions

Enterprise issues expand on the cross-application issues, especially as development teams become separated over greater distances. In developing client/server applications, the focus on consistency switches to a central data repository. In some ways, this situation is a benefit because it becomes easier for everyone to determine what field names have already been used and how they have been defined. On the other hand, no system has the internal intelligence to prevent the types of situations mentioned earlier in this chapter.

One of the greatest potential areas for problems is development of applications in different departments of the same company, because there usually is little coordination between application developers in each department. As a result, the risk of naming inconsistencies increases dramatically. As long as each department operates independently of the other, these problems never surface. But as soon as two departments are required to work together on a common system, the naming inconsistencies create significant problems. A company-wide naming convention will not eliminate all these problems, but it will reduce them.

Other Advanced Features of Visual FoxPro's Database Container

In Chapter 3, "Defining Databases, Tables, and Indexes," we mentioned a few of the advanced features that Visual FoxPro's data container offers at the field level in addition to its capability to assign 128-character field names. Although this situation tremendously improves the 10-character limitation of free tables, it comes with a price: When you begin using 128-character field names, going back to 10-character names is difficult. All programs, forms, reports, and other files that reference the table will require changes to referenced, shortened field names.

Using Record-Level Validations

You can define additional properties at table level by clicking the Table Properties button. Figure 4.1 shows the Table Properties dialog box with its six additional fields.

FIGURE 4.1

The Table Properties dialog box shows a record-level validation rule.

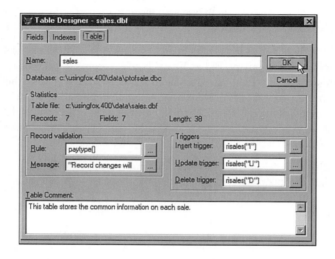

The validation rule in this dialog box is a record-level validation. Visual FoxPro triggers this rule when you change any value in the record and attempt to move to another record. When you are in a browse window, form, or other interface feature that enables scanning of records, you can move between records without triggering the validation only if you don't make changes.

When you use record-level validation, the validation code cannot change any field in the current record or move the record pointer. It can, however, compare the values of one field with those of another, as follows:

```
(dHireDate - dBirthDate) > 18 * 365.25
```

The code can also perform a lookup validation against another file:

```
SEEK(cCustId, 'CUSTOMER')
```

In Figure 4.1, the record validation is more complex than a single expression. Therefore, a user-defined function (UDF) calls the validation code that is saved as a stored procedure in the database.

N O T E Before you can enter a UDF for a validation rule, the stored procedure must exist.
Otherwise, Visual FoxPro rejects the UDF reference. Therefore, choose Edit Stored Procedure
from the Database pull-down menu before adding the validation clause to the table structure. You can
also open the stored procedures anytime the database is open by typing **MODIFY PROCEDURE** in the
Command window. ▪

Any validation expression or function call must evaluate to a logical result. If the field validation
returns .F., Visual FoxPro keeps the record pointer in the same record and does not save any
changes made to it; it also displays the validation text. Following is the full text for the validation text that was cut off in Figure 4.1:

```
"Record changes will not be accepted!"
```

To validate the records, you need to use a new Visual FoxPro function called GETFLDSTATE.
This function determines whether a field in a table or cursor has changed during the current
command or whether the delete status has changed. The basic syntax of this command is

```
GETFLDSTATE(cFieldName¦nFieldNumber [,cTableAlias¦nWorkArea])
```

N O T E Row or table buffering must be enabled with CURSORSETPROP() before GETFLDSTATE()
can operate on local tables. ▪

If you include a field name or number, GETFLDSTATE returns one of the values listed in Table 4.5
indicating the status of that field. The validation text in Listing 4.2 uses GETFLDSTATE to determine which error message to display based on whether the sales-total field has changed.

Table 4.5   Return Values for GETFLDSTATE

Return Value	Edit/Delete Status
1	Field has not changed value and deletion-status flag has not changed.
2	Either field or deletion-status flag has changed.
3	Field in appended record has not been changed and its deletion status has not changed.
4	Field in appended record has changed or the deletion-status flag has changed.

N O T E Visual FoxPro returns this information only for tables in a database. ▪

You can also return the information about all fields in the current table with GETFLDSTATE(-1).
This command returns a string. Its first value represents the deletion-status flag, which is
followed by one return value for each field in the record.

Calling GETFLDSTATE() with an argument of 0 returns a single value that represents the status of the deletion flag.

> **CAUTION**
>
> When you are evaluating return values from GETFLDSTATE(), all options other than –1 return a numeric value. Option –1 returns a string.

The code segment in Listing 4.2 shows the complete validation code associated with the record-validation function shown in Figure 4.2.

FIGURE 4.2

The Edit Relationship dialog box, used by the Database Designer, defines which fields connect the tables.

Listing 4.2   04CODE02.PRG—A Record Validation Function Called by the Valid Event of the Total Order Amount Field

```
FUNCTION PAYTYPE
* This function checks the payment type as a function
* of the total order amount to validate the record.
LOCAL llReturnCode, lnChangeCheck

* Check if any changes were made to either the sales total or
* the payment method.
* Check if customer attempts to pay < $10 by credit card.
  IF (MOD(GETFLDSTATE('nSalesTotal'),2) = 0 OR ;
      MOD(GETFLDSTATE('cPaymentMethod'),2) = 0) AND ;
      nSalesTotal < 10.00
    * Check for payment method of 'CA' - Cash
    IF cPaymentMethod # 'CA'
      = MESSAGEBOX('Orders of less than $10 must be cash')
      RETURN .F.
    ENDIF
  ENDIF

* If paid by credit card, Check if credit card was approved.
  IF (MOD(GETFLDSTATE('nSalesTotal'),2) = 0 OR ;
      MOD(GETFLDSTATE('cPaymentMethod'),2) = 0) AND ;
      cPaymentMethod # 'CA'
    * Ask if card was approved. If not reject record.
    IF MESSAGEBOX('Was card approved?', 36) = 7
      = MESSAGEBOX('Cannot accept a credit card ' + ;
        'order without approval')
      RETURN .F.
    ENDIF
```

```
        ENDIF

    RETURN .T.
```

Notice that the function first checks to see whether the change that triggered the validation occurred to either the sales-total or payment-method field. Remember that a change to any field triggers the record validation. Therefore, you should determine whether to perform the validation because you certainly don't want to perform the validation for every field that changes.

> **CAUTION**
>
> While you are in the validation-rule code, do not attempt to move the record pointer for the current table. Any change could result in a series of recursive calls that could create more error conditions. For this reason, VFP prohibits changes to any field in the current table. Therefore, you cannot use the record validation to "correct" an error.

Even if you don't move off the current record, but instead attempt to close the browse window or form after making a change to a field, Visual FoxPro still performs the record validation.

> **CAUTION**
>
> Visual FoxPro stores all validation code and text in the database. Freeing a table from a database removes the link to these definitions. The stored procedures remain in the database, but the links to the table are broken.

 TIP You can add, modify, or delete a record validation with the CHECK or DROP CHECK clause in ALTER TABLE.

Maintaining Referential Integrity

In general, referential integrity defines which operations are permissible between tables that are connected with relations. The basic premise is that a primary key value in the parent table must have a corresponding lookup or foreign key in another table (called the *child table*). Referential integrity treats records that do not meet these criteria as invalid.

You can implement referential integrity in several ways; you need to decide what method best suits the data. Consider the basic relation between general order information and detailed order information, for example. The Tasmanian Trader example provided with Visual FoxPro represents these files as ORDERS.DBF and ORDITEMS.DBF, respectively.

The orders table contains information that is unique to the order as a whole. This information includes Order_Id, Order_Date, Customer_Id, and many other fields. The order detail table contains specifics on individual items ordered, such as Order_Id, Product_Id, Quantity, and Unit_Price. The relation that ties these two tables together is based on Order_Id.

When you add a record to ORDERS.DBF, you do so with the intent of adding details to ORDITEMS.DBF. After all, an order without details is not a complete order. Similarly, you would never think of adding details to ORDITEMS.DBF without also adding an order record to ORDERS.DBF. These files reference each other in a parent/child relation: ORDERS.DBF represents the parent and ORDITEMS.DBF is the child. The analogy is that you can have a parent without a child, but you cannot have a child without a parent.

Forming Persistent Relations

Persistent relations define relations between two tables, and are stored in the Database Designer. Visual FoxPro automatically uses them each time the tables are opened. This feature is especially useful for automatically setting the relations between tables in SQL statements and for creating lookups, validations, and the data environment of forms and reports.

Persistent relations are sometimes called permanent relations, as opposed to temporary relations created with the SET RELATION command. The reason that SET relations are temporary is that FoxPro dissolves them when you exit FoxPro or issue the SET RELATION command by itself. Persistent relations remain in place between applications.

Creating Relations Among Tables   To create a relation between tables, return to the Database Designer window. Figure 4.2 shows two tables between which you need to define relations.

Create the following indexes using the Table Designer dialog box, if you do not have them already:

In CUSTOMER.DBF:

TAG: CUSTID	PRIMARY	INDEX ON: cCustomerId
TAG: CUSTNAME	REGULAR	INDEX ON: cLastName + cFirstName
TAG: COMPANY	REGULAR	INDEX ON: cCompanyName + STR(cOutstandingBillsTotal, 9, 2)

In SALES.DBF:

TAG: ORDERID	PRIMARY	INDEX ON: cOrderId
TAG: CUSTID	REGULAR	INDEX ON: cCustomerId
TAG: SALESMAN	REGULAR	INDEX ON: cSalesmanId
TAG: SALES	CANDIDATE	INDEX ON: DTOC(dSaleDate)+cOrderId

In DETAILS.DBF:

TAG: DETAILS   PRIMARY INDEX ON: cOrderId+cItemId

Use the scrollbars of each table to display the index list at the bottom. To form a relation, simply click the index name in one of the tables and drag it to an index in another table. Suppose that you want to find the sales information for each customer. Click CUSTID in the CUSTOMER table and drag it to CUSTID in the SALES table. FoxPro displays the Edit Relationship dialog box (refer to Figure 4.2).

Because you dragged the index from one table to another, FoxPro automatically fills in the customers' names. FoxPro also defines the relationship as one-to-many, because there can be many sales orders for each customer. Finally, to accept the relation, simply click OK.

FoxPro follows a few simple rules to define the relation type. First, it assumes that the start table, or "from" table, is on the "one" side and must be a candidate or primary index. (You cannot start a persistent relation from a unique or regular index.) If you then connect to a primary, or candidate, index in the related table, FoxPro knows that it must be a one-to-one relation because these are unique indexes that include every record in the table. Connecting to any other index (regular or unique) enables more than one record on the "to" side; therefore, FoxPro assumes a one-to-many relationship. Remember that a unique index does not prohibit multiple records that have the same index value, it merely keeps a pointer to only the first one.

Create a similar relation between ORDER_ID in SALES.DBF and ORDER_ID in DETAILS.DBF. The details side of this relation defines a many relation because each order can contain many ordered items.

In the Database Designer window, you now see a connecting line between the indexes. FoxPro displays the "one" side of a relation with a single line coming out of the table. The "many" side has three lines leading from the index.

Breaking a Relation To break a relation that is no longer needed or defined incorrectly, merely click it and press the Delete key. You can also right-click and then choose Remove Relationship from the shortcut menu.

Creating Self-Referential Relations A self-referential relation relates one field in a table to another field in the same table. An example that illustrates this concept involves the relation between a supervisor and an employee. An employee table contains a record for each company employee, identified by an employee ID. Each record has one field that identifies the ID of the employee's supervisor. That ID is also the supervisor's employee number. Thus, by referencing the employee's number, you can get the supervisor's name, the name of that supervisor's supervisor, and so on.

Figure 4.3 shows the Database Designer after the formation of the relation between two records within empl2. In this case, custid is defined as the primary index and superv is defined as a regular index.

Although queries have not been discussed yet, the following is a query that lists every employee and his or her supervisor's name using the self-referencing relation in EMPL2:

```
SELECT A.EmplId, ;
    A.LastName AS EMPLOYEE_LAST_NAME, ;
    A.FirstName AS EMPLOYEE_FIRST_NAME, ;
    B.LastName AS SUPERVISOR_LAST_NAME ;
    B.FirstName AS SUPERVISOR_FIRST_NAME ;
    FROM EMPL2 A, EMPL2 B ;
    WHERE A.Supervisor = B.EmplId
```

FIGURE 4.3
This Database Designer view shows a self-referencing relation.

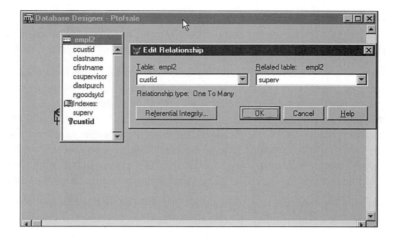

Using the Referential Integrity Builder

Visual FoxPro adds a powerful new feature by providing engine-based referential integrity. To access the Referential Integrity (RI) Builder:

- Open the database that contains the tables for which you want to define referential integrity rules.

- Right-click the persistent relation, or double-left-click the relation to display the Edit Relation box.

The first method displays a menu that contains the Referential Integrity option; the second method displays a command button. Choosing either option displays the builder shown in Figure 4.4.

FIGURE 4.4
Referential Integrity Builder opened for database
\VFP\SAMPLES\
TASTRADE\DATA\
TASTRADE.DBC,
showing all the table relations and their current RI rules.

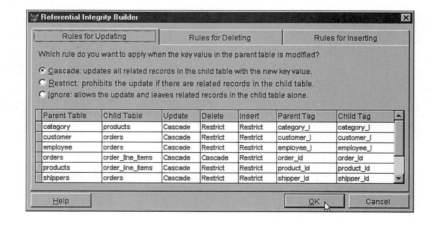

The bottom half of the builder lists each relation on a separate line or row. The columns across the row name the parent and child tables. Next are three columns for the Update, Delete, and Insert integrity rules. Initially, all these columns say Ignore. However, you can define rules for each relation and action. Finally, the last two columns define the parent and child tags involved in the relation.

Only the referential-rule columns can be modified. If you select any of these columns by clicking them, a drop-down-arrow button appears; when clicked, that button displays the referential options. These options are also defined in the page frame in the top half of the builder.

Each referential action has its own page, which lists the available options. The referential options available when you are updating the key value in a parent table include the following:

- *Cascade*. This option updates all child records with the new parent key value that had the same old parent key value.
- *Restrict*. This option checks to see whether any child records exist with the current parent key value. If so, FoxPro prohibits you from changing the parent key value.
- *Ignore*. This option performs no referential integrity and enables changes to the parent key without regard to any related child records.

As you can see, each of these options has an option (radio) button. Clicking the button changes the selected rule for the highlighted relation in the top half of the builder. Thus, you have two ways to select the referential rules.

The rules for deleting parent records are similar to those for updating. The rules for inserting records, however, apply from the child side of the relation. The two possible rules provided here are:

- *Restrict*. This rule prevents the insertion of a child record if a parent record with the same key value does not exist.
- *Ignore*. This option performs no referential-integrity checks.

After you define the referential integrity rules for each relation and action, click OK to exit the builder. You might want to cascade key updates made in the CUSTOMER table to the ORDERS table. On the other hand, you might want to restrict deletion of CUSTOMER records if ORDERS records exist. Finally, you want to restrict the entry of an ORDERS record if the customer key does not exist in CUSTOMER.

When you click OK, the builder displays a dialog box that asks you to save your changes, generates the RI code, and exits. This process creates a set of triggers and stored procedures in the database. If the database previously defined triggers or a stored procedure, it makes a backup copy before overwriting it. If you defined stored procedures for other features, such as validations, you need to manually copy them from the backup to the new stored procedures.

After the RI Builder completes this task, you can open the Table Designer and select Table Properties to view the added triggers. Alternatively, you can view the stored procedures by clicking the Edit Stored Procedure button on the Database Designer toolbar.

> **CAUTION**
>
> If you change any of the tables that are involved in referential integrity, their indexes (or persistent relations) rerun the RI Builder. This action revises the code as appropriate due to the changes made.

Although the Referential Integrity Builder is a fast and easy way to add common referential integrity rules to your database relations, you define referential integrity in many ways. Some of these ways are discussed in the following section.

Building Your Own Referential Integrity

To illustrate some of these principles, the Web site Que has set up to accompany this book contains a database called PTOFSALE (for point-of-sale). This database is a modification of the Tastrade files, which show one way of implementing referential integrity.

The following section examines referential integrity rules created for two files in the database: SALES.DBF and DETAILS.DBF. These files loosely resemble ORDERS.DBF and ORDITEMS.DBF, from Tasmanian Traders, but with fewer fields and records to help illustrate the points. By using separate files, you can experiment with triggers without worrying about potential damage to your Tasmanian Trader example. Table 4.6 displays the field structure for SALES.DBF; Table 4.7 displays the field structure for DETAILS.DBF.

Table 4.6   Field Structure for SALES.DBF

Field Name	Type	Width	Decimals	Null
dSaleDate	Date	8		No
cCustomerId	Character	4		No
cSalesmanId	Character	4		No
cOrderId	Character	6		No
nSalesTotal	Numeric	9	2	No
cPaymentMethod	Character	2		No
cShipperId	Character	4		No

Table 4.7   Field Structure for DETAILS.DBF

Field Name	Type	Width	Decimals	Null
cOrderId	Character	6		No
cItemId	Character	6		No
nQuantity	Numeric	4	0	No

Field Name	Type	Width	Decimals	Null
nUnitPrice	Numeric	8	2	No
lTaxable	Logical	1		No

N O T E These two files use the standard recommended naming convention for table variables, which includes a single-character type prefix. The convention also uses initial caps for words within the field name where Visual FoxPro recognizes them, such as within code to help make reading the names easier. ▓

Using Triggers

The next three options after Record Validations in the Table Properties dialog box are called *triggers*. Visual FoxPro executes these triggers when you insert, update, or delete a record in the table. As is true of record validation rules, you need to store the code for triggers as stored procedures in the database.

You can use triggers for additional calculations or validations when you perform any of these three operations. You could send an email message to Purchasing when the inventory of any item falls below a predefined stock value, for example. You could also log all changes made to a table or create your own referential integrity rules. However, you cannot do several things with them. You can't do the following:

- Move the record pointer in the current work area
- Change the value of any field in the current record
- Close the current work area or open another file in the same work area

The most common use for triggers is to implement referential integrity.

Initializing the Stored Procedures for Triggers In this section, you learn how to define the triggers. Figure 4.1 shows the extended options for triggers in SALES.DBF, defined as follows:

Insert Trigger:	RISALES("I")
Update Trigger:	RISALES("U")
Delete Trigger:	RISALES("D")

Next, define a similar set of triggers for DETAILS.DBF:

Insert Trigger:	RIDETAILS("I")
Update Trigger:	RIDETAILS("U")
Delete Trigger:	RIDETAILS("D")

Notice that in both cases, triggers for each table call the same function, merely passing it a different single-character parameter to identify the operation. The reason is that referential integrity requires some common additional support, or housekeeping tasks. These tasks are called from RIDETAILS and RISALES, so they do not have to be repeated. Each of these requirements is examined later in this chapter; the following section starts by examining RISALES().

Part
II

Ch
4

Defining Triggers for the Parent Table   Whenever Visual FoxPro senses the insertion, updating, or deletion of a record, it checks to see whether a trigger for that event exists. If it does, as in this case, VFP executes the trigger. All triggers for the table SALES.DBF call function RISALES(), as shown in Listing 4.3.

Listing 4.3   04CODE03.PRG—Referential Integrity Code Generated by the RI Builder Called on by VFP in the Event of a Delete, Insert, or Modify

```
****************
FUNCTION RISALES
* This routine is called by the triggers in SALES.DBF
LPARAMETERS lcAction
LOCAL llReturnValue, Dummy

* Start Transaction
  Dummy        = IIF(TYPE("nLevel")<>"N" OR nLevel=0, ;
                     RISTART(), "")
  nLevel       = nLevel + 1
  llReturnValue = .F.

* Perform action
  DO CASE
    CASE TYPE('lcAction') # 'C' ;
         OR !UPPER(lcAction) $ 'DIU' ;
         OR LEN(lcAction)>1
      ERROR 'Invalid action code passed to RISALES'
    CASE UPPER(lcAction) == 'D'
      llReturnValue = SALEDEL()
    CASE UPPER(lcAction) == 'I'
      llReturnValue = SALEINS()
    CASE UPPER(lcAction) == 'U'
      llReturnValue = SALEMOD()
  ENDCASE

* End transaction
  nLevel = nLevel - 1
  Dummy  = IIF(nLevel = 0, RIEND(llReturnValue), 0)

RETURN llReturnValue
```

Notice that this routine begins by assigning the passed character to a local parameter (LPARAMETER) called lcAction. It then defines a local variable, which it uses to return a logical value to the trigger, llReturnValue.

This function itself has three parts. The first part initializes a transaction by checking the current value of variable nLevel. If you object that nLevel is not defined yet, you are correct. That is the purpose of the first conditional test in the IIF statement: It takes advantage of the way Visual FoxPro evaluates expressions. When a conditional statement has more than one expression, VFP evaluates them one at a time from left to right. As soon as VFP can evaluate the expression, it stops, even if it does not evaluate all conditions.

In this case, IIF() contains two conditions connected with OR. The logical result of this expression is true as long as one or the other condition is true. Visual FoxPro knows this. It evaluates the first expression, and because nLevel is undefined, it returns a type of "U". Therefore, the first condition is true. Because this is all that FoxPro needs to evaluate the entire expression, it never checks to see whether nLevel is equal to zero. If nLevel were equal to zero, it would generate an error because nLevel is undefined. Thus, FoxPro executes function RISTART() when the expression is true, as occurs at the start of the first trigger event.

> **N O T E** When defining conditional expressions, define the evaluation order so as to minimize the work that Visual FoxPro must do. Put the most critical condition first. This action saves VFP time; it also enables you to include in the second part of the test conditions that are not otherwise valid. ▨

T I P When you are connecting two expressions with OR, put the one that is most likely to pass first. When you are connecting two expressions with AND, put the one that is most likely to fail first.

This first section also increments the value of nLevel, which RISTART() initializes to zero. This variable tracks how many triggers have been set and which one is being processed. An nLevel value of 1 indicates that processing should execute code related to the primary trigger event. Higher values of nLevel evaluate cascade events.

The second portion of RISALES() uses a CASE statement to determine whether the parameter passed is valid and then to branch to the correct function. Notice, again, that a compound test is used in the first CASE statement. If the TYPE of lcAction is not Character, Visual FoxPro ignores the rest of the conditions—which only makes sense because lcAction should be Character.

Finally, the last section performs a cleanup. First, the section decreases the trigger level. If it has executed all the triggers (nLevel=0), it executes one final function: RIEND().

Now examine RISTART, shown in Listing 4.4.

Listing 4.4 04CODE04.PRG—The RISTART Code

```
****************
FUNCTION RISTART
* Call this program when starting Referential Integrity.
* It initializes several variables.
  IF TYPE("nLevel") <> 'N'
    PUBLIC nLevel
    nLevel = 0
  ENDIF

  IF TYPE("cCursors") <> "C"
    PUBLIC cCursors
  ENDIF

  IF nLevel = 0
```

continues

Listing 4.4 Continued

```
      BEGIN TRANSACTION
      PUBLIC cOldError, nError
      cCursors  = ""
      cOldError = ON("ERROR")
      nError    = 0
      ON ERROR nError = ERROR()
   ENDIF
RETURN
```

As you can see, the routine initializes nLevel to zero and makes it a public variable. This routine also initializes two other variables. The first variable, cCursors, tracks the names of cursors opened by the code in the triggers. The second variable, cOldError, stores the current ON ERROR action.

The following statement is very important:

BEGIN TRANSACTION

This statement defines the beginning of a transaction and tells Visual FoxPro to buffer all record changes that are made until it executes an END TRANSACTION. END TRANSACTION writes the changes from the buffer permanently to the file. If you decide to cancel changes, you can use ROLLBACK or TABLEREVERT() to back out or discard changes. Function TABLEREVERT() has the following syntax:

TABLEREVERT([lAllRows][,cTableAlias¦nWorkArea])

The first parameter, when it is set to true, discards changes made to all records in the current table or in the table referenced by an alias or work-area number. When it is set to false, the parameter discards only changes made in the current record.

Up to this point, the routines used have been fairly generic. In fact, you could use them in your own applications virtually unchanged, except for the functions called by the CASE statement in RISALES. The following section examines the first function that performs the real action of the trigger.

Defining a Cascade Delete Trigger   The SALEDEL() function defines the trigger action when Visual FoxPro senses the deletion of a record in SALES.DBF. The purpose of this routine is to cause a delete cascade to remove all order details associated with the deleted order record. After all, when the parent order record no longer exists, the child details are no longer valid. Listing 4.5 shows the code required to accomplish this task.

Listing 4.5   04CODE05.PRG—Referential Integrity Code Generated by the RI Builder Called on the Event of a Delete

```
****************
FUNCTION SALEDEL
* If deleting a sales record, delete all details
LOCAL  llReturnValue, lcOrderId, lnDetArea

  llReturnValue = .T.
```

```
IF nLevel = 1
  lcOrderId     = cOrderId
  lnDetArea     = RIOPEN('DETAILS')
  SELECT (lnDetArea)
  SCAN FOR cOrderId = lcOrderId
    llReturnValue = RIDELETE()
  ENDSCAN
  SELECT sales
ENDIF

RETURN llReturnValue
```

This relatively short routine starts by storing the order ID from the sales record in lcOrderId and then uses RIOPEN() to safely open a copy of DETAILS. The routine opens DETAILS.DBF without setting a tag so that Rushmore can fully optimize the FOR clause. The code uses SCAN FOR to find all records with a matching order ID; it then deletes each matching record by calling the RIDELETE() function.

The SALEDEL() function introduces two new functions, both of which are generalized functions that you can use in any referential integrity situation. In fact, triggers from the DETAILS table also use them. The following section discusses RIOPEN().

Using a Common Procedure to Open Cursors   The RIOPEN() function supports two parameters: one for the table name and the other for an optional tag name. Listing 4.6 shows the RIOPEN() code.

Listing 4.6   04CODE06.PRG—The RIOPEN() Code

```
***************
FUNCTION RIOPEN
* This procedure opens cursors for use during Referential
* Integrity checks since operations that perform record
* pointer moves are not allowed directly.
LPARAMETERS lcTable, lcTag
LOCAL lnNewArea, nInUseArea

  nInUseArea = ATC(lcTable+"*", cCursors)

* Open reference table
  IF nInUseArea = 0
    SELECT 0
    lnNewArea = SELECT()
    IF EMPTY(lcTag)
      USE (lcTable) ;
          ALIAS ("RI_"+LTRIM(STR(lnNewArea))) ;
          AGAIN SHARE
    ELSE
      USE (lcTable) ;
          ORDER (lcTag) ;
```

continues

Listing 4.6 Continued

```
            ALIAS ("RI_"+LTRIM(STR(lnNewArea))) ;
            AGAIN SHARE
   ENDIF
   cCursors = cCursors + UPPER(lcTable) + "?" + ;
            STR(lnNewArea,5)
ELSE
* Retrieve work area of referential integrity cursor
   nNewArea = VAL(SUBSTR(cCursors, ;
            nInUseArea + LEN(lcTable) + 1, 5))
   cCursors = STRTRAN(cCursors, ;
            UPPER(lcTable) + "*" + STR(nNewArea,5), ;
            UPPER(lcTable) + "?" + STR(nNewArea,5))
ENDIF

RETURN (lnNewArea)
```

This routine begins by checking variable cCursors to see whether the table has already been opened for use by the referential integrity routines. Variable cCursors has the following structure:

■ Table name

■ Character to identify whether the table is in use for another trigger

■ Work-area number where table is open

Actually, cCursors is a string that repeats the preceding structure for each open table. If the table is already open, all that the routine needs to do is retrieve the work area that it is in and change the in-use character flag from * to ?. Then, RIOPEN() returns the work-area number. This tracking is required to keep track of which tables are open and can have their record pointer moved. Remember that you cannot move the record pointer of tables that are directly involved in the current trigger.

If the table is not open, RIOPEN() selects the next available work area with SELECT 0 and opens the table with the AGAIN and SHARE clauses. The AGAIN clause creates a cursor that enables you to open the table multiple times. The table could already be open, but referential integrity requires a separate copy with its own tag and record pointer. Systems developed for use on a network require the SHARE clause so that multiple users can have the same file open at the same time.

The last thing that RIOPEN() does is update variable cCursors with the following information:

■ The name of the table

■ The ? character, indicating that the file is in active use

■ The work-area number

The other routine used by SALEDEL() is RIDELETE(), which performs the actual deletion of records referenced by triggers. In this case, SALEDEL() has already changed the default work area to DETAILS.DBF and points to a record to delete. However, RIDELETE() cannot simply delete the record, it first checks to see whether it can get a record lock. If not, REDELETE() begins a rollback process by returning a false value in llReturnValue. This value eventually works its way back up to the trigger, which cancels the deletion of the parent record and any child records deleted for this parent since the trigger began.

Listing 4.7 shows the code for RIDELETE().

Listing 4.7   04CODE07.PRG—The RIDELETE Code

```
*****************
FUNCTION RIDELETE
* Delete the current record in the current area
LOCAL llReturnValue

llReturnValue = .T.
* Attempt to get a record lock
  IF (UPPER(SYS(2011))='RECORD LOCKED' and !DELETED()) OR !RLOCK()
    llReturnValue = .F.
  ELSE
  * If not deleted, delete it.
    IF !DELETED()
      DELETE
      nError = 0
      UNLOCK RECORD (RECNO())
      IF nError <> 0
        = TABLEREVERT()
        UNLOCK RECORD (RECNO())
        llReturnValue = .F.
      ENDIF
    ENDIF
  ENDIF
RETURN llReturnValue
```

When it obtains a record lock, RIDELETE() checks to see whether the record has already been deleted. (It hardly makes sense to delete it twice.) The function then deletes the current record in the current table. If an error occurs, it executes a function called TABLEREVERT(), which cancels the delete. RIDELETE() passes the llReturnValue back to the trigger to cancel any related deletions.

If everything deletes successfully, llReturnValue passes a value of true back to the trigger and the event ends. Although the trigger on the SALES file can perform other actions, it is the programmer's responsibility to determine appropriate actions in each situation.

After a procedure is performed by means of a cursor, the procedure can close it. On the other hand, leaving it open until the end of the transaction enables other functions in the program to reuse it. The special character (?) after the table name in variable cCursors indicates that the cursor is currently in use. If so, subsequent functions cannot reuse the cursor because another routine might need the current record-pointer position. (Remember that you cannot move the record-pointer position of a table that is currently involved in a trigger or validation.) When you are done with the cursor, change this character to a different character (*) in variable cCursors to tell the program that it can reuse the cursor. That is the purpose of RIREUSE(): It changes the special character from a question mark (?) to an asterisk(*) to indicate that the cursor can be reused. Listing 4.8 illustrates the code to perform this action.

Listing 4.8 04CODE08.PRG—Referential Integrity Code Generated by the RI Builder Called at the End of Every Trigger

```
****************
FUNCTION RIREUSE
* This routine allows reuse of exiting cursor
LPARAMETERS lcTable, lcArea
   cCursors = STRTRAN(cCursors, ;
             UPPER(lcTable) + "?" + STR(lcArea,5), ;
             UPPER(lcTable) + "*" + STR(lcArea,5))
RETURN .T.
```

Triggers Performing No Action   The insert trigger for SALES calls the SALEINS() function, which simply returns a value of true as shown in the following code. When you are adding a new sales order, there is no reason to check DETAILS.

```
****************
FUNCTION SALEINS
* No referential action required when adding a parent
RETURN .T.
```

> **N O T E**   Actually, there may be a reason for adding code to the insert trigger of SALES. Visual FoxPro executes this trigger not only when you add a new record to the table, but also when you recall a deleted one. When a sales order is recalled, you may want to recall its details automatically.

Performing a Cascade Modify   The last trigger in SALES.DBF occurs when you change any field value in a record. This routine begins by initializing the return variable to true, and then it checks to see whether it is in the first trigger level. This means that you are modifying a SALES record directly, not as a result of deleting DETAIL records for the same order ID.

Next, the routine stores the current order ID in a local variable, along with the "pre-change" order ID. When a transaction begins, think of Visual FoxPro as storing the changes to the current record in a buffer. You can access the changed values of any field by using the variable name directly. However, to access the original values of any field, you need to use the OLDVAL() function.

The SALEMOD() function retrieves both values to determine whether the relational fields (cOrderId, in this case) have changed. If they have not changed, the function exits with a return value of true. Otherwise, this function locates the matching records in DETAILS.DBF and updates the old key values to the new one. This portion of the routine is similar to SALEDEL(), with the exception that it uses a REPLACE statement instead of a call to RIDELETE().

Listing 4.9 shows the code for SALEMOD().

Listing 4.9   04CODE09.PRG—Referential Integrity Called on a Modify to Modify All Related Records Automatically

```
****************
FUNCTION SALEMOD
* If modifying a sales record, modify all details
LOCAL  llReturnValue, lcOrderId, lcOldValue, lnDetArea

  llReturnValue = .T.
  IF nLevel = 1
    lcOrderId    = cOrderId
    lcOldValue   = OLDVAL('cOrderId')

  * If key value changed, updated the child records
    IF lcOrderID <> lcOldValue
      lnDetArea = RIOPEN('DETAILS')
      SELECT (lnDetArea)
      SCAN FOR cOrderId = lcOldValue
        REPLACE cOrderId WITH lcOrderId
      ENDSCAN
      SELECT sales
    ENDIF
  ENDIF
RETURN llReturnValue
```

Another way to see whether the foreign key has changed uses the GETFLDSTATE() function. However, the function still needs OLDVAL() to find and replace the key value in the child records.

Using Triggers for the Child Table   DETAILS.DBF also has three triggers. Each trigger calls a single routine called RIDETAILS(), with a single-character parameter to identify the trigger. The code of RIDETAILS(), which appears in Listing 4.10, shows that except for the function calls in the CASE statement, it mirrors RISALES().

Listing 4.10   04CODE10.PRG—Referential Integrity Code Generated by the RI Builder Called on a Modification to Update All Related Records

```
******************
FUNCTION RIDETAILS
* This routine is called by the triggers in DETAILS.DBF
LPARAMETERS lcAction
LOCAL llReturnValue, Dummy

* Start Transaction
  Dummy        = IIF(TYPE("nLevel")<>"N" OR nLevel=0, ;
                 RISTART(), "")
  nLevel       = nLevel + 1
  llReturnValue = .F.
```

continues

Listing 4.10   Continued

```
* Perform action
  DO CASE
    CASE TYPE('lcAction') # 'C' ;
         OR !UPPER(lcAction) $ 'DIU' ;
         OR LEN(lcAction)>1
      ERROR 'Invalid action code passed to RIDETAILS'
    CASE UPPER(lcAction) == 'D'
      llReturnValue = DETAILDEL()
    CASE UPPER(lcAction) == 'I'
      llReturnValue = DETAILINS()
    CASE UPPER(lcAction) == 'U'
      llReturnValue = DETAILMOD()
  ENDCASE

* End transaction
  nLevel = nLevel - 1
  Dummy  = IIF(nLevel = 0, RIEND(llReturnValue), 0)
RETURN llReturnValue
```

Using a Trigger to Delete Parent When Last Child Is Deleted   When a user deletes an order detail record, you may want to know whether he deleted one of many detail records for the order or the last one. In this case, you should delete the parent record if you delete the last or only child record. However, not every application should delete the parent record. Just because you delete all the employee's projects, for example, does not mean that you delete the employee as well. So the developer must take an active role in determining the expected functionality of each trigger. The code shown in Listing 4.11 implements a trigger that deletes the parent record when the last child is deleted.

Listing 4.11   04CODE11.PRG—Code that Deletes the Parent Record When the Last Child Is Deleted

```
******************
FUNCTION DETAILDEL
* Check if all order details are deleted, then delete parent
LOCAL cnt, lcOrderId, lnCurrentArea, ;
      lnSalesArea, lnDetArea, llReturnValue

  llReturnValue  = .T.
  lcOrderId      = cOrderId
  lnCurrentArea  = SELECT()

  IF !EMPTY(lcOrderId)
    lnDetArea     = RIOPEN('DETAILS')
    cnt           = 0
    SELECT (lnDetArea)
    SCAN FOR cOrderId = lcOrderId AND !DELETED()
      cnt         = cnt + 1
    ENDSCAN
```

```
   IF cnt = 1 AND nLevel =1
     lnSaleArea  = RIOPEN('SALES', 'ORDERID')
     IF SEEK(lcOrderId)
       llReturnValue = RIDELETE()
     ENDIF
     = RIREUSE('SALES', lnSaleArea)
   ENDIF
   SELECT (lnCurrentArea)
 ENDIF
RETURN llReturnValue
```

This routine first checks to see whether the OrderId exists before proceeding so that the user can delete a blank record without going through the rest of the validation. Then, the routine opens a second occurrence of DETAILS and counts the number of active records that have the same OrderId. If this number is greater than 1, and if the trigger sequence began by deleting details, it looks for and deletes the parent record.

Why check for a count greater than 1 if the conditional string contains the function NOT DE-LETED()? During a transaction, the record is not recognized as deleted until you commit the transaction.

The reason why you have to check the level is that SALEDEL() can also call DETAILDEL(). When SALEDEL() initiates a DETAIL record delete, the function does not have to go back to SALEDEL() a second time, which could potentially lead to an endless loop. But when the trigger initiates the detail delete, you do want to check SALEDEL() when you delete the last child.

Using an Insert Trigger that Checks for a Parent Record   The second trigger for file DETAILS occurs when you add a record or recall a deleted one. Remember that Visual FoxPro triggers the insert trigger when you add a new record, not after you fill in its fields. Therefore, FoxPro triggers for a new, blank record. Because you do not want to check for a blank foreign key in SALES.DBF, the DETAILINS() function tests for an empty OrderId. When that field is empty, the function simply skips the check.

On the other hand, a recalled record should have a corresponding parent. Therefore, when OrderId exists, the following routine uses it to search a copy of SALES.DBF (see Listing 4.12). If the routine finds a matching order record, it completes the record recall; otherwise, the record remains deleted. When this happens, a message box appears telling the user that there is No corresponding order for this detail.

Part

II

Ch

4

Listing 4.12   04CODE12.PRG—**Referential Integrity Can Insert a Detail Record on the Insert of a Parent Record Automatically**

```
*******************
FUNCTION DETAILINS
* Insert a detail record only if a sales record exists
LOCAL lcOrderId, lnSaleArea, llReturnValue, lnCurrentArea

  llReturnValue =  .T.
```

continues

Listing 4.12   Continued

```
 lcOrderId    = cOrderId
 lnCurrentArea = SELECT()

 IF !EMPTY(lcOrderId)
   lnSaleArea    = RIOPEN('SALES', 'ORDERID')
   llReturnValue = SEEK(lcOrderId, lnSaleArea) AND ;
                   !DELETED(lnSaleArea)
   = RIREUSE('SALES', lnSaleArea)
   IF !llReturnValue
     = MESSAGEBOX('No corresponding order for this detail')
   ENDIF
   SELECT (lnCurrentArea)
 ENDIF
RETURN llReturnValue
```

If triggers cannot guarantee that a new detail record has a corresponding sales record, how can you guarantee it? One method uses the VALID clause on the cOrderId field, and it performs a SEEK against cOrderId in SALES. Barring that, consider checking for a SALES record in the update trigger of DETAILS. After all, filling in a blank field is still an update.

The following section examines the final trigger for DETAILS: the update trigger.

Using a Modify Trigger that Also Checks for a Parent Record   The update trigger, named DETAILMOD(), makes sure that cOrderId in DETAILS matches cOrderId in SALES. The trigger also checks to see whether any other detail records exist with the old cOrderId value. If not, it deletes the parent record that has the old ID.

Of course, there are other ways to handle an order ID modification. The first is to change all records with matching order IDs in DETAILS to the new value. Also, you can change the order ID in the parent record. If a corresponding parent record does not exist for the new order ID, find the SALES record with the preceding order ID and change it first. Then change all corresponding records in DETAILS to match the new order ID.

The code in Listing 4.13 shows the DETAILMOD() function.

Listing 4.13   04CODE13.PRG—Referential Integrity Can Check for a Matching Parent Key Value on the Modification of a Child Key Value and Delete the Child if the Child's Key Value Has No Match to a Parent

```
******************
FUNCTION DETAILMOD
* Allow key value change if it matches another parent
* If no more child records for this parent, delete it
LOCAL cnt, lcOrderId, lcOldValue, ;
      lnSalesArea, llReturnValue, lnDetArea

  llReturnValue   = .T.
```

```
IF nLevel=1
   lcOrderId      = cOrderId
   lcOldValue     = OLDVAL('cOrderId')

* First check if new value is a valid parent key
   lnSaleArea     = RIOPEN('SALES', 'ORDERID')
   llReturnValue  = SEEK(lcOrderId, lnSaleArea) AND ;
                    !DELETED(lnSaleArea)
   IF !llReturnValue
     = MESSAGEBOX('No corresponding order for this detail')
   ENDIF

* New order id is valid, check for other child records in old order
   IF llReturnValue
      cnt          = 0
      lnDetArea    = RIOPEN('DETAILS')
      SELECT (lnDetArea)
      SCAN FOR OLDVAL('cOrderId') = lcOldValue AND !DELETED()
        cnt = cnt + 1
      ENDSCAN
      = RIREUSE('DETAILS', lnDetArea)

* If no other child records, delete the parent
      IF cnt = 1
        SELECT (lnSaleArea)
        IF SEEK(lcOldValue)
           llReturnValue = RIDELETE()
        ENDIF
      ENDIF
   ENDIF
   SELECT DETAILS
ENDIF
= RIREUSE('SALES', lnSaleArea)
RETURN llReturnValue
```

Again, this routine first checks to see whether DETAILS.cOrderId exists in the parent file SALES.DBF. If not, the routine displays a message and exits with a return value of false. However, if the order ID does exist, the routine first counts the number of active DETAIL records with the old order ID. If no others exist, the routine opens SALES.DBF and deletes the parent record.

Using a Cleanup Routine   Only one routine remains. When Visual FoxPro completes any of these six triggers, it returns to either RISALES() or RIDETAILS(). FoxPro then executes the RIEND() routine, which takes the return value from the trigger and determines whether to commit the transaction or roll it back. To commit the transaction, FoxPro executes END TRANS- ACTION.

You have a choice, however. You can use ROLLBACK, which discards every change made since the transaction began in the RISTART() function. Alternatively, you can roll back incrementally using TABLEREVERT(). This command rolls back individual (or all) records in one table at a time, as shown in Listing 4.14.

Listing 4.14 04CODE14.PRG—**Referential Integrity Can Call a Routine to Perform the Appropriate Action After a Check**

```
**************
FUNCTION RIEND
* Call this routine to exit the referential integrity check
* It saves changes or reverts to original values depending
* on the value passed to it.
LPARAMETER llSuccess
LOCAL lnXx

* Complete transaction or roll it back
  IF !llSuccess
    IF USED('SALES')
      = TABLEREVERT(.T., 'SALES')
    ENDIF
    IF USED('DETAILS')
      = TABLEREVERT(.T., 'DETAILS')
    ENDIF
  ENDIF
  END TRANSACTION
* or use this code:
*   IF llSuccess
*     END TRANSACTION
*   ELSE
*     ROLLBACK
*   ENDIF

* Reset on error
  IF EMPTY(cOldError)
    ON ERROR
  ELSE
    ON ERROR (cOldError)
  ENDIF

* Remove cursors and reset variables that track them
  FOR lnXx = 1 TO OCCURS("?", cCursors)
    cFound = ATC('?', cCursors, lnXx) + 1
    USE IN (VAL(SUBSTR(cCursors, cFound, 5)))
  ENDFOR
  FOR lnXx = 1 TO OCCURS("*", cCursors)
    cFound = ATC('*', cCursors, lnXx) + 1
    USE IN (VAL(SUBSTR(cCursors, cFound, 5)))
  ENDFOR
  STORE "" TO cCursors
RETURN .T.
```

This routine reads cCursors to remove the cursors created by referential integrity so that functions can move the record pointer.

In the past, you could easily have programmed these functions into forms. But you could not have done anything about users who directly edited the tables using browse windows or other commands directly from the Command window. Now, by adding triggers to critical tables, you can protect referential integrity even from users who prefer to edit files directly rather than to use forms.

As you can see from these routines, writing your own referential integrity rules is certainly possible—and even necessary, if you want to handle changes differently from the VFP defaults. If you can accept the rules defined by VFP's own Referential Integrity Builder, however, your task will be much easier and more error-proof. ●

Selecting, Viewing, and Ordering Data

Opening a Data Table

A fundamental operation of any data-management system is opening tables and viewing the data that they contain. With Visual FoxPro 6, the way that you open and view data is determined by how you store data. In this new release, you have the capability to store tables of information either as free tables or as part of an associated group of tables called a database. Although a database offers many new data-management options that previously were unavailable to FoxPro users, you might find yourself supporting many existing applications that still use the standalone table model. Fortunately, working with tables bound into databases is not much more difficult than working with free tables. In fact, databases provide additional features, such as persistent relations, that make working with them easier.

Critical to the viewing of data is the effective use of indexes. The use (and misuse) of indexes greatly affects the way that you retrieve and view data from a table. Visual FoxPro 6 supports three major types of indexes: independent single-index files, structural compound indexes, and non-structural compound indexes.

Indexes serve two primary purposes. You use some indexes primarily to form relations between tables; you use others to help retrieve data and to improve the performance of queries and reports.

Opening Tables in Work Areas

Before you view data that is stored in a table or work with table data in any other way, you need to open the table in a work area. Visual FoxPro 6 supports 32,767 work areas. Each work area can hold one table and its related indexes, both independent and compound. It is unlikely that you will ever need to use all 32,767 areas—at least, not at the same time. Other system restrictions typically restrict most users to fewer than 256 files.

N O T E   Visual FoxPro does have more than 32,767 work areas available. If you use private data sessions, you will have 32,767 available in each private data session you open. See Chapter 9, "Creating Forms," and Chapter 10, "Creating Reports," for more information about private data sessions. ▨

Opening Free Tables

How do you open a table to look at it? If the table is a free table, select one of the 32,767 areas and issue a USE command, as shown in this example:

```
SELECT 2
USE CUST
```

The first command tells Visual FoxPro 6 to use the second work area. The second command tries to open CUST.DBF from the current directory. If CUST.DBF is not there, Visual FoxPro 6 displays the following message, which includes the current drive and directory:

```
File '<current directory>\CUST.DBF' does not exist
```

You can also retrieve the current directory with this command:

```
? CURDIR()
```

A safer way to open a file is to first test to see whether it exists before issuing the USE command. You can do this with the FILE function, as shown in Listing 5.1.

Listing 5.1   05CODE01.PRG—The FILE Function

```
* Program 5.1 - Testing if a file exists before using it
SELECT 2
IF FILE('CUST.DBF')
     USE CUST
ELSE
     = MESSAGEBOX('File CUST.DBF does not exist in ' ;
      + CurDir())
ENDIF
```

Of course, you can include a drive and directory with the table's name to open it:

```
USE C:\VFP5BOOK\DATA\CUST
```

The preceding examples select the second work area without first checking to see whether another file is open there. Visual FoxPro 6 automatically closes any file that is open in the selected area when you issue a USE command, whether the command succeeds or not. This means that even if the file being opened is not in the current directory or if VFP cannot open it, VFP closes the file that was open in the selected area. Therefore, you should find out whether the work area contains a file before you use it. Use the ALIAS function, which returns the alias name of a file when present, to test whether a work area is empty, as shown in Listing 5.2.

Listing 5.2   05CODE02.PRG—The ALIAS Function

```
* Program 5.2 - Use ALIAS to see if table is already open
* Check if work area 2 is available (empty)
  IF EMPTY(ALIAS(2)) && Returns .T. If no file is open in area 2
     SELECT 2
  ELSE
     = MESSAGEBOX('Work area 2 is in use')
  ENDIF
```

Of course, you should test successive work areas to find an empty one. Although you could write the code to perform such an iteration, there is a faster way. If you use SELECT 0, rather than open a specific work area, Visual FoxPro 6 begins with work area 1 and continues searching until it finds the first empty one. You do not really need to know in which work area VFP opens a file. Visual FoxPro assigns an alias name to a work area when a table is open in it. This alias name is usually the same as the table's name, but it doesn't have to be. Always reference work areas by their alias name after opening them instead of using their work-area numbers.

Part

II

Ch

5

You don't even need a separate SELECT statement to open a table. Select the work area and open the table at the same time by adding the IN clause to the USE statement. But before I show you the modified code that you use to open a file this way, consider an additional enhancement. If the file is not in the current or specified directory, open a dialog box to enable the user to locate the file. The GETFILE function, shown in Listing 5.3, provides this capability.

Listing 5.3   05CODE03.PRG—The GETFILE Function

```
* Program 5.3 - Use ALIAS and FILE to open table in next
*               available work area.
*
* Open CUST.DBF in the next available work area
  IF FILE('CUST.DBF')
     USE CUST IN 0
  ELSE
     = MESSAGEBOX('File CUST.DBF does not exist in ' ;
     + CURDIR())
     lcNewFile = GETFILE('DBF', 'Pick table:', 'Select', 1)
     IF !EMPTY(lcNewFile)
        USE (lcNewFile) IN 0
     ENDIF
  ENDIF
```

Notice that GETFILE() enables you to select a table from any drive or directory and returns the fully qualified pathname to the variable lcNewFile. Use this variable in USE to open the file. The parentheses in this statement tell Visual FoxPro 6 to use the contents of the variable pcNewFile, rather than the name pcNewFile itself.

What if the file that you want to open is already open in a different work area? By default, Visual FoxPro 6 considers this situation to be an error and displays the message File is in use.

Test for this condition with the USED() function, which requires the file alias as its parameter. As shown in Listing 5.4, the function checks to see whether the file alias exists in any work area.

Listing 5.4   05CODE04.PRG—USED() Function

```
  CLOSE DATABASES
  CLEAR

* Test if CUST is already in use
  IF USED("CUST")
    = MESSAGEBOX("File CUST.DBF is already in use.")
    SELECT CUST
  ELSE
  * If file CUST.DBF exists, open it
    cCurDirectory = CURDIR()
    CD \VFP5BOOK\DATA
    IF FILE("CUST.DBF")
```

```
      USE CUST.DBF IN 0
      = MESSAGEBOX("File CUST.DBF successfully opened.")
  ELSE

    * File CUST.DBF is not in default drive,
    * ask user to locate it
      = MESSAGEBOX("File CUST.DBF does not exist in ";
        + CURDIR())
      lcNewFile  = GETFILE("DBF", "Select a table:", "Select", 1)
      lcFileName = SUBSTR(lcNewFile, RAT("\", lcNewFile) + 1)
      lcRootName = LEFT(lcFileName, LEN(lcFileName) - 4)

    * Check if used selected file is already open.  If not, open it
      IF !EMPTY(lcNewFile)
        IF USED(lcRootName)
          = MESSAGEBOX("File " + lcNewFile + " is already in use.")
          SELECT(lcRootName)
        ELSE
          USE (lcNewFile) IN 0
          = MESSAGEBOX("File CUST.DBF successfully opened.")
        ENDIF
      ENDIF
  ENDIF
  CD &cCurDirectory
ENDIF
```

Notice that you have to extract the filename from the value returned by GETFILE before you can use USED() to test for it.

N O T E   If you ever try to open a table in an empty work area and VFP tells you that the file is in use, but you don't see that file listed when you use the View window to look at the work areas, don't panic. Remember that USED() looks for files based on their alias names. If you open the file CUST.DBF and assign an alias of BUYERS to it, USED('CUST') returns false, even though any attempt to open CUST.DBF a second time in a different work area fails with a File is in use error message. If you open tables with alias names other than their filenames, document this information in the program so that other programmers can find it. ▪

Opening Tables More Than Once

At times, you might want to open a file twice, such as when you perform a recursive reference on a file. Chapter 3, "Defining Databases, Tables, and Indexes," includes an example of a self-referencing relation that finds the supervisor of every employee. That example uses a query and the relation to find each supervisor's name. You can achieve the same result by opening the file in two different work areas using the AGAIN clause of USE. AGAIN enables you to open a file more than once. The advantage is that you can use different indexes and move the record pointer independently in each work area. The following two lines show how to open a table a second time:

```
USE empl1 IN 0
USE empl1 IN 0 AGAIN
```

Although Visual FoxPro 6 enables you to open a file multiple times by including the AGAIN clause in USE, remember that it is really the same file. You can even turn an index on in one area and set a relation to it from the other; the record pointer is independent in each work area. Therefore, you can step through the first file to read the employee information, including supervisor IDs, and then you can switch to the second work area to search for the employee who has the first employee's supervisor ID and report their name. Listing 5.5 shows this technique.

Listing 5.5 05CODE05.PRG—Including the AGAIN Clause in USE

```
CLOSE DATABASES
CLEAR

* Open EMPL1.DBF in two work areas
SELECT 0
USE \VFP5BOOK\DATA\EMPL1
SELECT 0
USE \VFP5BOOK\DATA\EMPL1 AGAIN ;
    ALIAS SUPERVISOR ;
    ORDER EMPLOYEEID

* Step through the first area
SELECT Empl1
SCAN
  ? EmplID, ;
    LastName FONT "Foxfont", 10, ;
    FirstName FONT "Foxfont", 10, ;
    Supervisor FONT "Foxfont", 10
* Now find the employee corresponding to the supervisor id
  IF SEEK(Supervisor, 'SUPERVISOR')
    ?? supervisor.LastName FONT "Foxfont", 10, ;
       supervisor.FirstName FONT "Foxfont", 10
  ENDIF
ENDSCAN
```

Opening Tables Bound to a Database

If you try to open a table that is bound to a database without first opening the database, VFP uses a *back link* to identify and open the corresponding database automatically.

VFP stores this back link in the table to identify its parent database. It stores this information at the end of the field list in the table header. The reference includes the name of the database and a relative path to the database from the table. If you open the table with a full pathname, VFP bases its relative path search for the database on that pathname rather than the current directory.

If you ever attempt to open a table and VFP reports that it cannot locate the database, one of two things probably happened: Either you moved the table relative to the database, or you moved the database relative to the table.

Suppose that you begin with database PTOFSALE and table CUSTOMER in the same directory. In this case, the back link in CUSTOMER simply is PTOFSALE.DBC. In other words, VFP looks in the same directory as the table for the database.

On the other hand, suppose that you store the database as \app1\PTOFSALE.DBC and the table as \app1\data\CUSTOMER.DBF. Now the back link is ..\PTOFSALE. In this case, the double dot at the beginning of the back link means to return to the parent directory of the current directory.

Similarly, suppose that you store the database as \app1\database\PTOFSALE.DBC and the table as \app1\data\CUSTOMER.DBF. Now the back link becomes ..\database\PTOFSALE. In this case, the back link returns first to the parent directory and then goes down a different branch: the \database subdirectory.

Following this logic, you can see that moving the entire tree structure that contains the database and table continues to work because the relative paths remain the same. You can even move the tree to a different directory or drive without a problem. You cannot move the tables relative to the database, however.

To be more explicit in your coding, precede commands that open a bound table with a command that opens the database, as shown in the following example:

```
OPEN DATABASE C:\VFP5BOOK\DATA\PTOFSALE
USE C:\VFP5BOOK\DATA\CUSTOMER
```

VFP requires the database to be open because bound tables can use long table names, validation rules, triggers, or other database enhancements. Visual FoxPro would know nothing about these new features unless it opened the database first.

Listing Data to the Screen or Printer

Visual FoxPro has two commands—DISPLAY and LIST—that create simple data listings. Following is the syntax for both commands:

```
DISPLAY
        [[FIELDS] FieldList]
        [Scope][FOR IExpression1][WHILE Iexpression2]
        [OFF]
        [TO PRINTER [PROMPT]¦TO FILE FileName]
        [NOCONSOLE]
        [NOOPTIMIZE]

LIST
        [FIELDS FieldList]
        [Scope][FOR IExpression1][WHILE Iexpression2]
        [OFF]
        [TO PRINTER [PROMPT]¦TO FILE FileName]
        [NOCONSOLE]
        [NOOPTIMIZE]
```

In addition to listing the contents of tables, Table 5.1 lists other clauses that are available with LIST and DISPLAY.

Table 5.1   Clauses of LIST and DISPLAY

Clause	What It Lists
CONNECTIONS	Information on named connections to external data sources, such as SQL Server, Access, dBASE, and Paradox
DATABASE	Information about the current database
FIELDS	Contents of table fields
FILES	Filenames
MEMORY	Contents of memory variables
OBJECTS	Information about objects
PROCEDURES	Information on stored procedures
STATUS	System status
STRUCTURE	File structures
TABLES	Tables in an open database
VIEWS	Information on SQL views

DISPLAY with no additional clauses shows the current record of the current table. On the other hand, LIST shows all the records from the current table, beginning with the first one. You can modify the scope of either command with ALL, NEXT, RECORD, or REST.   Table 5.2 defines these modifiers.

Table 5.2   Record Scope Modifiers

Scope	What It Includes
ALL	Every record in the table
NEXT n	The next n records, where n can be any integer, beginning with the current record
RECORD n	The nth record in the table (based on physical record numbers, not logical orders defined by a sort)
REST	All records from the current one to the end of the table

You can also specify a subset of fields by using the FIELDS clause for both commands. You need to list only the fields; the keyword FIELDS is optional. Following are the various syntax forms for these two commands:

```
USE C:\VFP5BOOK\DATA\CUST
DISPLAY            && Displays the first record only
LIST               && Lists all records, scrolling if necessary
DISPLAY NEXT 4     && Displays the next four records
```

```
DISPLAY REST      && Display the rest of the record in the table
                  && from the current record pointer position
DISPLAY ALL       && Display all the records in the table
LIST cLast, cFirst     && List the last and first names of
                       && every record in the table
```

Another difference between these two commands appears when you are displaying more records than will fit onscreen. When LIST reaches the bottom of the screen, it does not stop; it simply clears the screen and begins again from the top without pausing. DISPLAY pauses when it reaches the bottom of the screen and waits until you press a key to continue. Therefore, you might want to use LIST with the TO PRINTER clause to redirect output to the printer so that Visual FoxPro 6 does not pause. On the other hand, when you are viewing records onscreen, use DISPLAY to see each record. You can also list records to a file by using the TO FILE clause.

To display records onscreen, use the following:

```
DISPLAY ALL cCustId, cCompany
```

To list records to the printer, use the following:

```
LIST cCustId, cCompany TO PRINTER
```

To list records to a file, use the following:

```
LIST cCustId, cCompany TO FILE CUSTOMER.TXT
```

> **CAUTION**
>
> When you issue a LIST REST, you might not get all the records that you expect to get. The scope modifiers REST and NEXT both begin retrieving records from the current record pointer. If you move the record pointer before issuing either of these commands, you might not get the records that you expect.

Part II
Ch 5

Finding Records with LOCATE

If you have only a few records in a table, listing or displaying all records in a table to find the one that you want might not seem to be a bad idea. As tables grow to hundreds or thousands of records, however, LIST and DISPLAY by themselves become impractical. You need to jump immediately to the record or records that match the desired condition.

LOCATE helps you find records for a specific condition, even if the records are scattered throughout the table. Suppose that you want to see records for customers who have outstanding bills. Unless you have a really bad collection history, you really do not want to see every record. The following statement jumps to the first record that matches the search condition:

```
SELECT CUST
LOCATE FOR cBillDue > 0
```

LOCATE always begins at the first record in a file and checks records sequentially until it finds the first one that passes the condition test. To see more information about this customer, use DISPLAY by itself to print to the screen all fields for the current record. You can also use LIST NEXT 1.

But suppose you suspect that more customers have outstanding bills. If you reissue the LOCATE command, Visual FoxPro 6 merely displays the same record because it always begins its search from the top of the file. If you use CONTINUE instead, the search begins at the record immediately after the current one and finds the next record that matches the condition. In fact, you can continue issuing CONTINUE until VFP reaches the end of the file. The code segment in Listing 5.6 shows you how to use these commands to view all customers who have outstanding bills.

Listing 5.6 05CODE06.PRG—Using LOCATE and CONTINUE

```
* View customers with outstanding bills
USE CUST
LOCATE FOR cBillDue > 0
DISPLAY OFF cCustId, cBillDue
DO WHILE !EOF()
  CONTINUE
  IF NOT EOF()
    DISPLAY OFF cCustId, cBillDue
  ENDIF
ENDDO
```

TIP When you use LOCATE or CONTINUE, EOF() remains .F. until the search fails to find additional records that match the condition. Alternatively, you can use FOUND(), which returns .T. as long as records are found.

The advantage with LOCATE is that you can define a condition on any field or portion of a field in the table; it does not need an index. To find all customers who have the word CONSULTANTS in their company names, use the commands in Listing 5.7.

Listing 5.7 05CODE07.PRG—Putting Them All Together

```
* Locate all customers who are consultants
USE CUST
LOCATE FOR 'CONSULTANTS' $ UPPER(cCompany)
LIST OFF cCompany
DO WHILE !EOF()
  CONTINUE
  IF FOUND()
    LIST OFF cCompany
  ENDIF
ENDDO
```

TIP When you compare strings, convert both sides of the string to all uppercase or all lowercase before comparing them to make comparisons independent of case.

TIP Even though the LOCATE command does not require that any indexes exist, it is a good idea to maintain indexes on all the fields that you refer to in your LOCATE commands. This is because the optimizing technology in Visual FoxPro 6, Rushmore, uses available indexes to improve the speed at which it can evaluate your FOR clause on the LOCATE command.

You can even use LOCATE with a condition that combines several fields. Although LOCATE does not require an index, if one exists that matches the form of the condition, LOCATE automatically optimizes the search for matching records. What this means to you is improved performance with almost instantaneous response, even in tables that have millions of records.

Seeking Records on Index Values

Another command that you can use to find selected records in a table is SEEK. Unlike LOCATE, SEEK requires the use of an index. Furthermore, if the index is a compound one, or if you open multiple simple indexes, SEEK works only with the current one. Therefore, first SET ORDER TO the index that you want SEEK to use. SEEK has a simple syntax. Simply follow SEEK with the value that you want it to find. To find CUSTOMER 0025, enter the code shown in Listing 5.8.

Listing 5.8 05CODE08.PRG—Using SEEK

```
* Locate customer '0025'
USE CUST
SET ORDER TO TAG custid
SEEK '0025'
IF FOUND()
  DISPLAY
ELSE
  = MESSAGEBOX('CUSTOMER 0025 was not found')
ENDIF
```

SEEK requires a value of the same data type as the current index. A seek expression does not always have to match the index value exactly, however. If SET EXACT is OFF, the index value needs to match character-for-character for only as many characters as are in the seek value. Suppose that you want to search CUST.DBF for a company whose name begins with Laser. Use the following code:

```
USE C:\VFP5BOOK\DATA\CUST
SET ORDER TO TAG company
SEEK 'Laser'
```

If SET EXACT is OFF, Visual FoxPro 6 finds the record. If SET EXACT is ON, the seek value must match the index value exactly, in total number of characters as well as each individual character. Thus, if you index CUSTOMER.DBF by company and perform the following SEEK with SET EXACT OFF, VFP places the record pointer at the first company whose name begins with L:

```
SET EXACT OFF
SEEK 'L'
```

Part

II

Ch

5

The SET EXACT command also works for other conditional tests, such as in the FOR clause described earlier in this chapter. In these cases, however, an inexact search matches characters from left to right until a mismatch is found or until the expression on the right side of the = operator ends. You can temporarily override inexact comparisons for a single conditional test by using the == operator. Therefore, the following two LOCATEs are equivalent:

```
SET EXACT ON
LOCATE FOR cFirst = 'NATASHA    '
```

and

```
SET EXACT OFF
LOCATE FOR cFirst == 'NATASHA    '
```

N O T E Even though == and SET EXACT ON seem to be equivalent, they are slightly different. SET EXACT ON compares two strings until the one on the right side of the = is exhausted, and then checks to see if both strings are of equal length. ==, on the other hand, pads the shorter string with spaces to force it to be the same length and then checks the two strings to see if they are the same.

The following code listing explains the difference:

```
LcVar1 = 'SMITH'
LcVar2 = 'SMITH     '
? lcVar1 == lcVar2 && Displays .T. that they are equal
SET EXACT ON
? lcVar1 = lcVar2 && Displays .F. that they are not equal
```

Normally, when a LOCATE or SEEK fails, Visual FoxPro 6 leaves the record pointer at the end of the table. In some cases, however, you might not know exactly what value to search for, so you guess. You want the pointer to stop at the next record after the position of the search value, if that value exists.

Suppose that you don't know the exact name of the company, but you think that it's Golf Heaven, so you write the code shown in Listing 5.9. If no company name in CUST.DBF has this exact spelling, the record pointer moves to the end of the file. If you first enter the command SET NEAR ON, however, VFP stops at the first company name that alphabetically follows Golf Heaven: Goofer's Arcade Heaven in table CUST.DBF.

Table 5.3 might help clarify interpreting a SEEK with SET NEAR ON and SET EXACT OFF.

Table 5.3   Results of SEEK with SET NEAR ON and SET EXACT OFF

EOF()	FOUND()	Search Result
.F.	.T.	Exact match of search string found.
.F.	.F.	No exact match found, but record pointer is on the next record alphabetically.
.T.	.F.	No exact match found; search string is beyond the last value in the table.

Listing 5.9 05CODE09.PRG—Results of SEEK with SET NEAR ON

```
* Locate customer data for GOLF HEAVEN
* Open table and set tag to COMPANY
  USE C:\VFP5BOOK\DATA\CUST
  SET ORDER TO TAG company

* Save current setting of NEAR, and turn NEAR ON
  curnear = SYS(2001, 'NEAR')
  SET NEAR ON

* Find record closest to 'GOLF HEAVEN'
  SEEK 'GOLF HEAVEN'

* If search goes beyond last records, display last record.
  IF EOF()
     GOTO BOTTOM
  ENDIF
  DISPLAY

* Reset NEAR to original value
  SET NEAR &curnear
```

N O T E Use SET EXACT ON only if you search or compare with strings of the same length as the index or comparison field. Otherwise, SET EXACT OFF enables you to search by entering a substring. If you know that the substring that you want to search with matches a field in the table character for character, you can SET NEAR OFF. Otherwise, SET NEAR ON finds the next record alphabetically after the substring.

Whenever you use a SET command in a program, consider capturing the current state of the SET parameter by using the SET() function. Remember to restore the parameter to its original value when you leave the program. Always begin programs with a common SET definition. Then program by exception only those SET parameters that must change from this default. ■

Part
II

Ch

5

If you are not sure that an entered value will exactly match a value in the table, use SET NEAR ON to find the next record alphabetically. Use this technique when you are setting ranges for parameters in reports. On the other hand, if you need to create a relation between customer ID in the order file and in the customer file, you want an exact match and should use both SET EXACT ON and SET NEAR OFF.

Selecting Groups of Records

Many operations call for a subset of the table that is being used. Perhaps you want to see only the customers in Pennsylvania or those customers in California who have outstanding bills. In either case, define a filter condition using the SET FILTER TO command followed by LIST or DISPLAY, as follows:

```
USE C:\VFP5BOOK\DATA\CUST
SET FILTER TO cBState = 'PA'
LIST
```

TIP   Even though it does not use a FOR clause, SET FILTER is Rushmore-optimizable.

You have the same capability to filter records directly from within both LIST and DISPLAY. The FOR clause enables you to define a condition that selects records from the table. To select records for Pennsylvania customers, for example, use an expression like the following:

```
FOR cBState = 'PA'
```

Use the following expression to DISPLAY the results:

```
DISPLAY ALL cCustId, cCompany FOR cBState = 'PA'
```

This command steps through the records sequentially from the first record and displays only those that match the condition of the FOR expression. The potential problem with this method is apparent if you envision that the customer records will be sorted but not indexed by state: Visual FoxPro reads more records than it needs to. When Visual FoxPro reads the table using a FOR clause, it tests each record to find the Pennsylvania ones. Furthermore, even after VFP displays the last record for Pennsylvania customers, it continues reading records until it reaches the end of the file. The FOR clause makes no assumptions about sort orders; it is a brute-force way of processing all records that match the condition.

N O T E   If the FOR expression is Rushmore-optimizable, performance is greatly improved. If the FOR expression is not optimized, it can be extremely slow because it reads every record in the table. The programmer has the responsibility of ensuring that the FOR expression is Rushmore-optimizable. ■

Processing Records with WHILE

An alternative method of finding records that match an expression uses the WHILE clause. To begin, open a table and an index that uses the same order as the search condition. Next, find the first record that matches the search condition. To do so, use LOCATE or SEEK. If EOF() returns .T. or FOUND() returns .F., no records match the search condition. Having found the first record that matches the condition, you know that all additional matching records in the table follow it sequentially. Read these records one at a time, using a simple loop such as DO WHILE or SCAN, until the search condition fails. Then you can ignore the rest of the table without searching it because you know that no other records will match.

Listing 5.10 shows a variation on the preceding search. It requires a nonoptimizable search, because it uses a substring expression to find a customer whose name begins with the letter M.

Listing 5.10   05CODE10.PRG—Using WHILE

```
SELECT CUST
SET ORDER TO TAG COMPANY
LOCATE FOR LEFT(cCompany,1) =  'M'
```

```
SCAN WHILE LEFT(cCompany,1) = 'M'
  ? cCustId, cCompany
ENDSCAN
```

N O T E The real difference between FOR and WHILE is that FOR will check every record in the command scope and only affect those that meet the condition. WHILE will affect records until it encounters one that does not meet the condition. This means that WHILE is always faster than FOR because it deals with fewer records. ▪

You can combine FOR and WHILE clauses in the same command line. For example, if you want to see the customers in Texas that owe you more than $1,000, you could use the following:

```
USE Customer ORDER TAG State
SEEK 'TX'
DISPLAY WHILE State = 'TX' FOR Balance > 1000
```

You might wonder which condition is best to put in the WHILE and which in the FOR. You want to put the most restrictive condition—that is, the one that provides the smallest number of records—in the WHILE. In the preceding example, if there were 20,000 customers in Texas and 1,000 that owe more than $1,000, the fastest way would be the following:

```
USE Customer ORDER TAG Balance
SEEK 1000
DISPLAY WHILE Balance>1000 FOR State = 'TX'
```

N O T E If you need to retrieve records based on an expression that does not have a corresponding index, you probably need to use a nonoptimized FOR. Because such expressions are slow, you might want to consider creating a separate index for this situation if it occurs frequently. ▪

Using SEEK and a WHILE clause provides performance that is better than that of a Rushmore-optimized FOR expression.

One additional enhancement can be added to this example. SEEK has an equivalent function call that returns .T. when it finds a match. You can place this function directly in the DO WHILE statement, as shown in Listing 5.11.

Listing 5.11 05CODE11.PRG—Using SEEK and DO WHILE

```
SELECT CUST
SET ORDER TO TAG CUSTSTATE
IF SEEK('PA')    && Execute the code block on if PA is found
  DISPLAY REST cCustId, cCompany ;
       WHILE cBState = 'PA'
ENDIF
```

N O T E In the example in Listing 5.11, notice the scope word REST used on the DISPLAY command. This scope word is optional in this situation because a WHILE clause implicitly includes a scope of REST. ▪

Sorting Data in the Table

You can sort data in a table in two fundamental ways. The first is a *physical sort*, also called a *permanent sort*. To create a physical sort, you need to rewrite the table in the desired sort order. The advantage of this method is that you need no additional file other than the data file itself. The disadvantage is that the sort order is difficult to maintain if users make frequent updates to the data. A physical sort requires more code to maintain or requires frequent re-sorting.

> **CAUTION**
>
> A further disadvantage to sorting occurs with large files. If your tables get large, a sort will take considerable time to execute.

The second type of sort uses a second file called an index. An *index* stores values for the indexed field(s) and pointers to the location of those values in the database. The *pointer* is a record number. Visual FoxPro 6 stores the indexed field values in a b-tree (balanced binary tree) structure that it can search quickly.

Creating Permanent Sortings

As mentioned earlier in this chapter, you are unlikely to add records to the table in a sorted order. But if you do, what happens if you need more than one sort order? You certainly cannot have two physical sort orders in one table. The alternative—maintaining two or more separate copies of the data in tables with different sort orders—is a major nightmare. Yet at times, you want to store data in sorted order. Other than entering the records that way, how can you create a sorted table?

The SORT command creates another copy of the table and enables you to sort on any field or combination of fields. SORT's syntax is rather rich, as follows:

```
SORT TO TableName
    ON FieldName1 [/A][/D][/C]
    [FieldName2 [/A][/D][/C]...]
    [ASCENDING|DESCENDING]
    [Scope][FOR Iexpression1][WHILE Iexpression2]
    [FIELDS FieldNameList|FIELDS LIKE Skeleton
    |FIELDS EXCEPT Skeleton]
    [NOOPTIMIZE]
```

Suppose that you need to generate a report that lists customers alphabetically by state, and that within each state you want to list customers with the largest annual purchases first and continue to the smallest. You need an ascending sort on state and a descending sort on purchases. SORT can create this file with the following statement:

```
USE \VFP5BOOK\DATA\CUSTOMER
SORT TO STATSALE ON cBillingStateProvince /A/C + ;
        nPurchasesYearToDate /D
```

CAUTION

SORT creates a free table. Therefore, it truncates the long field names defined in the original table of the example to 10-character fields.

 You can create indexes that have different orders (ascending/descending) on the parts of the index, such as:

```
INDEX ON cState + STR(999999.99-nPurchases,9,2)
```

Another disadvantage of using SORT is the quick obsolescence of the data. As soon as you create the table, it begins to become obsolete. Someone else might immediately add, delete, or modify a record. One situation in which physically sorting the records in a table can benefit an application is when a table has a very large number of records and there is one primary order in which those records are used. In this case, it is beneficial to sort the table on that order whenever you are doing maintenance on the table (such as re-creating the indexes or something else).

In Chapter 6, "Creating Basic Queries," you learn to create CURSORS with the SQL SELECT command. Cursors provide the same advantages as SORT (sort directions by field). In addition, Visual FoxPro 6 automatically deletes cursors when you exit VFP or open another table in the same work area.

Creating Virtual Sorts with Indexes

Indexes are the best way to provide different sort orders for data. Visual FoxPro 6 can create, use, and maintain three types of indexes:

- Independent indexes (.IDX)
- Compound structural indexes (.CDX)
- Compound non-structural indexes (.CDX)

Indexes are not static in the same way that tables created with SORT are. Rather, indexes are dynamic. Indexes adapt automatically to added, deleted, and modified records, as long as you keep them open. The following is the syntax for the INDEX command:

```
INDEX ON eExpression ;
     TO IDXFileName¦TAG TagName [OF CDXFileName]
     [FOR lExpression]
     [COMPACT]
     [ASCENDING¦DESCENDING]
     [UNIQUE¦CANDIDATE]
     [ADDITIVE]
```

Chapter 3, "Defining Databases, Tables, and Indexes," discusses how to create compound structural indexes by using the index page of the Table Designer. You can also create and use any of the three indexes directly from the Command window or from within a program.

Simple Independent Indexes *Independent indexes* on a single expression were the first indexes used by FoxBase, the predecessor of FoxPro. For each index expression, you create a separate index file with its own name. The root names of the table (.DBF) and index (.IDX) do not have to be the same. In fact, if you have more than one simple index, it is not possible for all the indexes to have the same root name. Many programmers developed the habit of naming the primary index with the same root name as the table. The following lines use the INDEX command to create an independent index on customer ID in CUST.DBF, which has 10-character field names:

```
USE CUST
INDEX ON cCustId TO CUSTID.IDX
```

At this point, the table and index are open. But in most programs, you need to specifically open previously created indexes with the table, as in the following command:

```
USE CUST INDEX CUSTID
```

If you have more than one index for a table, open the indexes at the same time if you plan to make modifications to the records, as follows:

```
USE CUST INDEX CUSTID, COMPANY, ZIPCODE
```

If you do not open each index, VFP cannot maintain the indexes that are not open if you add, delete, or modify records. (Because the indexes can have any name, how would FoxPro know about them?) If you attempt to use the table with one of these indexes later, VFP might display records out of order or even point outside the table due to deleted records.

N O T E To get the best performance, use the COMPACT option with single indexes. Except for backward compatibility, continued use of independent indexes is not recommended. It is too easy for the indexes to get out of sync, and they are much slower than compact indexes. The exception is when you need to use an index temporarily and will delete it when the task is complete. ▦

CAUTION
Compact independent indexes are not compatible with older versions of FoxBase.

Compound Indexes Although independent indexes work, *compound indexes* are a better alternative for most indexing needs. These indexes enable an unlimited number of separate index expressions in one file. You cannot lose files or forget the names of all the index files that belong to one table. If you assign the same root name to the index files used by the table, you do not even have to worry about opening the index file; Visual FoxPro 6 opens that file automatically when it opens the table. These compound indexes have a special name: *structural indexes*.

When you are working with compound indexes, you need to know not only how to set a tag, but also which tag is current, the names of the defined tags associated with a table, and their index expressions. You saw earlier that SET ORDER TO sets the current index when you are using standalone index files and SET ORDER TO TAG sets the current tag for compound tags. But how can you determine which indexes are associated with a table?

> **N O T E** The TAG word in SET ORDER TO is optional. SET ORDER TO TAG City and SET ORDER TO City are equivalent as long as there is no simple index file named City.idx open. ▨

You can use a combination of TAG() and TAGCOUNT() to get a list of the index tags in a compound index. TAGCOUNT() tells you how many tags the index has and TAG() tells you name of each tag.

No relation exists between a table and its independent indexes or non-structural indexes. The only index that you can automatically associate with a table is its structural index. Even in the context of a program that opens independent and non-structural indexes with their table, you cannot be sure that you have opened all the indexes.

T I P For all the reasons just mentioned, it is recommended that you use structural compound indexes on your tables. The only exception is when you are creating a temporary index that will be deleted immediately after its use.

You can examine the indexes opened with a table, however, by using several functions. The NDX() function returns the names of any open .IDX files. (Originally, index files had an .NDX extension, and they still do in dBASE. Therefore, the function to list them became NDX(). The name NDX() remains the same in Visual FoxPro 6, even though its indexes have an .IDX extension.)

To find the names of open compound indexes, use the CDX() or MDX() functions. These two functions perform the same task. At minimum, each function requires a numeric parameter. A value of 1 returns the name of the structural index, if present. Subsequent values return the names of other compound indexes in the order in which they are opened. These two functions, along with NDX(), return an empty string when the index number exceeds the number of open indexes. Therefore, test for this condition to determine when to stop.

> **N O T E** Both the CDX() and MDX() functions support a second parameter that enables you to determine the index names associated with tables in another work area. Enter the second parameter as the work-area number or the file alias, as in the following example:
>
> ? CDX(1,'customer') ▨

When you know the names of the compound indexes, find their tag names. The TAG() function returns the name of each tag in the current compound index, as in the following example:

```
i = 1
DO WHILE !EMPTY(TAG(i))
      ? TAG(i)
      i = i + 1
ENDDO
```

You also can include arguments to specify the compound-index name, as well as the table name or work area.

NOTE Although the preceding functions help you define the index files and tag names that are associated with an open table, they do not tell you which index or tag currently controls the order. Two functions provide this information. ORDER() returns the controlling index tag name, and SET('ORDER') returns the controlling index tag name and the compound index file's name with the full path.

You can obtain the index expression easily with the KEY() function, which enables both a .CDX filename and a tag number relative to that file. ▪

Listing 5.12 provides a routine that documents the tables and indexes that are currently open in an application.

Listing 5.12 05CODE12.PRG—Determining Which Tables and Indexes Are Open

```
LOCAL lnCurArea, lnHighestArea, lnIwork, lnIndx, lnIcdx, lnItag
CLEAR

* Current information on open tables
* Save the current work area
  lnCurArea = SELECT()

* Find the highest work area in use
  SELECT 0
  lnHighestArea = SELECT(0) - 1

* Loop through the work areas
  FOR lnWork = 1 to lnHighestArea
    WAIT WINDOW "Examining workarea: "+STR(m.lnWork,5) NOWAIT
    SELECT (lnWork)
    IF EMPTY(DBF())
      LOOP
    ENDIF
    ? 'Work area ' + STR(m.lnWork,5) + ': '
    ? '  Table: ' + DBF()

* Next scan for simple indexes
    ? '  Simple Indexes'
    FOR lnIdx = 1 to 256
      IF EMPTY(NDX(lnIdx))
        IF lnIdx = 1
          ? '        NONE'
        ENDIF
        EXIT
      ENDIF
      ? '    Index: ' + NDX(lnIdx)
      ? '       Expression: ' + TAG(lnIdx)

* Check if this IDX is the master index
      IF ORDER(ALIAS(),1) = NDX(lnIdx)
```

```
      ? '       This is the MASTER index'
   ENDIF

ENDFOR

* Scan for compound indexes
 ? '  Compound Indexes'
 FOR lnCdx = 1 to 256
   IF EMPTY(CDX(lnCdx))
     IF lnCdx = 1
       ? '      NONE'
     ENDIF
     EXIT
   ENDIF
   ? '    Index: ' + CDX(lnCdx)

* Check if this CDX holds the master index
   IF ORDER(ALIAS(),1) = CDX(lnCdx)
     ? '     MASTER index:      ' + SYS(22)
     ? '            expression: ' + TAG(VAL(SYS(21)))
   ENDIF

* Loop for each tag in the compound index
   FOR lnTag = 1 TO 256
     IF EMPTY(TAG(CDX(lnCdx),lnTag))
       EXIT
     ENDIF
     ? '     Tag Name:       ' + TAG(CDX(lnCdx),lnTag)
     ? '         Expression: ' + KEY(CDX(lnCdx),lnTag)
   ENDFOR
   ?
 ENDFOR
ENDFOR

* Return to original area
 SELECT (lnCurArea)
```

N O T E   To keep the index tags balanced, Visual FoxPro 6 retains the old tags and marks them obsolete in a `.CDX` file after re-creating a specific tag. This arrangement causes the `.CDX` file to grow. To prevent this growth, `DELETE TAG ALL` for the table and re-create the tags using `INDEX ON`. How can you do this in a program? Use the concepts from the preceding program to save the tag names and expressions for your selected `.CDX` in an array; then delete the `.CDX` and re-create the tags from the array. ▨

CAUTION

When dealing with tables in a database, things can get tricky. The persistent relations stored in the database are based on index tags. If you use `DELETE TAG ALL`, you will destroy any persistent relationships for that table in the database. To solve this problem, you need to use `DbGetProp` to get all the relations for the table into memory variables or an array. After you create the index tags again, you need to use the `ALTER TABLE` command to reset all the persistent relationships.

Planning Indexes for Rushmore

Indexing is more than just sorting records for views or reports. Indexes have a more direct impact on the application's performance than ever before. Since the release of FoxPro 2.0, when Microsoft introduced Rushmore, this optimization technique has dramatically improved the performance of applications by locating records in large tables faster. Rushmore achieves this task through the use of indexes. It uses any index type—.IDX files, compact .IDXs, or .CDXs. In fact, it is common today to define indexes that you never intend to use for retrieving or viewing data; rather, these indexes exist solely to enhance the performance of SEEKs and REPORTs. Developers have reported search improvements 100 to 1,000 times faster when they use an optimizable Rushmore expression compared with a nonoptimized expression. The greatest improvements come from using compact .IDX or .CDX files, principally because VFP can read more of the index into memory at one time.

Listing 5.13 times how long it takes to count the number of zip codes in Pennsylvania.

Listing 5.13 05CODE13.PRG—Testing Index Search Time

```
CLOSE ALL
CLEAR

SET OPTIMIZE OFF
? "Counting the number of zip codes in Pennsylvania."
USE \VFP5BOOK\DATA\ZIPCODE
nStart = SECONDS()
COUNT FOR (STATE == 'PA') TO nZipCnt
nEnd   = SECONDS()
? '        COUNT WAS: ' + STR(nZipCnt, 12, 0)
? 'ELAPSED TIME WAS: ' + STR(nEnd - nStart, 8, 2)
SET OPTIMIZE ON
```

On a test system, it took 4.61 seconds to find 2,217 records out of 42,818. Elapsed time on your system will vary depending on the processor speed, drive speed, physical sector allocation, and other factors. If you remove both SET OPTIMIZE statements, the required time drops to 0.16 second. Although this figure is an increase of only 29 times, the sample table is small; improvements become more dramatic as the number of records grows. The difference can easily extend into minutes and even hours for large tables that have millions of records.

How can Rushmore provide such improved performance? First, by reading an index, it quickly locates the first record reference required by the condition and then reads the index only until the condition changes. Second, it reads only the index, rather than the table; it does not have to use the record pointer to read the actual table data. In the zip code table, Rushmore reads the index tag STATE, which contains an entry for each record in the table. This entry contains the state name and a pointer to the table record. There is no reason to go to the table. Because Rushmore can directly read the state name stored in the index, it can simply count the number of times that the state PA occurs.

N O T E   Rushmore must compare the index expression with a memory variable or constant. In other words, you can compare the index expression with a string, number, or date value, or store a value in a constant and use it. But Rushmore cannot optimize an expression that compares an index expression with another variable in the table. Suppose that you have a table that includes birth dates and hire dates. Rushmore cannot optimize an expression such as the following, which lists records for people 16-years old or older:

```
LIST FOR dHire_Date > GOMONTH(dBirth_Date, 16*12)
```

To use Rushmore, you don't need to know the details of how it works internally any more than you need to know the details of how an internal-combustion engine works to drive a car. But obviously, you need to know how to define indexes that Rushmore can optimize. More important, you need to know what Rushmore likes and dislikes.

This chapter has already mentioned a few rules that you must obey to use Rushmore successfully. Another rule is that Rushmore can optimize only those expressions based on regular, primary, and candidate indexes. These indexes (as mentioned in Chapter 3) contain a reference for every record in the table, even if the index value is not unique. If you think about it, how else would Rushmore count the number of zip codes in a state if you define the state index as unique? You would never get a value other than 0 or 1.

Rushmore also requires that any search or query exactly match the index key. This statement has led many developers to believe that they needed a separate index tag for every field in their tables. Then the developers realized that they also needed more complex index expressions for reports or other activities, so they created additional indexes. Before long, the total number of indexes grew out of control, and the size of the .CDX file rivaled or exceeded that of the data itself. Performance degrades not just because of the size of the .CDX, but because Visual FoxPro 6 has more indexes to maintain every time you add, delete, or modify a record.

Often, you can delete many of these indexes without seriously affecting the application's performance. Returning to the customer file, suppose that you have the following set of indexes (using short field names in CUST.DBF):

```
INDEX ON UPPER(cLast) TAG LASTNAME
INDEX ON UPPER(cFirst) TAG FIRSTNAME
INDEX ON UPPER(cCompany) TAG COMPANY
INDEX ON UPPER(cLast)+UPPER(cFirst) TAG STAFF
INDEX ON UPPER(cCompany) + UPPER(cLast) + ;
        UPPER(cFirst) TAG EMPLOYEES
```

Although these tags appear to cover every contingency, they affect performance when you add, delete, or modify records because VFP must change more information in more tags. An alternative method takes advantage of the fact that Rushmore can optimize concatenated indexes. If you use SET EXACT OFF, you do not need to supply every field as an index.

If you want to search on the company field, for example, you could use either the COMPANY or EMPLOYEES tag, as follows:

```
LOCATE FOR cCompany = 'RENARD CONSULTANTS'
```

Alternatively, you could use the following:

```
SET EXACT OFF
LOCATE FOR cCompany + cLast + cFirst = ;
           'RENARD CONSULTANTS'
```

In the first LOCATE, Rushmore looks at the index expression on the left and decides to use the COMPANY tag. In the second, LOCATE uses the EMPLOYEES tag. The second expression is only slightly slower than the first. The only consideration is that you must include the entire index expression on the left side.

A similar argument applies when you are searching for names and choosing between the tags STAFF and LASTNAME. The only individual field tag that you might still need is FIRSTNAME. Therefore, you can eliminate at least two of these five indexes, and maybe more, depending on what the application really needs to do.

> **CAUTION**
>
> Although Rushmore can optimize an expression that matches only a portion of the concatenated fields, when you have SET EXACT OFF, the shorter string must be on the right side of the expression. Also, there is no way to skip a field in a multiple-field index to search only for later components.

Notice that if you eliminate tags LASTNAME and COMPANY, Rushmore does not optimize a search like the following because the index expression no longer exactly matches an index tag:

```
LOCATE FOR cCompany = 'RENARD CONSULTANTS'
```

Other things that Rushmore does not like and will not handle include index expressions that contain NOT or !. Surprisingly, you cannot include NOT or ! in the FOR expression and have Rushmore optimize it.

Rushmore optimizes expressions that contain exactly equal relational operators (==), but not the contained-in operator ($), AT(), ATC(), or RAT(). It will not use indexes that include FOR conditions.

On the other hand, you can build compound FOR expressions that Rushmore can optimize (or at least partially optimize). A *compound expression* joins two or more simple expressions with an AND or an OR. In this case, each expression can reference a different index expression. When it is looking at compound expressions two at a time, Rushmore optimizes the entire expression only if it can optimize both individual expressions. If it can only optimize one of the expressions, and you join the expressions with AND, Rushmore executes the part that it can optimize first. Then Rushmore takes this intermediate result set and performs the nonoptimizable portion on it, rather than on the entire database. This arrangement usually results in some improvement over a completely nonoptimizable expression.

Visual FoxPro 6 will partially optimize a compound expression that contains one optimizable expression and one nonoptimizable expression joined with an OR because it still must read the entire table to evaluate the nonoptimizable expression. Finally, if both individual expressions are nonoptimizable, Rushmore cannot optimize any part of the expression.

Table 5.4 displays possible combinations of expressions and their results.

Table 5.4 Combining Optimizable Expressions

First Expression	Connection	Second Expression	Result
Optimizable	AND	Optimizable	Optimizable
Optimizable	OR	Optimizable	Optimizable
Optimizable	AND	Nonoptimizable	Partial
Optimizable	OR	Nonoptimizable	Nonoptimizable
Nonoptimizable	AND	Nonoptimizable	Nonoptimizable
Nonoptimizable	OR	Nonoptimizable	Nonoptimizable

Potentially, Rushmore can optimize every VFP command that supports a FOR clause. You must work with a single table, however, and follow the rules described earlier in this section. The following list shows the commands that Rushmore supports:

AVERAGE	DISPLAY	REPORT FORM
BROWSE	EDIT	SCAN
CALCULATE	EXPORT	SET FILTER TO
CHANGE	LABEL	SORT
COPY TO	LIST	SQL SELECT
COPY TO ARRAY	LOCATE	SUM
COUNT	RECALL	TOTAL
DELETE	REPLACE	

Remember that Rushmore works with these commands only if you use them with a single table. To query or gather data from multiple tables, use SQL SELECT. Only the SQL SELECT command supports Rushmore optimization across multiple tables.

NOTE If you have a simple SQL SELECT on a single table with no special functions, groups, or sort orders, Visual FoxPro 6 uses Rushmore to create a filter on the database that returns the result set extremely fast. VFP does use Rushmore on multiple-table queries, but only if you use SQL SELECT.

With the introduction of Rushmore, traditional accessing of files with deleted records exhibited a performance degradation. A simple solution exists, however: Merely add a tag to the structured index, using the function DELETED( ), but do not name it DELETED, which is a restricted keyword. Now Rushmore can use the index to determine whether to include a record, rather than having to check the deleted flag in the table.

Part II

Ch 5

Turning Rushmore Off

At the beginning of this section, you learned that SET OPTIMIZE OFF can turn Rushmore off. Why turn off a tool that usually results in better performance? You typically don't want to turn Rushmore off when you are using expressions that it can optimize. When you are using nonoptimizable expressions, however, leaving it on actually lowers performance. In such cases, Rushmore needs extra machine cycles just to know that it is not needed. Therefore, turn optimization off by using the SET OPTIMIZE statement or by adding the clause NOOPTIMIZE after the FOR expression, as follows:

```
LOCATE FOR cFirst = 'NATASHA' NOOPTIMIZE
```

Another reason for turning off optimization involves the particular command you are using; for example, the REPLACE command can have a FOR clause. If you were replacing one of the fields used in the Rushmore optimized FOR clause, the actual command itself would be causing the Rushmore selected set of records to be incomplete.

```
REPLACE ALL State WITH 'NY' FOR City = 'New York' ;
                OR State = 'NY'
```

Helping Rushmore Along

You can improve the performance of Rushmore by deselecting any default index or tag before executing a command that Rushmore can optimize. The following command leaves the index file open but turns off its active use:

```
SET ORDER TO 0
```

When there is an index order set, Rushmore must sort the records it finds on the index expression. This extra step will slow down the result. Although this is true, Rushmore-optimized expressions will still be faster than nonoptimizable expressions even with an index order set.

 T I P   As a general rule, you add as many indexes as necessary to search for and display data. You should periodically review whether you require all of them, however.

When an application's performance slows due to index overload, you need to identify indexes that you use only occasionally. You should delete those index tags and enable the program to re-create them as needed.

 T I P   To delete a tag, open the table and use the command DELETE TAG *tagname*.

You might want to create temporary indexes on a local rather than a network drive. You might even gain some performance by creating a cursor with a SQL SELECT statement to gather and sort the data for a report. Listing 5.14 shows a method that might appear to be awkward at first, yet yields quite respectable performance when the selected records are widely scattered and need to be reused. The routine begins by creating a temporary index; then it uses a Rushmore-assisted SEEK to find the first record. The routine processes the desired records using a SCAN loop; generates a report with the same index; and, finally, deletes the temporary index.

Listing 5.14 `05CODE14.PRG`—Using Rushmore

```
CLOSE DATABASES
CLEAR

* Open the customer table (free table)
USE \VFP5BOOK\DATA\cust

* Set NEAR ON to find first customer with more than
* $200 of outstanding bills
cCurNear   = SYS(2001, 'NEAR')
cCurExact  = SYS(2001, 'EXACT')
cCurSafety = SYS(2001, 'SAFETY')
SET NEAR   ON
SET EXACT  OFF
SET SAFETY OFF

* Create a temporary index on outstanding bills
* This assumes that you have previously created a directory
* with the name C:\TEMP
INDEX ON nBillDue TO C:\TEMP\BILLS.IDX

* Find records and change default billing method to cash 'CA'
SEEK 200
SCAN WHILE nBillDue >= 200
  REPLACE cPayMeth WITH 'CA'
ENDSCAN

* Create a report for sales representative of customer that
* must pay cash
REPORT FORM \VFP5BOOK\PROGRAMS\BillMeth ;
   FOR nBillDue => 200

* Reset environment
SET NEAR   &cCurNear
SET EXACT  &cCurExact
SET SAFETY &cCurSafety

* Delete temporary index
USE
ERASE C:\temp\bills.idx
RETURN
```

Part
II

Ch
5

A SEEK combined with SCAN WHILE structure always executes faster than Rushmore. Also notice the use of SET NEAR ON to find the first record above a specific value, just in case no records have a value of exactly 200.

The best indexing method varies from one situation to the next. Your choice depends on the specific task that you want to accomplish, the current organization of the data, the specific commands that you use, and (probably) the phase of the moon.

The BROWSE command illustrates this point. Reopen ZIPCODE.DBF and turn off the index, as follows:

```
USE C:\VFP5BOOK\DATA\ZIPCODE
SET ORDER TO
```

The natural order of this data is city within state. Thus, all the zip codes for Alaska appear first, and all the zip codes for Wyoming appear at the end of the file. Now try the following simple BROWSEs:

```
BROWSE FOR cBState = 'AK'
BROWSE FOR cBState = 'WY'
```

The first BROWSE comes up almost immediately. The second BROWSE opens a window immediately but takes several seconds to display the first screen of data. BROWSE displays the first screen of data as soon as it has enough records to populate it. Thus, the second command pauses with a blank window, while BROWSE searches through the file until it finds Wyoming.

Suppose you know that the selected data either appears very near the beginning of the file or that it encompasses the majority of the data (such as BROWSE FOR !DELETED()). A simple BROWSE statement without an index might appear to be as quick as one with an index using Rushmore, because BROWSE does not need to find every record that matches the criteria—only enough to display a screen of records. That explanation might be stretching the point just a little, but you should try several alternatives before you assume that Rushmore and another index tag provide the best performance. ●

Creating Basic Queries

What Is a Query?

According to the *American Heritage Dictionary*, a *query* is a question, an inquiry. So when you query a database, you are asking it questions about data. Using a sales file, for example, you might ask the following questions:

- What is the total value of all sales for last week? last month? last year?
- Are sales increasing?
- Which products sell the greatest quantity?
- Which products produce the most sales dollars?
- Which products are losing sales?
- How many sales are made to repeat customers?
- How are sales distributed by state?

With a little effort, you surely can come up with infinitely more questions. Although you might write programs to answer many of those questions, you cannot anticipate them all. Both queries and views are built to order for answering these types of questions. In this chapter, you will examine the Visual FoxPro query and learn how to use it. In subsequent chapters, you will learn about Visual FoxPro views and see how they are often more powerful and full-featured than the queries.

Queries and views are similar, but the differences are important. Queries are stored as program files with the extension .QPR. The QPR program contains a SQL SELECT command. Views are stored in a database and are also stored as a SQL SELECT command. However, views have two advantages over queries. First, they can be updated, meaning that they update their source tables when the view is updated. Second, they can be parameterized. Chapter 7, "Advanced Queries and Views," will present views for you. In this chapter, the discussion is limited to queries.

Selecting Tables for a Query

Open the Query Designer by choosing File, New from the system menu or by clicking the New button in the toolbar. Choose the Query option in the New dialog box, and click the New File button, as shown in Figure 6.1.

Adding a Table or View from a Database

TIP   You also can start a new query from the Command window by using the CREATE QUERY or MODIFY QUERY command.

TIP   You can create a query without first opening the database. In the File Open dialog box, just select one of the tables that is in the database, and Visual FoxPro opens the database for you.

FIGURE 6.1

Use the New dialog box to start a new query.

A query requires at least one table. However, Visual FoxPro does not assume that you want to query the table in the current work area; rather, it immediately opens a window displaying the Open Table dialog box and enables you to select the first table. Actually, VFP can open two windows, depending on whether a database is open. Figure 6.2 shows the Add Table or View dialog box, which lists tables in an open database. If more than one database is open, you can pull down the database combo list and change the current one.

FIGURE 6.2

The Add Table or View dialog box appears when you create a new query, allowing you to select a table.

For this set of examples, open the Tastrade database that comes with Visual FoxPro. In the Select area, you can choose either Tables or Views to use in the query. Tastrade has both tables and some predefined views. To start a new query definition, select from the available tables. Notice that the list of tables in this dialog box includes only tables that are defined in the Tastrade database.

TIP Keep in mind that the methods discussed in this chapter apply to views as well.

Part
II
Ch
6

Adding a Free Table

To use a free table, either start the Query Designer without first opening a database, or click the Other button in the Add Table or View dialog box (see Figure 6.2). VFP displays the standard Open dialog box, shown in Figure 6.3. In this dialog box, you can select a table from any directory or drive, including network drives. If the selected table really is bound to a database, Visual FoxPro automatically opens the database, too.

FIGURE 6.3

In the Open dialog box, you can select free tables or tables from databases that are not open.

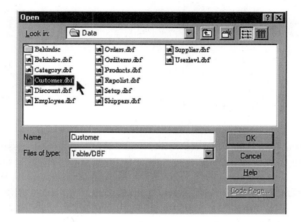

To begin the first query, return to the Add Table or View dialog box, and select the PRODUCTS table from the Tastrade database. A small window in the data source area (the top half) of the Query Designer displays the table's field names. The name of the selected tables always appears in the window header. Figure 6.4 shows the Query Designer at this point.

When the Query Designer opens, it also opens a toolbar (see Figure 6.5). The toolbar's six buttons perform functions that are specific to queries.

Suppose that you want to list products by suppliers. The PRODUCTS file has a supplier ID associated with every product. But the SUPPLIER table stores the details about each supplier, such as name and address. Therefore, you need to open both files. To add a second table, click the Add Table button in the query toolbar. VFP displays the View dialog box. Select the SUPPLIER table, and click Add.

FIGURE 6.4
The Query Designer, with two tables from the Tastrade database, is open in the source data area.

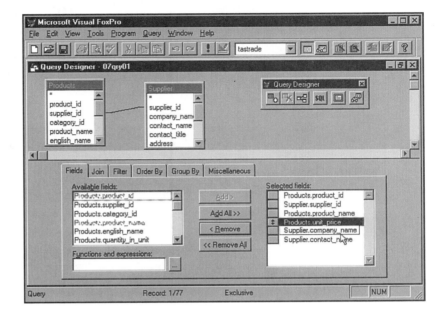

FIGURE 6.5
The Query Designer toolbox contains six buttons that provide fast access to some of the most common functions.

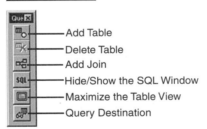

QUERY TOOLBOX

- Add Table
- Delete Table
- Add Join
- Hide/Show the SQL Window
- Maximize the Table View
- Query Destination

In Figure 6.6, notice that when Query Designer adds the SUPPLIER table to the table view area, it also draws a line between PRODUCTS and SUPPLIER. To be more specific, it draws the line between the field PRODUCTS.Supplier_Id and SUPPLIER.Supplier_Id. This line indicates that these two files share a field that relates records from one table to another. FoxPro knew to draw this line because of the persistent relation defined between these two files in the database. VFP also displays this *join condition* on the Join page in the bottom half of the Query Designer window.

FIGURE 6.6

The Query Designer is shown with two open tables.

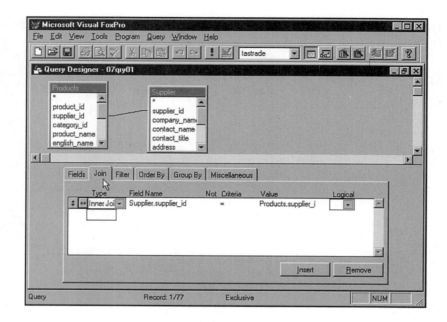

Perhaps you wonder what the two buttons to the left of the field name in the Join page do. The leftmost button, which points up and down, enables you to change the order of the selection expressions (if you have more than one). The second button, which points left and right, appears only when the criteria define the link between tables and allow modification to the type of join condition. Click this second button to display the dialog box shown in Figure 6.7. You can also open this dialog box by clicking the Add Join button in the toolbar or by double-clicking the line that links the two tables in the source data area.

FIGURE 6.7

Define the join criteria by using the Join Condition dialog box.

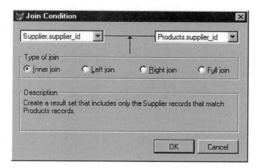

The Join page enables you to customize the join condition. You can select the type of join from the Type drop-down list, open the drop-down list for either field, and select fields to define the join relations. You can also change the connection criteria and reverse the logic by clicking the Not button. Join supports five criteria:

- Equal
- Like
- Exacly Like
- More Than
- Less Than

N O T E Join conditions that are established as the result of a persistent relationship between tables cannot be modified. If you try to modify such a join condition, you'll find that the drop-down lists are disabled. You must remove the join condition and then set it again from the Join page. Removing the join condition from the Join page does not affect the persistent relationships between tables. ■

The Join Condition dialog box enables you to select the type of join and describes each condition. The four types of joins are as follow:

- Inner join, which includes only the records from both tables that match the join condition.
- Left outer join, which includes all records from the table on the left and records that match the join condition from the table on the right.
- Right outer join, which includes all records from the table on the right and those records that match the join condition from the table on the left.
- Full outer join, which includes all records from both tables and combines those that match the join condition into one record in the result set.

To better understand the differences among these four join types, look at some sample ddata. Tables 6.1 and 6.2 show sample data from two tables.

Table 6.1 The Persons Tabls

PersonID	Name
1	Joe
2	John
3	Mary
4	Joan

Table 6.2 The Cards Table

CardID	PersonID	Reason
1	1	Birthday
2	2	Birthday
3	3	Birthday
4	0	Christmas

Notice that the Persons table has one person from whom we have never received a card, and the Cards table has one card that is not from any of the people. These two records are the ones that the various join types will affect.

The join criteria that we will use is Persons.PersonID = Cards.PersonID. Table 6.3 shows you the result of an inner join. Remember that an inner join contains only those records from the two tables that meet the join criteria.

Table 6.3 The Inner Join

CardID	PersonID	Name	Reason
1	1	Joe	Birthday
2	2	John	Birthday
3	3	Mary	Birthday

In Table 6.3, notice that Joan doesn't show up and that no card is shown for Christmas. These two records did not meet the join criteria. Joan didn't have a matching card, and the Christmas card had no matching person.

Table 6.4 shows the left outer join.

Table 6.4 The Left Outer Join

CardID	PersonID	Name	Reason
1	1	Joe	Birthday
2	2	John	Birthday
3	3	Mary	Birthday
0	4	Joan	

In the left outer join, you see that Joan is included even though she has no corresponding card record. The fields for the card data are empty.

Table 6.5 is an example of the right outer join.

Table 6.5	**The Right Outer Join**		
CardID	**PersonID**	**Name**	**Reason**
1	1	Joe	Birthday
2	2	John	Birthday
3	3	Mary	Birthday
4	0		Christmas

Notice that the Christmas card is included in the right outer join even though it has no corresponding person record.

Finally, consider the full outer join shown in Table 6.6.

Table 6.6	**The Full Outer Join**		
CardID	**PersonID**	**Name**	**Reason**
1	1	Joe	Birthday
2	2	John	Birthday
3	3	Mary	Birthday
4			Christmas
5	4	Joan	

Notice that both Joan and the Christmas card are included in the full outer join result.

CAUTION

A type of join not yet mentioned is the *Cartesian product*. The Cartesian product is the result of a join with no join criteria. This join combines every record in one table with each of the records in the other table, resulting in a number of records equal to the first table's record count times the second table's record count.

If you deal with tables that have large numbers of records, the Cartesian product can fill your disk drive in a heartbeat.

Part

II

Ch

6

Additional Filter Criteria

Record filters support three additional criteria: BETWEEN, IN, and IS NULL. BETWEEN defines an inclusive range of values. The following would include employees between 0100 and 0199, inclusive:

```
Employee_Id BETWEEN '0100' AND '0199'
```

On the other hand, IN defines a list of independent values. The following statement tells the query to include only records for these three employees:

```
Employee_Id IN ('0100', '0133', '0175')
```

You also can use IS NULL to find any records that do not have an employee ID entered. In this case, no Example value is necessary.

Criteria Comparison

The preceding sidebar shows the selection example as it appears in the resulting SQL statement. However, when you are entering the example for a criteria comparison, follow these rules:

- Do not enclose character strings in quotation marks. The Query Designer automatically adds the necessary quotes. If your comparison string contains multiple words that are separated by blanks, you might want to use the quotation marks for your own clarity. You also need to enclose the string in quotation marks if the text is the same as the name of a field in a table used by the query.

- If the example is the name of a field used by the query, the Query Designer treats it as such.

- Do not enclose dates in braces or use CTOD(). Simply enter the date in this format: 03/22/99.

- If the example is a logical value, include the periods before and after the value (.T.).

The Equality operator performs exactly like a simple equal sign between the strings on either side of the join. Thus, whether trailing blanks are considered in the comparison depends on the current setting of SET ANSI. If SET ANSI is ON, it pads the shorter string with spaces before comparing the strings, character for character, for their entire length. If SET ANSI is OFF, the strings are compared only until the end of the shorter string is reached.

The Like criterion performs a comparison equivalent to that of SET EXACT OFF. FoxPro compares the expression on the left, character by character, with the one on the right for as many characters as the expression has.

The Exactly Like criterion creates a more restrictive comparison. It compares the two strings character for character to see whether they match, and then it compares the two strings to see whether they are the same length. As you can see, this is slightly different than SET ANSI ON. It includes only those records whose criteria match exactly.

The More Than and Less Than criteria perform simple less-than and greater-than comparisons of the expression values. You can ask for product records with product unit prices more than $10, for example. In that case, only records whose product unit price is greater than $10 appear in the result set.

> **T I P** More Than and Less Than can be used to compare strings also. When you're comparing strings, the ASCII sort order for the string is used, so "A" comes before "B".

Because this example compares two fields in separate tables, each representing supplier ID defined the same way, choosing Like or Exactly Like generates the same results. Additional criteria in the form of record filters, however, might use these alternative comparison criteria.

Another option when you are defining the comparison criteria is the Not button. Clicking this button reverses the criteria's logic. Click Not with Exactly Like to create Not Exactly Like; choose it with More Than to create Less Than Or Equal To.

Finally, you can ignore the case of character strings by clicking the button on the right that appears below the Case heading. You might use it in record-selection criteria to ignore inconsistent case in field values.

Selecting Fields to Include in the Query

Having defined the relation between the two tables, you next define which fields to include in the results. Clicking the Fields tab in the Query Designer displays two lists: Available Fields and Selected Fields. Initially, all fields in all selected tables appear in the Available Fields list, and the Selected Output list is empty.

To include all fields in the Selected Fields list, click the Add All button. (You can also double-click the asterisk in the table's field list or drag the asterisk to the Selected Fields list.) However, you seldom need to see all fields when viewing data. To select individual fields, click them in the Available Fields list. Each time you click an available field, the Add button becomes enabled. Click this button to move the field to the Selected Fields list. You might find double-clicking a field to be a faster way to select and move it.

Other ways to move a field from the Available Fields list to the Selected Fields list include the following:

- Drag the field from the Available list to the Selected list.
- Click the field name in the table field list in the table view of Query Designer, and drag it to the selected list.
- Double-click the field name in the table field list in the table view of Query Designer.
- Hold down the Ctrl key, click on multiple fields, and choose the Add button.
- Drag or double-click the asterisk in the table field list in the table view to include all the table's fields.

> **N O T E** Selected Output fields initially appear in the order in which they are added. You can rearrange the order by dragging the mover button to the left of each field. The order of the selected fields determines the column order of the output view or file. ▪

To remove all the Selected Fields, placing them back in the Available Fields list, click Remove All. You also can remove fields one at a time by double-clicking a field in the Selected Fields list or by clicking on a field and then clicking Remove.

 TIP If you want to add more than half of the fields from the Available Fields list, the quickest way is to click Add All to move them to the Selected Fields list. Then select the individual fields that you don't want to use, and send them back by clicking the Remove button.

The No Duplicates check box, in the Miscellaneous page, checks to see whether the value of every selected field remains the same from one record to the next. If so, VFP includes the record only once. If at least one value in one field differs from record to record, VFP includes the record.

Ordering the Results

To see products alphabetically by description for each supplier, click the Order By tab. This tab, shown in Figure 6.8, provides options to customize the sort order of the results.

FIGURE 6.8
Define the sort order of the query results by dragging fields to the Ordering Criteria list in the order in which you want to sort the query results.

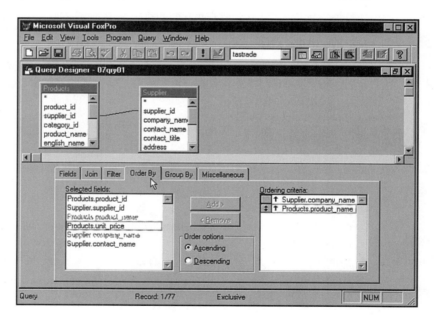

This page displays two list boxes that contain fields. The left box contains only the Selected fields. After all, you cannot sort on a field that is not included in the results. To begin the sort with the supplier's company name, click it and then click Add. As with adding fields, this action moves the selected field to the right list box. Notice that a small up arrow appears next to the field name in the Ordering Criteria list. This arrow indicates that the current sort order for this field is ascending. Change the field sort order to descending by selecting the field and then clicking the Descending option in the Order Options area. You can also select the order option before moving the fields to the Ordering Criteria list.

To see products alphabetically for each supplier, double-click Product_Name. The order in which you select fields for the ordering criteria determines their sort order. If you use the mover button to put Product_Name before Company_Name, the query sorts the records first by product name. Then, if the product has more than one supplier, the query lists them alphabetically.

Miscellaneous Tab Options

The Miscellaneous tab provides options for additional record-selection criteria:

■ No Duplicates enables you to show or to exclude duplicate records from your selection.

■ Cross-Tabulate outputs the result set into a cross-tabular format. It also automatically selects the Group and Order By fields.

■ Top enables you to select all records, several records, or a percentage of records to be returned. If you want to show the top 10 sales items, a query ordered by the units sold and limited to the top 10 would provide your top 10 items. Changing the order option from ascending to descending provides the bottom 10 sales items.

N O T E The Top option on the Miscellaneous tab can be a little confusing. The top ## result is the top ## values for the ORDER BY clause. So, if you have top 10 sales of $1,000, $900, $800, $700, $500, $400, $300, $200, $100, and $50, and for each, you have three items, the top 10 sales give you a result of 30 records, representing the records with the top 10 sales amounts.

Keep in mind that the top ## (including the percent option) is the top ## of the values and not the top ## of records. ■

Viewing the Results

To see the results of a query using the current query definition, click the Run button (the button with an exclamation point on it) in the toolbar. Visual FoxPro runs the query; gathers the records from the tables, based on the selection criteria; selects fields to display; and sorts the records. VFP then displays the results in Browse mode, as shown in Figure 6.9.

Notice that columns in the result set appear in the order in which you selected the fields. If you do not like this order, you can change it. Click the column heading, and drag it left or right. As you move the mouse, the column heading follows. Simply release the mouse button when you are satisfied with the new position.

Part
II
Ch
6

FIGURE 6.9
Display a view of query
results in Browse mode
at any time by clicking
the Run button in the
standard toolbar.

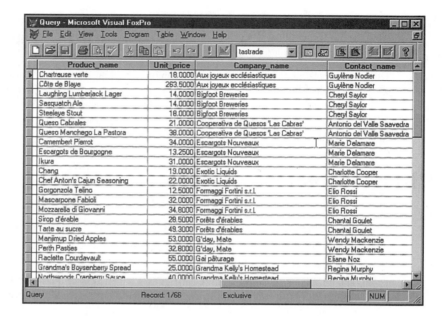

You also can adjust column widths to view more columns at one time. Place the mouse pointer
over any vertical bar that separates two column headings. The mouse pointer changes to a
thick vertical bar with a left and right arrow (see Figure 6.10). Click and drag this separator to
resize the column. If you make the column smaller than necessary to display its values, VFP
truncates the displayed values, not the actual data.

FIGURE 6.10
A split query window,
with the Product Name
column being resized.

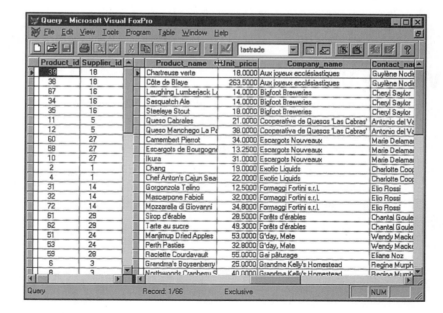

Because query results appear in an actual Browse window, they have a few additional features. Perhaps you have noticed that when you press Tab or use the scrollbars to view additional columns, columns on the other side of the screen scroll out of view. Often, the first few columns include fields (such as ID or name fields) that identify the rows. Sometimes, a query has so many columns that by the time you scroll to the ones you need, you forget which row you are in. Although you could manually move these columns together (or redefine the query with the columns closer together), you might need to view so many columns that moving them would simply not be practical.

N O T E   Clicking the arrows at the end of the horizontal scrollbars moves the view one field to the left or right. Clicking the arrows at the top and bottom of the vertical scrollbar moves up or down one record. ■

To view all the columns that you need to view, no matter how far apart they are, split the Browse window by using the browse splitter. Initially, the browse splitter appears as a thin black box in the lower-left corner of the window. To split the window, click the splitter and drag it horizontally. Immediately, the query window splits into two partitions, each with its own set of scrollbars (refer to Figure 6.10).

After you split the window, use the scrollbars to move through records or columns in either window. When you move between fields by pressing the Tab key or by using the horizontal scrollbar, the fields scroll horizontally in one window but remain unaffected in the other. Using this method, you can keep key fields displayed in one window to identify the record while you view the remaining fields in the other one.

Initially, moving between rows in one window automatically moves the corresponding record pointer in the other window and also scrolls both windows, if necessary, because Visual FoxPro maintains a link between the two windows. To break this link, deselect the Link Partitions option in the Table menu. Now VFP still moves the pointer in both windows, but it no longer scrolls the other window as you move between records. This feature helps you view records that are scattered throughout the table. If you later turn Link Partitions back on, VFP resynchronizes the two windows to match the selected record in the active partition.

You can also change the view from browse style to edit style for the entire window or just one partition. To change a partition to edit view, click the desired partition and then choose View, Edit.

For a query, you cannot modify the results in either the browse or edit style view.

To remove the partitioned window, simply drag the splitter bar back to the far-left side of the main Query window. Whatever view mode exists in the partition on the right side of the window remains in effect.

Using Multiple-Condition Filters

In this section, you return to the Query Designer and add a second condition to the filter criteria. Rather than view all products from a supplier, you can limit the view to products on order. To do so, click the Filter tab, pull down the Field Name list, and click the Units_On_Order field to select it.

 T I P Fields used for filter criteria do not have to appear in the results.

To limit selected records to those that have products on order, you should find records that have a Units_On_Order value greater than zero. Therefore, select > (more than) as a Criteria and enter 0 in the Example field.

Suppose that you also want to see items that sell for less than 25 percent above cost. First, move down to a new Filter Criteria line, and click the Field Name text area. At the bottom of the drop-down field list is an item called <Expression...>. This item opens the Expression Builder dialog box, in which you can create any valid FoxPro expression. Figure 6.11 shows the Expression Builder dialog box with the completed expression for profit margin. To complete these criteria, you want records that evaluate to < .25 (less than .25) because the profit-margin expression generates a fraction, not a percentage.

FIGURE 6.11
Calculate the profit margin of a product by building an expression with the Expression Builder.

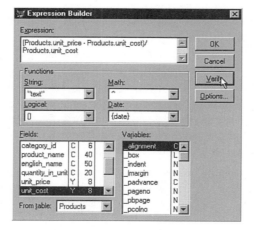

 T I P If .25 returns zero records in your record set, increase the fraction to .45.

Because the profit-margin expression includes division by one of the fields, you should eliminate records in which Unit_Cost is zero. You cannot lose money on a product that costs nothing unless you have to pay someone to take it. But more important, you cannot divide by zero. You accomplish this task with a separate filter criterion that selects only those records in which

`Unit_Cost` is greater than zero. To get VFP to evaluate this expression before the profit-margin expression, place it before the profit-margin expression.

Notice that VFP evaluates criteria sequentially. If a potential result record fails an intermediate criterion, VFP does not evaluate the remaining criteria. Thus, check to see whether the unit cost is zero before you use it as a divisor in a later expression.

Figure 6.12 shows the completed Filter page. This query now has one join on the Join tab, and three filter conditions on the Filter tab. The join criteria and the three filter criteria must evaluate to true before VFP will include the record in the results table.

FIGURE 6.12

The completed Filter tab shows several criteria for selecting records.

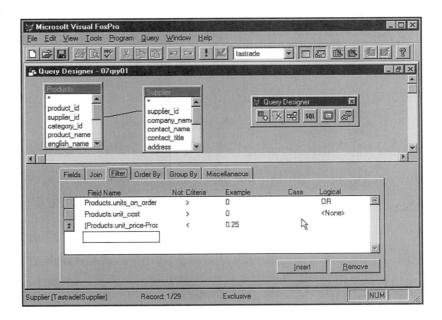

N O T E Place expressions that are most likely to eliminate records near the beginning (top) of the selection criteria list so that FoxPro does not waste time going through the other criteria. In this example, test for a zero value of `Unit_Cost` before performing the profitability calculation. ▪

Part
II
Ch
6

Running this query results in six selected records. This result means that of the items on order, six of them have profit margins of less than 25 percent. Looking at the query results, the store manager might decide to discontinue stocking these items.

But what if you want to know how many items from the entire inventory had profit margins of less than 25 percent or were on reorder? To find out, you need to connect the last two expressions with OR instead of AND. Click the Logical drop-down list for the first Field Name—`Products.units_on_order`—and select OR. Rerunning the query retrieves 17 records.

Remember that the Query Designer merely checks the syntax of the criteria; it has no knowledge of what makes sense. You can easily define a meaningless set of conditions or a set that eliminates all records. You control the criteria's meaning.

> **CAUTION**
>
> Although you can easily define a query that uses legal FoxPro syntax, the query might be meaningless. FoxPro enables users to create any query, no matter how ridiculous, as long as it has valid syntax. For example, Visual FoxPro doesn't care if you make a query that has `State = "NY" AND State = "CA"` when any record can have only one state. In this case, Visual FoxPro faithfully returns no records as the result. Remember, you get what you ask for.

> **CAUTION**
>
> Adding `OR` in the middle of a series of conditions automatically groups the expressions that come before and after it. Only then does VFP compare the logical results of the groups. As long as one of the groups on either side of the `OR` evaluates to true, the query includes the record. This grouping ignores clauses that are used to join files.

Finally, the Insert and Remove buttons permit you to add or remove expressions from the Join tab and Filter tab criteria lists. To add a criterion to the bottom of the list, just use the empty Field Name box provided by the Query Designer. To insert a criterion between existing criteria, select the lower criterion and click the Insert button. Insert adds a blank line above the selected criterion. Alternatively, you could always add the criterion to the bottom of the list and move it up with the mover button.

Routing the Query Results

So far, all the examples in this chapter have written the query results to a Browse or Edit window onscreen. You might want to keep some query results around a little longer, perhaps saving them or using them in a report. To change the query destination from onscreen to a file or printer, click the Query Destination button in the Query toolbar.

FoxPro displays the Query Destination dialog box (see Figure 6.13), which includes the options shown in Table 6.7.

FIGURE 6.13
The Query Destination dialog box provides seven ways to display the query results.

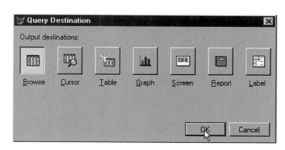

Table 6.7   Query Destination Options

Destination	Definition
Browse	View query results in a Browse window only
Cursor	Create a temporary table or cursor with query results
Table	Create a permanent table
Graph	Use query results to produce a graph with Microsoft Graph
Screen	Display results to screen only
Report	Use query results as a data source for a report
Label	Use query results as a data source for labels

By default, the Browse button is selected. When you generate results to a Browse window, FoxPro creates a temporary table that contains the query results (usually, in memory), opens the Browse window, and displays the table. As soon as you close the Browse window, Visual FoxPro erases the temporary table. If you need only a quick view of data that matches certain conditions, sending the query results to a Browse window is fine, and it saves a tree. You don't need to define anything else with this option because it is VFP's default and needs no special parameters.

Output to a Cursor

The next output-destination option in the Query Destination dialog box creates a cursor. Cursors are also temporary files, but they remain open and active for as long as you choose. When cursors are closed, however, Visual FoxPro deletes them. Other than in the actual process of creating a cursor, you cannot write to one created as output from a query. After a cursor is created, you cannot replace values or add or delete records.

Cursors have only one additional, required attribute: Despite their temporary status, cursors must have names. The Query Destination dialog box provides a suggested cursor name, based on the query name. You can accept the name or provide your own name. The assigned name then serves as an alias, allowing you to reference it from within a program or other command lines.

N O T E   Cursor names are actually alias names; if Visual FoxPro needs a disk file to store the cursor, it assigns that file a unique name. The files for cursors are always stored in the temp directory for the computer on which the query was run. Because the cursor's name is its alias and FoxPro uses a unique filename, you need not concern yourself with unique names for cursors. You can use names that make sense in your program. ■

N O T E   You might find it interesting to know where the word *cursor* comes from. It is an acronym for *CUR*rent *S*et *O*f *R*ecords. ■

Output to a Table

Sending query results to a table is similar to sending them to a cursor, with one major exception: A table, by definition, has a physical existence on your disk and, therefore, can exist after the current Visual FoxPro session. You can close and reopen tables. You can add, delete, and modify records in a table. When you select Table in the Query Destination dialog box, you can directly enter a table name or click the button containing an ellipsis (...). This button opens the Open dialog box, in which you can select tables from any directory and drive. This action causes the query results to overwrite existing tables. You might want to open the directory to ensure that the table name that you enter does not already exist.

N O T E   In a networked environment, querying into a table requires that you supply a unique name for that table. Using a cursor instead of tables is recommended. The only limitation on a cursor from a query is that you cannot update it, but you can overcome that limitation by using views (which are discussed in Chapter 7). ∎

Output to a Graph

To show the output, the query was changed (see Figure 6.14) to select only three fields from the Product file: `Product_Id`, `Unit_Cost`, and `Unit_Price`. Open the Query Destination dialog box, and select Graph. Finally, run the query.

FIGURE 6.14
This query on just the Products table extracts product information to display as a graph.

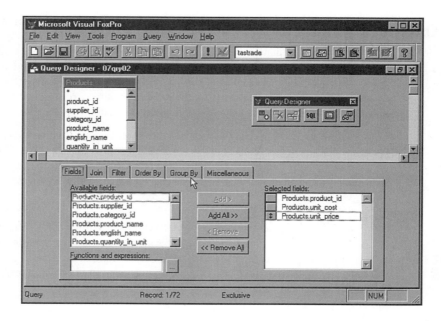

When the query runs, it opens the Graph Wizard to help define the graph. The query skips the first step of this wizard because the fields have already been selected in the query; it begins with the layout step. In this step, you assign fields to desired locations on a graph. In this example, you can use `Product_Id` as the axis variable. You also have two data series to plot: `Unit_Cost` and `Unit_Price`. Your Graph Wizard dialog box should look like Figure 6.15 after you make these selections.

FIGURE 6.15

Use the layout step of the Graph Wizard to assign fields to various graph locations.

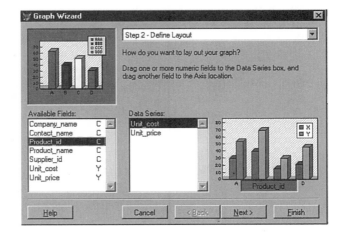

Move to the next step by clicking Next or by choosing Step 3 from the step drop-down list. In this step, you can choose any of 12 predefined graph styles, as shown in Figure 6.16. To select a style, click the button that displays a picture of the style that you want to use.

FIGURE 6.16

Choose one of the 12 available graph styles.

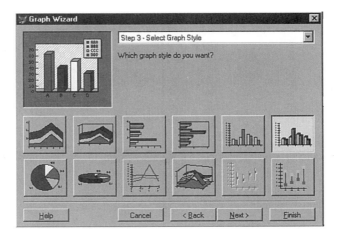

Part

II

Ch

6

In the last step of the Graph Wizard, you can display null values, add a legend to the graph, and preview the graph before you click Finish. The legend identifies the data series with the field name. You also can enter a title to display at the top of the graph. Figure 6.17 shows these options.

FIGURE 6.17

In the last step of the Graph Wizard, you can include a legend and graph title before saving the graph.

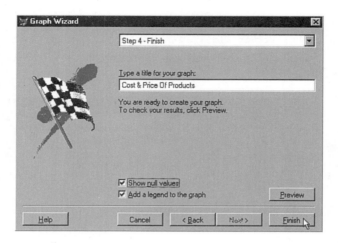

When you click Finish, the Graph Wizard prompts you for a table name under which to save the graph. After you save the graph, the Graph Wizard displays the result.

Before completing Step 4—Finish, you can click the Back button to change the features of your graph and then click the Preview option to see the results. This way, you can preview several graph styles before committing to a final one.

Output to the Screen

Figure 6.18 shows the options that are available when you output query results to the screen.

FIGURE 6.18

The Query Destination dialog box displays options for outputting query results to the screen.

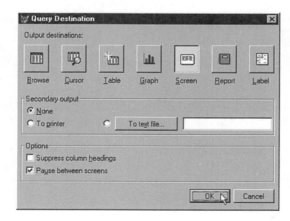

First, you can define a secondary output destination. Why? Because FoxPro does not retain the query results after writing them to the screen. Therefore, you can use a secondary output destination to create a more permanent copy by selecting To Printer or To Text File. When you are outputting to a printer, be aware that fields within a record wrap across multiple lines if they do not all fit on one line. When you select To Text File, you must also supply a filename, using the Open dialog box. If you know the fully qualified text-file name, you can enter it directly in the text box. Notice that you cannot choose both the printer and a text file as a secondary output destination.

Additional options include the capability to Suppress Column Headings and Pause Between Screens. To view the data, be sure to check the Pause Between Screens check box; otherwise, the data scrolls past faster than you can read it.

> **CAUTION**
>
> During pauses between screens, output directed to a secondary source repeats the column headings every time Visual FoxPro starts a new screen.

Output to a Report

When you are outputting to a report, Visual FoxPro provides a wide selection of options, as shown in Figure 6.19.

FIGURE 6.19
The Query Destination dialog box lists the options for sending query results to a report.

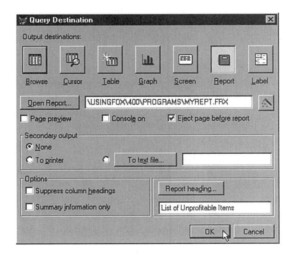

To use an existing report definition with the new query results, click the Open Report button, and select an existing report in the Open dialog box that appears. You can also use the Open dialog box to ensure that the report name that you supply does not currently exist if you intend to create a new report. If you know the report's filename without opening the Open dialog box, enter it directly in the text box.

The button on the right side of the dialog box that looks like a magic wand opens the Report Wizard. Use this wizard to create a new report in seconds.

If you click Page Preview, VFP outputs the report in a window for review. Notice that if you select Page Preview, you cannot simultaneously output the report to a secondary destination. This feature is best used for the following purposes:

- To test reports during development
- To view reports when you need to see a few results and do not keep a hard copy
- To review reports when you don't want to walk up three flights of stairs and down four halls to retrieve the report output from the only network printer
- To preview a report before printing to see how it will look and to decide whether you want to print it
- To view reports when you do not have access to a printer, either because it temporarily does not work or is busy printing past-due notices to clients

Console On echoes the report output to the current window, and Eject Page Before Report sends a page-eject command to the printer before beginning a report to ensure that the report starts at the top of the form.

N O T E   Some printers store one or more lines of output in a buffer. This arrangement sometimes prevents the printer from printing the last line, or even the entire last page, until another print job starts. If that print job does not use a page eject at the beginning, it most likely appends to the end of the report. One solution to this problem is to use the Report Designer to add a page eject after the report as well.

As you can see when you send output to the screen, you can define a secondary output destination. (The primary destination for a report is the screen.) Choose None, To Printer, or To Text File. When you choose the last option, Visual FoxPro displays the Open dialog box, in which you can enter or choose a file. If you select a file that already exists and SAFETY is OFF, VFP overwrites the old file automatically. When SAFETY is ON, VFP displays a warning and enables you to decide whether to overwrite the file. You can also enter a text-file name in the edit box next to the To Text File button.

In the Options area, you can choose Suppress Column Headings or create a report by choosing Summary Information Only. When you choose Summary Information Only, Visual FoxPro suppresses all detail lines and prints only Title, Group, Page, and Summary bands.

Finally, you can add a separate report heading that appears at the top of each page, in addition to any heading that is already in the Page Header band of the report. Clicking the Report Heading button opens the Expression Builder dialog box. Use this dialog box to define a heading that includes memory variables, table fields, and calculated results.

Output to a Label

Outputting options for labels are similar to those for reports, as shown in Figure 6.20.

FIGURE 6.20
The Query Destination dialog box lists the options for sending query results to a label.

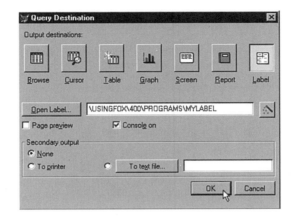

To use an existing label definition with the new query results, click the Open Label button and select an existing label from the Open dialog box. You also can use the Open dialog box to ensure that the label name that you supply does not currently exist, if you intend to create a new label. If you know the label's filename without opening the Open dialog box, enter it in the text box.

When Page Preview is selected, Visual FoxPro outputs the label in a window for review. Notice that when you select Page Preview, you cannot simultaneously output the label to any other destination. This feature is best used for the following purposes:

- To test labels during development
- To ensure that the labels are correct before rerunning the query and sending the output to a printer

The Console On option echoes the label output to the screen when the label output is created.

As you can do with reports, you can define a secondary output destination. (The primary destination for a label is the screen.) Choose None, To Printer, or To Text File. If you choose the last option, Visual FoxPro displays the Open dialog box, in which you can enter or choose a file. If you select a file that already exists and SAFETY is OFF, VFP overwrites the old file automatically. When SAFETY is ON, VFP displays a warning and enables you to decide whether to overwrite the file. You also can enter a text-file name directly in the edit box next to the To Text File button.

Part
II

Ch
6

Using Query Designer Versus Manually Created SQL SELECT Statements

By now, you have seen how easily you can query data by using the Query Designer. You might not realize that you have been creating SQL SELECT statements throughout this entire chapter. If you have been hesitant to write your own SQL statements because you thought they were too complex, continue reading to explore the world of SQL SELECT statements.

The simplest query grabs every field and every record from a single table and displays them in a Browse window. The following code shows this query command used in the CUSTOMER.DBF table (in the Tastrade example provided with Visual FoxPro):

```
USE \VFP\SAMPLES\ DATA\CUSTOMER
SELECT * FROM TASTRADE!CUSTOMER
```

N O T E If the table is part of a database that is not open, VFP uses the information in the table header to open the database. If the table is a free table, VFP opens the Open dialog box to allow you to select it. ▪

The asterisk immediately after the SELECT keyword tells Visual FoxPro to get all fields in the table referenced by the FROM clause. If you do not want to see all the fields, list the ones that you do want to see, as in the following:

```
SELECT Customer_Id, Company_Name FROM TASTRADE!CUSTOMER
```

Notice that commas separate the field names. To see the companies that begin with the letter *A*, add a WHERE clause, as shown in the following command (which assumes that SET ANSI is OFF):

```
SELECT Customer_Id, Company_Name FROM TASTRADE!CUSTOMER ;
    WHERE Company_Name = 'A'
```

To perform an exact search, use the == operator.

With that introduction, let's return to the SQL SELECT statements that were generated by FoxPro while using the Query Designer that we created earlier.

Any time while you are in the Query Designer, you can view the SQL that Visual FoxPro continuously builds in the background. Simply click the SQL button in the SQL toolbar. Actually, this button alternately shows and hides the SQL window. After you click it, the button stays down until you click it again or use the Window menu to switch the active window.

 T I P Add a comment to your SQL SELECT statement by choosing Query, Comments and entering text in the dialog box that appears.

When you started the first query in this chapter, you selected two tables: PRODUCTS and SUP-PLIER. A persistent relation on the field Supplier_Id joined those tables. You also selected several fields to display: PRODUCTS.Product_Id, PRODUCTS.Supplier_Id,

PRODUCTS.Product_Name, and SUPPLIER.Company_Name. This information defines a simple query. If you click the Run button, a Browse window pops up and displays the query results. But what SQL SELECT statement did FoxPro actually use to produce this output? If you click the SQL button in the toolbar, you should see something similar to Figure 6.21.

FIGURE 6.21

Here is the SQL SELECT statement in which the inner join is used to create the relationship.

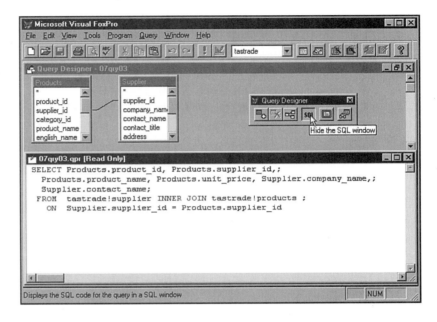

SQL SELECT commands begin with the SELECT keyword. You immediately follow SELECT with a list of fields to include in the results. Notice that Visual FoxPro qualifies each field with the alias name for the table. Strictly speaking, you do not need to qualify every field—only those fields that exist in both tables, such as Supplier_Id. Qualifying every field, however, helps you document the table to which the field belongs. When you are writing a SQL SELECT that uses a single table, you do not need to qualify the fields.

NOTE The examples used in this chapter prefix fields with their table name. You can also equate a field name to a local alias. Although this method makes the SQL a little more difficult to read, it might make entering the SQL a little easier by reducing the amount of typing. The following simple example shows you how to assign a one-letter alias:

```
SELECT Or.Customer_Id, Cu.Customer_Id ;
    FROM TASTRADE!ORDERS Or, TASTRADE!CUSTOMER cu
```

Although local aliases can be a single character, using only one character is not recommended. Single-character local aliases can, under certain circumstances, conflict with Visual FoxPro's default work area aliases. ▪

Although a SQL SELECT command is one line of code, you might want the SELECT statement to show on multiple lines of text. Just remember to end each line (except the last) with a

Part

II

Ch

6

semicolon. The field order in the SQL SELECT statement determines the field output order in the results table.

The SQL SELECT statement requires the FROM clause to identify the table or tables containing the fields. Notice that when a table belongs to a database, its name is preceded by the database name, separated by an exclamation point.

 TIP When you are creating a SQL SELECT statement in the Command window or a program, precede the database name with its full pathname so that the query will work from any directory.

You can use a WHERE clause to limit the records included in the result set. The WHERE clause of the SQL SELECT statement corresponds to the filter criteria you supplied in the Query Designer.

After you define it, use the SQL SELECT statement in the Command window, or embed it in a program. No matter where you use it, the statement creates the same results as it does when you use it from the Query Designer.

N O T E Use the Query Designer to create SQL SELECT commands visually. Then copy the commands from the SQL window to the Command window or the program's Edit window, where you can customize them further or run them as they are. Alternatively, save the query and run the QPR file, using DO. ■

Figure 6.22 expands the SELECT statement to include more fields and conditions. First, notice the DISTINCT clause added after SELECT. This clause, which corresponds to the No Duplicates check box in the Miscellaneous tab, appears only at the beginning of the field list but applies to all fields. The clause means that if all selected fields have the same value as they did in the preceding record, the current record is not included in the results.

 TIP In some situations, you know that your WHERE clause will allow only unique records into the result. In these cases, *do not* use the DISTINCT option, as it will slow down your SELECT considerably while Visual FoxPro searches for duplicates that do not exist.

A second condition is added to the WHERE clause in Figure 6.22. This expression examines the value of the field Units_On_Order in the PRODUCTS table and includes records only if this value is greater than zero. By default, Visual FoxPro connects all criteria with AND. This means that the records must pass all the criteria before they are added to the result set. In this example, VFP would create a result set of unprofitable products that are also on order. However, suppose that you want to see all the products that are on order or the unprofitable products. To do so, you need to add a logical OR operator. In other words, you want to see records for those products that have outstanding orders and for those that are unprofitable.

Finally, the ORDER BY clause defines a sort order for the results. In this case, you want to sort records first by company and then by product name. Each field in the ORDER BY clause can have a different sort direction. By default, the sort order is ascending. However, you can follow the field name with DESC to define a descending sort or ASC to ensure an ascending sort.

FIGURE 6.22
Add conditions to the
SQL SELECT statement
to filter and sort results.

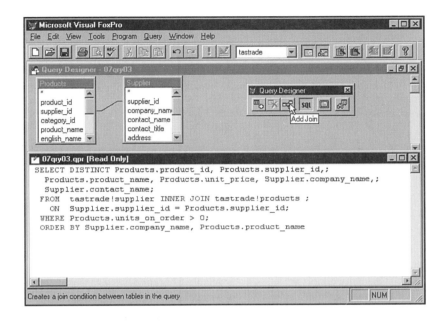

Now look at the SQL SELECT statement generated at the end of the Query Designer session
(see Figure 6.23).

FIGURE 6.23
This is the final SQL
SELECT created to
select items with profit
margins less than 25
percent.

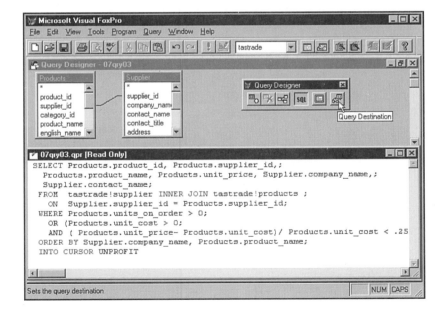

Part
II

Ch
6

This expression adds additional filter clauses to limit the on-order product list to products that have low profit margins. Notice that with the OR condition between the second and third condition, Visual FoxPro groups the last two expressions together, using parentheses. This result is exactly what you want because you should perform the profitability calculation only for records that have a unit cost greater than zero.

By default, VFP sends all queries to a Browse window. The INTO clause specifies where to redirect the query results. In Figure 6.23, the results are output to a cursor named UNPROFIT. However, you can select several other destinations, including the following:

- An array (INTO ARRAY <arrayname>)
- A different cursor (INTO CURSOR <cursorname>)
- A table or .DBF file (INTO TABLE <dbfname>)
- A printer (TO PRINTER)
- The screen (TO SCREEN)
- A file (TO FILE <filename>)

The array option, which is not available from the Query Designer, adds the query results to a memory variable array. VFP does not create the array if the query does not return at least one record. Therefore, before you attempt to use the array variable, test how many records the query returned by checking the value of _TALLY. This system memory variable records the number of records processed by the most recent table command. The variable also works with the following commands:

APPEND FROM	PACK
AVERAGE	REINDEX
CALCULATE	REPLACE
COPY TO	SELECT - SQL
COUNT	SORT
DELETE	SUM
INDEX	TOTAL
JOIN	UPDATE

If _TALLY equals 0, the query found no records.

When storing the query results to a cursor or table, VFP prompts you before overwriting existing tables with the same name if SET SAFETY is ON. The Alert dialog box displays the following text:

```
<filename>
This file already exists
Replace existing file?
```

Click the Yes or No button to replace or not replace the existing file. When SET SAFETY is OFF, Visual FoxPro overwrites existing files automatically. In most programming environments, unless the user specifies the filename, you probably want SET SAFETY OFF to overwrite existing files.

Specifying TO FILE together with a filename is not the same as creating a cursor or table. Sending query results to a file creates an ASCII text file, not a table. You can print this file directly to the printer or screen from DOS by using the TYPE command. You can also append the file to other documents that read text files.

Another option, NOCONSOLE, suppresses echoing the query results to the screen. This capability is especially useful when you are directing output to a file or printer. Sending query results to a cursor or table never echoes the results to the screen; therefore, this option is not needed. PLAIN removes the column headings from the output. Use this option if you intend to send the query results to a file and later use that file as input to another program.

We hope that by seeing how the Query Designer sessions result in SELECT statements, you will not think of SQL statements as being difficult. Just remember to break the SELECT into individual clauses when you try to understand it.

Grouping Records to Summarize Data

Before you leave this introductory chapter on queries and SQL, return to the Query Designer one more time to see how to group records to provide summary information.

This example requires three tables from the Tastrade database: ORDERS, ORDER_LINE_ITEMS, and PRODUCTS. Using the previously defined persistent relations, notice that ORDERS relates to ORDER_LINE_ITEMS through the Order_Id field. Similarly, ORDER_LINE_ITEMS relates to PRODUCTS through the Product_Id field. Figure 6.24 shows the inner joins and the persistent relations. A separate filter that limits the result set to orders taken in a one-year period has been set in the Filter tab.

FIGURE 6.24
The inner joins used in the Query Designer to join ORDERS, PRODUCTS, and ORDER_LINE_ITEMS.

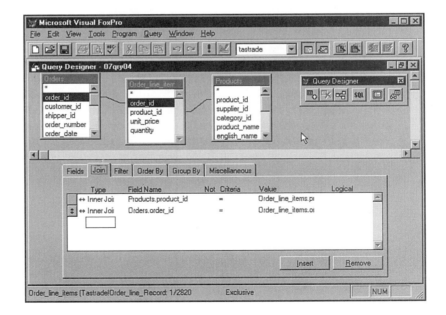

This report requires as output the product name, the quantity sold, and a price analysis. In fact, you want to see only one record for each product—a record that sums the number of units sold for that product. In a report, you would group the output records by product ID or product name, sum the quantity field for each detail record, and print the resulting sum after the last record for that product.

In the Query Designer, you accomplish something similar by using options in the Group By tab. Move the Product_Id field from the Available Fields list to the Grouped Fields list. This operation tells the Query Designer to output only a single record for each product ID. Figure 6.25 shows the Group By definition in the Query Designer.

FIGURE 6.25

Group selected records by Product_Id, using the Group By tab of the Query Designer.

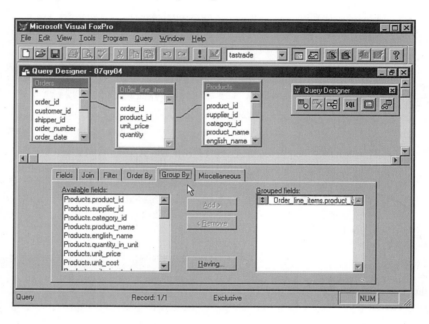

When you are looking at the field values for a group of records for the same product ID, some values change, and others remain constant. If, as in this case, the product ID identifies the group, the ID value remains constant, but so do other fields, such as description. Do not worry about these fields. In the quantity field, however, each detail record represents a different transaction. Because you need to include this field in the query, you must tell Visual FoxPro what to do with it. Otherwise, VFP outputs to the results table the values in the last record that it processes for each group.

In this query, you can sum the quantity sold in each transaction. Going to the Fields tab, click the button to the right of the Functions and Expressions field. This button displays the Expression Builder. The grouping functions are listed in the Math drop-down list; Table 6.8 defines them.

Table 6.8 Grouping Functions

Grouping Function	Description
COUNT()	Counts the number of records in a group
SUM()	Sums the field value for records in a group
AVG()	Averages the field value for records in a group
MIN()	Specifies the minimum field value for records in a group
MAX()	Specifies the maximum field value for records in a group
COUNT(DISTINCT)	Counts distinct records in a group
SUM(DISTINCT)	Sums the field value for distinct records in a group
AVG(DISTINCT)	Averages the field value for distinct records in a group

Click SUM() to calculate the total quantity of a numeric field. Visual FoxPro immediately displays "SUM(expN)" in the Expression text area. Select Order_line_items from the From Table drop-down list. Then select ORDER_LINE_ITEMS.Quantity in the Fields list (see Figure 6.26). The required expression appears in the text area. Clicking OK adds the expression to the Functions and Expressions field. Finally, select the new function and add it to the Fields list by clicking the Add button.

FIGURE 6.26
Open the Fields tab of the Expression Builder to define a calculation method and a field for a query.

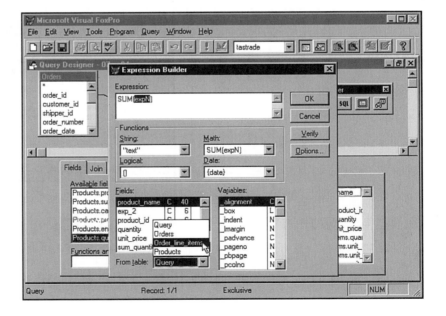

Because the selected data spans a year, you expect that prices will change at least for some products. Thus, although Unit_Price (stored in PRODUCTS) represents the current price, it might not equal the price for previous orders. Because the program saves the Unit_Price with each order in the order details file (ORDER_LINE_ITEMS), however, you can determine the minimum, maximum, and average price throughout the year. To retrieve these other prices for the report, use the Fields page of the Expression Builder. The new calculated fields for this query include the following:

- SUM(ORDER_LINE_ITEMS.quantity)
- MIN(ORDER_LINE_ITEMS.unit_price)
- MAX(ORDER_LINE_ITEMS.unit_price)
- AVG(ORDER_LINE_ITEMS.unit_price)

Figure 6.27 shows the SQL SELECT statement for the completed query.

FIGURE 6.27
Here is the complete query to analyze Tastrade product prices.

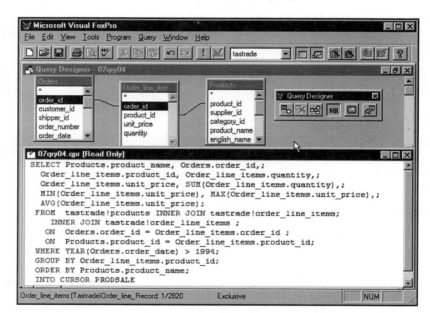

Using Queries in Programs and Forms

When you are using the Query Designer to create a query that you later want to use in a program or form, remember to save the query after testing it. Visual FoxPro saves the SQL SELECT statement in a file with the extension .QPR. You can execute the SQL directly from the Command window, program, or form by using a simple DO command, such as the following:

```
DO SALBYPRD.QPR
```

Because the Query Designer does not automatically include drive or path prefixes for databases or tables, you must do one of the following things:

- Run the query from the directory that contains the databases or tables.
- Add a SET DEFAULT TO or SET PATH TO command to change to the directory that contains the data.
- Modify the query manually to contain the drive and path information.

The following SELECT statement shows a simple example:

```
SELECT * ;
    FROM C:\VFP\SAMPLES\ \DATA\TASTRADE!CUSTOMER
```

From within a form control, simply attach a DO statement like the preceding one to the Click event. Visual FoxPro executes the query whenever someone clicks the control.

Editing the Generated SQL SELECT Statement

The .QPR file is a text file. just like a .PRG. Therefore, you can edit it with either of the following commands:

```
MODIFY COMMAND SELBYPRD.QPR
```

```
MODIFY FILE SELBYPRD.QPR
```

Both commands open an Edit window and load SELBYPRD.QPR into it. The following are some additional reasons that you might edit the SQL SELECT statement directly, as opposed to using the Query Designer:

- Faster editing of minor changes, such as adding or deleting a field or changing a condition test value.
- Creating more complex queries. After all, the Query Designer is still an end user's tool and lacks the robustness available with direct creation of SQL SELECT statements.

Creating Complex Queries

The first part of this chapter concentrated on using the Query Designer to create the SQL SELECT statements. The Query Designer has enough power for many basic queries, and it helps teach you query design in a visual environment in which you can concentrate on what you want to do, not on how to do it. If you plan to write your own SQL SELECT statements from scratch, you need to know the syntax. The following shows the complete syntax for creating SQL SELECT statements:

```
SELECT [ALL ¦ DISTINCT] [TOP nExpr [PERCENT]]
 [Alias.] Select_Item [AS Column_Name]
 [, [Alias.] Select_Item [AS Column_Name] ...]
FROM [FORCE] [DatabaseName!]Table [LocalAlias]
 [[INNER ¦ LEFT [OUTER] ¦ RIGHT [OUTER] ¦ FULL [OUTER] JOIN]
 [, [DatabaseName!]Table [Local_Alias]
 [[INNER ¦ LEFT [OUTER] ¦ RIGHT [OUTER] ¦ FULL [OUTER] JOIN] ...]
```

```
[ON [DatabaseName!]Table [Local Alias] .Column_Name =
[DatabaseName!]Table [Local_Alias] .Column_Name]

[[INTO Destination]
 ¦ [TO FILE FileName [ADDITIVE] ¦ TO PRINTER [PROMPT]
 ¦ TO SCREEN]]
[PREFERENCE PreferenceName]
[NOCONSOLE]
[PLAIN]
[NOWAIT]
[WHERE FilterCondition [AND ¦ OR FilterCondition ...]]]
[GROUP BY GroupColumn [, GroupColumn ...]]
[HAVING FilterCondition]
[UNION [ALL] SELECTCommand]
[ORDER BY Order_Item [ASC ¦ DESC] [, Order_Item [ASC ¦ DESC] ...]]
```

Many of these clauses are described earlier in this chapter. As you can quickly tell, not all of these clauses appear in the Query Designer. Two primary clauses that are not included are the use of subqueries and UNIONs. The balance of this chapter is devoted to subqueries. Chapter 7, "Advanced Queries and Views," picks up with a discussion of UNIONs.

Using a BETWEEN Clause to Filter a Range of Values

The BETWEEN clause enables you to define a value range for a field by using a single condition statement rather than two. However, you will experience very little difference in performance whether you use the BETWEEN clause or two separate conditions. Suppose that you want a list of order details for products that have product IDs between 10 and 19. You could write a two-condition SELECT, as follows:

```
SET ANSI ON
SELECT * ;
  FROM order_line_items ;
WHERE ALLTRIM(Product_Id) >= '10' AND ALLTRIM(Product_Id) <= '19'
```

SET ANSI and SQL

SET ANSI determines the way that SQL commands compare strings connected with the = operator. The default is OFF, in which case SQL compares strings character for character until reaching the end of the shorter string. The following table provides examples of how SET ANSI affects comparisons:

SET ANSI	OFF	ON
'10' = '1'	True	False
'1' = '10'	True	False
'' = '1'	True	False
'1' = ''	True	False
'10' = '10'	True	True
'10' == '101'	False	False
'10' == '1'	False	False
'10 ' == '10'	True	True
'10' == '10 '	True	True

With SET ANSI OFF, a single character matches any field value that begins with that character, and empty fields match everything. Although you can use == in place of the = operator to force an exact comparison, you cannot replace >= with >===. In these situations, you must exercise extra caution. One solution changes SET ANSI to ON, as shown in the preceding table. To see the effect with real data, run the preceding SELECT with SET ANSI OFF, and compare the results table to the one generated with SET ANSI ON.

CAUTION

When you are comparing a field (such as CAT_ID) to a character string, be aware of whether the field is left- or right-justified when the comparison values do not have to use all character positions. Use ALLTRIM on the field to prevent problems, or pad the comparison value to the full field size.

Combining these two conditions with BETWEEN results in the following statement:

```
SET ANSI ON
SELECT * ;
  FROM order_line_items ;
 WHERE ALLTRIM(Product_Id) BETWEEN '10' AND '19'
```

You will find little difference between the times that it takes these two statements to find 31,280 records out of 225,840 (in a modified version of the ORDER_LINE_ITEMS table). In fact, the first statement ran only slightly faster on the test machine, requiring 44.00 seconds, compared with 44.87 seconds for the second statement. Perhaps the difference is that the first statement eliminates some records that have only a single comparison expression. The difference is minimal, however.

SQL Performance Testing

The timings of different SELECT versions probably will vary on your system. Many factors affect the overall SELECT speed, including the system CPU, the storage medium that is being used for the file, the access rate for that storage medium, the controller card, and the transfer method for that storage medium. However, the basic overall pattern of which method is fastest should remain the same.

Visual FoxPro attempts to keep Rushmore-related information about a completed SELECT in memory. Therefore, if you repeat the same or similar SELECT, the relative number of times decreases. One sure way to ensure that no residual Rushmore information exists in memory is to exit Visual FoxPro between tests.

For many of the SQL examples used in this section, the files from Tastrade were artificially bloated to create files with more records. This procedure involved first copying a file to a new filename and then opening the new file and repeatedly appending the original table to it. This technique works for SQL tests that require extracting a subset of records based on a field value that extracts records based on a product ID range. If you need to test a SQL statement that joins two files, however, this technique might lead to unexpected and incorrect results, with multiple "matches" between the files.

Because the field used in this condition contains only digits, you could also write the condition as follows:

```
SET ANSI ON
SELECT * ;
  FROM products ;
 WHERE VAL(Product_Id) BETWEEN 10 AND 19
```

The performance of this query is significantly slower than that of the first two. Perhaps this fact reflects on the inefficiency of converting the string to a numeric value first before performing the comparison. This SELECT requires 47.35 seconds on the test system. The problem in each case is that the field criteria do not match an index definition. The index on the product ID uses no special functions. Therefore, the only way to obtain better performance from a query is to eliminate all functions used in the WHERE clauses. The following example, which carefully formats the test values as right-justified six-character fields, executes in 31.47 seconds (still a long time, but the query is retrieving 32,180 records out of 225,840):

```
SELECT * ;
  FROM order_line_items ;
  WHERE product_id >= '    10' AND product_id <= '    19'
```

This procedure also averts any potential problems caused by having SET ANSI ON or OFF.

N O T E   The preceding SELECT statement was tested after setting the order to the tag based on
Product_Id. Many developers who think that they can help SELECT work faster by presetting the "correct" tag make this common mistake. In this case, the query required 32.35 seconds—almost a second longer, just because a tag was set. ▪

N O T E   You also can write the preceding SELECT command the following way with the same improvement in performance:

```
SELECT * ;
  FROM order_line_items ;
 WHERE Product_id BETWEEN '10' AND '19'
```
▪

Using an IN Clause to Filter Selected Values

The IN clause enables you to specify a discrete set of values that do not constitute an inclusive range. Suppose that you want to see only the customers from Canada, Mexico, the United Kingdom, and the United States. CUSTOMER.DBF has a Country field that you can use, but testing for each country separately would be awkward, as in the following example:

```
SELECT Company_Name ;
  FROM CUSTOMER ;
  WHERE UPPER(Country) = 'CANADA' OR ;
       UPPER(Country) = 'MEXICO' OR ;
       UPPER(Country) = 'UK' OR ;
       UPPER(Country) = 'USA' ;
  ORDER BY Country, Company_Name
```

You can perform the same query faster by using an IN clause that lists the possible values, as follows:

```
SELECT Company_Name ;
  FROM CUSTOMER ;
  WHERE UPPER(Country) IN ('CANADA', 'MEXICO', 'UK', 'USA') ;
  ORDER BY Country, Company_Name
```

This second expression required less time than the first: 4.67 seconds for the first versus 4.07 seconds for the second to find 1,540 records out of 5,005. (An inflated version of CUSTOMER was used.) The performance difference becomes even greater the more values that Visual FoxPro needs to compare. This fact implies that if you need to compare a field with several values, using the IN clause is more efficient.

> **N O T E** Another feature of this second query is that it includes Country in the sort order, even though it does not output this field in the results. SQL SELECT enables this sorting. ▪

Defining Subqueries

The filter conditions used in queries earlier in this chapter had this basic structure:

```
<field expression> <operator> <field expression or value>
```

You can create more complex conditions that use a subquery to limit the values. A subquery is simply a query within a query. You use subqueries primarily for two reasons:

- ▪ To define a set of values, of which a field must be a member, before including the record in the result table
- ▪ To determine whether a field value exists in another table

Suppose that you want to produce a list of customers who did not make any purchases during a given year, such as 1998. Producing a list of customers who did make purchases is easy. Simply enter the following command:

```
SELECT DISTINCT CUSTOMER.Company_Name ;
  FROM CUSTOMER, ORDERS ;
  WHERE CUSTOMER.Customer_Id = ORDERS.Customer_Id AND ;
      YEAR(ORDERS.Order_Date) = 1998
```

Notice that the DISTINCT clause prevents the company name from appearing more than one time. On a test system using Tastrade data, this query took 1.15 seconds to retrieve 87 records out of 91. To get those 87 records, the query had to examine 929 order records.

You can also write this query using a subquery. The subquery creates a list of customer IDs for customers who placed orders in 1998. The main query retrieves the company name for customer IDs in the subquery list, as follows:

```
SELECT Company_Name ;
  FROM CUSTOMER ;
  WHERE Customer_Id IN (SELECT Customer_Id ;
                  FROM ORDERS ;
                  WHERE YEAR(Order_Date) = 1998)
```

This complex query retrieves the same data as the preceding one, but it requires 5.11 seconds. Notice that a complex query takes more time than a simple one does. In almost all cases, a simple query outperforms a complex query.

The problem is that neither command answered the real question: What are the names of the customers who did not place orders? You would have trouble attempting to modify the first query to answer this request. You can modify the second query, however, by adding a single word, as follows:

```
SELECT Company_Name ;
  FROM CUSTOMER ;
  WHERE Customer_Id NOT IN (SELECT Customer_Id ;
                       FROM ORDERS ;
                       WHERE YEAR(Order_Date) = 1998)
```

Adding NOT before IN changes the meaning of the query to answer the question correctly. In case you are interested, this query ran in 5.27 seconds.

Sometimes, writing a single SQL statement is just not convenient because SQL generates a results table with duplicated fields. Suppose that you want to retrieve only orders from outside the United States. You might write the following command:

```
SELECT * ;
  FROM ORDERS, CUSTOMER ;
  WHERE CUSTOMER.Customer_Id = ORDERS.Customer_Id AND ;
       UPPER(CUSTOMER.Country) # 'USA'
```

A problem occurs when SQL sees the potential for duplicated field names; it renames both fields by appending an underscore and letter to them. You could manually list each field that you want to be prefixed by its table name, thereby averting duplicate references, but for tables that have a large number of fields, this method requires a great deal of extra work.

N O T E   One way to get around the problem of duplicate field names is to use the AS clause. You could rename a field for the query by using the following clause:

```
SELECT id AS customer_id, name AS cust_name ...
```

You can even add "new" or calculated fields, such as the calculated tax amount based on the sales total and a tax rate, as follows:

```
SELECT order_amt, order_amt*.07 AS sales_tax, ;  order_amt*1.07 AS sale_total,
... ▪
```

Another solution splits the query into two pieces. The inner query creates a list of customers who are not from the United States. The outer one retrieves records from ORDERS only if the inner query returns any records.

```
SELECT * ;
  FROM ORDERS ;
  WHERE EXISTS (SELECT Customer_Id FROM CUSTOMER ;
                   WHERE CUSTOMER.Customer_Id = ORDERS.Customer_Id AND ;
                       UPPER(CUSTOMER.Country) # 'USA')
```

The second query takes longer than the first simple one (2.20 seconds, compared with 1.65 seconds, for 931 records out of 1,080), but it has no problem with renamed fields.

This type of complex query is called an existence or correlated query. When executed, the inner query must reference a field from the outer query (ORDERS.Customer_Id, in this case). As a result, VFP performs the inner query for each record in the outer query, which slows performance.

Because EXISTS merely checks to see whether any records exist, it doesn't matter what fields it returns. EXISTS can even return all fields with an asterisk (*), although using a single field results in slightly better performance.

A better subquery than the preceding method uses IN. IN does not require re-executing the query for each row in the outer query; therefore, it is called a *noncorrelated subquery*. Because it uses a subquery, however, it does take longer (2.14 seconds) than a simple query.

```
SELECT * ;
  FROM ORDERS ;
  WHERE Customer_Id IN (SELECT Customer_Id FROM CUSTOMER ;
                WHERE UPPER(Country) # 'USA')
```

N O T E Even though we have told you that subqueries are longer than simple WHERE clause that do the same thing, not all subqueries can be replaced by a simple WHERE clause. ■

The EXISTS clause compared a value in one SELECT against all values in another SELECT. Suppose that you want to find out which products, if any, have not been purchased since the last price increase posted in PRODUCTS.DBF. In this case, use an inner SQL SELECT to create a list of all product prices for orders by Product_Id. Then, using the outer SELECT, check to see whether the current unit price in PRODUCTS is greater than all values in the first list. The following query result displays the product name and ID of any such products:

```
SELECT DISTINCT PRODUCTS.Product_Name, PRODUCTS.Product_Id ;
  FROM PRODUCTS, ORDER_LINE_ITEMS ;
  WHERE PRODUCTS.Product_Id = ORDER_LINE_ITEMS.product_id AND ;
        PRODUCTS.Unit_Price > IN (SELECT DISTINCT Unit_Price ;
            FROM ORDER_LINE_ITEMS ;
            WHERE ORDER_LINE_ITEMS.Product_Id = PRODUCTS.product_id);
  ORDER BY PRODUCTS.Product_Id
```

Finally, use SOME or ANY to compare the value of a field in the outer query with at least one or more of the values selected by the inner query. Suppose that you want to know whether any products have a current price that is more than 50 percent greater than that of their first order. Modify the preceding query by using SOME, as follows:

```
SELECT DISTINCT PRODUCTS.Product_Name, PRODUCTS.Product_Id ;
  FROM PRODUCTS, ORDER_LINE_ITEMS ;
  WHERE PRODUCTS.Product_Id = ORDER_LINE_ITEMS.Product_Id AND ;
        PRODUCTS.Unit_Price/1.5 > SOME (SELECT DISTINCT Unit_Price ;
            FROM ORDER_LINE_ITEMS ;
            WHERE ORDER_LINE_ITEMS.Product_Id = PRODUCTS.Product_Id);
  ORDER BY PRODUCTS.Product_Id
```

Part

II

Ch

6

The point of all these examples was not only to show you some of the other clauses that SQL SELECT supports, but also to show you that different ways of expressing a query can lead to different query times. A method that might provide the best performance for small tables in which the selected records are relatively concentrated might not be the best when the tables become large and the data more scattered. The best advice is to experiment with various ways of writing the SQL SELECT statement to find out which method yields the best performance. ●

Advanced Queries and Views

Joining the Results of Multiple Queries

Several examples in Chapter 6, "Creating Basic Queries," used subqueries to define subsets of data from which to draw records in the main SELECT statement. However, what if you need to combine the results of two separate SELECT statements?

Suppose that it is time to send out invitations to the Tasmanian Annual Appreciation Picnic. You want to send invitations to all current customers (ones who bought something this year), suppliers, and employees.

Retrieving Current Customer Records

You have customer information stored in table CUSTOMER.DBF of the database TASTRADE.DBC. Table 7.1 shows the appropriate customer fields.

Table 7.1 Customer Mailing Information Fields

Field	Type	Size
Customer_Id	Character	6
Contact_Name	Character	30
Company_Name	Character	40
Address	Character	60
City	Character	15
Region	Character	15
Postal_Code	Character	10
Country	Character	15

Because you want to include only customers who made purchases in the current year, you need to use ORDERS.DBF to identify records for current year purchases. Then match the customer ID field, Customer_Id, with a record in CUSTOMER.DBF. The SQL SELECT statement in the following example extracts the needed records:

```
SELECT Customer.contact_name, Customer.company_name, Customer.address,;
  Customer.city, Customer.region, Customer.postal_code, Customer.country;
  FROM   tastrade!customer INNER JOIN tastrade!orders ;
   ON  Customer.customer_id = Orders.customer_id;
 WHERE YEAR(Orders.order_date) = 1998 ;
INTO CURSOR MyResult
```

TIP By fully qualifying the table names, you can successfully run SELECTs from any directory.

These commands display the records in a browse window. The first thing to observe is the use of an alias name, as defined in the database, rather than the table name when specifying the fields. Instead of repeating the table name with each field, you can use a local alias to reduce the amount of typing and the spelling errors associated with typing SQL SELECT statements. Note that this alias is independent of the work-area alias.

Observe also that the selected records do not appear in any particular order. If you want to see the customers in order by name, you need to add the following clause to the SELECT statement:

```
ORDER BY Customer.Contact_Name
```

Using DISTINCT Versus GROUP BY

After putting the records in order, you see that the names of many customers occur several times. You get this result because the SELECT statement includes a record for each customer order in ORDERS.DBF during 1995. Adding the DISTINCT clause at the beginning of the field list includes each customer one time only. The SELECT now looks like the following:

```
SELECT DISTINCT Customer.contact_name, Customer.company_name, ÂCustomer.address,;
   Customer.city, Customer.region, Customer.postal_code, Customer.country;
 FROM   tastrade!customer INNER JOIN tastrade!orders ;
   ON   Customer.customer_id = Orders.customer_id;
 WHERE YEAR(Orders.order_date) = 1995;
 ORDER BY Customer.contact_name ;
INTO CURSOR MyResult
```

This command generates a list of all active customers in 1995, listed alphabetically by contact name. However, the ORDER BY clause is no longer needed. When you include DISTINCT, SELECT automatically orders the records alphabetically based on the field sequence. As long as you place the fields in order beginning with the first one you want to sort on, you do not need a separate ORDER BY clause.

You can perform the same SELECT with improved performance in yet another way. Rather than use SELECT DISTINCT, select all the records and then include a GROUP BY clause. When SELECT uses DISTINCT, it checks all the fields in the added record to see whether anything has changed. On the other hand, GROUP BY works with the result table and combines records with the same selected group field or fields. In this case, group on CONTACT_NAME. The resulting SELECT, shown in the following example, executes faster:

```
SELECT Customer.contact_name, Customer.company_name, Customer.address,;
   Customer.city, Customer.region, Customer.postal_code, Customer.country;
 FROM   tastrade!customer INNER JOIN tastrade!orders ;
   ON   Customer.customer_id = Orders.customer_id;
 WHERE YEAR(Orders.order_date) = 1995;
 GROUP BY Customer.contact_name ;
INTO CURSOR MyResult
```

Part
II

Ch
7

Retrieving Supplier Records Corresponding to Purchases

Using similar logic, you can retrieve records of suppliers from which you purchased products during the year. Table 7.2 shows the appropriate Supplier fields.

Table 7.2   Supplier Mailing Information Fields

Field	Type	Size
Supplier_Id	Character	6
Contact_Name	Character	30
Company_Name	Character	40
Address	Character	60
City	Character	15
Region	Character	15
Postal_Code	Character	10
Country	Character	15

The required SELECT statement to retrieve supplier names and addresses selects suppliers based on which products Tasmanian Traders sold during the year. Product-supplier information appears in the Products file. Therefore, you need to work from ORDERS, through ORDER_LINE_ITEMS, and then Products to identify the current suppliers. The following SELECT captures this information:

```
SELECT Supplier.contact_name, Supplier.company_name, ;
       Supplier.address, Supplier.city, Supplier.region, ;
       Supplier.postal_code, Supplier.country;
 FROM  tastrade!supplier INNER JOIN tastrade!products;
   INNER JOIN tastrade!order_line_items;
   INNER JOIN tastrade!order_line_items ;
  ON  Orders.order_id = Order_line_items.order_id ;
  ON  Products.product_id = Order_line_items.product_id ;
  ON  Supplier.supplier_id = Products.supplier_id;
 WHERE  YEAR( Orders.order_date) = 1995;
 GROUP BY Supplier.contact_name ;
INTO CURSOR MyResult
```

This SELECT is similar to the customer SELECT, except that it requires several files to determine which suppliers to invite. Both SELECT statements use fields in tables to select records for the result table, even though those fields do not appear in the result. This is not a problem. Selection criteria looks at the source tables, not the result table.

Retrieving Employee Records

Finally, you need an employee list. Table 7.3 shows the appropriate Employee fields. Unfortunately, the Employee table includes only a hire date; it doesn't include a termination date.

Perhaps everyone is so happy working for Tasmanian Traders that no one ever leaves, and all the employees are model employees.

Table 7.3   Employee Mailing Information Fields

Field	Type	Size
LAST_NAME	Character	20
FIRST_NAME	Character	10
ADDRESS	Character	60
CITY	Character	15
REGION	Character	15
POSTAL_CODE	Character	10
COUNTRY	Character	15

This SELECT is the simplest of the three:

```
SELECT Employee.last_name, Employee.first_name, ;
      Employee.address, Employee.city, ;
      Employee.region, Employee.postal_code, ;
      Employee.country;
 FROM tastrade!employee;
 GROUP BY Employee.last_name, Employee.first_name ;
INTO CURSOR MyResult
```

You can now run each of these three SELECT statements and obtain three separate mailing lists. However, what you really want is a single list. For that job, the UNION clause helps.

Using UNION to Join SELECT Results

UNION combines information from two or more separate SELECT statements in a single cursor or table. To use UNION to combine the result sets of multiple SELECT commands, you must follow these rules:

- You can have up to 10 UNIONs in a SELECT command, connecting each SELECT to the preceding one. The important point to remember is that the result set created by the first SELECT determines the required structure of the rest.

- The order, number, size, and type of fields in the first SELECT define the structure required in all subsequent SELECTs. Visual FoxPro 6 does not require that the corresponding fields in each SELECT have the same names. However, the first SELECT does define the field name used in the result set. It uses the field order to determine how to combine two or more SELECTs. This means that if you accidentally switch the order of two fields, Visual FoxPro appends the data that way. If this operation results in the wrong field type, Visual FoxPro generates this vague error: SELECTs are not UNION-compatible. (Could SELECTs be a synonym for management?)

Part

II

Ch

7

Observe that the SELECTs for CUSTOMER and SUPPLIER have a contact name of 30 characters, which includes both the first and last names. On the other hand, EMPLOYEE uses a separate field for first and last names, although the sum of their lengths is also 30. Another difference is that CUSTOMER and SUPPLIER have a company field; EMPLOYEE does not.

To combine these result sets, you must reconcile these differences. Listing 7.1 combines the three SELECTs to   create a single result table.

Listing 7.1   07CODE01—Using UNION to Join Multiple SELECT Statements

```
* Creates an annual picnic invitation list from customers,
* suppliers, and employees for Tasmanian Traders

* Create mailing list of employees, suppliers and customers
SELECT Customer.contact_name, Customer.company_name, ;
       Customer.address, Customer.city, ;
       Customer.region, Customer.postal_code, ;
       Customer.country;
  FROM  tastrade!customer INNER JOIN tastrade!orders;
    ON  Customer.customer_id = Orders.customer_id;
 WHERE YEAR(Orders.order_date) = 1995;
 UNION ;
 SELECT SPACE(40) AS Company_Name, ;
    PADR(ALLTRIM(Employee.first_name) + ' ' + ;
         ALLTRIM(Employee.last_name),30) AS Contact,;
    Employee.address, Employee.city, Employee.region, ;
    Employee.postal_code, Employee.country ;
 FROM tastrade!employee ;
 UNION ;
 SELECT Supplier.contact_name, Supplier.company_name, ;
        Supplier.address, Supplier.city, Supplier.region, ;
        Supplier.postal_code, Supplier.country ;
  FROM  tastrade!supplier INNER JOIN tastrade!products ;
    INNER JOIN tastrade!order_line_items ;
    INNER JOIN tastrade!order_line_items ;
    ON  Orders.order_id = Order_line_items.order_id ;
    ON  Products.product_id = Order_line_items.product_id ;
    ON  Supplier.supplier_id = Products.supplier_id ;
 WHERE YEAR(Orders.order_date) = 1995 ;
INTO CURSOR MyResult
```

Notice the use of the following clause:

```
SPACE(40) as Company
```

This expression is a placeholder that corresponds to the company field in the CUSTOMER and SUPPLIER files. This clause fills the company field in the combined result table with spaces because the EMPLOYEE file has no company field. Without it, Visual FoxPro cannot perform the UNION correctly, and an error occurs.

You must put a placeholder in any SELECT statement in which you need to satisfy the rule that all fields, data types, and widths must match. You can put it in the first SELECT statement of a group to reserve space for a field that exists only in later SELECTs. Alternatively, as in this example, you can include it in a later SELECT to match the columns of the first (master) SELECT.

To ensure that employees are not confused with customers or suppliers, you could replace the preceding clause with the following:

```
PADR("Tastrade",30) AS Company_Name
```

Next, the SELECT statement concatenates the employee first- and lastname fields to match the contact names in CUSTOMER and SUPPLIER. It uses ALLTRIM with the employee's first name to remove trailing blanks and uses the PADR() function to produce a field that is of equal length to the other SELECTs. However, a blank must then be added to separate it from the employee's last name. The employee first name can store up to 10 characters, and the last name can have 20 characters, according to the Employee table structure. Thus, with the addition of a blank between these two fields, the total field size might exceed the 30-character limit of CONTACT. In that case, Visual FoxPro truncates the last character.

You can define placeholders for variables of other types as well. The following are some examples:

```
.T. AS InStock

000.00 AS UnitPrice

00000 AS OnHand

{//} AS OrderDate
```

Observe that in the case of numeric values, the picture used determines the size of the field and number of decimal places.

Sometimes, a field exists in all SELECTs combined with UNIONs, but the field sizes differ. Suppose, for the sake of this example, that the Employee files use a 30-character address field. The Address field in CUSTOMER and SUPPLIER has 60 characters. Although you do not have to do anything when subsequent fields are smaller, you could pad the employee address in the third SELECT with 30 trailing blanks, as follows:

```
PADR(AEmployee.Address,30) AS Address
```

 TIP Make sure that field definition in the first SELECT is large enough for its associated fields in the other SELECTs. If it is not, Visual FoxPro truncates the data.

N O T E   A set of SELECT statements combined by multiple instances of UNION is actually one line of code. Therefore, any error occurring anywhere within a set of SELECTs connected with UNION causes the entire statement to fail. Often, you cannot easily determine which SELECT caused the failure. Therefore, consider testing each SELECT individually before combining them with UNION. ▓

The following are some other considerations in combining SELECTs with UNION:

- Because ORDER BY and INTO clauses work with the final result set, they can appear only in the final SELECT. After all, it would not make sense to UNION result sets sorted by different fields or output to different files or devices.

- On the other hand, GROUP BY and HAVING work with the selected records in creating the final result set. Because each SELECT creates an intermediate result set before UNION combines them, these clauses can appear in each SELECT. They affect only records from the SELECT that they are in.

CAUTION

Surprisingly, you can put a single ORDER BY or INTO clause in any of the SELECT statements, and Visual FoxPro uses it appropriately for the entire result table. However, if more than one SELECT has an ORDER BY or INTO clause, Visual FoxPro displays the nonspecific error message Unrecognized phrase/keyword in command.

N O T E To sort the output of the company picnic list, you could include the clause ORDER BY Company_Name. However, the program would fail. In individual SELECT statements, you can sort the result table by adding an ORDER BY clause, followed by the name of the field, as follows:

ORDER BY Company_Name

However, when combining SELECT results with UNION, you must refer to the relative field position of the column to sort on, such as

ORDER BY 2

to sort on one field, or

ORDER BY 6, 2

to sort on multiple fields. Attempts to reference a field by its name in one of the original tables will result in the error SQL Invalid ORDER BY. ■

Perhaps you also noticed that the records in the result set were already sorted by contact name. Whenever you create a UNION between two or more SELECTs, and you do not specify a sort order, Visual FoxPro automatically sorts them, using the selected field order to define a default sort. Thus, the Tasmanian Trader picnic SELECT sorts by contact.

Unlike the basic SELECT statement, which automatically includes duplicate records as long as they match the selection criteria, UNION performs an automatic DISTINCT. This means that it checks each record added to the result table to ensure that no other records in the result table match it exactly, field for field. Obviously, this process takes additional time. To help, VFP places the records in a default sorted order if the code does not specify an order.

If you know that the SELECT statements do not create duplicate records, or you don't care about the duplicates that might be created, you can replace UNION with UNION ALL. Adding ALL eliminates the test for duplicates, thus reducing the overall execution time.

Visual FoxPro uses UNION only between queries, not subqueries. Suppose that you want to see the names of all employees who do not live in a country where you have suppliers or customers. (Pink-slip time!) You might want to perform the following query:

```
SELECT Em.First_Name, Em.Last_Name ;
  FROM \VFP\SAMPLES\MAINSAMP\DATA\TASTRADE!EMPLOYEE Em ;
WHERE Country NOT IN (SELECT customer.Country ;
        FROM \VFP\SAMPLES\MAINSAMP\DATA\TASTRADE!CUSTOMER, ;
        UNION ;
        SELECT supplier.Country
          FROM \VFP\SAMPLES\MAINSAMP\DATA\TASTRADE!SUPPLIER) ;
INTO CURSOR MyResult
```

Visual FoxPro does not support this use of UNION. In fact, it generates the error SQL Invalid use of union in subquery. Rather, you need to ask the following:

```
SELECT Em.First_Name, Em.Last_Name ;
  FROM EMPLOYEE Em ;
 WHERE Country NOT IN (SELECT customer.Country) ;
        FROM \VFP\SAMPLES\MAINSAMP\DATA\TASTRADE!CUSTOMER) ;
          OR Country NOT IN (SELECT supplier.Country ;
        FROM \VFP\SAMPLES\MAINSAMP\DATA\TASTRADE!SUPPLIER) ;
INTO CURSOR MyResult
```

Following is a summary of Visual FoxPro's UNION rules:

- Any field included in the first field list must be represented by a field or placeholder in subsequent field lists.
- Any field from a subsequent field list that is not part of the first field list must be represented by a placeholder in the first field list.
- No calculated fields can appear in the first field list.
- ORDER BY and INTO clauses can appear in any SELECT in the UNION, but only one time, and they apply to the entire result.
- ORDER BY must reference the column by numeric position rather than by name.
- If no ORDER BY clause exists, Visual FoxPro uses the field order as the default order.
- GROUP BY and HAVING clauses can appear in each SELECT in the UNION, and they apply to only the partial results generated by that SELECT.
- You are limited to 10 UNION clauses.
- UNION cannot combine the results of subqueries (SELECTs used within the WHERE clause of other SELECTs).

Creating Inner Joins

Actually, you have been creating inner joins for the past chapter and a half. An inner join includes only the records from each table that match a join condition.

The following SQL SELECT command from Visual FoxPro 6 shows the syntax that supports the JOIN argument:

```
SELECT Customer.contact_name, Customer.company_name, ;
       Customer.address, Customer.city, ;
       Customer.region, Customer.postal_code, ;
       Customer.country;
 FROM  tastrade!customer INNER JOIN tastrade!orders;
  ON Customer.customer_id = Orders.customer_id ;
INTO CURSOR MyResult
```

These SELECTs include records for customer IDs that exist in both CUSTOMER.DBF and ORDERS.DBF.

Creating Outer Joins

In an inner join, Visual FoxPro gets from the first table the records that have at least one corresponding record in the second table.

Suppose that you want to create a SQL SELECT that sums the quantity of each product sold by Tasmanian Traders. The following SELECT counts the sales, using ORDER_LINE_ITEMS:

```
SELECT Oi.Product_ID, SUM(Oi.Quantity) AS Total_Sales, ;
       Pr.Product_Name ;
  FROM \VFP\SAMPLES\MAINSAMP\DATA\TASTRADE!ORDER_LINE_ITEMS Oi, ;
       \VFP\SAMPLES\MAINSAMP\DATA\TASTRADE!PRODUCTS Pr ;
 WHERE Oi.Product_ID = Pr.Product_ID ;
 GROUP BY Oi.Product_ID ;
INTO CURSOR MyResult
```

The problem with this SELECT is that it includes only records for items with sales. You might have products without sales. To include them, you need an outer join.

Outer joins come in three flavors: *left outer join*, which includes all records for the table on the left side of the join statement and only matching records from the table on the right; *right outer join*, which includes all records from the table on the right side of the join condition and only matching records from the table on the left; and *full outer join*, which includes all records from both tables and matches up those that it can.

Left Outer Join   One way to implement a left outer join is to perform two SELECTs: one for all records with children and one for all records without children. Then combine the results of these two SELECTs with a UNION. Listing 7.2 creates the necessary list.

> **N O T E**   To show that this example really does include products without sales, modify the PRODUCTS.DBF table in \VFP\SAMPLES\DATA before running this program. Add a few records with new Product_ID values. Include at least product names (for example, Discontinued Product #1) to help you identify the ones that were added. ∎

Listing 7.2   07CODE02—A Simple Left Outer Join

```
* Creates an outer-join to list all products and their sales.

  SELECT Oi.Product_ID, SUM(Oi.Quantity) AS TotalSales, ;
         Pr.Product_Name ;
```

```
      FROM \VFP\SAMPLES\MAINSAMP\DATA\TASTRADE!ORDER_LINE_ITEMS Oi, ;
           \VFP\SAMPLES\MAINSAMP\DATA\TASTRADE!PRODUCTS Pr ;
    WHERE Oi.Product_ID = Pr.Product_ID ;
    GROUP BY Pi.Product_ID ;
    UNION ALL ;
    SELECT Pr.Product_ID, 0, Pr.Product_Name ;
      FROM \VFP\SAMPLES\MAINSAMP\DATA\TASTRADE!PRODUCTS Pr ;
    WHERE Product_ID NOT IN (SELECT DISTINCT Product_ID ;
           FROM \VFP\SAMPLES\MAINSAMP\DATA\TASTRADE!ORDER_LINE_ITEMS) ;
INTO CURSOR MyResult


*/ Using a JOIN clause
SELECT Products.product_id,;
  SUM(Order_line_items.quantity) AS totalsales, Products.product_name;
 FROM  tastrade!products LEFT OUTER JOIN tastrade!order_line_items ;
   ON  Products.product_id = Order_line_items.product_id;
  GROUP BY Products.product_id ;
INTO CURSOR MyResult
```

TIP A left outer join should never have an overlap of records. Therefore, use UNION ALL to optimize performance when you're combining the two record sets.

Right Outer Join A right outer join is required when you want all the records from the table on the right side of the join criteria. The following example shows the use of a right outer join:

```
SELECT Customer.Cust_id,;
  SUM(Invoice.Amount) AS totalsales ;
 FROM  Customer RIGHT OUTER JOIN Invoices ;
   ON  Customer.Cust_id = Invoices.Cust_id;
  GROUP BY Cust_id ;
INTO CURSOR MyResult
```

N O T E A right outer join combines all the records that satisfy the relational criteria, as well as all child records without parent records. ▪

This example will produce a result that includes only the names of customers who have invoices, but it also includes any invoices that have no corresponding customer records.

N O T E You might object to the right outer join, saying that sound referential integrity would prevent "orphaned" invoice records. The answer to your objection would lie in the business rules for the system. Some businesses might, for instance, want to record cash sales as invoices without customers. ▪

Full Outer Join What happens if you want all customers and all invoices, and you want the ones that match to be combined? The answer lies in the full outer join. The following example shows the full outer join syntax:

```
SELECT Customer.Cust_id,;
  SUM(Invoice.Amount) AS totalsales ;
```

```
 FROM  Customer FULL OUTER JOIN Invoices ;
   ON  Customer.Cust_id = Invoices.Cust_id;
 GROUP BY Cust_id ;
INTO CURSOR MyResult
```

This type of join will produce a set of records that includes all customers and all invoices, and for those invoices that have customers, the data will be combined into one record.

Creating a Self-Join

A *self-join* is a query that needs to form a relation between two fields in the same table. See the section "Creating Self-Referencing Relations" in Chapter 4, "Advanced Database Management Concepts"; there, you used a self-join in an employee file to find the names of each employee's supervisor. Listing 7.3 shows the necessary SELECT statement to generate the required result.

Listing 7.3   07CODE03—A Simple Self-Join Example

```
* Creates a self-join to find the suppliers
* of both products 16 and 17.


   SELECT E1.cEmpId, ;
          E1.cLastName AS Employee_Last_Name, ;
          E1.cFirstName AS Employee_First_Name, ;
          E2.cLastName AS Supervisor_Last_Name, ;
          E2.cFirstName AS Supervisor_First_Name ;
     FROM \USINGFOX.300\DATA\PTOFSALE!EMPL2 E1, ;
          \USINGFOX.300\DATA\PTOFSALE!EMPL2 E2 ;
    WHERE E1.cSupervisor = E2.cEmpId ;
INTO CURSOR MyResult
```

Observe that to form a self-join, you must open the table more than once, with a different alias for each occurrence. This example opens the file EMPL2.DBF, using the simple character aliases E1 and E2. It then forms a relation between the supervisor ID in one instance and the employee ID in the other.

Another situation that calls for a self-join occurs when you need to find records that match two or more occurrences of the same field. Suppose that you want to know which Tasmanian Traders supplier, if any, provides both product ID 16 and 18. Because this request requires comparing products across multiple records, a simple query will not solve it. Listing 7.4 opens PRODUCT.DBF twice, once to find each product. If the supplier ID for both is the same, it retrieves the name of the supplier for the result table.

Listing 7.4   07CODE04—An Advanced Self-Join Example

```
* Creates a self-join to find the suppliers of both products 16 and 18.
* Ensure the Products.Supplier_Id for both products 16 and 18 are the same.

  SELECT Pa.Product_Name, Pb.Product_Name, ;
         Su.Company_Name, Pa.Product_ID, Pb.Product_id ;
```

```
      FROM TASTRADE!PRODUCTS Pa,;
           TASTRADE!PRODUCTS Pb,;
           TASTRADE!SUPPLIER Su ;
     WHERE Pa.Product_ID = '     16' AND ;
           Pb.Product_ID = '     18' AND ;
           Su.Supplier_ID = Pb.Supplier_ID AND ;
           Pa.Supplier_ID = Su.Supplier_ID ;
 INTO CURSOR MyResult

 * Visual FoxPro 6.0
 CLOSE ALL
 SELECT 0
 USE products ALIAS products
 SELECT 0
 USE products ALIAS products_a AGAIN
 SELECT 0
 USE supplier
 SELECT Products.product_name, Products_a.product_name, ;
   Supplier.company_name, Products.product_id, Products_a.product_id;
  FROM  tastrade!products INNER JOIN tastrade!supplier;
    INNER JOIN tastrade!products Products_a ;
    ON  Products.supplier_id ==Supplier.supplier_id ;
    ON  Products.supplier_id == Products_a.supplier_id;
  WHERE Products.product_id == '     16';
    AND (Products_a.product_id == '     18');
  ORDER BY Products.product_id ;
 INTO CURSOR MyResult
```

Optimizing Query Generation

A poorly designed query can require minutes or even hours to return a result set that a properly designed query can return in seconds. This section examines techniques that improve the performance time of queries.

Basic Rules for Using Rushmore

Rushmore can improve the performance of most queries when used properly. However, many developers don't understand how Rushmore really works; therefore, they create queries that do not perform at their optimal level.

Rushmore uses existing indexes whenever possible to process a query. If an index does not exist, Rushmore creates a "virtual" index in memory for the request. However, creating an index takes more time than using an existing one.

Many developers, knowing that Rushmore uses indexes, try to "help" it along by setting the order of the tables before running the query. In commands that use the Rushmore optimizable FOR clauses, such as BROWSE, LIST, and SCAN, this practice slows the command. It does not turn off Rushmore, however. Rushmore finds the records that match the criteria; then it has to go back to the index to determine the order in which to display them.

Part

II

Ch

7

When you create queries using SELECT, Visual FoxPro ignores any established order for selected tables. Therefore, you do not need to go back and turn off indexes to benefit from Rushmore. But setting them doesn't help either. You still have to phrase all WHERE clause criteria using Rushmore-optimizable clauses for the best performance.

The main criterion in determining whether a clause is Rushmore-optimizable is whether it exactly matches a current index expression. If it does, Rushmore optimizes the expression. For this reason, many developers create a separate index tag on each field in the table (this process is called *inverting* the table). Consider this example:

```
INDEX ON Company_Name TAG company
INDEX ON Employee_ID TAG employee
```

Here, Visual FoxPro must update each index every time it adds, changes, or deletes a record. Alternatively, you can define a concatenated index like the following:

```
INDEX ON Company_Name + Employee_Id TAG employee
```

This index performs searches only slightly slower than indexes on individual fields. It reduces the total number of indexes that Visual FoxPro must maintain, however. If you look at your applications, you usually don't need indexes on every field. In fact, only a few indexes might really be necessary to form relations and queries. A good goal is to minimize the total number of indexes while providing an index for every defined need.

On the other hand, if you need individual indexes on Company and Employee ID, don't create a third index on the concatenation of the two; doing so actually slows Rushmore.

Even a seemingly minor change to the index expression can turn off Rushmore. Using the preceding index expression on Company_Name, for example, Rushmore will not optimize the following expression:

```
UPPER(Company_Name) = 'FRANS'
```

The function UPPER() invalidates the use of Rushmore. On the other hand, if you know that the application stores all company names in uppercase, Rushmore will optimize the following expression:

```
Company_Name = UPPER('frans')
```

 TIP Don't control case in conditional statements. Use the InputMask or Format properties of the data input objects to control case.

If the WHERE clause contains several conditions connected with AND, Rushmore optimizes each condition separately. This situation can result in a *partially optimized expression* when all the expressions connected with AND are Rushmore-optimizable.

Unless you want to display all records in the table regardless of their delete status, you should create an index on DELETED(). Rushmore uses this index to determine which records it can use when SET DELETED ON is set. If Rushmore has to read the table to determine the delete flag on each record, the SELECT cannot be fully optimized.

N O T E You might not have realized that deleted records can cause a problem for Rushmore. `SET DELETED ON` is equivalent to `SET FILTER TO NOT DELETED()`. Remember that the command `SET DELETED ON` can be set elsewhere in the current program, a previous program, the FoxPro `CONFIG.FPW` file, or even interactively. If you want to skip deleted records and want optimal performance from Rushmore, you must have a tag defined on the `DELETED()` function. ▨

Rushmore will not use indexes that contain `NOT` or `FOR` when optimizing an expression. However, you can use `NOT` in the condition. For example, you can have a `SELECT` like the following:

```
SELECT Company_Name FROM customer WHERE NOT (State='TX')
```

As long as an index exists on the field `STATE`, Rushmore will optimize the expression.

Sometimes, you can benefit from previous Rushmore optimization. Suppose that you begin by searching the `ORDERS` table for all orders in 1995, as follows:

```
BROWSE FOR YEAR(Order_Date) = 1995
```

Next, suppose that you need only orders from customer `'FRANS'` in 1995:

```
BROWSE FOR YEAR(Order_Date) = 1995 AND Customer_ID = 'FRANS'
```

Now, assume that the following indexes exist:

```
INDEX ON YEAR(Order_Date) TAG year
INDEX ON Customer_ID TAG customer
```

In this case, Rushmore optimizes the first expression, finding all orders for 1995. When it begins the second browse, it recognizes that it already has information about orders in 1995. Therefore, it examines those records only for customer `'FRANS'`.

The biggest potential danger with Rushmore is that it creates a solution set for any given optimizable expression only once. If you use a `SCAN FOR` clause, Rushmore determines which records to process the first time it executes the `FOR`. In a shared environment, another user could make a change that would affect Rushmore's solution set while `SCAN` is processing. However, because Rushmore does not check for changes, you might process the wrong records. For the average application, the benefits of using Rushmore outweigh this remote but possible problem. However, you should be aware of it if you have very high transaction rate tables. If you decide that the potential danger is too great, turn optimization off by using the `NOOPTIMIZE` option on the command you are using to get the data.

Suppose that you need to reference selected records from a single table and need no special column functions, groups, or orders. `SELECT` creates a special cursor that effectively reopens the table in a different work area and applies a filter to it. It performs this activity almost instantaneously. Therefore, rather than use this code

```
SELECT orders
SCAN FOR Customer_Name = 'TAZMAN'
  << commands that process each selected order >>
ENDSCAN
```

Part

II

Ch

7

you might instead use this code

```
SELECT * FROM orders WHERE Customer_Name = 'TAZMAN'
SCAN
  << commands that process each selected order >>
ENDSCAN
```

N O T E   Rushmore will not use a UNIQUE index, and you shouldn't, either. In Chapter 3, "Defining Databases, Tables, and Indexes," I explained why UNIQUE indexes are not recommended except for the rare situation in which you might create one, use it, and then erase it. ▪

Minimizing Fields in a Query

All too often, it seems easy to just include the * character in a SELECT statement to include all the fields in a table. However, you should include only the fields that you absolutely need. The most time-consuming aspect of any SELECT is getting the data for the result, and the fewer fields you ask for, the faster the SELECT will get them.

If you want only DISTINCT records, SELECT compares every field in every record to determine whether the new record is distinct. This process consumes time. Reducing the number of fields in the SELECT reduces the number of comparisons. However, a better solution is to use the GROUP BY clause wherever possible.

Another trap is the assumption that forming relations between SELECT results and other existing tables is easier than including all the fields in the SELECT. Actually, the most likely reason for doing so is reluctance to include all the field references. It is true that large multiple-table SELECTs consume a great deal of memory and often need to be stored partially on disk. Further, the more fields included in the SELECT, the more memory it needs or the more disk access time it requires. Of course, any disk access slows a SELECT considerably. You might be tempted to include only those fields that are necessary to uniquely identify the records in the SELECT and then form relations to other physical tables. This solution generally is not good. The main reason is that accessing all the other physical tables to form and access the relations definitely involves slower disk access.

Creating Cross-Tabs

Cross-tabs are special types of queries in which you define column and row headings of a table and calculate results for the intersecting cells. Suppose that you want to create a monthly sales summary, by customer, for Tasmanian Traders. This report needs to display 12 column headings, each one representing a different month. Each row represents a different customer. You probably would not normally store a table with a structure like the following:

```
CustomerId      Character       8
JanuarySales    Numeric         8    2
FebruarySales   Numeric         8    2
MarchSales      Numeric         8    2
AprilSales      Numeric         8    2
MaySales        Numeric         8    2
```

JuneSales	Numeric	8	2
JulySales	Numeric	8	2
AugustSales	Numeric	8	2
SeptemberSales	Numeric	8	2
OctoberSales	Numeric	8	2
NovemberSales	Numeric	8	2
DecemberSales	Numeric	8	2

Instead, the data file looks like this:

CustomerId	Character	8	
SalesDate	Date	8	
SalesAmt	Numeric	8	2

How do you get from the first form to the second? Visual FoxPro includes a special program called VFPXTAB, which converts a SELECT cursor that contains the necessary information to a cross-tab table. To gather the necessary information for the cross-tab, you first need a cursor with three fields:

- The row headings
- The column headings
- The row-column intersection values

The first SELECT statement in Listing 7.5 gathers the required data for 1994 and stores it in a cursor named MyTab. The second SELECT creates the cross-tab, using the data from MyTab to provide the row, column, and data. Function SYS(2015) generates a unique name for the cursor.

Listing 7.5 07CODE05—Creating a Cross-Tab from a SELECT Cursor

```
* Creates a cross-tab


*/ Create the source information for row, column, and data
  SELECT Or.Customer_id, Pe.Monthid, ;
         (Oi.Unit_Price*Oi.Quantity) AS Order_Net ;
    FROM TASTRADE!ORDERS Or, ;
         TASTRADE!ORDER_LINE_ITEMS Oi, ;
         PERIOD Pe ;
   WHERE YEAR(Oi.Order_Date) = 1994 AND ;
         MONTH(Oi.Order_Date) = Pe.MonthId AND ;
         Oi.Order_Id = Or.Order_Id ;
   GROUP BY Oi.Customer_Id, Pe.MonthId ;
    INTO CURSOR MyTab

  */ Create the cross-tab
  SELECT MyTab.customer_i, MyTab.monthid, SUM(MyTab.order_net);
  FROM MyTab;
  GROUP BY MyTab.customer_i, MyTab.monthid;
  ORDER BY MyTab.customer_i, MyTab.monthid;
  INTO CURSOR MyXTab
  DO (_GENXTAB)
BROWSE NOMODIFY
```

Part
II

Ch
7

N O T E In Listing 7.5, you might notice the use of _GENXTAB. This system memory variable, which is created by Visual FoxPro, holds the name of the program to use for creating cross-tabs. The default program is VFPXTAB.PRG, but you can replace that program with one you've written by adding the following in the command window:

```
_GENXTAB = "C:\VFP\MyXTab.prg"
```

This SELECT requires a special table that is not included with the Tasmanian Trader example. You can quickly create this table, based on the structure shown in Table 7.4. Table 7.5 shows the contents of all 12 records. Place this table in directory \USINGFOX.500\DATA.

Table 7.4   Table Structure for PERIOD.DBF Used in the Cross-Tab

Field	Type	Size
MonthID	Numeric	2
MonthName	Character	10

Table 7.5   Records in PERIOD.DBF

Record #	MonthID	MonthName
1	1	January
2	2	February
3	3	March
4	4	April
5	5	May
6	6	June
7	7	July
8	8	August
9	9	September
10	10	October
11	11	November
12	12	December

The SELECT in Listing 7.5 creates a cursor with one record for each customer-month combination. It first has to link ORDERS with ORDER_LINE_ITEMS to calculate the product of the Unit_Price and Quantity. It stores this product in the result set field ORDER_NET. The GROUP BY clause then sums ORDER_NET if the customer ordered more than one item in any month.

The result table from this SELECT is not a cross tabulation. However, you can create a cross-tab report with it if you sort and group by customer ID. First, you need to define report variables such as the following:

```
JanSales = IIF(MonthName = 'JANUARY', Order_Net, 0)
```

This expression totals sales for January. You need to create 11 similar expressions, defining total sales for other months. Then add these report variables to the customer ID group footer, and set the calculation method to SUM. This report does not need detail lines—only group footers.

This solution works for a report. However, displaying the information in a form, using the results with another table, or generating a graph would not be as easy. For that reason, you need to use VFPXTAB.

VFPXTAB reads the cursor created by the preceding SELECT and determines the number of distinct columns. Next, it creates a new table with the same first column (Customer_Id, in this case) and columns for each distinct value in the cursor's second field. Then it creates one record for each customer and puts the corresponding total sales in the correct column. The net result is a cross-tab table with 13 columns and 1 row for each customer. Now you can directly use this table to generate reports or graphs.

To execute VFPXTAB, you can call it directly, as follows:

```
DO \VFP\VFPXTAB
```

This statement assumes that the root directory for Visual FoxPro is \VFP\. If your root directory is different, adjust this statement appropriately. If you have never run VFPXTAB before, Visual FoxPro must first compile it.

VFPXTAB uses, as input, the table in the current work area. Therefore, the table does not have to be named in the command that executes VFPXTAB. However, VFPXTAB has nine other possible parameters. All these parameters have default values and can be omitted. The parameters are as follow:

Parm1	Specifies the output file/cursor name (default: XTAB.DBF)
Parm2	Creates a cursor only (default: .F.)
Parm3	Closes the input table after use (default: .T.)
Parm4	Shows a progress thermometer (default: .T.)
Parm5	Specifies the row field (field number to use as row) (default: 1)
Parm6	Specifies the column field (field number to use as column) (default: 2)
Parm7	Specifies the data field (field number to use as data) (default: 3)
Parm8	Calculates the row total) (default: .F.)
Parm9	Indicates the totaling options (0: sum, 1: count, 2: % of total)

The following command creates a cross-tab with one row per customer; then it sums all the customer's sales by month and displays one column per month:

```
DO \VFP\VFPXTAB WITH 'CUSTSALE.DBF', .F., .F., .T., 1, 2, 3, .T.
```

Part
II

Ch
7

The eighth parameter has been set to .T.; thus, it creates an additional column at the end to total all the sales for the preceding columns. In this case, because the SELECT limited records to a single year, this column represents the annual sales to each customer.

When you add 2 as the ninth parameter, the cross-tab calculates the percentage of total sales attributed to each customer during the year. Then you can sort the resulting cross-tab table to display the customers in order of total sales percentage, as follows:

```
DO \VFP\VFPXTAB WITH 'CUSTSALE.DBF', .F., .F., .T., 1, 2, 3, .T., 2
```

CAUTION
A maximum of 254 unique values are allowed for the "columns" side of the cross-tab.

Using Views and Updatable Queries

Views and queries are almost the same thing. The principal difference is that you can use views to update data in the source tables. Also, Visual FoxPro stores views in the database, not as separate .QPR files; as a result, you can access them only while the database is open. Because you can update data in a view, views provide an excellent way to access and edit data stored in multiple related files. They also provide access to remote data on the same machine or on a remote server. When you are working with server data, you do not have to download all the records to your local machine to accomplish a change. The view can retrieve a subset of data, process it, and return it.

Views of Local Data

This section starts by showing you how to create views of local data. Creating a view is similar to creating a query. You can create a view in two primary ways:

- Choose File, New, View from the system menu.
- Type CREATE VIEW in the command window.

Both methods open the View Designer. The View Designer is similar to the Query Designer, with the addition of an Update Criteria Page. Suppose that you want to create a view between tables CUSTOMER and ORDERS in Tasmanian Traders. Figure 7.1 shows the opening screen of the View Designer, with the Add Table or View dialog box open and ready to add the second table.

The first five pages and the last page in the page frame provide the same options as queries. For further information about how to use these pages, refer to Chapter 6, "Creating Basic Queries."

FIGURE 7.1
To begin a view, open the Add Table or View dialog box, and add the tables or views that will be the data source for the view you are creating.

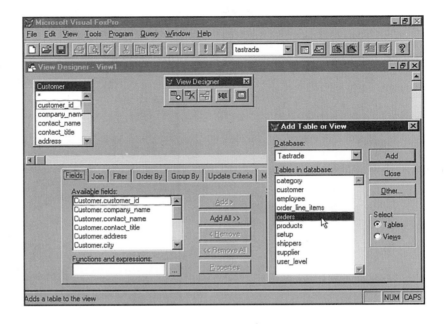

The first page, shown in Figure 7.2, displays a list of selected fields.

FIGURE 7.2
The Fields page of the View Designer enables you to select fields from the available tables and to rearrange their order.

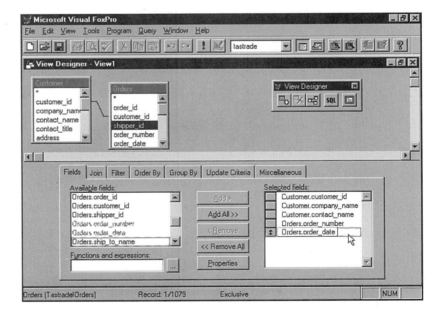

Part
II
Ch
7

You can add or remove fields from this list by doing the following:

- Double-clicking the field name in the Table View area. Double-clicking the asterisk at the top of each table copies all fields to the output list.
- Dragging the selected fields from the Table View area to the Selected Fields list.
- Double-clicking the field names in the Available Fields list and Selected Fields list, or clicking the buttons that are positioned between the lists.

The order in which you select fields becomes the fields' default order in the selected output list. You can easily change this order by clicking and dragging the button to the left of each field name, moving it up or down in the list. Defining the field order is important because it defines the field order in the result set.

Figure 7.3 shows the Properties dialog box that appears when you click the Properties button in the Fields page. In this dialog box, you can specify validation, display, and mapping options, as well as enter a comment for each field in the view.

FIGURE 7.3

The View Field Properties dialog box provides field-property options.

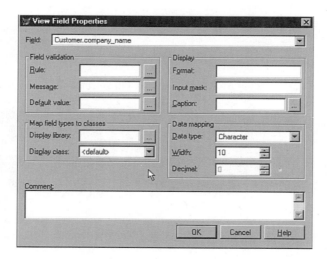

On the Join page of the View Designer, you can set up inner, left, right, and full joins when a view or query has more than one table (see Figure 7.4).

There are two check boxes on the Miscellaneous tab of the View Designer. The one labeled No Duplicates creates a DISTINCT result set, and the one labeled Cross Tabulate creates a cross-tab result. Thus, you can use the Query or View Designer to create the necessary intermediate table for VFPXTAB, described in the preceding section. This check box is disabled if the memory variable _GENXTAB is empty (Visual FoxPro, by default, points _GENXTAB to the VFPXTAB program). You also have to select at least three fields.

On the Filter page, you enter the conditions that are expressed in the WHERE clause of the SE-LECT statement (see Figure 7.5). Fields do not have to be included in the Selected Fields list to be used in filter conditions.

FIGURE 7.4

The Join page displays the join condition(s) for the tables in the top pane of the designer.

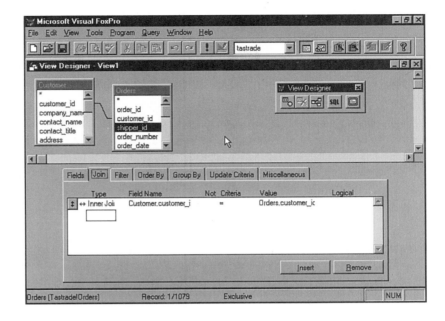

FIGURE 7.5

Exclude records from the view by selecting filter conditions.

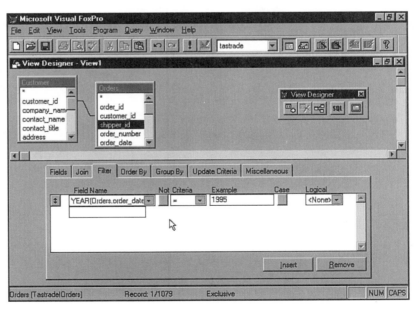

The Order By page (see Figure 7.6) determines a sort order for the fields. Order criteria enable you to establish a sort order based on selected fields and expressions. You can sort each selected field in ascending or descending order. The order of the fields in the Ordering Criteria list determines the sort hierarchy. To change the sort hierarchy, simply click and drag the button to the left of each field name.

FIGURE 7.6
Define the order of the records in the result set by selecting fields in the Order By page of the View Designer.

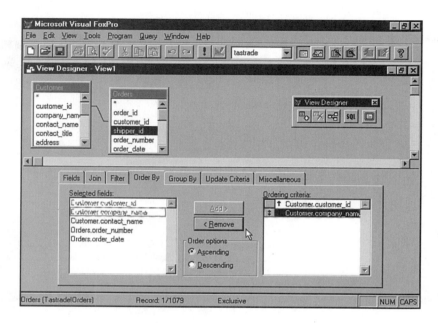

The Group By page (see Figure 7.7) provides an alternative to using No Duplicates.

FIGURE 7.7
Use the Group By tab of the View Designer to sum records by one or more of the selected fields.

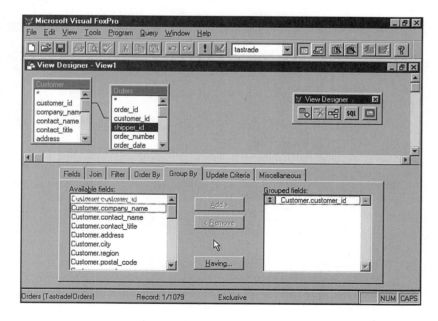

The section "Using DISTINCT Versus GROUP BY" earlier in this chapter describes the advantage of using GROUP BY over the DISTINCT clause in SQL statements. The Group By page also enables you to add a HAVING clause by clicking the Having button. Remember that the HAVING clause operates on the selected records in the result set. Therefore, you can use GROUP BY to collect and sum records by customer ID. Then you can select customers who made total purchases of more than $1,000 by using a HAVING clause such as the following:

```
HAVING TotalPurchases > 1000
```

For a local table view, Visual FoxPro supports only buffering. All views are buffered with optimistic row buffering by default. By using the CURSORSETPROP() function, however, you can change the buffering mode to one of the following values:

1   Pessimistic row buffering on
2   Optimistic row buffering on (Default)
3   Pessimistic table buffering on
4   Optimistic table buffering on

N O T E   You cannot turn buffering off for a view.

To use buffering, you must first turn on MULTILOCKS. Then, using the CURSORSETPROP() function, you can select one of the buffering methods. The following code turns on optimistic table buffering for the CUSTOMER table:

```
SET MULTILOCKS ON
CURSORSETPROP('BUFFERING', 5, 'CUSTOMER')
```

Notice that this function requires three parameters. The first tells CURSORSETPROP() which cursor property you want to change; in the example, we are changing the BUFFERING property. The second is a numeric value to identify the new value for the property; acceptable values depend on the property being changed. The last parameter identifies the alias to be affected.

N O T E   The Miscellaneous page of the View Designer contains check boxes for the duplicate-records and cross-tabulate options. The cross-tabulate option is enabled when you select three fields. These fields must represent the X axis, the Y axis, and data for the cross-tab. Record selections include all records, a specified number of values, or a percentage of the values that meet the selection criteria. (See Figure 7.8.)

View Update Options

The Update Criteria page of the View Designer page frame contains options that are specifically related to the capability of views to update the data that they represent. Figure 7.9 shows the options on this page.

FIGURE 7.8

The Miscellaneous page of the View Designer specifies duplicate records, cross-tabular format, and how records are selected for the result set.

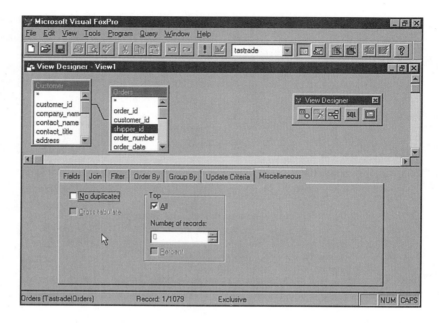

FIGURE 7.9

The Update Criteria page of the View Designer defines how Visual FoxPro updates the tables when changes are made to the view result set.

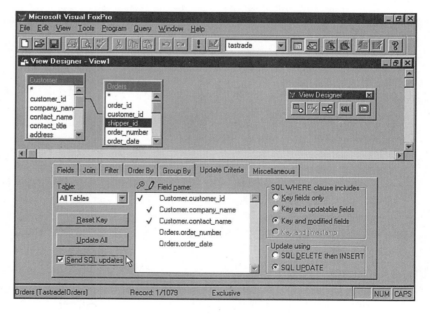

Within a view, you can control which tables and fields the user can update and how Visual FoxPro performs the updates. By default, Visual FoxPro prohibits all field updates in the view. To enable updates, first select the table to which the field belongs, using the table combo box in the upper-left corner of this page. You can select individual tables or all tables involved in the view. When you select a table, Visual FoxPro displays its fields in the center list box. Observe that it does not display all the fields from the table—just those that are included in the output set.

If a table has a primary index, and if that field appears in the output set, a check mark appears in the first column, below the key symbol. You can change the field(s) used to uniquely identify records in the original table. However, you should select only the primary-key field or a candidate-key field. These fields must appear in the selected fields.

The Reset Key button immediately below the table combo box returns the key-field status to the original setting used by the source table.

The Update All button places check marks in the second column of the field list, below the pencil icon. This column determines which fields VFP will update. You can select individual fields for updating by clicking the button in this column next to the field name. Conversely, you can click the Update All button and turn off individual fields that you do not want to update.

By default, the Update All button does not select the key field as an updatable field. Although you can mark the key field as updatable by manually clicking its second column, you normally do not want to update the key field. Before enabling updates to a key field, you should define referential-integrity rules by using the RI Builder or by using the append, delete, and update triggers. Then you should enable updates only from the primary table field.

Even if you mark fields as updatable, SQL does not send the updates back to the original files unless you also select the Send SQL Updates option. When you enable updates, you must also select one of the four update options shown in Table 7.6.

Table 7.6   Update Options for the SQL WHERE Clause

Option	Description
Key Fields Only	Tells VFP to use only the key field in finding records to update in the source data.
Key and Updatable Fields	Tells VFP to use the key field and all the updatable fields, even if they haven't been changed, to locate records to be updated.
Key and Modified Fields	Tells VFP to use the key and any modifiable fields that have been modified to locate records to be updated.
Key and Timestamp	Causes the update to fail if the key value or the time stamp in the original table has changed. (Not all database servers support a time stamp.) This option is disabled for local views.

N O T E In all the options in Table 7.6, the original value for the referenced fields is used to find a record to update. Even the Key and Modified option uses the original values of the modified fields. ■

Observe that the most severe test in this sequence is the last one, but it is also the safest. It can cause an update to fail even if the only field in the original table to change is one that is not selected as updatable in the current view.

The next-most-severe test checks the key and updatable fields. Usually, this test does not cause a problem because views cannot update nonupdatable fields. Therefore, changes made by other users are safe.

The option that checks only modified fields leaves open the possibility of overwriting changes to updatable fields in the original table. Overwriting occurs if you do not change an updatable field that someone else changes before you send the update back.

A similar problem occurs if you check only whether the key field has changed—the least severe test. Another user could change one of the other updatable fields, and you could easily overwrite these changes. However, if other users have only add or delete rights to a file, this less restrictive update test performs better because it has fewer fields to check for changes.

The last two options in the Update Criteria page determine which technique to use when the original data is updated. SQL can either delete the original records first and then insert a new one or simply update the existing record. The reason for two methods is to enable for the fact that certain database servers are much faster at deleting and inserting records than they are at updating records. This option creates SQL DELETE and SQL INSERT commands to update the data. For local views, you can choose either of these methods, but there is little reason to use the delete and insert method.

Updating the existing record creates a SQL UPDATE command to update the source table. This option preserves changes to fields that are not used in the SQL WHERE clause.

N O T E Although you can include a memo field in a view, it is not updatable. ■

Creating a SQL View in Code

You also can create a view directly within your program code by first opening the database and then using the CREATE SQL VIEW command, as follows:

```
OPEN DATABASE \VFP\SAMPLES\MAINSAMP\DATA\TASTRADE
    CREATE SQL VIEW CustInfo_View AS ;
    SELECT Customer.customer_id, Customer.company_name,;
     Customer.contact_name, Orders.order_number, Orders.order_date;
    FROM  tastrade!customer INNER JOIN tastrade!orders ;
    ON  Customer.customer_id = Orders.customer_id;
    WHERE YEAR(Orders.order_date) = 1995;
    GROUP BY Customer.customer_id;
    ORDER BY Customer.customer_id
```

To make this view updatable, you must set table properties with the DBSETPROP() function. You can easily create the view ahead of time and then just open the database and USE the view. This method has the added advantage of enabling you to define the table properties more easily.

Using Memory Variables in Selection Criteria

In all the examples so far, the selection criteria used to limit the selected records used actual values in the sample portion of the criteria. Unfortunately, this approach limits the query to extracting only a fixed set of records each time the query is run, unless you modify the query. You might perform the following query, using the field Region to select records from the table CUSTOMER of TASTRADE:

```
SELECT CUSTOMER.Customer_Id, CUSTOMER.Company_Name, ;
       CUSTOMER.Region, CUSTOMER.Max_Order_Amt ;
  FROM TASTRADE!Customer ;
 WHERE CUSTOMER.Region = "PA";
INTO CURSOR MyResult
```

This WHERE clause returns those records for customers from Pennsylvania (PA). Every time you run the query, however, it returns the same records. To change the records that are returned, you have to modify the statement.

This operation might be fine for users who are familiar and comfortable with working in interactive mode. However, suppose that you need to put the query in a program. Further suppose that you want the user to still be able to select from which state to retrieve records.

One solution involves the use of memory variables. You must define a memory variable to hold the state code. Then you need to create a way to enable the user to enter a state code in this variable. The easiest way is to give the user a simple form that asks for the state. Alternatively, you can give the user a list from which he or she can pick valid state codes.

In either case, the next step is for you to redefine the SELECT statement with a memory variable that holds the selection for the criteria's example rather than use a fixed value. The following statement shows the new SELECT, assuming that the user enters the state code in the lcGetState variable:

```
SELECT CUSTOMER.Customer_Id, CUSTOMER.Company_Name, ;
       CUSTOMER.Region, CUSTOMER.Max_Order_Amt ;
  FROM TASTRADE!Customer ;
 WHERE CUSTOMER.Region = lcGetState ;
INTO CURSOR MyResult
```

You can try this example interactively simply by assigning a value to lcGetState through the Command window before executing the SELECT. In a program, this technique enables the user to customize the records returned by the SELECT.

This method works for both queries and views. However, views support another way to obtain a value from the user.

Parameterized Query Criteria

Fixing the record-selection criteria at design time is not always possible, or even desirable. Neither do you necessarily want to create a separate form just to prompt for criteria values. Yet you still want the user to determine the condition. You can do so relatively easily by using a view.

First, you need to define a view parameter by choosing Query, View Parameters. In the View Parameters dialog box, you can enter any valid variable name, along with its type. Then click OK to save it. In Figure 7.10, the parameter GroupDiscount has been defined as numeric.

FIGURE 7.10

To enable the user to control the criteria values used in the selection criteria of a view, you must define the criteria with a view parameter.

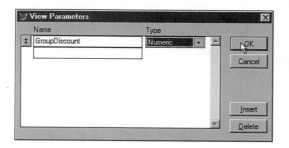

After you define the parameter, place the view parameter in the Example box of the appropriate selection criteria. To tell Visual FoxPro that this parameter is a view parameter, precede it with a question mark. Do not put a space between the question mark and the parameter. For example, you enter the GroupDiscount parameter as follows:

```
?GroupDiscount
```

A view parameter is a memory variable. The only difference is that when a view is opened, if the variable does not exist, Visual FoxPro will prompt the user for a value to replace the parameter.

When the view runs, a dialog box appears, asking the user to enter a value of the view parameter. VFP then uses the entered value to select records for the view. If you run the view and respond with a value of 2, VFP creates a view of customers who have a 2 percent discount.

 You might want to use a parameterized view in a form and not want the user to be prompted for the value while the form loads. In this case, you can change the NODATAONLOAD property for the view in the form's data environment to .T., thus not running the SELECT for the view when it is initially opened. Then, at a later time after you have created the variable and assigned the proper value to it, you can use the Requery() function to execute the SELECT statement that makes up the view definition.

Actually, you can requery a view any time you want by using the Requery() function. The most likely time to do so is when the value of the parameters change. The Requery() function takes one argument: the name of the view to be requeried.

CHAPTER

8

Accessing Remote Data

Introduction to Remote Data Access

Visual FoxPro has a very powerful database engine built into it. When you deal with data stored in the Visual FoxPro dbf tables, you are using what is called *local data*. Even though Visual FoxPro has this local data engine, in some situations the data you need to deal with is not stored in local tables. At these times, the remote data handling capabilities of Visual FoxPro 6 will save your day.

In this chapter, you will see that Visual FoxPro has a variety of options for dealing with remote data. You can use ODBC data sources, Connections, ADO, or RDO to get at data that is stored outside Visual FoxPro. The best method depends on a number of factors, which are discussed in this chapter.

There is no single correct method. Each method has it own strengths and weaknesses. This chapter covers the strengths and weaknesses of each method so that you have the information to make decisions for your particular projects.

What Is Remote Data?

Remote data refers to any data that is not being accessed directly by Visual FoxPro. In most cases, remote data refers to data stored in products such as Microsoft SQL Server or Oracle or any of the many other database server products. However, database servers are not the only kind of remote data.

You might need to access data stored in a Microsoft Access database file. You can even access a Visual FoxPro database remotely.

In using local data, you usually put the tables you want in a form's data environment. Then the form's data environment will USE those tables for you when you run the form. With remote data, you cannot place the table directly into the data environment; you must handle accessing the data externally to the form by using remote views or SQL Pass Through.

Visual FoxPro 6 can use two different technologies to access remote data. The two technologies have a lot in common, as one uses the other internally. The two technologies available are Open Database Connectivity (ODBC) and Distributed Component Object Model (DCOM).

DCOM uses ODBC to access its data. In Visual FoxPro, you can either use ODBC directly, or you can leverage the bigger feature set of DCOM and use ODBC indirectly.

ODBC

As you saw in the preceding section, *ODBC* is an acronym for *Open Database Connectivity*. ODBC is a technology, built in to the Windows 95/98 and Windows NT environments, which enables two different database systems to share data with each other.

ODBC works based on the ODBC engine in Windows. The ODBC model is divided into three separate layers. One layer is the ODBC engine in Windows. The other two are referred to as ODBC drivers, one for the data consumer and the other for the data source.

The specifications of ODBC make it possible for a vendor, such as Microsoft, to provide an ODBC consumer driver without having specific knowledge of the data source that will be used. This is possible because the ODBC specifications deal only with the consumer talking to the ODBC engine.

Vendors of data sources can also provide ODBC source drivers without knowing what the consumer will be because the ODBC data source driver has to communicate only with the ODBC engine. The ODBC engine is a switchboard of sorts that receives requests from an ODBC consumer driver and passes them on to an ODBC data source driver.

Figure 8.1 is a block diagram of the ODBC process.

Part
II

Ch
8

FIGURE 8.1

A block diagram of how ODBC works.

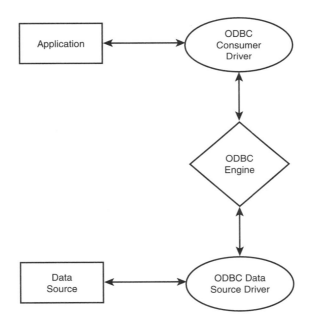

Data Sources   Because ODBC is a service of Windows, before you can access any ODBC data sources, you must first set up the data source driver in Windows.

ODBC drivers are usually available with the data sources you have, or you can find third-party vendors that sell ODBC drivers for many products. The speed of data access through ODBC is a direct result of the drivers being used. If ultimate speed is a goal, you might be well served to evaluate the third-party drivers available.

The process of setting up an ODBC driver is not difficult, although you will need to know some information about the data source that the driver will access.

The ODBC Administrator   To set up an ODBC driver, you use the Windows ODBC Administrator. Figure 8.2 shows the 32-bit ODBC Administrator.

FIGURE 8.2

The ODBC Administrator with the User DSN tab visible.

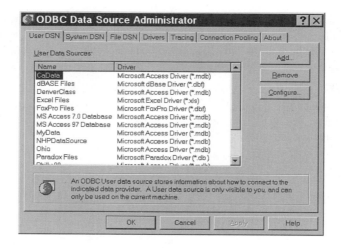

In the ODBC Administrator, choose the Add button. The dialog box you get will look similar to Figure 8.3.

FIGURE 8.3

The ODBC driver selection dialog box in the ODBC Administrator.

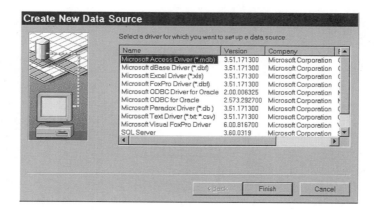

The first step in setting up an ODBC data source is to select the ODBC driver that you want to use. The available drivers on your computer might be quite different from those you see in Figure 8.3 because the list shows the ODBC drivers that have been installed on the computer. You might need to use the installation disks from the data source vendor to install the appropriate ODBC drivers before starting this process.

For this example, use the Microsoft Access driver. Figure 8.4 shows the dialog box we get after selecting the Microsoft Access driver.

The setup dialog box that you get depends on the ODBC driver you've chosen. For the example, you only have to choose the Select button under the Database prompt. This action brings up the dialog box shown in Figure 8.5.

FIGURE 8.4

The setup dialog box for the Microsoft Access ODBC driver.

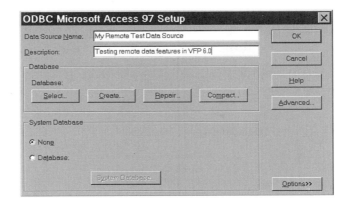

FIGURE 8.5

The database selection dialog box for the Microsoft Access ODBC driver.

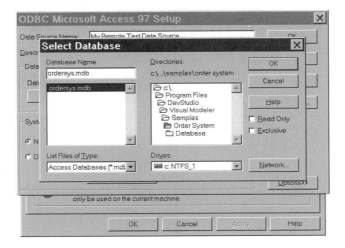

In Figure 8.5, I selected an Access database that is installed on my computer. You might or might not have that same database installed on your computer.

After you select the database, click OK in the database dialog box and also click OK in the ODBC driver setup dialog box. Figure 8.6 shows how the ODBC Administrator looks now on my computer.

That is all there is to creating a data source in ODBC. As an example of another ODBC driver setup dialog box, Figure 8.7 shows the one for Microsoft SQL Server.

The process of setting up the driver for Microsoft SQL Server involves a number of steps sufficient for the driver to use a wizard to assist you. Included in the steps are elements such as a login name and password, and whether you want the data source to display SQL Server dialog boxes when it attempts to connect to the SQL Server database. The issues that are addressed by the setup process will vary based on the requirements of the particular data server you are using.

FIGURE 8.6
The ODBC Administrator after I added our new data source.

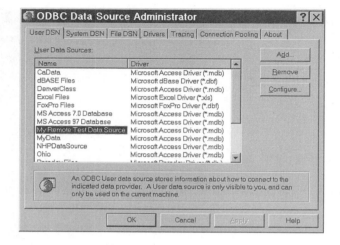

FIGURE 8.7
The first page of the Microsoft SQL Server ODBC Driver Setup Wizard.

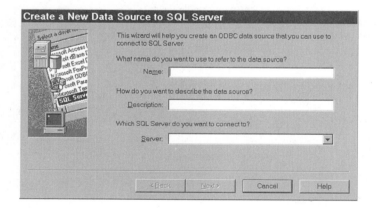

Oracle's setup dialog box would be different from the SQL Server dialog box shown in Figure 8.7. It is beyond the scope of this book to present and explain every possible ODBC driver you might encounter. Look to the documentation of the product you are connecting to get the information you need to set up its ODBC driver.

Creating Remote Views in Visual FoxPro 6

Now that your data source is set up in ODBC, you can create a remote view in Visual FoxPro. To do so, open a database in the Database Designer, and right-click the designer. The shortcut menu you get is shown in Figure 8.8.

Select the New Remote View option. If you see a dialog box asking whether you want the View Wizard or a new view, choose New View. Figure 8.9 shows the next dialog box.

FIGURE 8.8
The Database Designer
shortcut menu.

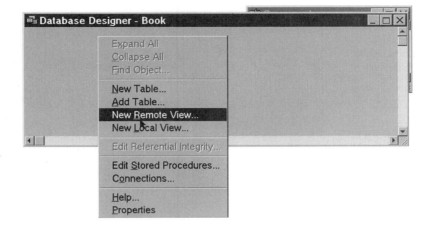

FIGURE 8.9
The data source and
connection selection
dialog box.

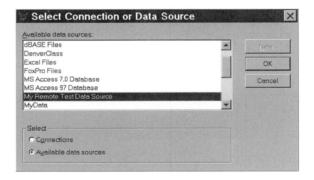

Using a Data Source

In Figure 8.9, notice that we have selected the Available Data Sources radio button to get the dialog box to show us the data source we have created with the ODBC Administrator. For now, don't concern yourself with connections; we will cover them later in this chapter.

At this point, select My Remote Test Data Source and click OK. You will see the Open dialog box shown in Figure 8.10.

From this point forward, creating a remote view is exactly the same as creating a local view. You are now in the Visual FoxPro View Designer. The only difference is that the data is coming from a remote source through ODBC.

You finish creating the view by doing the same things you did in Chapters 6, "Creating Basic Queries," and 7, "Advanced Queries and Views." You select the tables, set the joins, select the fields, set the filter criteria, and set all the other options you want for this view.

FIGURE 8.10

The Open dialog box with the tables from the My Remote Test Data Source database.

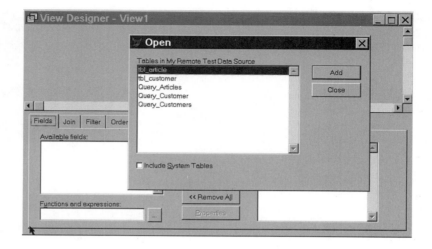

Figure 8.11 shows our database after we have created two remote views from the Northwind.mdb sample database that Microsoft supplies with Access. The two remote views are named rvcust and rvorders. We use the naming convention of prefixing local views with lv and remote views with rv.

FIGURE 8.11

The Database Designer with two remote views in it.

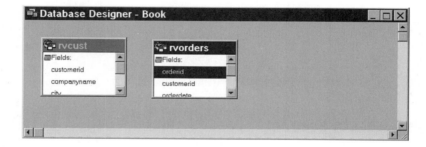

Now we are going to create a local view that joins the two remote views. To do so, right-click the Database Designer, and select New Local View. When the Add Table or View dialog box appears, change the Select option from Tables to Views, as is done in Figure 8.12.

You see the views that are in the database in the list. Select rvcust by double-clicking it; then select rvorders the same way. After you select the two views, choose Close to close the dialog box. Figure 8.13 shows the Join Condition dialog box, which you will see next.

Notice that the dialog box contains a default join condition that is based on the customerid field in rvcust_b being joined to the customerid field in rvorders. Where did Visual FoxPro come up with this? VFP makes this assumption because the two fields share the same name and data type. Because these views get their data from outside Visual FoxPro, they have no persistent relations that VFP can use to determine a default join condition. Accept the join shown, and click OK.

FIGURE 8.12
The Add Table or View dialog box with the Views option selected.

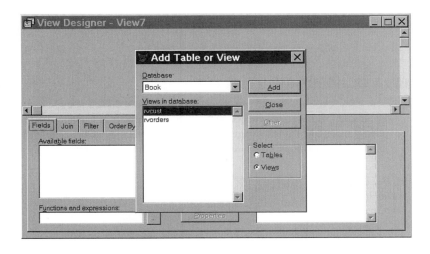

FIGURE 8.13
The Join Condition dialog box with the join condition for the two remote views.

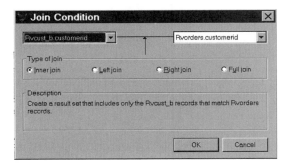

Now simply do the same things you would for any other local view. Select fields, filter conditions, group by conditions, and order by conditions.

To see the results of the local view, right-click it and select Browse. Figure 8.14 shows the browse that we saw.

FIGURE 8.14
The browse of our local view.

Companyname	Country	Orderid	Orderdate	Requireddate	Shippeddate
Vins et alcools Chevalier	France	10248	07/01/93 12:00:00 AM	07/29/93 12:00:00 AM	07/13/93 12:00:00 AM
Toms Spezialitäten	Germany	10249	07/02/93 12:00:00 AM	08/13/93 12:00:00 AM	07/07/93 12:00:00 AM
Hanari Carnes	Brazil	10250	07/05/93 12:00:00 AM	08/02/93 12:00:00 AM	07/09/93 12:00:00 AM
Victuailles en stock	France	10251	07/05/93 12:00:00 AM	08/02/93 12:00:00 AM	07/12/93 12:00:00 AM
Suprêmes délices	Belgium	10252	07/06/93 12:00:00 AM	08/03/93 12:00:00 AM	07/08/93 12:00:00 AM
Hanari Carnes	Brazil	10253	07/07/93 12:00:00 AM	07/21/93 12:00:00 AM	07/13/93 12:00:00 AM
Chop-suey Chinese	Switzerland	10254	07/08/93 12:00:00 AM	08/05/93 12:00:00 AM	07/20/93 12:00:00 AM
Richter Supermarkt	Switzerland	10255	07/09/93 12:00:00 AM	08/06/93 12:00:00 AM	07/12/93 12:00:00 AM
Wellington Importadora	Brazil	10256	07/12/93 12:00:00 AM	08/09/93 12:00:00 AM	07/14/93 12:00:00 AM
HILARIÓN-Abastos	Venezuela	10257	07/13/93 12:00:00 AM	08/10/93 12:00:00 AM	07/19/93 12:00:00 AM
Ernst Handel	Austria	10258	07/14/93 12:00:00 AM	08/11/93 12:00:00 AM	07/20/93 12:00:00 AM
Centro comercial Moctezuma	Mexico	10259	07/15/93 12:00:00 AM	08/12/93 12:00:00 AM	07/22/93 12:00:00 AM
Ottilies Käseladen	Germany	10260	07/16/93 12:00:00 AM	08/13/93 12:00:00 AM	07/26/93 12:00:00 AM
Que Delícia	Brazil	10261	07/16/93 12:00:00 AM	08/13/93 12:00:00 AM	07/22/93 12:00:00 AM
Rattlesnake Canyon Grocery	USA	10262	07/19/93 12:00:00 AM	08/16/93 12:00:00 AM	07/22/93 12:00:00 AM

As we just joined data from two remote views into a local view, you can also join data from a remote view and a local view or even from a remote view and a local table. These joins can be done in local views as long as the proper relationships exist in the data.

Using a Connection

The next method you will see for accessing remote data is using a connection. A *connection* is a predefined remote data source that has been stored in a Visual FoxPro database. You create connections by using the Connections option on the database shortcut menu (as shown earlier in Figure 8.8). Choosing this option brings up the dialog box in Figure 8.15.

FIGURE 8.15

The Visual FoxPro Connections dialog box used to select a connection for a remote view.

In this dialog box, you should select New to access a dialog box like the one in Figure 8.16.

FIGURE 8.16

The Visual FoxPro Connection Designer.

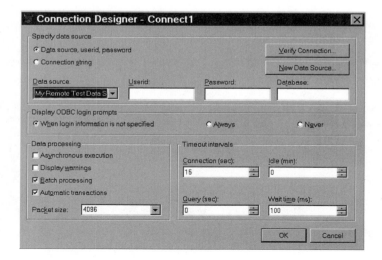

The first area to investigate in the Connection Designer is in the upper-left corner directly under Specify Data Source. There, you'll find two option buttons: Data Source, Userid, Password and Connection String. These options will control how you go about defining the connection. First, we will use the Data Source, Userid, Password option.

With this method, the next thing you need to do is select a data source from the Data Source combo box below the option buttons. The data sources listed in that combo box are those that have previously been set up using the ODBC Administrator described earlier in this chapter.

If you change the Specify Data Source option to Connection String, the set of text boxes for Data Source, Userid, Password, and Database are replaced with one large text box. In the large text box, you type the connection string exactly as it should be sent to the database server you are going to connect to.

The three text boxes beside the Data Source combo box are used to enter a user ID, password, and the name of the database you want to use, respectively. Some remote data sources require that a login is accomplished before the data can be accessed. In these cases, the user ID and password are used to log in to the database server. The values you use here, in the Connection Designer, will be given to you by the database administrator in charge of your database software. Both the user ID and the password can be supplied at a later time when you try to use the connection.

Just below the data source information is a section titled Display ODBC Login Prompts. There, you'll find three choices: When Login Information Is Not Specified, Always, and Never. These options correspond to showing the login dialog box from ODBC when the connection did not specify a user ID and password, always showing the login dialog box, and never showing the login dialog box. The option you choose here depends on the design of your data access for your application.

Some applications are designed with a user ID and password for the application set up in the database server. In these applications, you should probably choose Never, as you would supply the user ID and password in the connection definition.

In other designs, each user of the system might have his or her own user ID and password within the database server. In these cases, you might or might not want the login dialog boxes to appear, depending on whether you are storing the user IDs and passwords and supplying them at the time you connect to the server.

You might want to use the first option to handle situations in which your system doesn't have login information for a user. The first option will display the login dialog box if, and only if, you don't supply the user ID and password when you try to connect.

Table 8.1 describes the options available to you in the Data Processing section in the lower left of the Connection Designer dialog box.

Table 8.1   The Data Processing Options of the Connection Designer

Option	Description
Asynchronous Execution	Enables the data for this connection to be fetched in the background. This setting can be very valuable when a remote view might need to fetch a large number of records from the data source and you want your application to continue while the fetching goes on in the background. Unchecking this option will cause any remote view to completely get all its data before your application code will continue.
Display Warnings	Determines whether ODBC warning dialog boxes will be displayed when using this connection. You would set this option off if you are using error handling in your application to deal with the warning conditions that might arise during a remote connection.
Batch Processing	Determines if the view will return all records together or if it will receive records a few at a time. With Batch Processing on, your view will not get any records until the data source has finished processing your SELECT command and is ready to send you all the records. Turning Batch mode off will allow the data source to return partial results as it gets them ready for you.
Automatic Transactions	Turns on or off automatic transactions. Some database servers can use automatic transactions when processing table updates, deletes, and inserts. If you are connecting to a data source that can use automatic transactions, this option either turns them on or off. You will most likely want this option turned on unless you are using SQL Pass Through and not remote views. (SQL Pass Through is discussed later in this chapter.)
Packet Size	Controls the size of the data packets sent back and forth on the connection. You can use this setting to optimize the connection for performance based on the probable size of the various queries that might hit the connection. Increasing the packet size will cause more data to be sent in each packet. Decreasing it will reduce the packet size. What size is best depends on a number of issues—among them, what is the average size of a record or set of records being retrieved over this connection. If the data size is large, then increase the packet size so the connection uses fewer packets. If the data size is small, then reduce the packet size so the connection uses the bandwidth of the network more efficiently.

The last set of options in the Connection Designer consists of the Timeout Intervals in the lower-right corner of the dialog box. Table 8.2 describes these options.

Table 8.2   The Timeout Intervals in the Connection Designer

Option	Description
Connection (sec):	The time in seconds before Visual FoxPro will report a connection timeout error.
Idle (min):	The Idle timeout period in minutes after which Visual FoxPro will break the connection. The connection is not broken if the connection is in manual transaction mode and a transaction is in process.
Query (sec):	The time to wait, in seconds, before reporting a general timeout error.
Wait Time (ms):	The time, in milliseconds, that Visual FoxPro will wait before checking to see whether the SQL statement has completed.

By setting all these options, you can customize the connection that will be used for your remote views. After you have completed these settings, you can click OK. In the next dialog box you see, you can give the connection a name. We named ours MyTest.

If you now right-click the Database Designer and select New Remote View, you will see that your connection is listed in the Select Connection or Data Source dialog box. You can select the connection and then go on to the View Designer to define the view.

When you use one of these remote views, Visual FoxPro will make a connection through ODBC to the database server's ODBC driver and execute the SELECT statement defined by the view. The data retrieved will be in a Visual FoxPro cursor, and you can work with the contents of that cursor as you choose.

Remote views are capable of everything that local views are. You can update them, you can use the Top-N features, and so on.

In the next section, you will see how you can directly manage everything that is going on with remote data access by using SQL Pass Through.

Using SQL Pass Through Functions

In Visual FoxPro, *SQL Pass Through* is a set of functions that allow you to send commands directly through ODBC. The code in Listing 8.1, which comes from the program SQLPT.prg, uses SQL Pass Through to access the data source you saw earlier in this chapter.

Listing 8.1 08CODE01—Using SQL Pass Through to Access the My Remote Test Data Source

```
LOCAL lnHandle
lnHandle = SQLConnect("My remote test")
IF lnHandle > -1
    SQLExec(lnHandle,"SELECT * FROM Customers","Results")
    SELECT Results
    BROWSE
    SQLDisconnect(lnHandle)
ENDIF
```

In Listing 8.1, you can see the use of the SQLConnect() function to establish a link to the data source. The handle to this connection is saved in the variable lnHandle. The IF checks to see whether the connection was successful. If the handle is a negative number, it indicates that the connection was not successful.

If the connection was successful, the SQLExec() function is used to pass a SELECT statement to the data source, and the results of that SELECT are stored in a cursor named Results. Finally, the Results cursor is selected and browsed. When the browse is closed, the SQLDisconnect() is issued to drop the connection to the data source.

In Listing 8.1, you see three SQL Pass Through functions being used: SQLConnect(), SQLExec(), and SQLDisconnect(). Many more SQL Pass Through functions than these three are available. For example, the SQLStringConnect() function uses a connection string rather than a data source. Table 8.3 lists all the SQL Pass Through functions and describes their use.

Table 8.3 The SQL Pass Through Functions

Function	Description
SQLConnect()	Creates a connection to an ODBC data source. Takes one or three arguments. If using a connection stored in the current Visual FoxPro database, a single argument of the connection name can be used. When not using a connection name, the three arguments are the Data source name, the user ID, and the password. SQLConnect returns a connection handle or -2 to indicate that the connection was unsuccessful.
SQLStringConnect()	Similar to SQLConnect(), but it uses a single argument of a connection string. Like SQLConnect, it returns a connection handle or -2 for failure.
SQLDisconnect()	Accepts a single argument of the connection handle to disconnect. Shuts down a connection. Returns 1 if successful, -1 if an error occurred with the connection, and -2 if an error occurred with an environment error. SQLDisconnect will cause an error if you try to disconnect from a connection that has a transaction in process.

Function	Description
SQLCancel()	Requests cancellation of an executing SQL command. Return types are the same as SQLDisconnect. The single argument is the handle for the connection to cancel.
SQLExec()	Sends a SQL command to the data source for the connection. Takes three arguments: the first is the connection handle, the second is the command to be executed, and the third is the name of the Visual FoxPro cursor to hold the results. The return value is 1 for a successful execution and -1 if an error occurred.
SQLMoreResults()	Returns more results from a command executed with SQLExec() when in non-batch mode. This function accepts the connection handle as an argument and returns 0 if the command is still executing, 1 if the command is finished executing, and 2 if it finds no more results sets to get. A return of -1 indicates an error on the connection, and -2 indicates an error in the environment.
SQLPrepare()	Prepares a SQL command for execution with SQLExec(). SQLPrepare() takes three arguments: the connection handle, the SQL command to prepare, and the name for the results cursor. This function can be used to prepare a parameterized view in the data source. All parameters must exist before issuing the SQLPrepare() function call. To use the prepared command, issue the SQLExec() and supply only the connection handle.
SQLCommit()	Commits a transaction on the data source. Takes one argument of the connection handle. Returns 1 if the commit was successful and returns -1 if an error occurred. You can use AERROR() to get information about the error that occurred.
SQLRollback()	Cancels a transaction in the data source. Takes the same argument and returns the same values as SQLCommit().
SQLColumns()	Stores the field names in a Visual FoxPro cursor. Takes three arguments: the connection handle, the table name from which to return fields, and either FOXPRO or NATIVE to specify the format of the field information. FOXPRO is the default format. The resulting cursor has four fields in it for Field_Name, Field_Type, Field_Len, and Field_Dec. When you're using the NATIVE format, the fields of the cursor will vary depending on the data source for the connection. Returns 1 when finished successfully, 0 while still executing, -1 for a connection error, and -2 for an environment error. Consider this example: SQLTables(lnHandle, "'VIEW', 'SYSTEM TABLE'", "Results"). In this example, we are getting a list of all Views and System Tables from the data source.
SQLGetProp()	Takes two arguments: the connection handle and the setting you want returned. Used to read the properties of the remote connection.

continues

Table 8.3 Continued	
Function	**Description**
SQLSetProp()	Takes three arguments: the connection handle, the setting you want to change, and the new value for the setting. The settings that can be changed using SQLSetProp() are listed in the Visual FoxPro help file.

The big question you should be asking now is, "When should I use SQL Pass Through instead of remote views?" In answering this question, you need to know about the data source and its capabilities and the way in which you plan to use the data from that source.

The advantages of SQL Pass Through are as follows:

- A remote view is limited to only the SQL SELECT command, whereas SQL Pass Through can pass any valid command to the data source, allowing you to take advantage of the features of the data source.

- A remote view fetches only one result set, whereas SQL Pass Through can fetch multiple result sets.

- With remote views, you cannot access the transaction handling features of the data source, whereas with SQL Pass Through, the transaction handling is available if the data source supports it.

The disadvantages of SQL Pass Through are as follows:

- SQL Pass Through result cursors are not updateable by nature. You can set them to be updateable by using the SQLSetProp() function after the cursor exists. With remote views, you set the updateable properties when you design the view.

- With SQL Pass Through, you have no way of using the visual View Designer; you must write the SQL commands in program code.

- You create the connection to the data source, and you must manage that connection in your program code.

Based on the advantages and disadvantages of SQL Pass Through, you should be prepared to decide when to use the technology and when to use remote views. Although SQL Pass Through gives you more complete control over the access of data in a remote data source, it also requires that you manage the connections.

When comparing SQL Pass Through to an equivalent remote view, you will find no noticeable difference in speed. In fact, Microsoft has said that remote views might be the faster of the two approaches in most cases. However, using the SQLPrepare() function to establish a remote parameterized view that is precompiled on the server can cause a performance improvement with SQL Pass Through.

SQL Pass Through also enables you to take advantage of certain features of the data server that remote views cannot access. They include data definition, administration of the server, and other features that are unique to the particular data server you are connecting to.

Using DCOM

DCOM is an acronym for *Distributed Component Object Model*. DCOM is the Microsoft technology that enables you to create an object that is running on another machine as an ActiveX, or COM, object and then access the properties and methods of that object.

ADO Versus RDO

COM, which is an acronym for *Component Object Model,* is the predecessor of DCOM. COM objects are created on the same machine that uses them, whereas DCOM objects might be created on a different machine.

The data access technologies that COM and DCOM use are named Active Data Object (ADO) and Remote Data Object (RDO), respectively. RDO, which is an expansion of ADO, enables access to data that is stored on another machine. Both ADO and RDO can be used in Visual FoxPro 6 for accessing data.

In this section, we will build a form that uses RDO to access the data in our My Remote Test data source. To the form, we add a property named oRDS to hold an object reference to the RDO. We also add properties for Company and Contact with assign methods. Listing 8.2 shows the form's Init event.

Listing 8.2 08CODE02—The Form's Init Method Code

```
This.oRDS = CreateObject("RDS.DataControl")
If Type("This.oRDS") <> "O"
    MessageBox("oRDS not created")
Else
    With This.oRDS
        .Connect = "dsn=My Remote Test"
        .SQL = "Select * from customers"
        .ExecuteOptions = 1
        .FetchOptions = 2
        .Refresh
    EndWith
    This.ShowValues()
EndIf
```

This code starts by creating an instance of the RDS.DataControl class, which is the class for Remote Data Sets. The IF checks to see whether the RDS was successfully created. If it was, then the code in the ELSE is executed.

The ELSE code sets some properties of the RDS object. The properties being set are Connect, which stores the name of the data source to connect to; SQL, which holds the SELECT command to be run; ExecuteOptions, which controls how the SQL results will be processed; and FetchOptions, which controls the fetching method used. All these properties are described later in this section.

Notice the call to the form's ShowValues method. The ShowValues method was added to the form, and the code for it is shown in Listing 8.3.

Listing 8.3 08CODE03—The Form's ShowValues Method Code

```
With This
    .txtCompany.Value = ;
    .oRDS.Recordset.Fields("CompanyName").Value
    .txtContact.Value = ;
    .oRDS.Recordset.Fields("ContactName").Value
EndWith
This.Refresh
```

This method requests data from the RDS by referring to its Recordset.Fields(#).Value property and storing the fields value in the Value property of the text boxes. We are only using two of the fields in the recordset: CompanyName and ContactName.

The Company property of the form is used to set the CompanyName for the current record in the RDS record set. The assign method for the Company property is shown in Listing 8.4.

Listing 8.4 08CODE04—The Company_assign Method Code

```
LPARAMETERS vNewVal
*To do: Modify this routine for the Assign method
THIS.COMPANY = m.vNewVal
This.oRDS.Recordset.Fields("CompanyName").Value = ALLTRIM(vNewVal)
```

You can see that the code here is storing the value to the Company property of the form and updating the RDS CompanyName field with the value as well. The RDS field is updated by referring to the Recordset.Fields("CompanyName").Value property.

The navigation buttons in the form have code in them to tell the RDS to go to a new record. Listing 8.5 shows the code from the Next button's Click event.

Listing 8.5 08CODE05—The Next Button's Click Event Code

```
ThisForm.oRDS.RecordSet.MoveNext
If ThisForm.oRDS.RecordSet.Eof
    ThisForm.oRDS.RecordSet.MoveLast
EndIf
ThisForm.ShowValues
```

This code calls the RDS RecordSet.MoveNext method and then checks to see whether the end of file was encountered. If end of file was encountered, it moves to the last record. The code finishes by calling the form's ShowValues method, just like before. The code in the other navigation buttons is similar except for the record movement itself.

The Save button has one line of code in it:

```
ThisForm.oRDS.SubmitChanges()
```

This line calls the RDS `SubmitChanges()` method, which submits the changes to the data source.

To better understand the power of RDO, review Table 8.4 to learn the RDS properties and Table 8.5 to learn the RDS methods.

Table 8.4   The RDS Properties

Property	Description
Connect	Connects to a data source. Takes three arguments: data source name, user ID, and user password.
ExecuteOptions	Sets the synchronous or asynchronous mode for executing the SELECT command. A value of 1 is synchronous, and a value of 2 is asynchronous.
FetchOptions	Sets the type of asynchronous fetching. Accepts three values: 1 to fetch up front, 2 to fetch in the background, and 3 to fetch asynchronously.
FilterColumn	Sets or returns the column for the filter criterion. The actual criterion is specified in the FilterCriterion property.
FilterCriterion	Sets or returns the filter criterion as a string. The values available are <, <=, >, >=, =, and <>.
FilterValue	Sets or returns the filter string. Holds the value with which to apply FilterCriterion.
InternetTimeout	Sets the number of milliseconds to wait before timing out a request.
ReadyState	Represents the progress of RDS.DataControl as it fetches its results. Can be one of three values: 2, the query is still loaded and no records have been fetched; 3, the initial set of rows has been fetched, and the remaining rows are still being fetched; or 4, all rows have been fetched.
RecordSet and SourceRecordSet	Sets the RecordSet returned by the SQL SELECT command. You can manipulate the data in the recordset by manipulating the RecordSet property of the RDS.
Server	Sets or returns the Internet Information Server name and protocol for the data source.

continues

Table 8.4   Continued

Property	Description
SortColumn	Sets or returns the column used for sorting the records in the recordset.
SortDirection	Sets or returns a logical value of .T. for ascending sort or .F. for descending sort.
SQL	Sets or returns the SQL SELECT command used to retrieve the recordset.
URL	Sets or returns the location of a file that stores the persistent or saved recordset.

Table 8.5 contains the methods of the RDS.DataControl.

Table 8.5   The Methods of the RDS.DataControl

Method	Description
Cancel	Cancels the currently running asynchronous fetch.
CancelUpdate	Cancels all updates made to the recordset, restoring the recordset to its state at the last refresh.
CreateRecordSet	Creates an empty recordset.
MoveFirst	Moves to the first record in the current recordset.
MoveLast	Moves to the last record in the current recordset.
MoveNext	Moves to the next record in the current recordset.
MovePrevious	Moves to the previous record in the current recordset.
Refresh	Requeries the record source and updates the recordset.
Reset	Executes the filter and sort criteria for the recordset on the client side. Takes one argument of logical: .T. uses the current filtered rowset; and .F. uses the original rowset, discarding any previous filter options.
SubmitChanges	Updates the data source from the current cached recordset.

Using these properties and methods, you can manage the data returned in an RDS.DataControl.

User Interface Concerns with Remote Data

Any discussion would be incomplete if we were to describe remote data access and not describe the impact remote data access has on user interface design. The issue in user interface design related to remote data access is that a remote data source might have a very large number of records in it.

Imagine a Microsoft SQL Server database that has 10,000,000 customer records in it. Retrieving all the customer records with remote data access is not practical or desirable. Instead, your user interface should provide a method for the users to specify which customer records they want and then only get that number of records from the data source.

This type of interface design precludes this old style:

```
USE Customer
BROWSE
```

Instead, you need to provide controls for the users to specify criteria for selecting the customer records desired and then use a parameterized remote view or an RDS.DataControl with a filtered SELECT statement to retrieve the records. ●

Creating a Graphical User Interface

Creating Forms

Anatomy of a Form

Nearly every application or user utility that you write in Visual FoxPro will include at least one form (and probably quite a few). Forms are the powerful descendants of pre-Visual FoxPro screens, and they serve as the primary points of user interaction with both the underlying data and business logic in most applications. The days of simple, two-dimensional, programmer-directed dialog boxes are over. User expectations have changed dramatically in recent years, and odds are you'll be expected to provide your customers with event-driven, user-controllable, Windows-standard graphical user interfaces (GUIs). The most thorough database design and most powerful programming paradigm in the world probably won't stand a chance of winning over clients if the application interface consists of white-on-blue modal screens in a Courier 12 font. Luckily, Visual FoxPro 6 includes a powerful and flexible Form Designer to assist developers in the creation of slick, flexible, fully object-oriented forms for any size application. And, as you'll see, creating and maintaining forms can be remarkably simple and straightforward.

The Visual FoxPro *form* is a container class, capable of holding any number of other controls or containers such as text boxes, command buttons, check boxes, pageframes, or grids. Because the form is simply a specialized container class, it supports every aspect of Visual FoxPro's powerful and thorough object-oriented programming paradigm. Forms have over 100 base properties and 60 base methods and support the addition of an unlimited number of user-defined properties or methods to augment their functionality. Forms can be inherited from specialized form subclasses or can serve as a superclass of other forms. In fact, you'll find only two major differences between forms and most other container classes: Forms can assume their own visual presence on the user desktop, and forms (like toolbars) can draw their information from a private data session.

Despite all this power, basic forms are remarkably easy to create, edit, and run. Figure 9.1 shows a basic sample form, consisting of two general sets of visual components:

- The form itself
- Controls on the form

FIGURE 9.1

A basic form presents information in an easy-to-read manner.

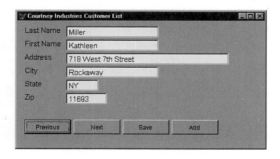

The form itself consists of the background, on which most of the functional contents of the form will sit. I say "most" because it is important to remember that the form itself responds to a set of Windows events: mouse clicks, activation, resizing, and moving. But, in most cases, the core user functionality will be provided by the controls within forms. Back in FoxPro 2.6 and earlier versions, controls were placed within user-defined windows with @SAY and GET style commands and were generally quite limited in their capability to respond to user events. Starting with Version 3, Visual FoxPro extended its set of native controls and even allowed support for ActiveX components. Table 9.1 includes a listing of native Visual FoxPro controls that are used in forms, along with brief descriptions.

Table 9.1   Visual FoxPro Form Controls

Control Name	Description
Check box	A control that shows an On/Off state.
Combo box	A control that presents a list. Only the currently selected value is shown, but the rest of the list can be expanded by the user.
Command button	A button that the user can click to make something happen.
Command button group	A group of command buttons that work together.
Edit box	A box that enables the user to enter long strings of information.
Grid	A control that browses a table on a form.
Image	A control that shows a picture on a form.
Label	A control that displays text.
Line	A line drawn on a form.
List box	A box that shows a list of items.
OLE bound control	A control that has as its source a general field in a table.
OLE container control	A control for OLE objects and controls.
Option group	A series of options, from which the user can select only one.
Page frame	A control that enables the user to pick one of some number of tabs, each of which has a different set of controls.
Shape	A drawn shape.
Spinner	A combination of a text box and up and down controls, enabling the user to increment numeric data.
Text box	A control that enables the user to enter information, usually to be saved to a character, numeric, or date field.
Timer	A control that runs a command or series of commands at predetermined intervals.

NOTE Forms are stored in .SCX and .SCT files, which are identical in structure to the class library's .VCX and .VCT files. A form, in fact, is simply a class library with only one class—the form itself. And, unlike its pre-Visual FoxPro cousin, the screen, the form doesn't need to be generated into code in order to be run. A form is a full-fledged Visual FoxPro object. ▪

Creating Forms

The simplest and most common way to create a form is with one of the following commands:

CREATE FORM *file name*

or

CREATE FORM *file name* AS *superclass name* FROM *base library name*

However, you can use one of several additional ways to create a form in Visual FoxPro. Here are just a few:

- Select File, New, Form from the system menu.
- Enter the command MODIFY FORM *formname*, or enter MODIFY FORM followed by an entry in the File, Open dialog box.
- Select the New button from the toolbar, and select Form in the resulting dialog box.
- Select the Docs tab of the Project Manager, click on Forms, and select New (you will be asked whether you want to use a Form Wizard or go right to creating a new form).
- Use the Component Gallery or the Class Browser.
- Enter the command

  MyForm = CREATEOBJECT(<form subclass name or "Form" for base class>)

  followed by

  MODIFY FORM "MyForm"

- Use one of the Visual FoxPro Form Wizards or a developer-defined Form Wizard.

The approach you use for creating new forms will depend on your own personal preference, as well as that of your fellow developers if you work in a team programming environment. You will examine the Form Wizard in the section titled "Using Form Wizards and Builders" later in this chapter. In the meantime, let's explore Visual FoxPro's Form Designer.

TIP Many of the approaches specified use the default setting to determine the class on which the form should be based. If you do not want to use the Visual FoxPro base class, you will need to set your default by first choosing Tools, Options. Click on the Forms tab, and then check the Form check box in the Template classes area. You will be prompted to select your preferred template class. You can change this setting at any time by returning to this screen and clicking the ellipsis next to the filename (see Figure 9.2).

FIGURE 9.2
You can set the form template class through the Forms tab of the Options dialog box.

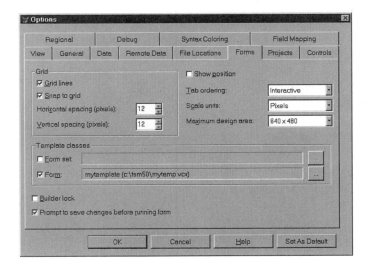

Working in the Form Designer

After you have created a new form, FoxPro will launch the Form Designer (see Figure 9.3). The most crucial elements of the Form Designer are the Form Canvas, the visual representation of the form container; the Properties Window, which shows all available property, event, and method (PEM) settings for the form and its controls; and the Form Controls toolbar, which makes available various controls that can be dropped onto the canvas. Each of these elements is covered in greater detail in this section. However, note that you can also add the following windows and toolbars to the Form Designer to assist in your design and development:

- The Color Palette toolbar—This toolbar enables you to easily set the colors on a form and any of its controls.

- The Layout toolbar—This toolbar provides the tools for properly aligning and sizing controls on the form, modifying the relative stacking order of overlapping objects, and resizing controls. (You can find more details about this toolbar in the section "Aligning Controls" later in this chapter.)

- The Form Designer toolbar—This toolbar operates at the control center, or meta-toolbar, and dictates which other Form Designer bars are shown. You can also control which toolbars are shown by selecting them from the View menu or by double-clicking their close boxes to release them.

- The Data Environment window—This window shows the specified elements of the Form's Data Environment. (You can find more details about this subject in the section titled "Setting the Form's Data Environment" later in this chapter.)

- The Code window—This window shows the code that has been added to any of the methods of the form or its controls.

FIGURE 9.3

Using the Form Designer, you can specify the placement of information, text, and graphics on your form.

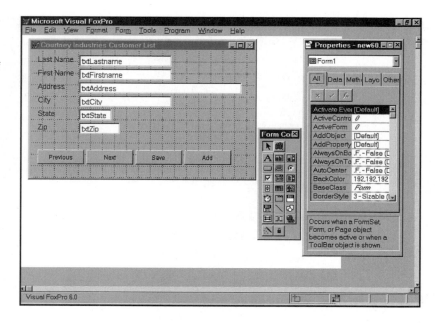

 T I P   Because the Form Designer enables you to view so many different components at once, you might want to consider increasing your resolution to maximize the available area. You will be shocked how much more screen real estate you gain by switching from 640×480, or even 800×600, to a 1024×768 resolution. And, luckily, FoxPro includes the capability to define the resolution for which you are developing, so you can see how much "real" space you have for your lower-resolution viewers (refer to Figure 9.2). One point of caution, however: When Visual FoxPro determines lower-resolution borders, it does not take into account any toolbars a user might have docked along some edge of the screen. Always leave a suitable margin, and if necessary, during your final screen testing, change your monitor's resolution to the desired settings to be sure that everything fits as you expected.

N O T E   Because forms are actually classes, you might not be surprised to learn that the Form Designer and Class Designer are quite similar. You cannot modify forms in the Class Designer, though you can view and modify forms through the Class Browser. See Chapters 15, "Creating Classes with Visual FoxPro," and 16, "Managing Classes with Visual FoxPro," for more information on using the Class Designer and Class Browser. ▪

Adding Controls to a Form

You can add controls to a form by clicking on the desired control and then clicking on the spot on the form canvas where you want the control to reside (more specifically, click the spot where you want the top-left corner of the control to start). Visual FoxPro gives the control a default size, which you can then change by clicking on one of the corner or side placeholders and dragging to the desired boundary. Or, if you prefer to add a control and resize it in one step, you can vary these steps slightly. Click on the control you want, as usual, but instead of clicking on the form canvas, drag the mouse to create a dotted area of the desired size. Then release the mouse button to drop the resized control into this area.

The Form Controls Toolbar

Figure 9.4 shows the Form Controls toolbar, which, like the Control Palette toolbar, consists of several sections. The top two buttons are not controls, but instead are tools to control the settings for the rest of the toolbar.

FIGURE 9.4

Using the Form Controls toolbar, you can include various types of form controls on your report.

The Select Objects Button   The Select Objects button (with the arrow icon), at the top left of the Form Controls toolbar, indicates whether a control is currently selected and ready to be dropped. If no control is selected, the arrow button is in the down, or on, position, indicating that your mouse serves as a pointer on the form canvas. After you select a control, and while you are still deciding where to drop the control, the arrow button is in the up, or off, position. This position indicates that the mouse is currently in the drop-control mode. If you decide you don't want to drop a control you have just selected, click on the arrow button to end the process and restore your mouse to a pointing device.

The View Classes Button   The View Classes button (with the bookshelf/library icon), at the top right of the Form Controls toolbar, enables you to toggle among any number of class libraries. The currently selected class library determines which controls are shown in the middle section of the toolbar. Three options are always available when you click on this button. Standard includes applicable controls from the FoxPro base classes, Active X includes Visual FoxPro's default Active X controls (such as the calendar control and the Microsoft progress bar), and Add enables you to add additional class libraries to the list. You can also add libraries to the list and assign your own names to them by selecting Tools, Options and clicking the Controls tab.

Available Controls   The middle section of the Form Controls toolbar includes all available classes from the currently selected class library. The controls show up under the icons assigned to them by Visual FoxPro (or by the developer during class design of a specialized control). The standard buttons (in the order they are shown in Figure 9.4) are as shown in Table 9.2.

Table 9.2   Form Control Toolbar Buttons

Label	Text Box	Edit Box
Command Button	Command Group	Option Group
Check Box	Combo Box	List Box
Spinner	Grid	Image
Timer	Page Frame	OLE Container Control
OLE Bound Control	Line	Shape
Separator		

The Builder Lock   The Builder Lock button (with the wand icon), at the bottom of the Form Controls toolbar, controls whether adding a control should automatically launch an associated builder. You can always call any available builders after dropping a control by right-clicking and selecting Builder. The Builder Lock simply makes this a one-step process. (You'll find more details on builders in the section titled "Using Form Wizards and Builders.")

The Button Lock   The default Visual FoxPro behavior is to enable you to choose and drop one instance of a control at a time. When the Button Lock button (with the padlock icon) is set on, you can click and add any number of the same controls to a form without having to return to the Form Controls Toolbar and click the control again. This capability can prove useful when you know you need 10 text boxes on a form; unfortunately, it can also prove quite irritating when you accidentally drop 17 pageframes onto the same form.

Working with Properties, Events, and Methods

Table Part 4 discusses Visual FoxPro's properties, events, and methods (PEM) model in some detail, but to take full advantage of the Form Designer, you need to have some understanding of these concepts. What follows is a brief discussion of objects, properties, events, and methods as they apply to form design.

A form, as I've mentioned, is a container object; it is a visible window that holds other controls. The form, like any object, is a distinct unit with attributes and behaviors—that is, with properties, events, and methods. The different objects available in Visual FoxPro have a range of properties, events, and methods. Some of them are particular to one type of object, some are available for many objects, and others are available to all types of objects. Table 9.3 presents the behaviors that Microsoft considers the "core events" of Visual FoxPro.

Table 9.3   Core Object Events in Visual FoxPro

Name of Event	Executes When...
Init	An object is created.
Destroy	An object is released from memory.

Name of Event	Executes When...
Error	An error occurs in an event or method of the object.
Click	The user clicks the object using the primary mouse button.
DblClick	The user double-clicks the object using the primary mouse button.
RightClick	The user clicks the object using the secondary mouse button.
GotFocus	The object receives focus through a user-initiated event or through code.
LostFocus	The object loses focus through a user-initiated event or through code.
KeyPress	The user presses and releases any key.
MouseDown	The user presses a mouse button while the mouse pointer is over the object.
MouseMove	The user moves the mouse over the object.
MouseUp	The user releases a mouse button while the mouse pointer is over the object.
InteractiveChange	The value of the object is changed by the user.
ProgrammaticChange	The value of the object is changed in a program.

With a firm understanding of these core events, you'll be well on your way to designing fully object-oriented Visual FoxPro forms. Of course, most Visual FoxPro objects offer you greater flexibility through additional events and methods, but these core events will give you the running start you need to begin working with forms.

As you might suspect, Visual FoxPro also has a number of common properties (see Table 9.4). The supported values and default values will differ by the type of object you are modifying.

Table 9.4   Common Properties in Visual FoxPro

Property Name	Description
Alignment	Specifies how text is aligned in a control.
AutoSize	Specifies whether the control is automatically sized to fit its caption.
BackColor	Indicates the background color of an object.
BackStyle	Specifies whether the background of an object is opaque or transparent.
BorderColor	Specifies the color of the border around an object.

continues

Table 9.4   Continued

Property Name	Description
Caption	Specifies the text displayed within an object.
Comment	Provides a comment about the object. Visual FoxPro doesn't use this property; it is a freebie for developers, and might be used to describe to other programmers the purpose of the object.
ControlSource	Indicates the source for the control's value. Can be a field or a memory variable.
Enabled	Determines whether a control is enabled or disabled.
Height	Specifies the height of the object.
Left	Specifies the leftmost coordinate of the object.
Name	Indicates the name of the object. This value determines how the object will be referenced by other object's methods or external code.
Tag	Provides an extra base property to hold any additional information about the property. Can be used at developers' discretion.
ToolTipTest	Holds the text that will be shown as a Windows ToolTip when the mouse cursor hovers over an object. Note that ToolTips are shown only when the ShowTips property is set to .T..
Top	Specifies the top coordinate of the object, relative to the top of the form.
Value	Indicates the value for the control. If ControlSource is populated, these two properties are always equal.
Visible	Specifies whether an object can be seen by users.
Width	Specifies the width of an object.

Changing Form and Control Properties

You can edit the properties of a form or its controls via the Properties window, which is shown in Figure 9.5. You can access the Properties window by selecting View, Properties from the system menu, or right-clicking and selecting Properties from the shortcut menu.

The Properties window consists of two parts: the Controls section and the PEM section. The Controls section, at the top of the window, consists of several important elements. The Object drop-down shows objects on the form in a hierarchical format and enables you to toggle easily to the properties, events, and methods of a particular control. The push pin enables you to force the Properties window to remain on top of any windows or toolbars in the Form Designer. The Builder Button activates the Builder for the currently selected object. (You'll learn more about Builders in the section titled "Using Form Wizards and Builders.")

FIGURE 9.5

Using the Properties window, you can view and, in most cases, change the properties of a form or an embedded control.

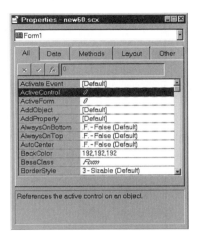

The PEM section lists the properties, events, and methods of the selected object and has five tabs: All, Data, Methods, Layout, and Other. Each tab includes only those properties, events, and methods that fall under the category specified in the heading. (As you might suspect, the All tab includes all properties, events, and methods.) Each of these tabs is reviewed in more detail later in this chapter.

Each tab consists of two columns: The left side (shown with a gray background) holds the name of the property, event, or method. The right side (in white) holds the value for properties, and the words Default or User Procedure for events and methods. Note that some properties, events, and methods are read-only during design time. They have values represented in *italic* text and, for properties, a disabled text box on the top of the tab.

Changing a Property

Generally speaking, changing a property is as simple as clicking the property and typing the value into the text box at the top of the tab. However, some native Visual FoxPro properties must evaluate to a particular data type, or a range of values. For instance, a logical property, such as the form's Visible setting, must be set to either .T. or .F. (and, in fact, double-clicking this property will toggle the value of such a property). Properties with a strict range of values, such as the form's WindowState property, can be entered using a combo box that will appear on top of the tab.

Does this mean that Visual FoxPro is now a strictly typed language? No, not really. You'll note that I specified that "some native Visual FoxPro properties" limit the user to a series of choices or a particular data type. User-defined properties and many native properties cannot be set up with such limitations. Keep in mind that the values for these less strictly typed properties can be entered as text (MyName), as a variable (=glMySetting), or as an expression (=3+4, or =MyFunction()). Expressions can be entered directly or can be created with some assistance from Visual FoxPro by clicking on the formula button on top of the Form Controls toolbar tab (the button marked `fx`). For user-defined properties, as well as some native properties, `.T.`, `.F.`, and `.NULL.` are acceptable entries. (These values must include periods on both sides to indicate to Visual FoxPro that you are referring to a value and not a variable.)

TIP You can enter a character value for, say, a label in the PEM window in several different ways. Any of the following entries will result in a label of `Last Name`:

`Last Name`	No quotation marks
`="Last Name"`	Quotation marks with an equal sign
`=FunctionCall()`	A function or procedure that is currently in scope and available
`= MyLabelVar`	A variable that is currently in scope

Many developers and programmers also choose to load the property value from the `Init()` event of the control or the form. This approach can make searching for values and debugging them easier, but remember that in version 6, it carries a small price: The property's associated `_Assign` method, if it exists, will fire. (For more details on the `_Assign` method, see the section "Access and Assign Methods" later in this chapter.)

Editing a Method

To edit the code behind a method, double-click the method name in the Properties window. When the Code window appears, you can type any code that should fire when the event occurs or the method is called. Note that you can also edit methods and events by choosing the desired object and method directly from the Code window; to do so, use the Object and Procedure pull-downs (see Figure 9.6).

FIGURE 9.6
You can select a method to edit by using the pull-downs in the Code window.

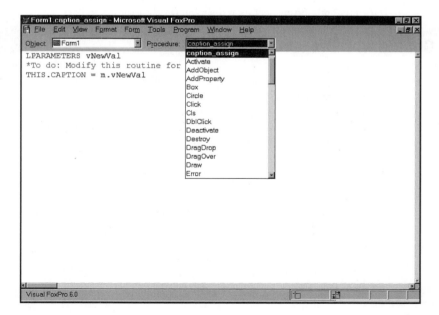

Default Values and Nondefault Values

After you've changed a property or a method from its default, it will appear in the Form Controls toolbar tab in **bold** type. To restore a property or a method to its default, right-click and select Reset To Default.

Suppose you change a label's `FontName` property from the Arial default to Courier, and then you change your mind and restore the property to Arial. You think it's once again set to the default, but the property value is still listed in bold. Manually resetting the original value is not the same as right-clicking and selecting Reset To Default.

Reset To Default tells FoxPro to once again accept the property's value from the object's parent. A manual resetting of `FontName` tells FoxPro that you want the Font property to be Arial, *even if the parent class `FontName` is one day set to, let's say, Times Roman.* Inheritance is discussed in greater detail in Part 4 of this book, but for now, remember that if you want to restore a property to the default value, the safest approach is right-clicking and selecting Reset to Default.

Part
III

Ch
9

PEM Tabs

The Properties window includes a pageframe that lets you limit the number of properties, events, and methods that you view at one time.

The All Tab   The All tab includes all PEM settings for the object specified, including user-defined properties and objects. Figure 9.7 shows the All tab for a form.

FIGURE 9.7
Using the All tab, you can view all properties, events, and methods.

The Data Tab   The Data tab shows only those properties related to the data for the control (see Figure 9.8). These properties vary according to the control being modified, but this tab might include the data control source, the control value, the input mask and format commands, and which columns of combo boxes or list boxes are bound to the underlying data. The form's Data tab includes information on the data session and buffering (see the section "Understanding Private Data Sessions" later in this chapter).

FIGURE 9.8

The Data tab shows all data-related properties.

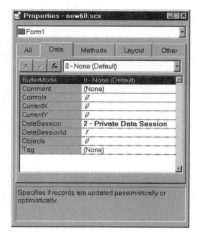

The Data tab also includes a control's `Tag` property and `Comment` property (where applicable), which serve as areas for the developer to include any additional data relating to the object that might need to be accessed. The developer can also add his or her own properties when designing a control subclass. The `Tag` and `Comment` properties have been included to provide at least one extra property on every single class, thereby adding a degree of flexibility to most controls, even those subclasses as high up in the class hierarchy as the FoxPro base classes.

The Methods Tab   The Methods tab shows all methods and events, including user-defined methods. Figure 9.9 shows the Methods tab for a form object.

FIGURE 9.9

The Methods tab shows all methods and events, but no properties.

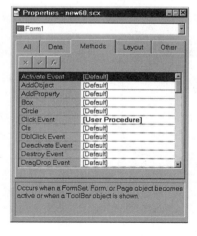

The Layout Tab   The Layout tab shows all the native Visual FoxPro properties related to the physical appearance of the object. Figure 9.10 shows the Layout tab for a form object.

FIGURE 9.10
The Layout tab shows properties related to a form or a control's layout.

The Other Tab   The Other tab shows all the native Visual FoxPro properties that do not fit logically into the Data or Layout categories. Figure 9.11 shows the Other tab for a form object.

FIGURE 9.11
The Other tab shows all miscellaneous properties.

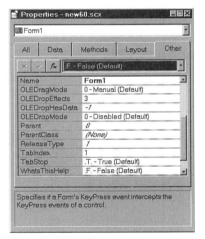

Coding with Properties, Events, and Methods

The sheer number of properties, events, and methods in Visual FoxPro might seem daunting to you, particularly when compared with software products with fewer PEM options. Don't feel overwhelmed just yet. You will soon find that the bulk of your coding will occur in a relatively small number of methods and that you will usually change only a limited number of properties.

TIP To find a property, event, or method in a Properties window list, you don't have to scroll through the entire list. If you know the name of the property you are looking for (or have an idea of the name), you can press Ctrl+Alt and the first letter of the name while the list has focus. The list will automatically reposition itself to the first property, event, or method starting with that letter. For example, to find the ControlSource property, press Ctrl+Alt+C when in either the All or Data tab, and the list will position to the first entry starting with the letter *C*.

Visual FoxPro's wide range of methods and properties allows for very precise fine-tuning (and in some cases, they have been retained for backward compatibility). Such flexibility has been a hallmark of FoxPro since its earliest incarnations, and Visual FoxPro's object model has greatly increased the number of available points of access and code execution. Enjoy the control you have as a programmer, and don't become overly entangled too quickly in the subtle differences between Valid, InteractiveChange, and LostFocus events. Use what you can (or what you already know), until you brush up against limitations and need to move on.

For instance, let's look for a moment at validation information entered in a text box. Pre-Visual FoxPro users will recognize the Valid event, but it has since been fully incorporated into the Visual FoxPro object-oriented model.

Validation of the data entered in a text box is accomplished by placing code in the Valid event. Figure 9.12 shows how to trap an invalid entry in a text box.

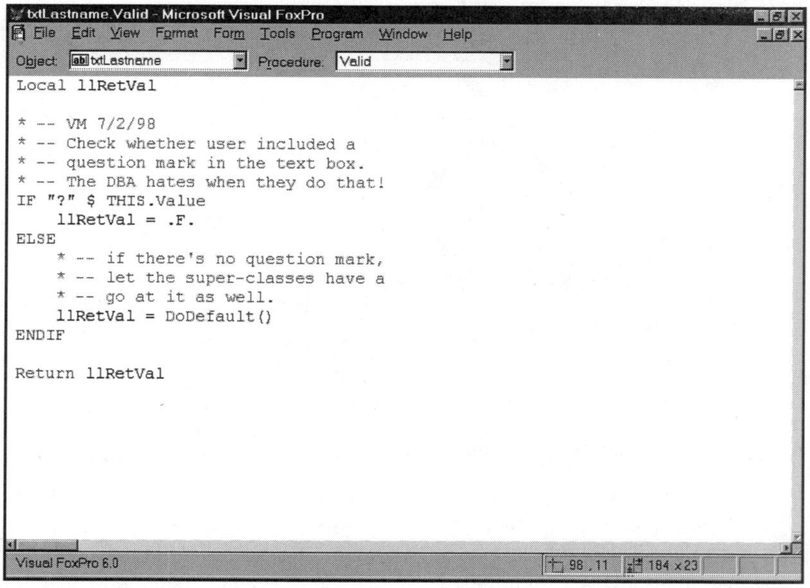

FIGURE 9.12

This example checks for invalid entry in a text box.

```
txtLastname.Valid - Microsoft Visual FoxPro
File   Edit   View   Format   Form   Tools   Program   Window   Help

Object   txtLastname          Procedure: Valid

Local llRetVal

* -- VM 7/2/98
* -- Check whether user included a
* -- question mark in the text box.
* -- The DBA hates when they do that!
IF "?" $ THIS.Value
    llRetVal = .F.
ELSE
    * -- if there's no question mark,
    * -- let the super-classes have a
    * -- go at it as well.
    llRetVal = DoDefault()
ENDIF

Return llRetVal



Visual FoxPro 6.0                                    98 . 11      184 x 23
```

You might notice that the Valid event contains no code for displaying an error message. The actual text to be returned goes in the text box's ErrorMessage method. This method is automatically triggered whenever the `Valid` method returns `False`. The code for `ErrorMessage` is shown in Figure 9.13.

FIGURE 9.13

You can specify a particular message to be shown when `Valid` returns `False` by including code in the object's `ErrorMessage` method.

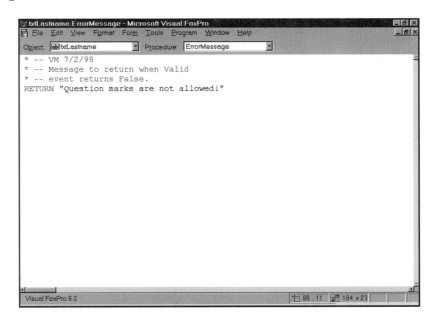

By the way, if you do not place code in the `ErrorMessage` method, the default error message of `Invalid Input` will appear (assuming that `Set Notify` is `On`).

Adding New Properties or Methods to a Form

To add a new property or method to a form, select Form, New Property or Form, New Method. A modal dialog box appears, into which you can enter the property or method name and description (optional), and click the Add button. The default value for a new property is a logical false (`.F.`). A new method defaults to an empty procedure; nothing will occur when this method is called until you actually add some code.

When you're adding a new property, you can tell Visual FoxPro to automatically create a new Access and/or Assign method corresponding to the new property (see Figure 9.14). You can also create an Access or Assign method at any time the same way as you would create any other new method. (For more details on Access and Assign methods, see the section titled "Access and Assign Methods.")

If you want to add a new array property, include array dimensions in the property name, even if you will later change these dimensions. Doing so automatically initializes the property as an array, which also makes the values read-only during development. You will need to write code (quite likely in your form's `Init` event) to fill this array property.

FIGURE 9.14

You can add new properties to a form.

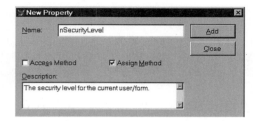

  Visual FoxPro assumes that you will want to add more than one property or method. In fact, after you have added a new property or method, Visual FoxPro keeps providing the same dialog box. To end this cycle and save the new properties or methods you have already added, just click Close or press Escape when you are shown the new dialog box.

Properties or methods added by the user appear in the Properties window in alphabetical order *after* all the native Visual FoxPro properties, events, and methods. User-defined property and method names always appear in lowercase (even hacking the underlying table doesn't help).

N O T E You cannot add new properties or methods to controls from the Form Designer. Instead, you must subclass the control and add your new class. (You'll find more details on subclassing in Part 4.) Remember, though, that every control has a Tag property that you can use. Think of it as a single-property freebie. ▪

Access and Assign Methods Beginning with version 6, Visual FoxPro's object model has been expanded through the addition of Access and Assign methods. These methods enable you to track every time a particular property is viewed, touched, or changed in any way. Let's say that your form includes a text box that is bound to a property on the form called .cLastName, and you want a certain action to occur whenever the property is changed. You can do just that by creating a method called cLastName_Assign. cLastName_Access would be even more thorough in its tracking; every time a piece of code "looked" at the property, this method would fire.

Confused yet? Don't be. You can accomplish a good deal of programming without ever using the Access or Assign methods. In fact, that's exactly what Visual FoxPro 5 developers have been doing all along! But if you do need greater protection against outside influence on your form, Visual FoxPro 6 now provides you with that flexibility.

Shortcut Options from the Properties Window

The Properties Window shortcut menu is among the most useful right-click menus in the entire product. Six options are available to you (seven if you count Help) and can prove quite useful when you're navigating the maze of properties, events, and methods (see Figure 9.15).

FIGURE 9.15

Using the Properties window shortcut options, you can easily take some common actions.

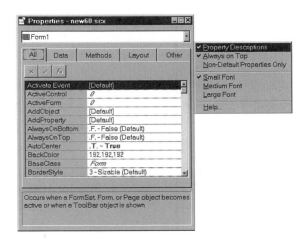

Property Descriptions   Property Descriptions, the first choice in this shortcut menu, indicates whether you want to view the property descriptions at the bottom of the window. Turning this feature off saves screen space, but turning it on can greatly ease development, especially if you are new to Visual FoxPro or if you are modifying a form originally designed by someone else (and containing a number of user-defined properties and methods).

Always on Top   Always on Top works just as it does throughout most of Visual FoxPro: Selecting this option guarantees that the Properties window will always be in the forefront of the screen while you are developing rather than lost beneath a maze of toolbars and other windows.

Non-Default Properties Only   Selecting Non-Default Properties Only limits what is shown in the Properties window to those properties and methods that have been changed for this form. This option can help you tell at a glance what has been changed on a given form, without fishing through the dozens of default PEM settings.

Font Settings   The Small Font, Medium Font, and Large Font selections enable you to choose the size of the font you want for the Properties window. The default is Small, and it's likely that you'll want to fit as many PEM settings as possible in the Properties window by keeping it that way. On a smaller monitor or a larger monitor with greater resolution, however, telling your MaxLeft from your MaxTop can be hard.

Working with Controls on a Form

Visual FoxPro provides a full range of tools and properties for formatting controls, and you definitely should make them a part of your programming life. It's true that most programmers are not expected to also act as graphic designers. However, you should still strive for a professional and slick look and feel, especially because creating it is so easy in Visual FoxPro. Remember that forms are the primary point of user interaction with your application, and to the user, running those first forms can be like checking out a used car. We all know that a tiny dent in the fender has no firm connection to engine performance, but what if the mirrors are cracked, the doors are different colors, and the gear settings are painted over? Well, you start wondering pretty quickly about what oddities lurk beneath the hood as well, no matter how many reassurances the salesman offers you.

Take pride in how your forms look and feel, and remember that to the many users, your forms *are* your application. Neatness counts!

Aligning Controls

Every control has a series of format properties to assist you in fine-tuning its location on the form. Visual FoxPro also provides a series of menu options under Format to ease this process. To align a series of text boxes, for instance, start by multi-selecting the text boxes (you can do so by holding down the Ctrl key as you click or holding down the mouse button and drawing a rectangular area around the controls you want to select). Then, while the controls are still selected, select Format, Align. You can choose how you want to align the select controls: left, right, top, bottom, centered vertically, or centered horizontally. This alignment process has no effect on the alignment of text within each control. Instead, it determines how the controls sit in reference to each other.

Visual FoxPro tries to take its best guess at exactly where you want the newly aligned group of controls to reside, but if you align controls that start out quite far apart, FoxPro might end up placing them a few pixels away from where you want them to be. In that case, while the controls are still multi-selected, you can move them together by using either the mouse or the arrow keys.

Size

The Format menu also includes a number of Size options, which enable the developer to easily size multiple controls to each other or to the gridline settings in the Form Designer. Choosing Format, Size, To Fit makes multiple controls the same height and width. Choosing Format, Size, To Grid snaps one or more controls to the same dimensions as the nearest Form Designer gridlines. The other options determine the size of multiple controls based on the tallest, shortest, widest, or most narrow selected control.

NOTE Notice that the Properties window changes slightly when you multi-select controls. The object pull-down contains the words *Multiple Selection*, and the window includes only properties common to all the selected controls. Changing a PEM setting changes the settings in all the selected controls. ■

Spacing

The Spacing options in the Format menu enable you to space three or more controls equal distances apart, either vertically or horizontally. You might not notice if a series of text boxes are a few pixels more or less apart from each other. On the other hand, a data entry clerk who stares at the screen all day certainly will.

TIP The View menu includes two options that might prove quite useful for creating an elegant form. The Grid Lines option fills in the form canvas with horizontal and vertical grid lines, enabling you to better gauge distances, as well as snap or size controls to the nearest gridlines. The Show Position option will show the exact size and location of the selected objects.

Tab Order of Controls

Even in our mouse-centric computer age, people still use keyboards. Personally, nothing ruffles my feathers more than opening a data entry form and trying to tab through the controls, only to find that focus jumps all over the page. Trust me: Your users will notice when this happens, and it will cost you more than a few points of credibility.

You can set tab order for controls in two ways, and the one you use will depend on your setting on the Forms tab of the Options dialog box (choose Tools, Options). The Tab Ordering pull-down includes two possible options: Interactive (the default) and By List. Selecting the Interactive option means that your controls will receive Tab focus in the order you specify in their TabOrder properties (in fact, choosing the View, Tab Order option will make the tab order visible right on the form). Selecting the By List option means that the View, Tab Order menu selection will present you with a dialog box. There, you'll see a list of controls and can manipulate the tab order as you want. Figure 9.16 shows the Tab Order dialog box.

FIGURE 9.16
In the Tab Order dialog box, you can specify the tab order of controls on your form.

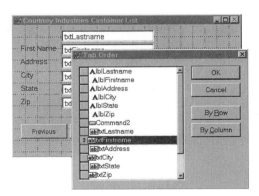

> **CAUTION**
>
> Visual FoxPro enables you to switch to any font currently on your system. Keep in mind that not all users' PCs will have the same fonts loaded as your own PC. You can include these fonts as long as you own royalty-free copies. Sticking to the most common typefaces—Arial, Courier or Courier New, and Times Roman—is probably safer unless you are certain of all your customers' configurations.

Part III

Ch 9

Naming Form Controls

When you drop a control onto the form canvas, Visual FoxPro automatically assigns the control a unique name, consisting of the control class and a numeric suffix (Command1, Label6, and so on). Most likely, the first property you will want to change is the control name. Many developers find it helpful to name controls in such a way that the control type and purpose are readily apparent: txtLastName, cmdProcess, chkSendMail, and so on.

Visual FoxPro does not enforce a naming scheme, outside of requiring unique names within a container and not allowing certain characters (spaces, slashes, hyphens, and punctuation). The naming convention you use will depend on your own preferences or, if you work in a team environment, existing standards. However, Microsoft does suggest the naming convention listed in Table 9.5. Many FoxPro developers use this scheme or one very similar to it.

Table 9.5   Microsoft Naming Conventions

Object Prefix	Object	Example
chk	CheckBox	chkReadOnly
cbo	ComboBox	cboEnglish
cmd	CommandButton	cmdCancel
cmg	CommandGroup	cmgChoices
cnt	Container	cntMoverList
ctl	Control	ctlFileList
<user-defined>	Custom	user-defined
edt	EditBox	edtTextArea
frm	Form	frmFileOpen
frs	FormSet	frsDataEntry
grd	Grid	grdPrices
grc	Column	grcCurrentPrice
grh	Header	grhTotalInventory
img	Image	imgIcon
lbl	Label	lblHelpMessage
lin	Line	linVertical
lst	ListBox	lstPolicyCodes
olb	OLEBoundControl	olbObject1
ole	OLE	oleObject1
opt	OptionButton	optFrench

Object Prefix	Object	Example
opg	OptionGroup	opgType
pag	Page	pagDataUpdate
pgf	PageFrame	pgfLeft
sep	Separator	sepToolSection1
shp	Shape	shpCircle
spn	Spinner	spnValues
txt	TextBox	txtGetText
tmr	Timer	tmrAlarm
tbr	ToolBar	tbrEditReport

Part
III

Ch
9

The Data Connection

Now that you've learned about designing the visual and code pieces of forms, you're ready to take a look at how FoxPro makes data available in the Form Designer. As is so often the case with Visual FoxPro, flexibility is the name of the game: Visual FoxPro enables you to access data as directly or indirectly as you want, and the Form Designer includes all the tools you need to follow your preferred approach.

Setting the Form's Data Environment

Perhaps the most radical enhancement to screen development (starting with Visual FoxPro 3) has been the inclusion of a flexible and visual Data Environment to each form you design. You are free to make as much or as little use of this Data Environment as you might like, though I think you'll find too many advantages to ignore it altogether.

Every form has a built-in Data Environment that exists as a child object of the form container. You won't be able to access this special object in the ways discussed here, though; the Data Environment cannot be selected through the Properties or Code windows and it cannot be clicked and selected from anywhere on the form canvas. Instead, you can access the Data Environment by selecting View, Data Environment or by right-clicking and selecting Data Environment from the shortcut menu.

Either way, you will be shown a visual representation of the Data Environment for the form, as shown in Figure 9.17, and you can choose to add tables, cursors, or views as you like. Each is added as a Cursor object, complete with its own set of properties, events, and methods. You can visually set relations between cursor objects or access the properties, events, and methods of tables, cursors, or relations via the Properties and Code windows.

FIGURE 9.17

Using the Data Environment of a form, you can specify and save the settings of the underlying data sources.

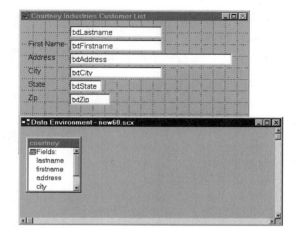

To add tables or views to the Data Environment, select Data Environment, Add, or right-click on the Data Environment designer and select Add. If a database is already open, that database and its tables or views will appear in the Add Table or View dialog box (see Figure 9.18). If no database is currently opened, or if you choose Other, a GetFile dialog box will appear for you to choose a table. If you select a table that is part of a database that is not yet open, Visual FoxPro backlinks the table to the database and opens the database automatically.

If you want to work against a view instead of a table, select the Views option button, and the list of tables will be replaced by a list of views in the database.

FIGURE 9.18

You can add tables or views to the form's Data Environment.

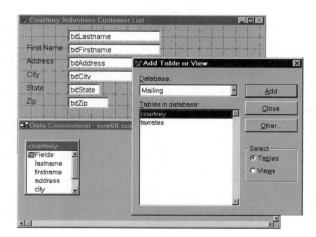

After you add the table or view to the Data Environment, you can browse it by right-clicking on the table or view and selecting Browse from the shortcut menu. You can also select Data Environment, Browse from the system menu, but only if the table or view has already been selected (you select it by clicking it).

Cursor objects include a logical property called .NoDataOnLoad. Setting this property to True for a cursor with an updateable view as its source will cause the cursor to start out empty. In forms designed to query specific data sets, this feature can be quite useful because it greatly enhances form loading performance. This property has no effect on local tables.

Working with Relationships in the Data Environment Designer

You can easily create a relationship between two cursor objects in the Data Environment. To do so, select the relation field from the parent data source, and drag it onto the child cursor. The child table must have an index on this field. If it doesn't, FoxPro offers to create one for you (see Figure 9.19).

FIGURE 9.19
Here, you must confirm whether to create a Data Environment index.

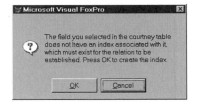

Data Environment: A Final Word

You can switch back and forth in your form between the Data Environment and the form canvas by clicking on either. Any tables you add to a form's Data Environment will be automatically opened whenever you run the form and automatically closed after the form is destroyed. If you have set relations between several tables or cursors, these relations are reset for you each time you run an instance of the form. Gone are the days of Open_File and Close_File style functions, with file alias assignments and tag order settings and those seemingly endless strings of Set Relation To *childtable* Additive commands. Now, you set your Data Environment at the same time as you design your form and then (practically) never worry about it again.

> **CAUTION**
>
> In addition to filling your Data Environment with visual cursor and relation objects, you can also enter code in any of the DE events, including BeforeOpenTables, Init, and AfterCloseTables. Be careful, though, about mixing and matching visual objects and code in this case. Stumbling into a web of cyclical relations and hard-to-debug anomalies is very frustrating. FoxPro attempts to undertake a certain set of low-level events when you enter objects visually into the Data Environment (and in fact, they fire more quickly than your code will). As you become comfortable with using Data Environments, you might want to augment their functionality. Until then, try using the visual Data Environment tools for all that you can.

Dragging and Dropping Data Controls onto Your Form

The Data Environment would be a helpful feature of Visual FoxPro's Form Designer even if its functionality stopped there. But it doesn't. Perhaps best of all, Visual FoxPro enables you to drag and drop data controls from the Data Environment directly onto your form, where they are instantiated as text boxes, spinners, or check boxes, along with field descriptions or names as corresponding labels. To move a field onto a form, add a table to the Data Environment, and click on the field you want to add. Drag and drop the control onto the form, and you'll notice that a label and a control appear. The label is the field description, or the field name if there is no description, and the control is precoded to be bound to the field you specified. The type of control that is created during drag-and-drop depends on the `DisplayClass` and `DisplayLibrary` settings in the Field tab of the Table Designer. (See Part 2 for more information on working with data.)

To drag multiple fields onto a form, just multi-select them by holding down the Ctrl key while clicking. To select all the fields in a view or table as individual fields, click on the word *Fields* on top of the table representation. To select all fields into a grid on the form, grab the title bar of the cursor object and drag and drop.

Bound Versus Unbound Controls

Adding controls to the form by dragging them from the Data Environment results in controls with `ControlSource` properties pointing to field references. That is, they are *bound* controls; they are directly tied to underlying tables or views, and changing the value of the control results in a corresponding change in the relevant field. Visual FoxPro makes it very easy to create forms with bound controls, and most developers choose to do so. However, Visual FoxPro also supports data manipulation through *unbound* controls. In other words, FoxPro lets you manipulate controls with no `ControlSource`, or with variables or properties as the `ControlSource`, and then programmatically change your data based on the control properties.

Many developers and OOP aficionados feel quite strongly one way or the other. My advice is to use what works for you: Bound controls offer many advantages, including the wonders of drag-and-drop. Unbound controls can provide you greater flexibility when you're dealing with a multitier environment, where you keep special business rules or validation methods in a separate layer of code, and let those objects take care of actually writing down data.

> **CAUTION**
>
> When you're deciding whether to bind your controls, keep in mind your current framework (if any) and your fellow developers (if any). Nothing gets muddier more quickly than a set of forms with varying approaches to the binding and writing of data. Remember that any code that relies on `GetNextModified()` or other commands that read from the underlying data source will *not* be privy to changes in unbound controls.

Understanding Private Data Sessions

One of the issues to deal with when you're working with forms that modify data is the issue of *data sessions*. In days gone by, FoxPro programmers jumped through a lot of hoops to guarantee that changes made to record pointers, relations, and so on, in one form did not change the settings in any other forms. Virtually anyone who programmed in FoxPro during the pre-3.0 days knows what I am talking about: macro-expansion aliases, saved and restored memory variables with every setting, and any number of less elegant and less efficient approaches.

Part
III

Ch
9

We can be thankful that all those approaches changed with the advent of the Visual FoxPro data session. A *data session* is an environment of work areas and data settings. Each data session has 32,767 available work areas and a number of FoxPro settings particular to its own area of your application. In other words, a data session is a small, relatively well-protected area of your application, enabling a form to change record pointers, index orders, relations, or any other setting without affecting other forms.

Private data sessions are a very powerful feature. Basically, private data sessions enable the developer to encapsulate a form's Data Environment within itself.

You can easily assign a form its own data session. Just set the `DataSession` property of the form to `2 - Private Data Session`.

A good way to view private data sessions in action is to run a form with the `DataSession` property set to `2` and then access the View window, by selecting Windows, View or typing `Set` in the command window. Expand the Current Session drop-down list (as shown in Figure 9.20). Note that you now have two sessions that are independent of each other. Opening or closing tables in one session will have no effect on any other data session.

FIGURE 9.20
You can switch data sessions from the View window to debug multiple forms.

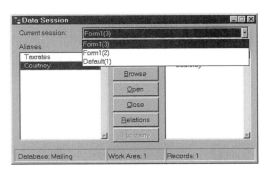

So, Who Controls the Data?

With all this talk of Data Environments, bound controls, and private data sessions, you might be wondering how it all fits in with the settings in the database container. The answer is actually quite simple: After you've set up your underlying database, the form's Data Environment enables you to maintain any relevant pieces of the database within the form's own private data session. At the form level, you can change certain general data properties, such as the level of data buffering. At any point in the form code, you can change a particular data-related setting, such as `Set Century On`, and it will affect all data accessed in the form's session.

You'll find that the database, the Data Environment, and the form itself can each be put to use to fine-tune your data access on each form. And it doesn't stop there! You can even drag tables from the Project Manager into your Data Environment or form. Just remember, whatever exists in the Data Environment, whether visually or through code in the Data Environment `Init` method, will be opened every time the form is run and closed each time the form is destroyed.

Running a Form

Now that's you've created a form, using it is quite easy. Just type the following command in the command window, or include it in your code:

```
DO FORM MyForm
```

Is running the form really that easy? Well, yes and no. As is so often the case, Visual FoxPro offers a good deal of flexibility in referencing and releasing forms. The `Name` keyword enables the user to specify an alternative name for a form:

```
Do Form MyForm Name MyGreatForm
```

A form created in this manner can be manipulated by calls to `MyGreatForm`. You'll soon notice, though, that a `Release MyGreatForm` command will have no effect on the form. It's almost as if the `Name` clause creates a form alias but doesn't bind the form entirely to the object reference. Fortunately, the `Linked` clause does just that: It strengthens the form's bind to the named object reference, above and beyond simple naming and reference. Instead, the form is represented by the variable and shares its scope:

```
Do Form MyForm Name MyGreatForm Linked
```

A form created in this manner can be released by setting `MyGreatForm` to `.Null.` or by releasing the variable.

Suppose, however, that you run an instance of a form named `MyMainForm` by using `Do Form MyMainForm Name MyForm`. Then you release the `MyForm` variable and even set it to `.NULL.`, but the screen doesn't close. The problem is that you must include the `Linked` keyword to bind a form to its object reference. Keep in mind that binding a form to a variable in this way introduces a pitfall: You must use caution when creating a form that is linked to a local (or private) variable. As soon as the variable goes out of scope, the form will be released.

Other Features of Forms

By now, you should have a pretty good idea of the power (and relative ease) of the Form Designer. Now, let's turn our attention to a few important additional notes on designing and running forms, including details of some features that are brand-new to Visual FoxPro 6.

Using Multiple Instances of a Single Form

Visual FoxPro enables you to run multiple instances of forms at the same time. This feature might be needed in an application for many reasons. For instance, a phone operator might be entering information for one customer when he or she is interrupted with a request to look up data for a second customer. You don't need to adjust any special settings for FoxPro to enable multiple instances of the same form; in fact, it's the default behavior. You'll want to be sure to use private data sessions for those forms, though. Otherwise, changes to the environment made by one form will be reflected in the other (record pointers, most notably). Then you'll have to write code to deal with potential record pointer changes in your Activate() and Deactivate() commands. And no VFP programmer I know *ever* wants to deal with all that again.

Part

III

Ch

9

 Visual FoxPro's support of multiple form instances presents an often-overlooked fringe benefit. Programmers and developers can use this feature, along with private data sessions, to test for multiuser contention right on their own PCs. Multiple data sessions basically imitate multiple user behavior, and by firing up a few copies of your form, you can easily do what used to be so difficult: test the exact behavior your user will encounter during most cases of multiuser contention.

Form Sets

Form sets were included in Visual FoxPro mainly for backward compatibility issues (they are very similar to pre-3.0 screen sets), but they have since proven useful to many programmers. Form sets have several advantages over individual forms:

- Developers can show or hide multiple forms at once. Of course, you could also write a little loop to scan through active forms, but if you'll be calling such code often, why not let Visual FoxPro do the work for you?

- Forms in a form set can share the same private data session, which can be quite useful when multiple forms need to keep record pointers in sync.

- If you want a group of forms to show up in a particular arrangement, form sets enable you to make such an arrangement much more quickly than you could if you were developing each form one-by-one.

So what's the downside? Well, some programmers feel that form sets muddy the water by adding an extra level of control and removing control of some properties from our friend, the form, into its bullying higher-level cousin. But, once again, you can turn FoxPro's flexibility to your advantage. Use form sets if you find a need, and keep using them if you find them useful. Or ignore them altogether, and dive right into the single-form development paradigm.

The LockScreen Property

If you have a control-laden form running against a large data source, you might notice a quick flicker across the form when the screen refreshes. Visual FoxPro forms include a special logical property, called `LockScreen`, that indicates whether the user's changes to the form are visible to the user. Typically, developers take advantage of this property as follows:

```
THISFORM.LockScreen = .T.
* -- a series of checks, refreshes, and data queries
THISFORM.LockScreen = .F.
```

Be careful when using this property. If you leave a form's `LockScreen` property set to `True` and do not include code to set it back to `False`, the form will remain locked and no subsequent changes will show. Also, be careful when using the `LockScreen` property when you're working within embedded methods. A calling procedure might have set `LockScreen` on or off and will expect it to return to that state when your code returns control. Follow the cardinal rule of programming: Restore anything in the environment that you have changed. The following code is a vast improvement on the preceding code:

```
Local llOldLockScreen
llOldLockScreen = THISFORM.LockScreen
THISFORM.LockScreen = .T.
* -- a series of checks, refreshes, and data queries
THISFORM.LockScreen = llOldLockScreen
```

Creating Modal Forms

As much as we strive to give users control over their environment, sometimes a crucial question still must be asked or a key piece of information must be entered or verified before any application functions can continue. At those moments, you can make use of Visual FoxPro *modal forms*.

Even younger and/or less-experienced computer users have grown used to the distinction between forms that let you "leave" or switch to another form, and those that stop you dead in your tracks and demand an answer. Modal forms are still an accepted application tool, *in moderation*. When you do need to develop a modal form, you can do so quite easily. Just set the form's `WindowType` property from `0` - `Modeless` (the default) to `1` - `Modal`. Voilà! You've created a modal form.

> **N O T E**   Another way of making a form modal is by calling its `Show` method with an optional parameter of `0` for Modeless or `1` for Modal. The parameter overrides the `WindowType` setting. The only hitch, as shown next, is that you must first hide the form to override the property. Consider this code:
>
> ```
> DO FORM MyModelessForm    && form opened modeless
> MyModelessForm.Hide()     && hides the form from view
> MyModelessForm.Show(1)    && shows the form as a modal form
> ```
>
> You could also have executed this code as follows:
>
> ```
> DO FORM MyModelessForm NoShow  && form is in memory, but not yet shown
> MyModelessForm.Show(1)         && shows the form as a modal form
> ```
>
> In this way, you can easily call any of your existing forms as modal forms. ■

Modal forms are often called in circumstances in which the programmer needs some sort of response from the user. Calling the forms is quite easy in Visual FoxPro. You can use a special version of the DO FORM command that looks like this:

```
Do FORM frmname to varname
```

The return statement, specifying the value to return, should be placed in the modal form's Unload method.

Using Form Wizards and Builders

Visual FoxPro includes two sets of powerful tools for facilitating Rapid Application Development of forms. The Form Wizards create a form for you, complete with fully functional pushbutton controls for editing and navigation. The builders help you quickly design and format a particular object through a series of wizard-like questions.

Creating a Form with the Form Wizard

Like other FoxPro wizards, the Form Wizards step you through the process of form creation by asking a series of questions about the desired form. The Form Wizards were designed to be quite easy to use and require little in the way of formal offline instruction. Let's take a few moments now to detail the process.

From the Tools menu option, select Wizards, Form. Visual FoxPro ships with two available types of Form Wizards: a basic one-record form and a one-to-many form. They are shown in the dialog box featured in Figure 9.21.

FIGURE 9.21
You can choose from two types of Form Wizards.

Let's assume that you want a form that is based on a single table, query, or view. Choose Form Wizard from the dialog box and click OK. You then see the first of the Form Wizard dialog boxes, as shown in Figure 9.22.

Select the desired database and associated table under the Databases and Tables options on the left. You will then see a list of available fields. You can click on the right-arrow command button to move the fields you want into the Selected Fields list, in any order you like. The double right-arrow button will move all available fields into the Selected Fields list.

FIGURE 9.22

In the first step of the Form Wizard, you can select fields for your form.

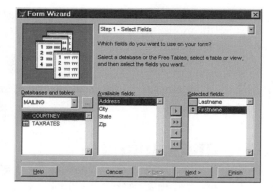

The next dialog box presented by the Form Wizards asks which style you want for the form (see Figure 9.23). Your choices are Standard, Chiseled, Shadowed, Boxed, or Embossed. The magnifying glass view at the top left of the screen will change with each selection to show you an example of the style you have just selected.

FIGURE 9.23

You can choose from various common form styles.

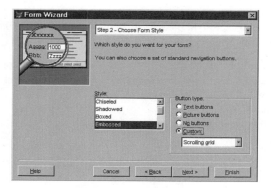

In this screen, you also choose which style navigation buttons you prefer or whether you would like to use scrolling grid to navigate through your table.

The next dialog box will ask you for the sort order of the data. You can add up to three fields on which to sort by clicking each desired field in the Available Fields list and then clicking the Add button (see Figure 9.24). You can choose from fields or from any existing index tags.

The last dialog box requests whether you want to save the form, save the form and immediately run it, or save the form and immediately begin modifying the form (see Figure 9.25). You can also decide whether you would like a pageframe form if the number of fields selected cannot fit on the main form canvas. Creating forms is that simple.

FIGURE 9.24

You can sort your form by an index or a field specification (up to three different fields).

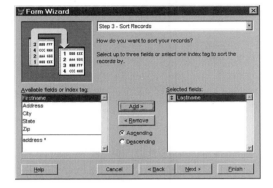

FIGURE 9.25

When you are finished with the Form Wizard, you can choose to run the form, save it, or modify it.

 The Form Wizard can be a useful tool for creating a simple form, prototyping a form, or just learning more about controls and how they work. The ease of use, however, carries with it an associated loss of control. After you become more comfortable with the Form Designer, you might begin to steer clear of the Form Wizards altogether. The choice is up to you.

Using Builders to Develop Forms

Whether you've started your form design from scratch or used a wizard to get a running start, you will probably want to take advantage of Visual FoxPro's builders. Simply put, a builder is kind of like a wizard: It's a dialog box that enables you to quickly and easily define some of the basic behaviors and formats of a form and its controls. Unlike wizards, though, builders can be run again and again against the same controls. You can use builders not just to create, but to edit.

You can use the following builders in the Form Designer:

> AutoFormat Builder
> ComboBox Builder

Command Group Builder

Edit Box Builder

Form Builder

Grid Builder

List Box Builder

Option Group Builder

Text Box Builder

You can run the builder associated with an object in two ways:

- Select the Builder Lock button on the Form Controls toolbar. Every time you drop an object on the form canvas, the associated builder (if it exists) will run.

- Right-click the object you want to build, and select Builder from the shortcut menu.

The Text Box Builder   Builders range in complexity based on the object being built. The Text Box Builder, shown in Figures 9.26 through 9.28, has three tabs of information enabling you to define how the text box should behave, including how it should look and what field in a table the text box should be bound to.

FIGURE 9.26

Use the Format tab of the Text Box Builder to specify input masks and the behavior of your text box at runtime.

FIGURE 9.27

On the Style tab of the Text Box Builder, you can select the size, border style, and alignment of your text box.

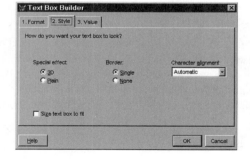

FIGURE 9.28

On the Value tab of the Text Box Builder, you can indicate the source of your data.

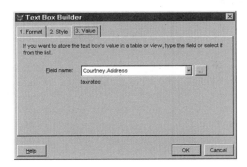

The Grid Builder   The Grid Builder, shown in Figures 9.29 through 9.32, makes the formatting and design of a grid a snap. The Grid Items tab, shown in Figure 9.29, like the Form Wizard, enables you to select the fields you want to include in the grid.

FIGURE 9.29

On the Grid Items tab of the Grid Builder, you can select the fields to be included in the grid.

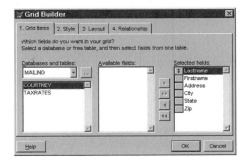

The Style tab, shown in Figure 9.30, enables you to select a particular style, including a "Ledger" style that alternates white and green rows.

FIGURE 9.30

On the Style tab of the Grid Builder, you can select a style for the grid.

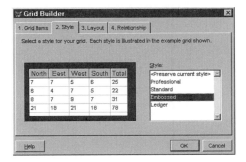

On the Layout tab, shown in Figure 9.31, you can specify column captions, as well as the control that will be used within the grid to show the data. For instance, you can choose here to have a spinner or an edit box embedded inside the column to show numeric or memo field data.

FIGURE 9.31

On the Layout tab of the Grid Builder, you can specify the layout of the grid.

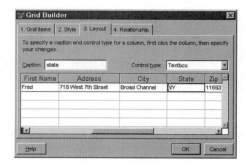

Finally, the Relationship tab (see Figure 9.32) helps you to define the relationship the table in the grid has with a parent table on the form. This capability is very useful when you're creating one-to-many forms.

FIGURE 9.32

On the Relationship tab of the Grid Builder, you can specify the relationships on a one-to-many form.

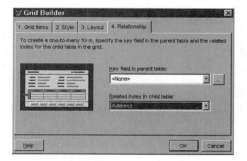

The AutoFormat Builder   Most builders work on one object in the Form Designer, but the AutoFormat Builder enables you to apply a particular style to multiple controls. Just multi-select various controls, right-click, and select Builder. Figure 9.33 shows the resulting dialog box.

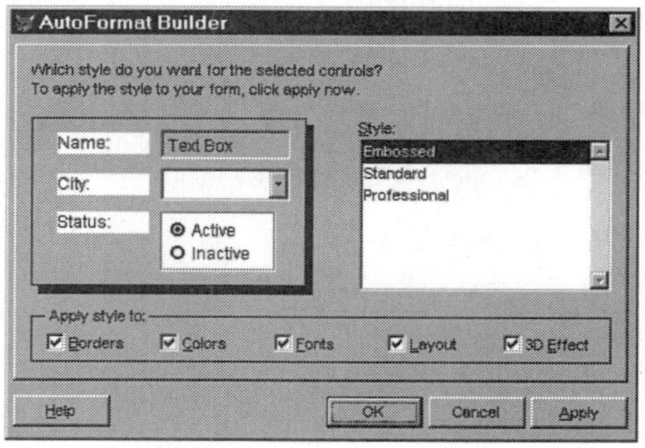

FIGURE 9.33

Using the AutoFormat Builder, you can specify a style for multiple controls.

Some Brand-New Form Options

Visual FoxPro 6 offers a couple of brand-new form features, which are discussed in the following sections.

Form Scrolls

One of my favorite new Visual FoxPro 6 form features is the capability to create forms with scrollbars on the side or bottom, enabling users to scroll through your form just as they would scroll through a grid, a word processing document, or an HTML page. In earlier versions of Visual FoxPro, developers had just a few choices when a form grew too long for a certain screen resolution. You could move some of the controls out to a new form (and perhaps include these forms in one FormSet), use pageframes, or take advantage of the ActiveX slider that ships with FoxPro and roll your own scrollbar-forms. The third option was quite attractive but required some specialized coding, and more important, some problems were documented with the slider control on PCs using multiple Microsoft products (newly installed products often overwrote Registry entries for previously installed sliders).

Part

III

Ch

9

Now, scrollable forms are a native Visual FoxPro feature. The default behavior of a form is to have no scrollbars, but you can choose to include vertical scrollbars, horizontal scrollbars, or both. The Scrolled event fires every time a scrollbar is used, and VscrollSmallChange and HscrollSmallChange let the user determine how much the form scrolls for each click. ContinuousScroll indicates whether the user sees the scroll commence as soon as the scroll cursor begins moving or whether the scrolling waits until the move is done to adjust the screen (this is analogous to the form's LockScreen properties).

If your form is Sizable, Visual FoxPro takes care of activating and deactivating the scrollbars as necessary. As soon as the user makes the screen too small to fit all the controls, the scrollbars become visible.

Title Bars

Visual FoxPro 6 includes a new property, TitleBar, that indicates whether the form includes a title bar. Savvy developers had managed to remove title bars in versions 3 and 5, but only by manipulating a particular sequence of properties and events (shades of 2.x). The TitleBar property simplifies matters a great deal.

On the downside, when you lose the title bar, you lose some of the built-in functionality users might have come to expect. They can't minimize, maximize, resize, or move the form with the mouse any longer.

The Last Word

If you're like most Visual FoxPro programmers and developers, you'll spend a remarkable amount of time working inside the Form Designer. Fortunately, VFP's object-oriented programming model makes it possible to create flexible, powerful, slick forms for your applications.

The tools included in the designer—from toolbars to formatting options to wizards and builders—simplify your coding and help to make VFP a true RAD tool.

Keep in mind that no VFP tool is an island. Your forms and form development process will really begin to zing after you've become familiar with other facets of Visual FoxPro. The Form Designer enables you to set some data-related properties, but even the Data Environment is no substitute for the Database Designer. Your VFP 5 code might have been remarkably quick and flexible, but odds are that your various form methods will benefit from some of the new language extensions of VFP 6. The better grasp you have of Visual FoxPro's OOP implementation, the better use you'll make of the Form Designer.

Try to find time to really delve into the Form Designer. Microsoft has packed an awful lot into it, and the more you learn about it and experiment with it, the better your applications will become. ●

Creating Reports

You've seen that Visual FoxPro provides a powerful tool for creating forms to give your users a way to put information *into* a database application. Not surprisingly, Visual FoxPro offers a number of ways to get data *out* of a system. Savvy users might learn a few simple Visual FoxPro commands for showing data: They could List the contents of a table, open simple Browse windows, maybe even execute basic SELECT statements. They might use ODBC technology to open Visual FoxPro data in another application. But most of your users will rely on reports to gather and present information.

Visual FoxPro's Report Designer is a visually oriented interface for manually designing reports and mailing labels. You create a report by placing different objects, such as fields, text, graphics, and expressions, onto the report wherever you want. The Quick Report menu option can speed the process by creating a default layout for the report. And the Report Wizards, like the Form Wizards, can help you quickly prototype and produce reports that you can later modify yourself.

Types of Reports

Reports in Visual FoxPro can present information in a number of ways. Data can be aligned into distinct columns, in a format reminiscent of spreadsheets or grids (see Figure 10.1). Or data for one record can be shown from top to bottom, much as a user might see it on a form (see Figure 10.2). Data can be presented as is, without much fanfare, or information can be grouped, totaled, and subtotaled. Any available font can be used. Graphics can be included to represent data, and different graphics can even be swapped out to represent different values. Your reports can be run off underlying tables, views, queries, or cursors. You could go so far as to include calculated fields on a report, or for that matter, you might insert the results of user-defined functions.

Creating Reports via Quick Report

Visual FoxPro's Quick Report option provides you with a quick way to create simple reports, letting Visual FoxPro handle most of the initial design decisions for you. Using Quick Report is easy:

1. Open the table with the data you want to include on the report (Choose File, Open and select the table name in the dialog box, or use the USE *tablename* syntax in the command window).

2. From the system menu bar, choose File, New, and then click Report. Then click New File. (Alternatively, you can enter Create Report in the command window.)

FIGURE 10.1

A column-style report presents lines of information one after another, in a style reminiscent of a spreadsheet.

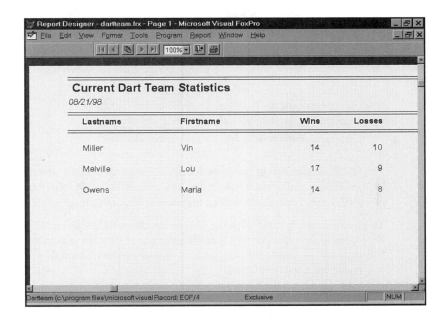

FIGURE 10.2

A row-style report presents the various pieces of information for each record on separate lines and starts over with each new record.

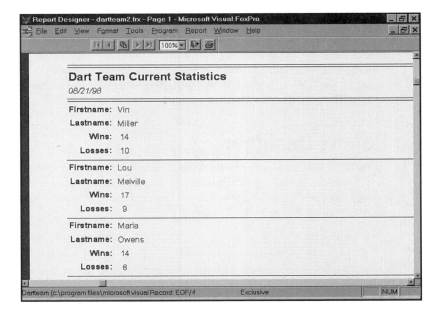

3. Select Report, Quick Report. The Quick Report dialog box appears (see Figure 10.3).

4. Choose the field layout you prefer, and click any other desired options for your report (see the following description). Then click OK.

FIGURE 10.3

In the Quick Report dialog box, you can specify the style for your report.

The Quick Report dialog box includes several major reporting layout options. The Field Layout buttons enable you to choose between a column-style layout, with data across the page, and a row-style layout, with data running from top to bottom for each record.

The Titles check box includes the field name above or beside each field (depending on the field layout). On most reports, you will want some identifying marker for each field and should keep this box checked. But, for instance, if your report is a simple list of names and addresses, you might not need field definitions.

The Add Alias check box indicates whether alias names are automatically added to the expressions for each field. In other words, this option indicates whether the field name should be listed as `lastname` or `mytable.lastname`. You will probably want the alias names turned on, particularly if you plan to run reports against a set of related tables. On the other hand, if you do not add an alias, you could later use the same report against any table with a field called `lastname`.

The Add table to Data Environment option adds the current table to the Data Environment window. You'll learn more about the Data Environment in the section titled "Taking Advantage of Data Environments and Data Sessions."

The Report Designer

Even if you use the Quick Report option, you will still probably make extensive use of the Report Designer in your applications. You've already learned about creating a report as a part of using the Quick Report feature. But you can create a new report in several ways. Here are the most common:

- Choose File, New. Click the Report button, and then click New Report.
- From the Project Manager, click the Documents tab, select the Report icon in the document list, and click on the New button. Then select New Report.
- From the command window, type `Create Report` or `Modify Report` *newname*.
- Use the Report Wizards to create a report, and then save it to return to and modify.

You'll learn about using the Report Wizards in the section titled "Creating a Report with the Report Wizards." In the meantime, let's explore Visual FoxPro's Report Designer.

No matter how you create your new report, Visual FoxPro will launch the Report Designer (see Figure 10.4). The Report Designer has several components:

- The *report canvas* is the visual representation of the report you are designing, the area onto which you place fields, labels, or graphics.
- The *Report Designer toolbar* enables you easy access to all the report toolbars and several important functions.

 TIP The Visual FoxPro Report toolbars have ToolTips attached to them to help you remember each bar's purpose. Hold the mouse cursor over the toolbar for just a moment, and a short explanation appears.

- The *Report Controls toolbar* enables you to drop any of six types of controls or objects onto your report: labels, fields, lines, rectangles, rounded rectangles, and ActiveX/OLE bound picture controls.
- The *Color palette* enables you to specify colors for the background or foreground of any control.

Part III

Ch 10

FIGURE 10.4
The Report Designer here is in its most basic mode.

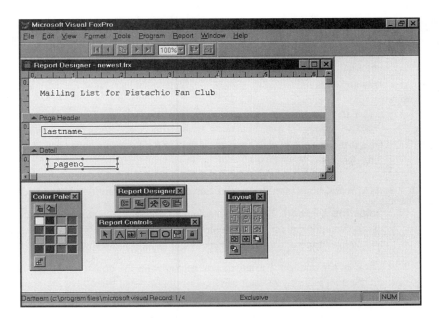

CAUTION
Be careful when you assign colors to your report. Not all users have color printers, and even those who do might rather have a quicker-printing report than one with a lime green background. On the other hand, judicious use of color can visually represent important points or notes.

- The *Layout palette* enables you to align or size one or more controls (see "Formatting Report Controls").

- The *Data Grouping* and *Data Environment* buttons give you quick control over the presentation of your data. You'll learn more about these controls throughout this chapter.

T I P   You can dock toolbars by dragging them onto the area just below the FoxPro menu. You can also stretch them (within limits) to suit your own taste by resting your mouse cursor over the edges and dragging to the size you want.

Working with Controls on the Report Canvas

The Report Designer supports three types of objects, or controls: text objects, field objects, and graphics objects. These objects are analogous to certain form controls, but they do differ in some important ways. Report controls cannot be derived from subclasses. They include a much more limited set of formatting and data properties. They cannot be referenced in code. And, by nature, they are not interactive: Users cannot enter text into a report.

Report objects are relatively easy to work with but flexible enough to enable for the design of sophisticated and professional reports. Text objects contain text that you type directly onto the Report Designer. Field objects are used to display data stored in fields or data supplied by calculations, expressions, or user-defined functions. Graphics objects are pictures, lines, or rectangles.

N O T E   Visual FoxPro report pictures can be stored in a table's general fields or on disk in any number of graphics formats: `.BMP`, `.ICO`, `.ANI`, `.JPG`, `.GIF`, or `.CUR`. This capability is a great improvement over earlier versions of the software, which supported only Windows Paintbrush `.BMP` files.

As you add objects to the report canvas, you can manipulate them in different ways.

Selecting a Report Object   To select an object, make sure the Select Objects button (the upward-pointing arrow) is selected in the Report Controls toolbar. Then point to and click on the desired type of object. The object will be highlighted with small rectangles, or handles.

Click on the spot on the canvas where you want the object to appear (or, more accurately, click on the spot where you want the upper-left corner of the object to appear). The object will start out with a default size assigned by Visual FoxPro; you can then resize as necessary. However, you could drop the object and resize it all in one step. To do so, click on the object you want to add to the canvas and resize. Drag the mouse across the canvas to create the right size rectangle, and then release the mouse. The control will be added to fit the area you've just highlighted.

Deleting a Report Object   To delete an object, select the object on the report canvas and then press the Delete key or choose Edit, Cut. Note that this procedure also works for multiple selected items.

Copying a Report Object   To duplicate an object, select the object on the report canvas, choose Edit, Copy (or Ctrl+C), and then choose Edit, Paste (or Ctrl+V). When you do so, a copy of the object appears near its original location. You can click the object and, using the arrow keys or the mouse, move it to a new location.

 TIP   The easiest way to resize a report object is to select the object, hold down the Shift key, and press an arrow key. With each arrow keypress, the object expands or contracts by one pixel or scale unit. You can also hold down the Shift key and use the mouse to resize an object, though being very precise is difficult when you use this technique.

Working with Fields   Text and graphics objects are quite powerful and important, but odds are that your users are really looking for the *data* included on your reports. To show data on a report, use the text box object to add a field, a variable, an expression, or a user-defined function.

To add a field to the report canvas, select the textbox/field control from the Report Controls toolbar. When you click on the report canvas to add the control, the Report Expression dialog box appears, as shown in Figure 10.5. Note that you can also access this dialog box at any later time by right-clicking on a field control and selecting Properties from the shortcut menu.

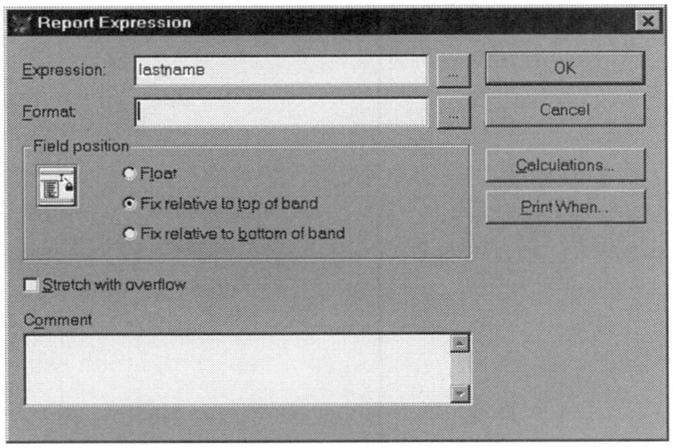

FIGURE 10.5
In the Report Expression dialog box, you can enter or build an expression that will evaluate to the data shown in the report.

In the Report Expression dialog box, you can specify several key properties, described in the following sections.

Changing Field Expressions   The Expression text box includes the expression, field name, or function call that will evaluate to the data you want to show. You can type a field or expression into the box yourself, or you can use the ellipsis at the right to bring forward the Expression Builder (see Figure 10.6). The Expression Builder includes a number of tools for helping you add data to your report, including a list of available fields, Visual FoxPro functions, and Visual FoxPro system variables.

FIGURE 10.6
The Expression Builder
enables you to select
from currently available
fields or system
variables or insert your
own expression.

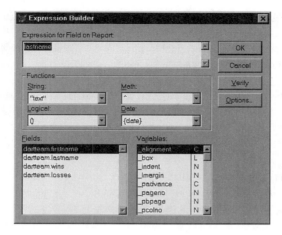

You can include any variable name or function call in the Expression entry, but remember, these variables and functions *must be in scope* when the report is running; otherwise, an error results.

 You can also include immediate If statements in the following format in the expression text box:

IIF(*condition*,*result if true*, *result if not true*)

These statements can be remarkably useful. You can change the True or False of a logical field, for instance, into something more informative or eye-catching with the following expression:

IIF(situation = .T.,"Absolutely!","No way, Jack!").

Changing Field Formats   In the Format field of the Report Expression dialog box, you can enter formatting guidelines for the resulting text or numeric data. Clicking the ellipsis for this property accesses the Format dialog box shown in Figure 10.7. You can use this dialog box to quickly format the data you are showing on your report and then return to the Report Expression dialog box.

FIGURE 10.7
In the Format dialog
box, you can format the
information that's shown
on your report.

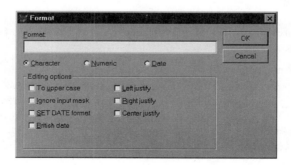

Field Position indicates where you want the field to lie in reference to its band. You can choose to have the field float, which means that its position is relative to other fields in the band. Or you can have the field position remain relative to the top or bottom of the detail band, which means that it is always some fixed distance from one of the band borders, despite the sizes of any other fields.

The Stretch with Overflow check box indicates whether the field control should grow large vertically enough to accommodate all text from the field or variable. Otherwise, only a portion of the expression result will print. This option is especially useful when you're printing data from memo fields.

The Calculations button enables you to specify a subtotal or a calculation. To create a subtotal for a field, click on this button, and then, in the Subtotal or Calculate Field dialog box, indicate the type of calculation and the scope of the calculation. In Figure 10.8, for instance, we are requesting a sum of the field to occur at the bottom of each page. We would then place this control in the Page Footer band.

FIGURE 10.8
In the Calculate Field dialog box, you can choose from a number of different numeric calculations.

The Print When button in the Report Expression dialog box enables you to limit when the field prints on the report. Clicking this button opens the Print When dialog box (see Figure 10.9). By default, an object is printed whenever the contents of its band are printed, but you can change the default. For example, you can choose not to print values that repeat, or in a report with grouping, you can choose to print the field only when the basis for the group changes. The Print Only When Expression Is True text box enables you to define another expression that determines whether the field prints. You could use this field, for instance, to limit printing some fields to certain security levels. Or you might print the results of a memo field only when some other field in the data source is set to True.

You can use the Comment portion of the Report Expression dialog box to enter comments for your own reference or to store notes to other programmers or developers. The comments do not appear anywhere in the report.

Working with Report Variables   You can define variables to be used in your reports by selecting Report, Variables (see Figure 10.10). Why use report variables? Well, you might want to keep running tallies that extend beyond the scope of the field calculations.

FIGURE 10.9
In the Print When dialog box, you can specify the conditions under which the report expression will actually appear.

FIGURE 10.10
In the Report Variables dialog box, you can create and use memory variables in your report.

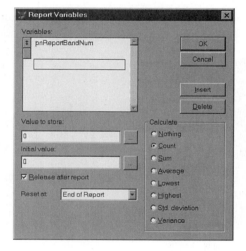

If you select the Release After Report check box in the dialog box, the Report variables are scoped privately (which means that any user-defined function you call can access them). If you don't check this box, the variables will remain in memory as public variables. It's unlikely you would ever need to retain the variables in such a global scope.

Working with Shapes and Text

You can easily add a shape or a line of text to a Visual FoxPro report: Just select it and drop it, as you would any of the controls. But you can also determine the behaviors of shapes and text on a report (just as you can determine field properties).

Double-click on a text object in a report, and the Text dialog box appears (see Figure 10.11).

Clicking the Print When button opens the Print When dialog box (shown earlier in Figure 10.9). Using this dialog box, you can exert the same control over text and shapes as you have over fields. The same is true of a text or shape control's object position: Use the Object Position option group to determine these properties.

FIGURE 10.11

In the Text dialog box, you can control the style and behavior of a text object in a report.

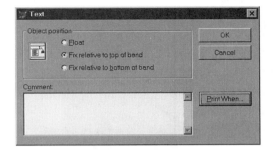

The Rectangle and Line controls have a few additional options above and beyond those present for text objects (see Figure 10.12). If you double-click a line in a report, you can also indicate how the line stretches relative to the band it is in. The No Stretch option restricts vertical lines or rectangles from stretching. The Stretch Relative to Tallest Object in Group option enables a vertical line or rectangle to stretch to the height of the tallest object in the group, and the Stretch Relative to Height of Band option enables the vertical line or rectangle to stretch in relation to the height of its band.

FIGURE 10.12

In the Rectangle/Line dialog box, you can control the style and behavior of rectangles and lines on your report.

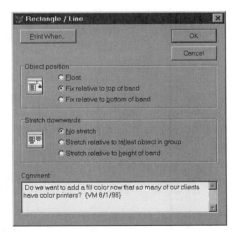

The Round Rectangle control has a similar dialog box, but it also contains five different buttons that indicate various styles (see Figure 10.13).

Working with Pictures and Graphics

Adding text and shape objects is useful, but when you really want to spruce up your report, attract attention to a particular piece of information, or just include a company logo, you can turn to full-fledged graphics. You can add graphics to a report from the general field of a Visual FoxPro table or from a file on disk. For example, Figure 10.14 shows a report with a special feature in the title: Everyone's favorite logo.

FIGURE 10.13

In the Round Rectangle dialog box, you can control the style and behavior of rounded rectangles on your report.

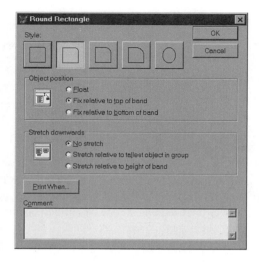

FIGURE 10.14

Visual FoxPro reports can include graphics.

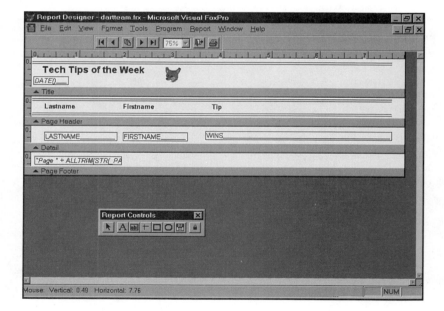

You can easily add a picture to a report by following these steps:

1. Select the Picture / OLE Bound Control icon in the Report Controls toolbar.

2. Click at the starting point for the graphic, and drag until the frame reaches the desired size for the picture. When you release the mouse, the Report Picture dialog box appears (see Figure 10.15).

3. Set the options (discussed in the following paragraphs) to tell Visual FoxPro where to find the picture and how to size it relative to the band it's in.

4. Click OK. The picture then appears right in the report's design.

FIGURE 10.15

In the Report Picture dialog box, you can set options for embedded pictures.

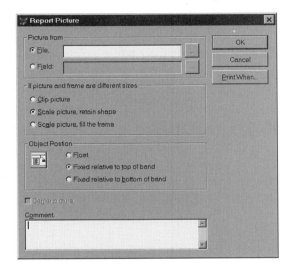

The Picture From area of the dialog box includes File and Field buttons and corresponding fields to enter the source of the picture. To include a single picture from a file in your report, click the File button. Then click the ellipsis to open a dialog box, and point to your file. You can also type the name directly into the text box. To base the picture on the contents of a table's general field, click the Field box, which you can use to select the field.

The If Picture and Frame Are Different Sizes area has three options: Clip Picture; Scale Picture, Retain Shape; and Scale Picture, Fill the Frame. When the picture is larger than the frame you added to the report, the Clip Picture option tells Visual FoxPro to clip the picture at the right and bottom as necessary to fit the picture. The Scale Picture, Retain Shape option tells Visual FoxPro to show the entire picture, filling as much of the frame as possible while keeping the relative proportions of the bitmap picture. The Scale Picture, Fill the Frame option shows the picture, filling the frame completely even if doing so distorts the picture.

The Center Picture check box is used with pictures stored in a table's general fields. Pictures in files on disk are not affected by this option. If the picture from the field is smaller than the frame, checking this box will center it within the frame.

The Print When button works similarly with pictures as it works with the other controls. You can choose to show a picture only when certain criteria are met. For instance, many developers add two pictures to a report, aligned one atop the other, with a logical flag determining which is printed. In this way, you can graphically indicate the value of a variable.

The Object Position area of the dialog box has three options: Fix Relative to Top of Band, Fix Relative to Bottom of Band, and Float. The Fix Relative to Top of Band option maintains the text's position in relation to the top of the band and does not enable field stretching to accommodate a different size picture. The Fix Relative to Bottom of Band *will* enable field stretching to accommodate lengthy data but will maintain the picture's position in relation to the bottom of the band. The Float option enables the text to float in relation to the bands' position.

You can use the Comment portion of the dialog box to add comments about the picture, for your own reference or for your fellow programmers. Comments do not affect the printed report.

Formatting Report Controls

When you are working in the Report Designer, a new menu option appears: Reports. In addition, certain options on other menus are enabled or take on a special meaning. Some of these options are also available through toolbar choices. For instance, the Format menu includes several tools to align and size data, which duplicate the functionality of the Layout toolbar.

Alignment

To align a series of text boxes, for instance, start by multiselecting the text boxes (you can do so by holding down the Ctrl key as you click or holding down the mouse key and drawing a rectangular area around the controls you want to select). Then, while the controls are still selected, choose Format, Align. You can choose how you want to align the select controls: left, right, top, bottom, centered vertically, or centered horizontally. This alignment process has no effect on the alignment of text within each control. Instead, it determines how the controls sit in reference to each other.

Visual FoxPro tries to take its best guess at exactly where you want the newly aligned group of controls to reside, but if you align controls that start out quite far apart, FoxPro might end up placing them a few pixels away from where you want them to be. In that case, while the controls are still multiselected, you can move them together by using either the mouse or the arrow keys.

Size

The Format menu also includes a number of Size options, which enable the developer to easily size multiple controls to each other or to the grid line settings in the Report Designer. Choosing Format, Size, To Grid snaps one or more controls to the same dimensions as the nearest Report Designer grid lines. The other options determine the size of multiple controls based on the tallest, shortest, widest, or most narrow selected control.

Spacing

The Format, Spacing options enable you to space three or more controls equal distances apart, either vertically or horizontally. You might not notice if a series of text boxes in a report are a few pixels more or less apart from each other. But an accountant who is proofing data with a ruler most certainly will. Try to use all the Format features at every opportunity. Doing so will only make your reports all the more attractive and professional.

Group

The Format, Group option lets you treat two or more controls as one single control. This capability is particularly useful when you're centering controls. If you multiselect controls in the Report Designer and select one of the centering features, each and every control is centered, which means that they will all end up overlapping one another. But if you first group these items and then center them, you will get the result you probably were looking for: The controls, as a group, will be centered on the page.

If you select a control that has already been grouped, this option changes to Ungroup.

Snap to Grid and Grid Scale

The View, Grid Lines option fills in the report canvas with horizontal and vertical grid aligns, enabling you to better gauge distances. Two options under Format—Snap to Grid and Grid Scale—enable you to change the length and width of the grid areas, and to snap a control to the nearest horizontal or vertical line.

 TIP Visual FoxPro enables for very precise placement of objects on a report. In addition to snapping objects to grids and aligning them through the menu or toolbar options, you can use the arrow keys to move them very slightly. Click the object, and then press the arrow keys. Every keypress moves the object 1/100th of an inch in the direction of the arrow.

Text Options

The Format, Font option enables you to specify a font for a control or a group of controls. You can use any available Windows font.

> **CAUTION**
>
> Sometimes a report you've designed looks just fine on your own machine, but when you send it to a client, certain letters are out of alignment or even missing. Keep in mind that your report will only print the way you designed it when it is run on a PC with all the necessary fonts available. Otherwise, the appearance will range anywhere from "off just a bit" to "bearing no resemblance whatsoever." For that reason, sticking to basic and widely used fonts such as Arial, Times Roman, or Courier is safest, unless you have acquired the legal rights to distribute a font with your applications or are certain that all your customers already have a particular font installed.

Text alignment determines the text alignment within a control. The Format, Align options determine the positioning of the controls relative to one another. The text alignment options let you justify the text to the right, left, or center. The Reading Order option is available only in BIDI versions of Visual FoxPro.

The Fill and Pen Options

The Fill and Pen options provide a quick mechanism for changing the internal (fill) or border (pen) patterns and sizes. The Fill option displays a submenu (see Figure 10.16) that includes hatched and crosshatched patterns, or a default setting of no fill pattern. The Pen option launches a submenu of pen widths (from hairline to 6 point) and types of outlines (no outline, dotted lines, dashed lines, and combinations).

The Mode option determines whether a control's background is transparent or opaque. It affects only text objects, rectangles, and rounded rectangles that have been assigned fill patterns.

FIGURE 10.16

Using the Fill menu, you can specify the background of a control.

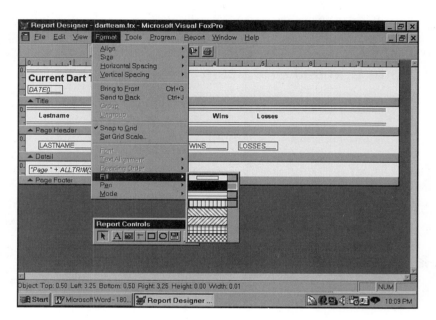

Report Bands

Visual FoxPro's Report Designer uses the *band-oriented* approach that has become so popular among report-writing products in recent years. Different *bands* represent different sections of the report, some of which repeat at different intervals than others.

The Major Report Bands Nearly every report you design will have a *detail band*, which contains the data that prints in the main portion of the report. The controls in this section probably represent the "heart" of the report. Controls placed in this band will print once for each record in the underlying data source (or, more accurately, each record included after any filters, keys, and the like are applied). So, including a "lastname" control in this band means that Visual FoxPro will print the `lastname` field from every record in this area, fitting as many as it can on a page, given the font and spacing you have used and the sizes of the other bands.

Controls in the *title band* are printed only once, on the first page of the report, whereas controls in the summary band will appear only at the end of the report. Title bands are commonly used for titles and such report-level information as the current data and time. Summary bands are used for summary information such as grand totals of numeric fields, counts of the number of records included in the report, or "for more information..." style report trailers.

 Unlike many database and reporting products, Visual FoxPro enables you to drag controls from one band into another. In other words, if you've added a field to the title band and then realize that you must instead show it on every page, just drag it to the page header band.

The *page header band* will print on the top of each and every page, and the *page footer band* should include only those objects that you want to appear on the bottom of each page.

 Page footers are a good place for page numbers, dates, report names, location codes, or any other information that users might need if pages of a report become loose or are stored out of order.

Other Report Bands If you choose to group your data, you will also be able to place information in the *group header* and *group footer* bands. Group header and group footer bands let you arrange reports by groups, and to indicate information about those groups. For example, you might sort a list of hospital patients by type of health insurance. One option would be to list each name and insurance type, but a better option might be to group the data, listing the insurance type only once for many names (compare Figures 10.17 and 10.18).

FIGURE 10.17
An ungrouped report includes details of information without any summary information.

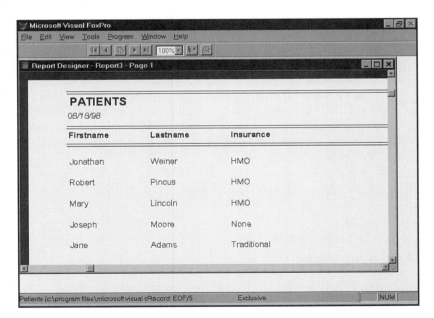

FIGURE 10.18

A grouped report presents summary information as well as details.

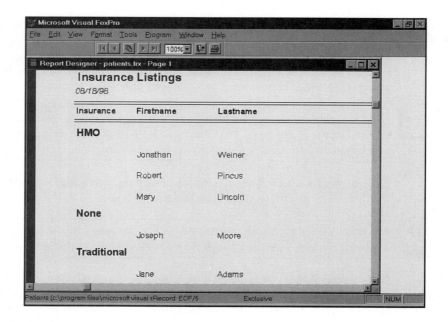

In Figure 10.18, the insurance types are listed once for each group, so we have placed that control in the group header band. The title of the report appears only once, so we have dropped that field control onto the title band. The Insurance, Firstname, and Lastname titles appear on each page, so we have placed them in the page header band. The real heart of the report, of course, is the list of patient names, which appear under each insurance type. They are placed in the detail band.

See Figure 10.19 for a look at the design of the report from Figure 10.18.

If you choose to create a multiple column report, you might also include column headers and footers. To create a report with multiple columns, select File, Page Setup and enter the number of columns in the dialog box, as well as the width of the columns and the space between them. This dialog box (see Figure 10.20) also includes a number of other useful items, detailed in Table 10.1.

FIGURE 10.19
Designing a grouped report is easy.

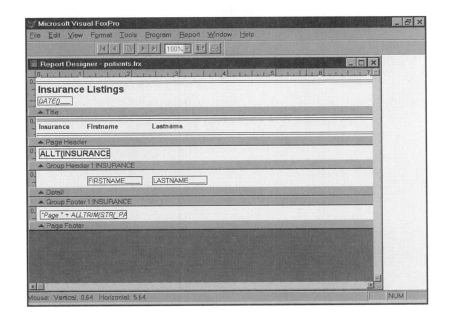

FIGURE 10.20
You can specify the number of columns on a report through the File, Page Setup options.

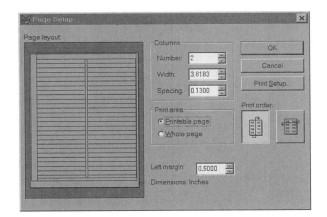

Table 10.1 Page Setup Dialog Box Controls

Control	Description
Number spinner	Use this spinner to increase or decrease the number of columns in your report. You can change the value by clicking the spinner's up and down arrows or by typing the number in the text box.

continues

Part III
Ch 10

Table 10.1   Continued

Control	Description
Width spinner	Use this spinner to set the width of the columns. You can change the value by clicking the spinner's up and down arrows or by typing the value in the text box.
Spacing spinner	Use this spinner to set the width of the space between columns. You can change the value by clicking the spinner's up and down arrows or by typing the value in the text box.
Print Area options	Use these options to determine how printer margins are handled in the report. If you select Printable Page, the printed area of the page is determined according to the default printer specifications and is shown in the Page Layout area of the dialog box. If you select Whole Page, your report fills the whole page.
Print Setup button	Use this button to open the Windows Print Setup dialog box, where you can change the default printer setup for the printer installed under Windows.
Print Order buttons	Use these buttons to determine whether vertical columns are filled from top to bottom beginning at the left side of the page or whether horizontal rows are filled from left to right starting at the top of the page.
Left Margin spinner	Use this spinner to set the width of the left margin. You can change the value by clicking the spinner's up and down arrows or by typing the value in the text box.

Ordering and Grouping Your Reports

The data in your reports will print in the order of the underlying data source. You cannot set a distinct order for printing data in a report, but instead, you should set the order or index tag of the underlying table, cursor, or view.

With most column-oriented reports, you should subdivide the data into groups. For example, in the preceding example, we grouped the records by the type of insurance.   To group data in your reports, order the data based on the grouping criteria, and then select Report, Data Grouping to add your groupings (see Figure 10.21).

You can add a group by clicking the Insert button. Type the expression into the text box, or click the ellipsis button to open Visual FoxPro's Expression Builder. When groups are used, the report begins a new group each time the basis of the group expression changes. For this reason, the underlying data source must be ordered according to the grouping criteria: Visual FoxPro cannot jump around the data source and collect all records relevant to a group. As soon as the result of the grouping expression changes, any group subtotals are made, the group bands print, and a new group begins.

FIGURE 10.21
Use the Data Grouping
dialog box to specify
the different groups on
your report.

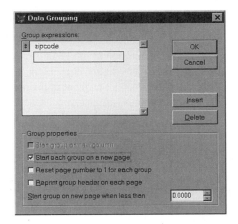

 The Group expression will often be a field, but it can also be a variable or a user-defined function. In fact, it can also be a concatenated expression, combining two fields (such as `lastname + firstname`).

The Group Properties area indicates the behavior on each group change. If your report has more than one column, the Start Group on New Column box starts a new column each time the group expression changes. Start Each Group in a New Page inserts a page break whenever the group expression changes. Reset Page Number to 1 for Each Group indicates that the page count will restart with each new group. This capability is useful if a report is to be split and sent to several different recipients. The Reprint Group Header on Each Page box, when checked, tells Visual FoxPro to reprint the group header on each page spanned by the group.

The Start Group on New Page When Less Than spinner control helps prevent a group header showing up too close to the bottom of a page. Use the spinner to choose the minimum distance from the bottom of the page that a group header should print. The default setting of zero means that the header will print as far down on the page as it ends up situated.

When you are done defining groups, click OK to close the dialog box. The bands for the new groups will appear in the report. However, by default, they occupy no space. You will need to increase the width of the new bands to the spacing you want by clicking and dragging them. Changing the width will enable you to drop any controls such as column headers or footer subtotals.

Taking Advantage of Data Environments and Data Sessions

In Chapter 9, "Creating Forms," I discussed the use of Data Environments and private data sessions in forms. Fortunately, these tools are available in the Report Designer as well. To open the Report Designer Data Environment window, choose View, Data Environment, or right-click on the report canvas and select Data Environment from the shortcut menu.

Either way, you will be shown a visual representation of the Data Environment for the form, as shown in Figure 10.22, and you can choose to add tables, cursors, or views as you want. Each of them is added as a cursor object, complete with its own set of properties, events, and methods. You can visually set relations between cursor objects, or access the properties, events, and methods of tables, cursors, or relations via the Properties and Code windows.

FIGURE 10.22

The Report Designer Data Environment enables you to specify and save the sources of information for your report.

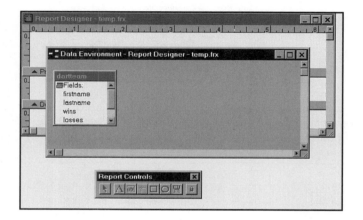

To add tables or views to the Data Environment, select Data Environment, Add, or right-click on the Data Environment designer and select Add. If a database is already open, that database and its tables or views will appear in the Add Table or View dialog box (see Figure 10.23). If no database is currently opened, or if you choose Other, a GetFile dialog box will appear for you to choose a table. If you select a table that is a member of a database that is not yet open, Visual FoxPro backlinks the table to the database and opens the database automatically.

If you want to work against a view instead of a table, select the View option button, and the list of tables will be replaced by a list of views in the database.

Once the table or view has been added to the Data Environment, you can browse it by right-clicking on the table or view and selecting Browse from the shortcut menu. You can also select Data Environment, Browse from the system menu, but only if the table or view has already been selected (select it by clicking it). From there, you can drag and drop fields onto the report canvas.

After a table or view has been added to the Data Environment, you can access its properties through a Properties window, just as if it were part of a class or form. And, the data source will be opened automatically whenever the report is called, rather than requiring the programmer to re-create the area.

FIGURE 10.23
In the Add Table or View dialog box, you can add different tables or views to the Report Designer Data Environment.

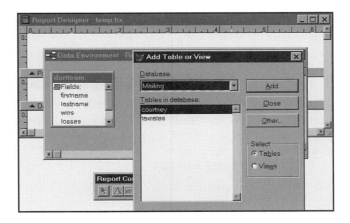

Part III
Ch
10

Working with Relationships in the Data Environment Designer

Creating a relationship between cursor objects in the Data Environment is easy. Select the relation field from the parent data source, and drag it onto the child cursor. The child table must have an index on this field. If it doesn't, Visual FoxPro offers to create one for you.

Just as the Data Environment makes running your report easier, private data sessions make cleaning up after your report a virtual nonissue. When a report runs, it moves record pointers in the underlying table. In pre-Visual FoxPro days, running a report meant having to keep track of record numbers, index tags, and relationships, and resetting them after you were done. But now, none of that is necessary. A private data session is a small, relatively well-protected area of your application, allowing a report to change record pointers, index orders, relations, or any other setting without affecting the current form or environment.

You can easily assign a report its own data session. Just choose Report, Private Data Session from the system menu. Doing so toggles the private data session setting on or off.

Design Strategies

Proper planning can help you save wasted time and avoid reports that don't give users the needed information. When you design reports, your job is to take the raw data provided by a table or a query and transform it into a printed report that provides the information in a way that makes sense to the user. Here are some suggested steps for designing a report:

- Discuss the layout with your users, and if possible, acquire copies of existing or similar reports.
- Design the layout on paper, and make note of any grouping, subtotaling, or formatting questions.
- Decide whether you can use a Data Environment and private data session, or if you will create a cursor in the current area before calling the report.

- Design the report in Visual FoxPro.
- Preview or print the report, and get feedback.

Creating a Report with the Report Wizards

The Visual FoxPro Report Wizards provide an automated way to create a report in any of a number of common styles. To start the Report Wizard process, select Tools, Wizards, Report. The dialog box shown in Figure 10.24 will appear.

FIGURE 10.24
In the Wizard Selection dialog box, you can select the desired Report Wizard.

One-to-many reports are used to create relational reports, showing one record from the primary table along with any associated records from the secondary, or child, table. The standard one-source report brings in data as it appears on a single underlying data source.

Click the OK button or double-click to choose the type of report you want to create, and the dialog box shown in Figure 10.25 appears.

FIGURE 10.25
The first step of the Report Wizard lets you choose the fields for your report.

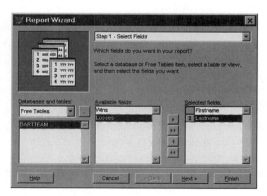

Select the desired database and associated table under the Databases and Tables options on the left. You will then see a list of available fields. You can click on the right-arrow command button to move the fields you want into the Selected fields list, in any order you like. The double right-arrow button will move all available fields into the Selected fields list.

The next dialog box, shown in Figure 10.26, enables you to group records on the report, up to three levels. In the Grouping Intervals dialog box shown in Figure 10.27, you can decide how closely something needs to match in order to be included in the same group: an absolute match of the entire field, the first digit, the first five digits, or anything in between.

FIGURE 10.26

The second step of the Report Wizard lets you group records for your report.

FIGURE 10.27

In the Grouping Intervals dialog box, you can specify the precision of your data groupings.

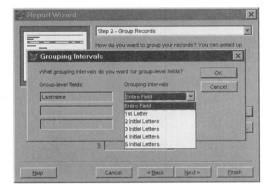

Using the Summary Options button on the Wizard's Step 2 dialog box, you can request one or more types of calculations on one or more of your report fields (see Figure 10.28).

FIGURE 10.28

The Summary Options button lets you request one or more types of calculation for your report fields.

In the next dialog box, you can select a style for your report from five common templates (see Figure 10.29). My favorite part of this box is the magnifying glass in the upper-left corner: As you select different styles, it changes to show you what the resulting report will look like.

FIGURE 10.29

The third step of the Report Wizard lets you specify the style of your report.

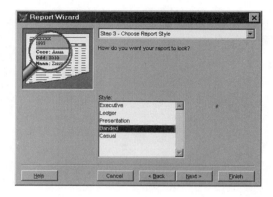

The Define Report Layout step (see Figure 10.30) lets you define whether a report is to be printed in landscape or portrait, how many columns the report should include, and whether the field layout is by rows or columns.

FIGURE 10.30

The fourth step of the Report Wizard lets you define the page layout of the report, including the number of columns.

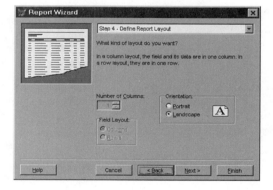

In the Step 5 dialog box, you can select the order for your report (see Figure 10.31). You can choose up to three nested layers of orders. Remember that your order must correspond to your group criteria if the grouping feature is to work correctly.

The last dialog box asks whether you want to save the report, save the report and immediately run it, or save the report and immediately begin modifying it (see Figure 10.32). You can also decide whether you want fields to wrap if they do not fit in the allowed space. If your source tables are database tables rather than free tables, you can also decide to use the display settings stored in the database.

FIGURE 10.31
The fifth step of the Report Wizard lets you specify the order of the underlying data source.

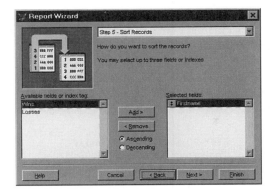

FIGURE 10.32
When you finish using the Report Wizard, you can run the report immediately, save it, or modify it.

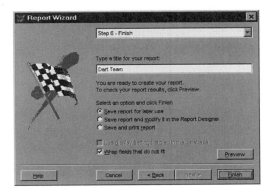

Part
III

Ch
10

TIP The Report Wizard can be a useful tool for creating a simple form, prototyping a form, or just learning more about Report Designer objects and how they work. I often use the wizard to get up and running with a general field layout and style and then modify the report extensively afterward.

Running Reports

You can print a completed report by using any of the following methods:

- From the Project Manager, click the Document tab, click and highlight a report, and then click the Print button from the Standard toolbar.

- From the command window (or from program code), use the `Report Form` command. This command has the following basic syntax:

```
REPORT FORM reportname TO PRINT ¦ PREVIEW ¦ TO filename ¦ FOR filter expression
```

Keep in mind that your reports will be formatted for the currently installed printer. If you run the same reports later to a different printer, some alignment and spacing might be off. Visual

FoxPro generally does a good job of resolving differences, if the printers used are both relatively standard and not very different from one another. However, you will want to test your reports from your users' printers if possible.

 TIP You might want to run your reports against an underlying cursor, which has already been filtered based on some programmer or user-defined criteria. Visual FoxPro also lets you filter data through a number of optional clauses of the `Report Form` command. The following commands will limit the data that is printed to the scope specified:

```
REPORT FORM MyReport TO PRINT FOR LastName = "Miller"
REPORT FORM MyOtherReport TO PRINT While Losses < 10
```

> **CAUTION**
>
> If you plan to distribute your reports as individual files, separate from your `.EXE` or `.APP` (many developers choose to do so), be sure to respect the network operating system's rules on file naming. Specifically, you might need to limit your names to an 8.3 format instead of using long filenames.

Choosing a Destination

Using the `Report Form` command, you can direct your output to one of several destinations. Most likely, you will want to print your report, in which case your command will look something like this:

```
REPORT FORM MyReport TO PRINT
```

You might want to preview the report, instead of sending it directly to a printer:

```
REPORT FORM MyReport TO PRINT PREVIEW
```

Of course, you might want to save the text of the report to an ASCII file. That's easy, too:

```
REPORT FORM MyReport TO FILE MyFile.txt ASCII
```

N O T E ASCII output loses most of the formatting and styles that you have specified but has the major benefit of enabling your users to access the resulting information through most word processing applications. ■

By default, report results echo to the screen while being generated. To prevent this from happening, attach the optional NOCONSOLE keyword.

N O T E Sometimes, a report will print with extra blank pages between each "real" page. This can happen when the length or width of a report exceeds the printable area. Visual FoxPro tries in such a case to print onto an additional page whatever portion of the report it couldn't fit on the first page. Then the actual page break fires. To resolve this problem, open the Report Designer and pull in the right and bottom edges of the report canvas as much as possible. Also, choose File, Page Setup and make sure that the margins are correct for your paper size—or try adjusting the margins. ■

Reports: A Final Word

To many users, the most important aspect of a database application is its reports. In fact, if you're designing an application for a large company, reports might be the *only* part of your system that the President or CEO will ever see.

Visual FoxPro's Report Designer allows you to create slick, powerful, graphically rich reports. Your report strategy might vary by application, but odds are that you'll include several Visual FoxPro reports in your final product.

Many developers augment Visual FoxPro's native Report Form capabilities by exposing report cursors to outside report writing products or by using ODBC technology to provide direct access to tables. If you and your users are comfortable with some approaches, then by all means pursue them. But don't overlook the capabilities of the Visual FoxPro Report Designer. More than once I've watched programmers take a second look at the Report Designer and comment that they might have spent too much time learning a third-party tool when there wasn't much need to do so after all. ●

Part
III

Ch
10

Creating Menus

Using the Menu Designer

As we've noted throughout this section of the book, the GUI is an extremely important part of an application because it is the element that your clients will see and work with each day. In the past few years, users have grown to expect slick, event-driven user interfaces, and fortunately, Visual FoxPro has kept pace through its various GUI design tools.

Just a few years ago, most users were satisfied with database applications that operated through a series of modal windows and hot keys. No more. Today, they want the same type of easy-to-use pull-down menus that they use in their other applications, from word processors to spreadsheets to Internet browsers. In fact, odds are that they'll even have a few expectations about just what appears on these menus and in what order.

Visual FoxPro 6 includes an easy-to-use *Menu Designer*, which enables you to center your application around a Windows-standard menu system. As you'll see, you can even use the same Menu Designer to create impressive right-click shortcut menus.

You can start the Menu Designer in the following ways:

- Choose File, New, and select the Menu option.
- Execute the `Create Menu` command from the command window. You'll be prompted to choose either a menu or a shortcut. Choose menu.
- From the Project Manager, select the Other tab, select Menus, and click on the New button.

Menu Designer Layout Window

No matter how you launch the Menu Designer, you'll see the same empty Menu Designer shown in Figure 11.1.

FIGURE 11.1

The Menu Designer provides an easy way to include standard Windows menus in your applications.

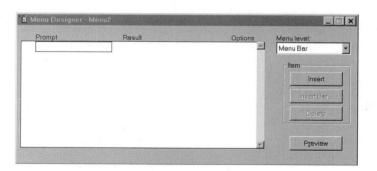

The Menu Designer is rather uncomplicated, especially compared to the Form Designer or the Report Designer. It contains a main list box area with three columns (Prompt, Result, and Options), a combo box indicating current menu level, and four pushbuttons (Preview, Insert, Insert Bar, and Delete). Note that when you start the Menu Designer, an additional menu, named Menus, appears on the Visual FoxPro system menu bar. Also, notice that two additional options (General Options and Menu Options) appear under the View menu whenever the Menu Designer is the active window.

Terminology

Let's take a moment to discuss Visual FoxPro's menu terminology. Menus are so easy to create and run in Visual FoxPro that you probably won't ever need to recall each of these definitions off the top of your head. But they will help you to follow the rest of this chapter, as well as the FoxPro documentation and various articles and news postings.

Menu bar refers to the top layer of a menu, the list of item names that remain visible throughout most or all of your application. If you work on applications that swap menus for different forms or reports, or for any other reason, you might find yourself referring to more than one menu bar (the primary menu bar versus the supervisor menu bar, and so on).

Menu pad is the next level in the hierarchy. Each of the item names in a menu bar represents a menu pad. Clicking on a pad can expand the pad to show any number of sub-options or can itself initiate some action. For instance, the File option on the FoxPro system menu (and most Microsoft product menus) represents one pad (the File pad), and the Windows option represents another (the Windows pad).

A *pop-up menu* is a vertical list of options that appears when you click on a menu pad. Clicking on the File pad in most applications will cause the File pop-up menu to appear. This pop-up usually includes options such as New, Open, and so on.

A *menu prompt* is a caption that appears on a menu pop-up. Clicking on a menu prompt might initiate an action or might lead to a *submenu* of other prompts.

The Prompt Column

Let's return to our Menu Designer. To create a new menu pad, type the text you want to appear in the Prompt column. Note that you can specify a hot key for this prompt by preceding one of the characters in the text with \< (see Figure 11.2).

Part
III

Ch
11

FIGURE 11.2
The Customers menu pad here has C indicated as its hot key and is set up to run a command.

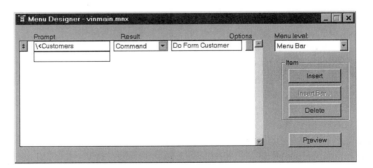

The Result Column

Next, specify a result. A *result* is what happens when the user clicks on the pad you've just specified or executes the hot key you have assigned to it. You can specify one of four result options: a Submenu, a Command, a Procedure, or a Pad Name.

Each of these options is used for a different purpose. If you choose to define a command, a text box appears, and you can type a valid Visual FoxPro command or function. Quite often, it will be a DO FORM *MyForm* command (as you saw in Figure 11.2), though it can also be a wait window, a user-defined function, or a MessageBox.

You can also enter an entire procedure that will be run when you activate the menu item. Choosing Procedure from the combo box results in a Create button beside the combo box. Click this button, and you can enter an entire procedure (sometimes referred to in this context as a code *snippet*). If a procedure already exists for this menu prompt, the Create button appears as an Edit button instead (see Figure 11.3).

FIGURE 11.3

You can include entire procedures within your menu pads.

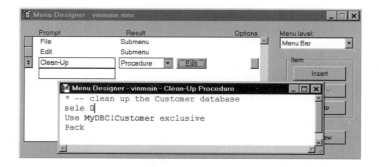

N O T E You might think that rather than entering a procedure right into the menu prompt, you could save it somewhere else and call it using the command option. This approach is often the better course of action, for various reasons. First, if your procedure might be used elsewhere in your application, storing it separately helps you maintain it as a reusable piece of code. Second, Visual FoxPro menus must be generated into code to be able to run (you'll see more details on this issue in the section "Generating Menu Code and Running Menus" later in this chapter). If you store your action as a procedure, you will have to regenerate the menu every time you want to change the action. If you store it as a separate program or function and call it as a command, you don't need to regenerate the menu code. But, as is so often the case with Visual FoxPro, you can use the approach that best meets your particular needs. ■

The Submenu option creates a new menu off the current pad or prompt. When you choose this option, a Create button appears to the right of the combo box. When you click this button, a new empty menu structure appears, enabling you to define the submenu. As with a procedure, the Create button changes to an Edit button after the submenu is designed.

The last available action in the Result column is Pad Name (when you are editing at the highest menu level) or Bar # (when you are editing at a pop-up or submenu level). This feature is very helpful for adding native Visual FoxPro behavior to one of your own menus. For instance, you can add cut-and-paste functionality by calling the Visual FoxPro bar numbers for Cut and Paste (see Figure 11.4).

FIGURE 11.4
Visual FoxPro 6 makes it easy to add cut-and-paste functionality to your menus.

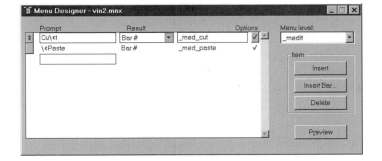

You can add Visual FoxPro functionality to your own menus in two ways. The hard way is to memorize bar number references and type them in yourself. The easy way is to use the Insert Bar button on the right side of the Menu Designer. Insert Bar offers you a dialog box with all the available native Visual FoxPro behaviors (see Figure 11.5). Select one, click Insert, and the prompt is inserted directly into your menu.

FIGURE 11.5
You can include VFP's native Copy functionality in your own menus, which is much simpler than coding that functionality from scratch.

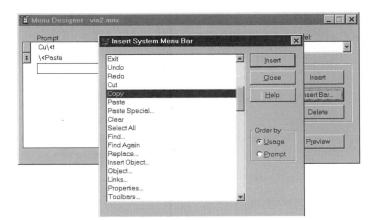

T I P When you select one of the Visual FoxPro menu bars, it inserts not only the bar number, but also the default prompt. There's no law that says you have to stick to this prompt caption. Editing the prompt does not alter the functionality. You could rename the Copy prompt to Copy Text, for instance.

Part
III

Ch
11

The Options Column

The Options column consists of a pushbutton for each item in the menu. When you click one of these buttons, the Prompt Options dialog box appears (see Figure 11.6). In this dialog box, you can take a number of actions, some to provide backward compatibility to prior versions of FoxPro, and some to provide easy access to advanced functionality.

FIGURE 11.6

In the Prompt Options dialog box, you can enter status bar messages, developer comments, and skip conditions.

In the Shortcut section, you can specify a keyboard shortcut (a hot key or shortcut key combination) for the menu option. In the Key Text box, you can indicate what description, if anything, should appear on the menu beside the prompt. Note that you can leave this box blank if you don't want the hot key assignment to show on the menu prompt itself.

The Negotiate section specifies the location of a menu item when you're editing an OLE object in your application. If you want one or more of your menu options to remain as part of the menu during an in-place OLE editing session, select an option in this section:

Option	Outcome
None	Menu title will not appear.
Left	Menu title is placed in the left group of menu titles on the menu bar.
Middle	Menu title is placed in the middle group of menu titles on the menu bar.
Right	Menu title is placed in the right group of menu titles on the menu bar.

If you are not using OLE components in your application, ignore the Negotiate section.

The Skip For option enables you to specify when the prompt is available to the user. Any FoxPro memory variable, property, or function call is valid, but keep in mind that the menu is polling for the value almost constantly. A complex function call could make your application feel quite sluggish to the user because it is hogging processor resources.

Also, keep in mind that the variable, property, or function call must be in scope to be able to function properly. Otherwise, a runtime error is generated when loading the menu, and the Skip For expression has no effect afterward (even if the variable comes back into scope). If the variable is in scope at the time the menu is created but later goes out of scope, a runtime error occurs.

In the Message box, you can specify a message that Visual FoxPro will display in the status bar whenever the pad or prompt is highlighted.

In the Pad Name box, you can specify a particular pad name, different from the Visual FoxPro default. Specifying a pad name is entirely optional, but it might assist you in referring to the menu option in code, if you ever do so.

The Comment edit box is for programmer use only. Nothing entered here has any effect on the menu at runtime. Use this area as you would use comments in your standard code.

The Menu Selection Combo Box

The Menu Selection combo box, in the upper-right corner of the Menu Designer, contains a list of the current menu and any higher-level menus. You can choose the level of the hierarchy that you want to view by selecting from this combo box.

The Menu Designer Pushbuttons

We have already discussed the Insert Bar pushbutton, but Visual FoxPro includes three other pushbutton options to assist your development. The Insert button inserts an empty prompt into the menu bar or pop-up you are currently editing. The Delete button deletes the prompt you currently have selected. Preview enables you to view the results of your efforts so far, without leaving the Menu Designer. After you click Preview, a box appears specifying the menu you are previewing. If you select a menu prompt, the box shows the command that would be executed if you were running the menu "live" (see Figure 11.7).

Part
III

Ch
11

FIGURE 11.7
You can preview your menu before you save it.

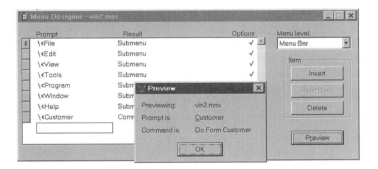

 TIP Whenever the Menu Designer is the active window, the Visual FoxPro system menu includes a new menu named Menu. This menu provides an alternative approach to accessing the Menu Designer's pushbutton functionality.

Other Menu Options via the View Menu

Whenever the Menu Designer is active, Visual FoxPro's View menu includes two additional items: General Options and Menu Options.

The General Options dialog box (see Figure 11.8) contains several useful features. The Procedure box specifies a default procedure that will run when a menu pad is selected. If no command is filled in for a given pad, the default procedure will be executed.

FIGURE 11.8

In the General Options dialog box, you can specify the location of the menu pads relative to any existing menus.

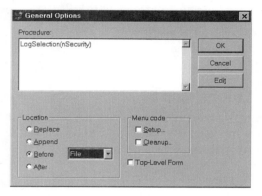

The Location section indicates whether this menu, when run, should replace any already-present menus, be appended after any existing menus, or be inserted before or after a particular existing menu pad.

The Menu Code check boxes open editing windows that enable you to enter startup and cleanup code that executes before loading and after unloading the menu, respectively.

The Top-Level Form check box indicates whether this menu can be used for a top-level (SDI) form or whether it is restricted to the FoxPro frame.

 The quickest way to get started with menus is to choose Menu, Quick Menu. This command basically creates a copy of the Visual FoxPro menu that you can then modify for your own purposes. It's a great learning tool and is also extremely useful when you plan to include a good deal of native Visual FoxPro functionality within an application.

The Menu Options dialog box (see Figure 11.9) specifies a default procedure that will run when a menu option (from a pop-up) is selected. If no command is filled in for a prompt, this procedure will be executed.

FIGURE 11.9

In the Menu Options dialog box, you can specify a default procedure for any menu options that have no actions specified.

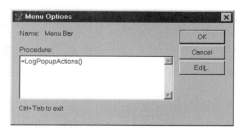

Designing Shortcut Menus

Visual FoxPro makes it easy to create shortcut menus that can be called from anywhere in your application (usually by right-clicking a form control). Shortcut menus are essentially the same as standard menus, but they do not have a top menu bar attached to them. Instead, their highest level of hierarchy is a horizontal menu pad.

To create a shortcut menu, just type `Create Menu` in the command window, and select Shortcut from the resulting dialog box. The standard Menu Designer appears. Now, just create the menu, and save your file as you would a standard menu. That's all there is to this process.

To run a shortcut menu, include a call to Do `ShortCut`.MPR in the `RightClick` of an object or form, or in any method from which you want to call the shortcut menu. Figure 11.10 shows a shortcut menu in action.

FIGURE 11.10

Visual FoxPro makes it easy for you to create shortcut menus that can be called from virtually any visual control in your application.

Generating Menu Code and Running Menus

Unlike most Visual FoxPro components, menus are not object-oriented. In fact, to many developers, they seem a bit of a throwback to pre-Visual FoxPro days because they still require a code generation program that converts the menu entries you've indicated into FoxPro code.

Many of us debate the merits and/or drawbacks of this approach until we are blue in the face. But, at any rate, Visual FoxPro menus are easy to create and even easier to generate. Just select Menu, Generate, and specify a filename in the resulting dialog box. The new file has a default extension of .MPR and can be run like any Visual FoxPro program: Just enter Do `MyMenu`.MPR.

Another way of generating menu code is to use the Project Manager. Just select Build, and in the resulting dialog check the Rebuild All box. The menu code will be generated automatically.

N O T E Visual FoxPro menus are Windows menus, not FoxPro objects. Why does this distinction matter? For two reasons. First, you cannot define the color of the menu in your Visual FoxPro applications. The user, through the Windows Control Panel, specifies these colors. Second, any timers in your application will not fire while the menu is active. ▦

TIP If you've changed one of your menu options and regenerated the code, but the old menu still appears when you run the application, you might have a problem with extraneous files. Check whether an old copy of the .MPR or .MPX file created by the code generator has been mistakenly copied to another area in your path. As with any program, FoxPro runs the first copy it finds along its available path.

Extending Visual FoxPro Menus

Many programmers feel, mistakenly, that because menus are not object-oriented, they are not reusable and extendable components of Visual FoxPro. That's not really true. Menus are just reusable in a different way.

True, you cannot subclass a new menu from an existing menu. However, remember that you can run multiple menus at once, and by adjusting the View, General Options, you can control where the menus sit in relation to one another. You therefore could design your applications to include a separate menu file for each pad and pop-up and include code to launch any appropriate menus in each of your application startup routines.

Also keep in mind that you can use macro substitution in your menu prompts. Just use the ampersand (&) followed by a variable name in the prompt. The variables must be in scope when the menu is created but can be released after that.

Finally, some developers wrap pad names and definitions in custom classes, to emulate some features of object orientation. In this way, you can, in fact, inherit properties and behavior for a *NewPrompt* object (based on a custom class) from an *OldPrompt* superclass. Custom methods would control the addition and removal of specified pads from the menu. This process gets a little complicated, but if your environment requires you to generate many applications with similar menus, considering this approach might be worthwhile. Several custom frameworks, such as *The Visual FoxPro CodeBook*, take just this approach.

Whether you work with such complex designs or stick to the native Menu Designer functionality, you'll soon find menus an indispensable part of your Visual FoxPro toolbox. ●

Organizing Components of an Application into a Project

Finding Your Way Around the Project Manager

The Project Manager is Visual FoxPro's tool for organizing all your application files—forms, reports, menus, programs, include files, graphics, and even data—into a single command center. Most programmers who have worked with FoxPro over the years have grown increasingly reliant on the Project Manager. There are many reasons for this growing relationship. First, many programmers have found that once an application grows beyond the three-program, two-form, one-report stage, its various parts become increasingly difficult to keep track of. The Project Manager enables access to all of an application's files through a single tool. Second, many Visual FoxPro programmers now release their applications as .EXE or .APP files, and the Project Manager makes creating those files a snap. Third, the Project Manager has grown in its functionality and usability, and now, with the release of Visual FoxPro 6, it is a fully exposed object, complete with development hooks to help automate source control and testing.

If you're a current FoxPro developer who hasn't taken full advantage of the Project Manager, there's no time like the present! And if you're new to FoxPro, you'll find the Project Manager a very valuable tool in your effort to keep track of your various application files.

In this section, you'll review each aspect of the Project Manager's interface.

Using the Outline Control

The *outline control* is the heart of the Project Manager. It's an easy to use, expandable hierarchy that's reminiscent of the Windows Explorer and File Manager tools. A plus sign icon indicates that there are hidden levels that can be uncovered with a click. Clicking a minus sign icon hides all the nested, subordinate levels.

Creating a new project in Visual FoxPro is easy. Just select New, Project from the system menu, or type **Create Project** in the Command window. When you are prompted for a filename, enter a name and press OK. The Project Manager will appear (see Figure 12.1).

FIGURE 12.1

The Visual FoxPro Project Manager enables you to access all your application's files through one central tool.

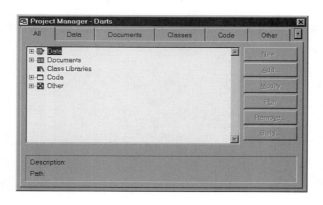

You can create a project as a late step in your application design and add existing files at that point. But to really take advantage of this tool, you should use it *while* you code and design, not after. I like to create a project at the same time as I create directories, and even before I create a main program for the application.

Types of Files Included in the Project Manager

The Project Manager window is reminiscent of the Properties window in the Form and Class Designers (and in the Data Environment of the Report Designer). Six different tabs are available, each of which shows a different subset of file types. The All tab, not surprisingly, shows all the project files. Let's take a moment to review each of the other tabs.

The Data Tab   The Data tab includes all databases, free tables, and queries (see Figure 12.2). It might shock you to learn that you can include data files in a project. But Visual FoxPro enables you to do so, which makes it easy to keep track of and quickly access the data your application runs against.

FIGURE 12.2
The Data tab includes all the data elements in your applications, including databases, free tables, and queries.

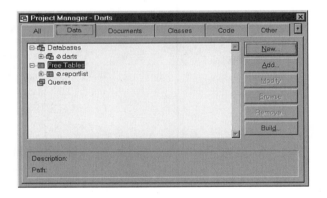

The Databases icon expands to show any databases in your project, but it doesn't stop there! The database icons each expand to differentiate among tables, local views, remote views, ODBC connections, and even stored procedures. Wherever possible, the Project Manager keeps expanding, showing more and more detail. So, for example, the Tables icon expands to show each table, and each table expands to show each field and index (see Figure 12.3).

Notice the small icon to the left of each table entry (a circle with a slash through it, known as the *Exclude icon*). This icon indicates that the file will not be included in any compiled .APP, .EXE, or .DLL created from the project. You'll learn more about compiling projects later in this chapter, but for now, keep in mind that there are some data or files you will probably distribute separate from your .EXE or .APP. Data files are a good example, and Visual FoxPro defaults to an exclude mode for these files. But you can also exclude other files or choose to include data files. Just choose Project, Exclude or Project, Include.

FIGURE 12.3
By expanding the icons on the Data tab, you can see each table in your application and even each field and index within tables.

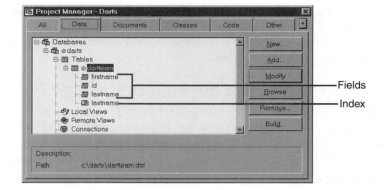

Fields

Index

The Documents Tab The Documents tab includes all document-style files, namely, forms, reports, and labels (see Figure 12.4). Again, expanding any of these icons results in a listing of all files of that type.

FIGURE 12.4
The Documents tab shows all forms, reports, and labels in your application.

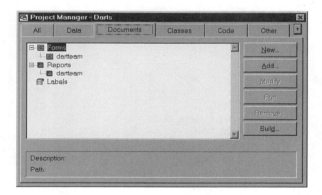

The Classes Tab The Classes tab includes all class libraries (see Figure 12.5). Class libraries can be expanded to show all member classes.

The Code Tab The Code tab shows all programs, API libraries, and applications (see Figure 12.6).

The Other Tab The Other tab shows all other types of Visual FoxPro files, such as menus, text files, or graphics files (see Figure 12.7).

 Text files usually consist of Include files, but can also include programmer documentation and tips. And remember, you can choose to exclude such files before compiling a program file by selecting Project, Exclude.

FIGURE 12.5

The Classes tab shows all class libraries in your application.

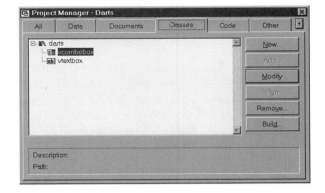

FIGURE 12.6

The Code tab shows all programs, API libraries, and external applications.

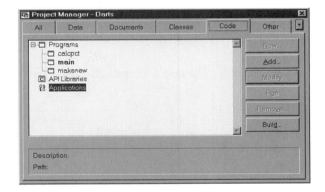

FIGURE 12.7

The Other tab shows all miscellaneous Visual FoxPro or external files.

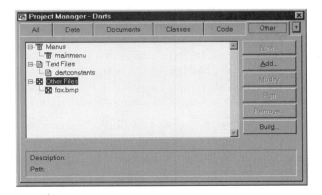

Part

III

Ch

12

Taking Advantage of the Project Manager's Functionality

If the Project Manager stopped there, it would still be useful; all the files you need are stored together in a nice hierarchical fashion, providing a self-documenting file management system. But the Project Manager also includes six buttons that are always present, no matter which tab or level of the hierarchy is selected, to enable you to modify, add, delete, or run files. These buttons will be enabled or disabled depending on what kind of file and level of hierarchy are selected. Here's a brief description of each:

- New—Adds a new file of the type currently selected.
- Add—Adds an existing file of the type currently selected to the project.
- Modify—Modifies the currently selected file.
- Run—Runs the currently selected file.
- Remove—Removes the currently selected file from the project, with an option to delete it from the disk.
- Build—Rebuilds the project, or builds an application, executable, or COM .DLL from the project.

 Some programmers find these options so useful that they find themselves never, or rarely, typing commands such as MODIFY FORM or Do *Program File*. Others mix and match techniques. Visual FoxPro lets you decide which approach works best for you and your team.

Creating Files Through the Project Manager

You can create any type of Visual FoxPro application file right from the Project Manager. Let's take a look at creating a program file. Click on the Code category and expand it. Visual FoxPro's Project Manager enables you to differentiate among three different types of code: programs, API libraries, and external applications (see Figure 12.8). Highlight Programs and click the New button to create a new program. A new program, with a default name of Program1, will appear (see Figure 12.9). Don't worry about the title in the Code window; when you save this program, you will be prompted for a more sensible name.

After you save the program, you can expand the Code, Programs outline branch to see it and any other programs you add to the project.

 You can expand or contract categories either by double-clicking the heading or by clicking the plus or minus icons.

FIGURE 12.8

You can expand the Code icon—or any icon—to indicate exactly what kind of file you want to add or create.

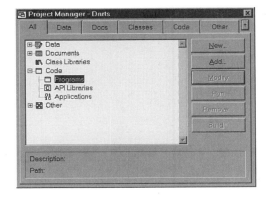

FIGURE 12.9

Creating a new program launches the Visual FoxPro Code window.

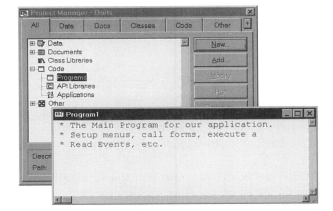

N O T E The very first program you create or add to the project is listed in bold type (see Figure 12.10). This indicates that the program is the main point of entry into the application, and it will be the first program code that fires when you start an application or project that you've created. You can always decide to use a different main program later by clicking on the file to highlight it and then selecting Project, Set Main. ■

Just as you use the New button to create a program file, you can use it to create a new form, menu, report, text file, or any other type of file. When you press the New button, Visual FoxPro looks at the file type selected and takes the appropriate behind-the-scenes action (Create Form, Modify Command, Create Report, and so on).

T I P You can include descriptions for each file in the project by highlighting the file and choosing Project, Edit Description.

FIGURE 12.10
The main program, or starting point, of your application is listed in bold type.

Adding Existing Files

You can also include preexisting files in your project. Just highlight the type of file you want to add and click the Add button. You'll be prompted to select an existing file from a GetFile() dialog box.

> **TIP** Remember that you can include the same file in several projects. The Project Manager just points to the underlying file. This is an extremely helpful tool for maintaining and making good use of reusable code and class libraries. But there's a downside: Remember that any changes you make to a program file, for instance, are reflected in any other projects using the program.

If you have decided to create a new project from a series of existing files and you're worried about having to add a hundred files in the manner demonstrated above, stop worrying! Just add the main file and when you rebuild the project (discussed below), Visual FoxPro will draw in any other called files. Of course, you might need to add a few references that Visual FoxPro could not pick up (such as any program that is called via macro-substitution, for instance), but you'll certainly get a running start.

Modifying Files

The Modify button, like the Add button, provides access to the native editor of the element you have highlighted. A Code window is brought forward for programs, the Form Designer for forms, and the Menu Designer for menus.

Visual FoxPro even activates the appropriate editor when you select an OLE component. Figure 12.11 shows what happens if you highlight a bitmap file and click Modify. This feature demonstrates the remarkable strength of the Project Manager. As the quantity and variety of multimedia, hypertext help, and other features in your applications increase, you will certainly be thankful for the ability to modify these files from one central development tool.

FIGURE 12.11
Whenever possible, Visual FoxPro lets you modify an OLE component through the associated application.

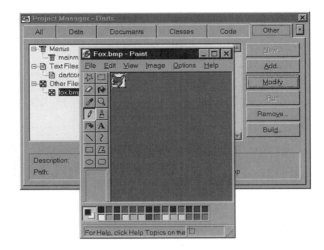

Running Programs and Forms and Previewing Reports

When you highlight a project element and press Run, Visual FoxPro runs the program or form for you.

This button's caption changes to Preview when you select a report. Of course, a particular program, form, or report can depend on certain variables or settings that might not be present. In that case, you might experience runtime errors. But, often, this is an extremely useful feature.

This button's caption changes to Browse when you select a table or a field. Clicking Browse will activate a browse window so that you can look directly at the table.

Removing Files

If you've worked with other project managers, you've probably been frustrated by the two-step (or more) process required for cleaning up and maintaining projects. After removing the file from the project, you still have to delete the actual file from disk. Visual FoxPro lets you handle both of these tasks at once. Just select the file and click Remove, and you will see the dialog shown in Figure 12.12.

> **CAUTION**
>
> While this procedure is very convenient, exercise caution! If there is any chance that the project might be associated with another project, choose to remove the file rather than deleting it entirely. (Of course, it's good practice to back up your files periodically, anyway.)

FIGURE 12.12
The Visual FoxPro Project Manager lets you remove a file from the project and even delete it from disk.

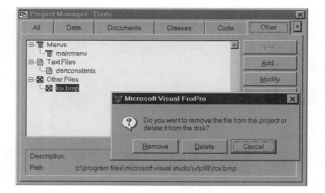

 The project files are actually special instances of .DBF and .FPT files. The Remove option deletes the element's particular record, but doesn't PACK the table. When you select Project, Clean Up Project, Visual FoxPro executes a PACK against the table.

Dragging and Dropping Project Elements

The Project Manager makes extensive use of drag-and-drop technology. With a little experimenting, you'll get a sense of just how powerful this feature will be in your development. For instance, you can drag and drop a control from one class library to make a copy of it in a second library. You can also drag a control from the Project Manager and drop it into the Form Designer to include an instance of it on a form.

Collapsing and Docking the Project Manager

For all its usefulness, the Project Manager is a big bulky window to have sitting on your desktop throughout your development. You can resize the window to some degree, just as you can most Visual FoxPro tools, but that's probably not enough in all cases. Fortunately, there is an alternative.

Click the up-arrow button in the upper-right corner (below the Close button) and the Project Manager is minimized. Only the tops of the tabs remain visible. This doesn't mean you've lost any functionality, though. If you click a particular tab, the tab expands downward and all your functionality returns. Figure 12.13 shows the Code tab dropped down. You can also continue to use the Project menu and right-click for certain shortcut options.

In this collapsed state, the Project Manager is a toolbar. If you drag it to the top of the screen, it docks there like any other toolbar. Additionally, you can drag a tab off the collapsed Project Manager down onto the Visual FoxPro screen. These torn-off tabs enable you to see only the parts of the Project Manager that you need. Figure 12.14 shows the Classes tab torn off; the rest of the Project Manager sits docked at the top of the screen. If you click the pushpin in the top right corner of the tab, it will stay on top. Just click it again to toggle it off and enable other windows to be moved above it.

FIGURE 12.13
Even when the Project Manager is minimized, all its options are available to you.

FIGURE 12.14
You can tear off one tab of the Project Manager and place it anywhere in your Visual FoxPro environment.

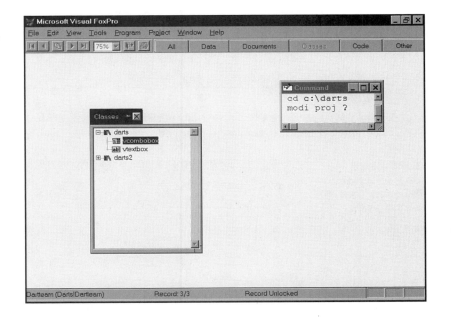

 TIP Torn-off tabs are particularly useful when you use the Form Designer. You can keep the Classes tab visible and active and drag classes into the Form Designer canvas.

The Project Information Dialog Box

The Project Information dialog box can be brought up by choosing Project, Project Info. The dialog box includes three tabs.

The Project tab enables you to specify information on the developer or company (see Figure 12.15). This tab also includes a setting for the home directory of the project and several compilation options, such as whether debug information is included and whether the compiled code is compiled. The Project Class check box and text box enable you to specify a `ProjectHook` class (the new project hook functionality is covered later in this chapter).

FIGURE 12.15

The Project tab holds information on the developer or company.

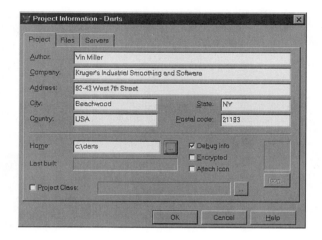

The Files tab includes a complete listing of all files in the project, the dates they were last modified, whether they are included, and the code page for the file (see Figure 12.16).

FIGURE 12.16

The Files tab includes a quick reference list of all files in your project.

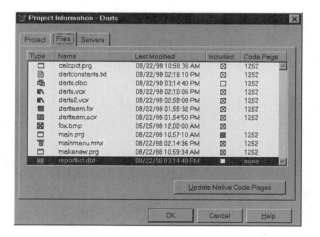

N O T E If the Included check box is blank, it is not included in any compiled `.APP`, `.EXE`, or `.DLL` files. If the check box is marked with an X, the file is included. If the check box is completely filled in, the file is the main file of the project. Remember, you can set the main file by highlighting the new main file in the Project Manager and choosing Project, Set Main. ▪

The Servers tab includes information on any classes (whether defined in code or visually) that are marked as OLE Public (see Figure 12.17). When you highlight a listed item, you see the library name and the name of the class. Also displayed is a description of the class name and a description of the library the selected class is based on. If you create your own help files and topic IDs, the filename and context ID are also shown. The public class's project name is displayed in the Project name box. The Instancing pull-down menu offers three choices:

- *Single Use.* This option indicates that you can create an instance of the class within or outside of Visual FoxPro using OLE Automation. Each instance requested causes a separate copy of the OLE server to open.

- *Not Creatable.* This indicates that you cannot create an instance of the server outside of Visual FoxPro.

- *Multi-Use.* This indicates that each requested instance uses the same copy of the OLE server to act as the server.

FIGURE 12.17
You can access information on OLE public classes through the Servers tab.

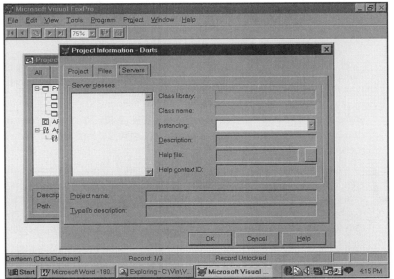

Part
III

Ch
12

Building Visual FoxPro .APP, .EXE, and COM .DLL Files

The Project Manager makes creating an application or executable file from your various program and document files a breeze. Just click the Build button on the right of the Project Manager. The dialog box shown in Figure 12.18 appears and enables you to choose from the following options:

- *Rebuild Project.* This option scans through all the files in the project, compiling where necessary or directed, generating source code, and checking for errors.

■ *Build Application.* This option builds the project, but then bundles all the files marked for inclusion into an .APP file. Anyone who wants to use this .APP file must have his or her own copy of Visual FoxPro.

■ *Build Executable.* This option builds and bundles the project just as Build Application does, but in addition, it places the Visual FoxPro runtime loader and an executable file header at the beginning of the file. Users can run the .EXE as long as they've loaded the runtime library and any other necessary .DLLs or .FLLs.

FIGURE 12.18

The Project Manager lets you rebuild the project, build a Visual FoxPro .APP file, or build an .EXE.

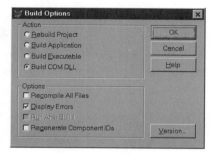

■ *Build COM DLL.* This option creates a Dynamic Link Library file that enables other applications to use your project as a server. You can learn more about Visual FoxPro's COM capabilities in Part V, "COM."

During any of the processes listed above, Visual FoxPro recompiles or regenerates any files that have been modified since the last build. The Recompile All Files option will force a recompile of all the files.

TIP Visual FoxPro does a pretty good job of knowing which files have to be recompiled, and as a result, I usually let it take the wheel and decide for itself what to recompile. But now and then, a file does not recompile (usually due to some action I've taken, such as restoring a backup .PRG without the corresponding .FXP). So, every few compiles, and definitely before I send anything out the door, I execute a recompile with a Rebuild All.

Visual FoxPro always maintains a log of compilation errors in a file with the same base name as your project and an .ERR extension. You can (and should) view this file right after a recompile by clicking the Display Errors option.

If you want your application to run right after the build, select the Run After Build option.

A Note on the Main File

As I discussed earlier in this chapter, the main file of your project is the file that gets called when a client runs your .APP or .EXE. It is easier to see in the list of Project Manager elements because it is always listed in bold. Although it can be a form, menu, or program, it is definitely best to make it a program. This program can be a very simple calling .PRG, but it will make your life much easier than starting with a form or menu. For instance, at its most simple, a main program might look something like this:

```
* setup code
DO MainMnu.MPR          && the menu code
DO Form StartUp.scx     && startup form
READ EVENTS             && VFP's internal event loop (kind(c)
* cleanup code
```

Including and Excluding Files from `.APPs` and `.EXEs`

Including and excluding files is sometimes a source of confusion, particularly for those new to Visual FoxPro. But it's really quite simple: Although you might want every file in your project to end up on clients' machines, you won't necessarily want them all to arrive there embedded in the `.APP` or `.EXE`. To begin with, anything included in the `.APP` or `.EXE` is read only, which means that some types of files should never be included. As a result, Visual FoxPro, by default, excludes databases, tables, `.FLLs`, `.DLLs`, and `.APPs`.

Wait a minute! It's easy to see why databases and tables shouldn't be included because you don't want them marked as read only, but why exclude `.FLLs`, `.DLLs`, and `.APPs`? Well, in those cases, the issues are more of a technical nature, and they have to do with the very nature of dynamic link libraries. Windows must be able to load a `.DLL` in to memory whenever it needs to, and if the files were embedded in your `.APP` or `.EXE`, that wouldn't be possible.

You'll have to make sure that you include any of these non-embedded files when you distribute your application. Fortunately, the Setup Wizard makes this easy to do.

You might also want to exclude Report Forms or other files that your clients might want to modify themselves. Even if your clients don't modify the reports you design for them, you might choose to deliver them separately as a part of your implementation strategy. Excluding reports will make your `.APP` or `.EXE` smaller, which means it will transmit more quickly. And, if you edit one report, you won't need to recompile and resend a large executable. Your decisions on which files to include will be based in part on your client base and the size and scope of your applications.

> **CAUTION**
>
> You can also create projects, `.APPs`, and `.EXEs` right from code, although there are very few reasons to do so. The `BUILD PROJECT`, `BUILD APP`, and `BUILD EXE` commands will do in code what you've already done in the examples above. But beware of the `BUILD PROJECT FROM` command! `Build Project MyProj` will rebuild the project, but `Build Project MyProj` from `Main` will overwrite the current project with a brand-new one, with `Main.prg` at its center. That is probably not the behavior you desire.

Building Setup Disks to Distribute Your Application

Creating setup disks is the final step in producing an application. But keep in mind that it is the first part of your product that your customers will see. And in this age of slick programs and rising user expectations, first impressions count.

Of course, programmers would rather put their time and energy into actual application development than slick setup procedures. And in fact, that should be the case. Fortunately, Visual FoxPro makes it easy to create professional setup programs without too much time or effort.

A slick interface is not the only reason to use Visual FoxPro's Setup Wizard. The simple fact of the matter is that a Visual FoxPro application is not a simple system to install. Gone are the days of batch files, a standalone .EXE, and a simple overlay file. These days, you need to install—and in many cases register with the operating system—the runtime modules, OLE files, .DLLs, and maybe even ODBC drivers.

At first glance, all of this might make you yearn for simple ZIP files and DOS paths. But then again, that would leave us with blue screens and modal forms. Visual FoxPro's power comes with a cost, but fortunately, Visual FoxPro comes with a powerful tool to assist you: the Setup Wizard.

Specifying Files to Include

Run the Setup Wizard after you build your .EXE. Then move the .EXE and any other files you want to distribute (reports, ReadMe.TXT files, and so on) to a separate subdirectory from the project. This subdirectory should include only the files you want to distribute and nothing more. To start the Setup Wizard, select Tools, Wizards, Setup, which brings forward the first page of the Setup Wizard (see Figure 12.19). This page requests one crucial piece of information: the directory location of the files you want to install. Press the ellipsis button to select a directory.

FIGURE 12.19

The first screen of the Setup Wizard requests the source directory for your setup files.

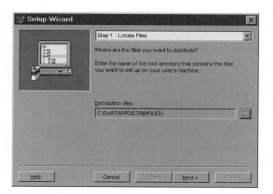

Specifying Components to Include

The second page of the Setup Wizard enables you to specify the components that must be distributed along with your executable file (see Figure 12.20). You will most likely want to include the Visual FoxPro 6 runtime (unless you know for sure that your users already have a Visual FoxPro 6 application installed on their machines). The chances are good that you will also want to include one or more other components. If your application includes graphs, select the Microsoft Graph 8.0 runtime option. If you use ActiveX components, ODBC connections, or HTML help, select these options.

FIGURE 12.20

The second screen of the Setup Wizard enables you to specify the additional system components that .EXE users require.

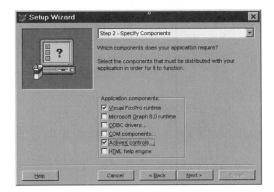

Notice that any of the check boxes with an ellipsis will prompt you for additional information. For example, when you click the ActiveX Controls option, Visual FoxPro will search your Registry for any current ActiveX components and bring forward a modal dialog box from which you can select any and all applicable items (see Figure 12.21).

FIGURE 12.21

The ActiveX Controls option enables you to specify which ActiveX controls are included in your application.

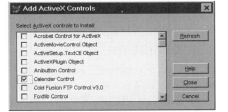

Part
III

Ch
12

Specifying Location of Setup Images

The third screen of the Setup Wizard enables you to choose the location for your installation images or directories and the type of installation images you would like to create (see Figure 12.22).

NOTE Creating setup files requires a file management decision, and maybe even an overall file management strategy. As I mentioned, you should not place the files you want to distribute in the same directory path as your actual project. In addition, you don't want to place the setup images in the same directory as the files. I keep a Setup Disk folder on my C:\ drive with a separate directory for each project. Each project folder, in turn, has two branches: Files and Distrib. You might find that some other approach works for you, but the important thing is to put at least a bit of thought into your strategy. ■

FIGURE 12.22

The third screen of the Setup Wizard requests a target directory for your setup files.

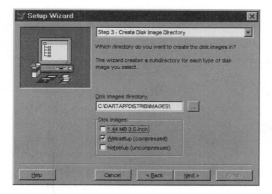

The type of installation image you want will depend on your distribution strategy. If you are distributing your application via several disks, choose the 1.44 Diskette option and Visual FoxPro will divide the files for you into several subdirectories, each representing one disk. This makes it easy to copy each directory directly to a disk. But, whenever possible, use the Websetup or NetSetup options. They each put all the setup files into one directory: Websetup compresses them a bit more tightly.

 TIP If you plan to distribute your application via CD-ROM, the preferred approach is probably NetSetup. After the files have been created, write them onto your CDs.

Specifying Setup Program Information

The fourth step in the Setup Wizard involves providing information that will be seen by the user during the setup (see Figure 12.23). This is a good place to include the application name, your company's name, and any copyright information. You can also choose to run a particular .EXE after the setup has completed on the client's machine. This might be a demo or a program that augments the setup functionality. In object-oriented terms, it is a hook process that runs after the main setup is complete.

FIGURE 12.23

The fourth screen of the Setup Wizard lets you provide information to users during the installation process.

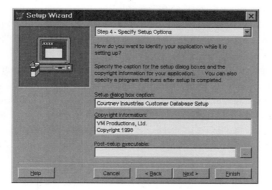

If you distribute your application via CD-ROM, you might consider writing a small program that sets the appropriate files back to a read/write setting. You could run this program right after setup by specifying it as the Post-setup executable.

Specifying the Application's Directory and Program Group

The fifth step of the process enables you to specify a default application destination and Windows program group (see Figure 12.24). You can also specify whether your customers can override your defaults. Your users will most likely have their own ideas on where application files should reside and from which branch of the Windows Start and Program menus they will call the program. You should make every attempt, during your programming as well as your setup disk creation, to permit them to do so. The boost in client relations will probably be well worth the additional programming cost. I know many computer users and very many IS professionals who raise their eyebrows at any application that insists on loading into a specified directory.

FIGURE 12.24
The fifth screen of the Setup Wizard lets you specify the default Windows group and application destination.

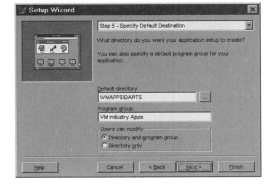

Part
III

Ch
12

Specifying File Directories

The sixth step in the process enables you to direct the ultimate destination of each of the files you are distributing (see Figure 12.25). You can choose to place a file in the Application directory, the Windows directory, or the Windows\System directory. The PM Item check box lets you add multiple icons to the program group from the same setup disks. For example, you might want your program group to include not just the icon for the application itself, but an icon for the Readme file. In that case, just click the PM Item check box for the Readme.txt file. You then can specify a name and an icon (see Figure 12.26).

FIGURE 12.25

The sixth screen of the
Setup Wizard lets you
specify different target
directories for files in
your application.

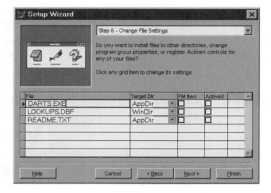

FIGURE 12.26

The Icon option lets you
specify names and
icons for the various
Project Manager items
that you install.

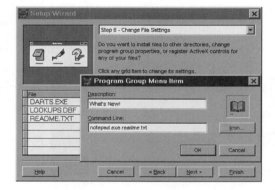

Launching the Setup Wizard

The seventh and final step puts FoxPro to work creating your files (see Figure 12.27). But first,
you can specify whether to create a Web executable. This is a nice way to enable installation of
an application right from your Web site, rather than requiring your users to first download your
setup files. This approach is very slick and avoids the problem of setup files cluttering your
users' disks following a standard NetSetup or Websetup download. On the other hand, remember that setup speed will vary by Internet connection speeds.

This screen also enables you to create dependency (.DEP) files. Select this option if you are
including new ActiveX files among your distribution files or if the version of the ActiveX file you
are installing might be newer from the one already on the client computer. This will help ensure that the ActiveX component is installed and registered correctly.

FIGURE 12.27
The final screen puts the Setup Wizard in motion creating and compressing the necessary files.

Press Finish and Visual FoxPro will build your image files (see Figure 12.28). The wizard does this in four passes:

- It checks your distribution tree for new or updated files.
- It updates its table of files.
- It compresses all new or changed files.
- It breaks these into separate setup files, and, in the case of a disk setup, creates separate directories for each required setup disk.

Don't be alarmed if the Setup Wizard takes a while to run. Remember, it's doing an awful lot behind the scenes.

FIGURE 12.28
The Setup Wizard lets you know its progress during file creation.

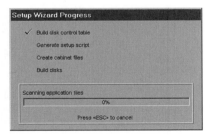

Part
III

Ch
12

Using Visual SourceSafe for Version Control in Team Development

One of the biggest headaches with a large product is managing the development and keeping track of changes to the source code. From one point of view, thorough object-oriented programming complicates this even further: If you have several objects designed to send messages back and forth to one another, and one of your programmers changes one object, the entire scheme can fall apart. Unless you've instituted a source control scheme, you might find it impossible to track down the rogue code (or the guilty programmer). Fortunately, Microsoft has a product that can be integrated quite tightly and smoothly with Visual FoxPro's development environment (and in particular the Project Manager).

Integrating Visual SourceSafe with Your Visual FoxPro Project

It's beyond the scope of this book to provide a complete discussion of source control tools, or even Visual SourceSafe itself. But source control is such an important part of team development that I hope to provide you with enough information to begin incorporating it into your projects. It can be quite comforting to have Visual SourceSafe looking over Visual FoxPro's shoulder during your development, helping to manage the process of team programming.

All you really need to do to get up and running is install VSS, with the server installation, on the server where the master files will be stored. Then install VSS for each client (that is, each programmer). After successful installations, Visual FoxPro 6 adds VSS to the source control options in the Tools, Options dialog box's Projects tab, as shown in Figure 12.29. From here, select Visual SourceSafe and set it as your default source control manager.

The additional options shown in Figure 12.29 in the Source Control Options area are essential to your VFP/VSS configuration. With them, Visual FoxPro defines whether files should be automatically checked out on modification, included in source control on addition to your local project, or removed from source control on removal from your local project. You are also given the option to automatically add new projects to source control. Don't worry: Even if you don't choose to add this feature, you can always go back and add an existing project to Visual SourceSafe.

FIGURE 12.29
You can choose how tightly to integrate Visual FoxPro and Visual SourceSafe in your development environment.

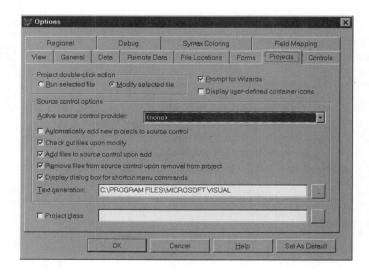

The Projects tab of the Options dialog box consists mainly of source control configuration items, but there are four other options.

Project Double-Click Action indicates what action should occur when you double-click a file inside the Project Manager. The default behavior is to modify the selected file, but you can change the setting so that the file runs on a double-click.

Prompt for Wizards indicates the action Visual FoxPro takes when you click the New button on the project. If this option is turned off, you proceed right to the appropriate editor for the file type. If this option is on, Visual FoxPro determines whether any wizards exist for the file type, and if so, gives you the choice of using them.

Display User-Defined Container Icons indicates whether or not the icons shown should be the default Visual FoxPro icons or user-defined and assigned icon files.

Project Class indicates a class to be used as the project hook. Project hooks are covered later in this chapter. Visual FoxPro 6

Creating a Source Control Project

As long as you have chosen to automatically add projects to source control, any project you create will automatically be managed by VSS based on the options that you have set. But as I noted earlier, if you want to go back and add an existing project to source control, that's easy, too. Just open the project you want to add and choose Project, Add Project to Source Control. You will be prompted for a login (see Figure 12.30). If you have not yet added usernames and passwords through the server version of VSS, just enter a login name of **Guest**, keep the password blank, and click OK.

FIGURE 12.30
You can choose to include login security to Visual SourceSafe.

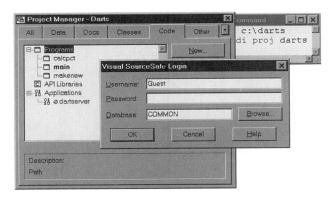

Part
III

Ch
12

N O T E   The Database text box in this dialog box has nothing to do with your Visual FoxPro databases or tables. Instead, it indicates the VSS database that will hold this project. The default setting is the Common database.

Figure 12.31 displays the Visual Sourcesafe dialog box for adding a project to source control. Click Create and then click OK. You will have the opportunity to enter a comment (see Figure 12.32). After entering a comment and clicking OK, you will be presented with a list of files from your project. Choose which of these should be kept under source control by clicking the check boxes to the left (see Figure 12.33).

FIGURE 12.31
It's easy to add a project to Visual SourceSafe control, even right within Visual FoxPro.

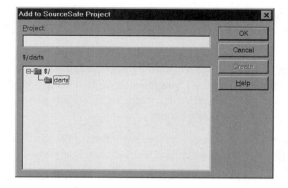

FIGURE 12.32
You can include comments on each project you add to Visual SourceSafe.

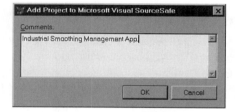

FIGURE 12.33
You can pick and choose which of your Visual FoxPro project files should be included under Visual SourceSafe version control.

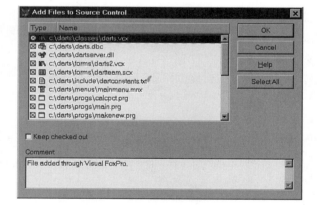

That's all there is to it! When you return to your project, any files that are under source control are displayed with a lock icon beside them. Whenever you modify a file, it is checked out by Visual FoxPro and the lock turns into a check mark. Figure 12.34 shows these icons in action.

FIGURE 12.34
Visual SourceSafe's lock and check mark icons provide visual clues to the status of your files.

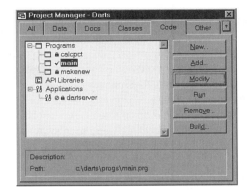

Files you have checked out remain checked out until you either check them back in or undo the checkout. Either of these actions can be performed by right-clicking the file and selecting the relevant shortcut option. When you check in a file, you are offered the chance to enter comments on the file or files you are checking in (see Figure 12.35). Try to determine a convention, with your team where applicable, and take care to follow it. Your comments will probably include your name or initials, the date, and perhaps some form of tracking ID. You might also include a brief synopsis of the changes you have made. The Keep Checked Out box will check in your changes, making them available to other programmers, but will keep the file checked out under your name.

FIGURE 12.35
Many development teams encourage comments for each check-in (such as programmer name, a tracking ID, and a summary of changes made).

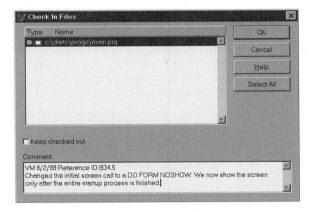

A Closer Look at Visual SourceSafe Terminology

Because both Visual FoxPro and Visual SourceSafe have collections of files called "projects," the terminology can get a bit confusing. In Visual SourceSafe, a *project* is a collection of files that you store under lock and key, checking them out in small bunches. These files are stored in Visual SourceSafe databases. Managing these files is accomplished through different combinations of the actions listed below. You'll find these options, and some lesser-used goodies, in several places in the Project Manager: the Project menu bar, the right-click shortcut menus, and even the Tools, Options menu:

- *Checking Files Out.* The check-out command places a file into the working directory with read/write access. After a file is checked out, it cannot be checked out by another user (actually, VSS can be configured to enable multiple checkouts, but it is not recommended). As you've seen, you can check a file out through the Project Manager by modifying it or using the right-click shortcut menu. You can also start SourceSafe directly and check out a file to your local disk, and then switch to Visual FoxPro to work on it.

- *Checking Files In.* When you have finished your changes, you will move the changes into the SourceSafe database, again through the right-click shortcut menu, the Projects menu, or directly through SourceSafe. VSS moves the file into its database and also copies the newly checked-in code down to the main project location. The file is once again made read-only in your personal programming area.

TIP   As you work with Visual SourceSafe through the Project Manager, it tracks its actions through commented lines in the Command window. This is a useful feature because it keeps an instant log of your session.

- *Undoing a Checkout.* This command undoes any changes, releases the checkout, and *overwrites your local copy of the file* with the master copy of the file.

- *Getting Latest Version.* You can choose to copy the most recent version of a file in the VSS database by getting the latest version instead of checking it out. Again, the easiest way to do this is through the right-click shortcut menu.

- *Tracking Versions.* Show History, Show Differences, and the Source Control Properties represent different facets of version tracking in Visual SourceSafe. These options enable you to compare the master copy to any previous copies. Visual SourceSafe assigns a version number to each file, and this number is incremented on each check-in.

- *Sharing and Branching.* Sharing enables VSS projects to access the same files. All actions that affect a shared file are automatically reflected in every project. Branching takes a shared file and breaks its link. You might want to do this to a shared file that has become specifically customized for one project.

- *Pinning.* Pinning is similar to branching, in that it takes a file shared by many VSS projects and removes the shared link. In this case, rather than create a new branch, you are pinning a particular version of a file within the project you are working with. You cannot edit this file until you unpin it. You can access this option through the Show History interface (see Figure 12.36).

- *Rolling Back Changes.* You can also choose to roll back to a particular version of a file through the Show History box. But beware: This feature deletes forever any changes that were made later than the version you restored.

FIGURE 12.36
The Show History
screen enables you to
pin a file, causing it to
remain static in the
project, even if it is
changed in other
projects.

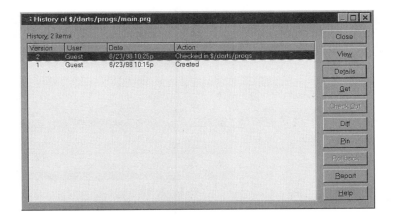

 Because Visual FoxPro 6 is so well-integrated with Visual SourceSafe, you might never need to enter
VSS through its own icon. But there are some options in Visual SourceSafe that you cannot access
through Visual FoxPro, so I suggest giving VSS a whirl when you're feeling adventurous. And, needless to
say, the server version of VSS includes many features not available through VFP or the client copy of
Visual SourceSafe.

Accessing the Project Manager as an Object

The discussion so far has focused on using the Project Manager as a visual development tool,
enabling programmers to interactively run, edit, and check out files, and making it easier to
create compiled applications and executable files. But there are many facets of the Project
Manager above and beyond what I've discussed. After all, everything I've talked about so far
has been useful and interesting, but it involves an awful lot of clicking, doesn't it? And, if you
are working in an environment where you create large numbers of small applications, you
probably don't want to dig in to your precious time by creating new project files every week.
You want a template or some other way to speed the process. Finally, if you are a team leader
or senior programmer working with a crew of less experienced VFP programmers, you might
want some way to automate some of the Project Manager's functionality or protect against its
misuse.

Fortunately, with Visual FoxPro 6, the Fox Team at Microsoft has greatly enhanced the Project
Manager by exposing it as a full-fledged object.

The Project Manager Object Design

You might never need to access the properties or methods of the Project Manager, and that's
just fine. FoxPro programmers have done so for years and have still made great use of many
facets of the Project Manager's functionality. But, you've also gotten used to jumping through
hoops to make this tool even more useful, or to fill in the gaps between its functionality and
your needs.

Part
III

Ch
12

As of version 6, Visual FoxPro fills in many of those gaps by enabling direct access to the Project Manager as an object (more specifically, as an OLE object). Figure 12.37 shows the Project Manager as it appears in the debugger.

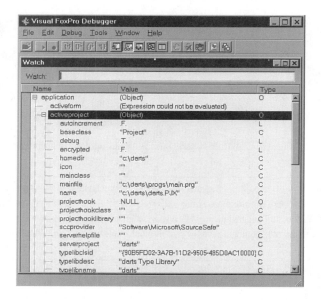

Accessing Project Methods and Properties

The Visual FoxPro application object (which can be referenced as _VFP or Application) now includes a new collection: Projects. It also includes a new object property, ActiveProject, which holds a reference to the current project.

To access a project, you can use the Count property or the Item method of the Applications.Projects collection. Or, you can use the Application.ActiveProject reference. The following two lines of code generate the same result as long as Darts.PJX is the only currently active project:

```
? Application.ActiveProject.Name
? Application.Projects[1].Name
```

If you have more than one project open, however, the Projects collection offers an advantage over the ActiveProject reference: It enables you to access all open projects as you would any other collection. For example, the following code is perfectly valid and will rebuild every open project:

```
FOR EACH oProject IN Application.Projects
     OProject.BUILD()
ENDFOR
```

Project Properties and Methods

Visual FoxPro's `Project` object includes over 25 properties, five methods, and two collections, all of which you can access programmatically just as you would with any other object. Some of the most useful properties include the following:

- `BuildDateTime`—The date and time of the last build.
- `Name`—The fully qualified path and name of the project (with a `.PJX` extension).
- `ProjectHook`—A reference to the project's ProjectHook (more below).
- `ProjectHookClass`—The `ProjectHook`'s class name (more below).
- `ProjectHookLibrary`—The library holding the `ProjectHookClass` (more below).
- `Visible`—Whether the Project Manager is displayed.

 The `Project` object also includes a family of `Version*` properties that hold your company name, comments, copyright information, description, version number, product, and trademarks.

`Project` also includes among its methods the following useful processes:

- `Build`—Executes a build, undertaking the same actions as if you had clicked the Build button itself. There are several parameters you can pass, the most important of which are the name of the new file (the first parameter) and the type of build (the second parameter: 1 is a project rebuild, 2 is an `.APP` build, 3 is an `.EXE` build, and 4 is a COM `.DLL` build.)
- `CleanUp`—Removes deleted references from the project.
- `Close`—Closes the project.
- `SetMain`—Sets the main file for a project. Just include the main file's name (with extension) as the parameter. Note that passing the name of a file not in the project, or even just a fake filename, does not result in a runtime error. Instead, the method returns `True` if its attempt at setting a main file was successful, and `False` if it was not.

 If you have a `Cleanup.PRG` or similar environment-clearing program or a Visual FoxPro backup routine, consider including calls to any open projects' `Cleanup` methods.

> **N O T E** The Project Manager uses a table to hold the information on its files (the table extension is `.PJX` and the associated memo field is held in a `.PJT` file). Many of us who worked with pre-Visual FoxPro 6 projects became somewhat used to opening these tables interactively to hack away—this was pretty much the only way to edit properties—or else we would open them in code to copy the projects to new locations, or create new projects from templates. With Visual FoxPro's new `Project` object model, there's no need to do this anymore (which is fine, because it never sat well with most of us to begin with). If your curiosity gets the best of you, you can still open project files as tables by executing a `USE ProjectName.pjx` command, but exercise caution. A hosed project is no fun at all. ▪

Part
III
Ch
12

File Properties and Methods

Your access to the Project Manager doesn't stop at the project itself! The `Project` object also includes two collections, `Files` and `Servers`. The `Files` collection holds one object for each file in the project. The `Servers` collection holds an object reference for every OLE Automation server in the project.

Most programmers will spend more time accessing `Files` properties than `Servers` properties. Here are some of the more useful `Files` properties:

- `Description`—The description shown in the Project Manager.
- `Exclude`—Whether the file is excluded from `.APP`, `.EXE`, and `.DLL` builds.
- `LastModified`—The date and time of the last modification to the file.
- `Name`—The fully-qualified name of the file.
- `Type`—The type of file:

B	Label
d	Database
D	Table
K	Form
L	API Library
M	Menu
P	Program file
Q	Query
R	Report
T	Text
V	Class library
X	Other (including bitmaps)
z	App

As with `Project` itself, the `Files` object includes a number of useful methods:

- `AddToSCC`—Puts the file under source control.
- `CheckIn`—Checks the file in.
- `CheckOut`—Checks the file out.
- `GetLatestVersion`—Gets the latest version of the file from the VSS (or other source control product) database.

With these exposed methods and properties, you can easily write quick utilities to rebuild projects (no more worrying about the steps you've missed). Below is some very basic code that gets the latest version of every file and recompiles the project. If you've ever struggled with a team recompile, you'll recognize the strengths of this approach.

```
* get the latest version of every file
```

```
    oFile.GetLatestVersion()
* Let's exclude all tables and databases
IF UPPER(oFile.Type) = "D"
oFile.Exclude = .T.
ELSE
oFile.Exclude = .F.
ENDIF
endfor


* now, clean up the project. No need
* to have deleted references clogging
* everything up
APPLICATION.ActiveProject.CleanUp()


* Finally, build the project.
APPLICATION.ActiveProject.Build("AutoBuild.APP",2)

* And, always view the error log!
MODI COMM AutoBuild.Err
```

Of course, you can (and will definitely want to) go much further. You should check for errors from each method, for example, and you will want to determine which files are under source control before trying to get the latest version of them. But the point is, these exposed properties and methods can be extremely powerful tools for project management and version control.

ProjectHooks

Visual FoxPro 6 enables you to further extend the Project object model through the use of its new ProjectHooks. Simply put, a *ProjectHook* is an object that includes several events that fire upon certain actions in the Project Manager. ProjectHooks are ActiveX objects, but again, Visual FoxPro 6 incorporates them so cleanly that you'll barely know the difference.

You can set a particular ProjectHook class for a given project in a couple of ways. You can open a project and select the Project page of the Project, Project Info menu option. Or you can set a ProjectHook default; refer to Figure 12.29 and recall that the Projects tab in the Options dialog (reached by choosing Tools, Options) includes an area to enter a ProjectHook class. If a ProjectHook class is entered here, it is used by any project that doesn't have its own ProjectHook class specified. Visual

TIP Actually, there's a third way to specify a project hook: by populating the exposed ProjectHookClass and ProjectHookLibrary properties on the Project object.

Project hooks do a pretty good job of taking care of themselves: they instantiate when the project is opened and are destroyed when the project is closed. The following ProjectHook events fire as you manipulate the project (whether interactively—the old-fashioned way—or via code):

- ▨ AfterBuild—Occurs after a project build finishes.
- ▨ BeforeBuild—Occurs before the build begins.

- ■ OLEDragOver—Occurs when a file is dragged over the project, but before it is dropped.

- ■ OLEDragDrop—Occurs when a file is dropped into the project.

- ■ QueryAddFile—Occurs just prior to a file being added to the project.

- ■ QueryModifyFile—Occurs just prior to a file in the project being modified.

- ■ QueryRemoveFile—Occurs just prior to a file in the project being removed.

- ■ QueryRunFile—Occurs just prior to a file in the project being run.

 T I P   The Query* events of the ProjectHook can be used to prevent the specific action from occurring by including NODEFAULT in the method code.

N O T E   Visual FoxPro 6 offers several new clauses for the MODIFY PROJECT command. The NOPROJECTHOOK clause opens the project without the associated ProjectHook class. NOSHOW opens both the Project Manager and the ProjectHook, but doesn't show the Project Manager window. This means that you can run your programs without even having the Project Manager visible. ■

Using ProjectHooks

Of course, you can choose not to use ProjectHooks at all. But if you decide to give them a shot, you won't have to look far to find uses for them. For example, you could clean up the project just prior to a build by including a call to the Project object's Cleanup method in the ProjectHook's QueryBeforeBuild. You could check that any file being added to the project conforms to naming conventions or filename length requirements by a check placed in the QueryBeforeAdd method. You could get the latest version of a file just prior to running it by calling a file object's GetLatestVersion method from the QueryBeforeRun. Or you could even utilize MAPI calls in the AfterBuild method to email your fellow programmers and inform them that the project has been freshly built (here's an even better idea: include the .ERR file if any errors occurred). ProjectHooks provide a tremendous degree of control over your projects and enable you to manipulate a project as you would almost any other object.

The Project Manager: A Last Word

The Visual FoxPro 6 Project Manager offers programmers a remarkable degree of control over the development environment. Your use of the Project Manager will depend on your programming experience, your interest, and your needs. You might choose to use the Project Manager simply as a file maintenance tool. Or, you might use a series of ProjectHook events and Project and File PEM calls to manage source control behind the scenes. Or, like most of us, the Project Manager's role in your development will fall somewhere between these extremes.

The bottom line is that the Project Manager is available, flexible, powerful, and easy to learn. Your clients will probably never see the Project Manager in action, but they, like you, will benefit from its presence on your desktop. ●

PART

IV

Object-Oriented Programming

Introduction to Object-Oriented Programming

In this chapter

Understanding Object-Oriented Programming

Object-oriented programming (OOP) revolutionizes nearly every aspect of application development with Visual FoxPro, from the analysis and design phases to the coding and testing of applications and application components. Object-oriented programming was introduced in Visual FoxPro Version 3.0 and has become one of its standard and most useful features.

This and the next four chapters discuss object-oriented programming with Visual FoxPro in detail and include the following information:

- This chapter discusses the basic concepts of object-oriented programming with examples shown in Visual FoxPro.
- Chapter 14, "OOP with Visual FoxPro," covers how to create classes with Visual FoxPro using programs and the Visual Class Designer.
- Chapter 15, "Creating Classes with Visual FoxPro," covers the different kinds of classes typically created in Visual FoxPro with examples of each.
- Chapter 16, "Managing Classes with Visual FoxPro," delves into the critical issue of managing class libraries and reviews the commands related to managing class libraries. The Class Browser, a powerful new addition to the FoxPro suite of tools, is also covered.
- Chapter 17, "Advanced Object-Oriented Programming," discusses some advanced topics related to OOP with Visual FoxPro.

Visual FoxPro, like Visual C++, is a *hybrid* language. This means that the developers have the option of developing applications using OOP methods or modular programming. If you develop applications in other languages, such as SmallTalk, you must use OOP.

If Visual FoxPro does not require the use of OOP, why should you consider leaving the warm comfort of developing the old way to go to the radically new mind-set of OOP? To answer this question, it is first necessary to review the background of what is called the *software crisis*.

The Software Crisis

Businesses today are experiencing a software crisis that stems from the inability of today's programming methodologies to adapt to the rapidly changing world of business. Applications developed in modular form often require a long development cycle, are based on marginally reusable code bases, and are frequently outdated before they hit the user's desk. The premise of modular development is to create software based on modules that are typically, by their very nature, different from business to business and even from department to department within a single company. In today's global business environment, companies need the diversity of an operating system or programming language that will enable them to develop programs or software that is cost efficient to produce and deploy in many working environments. For example, an inventory control program written to work in an American company might not have all the functionality that would be needed to work in a Mexican company. Visual FoxPro is one of the programming languages that is adaptable enough to enable the developer the versatility to quickly meet the needs of most companies in many situations.

Take the example of accounting applications. At the most basic level, they are the same: accounts receivable programs that manage and track the money owed to the company, accounts payable programs manage the bills owed by the company, and so on. However, when you drill down to the operations of the individual business functions, differences typically arise from organization to organization. For example, the format of a bill for a service organization is different from the format of a bill for a merchandising firm.

When software is developed in modules, as it was in FoxPro 2.x, individual programs are combined to create an application. If an application is brought from one company to another, or even from one department to another, typically the software is copied and the source code is modified to fit the requirements of the new users. Imagine what happens when an upgrade is released for the original software. The new users do not get the benefits of the new upgrade unless a second effort is made to incorporate the changes into the copied version. If a bug is found in one version of the software, the software must be fixed in two places. Obviously, this is not the best way to do things.

OOP takes a radically different approach. Software is created not in modules but rather in terms of *entities* (or objects). For example, using OOP, you do not create an accounts receivable module per se but instead create customer objects, invoice objects, and so on and then combine them into an application. In effect, *components* are developed that are put together to form an application.

Using this new method of development, you focus on the entities being modeled in the *problem domain* (a fancy term meaning the business problem you are trying to solve with software). The design of a customer object is based on the simple concept of trying to determine what a customer does and what a customer knows within the context of a business. "Within the context" means that you will come up with a *theoretical* model for the customer based on what the "customer" is within the business environment. For example, a customer knows his or her name, address, telephone number, and credit balance. The customer would also know how to print itself, save itself, and more. This does not mean that Joe Customer knows how to print his own record or save himself to the database. Rather, it means that a customer *object* would have these responsibilities.

If an application is taken from one business to another, the differences can be accommodated by basing new objects on existing ones (a process known as *subclassing*). The behaviors and attributes of the original object are automatically brought forward (*inherited*) and are changed as needed for the new software. This results in radically fewer code modifications. If changes are made to an original object, they are automatically brought forward to the new objects.

Why would you want to change to OOP from the familiar old world of modular programming? Because the old world is broken and OOP can fix it. Specifically, object orientation is designed to provide the following:

- Enhanced code reusability
- Enhanced code maintenance

Part IV

Ch 13

Now that you know what to look for from OOP, the following is an overview of the concepts that make up object orientation.

Objects and Encapsulation

If you've ever read a book or article about object orientation, you n ght have noticed many terms thrown about as if they were self-explanatory. Terms such as *inheritance, encapsulation,* and *polymorphism* are used to express OOP concepts. Because of these odd and difficult terms, OOP is often thought to be complex. The truth could not be more different.

The first and most important key concept in OOP is an object. An *object* is a package of information and actions. An object is self-contained. An object has things on the inside that only it knows about, characteristics that everyone can see, and ways of doing things.

Use an elevator as an example. An elevator is an object in that it has properties (such as a maximum weight load), it performs actions (such as opening and closing the door), and it has a public interface (the control buttons) that enables it to interact with the environment around it. An object has precisely these qualities.

The key to understanding objects is to view them like an elevator. When you think about an elevator, all you think about is the public interface: the buttons that tell the elevator where to go, the door that opens to let you in and out, and so on. However, there is a great deal more to the elevator that you never think about. For example, you probably don't know how the elevator interprets the buttons you press into a destination or how the elevator knows which floor it is on. And, for that matter, you probably don't care. These functions, although a significant part of the elevator, do not concern you.

This introduces a few more concepts. First, all the knowledge and behaviors of an object are contained within the object. This is known as *encapsulation*. An object knows what it needs to know and how to do what it needs to do without relying on the outside world. The data and behaviors are encapsulated within the object.

Properties

The data in an object is called a property. A *property* (in Visual FoxPro terms) is simply a memory variable that is attached and scoped to an object. You query the value and modify it by using the object name followed by a period (.) and then the name of the property. (For the record, properties are also called *member variables* in some texts.) Properties can have any data types that are valid for a plain old Visual FoxPro memory variable. A property exists as long as the object it is attached to exists.

For example, if you have a property called lIsNew that is attached to an object called oCust, you could query the value of the property by stating the following:

```
? oCust.lIsNew
```

Methods

In addition to having attached data, objects have actions to perform. These actions are coded in procedures that are attached to the object. These procedures are known as *methods*. There is little difference between a "regular" procedure and a method except in the way they are called. You call a method by stating the name of the object followed by a period (.) and then the name of the method. For example, the following line illustrates how to call a method named Print that is attached to the oCust object:

```
oCust.Print()
```

Technically, the parentheses at the end of the method name are only required if you expect a return value or if you are passing parameters to the method. I suggest that you always use the parentheses for consistency. It also makes it clear that you're calling a method.

Notice, by the way, the manner in which this method is called. Unlike Visual FoxPro procedures and user-defined functions, you do not have to use a DO-type syntax or specify the function with an expression. To call a method that is a procedure (assuming you do not expect a return value), all you need to do is call the method as shown in the previous example. If you expect a return value, you can use the old UDF-type syntax. For example, if the Print method returns a logical stating whether the customer was properly printed, you could capture the value with this:

```
llReturnValue = oCust.Print()
```

Events

Events are things that happen. For example, clicking the mouse is an event. Events can be caused by a user's action (such as clicking a mouse) or by the system itself (such as when an error occurs). When you are creating a class (such as a pushbutton) in Visual FoxPro, you can attach code (such as methods) to events. When the event happens (for example, the user clicks the left mouse button while on the object), the associated method (that is, the click method) is automatically called.

Events are not new. Developers have been using them since the advent of FoxPro 2.0. Valid clauses, for example, are simply procedures that are attached to an event (such as attempting to exit a modified field or clicking a pushbutton). Part of the power of using objects comes from attaching methods to an object that automatically execute when something specific happens. In Visual FoxPro, you can attach methods to all kinds of events: when the mouse is clicked, when the mouse is released, and so on. You can even attach code to events that execute automatically when the object is created (the Init event) and when the object is released (the Destroy event).

There is one major difference between events in an object-oriented development environment and the old Valid and When clauses. In FoxPro 2.6, there was no direct method for manually executing the code snippet attached to an event (well, there *was* a way, but it was a kludge). In other words, there was no single command that ran the procedure attached to a screen object's Valid event. In an object-oriented development environment you can do this easily by calling the event the same way you would call a method. For example, if you have a pushbutton called cmdOK, you could execute the code attached to the Click event (that is, the Click() method) at any time by issuing the following:

```
cmdOk.Click()
```

By attaching code to events, you greatly increase the control you have over the behavior of an object. In fact, with the myriad of events to which Visual FoxPro enables you to respond, you can have acute, pinpoint control over forms and objects.

So far, you have seen that you can create objects as well as assign properties to them and create methods for them. If you had to write code to fine-tune an object every time you created it, you would be in for a lot of coding. Fortunately, OOP has the answer for this as well—classes.

Classes

To this point, all of the discussion in this chapter has centered around the object. But, what is the basis for an object? How is an object coded?

Consider a candle for a moment. A candle maker typically creates a candle from a mold rather than creating each one individually by hand. If the design of a candle needs to change, where would it be changed? On every individual candle? Not likely. Instead, the mold would be changed. When the mold is changed, all new candles get the change automatically.

In object-oriented programming, objects are never coded. Rather, object molds (called *classes*) are coded. All objects are then *instantiated* (that is, created) from that class. All coding is done at the class level. Once an object is instantiated from a class, all you do is interact with it. You do not add methods or change existing methods in an object, but rather you add and change methods in a class.

Here's an example of a class:

```
DEFINE CLASS myClass AS Custom
     cName = ""
     cType = ""
     lIsNew = .F.

     PROCEDURE ShowVals
          ? this.cName
          ? this.cType

          IF this.lIsNew
               ? "I'M NEW"
          ELSE
               ? "I'M OLD"
          ENDIF
     ENDPROC
ENDDEFINE
```

A brief dissection of this block of code follows; however, for a more definitive description of the syntax associated with coding classes, refer to Chapter 14.

```
Define Class myClass as Custom
```

This line of code tells Visual FoxPro that you are defining a new class called MyClass that is based on another class called Custom, which is discussed in more detail later in the chapter.

```
cName = ""
cType = ""
lIsNew = .F.
```

The preceding lines are known as *declaration code*. In this part of the class definition, you list the member variables (properties) of the object and their initial values. If one of the member variables is an array, the DECLARE statement would be placed here.

```
PROCEDURE ShowVals
    ? this.cName
    ? this.cType

    IF this.lIsNew
        ? "I'M NEW"
    ELSE
        ? "I'M OLD"
    ENDIF
ENDPROC
```

This is a method definition. Calling a method executes all the code from the PROCEDURE line to the ENDPROC line. A method is very similar to a procedure in a FoxPro 2.x procedure file, except that the method is called through its object.

Instantiating Objects

An object is instantiated with the CREATEOBJECT() function. Here is the syntax for creating an instance of MyClass:

```
oMyClass = CREATEOBJECT("MyClass")
```

By the way, oMyClass is simply a memory variable of type Object.

In order to access the members of oMyClass, you could use the following commands:

```
? oMyClass.cName     && Initially blank
oMyClass.cName = "Menachem Bazian"
? oMyClass.cName     && Now shows "Menachem Bazian"
oMyClass.ShowVals() && Runs the showvals method
```

Referencing a Method or Property in a Class

An issue that arises with this method of development is that it is difficult to know what the name of an object's instance variable is inside a class. When coding the class, the name of the variable that holds the instance should be, and is, irrelevant.

In order to refer to an object's properties or methods within itself, the identifier THIS, in place of the object name, is used. (You saw this previously in procedure SHOWVALS.)

```
IF this.lIsNew
        ? "I'M NEW"
    ELSE
        ? "I'M OLD"
    ENDIF
```

The keyword THIS means that you are accessing the method or member variable of the object itself. It's that simple.

Subclassing—Basing a Class on Another Class

So far, you have learned just about all there is to know about objects, and you have also learned about properties, methods, and events. You have also seen how to create an object's blueprint with a class, which you then use to instantiate the object. However, one more important piece remains (the really exciting part as it turns out): creating classes based on prior classes.

Suppose you have a class called Light that models a light in a room. The class would need a method for turning the light on and off and a property for the current status of the light. It might look something like this:

```
DEFINE CLASS light AS custom
   status = "OFF"

   PROCEDURE Toggle
    IF this.status = "OFF"
      this.status = "ON"
    ELSE
      this.status = "OFF"
    ENDIF
   ENDPROC
ENDDEFINE
```

In the sample Light class, you create an object that basically has one property and one method. This works well for light switches that just turn on and off. But suppose you want to create a light switch that can dim as well? What do you do? Do you have to write a whole new class? The toggle is still applicable: the light can still be turned on and off. What you need is a modified version of the Light class that has all the same capabilities of the Light class plus the capability of dimming the light.

For the purposes of this illustration, I'll set the following rules: When you attempt to use the dimmer, it goes from full light to half light and then back again. In order to turn the light on or off, you still need to use the original light switch method.

Here's how you could accomplish this using an OOP model:

```
DEFINE CLASS dimmer AS light
   intensity = "FULL"

   PROCEDURE DimmIt
```

```
    IF this.status = "OFF"
      RETURN
    ENDIF

    this.intensity = IIF(this.intensity = "FULL", ;
             "HALF", "FULL")
    WAIT WINDOW "Lights are now "+this.intensity+" power."
  ENDPROC
ENDDEFINE
```

Notice the original DEFINE of the class. In the original DEFINE (class Light), I used Custom as the base class. Custom is the simplest base class that is built into Visual FoxPro; you use it when you are creating objects of your own from scratch. (In Chapter 15 you learn what Custom is in more detail and how you use it.) In the DEFINE used here, the base class is Light. This means that class Dimmer automatically *inherits* everything that Light has. Thus, although no code exists in the Dimmer class to handle the LightSwitch method and the Status property, Dimmer gets the method and property automatically because it is a subclass of Light. This process is known as *inheritance*.

In effect, a subclass (Dimmer) is a more specialized version of the *superclass* (Light).

Overriding Inherited Behavior

One of the nice things about inheritance is that you can accept what you like from the super-class and override the rest. A method is overridden when it is "recoded" in the subclass. Here is an example:

```
DEFINE CLASS offdimmer AS dimmer
    intensity = "FULL"

    PROCEDURE DimmIt
        WAIT WINDOW "Dimmer is DIsabled"
    ENDPROC
ENDDEFINE
```

In this case, the DimmIt method has been overridden. The DimmIt method from the Dimmer class is not called.

Suppose you want to run the method from the Dimmer class's DimmIt method and then add additional code. Here's how you could do it:

```
DEFINE CLASS AnotherDimmer AS offdimmer
    intensity = "FULL"

    PROCEDURE DimmIt
        Dimmer::Dimmit()
        OffDimmer::Dimmit()
        WAIT WINDOW "Isn't this cool?"
    ENDPROC
ENDDEFINE
```

The double colon operator (: :) is used to call methods from classes higher in the class hierarchy. Notice that you can only call methods from classes that have been inherited from.

Protecting Methods and Properties

When you create an object, you should take great care to decide what the public interface of the class is going to be. A class will typically have properties and methods that are intended for use inside the class only. Other properties and methods, if accessed from the outside, can have a disastrous effect on the inner workings of a class.

Consider the sample Light class and suppose that the Toggle method has code in it that turns the light on and off based on the Status property. If you modify the Status property by accessing it outside of the class, the Toggle method will not work properly.

The solution to this problem is to protect the methods and properties that should not be accessible outside of the class. When you code the classes you can protect the properties by adding PROTECTED *propertyname* definitions in the declaration section of the code. For methods, add the keyword PROTECTED to the PROCEDURE line. Here is an example:

```
DEFINE CLASS myClass AS Custom
     PROTECTED cName
     cName = ""
     cType = ""
     lIsNew = .F.

     PROTECTED PROCEDURE ShowVals
          ? this.cName
          ? this.cType

          IF this.lIsNew
               ? "I'M NEW"
          ELSE
               ? "I'M OLD"
          ENDIF
     ENDPROC
ENDDEFINE
```

In this example, both the cName property and the ShowVals method are protected. Attempts to access them from outside of the class will produce an error as if the property and method did not exist (and as far as the world outside of the class is concerned, they don't exist).

If a class has a property that has to be tightly controlled (such as the Status property, which can only be changed by the Toggle method), you should protect it. If the user needs to read the value of that property, provide a method that returns the value of the protected property. For example, in order to access the cName property in the sample class (shown previously) you might create a method called ShowName as follows:

```
FUNCTION ShowName
     RETURN (this.cName)
ENDFUNC
```

Understanding Polymorphism

Polymorphism is the next term that needs to be covered in this discussion. *Polymorphism* is the capability to give methods and properties in different classes the same name even if they mean different things.

For example, consider the `Light` objects. They all have a method called `Toggle`, which turns the light on and off. Suppose now that you were to create an entirely different object: a telephone. The `Telephone` object might not have anything to do with a `Light` object, but there is a method attached to it that is also called `Toggle`. The `Toggle` method in the `Telephone` class might or might not do anything like the `Toggle` method in the `Light` classes.

Compare the following commands:

```
oLight = CREATEOBJECT("Light")
oPhone = CREATEOBJECT("Telephone")
oLight.Toggle()    &&Runs the Toggle method from
                   &&the Light object
oPhone.Toggle()    &&Runs the Toggle method from
                   &&the Phone object
```

Notice how similar the code is between `oLight` and `oPhone`. You can call the `Toggle` method from either object in a similar fashion although they might do different things.

Polymorphism is an extremely useful way to develop classes. It enables you to put standards in place for naming methods that do similar things. For example, you can have a `Show` method for different objects that is designed to bring up the display portion of the object (for example, `oCust.Show()` might display the customer form, whereas `oInv.Show()` might display the invoice form). The beauty of this comes from a user perspective. It means that you can use the objects with much greater ease because you can develop a consistent interface when you work with your classes (imagine the difficulty you would have if the display method were called `Show` in one class and `Display` in another).

Messages, Messages, Messages

Everything you have learned so far that deals with working with OOP-based systems can be described as "sending a message." The following sections redefine previous examples of working with objects and discuss them in terms of messages.

Creating an Object

```
oInv = CREATEOBJECT("Invoice")
```

This line of code sends a message to the `Invoice` class telling it to create an object called `oInv` based on itself.

Getting the Value of a Property

```
lnAmount = oInv.nAmount
```

This can be described as sending a message to the oInv object and telling it to get the value of the nAmount property and to return it to lnAmount.

Calling a Method

```
oInv.Display && Show the Invoice
```

This can be described as sending a message to the oInv object and telling it to execute its Display method.

If you understand the concept of a message, a great deal of the gobbledygook you read in OOP literature becomes understandable. For example, polymorphism has been defined in OOP literature as "the capability to send the same message to different objects and have different actions take place." The practical definition of a message presented in this chapter means the same thing, but it is easier to understand than the OOP literature definition.

The moral of this story is this: Do not let the language throw you.

Encapsulation Revisited

Taking the concepts that you have seen so far in this chapter, the concept of *encapsulation* becomes clearer. Basically, encapsulation means that an object is a self-contained unit. The object contains data in the form of properties (also called *member variables*) and methods that are associated with the object to perform whatever actions need to be done.

You can also create a Customer class if you want. You can associate data and methods with it that encapsulate customer information and actions.

A Customer object's data could be items such as a name, address, phone number, credit limit, and so on. Methods associated with the object could be actions related to displaying customer data, enabling the user to edit or add customers, printing a customer, and so on. If you develop naming conventions for your object methods and properties, using the objects become a breeze.

Naming conventions means adopting standards for the names of the methods and properties. A good example would be a method that displays an object (for example, the form associated with a customer object). This method could be called Show(), Display(), ShowForm(), or even ShowTheFormForThisClassRightNow(). To a degree, what you call it really doesn't matter as long as you are consistent. The only area where you might have problems is with some of the more popular type of actions such as Print(). If Microsoft has a method that does the type of action the method does (such as the Show() method that shows a form), it might make sense to adhere to that standard. I am not suggesting that you are bound to someone else's standard, but imagine the tower of Babel–type development that will occur if one class calls the method Show(), another calls it Display(), and yet a third uses the name ShowForm(). This is not a situation I would want to be in.

To illustrate polymorphism, take a look at the following example, which uses two sample classes: `Customer` and `Invoice`. Notice how the code, in order to work with the two classes, can be exceedingly similar at this level. In fact, by using OOP, the developer who takes the objects and puts them together in the form of a system will have a much easier job.

```
oCust = CREATEOBJECT("Customer")
oCust.Show()        && Show the customer
oCust.Edit()        && Edit the Customer
oCust.Save()        && Save Customer
oCust.Print()       && Print the customer

oInv = CREATEOBJECT("Invoice")
oInv.Display()      && Show the Invoice
oInv.Edit()         && Edit the Invoice
oInv.Save()         && Save Invoice
oInv.Print()        && Print the Invoice
```

OOP and Its Effect on Development

Now that you have seen what objects are and what all the 10-dollar words mean, the next question is "Big deal. What does this do for me?"

OOP shifts the focus of development from coding procedures to the designing and defining of classes. Because objects are, in effect, complete and independent modules, it is possible to have developers who just work on classes of objects. The application developers can then use these classes, either directly or by subclassing them, and put them together to form a system.

Does this mean that after you have a library of classes you will never need to write code again? Not quite, but a class library will make your life a lot easier once it is developed, debugged, and ready to go.

Analysis and Design with OOP

Object-oriented programming does not start with code. Although the discussions in this chapter basically center around the implementation phase of writing objects, this step is the last step in creating object-oriented software.

Part

IV

Ch

13

The first step is to analyze the problem domain and to design the class hierarchies that make up the system. Sounds simple, right? In fact, object-oriented analysis and object-oriented design (*OOA* and *OOD*) are not difficult processes to perform, they just require discipline. Many different methodologies have been proposed and written about over the years. The more popular authors in this realm are Grady Booch, Ivar Jacobsen, and Rebecca Wirfs-Brock. Personally, I use the Wirfs-Brock method of CRC cards, but that is a whole different story. Her book, *Designing Object-Oriented Software*, should be required reading for all developers working on object-oriented analysis and design, in my opinion. But don't go by just what I recommend because others feel strongly about other authors.

Analysts have stated that as much as 70 percent of the time allotted for an object-oriented project is spent on analysis and design. That's a lot of time. Therefore, you should take the time you need to do your research and to find a methodology with which you are comfortable.

Whichever methodology you choose, the end result of object-oriented analysis and design is a coherent, well thought-out, logical class design that will clearly show the classes in the application as well as the public interface (that is, the unprotected properties and methods) and how they interact. When you have all this, coding can begin.

Multideveloper Issues with Object-Oriented Software

The focus of object orientation, which is based on objects rather than modules, has another interesting effect on the development process: It makes multi-developer situations much easier to handle. If the analysis and design phases have been properly done, the system is broken down into discrete pieces. The design will call for a particular class hierarchy and will state what each class can expect from other classes in the system. After you accomplish this, coding each class tree can be done independently of others in the system.

For example, the design document for a system calls for a Customer class and a Statement class. The Customer class calls the Statement class to create and print a statement that shows open invoices for customers. The design document states what methods and properties are available in the Statement class. There might be a Create() method that creates the statement and accepts a customer number as a parameter, a Print() method that prints the statement, and a property called cStatementNumber for the statement number. The developer of the Customer class could write the following method:

```
PROCEDURE CustomerStatement
    LOCAL loStatement

    *-- The next line creates the object
    loStatement = CREATEOBJECT("statement")

    *-- Now create the statement's contents.
    loStatement.Create(this.CustomerNumber)

    *-- Now print the statement
    loStatement.Print()

    *-- Finally, tell the user that we are done
    WAIT WINDOW "Statement number " + ;
                loStatement.cStatementNumber + ;
                " has been created and printed!"
ENDPROC
```

You can write this method without ever seeing a line of the Statement object's code. In fact, this is part of the whole point. Just like you could not care less what makes an elevator work, you could not care less what makes the Statement object tick. As long as the developer who created the Statement class did the job properly, you can rely on the design document to know how you need to interact with the class. That's all you need.

You can test the method by trading files. You should never have to modify someone else's code—it's none of your business.

By segregating development in this theoretical manner, OOP creates a situation that minimizes the need to modify shared code and, therefore, makes multi-developer teams easier to manage.

Of course, there is another issue to be dealt with here: the issue of integrating classes created by developers into the application's class libraries. This is the job of the class librarian. For more information on the class librarian, refer to Chapter 16.

System Maintenance with OOP

Users like to change things, right? Using the light example, suppose that the user changes the base definition of the light switch. In this example, a light switch has only one property (Status) and one method (Toggle). Suppose that the company redefined the base light switch (the Light class) to add another feature. Now, when the user turns the light off or on, the system tells the user what has been done.

In order to accomplish this, all you need to do is to modify the Light class definition as follows:

```
DEFINE CLASS light AS custom
    status = "OFF"

    PROCEDURE LightSwitch
        IF this.status = "OFF"
            this.status = "ON"
        ELSE
            this.status = "OFF"
        ENDIF
        WAIT WINDOW "Light is now " + this.status
    ENDPROC
ENDDEFINE
```

From this point on, all objects instantiated from the Light class get the changed method. In effect, you have changed the behavior of every object based on this class by adding one line of code to the class definition.

But wait, there's more. Not only have you modified all the objects based on the Light class, but you have also modified every object based on subclasses of light (Dimmer, for example). This is a powerful way to develop reusable code.

The flip side of this is that if you break a class, you might also break all the subclasses based on it, regardless of the application in which the class is used. If you have used a class in a production application, you'll need to be very careful with this. ●

OOP with Visual FoxPro

Creating and Using Classes with Visual FoxPro

In Chapter 13, "Introduction to Object-Oriented Programming," you briefly learned some of the issues related to creating classes in Visual FoxPro. All the work was done in code, which is a good way to look at creating classes because it provides a clear view of what you can do when you create classes.

The following sections provide a definitive look at the syntax of creating and using classes in Visual FoxPro.

Defining Classes

You define classes using the DEFINE CLASS/ENDDEFINE construct. Here is an example:

```
DEFINE CLASS <classname> AS <baseclass>
    *-- Declaration Code Here
    PROTECTED <list of member variables>

    PROCEDURE <methodproc> (param1, param2 ....)
        LOCAL <list of local variables>
        *-- Procedure Code Here
    ENDPROC

    FUNCTION <methodfunc> (param1, param2 ....)
        LOCAL <list of local variables>
        *-- Function code here
        RETURN <returnval>
    ENDFUNC
ENDDEFINE
```

In the following sections you read about each portion of the construct separately.

DEFINE CLASS <classname> AS <superclass>

This line of code tells Visual FoxPro that you are creating a class. All code between DEFINE and ENDDEFINE relates to this class. <classname> is the name of the class and <superclass> is the name of the class upon which the class is based. This can be a built-in class provided with Visual FoxPro 6 or one that you create or purchase.

The term *superclass* used here is in line with terminology used in most texts that discuss object orientation. Unfortunately, Microsoft uses the term *parentclass* to mean the same thing. Don't let the terminology throw you.

By definition, every class created in Visual FoxPro is a subclass of another class. At the highest level, classes created in Visual FoxPro are subclasses of what Microsoft calls *base classes*, the classes that ship with Visual FoxPro. Visual FoxPro 6 comes with the base classes shown in Table 14.1.

Table 14.1 Visual FoxPro 6 Base Classes

Class Name	Description	Visual	Form Control Toolbar	Subclass Only
ActiveDoc	An active document object that can be hosted in a host browser such as Internet Explorer.			√
CheckBox	A standard check box control similar to the check box created in FoxPro 2.x.	√	√	
Column	A column on a grid control.	√	√	
ComboBox	A combo box similar to the pop-up control in FoxPro 2.x.	√	√	
CommandButton	Equivalent to a pushbutton in FoxPro 2.x.	√	√	
CommandGroup	A group of command buttons that operate together. Equivalent to a group of pushbuttons in FoxPro 2.x controlled by one variable.	√	√	
Container	A generic object designed to hold other objects. This is useful when you are creating a class that has more than one object on it.	√		√
Control	The same as the container class with one major difference:	√		√

continues

Table 14.1   Continued

Class Name	Description	Visual	Form Control Toolbar	Subclass Only
	When the object in a container class is instantiated from the class, you can address all objects within the container. The Control class hides all internal objects and only allows communication with the control class.			
Cursor	A cursor definition in a data environment.			
Custom	Primarily used for objects that are not visual but might contain visual objects as members.			√
Data Environment	A collection of cursors and relations to open or close as a unit.			
EditBox	The equivalent of a FoxPro 2.6 edit region.	√	√	√
Form	A single "screen." This is a container object in that it can (and usually does) contain other objects. The equivalent of a FoxPro 2.x screen.	√	√	√
FormSet	A container-type object that has one or more forms as members. This is the equivalent of a FoxPro 2.x screen set.		√	√
Grid	A container-type object that allows display and editing of information in browse-type format.	√	√	√

Class Name	Description	Visual	Form Control Toolbar	Subclass Only
Header	The header of a grid column.	√		
Hyperlink Object	Provides button, image, or label object that when clicked, launches a Web browser and navigates to a hyperlink.	√	√	√
Image	A picture.	√	√	√
Label	The equivalent of placing text on a screen in FoxPro 2.x.	√	√	√
Line	A drawn line.	√	√	√
ListBox	The equivalent of the FoxPro 2.x scrolling list control.	√	√	√
OleControl	A control based on an OLE 2 object.	√	√	√
OptionButton	A single radio button-type object.	√		
OptionGroup	Multiple radio buttons that operate as a single control. This is the equivalent of a FoxPro 2.x radio button object.	√	√	√
Page	A single page within a page frame.	√		
PageFrame	A tabbed control. Each tab within a tab control is a separate page. The page frame control is a container-type control because it can (and usually does) contain many objects.	√	√	√

Part
IV

Ch
14

continues

Table 14.1   Continued

Class Name	Description	Visual	Form Control Toolbar	Subclass Only
ProjectHook	Creates instance of opened project that enables programmatic access to project events.			
Relation	A definition of a relation between two cursors in a data environment.			
Separator	Object that puts blank spaces between controls on a toolbar.	√	√	
Shape	A shape (such as a circle or a box).	√	√	
Spinner	The equivalent of the FoxPro 2.x spinner control.	√	√	
TextBox	The equivalent of a FoxPro 2.x "plain" GET control.	√	√	
Timer	A visual object that does not display on a form. This control is designed to allow for actions at certain timed intervals.		√	
ToolBar	A toolbar, which is a group of objects that can be docked at the the top, bottom, or sides of the desktop. When not docked, a toolbar looks something like a form.	√		√

As Table 14.1 indicates, classes can be categorized in three ways: "Visual," "Form Control Toolbar," and "Visual Class Designer Only." Classes can be visual or nonvisual. A visual class "displays," whereas a nonvisual class does not have a display component attached to it. In addition, some classes are not available from the Form Control toolbar. Finally, some classes are available only in the Visual Class Designer for subclassing, not for use as controls.

The Visual column specifies whether a base class is visual or nonvisual. Form Controls Toolbar specifies whether the base class is available on that toolbar. Subclass Only specifies those base classes that are intended for subclassing and provide little functionality on their own (for example, the Container class).

Most classes are available in the Form Designer from the Form Controls toolbar, but others are not. Some of those unavailable classes (such as Page, Header, and OptionButton) are unavailable because they are members of other objects. For example, Page is a member of PageFrame, Header is a member of Grid, and OptionButton is a member of OptionGroup. FormSet is not a control per se but a container of forms; it is created by combining multiple forms.

Finally, some classes are specifically designed for subclassing and are only available either in code or through the Visual Class Designer. You learn about the Visual Class Designer in the section "The Visual Class Designer" later in this chapter.

The classes that are controls available within the Form Designer are discussed in Chapter 9, "Creating Forms." In addition to the base classes included with Visual FoxPro 6, you can base classes on your own classes. Finally, the DEFINE CLASS/ENDCLASS structure must live on its own and cannot be nested within a loop or a decision structure (such as IF/ENDIF). Think of each class definition construct as its own "procedure" and you'll be fine.

*--Declaration Code Here/PROTECTED <list of member variables>   Declaration code declares your class member variables. Only the member variables listed here are properties of objects instantiated from this class (with the exception of member objects, which are discussed later in this chapter in the section "Creating Composite Classes"). If a member variable is an array, you would declare the array in this section of code.

Another important piece in this section is the declaration of protected members. A *protected member* is a member variable that is not visible outside the class. In other words, methods within the class can access and modify that variable, but the variable does not exist as far as the outside world (anything that is not a method of the class) is concerned.

You declare member variables protected by using the keyword PROTECTED and then listing the member variables that you want protected. The following example creates a protected member variable called cProtected:

```
PROTECTED cProtected
```

You must declare a property protected within the declaration section of the DEFINE CLASS construct.

An example of a member variable that would be declared PROTECTED? is a member that saves the state of the environment when the object is instantiated. The variable can be used to reset the environment when the object is released, but it serves no purpose to programs instantiating the object and interacting with it. As a matter of fact, you would not want this member variable to be changed by the outside world. Hence, you would protect it in the declaration section of code.

PROCEDURE <*methodproc*> **(param1, param2....)/ENDPROC FUNCTION** <*methodfunc*> **(param1, param2....)/ENDFUNC**   This line of code defines a method. <*methodproc*> and <*methodfunc*> refer to the name of the method. Note that you can call a method a FUNCTION or a **FUNCTION**—both syntaxes are equivalent. I like to use the **FUNCTION** syntax if the method is intended to return a value; otherwise I use **PROCEDURE**.

Parameters sent to a method can be accepted with a PARAMETERS statement (more typically LPARAMETERS), or the parameters can be accepted in parentheses after the name of the method. For example, if a method called ShowVals were to accept two parameters (Parm1 and Parm2), the code to accept these parameters would look like this:

```
PROCEDURE ShowVals
LPARAMETERS Parm1, Parm2
```

it might also look like this:

```
PROCEDURE ShowVals(Parm1, Parm2)
```

Of the two, I prefer the second syntax because I think it reads better. You can choose either one.

Be aware that parameters sent through to methods, whether the parameters are called as a procedure (such as loObject.Method(Parm1)) or a function (such as lcVar = loObject.Method(Parm1)), are treated like parameters sent through to a user-defined function: They are sent through by VALUE unless either SET UDFPARMS has been set to REFERENCE (I don't recommend changing the setting of SET UDFPARMS) or the name of the parameter is sent through with the @ sign.

For example, note the TSTPROC.PRG test procedure presented in Listing 14.1. The return values quoted assume the default setting of SET UDFPARMS.

Listing 14.1   14CODE01.PRG—**Test Procedure That Illustrates the SET UDFPARMS Command Settings**

```
lcText = "Menachem"
loX = CREATEOBJECT("test")

*-- Call testfunc first as a procedure and then as a method
*-- without specificying by reference.

loX.testfunc(lcText)      && "Proc" Syntax
? lcText                  && Shows "Menachem"

=loX.testfunc(lcText)     && Func Syntax
? lcText                  && Shows "Menachem"
```

```
loX.testfunc(@lcText)     && "Proc" Syntax
? lcText                  && Shows 10
lcText = "Menachem"         && Reset for next test

=loX.testfunc(@lcText)     && Func Syntax
? lcText                  && Shows 10
lcText = "Menachem"         && Reset for next test

loX.testproc(lcText)      && "Proc" Syntax
? lcText                  && Shows "Menachem"

=loX.testproc(lcText)      && Func Syntax
? lcText                  && Shows "Menachem"

loX.testproc(@lcText)      && "Proc" Syntax
? lcText                  && Shows 10
lcText = "Menachem"         && Reset for next test

=loX.testproc(@lcText)      && Func Syntax
? lcText                  && Shows 10
lcText = "Menachem"         && Reset for next test

DEFINE CLASS test AS custom
    FUNCTION testfunc (Parm1)
        Parm1 = 10
    ENDFUNC

    PROCEDURE testproc (Parm1)
        Parm1 = 10
    ENDPROC
ENDDEFINE
```

Methods can be protected like member variables—that is, they can only be called from other methods in the class—by adding the keyword PROTECTED before PROCEDURE or FUNCTION (PRO-TECTED PROCEDURE <methodproc>). Methods that are protected do not exist outside the class, and an error is generated if an attempt is made to call them.

As a general rule, methods should be protected if they are not intended for the "outside world." This saves you a lot of trouble down the road. For example, a method that is intended only to be called by other methods in the class would be protected.

If a method has to return a value, a RETURN statement precedes the ENDPROC/ENDFUNC statement as shown in the following example:

```
PROCEDURE ShowDate
    RETURN date()
ENDPROC

FUNCTION FuncShowDate
    RETURN date()
ENDFUNC
```

Methods are closed with the ENDPROC or ENDFUNC command; the command you use depends on the command used to start the method definition.

Part
IV

Ch
14

Instantiating Objects

Objects are instantiated from their classes with the CREATEOBJECT function. Here's the syntax:

```
loObject = CREATEOBJECT(<classname> [, <Parameter list>])
```

The CREATEOBJECT function returns an object reference that is stored in loObject. *<classname>* is a string indicating the class to be used for instantiation. Parameters follow in the CREATEOBJECT function; they appear one at a time and are separated by commas. Parameters are accepted in the object's Init method. (You learn the Init method and sending parameters later in this chapter in the section "A Technical Tip—Sending Parameters to an Object.")

In order to instantiate an object with CREATEOBJECT, the class definition has to be available when the CREATEOBJECT function is used. If you have manually coded your classes as opposed to using the Visual Class Designer (as shown in Chapter 15, "Creating Classes with Visual FoxPro"), the program that has the class definitions must be available. The program is made available with SET PROCEDURE or by placing the class definitions in a program that is higher in the calling chain.

You can release the procedure file once the object is instantiated if you use SET PROCEDURE. Visual FoxPro loads all the methods into memory when the object is instantiated.

Always remember that an instance is just a memory variable and follows almost all of the same rules as regular memory variables. Objects can be made local, public, or private and will lose or keep scope like any other memory variable.

There is one significant difference between an object (known as an *instance variable*) and other Visual FoxPro variables: Variables can be thought of as holding *values*, whereas instance variables do not hold values—they hold references to an object, which in turn holds the values.

This has three implications. First, an instance variable is always passed to procedures and functions by reference. Second, if an instance variable is copied into another variable, all changes in the second variable affect the same object. Finally, an object is not released until all references to it have been released. Here is an example:

```
loInstance = CREATEOBJECT("Form")
loInstance.Show()                        && Show the form
loVar = loInstance                       && loVar points to the form
➡too, now.
loInstance.Caption = "Hello"          && Caption changes
loVar.Caption = "There"                  && Caption changes again
RELEASE loInstance                          && Form does not disappear
RELEASE loVar                                && Now it disappears
```

Calling Methods

You always call methods by specifying the name of the instance variable, then a period, and then the name of the method. Here is an example:

```
loClass.MyMethod
```

Parameters are sent through to a method by listing them in parentheses after the method name. Here is an example:

```
loClass.MyMethod(Parm1, "StringParm2")
```

There is no DO syntax for a method. To call a method and get a return value, the syntax is almost identical. You specify a variable to accept the value:

```
lcRetVal = loClass.MyMethod(Parm1, "StringParm2")
```

If no parameters are sent through to the method, you can still use parentheses after the method name. Here is an example:

```
loClass.MyMethod
```

I use this syntax exclusively because it is much clearer that the member you are accessing is a method, not a property.

Base Events, Methods, and Properties

As you know from reading Chapter 9, different controls have different events, methods, and properties. For example, the Label control has a Caption property, whereas the TextBox control has a Value property.

Each control shown in the default Form Controls toolbar is a base class in Visual FoxPro and can be used as the basis for your own classes.

In addition to the classes shown in the Form Controls toolbar, there are four classes specifically designed to be used as the basis for user-defined classes. They do not show up on the Form Controls toolbar nor are they part of other classes (such as an OptionButton, which is part of an OptionGroup control). These classes are Container, Control, Custom, and ToolBar.

Although each base class supports its own set of events, properties, and methods, there is a common set of events, methods, and properties that apply to all base classes in Visual FoxPro.

Base Properties

The following list shows the properties that are common to all of Visual FoxPro's base classes.

Property	Description
Class	The name of the object's class
BaseClass	The name of the object's base class
ClassLibrary	The full path of the class library where this class is defined
ParentClass	The name of the class upon which this class is based

Part

IV

Ch

14

Base Events and Methods

The following list shows the events and methods that are common to all of Visual FoxPro's base classes.

Event	Description
Init	Invoked when the object is created. Accepts parameters sent through to the object. Returning .F. aborts object instantiation.
Destroy	Invoked when the object is released.
Error	Invoked when an error occurs inside one of the object's methods.

In the next chapter you learn the properties and methods of the four special base classes just mentioned.

The `Error` Method

The Error method is important and worthy of special note. The Error method is called in the event an ON ERROR-type error occurs in a class. The Error method takes precedence over the setting of ON ERROR, which is important because this enables you to encapsulate error handling where it belongs—within the class itself. You see examples of the Error method and its uses in the next chapter.

Creating Composite Classes

A *composite class* is a class that has members that are themselves instances of other classes. A perfect example of this is a class based on a container-type class, such as a form. When you think of it, a form itself is a class, yet the objects in it are classes, too. Therefore, you have one object that has other objects contained in it (hence the name container class).

When you work with code you can add object members in one of two ways. The first way uses the ADD OBJECT command and is called within the declaration section of code. Here is the syntax:

```
ADD OBJECT <ObjectName> AS <ClassName> ;
    [ WITH <membervar> = <value>, <membervar> = <value> ... ]
```

<ObjectName> is the name you want to give to the instance variable being added to the class. <ClassName> is the class upon which <ObjectName> is based. You can specify special settings for member variables of the added object by setting them after a WITH clause. Here is an example:

```
DEFINE CLASS Foo AS FORM
    ADD OBJECT myCommandButton AS CommandButton ;
        WITH    caption = "Hello", ;
                height = 50
ENDDEFINE
```

When class Foo is instantiated, a member variable called myCommandButton is added to the form with a height of 50 pixels and a caption of "Hello." When the form is shown, the command button will be happily waiting for you to click it.

The second syntax is the AddObject method. This method can be called from either inside the class or outside the class. This means that you can add objects to container-type objects on-the-fly. Here is the AddObject method's syntax:

```
<object>.AddObject(<Member Name>,<Class Name>[, Parameters])
```

To mimic the prior example (note that I do not even define a class for this one), I could do this:

```
loFoo = CREATEOBJECT("Form")
loFoo.AddObject("myCommandButton", "CommandButton")
loFoo.MyCommandButton.Caption = "Hello"
loFoo.MyCommandButton.Height = 50
loFoo.MyCommandButton.Visible = .T.
loFoo.Show
```

Accessing Child Member Variables and Methods

As far as Visual FoxPro is concerned, using the object names from the previous example, loFoo is a parent object and MyCommandButton is a child object. As you just saw, the properties of the child object, MyCommandButton, can only be accessed by going through its parent.

 TIP Composite objects can have members that are themselves composite objects. This can lead to a very long "path" to get to a member variable. If you want to cut through the keystrokes, copy a reference—to another memory variable—to the object you're trying to get to and work with it that way. For example, assume you have an object with the following hierarchy and you want to work with the text box for a little while:

```
MyForm.MyPageFrame.myContainer.myTextBox
```

Just use this code:

```
loMyObj = MyForm.MyPageFrame.myContainer.myTextBox
```

From here on you can access all the properties and methods of MyTextBox through loMyObj. This can save you a lot of typing. Remember, though, that you will not be able to get rid of any parent objects of myTextBox without first releasing loMyObj.

Differences Between ADD OBJECT and AddObject

A review of the code examples for ADD OBJECT and AddObject show some differences. First of all, ADD OBJECT enables you to set properties on the calling line, whereas AddObject does not. You have to access the member variables individually. Secondly, when a visual object is added to a container with AddObject, the object is hidden by default (its Visible property is set to .F.), which enables you to set the display characteristics before showing the control.

AddObject enables you to send parameters to the object's Init method, whereas ADD OBJECT does not. Finally, ADD OBJECT enables you to turn off the Init method when you instantiate the member object with the NOINIT clause; AddObject does not have this capability.

THIS Revisited

In the previous chapter you learned a special keyword called THIS. Its purpose is to enable a class to refer to itself. There are three additional keywords along this line that are applicable for composite classes only. Here is a list of these keywords:

THISFORM	This keyword is special for members of Form-based classes. It refers to the form on which an object lies.
THISFORMSET	This keyword is special for members of a form that is part of FormSet. It refers to the FormSet object of which the current object is a member.
PARENT	This keyword refers to the parent of the current object.

Note that you can move up the hierarchy with this.parent.parent.parent (you get the idea).

Adding Objects with `CreateObject`

Can you add an object to another object with CreateObject? In effect, can you do this:

```
DEFINE CLASS test AS custom
    oForm = .NULL.

    PROCEDURE INIT
        this.oForm = CREATEOBJECT("form")
    ENDPROC
ENDDEFINE
```

The short answer is yes and no. Sound confusing? Let me explain. The code snippet shown here does indeed create an object with a member called oForm that is an object. However, oForm is not a child of the object. oForm is a member variable that is an object. This might sound as if I'm splitting hairs, but there are some very important differences.

First, the PARENT keyword will not work with oForm. Second, because the member object is not a child object, you can do some interesting things. Take a look at this bit of code:

```
DEFINE CLASS foo AS form
    ADD OBJECT myForm AS Form ;
        WITH    caption = "Hello", ;
                height = 50
ENDDEFINE

DEFINE CLASS bar AS form
    PROCEDURE init
        this.addobject("myForm", "Form")
    ENDPROC
ENDDEFINE
```

```
DEFINE CLASS foobar AS Form
    oForm = .NULL.

    PROCEDURE init
        this.oForm = CREATEOBJECT("form")
    ENDPROC
ENDDEFINE
```

Neither class Foo nor Bar works. If you try to instantiate them, you get an error because you cannot add an object based on any descendant of the Form class to a form-based object. The last iteration, class FooBar, works just fine. You'll see a more practical example of this capability in Chapter 17, "Advanced Object-Oriented Programming."

How Classes Are Created in Visual FoxPro

So far, all the examples you have seen for creating classes in Visual FoxPro deal with code. In fact, as shown in Table 14.1 and further detailed in Chapter 15, there are some classes that can only be created via a coded program.

For the most part, however, creating classes is much more efficient using the Visual Class Designer—the tool provided with Visual FoxPro to make the job of creating classes easier.

Why a Visual Class Designer?

Why do you need a Visual Class Designer when you can easily create classes with code? There are three reasons the Visual Class Designer is integral to class development. The first reason is that it insulates you from the intricacies of code. Although you have learned the syntax for creating classes, you should not have to remember and type in the constructs and keywords related to the structure of a defined class. The Visual Class Designer handles this for you.

The second reason is that some classes can get complex rather quickly. This is especially true of some visual classes, such as forms (where the placement of the objects within the container are critical). Creating complex classes is best done visually.

Finally, only classes created with the Visual Class Designer can be managed with the Class Browser, a wonderful tool provided with the product. The Class Browser is discussed in Chapter 16, "Managing Classes with Visual FoxPro."

All three reasons are valid for using the Visual Class Designer. That's why I recommend that you use it whenever you can for developing classes.

The Visual Class Designer

The Visual Class Designer is a superset of the Form Designer. In fact, the Visual Class Designer is so much like a Designer that the metafile it uses to store the classes you create is a copy of the .SCX/.SCT file structure. The only difference here is that the extension given a class file is .VCX instead of .SCX, and a .VCX can hold many classes in one file as opposed to just one form (in an .SCX).

Part
IV

Ch
14

When you create classes visually, Visual FoxPro 6 gives you access to the Controls toolbar, the Properties window, and the visual canvas.

Figure 14.1 shows the Visual Class Designer when you are working on a command button–based class.

FIGURE 14.1

The Visual Class Designer.

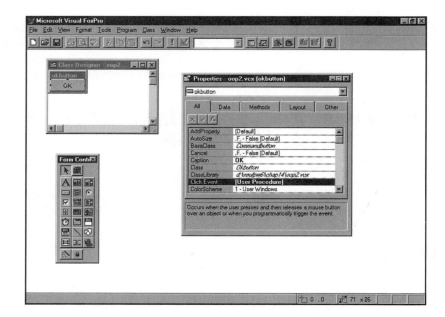

All the options on the menu operate in an almost identical manner to their counterparts on the Form Designer. Rather than cover the Visual Class Designer in detail, I only cover instances where it differs from the Form Designer.

Design Surface Differences

The first difference is the most apparent, but technically is not really a difference at all. The object being modified in the Form Designer is a form. A form is a container object and therefore can have many objects on it. Figure 14.1 only shows a CommandButton. That's because the class being designed is a subclass of CommandButton, which does not support adding other objects to it. Therefore, all you see is the single object on which you are working. If you are working on a Form type class in the Visual Class Designer, the canvas looks the same as it does in the Form Designer.

Menu Differences

Menu options that are specific to forms, such as Create Form Set and Remove Form Set are not on the Visual Class Designer's class menu. The Visual Class Designer does add one menu option, Class Info, and the operation of New Methods and New Properties is slightly changed. These changes are discussed first.

Adding Properties and Methods

The New Property and New Method menu options work as they do in the Form Designer, with one important change: There is a new check box control on the dialog box that enables you to protect new methods and properties. Checking this box means that the property or method is protected. To "unprotect" a method or property, you need to use the Edit Property or Edit Method option. Note that a property or method, once protected, cannot be unprotected in a subclass. It must be unprotected on the level at which it was added to the class hierarchy.

A Technical Tip—Adding Member Arrays to a VCX Class

Suppose you want to add a property to a class that is an array. This is not a problem in code because you have access to the declaration section. However, you do not have access to the declaration code with visually designed classes. The trick is to specify the name of the array with its default length in the New Properties dialog box. For example, to add a property called aProp to a class, the name of the property you type in would be this:

```
aProp[1]
```

The array subscript tells Visual FoxPro that the property you are adding is an array. If you look at the new property in the Properties window, you'll notice that the new array is read-only. Don't worry about this; it just means that you have to work with the array in code. There is no provision for setting values in arrays in the Properties window.

Accessing Class Information

The Class Info menu option gives the developer access to information about the class being modified with the dialog box shown in Figure 14.2.

FIGURE 14.2
The Class Info dialog box.

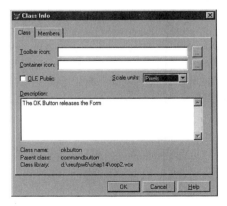

The Class tab on this page frame shows some basic information about the class. Here is a list of the options:

Toolbar Icon
This modifiable option specifies which icon will show in the Form Controls toolbar when the .VCX file is loaded. Clicking the command button to the right of the text box displays a GETPICT dialog box that enables you to select a graphics file.

Container Icon
This is the same idea as Toolbar Icon except that it deals with the icon shown for this class in the Class Browser. The Class Browser is discussed in Chapter 16.

OLE Public
If this option is set, whenever a program containing this class is built using the Project Manager, a custom automation server and a GUID (Globally Unique Identifier) are generated.

Scale Units
This option determines whether the grid is measured in terms of pixels or foxels.

Description
This is an EditBox in which the developer can enter a description of the class.

Class Name
This is the name of the class being modified.

Parent Class
This is the name of the class upon which this class is based (that is, the immediate superclass).

Class Library
This is the name of the .VCX file in which the class is stored.

The next tab is Members, which it shows the members of the current class. Members of the class can be properties, methods, events, or objects. Object members occur if the class is a composite (container-type) class.

This tab, which is shown in Figure 14.3, has a list of all the members of the class and enables the developer to protect any or all of them by checking the box in the Protected column. The No Init column is only applicable for object members and tells Visual FoxPro whether to run the Init event for this object when it is added at runtime. Checking the box means that the Init event is skipped.

FIGURE 14.3
The Members tab for the Class Info dialog box.

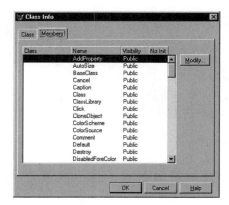

Now that you have seen how to use the Visual Class Designer, the next step is to look at the syntax involved in getting into the Visual Class Designer. Obviously, there are two modes: CREATE and MODIFY.

Creating a Class

A new class can be created with the CREATE CLASS command. Issuing CREATE CLASS with no additional information presents the dialog box shown in Figure 14.4.

FIGURE 14.4

The New Class dialog box.

Classes can be based on Visual FoxPro base classes (listed in the drop-down list box) or on any class you create. In order to base your new class on a class you have created (as opposed to one Visual FoxPro supplies for you), click the ellipses (...) CommandButton. A dialog box will enable you to select the class you want to use (shown in Figure 14.5). The left portion of the dialog box is a GETFILE type display that enables you to select a .VCX file. Once you select a .VCX file, the classes it contains shows in the list to the right. You can then select a class to open and click the Open CommandButton; the Visual Class Designer comes up.

FIGURE 14.5

The dialog box in which you can select a class.

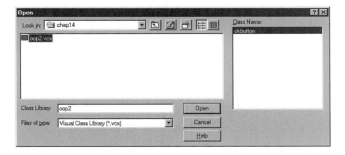

Note that you can only use a class stored in a .VCX file as the base class for another VCX-stored class. Figure 14.6 shows the New Class dialog box once the parent class has been selected.

FIGURE 14.6

The New Class dialog box for the VCX subclass.

Another way to create a class and bypass the dialog box is to provide all the information needed to create the class on the command line. Here's the syntax for this:

```
CREATE CLASS <ClassName> OF <ClassLibraryName1>     ;
     AS cBaseClassName [FROM ClassLibraryName2]
```

ClassName is the name of the class to create. *ClassLibraryName1* is the name of the .VCX file in which to store the class. If the .VCX file does not exist, Visual FoxPro creates it for you (note that you can create a class library, too, with the CREATE CLASSLIB command). cBaseClassName is the name of the class on which to base the new class. This can be a Visual FoxPro base class or a class you create. If it's a class you have created, you must specify the .VCX file it is stored in with ClassLibraryName2. You need to specify the class library name from where the super-class is coming even if it comes from the same .VCX file where the new class is stored.

Modifying Classes in a .VCX File

Classes are loaded for modification into the Visual Class Designer with the MODIFY CLASS command. Here's the basic syntax:

```
MODIFY CLASS <ClassName> OF <ClassLibraryName>
```

ClassName is the name of the class to modify, and *ClassLibraryName* is the name of the .VCX file containing the class to be modified. If you prefer a more visual method of selecting a class to edit, you can issue this without any additional information:

```
MODIFY CLASS
```

Visual FoxPro displays the same dialog box shown in Figure 14.5.

Using Classes in a .VCX File

Classes created with the Visual Class Designer are stored in a .VCX file (also called a *class library*). The structure of the table is the same as the structure of the .SCX file.

In order to instantiate an object from a class stored in a .VCX file, the class library must be loaded with the SET CLASSLIB command. Here is the syntax:

```
SET CLASSLIB TO <vcxFileName> [IN APPFileName ¦ EXEFilename]
   [ADDITIVE] [ALIAS AliasName]
```

After the class library is loaded, any classes in the class library can be used for instantiating objects.

Be careful of one thing. As you saw previously in this chapter, a class in a .VCX file can be a subclass of a class stored in another class library. Make sure that all the .VCX files you need are loaded with SET CLASSLIB before you instantiate objects. A good strategy is to load all the .VCX files used in an application at the beginning. This way you are sure not to miss a .VCX file when you need it. If the visual class library is in a Visual FoxPro application or Visual FoxPro execut-able file, you can include the IN clause to designate the filename. In addition, be sure to use the ADDITIVE keyword when adding class libraries, or else those already loaded will be released.

You can designate an ALIAS name for your visual class library. You can then use the alias name to reference the specified visual class library. This is especially useful if your visual class library's filename is long, such as "My Very Own Excellent Visual Class Library." Here is an example:

```
SET CLASSLIB TO "My Very Own Excellent Visual Class Library" ;
    ALIAS Mine
oMyForm = CREATEOBJ(Mine.SpecialForm)
```

Use the RELEASE CLASSLIB command to release a single class library. To release all the class libraries, issue a SET CLASSLIB TO command without specifying a class library file. By the way, if all of this syntax looks familiar, it should. This is one thing Microsoft did really well—it kept the syntax for similar commands, such as SET LIBRARY and SET PROCEDURE, virtually identical.

A Technical Tip: Sending Parameters to an Object

When you instantiate an object it may be necessary to send parameters through to the object. For example, if you were creating an object that displays a message (I know there is a MessageBox function, but please bear with me), you might want to send parameters through that indicate the message text, the form caption, and so on.

The syntax for sending parameters through when instantiating an object is simple—all you do is add the parameters (separated by commas) after the name of the class from which you are instantiating. Here is an example:

```
loForm = CREATEOBJECT("MyMsgForm", "Hello. This is a message.")
```

This line of code instantiates an object called loForm from the "MyMsgForm" class and passes through the string "Hello. This is a message." as a parameter.

The next question is where do you accept the parameters? The answer is in the Init method. Beware, however, because unlike sending parameters through in FoxPro 2.6, parameters in Visual FoxPro that are accepted in the Init method are released when the Init method completes. Don't forget that Init is a procedure and thus causes its parameters to lose scope when it returns from where it was called.

How do you keep the parameters around? If the parameters are intended to be sent through by value (which is usually the case) you can move the parameters' values into the object's custom properties. You can't pass a parameter and have it stick around to be modified.

Managing Instances with AInstance

Visual FoxPro can give you a list of instances created for a particular class with the AInstance function. Here is this function's syntax:

```
lnNumInstances = AInstance(<ArrayName>, <ClassName>)
```

The AInstance function returns a numeric value: the number of instances found.

For example, you would issue the following command in order to determine how many instances have been created for class FORM:

```
lnNumInstances = AInstance(laInstances, "Form")
```

The variable lnNumInstances has the number of instances found, and the array laInstances has a list of the instance variables instantiated from class Form.

Note that this function only returns member variables created with CREATEOBJECT that are not themselves members of other objects. For example, if you have an instance of class Form that is a member of another object, this instance does not show up with AInstance.

AInstance can have many uses. A more common one is to use it to manage multiple instances of a class (a form, for example). The following example illustrates such a use. In this form class' Init method, the AInstance function checks for the number of instances of this class. Each instance of the class has a custom property called nInstanceNumber, which holds the instance number of the form. The Init method determines the instance number for this instance and then adds the instance number to the caption of the form. (Note that if this is the first instance of the form, the caption remains unmodified.) The Init method could do more. For instance, many developers adjust the Top and Left properties to cascade the form on the desktop. The code is presented in Listing 14.2.

Listing 14.2   14CODE02—**The Multform Class That Illustrates How to Pass Arguments to a Class's Init Method**

```
*   Class.............: Multform
*   Author............: Menachem Bazian, CPA
*   Notes.............: Exported code from Class Browser.


**************************************************
*-- Class:          multform (d:\data\docs\books\vfu\code\oop2.vcx)
*-- ParentClass:     form
*-- BaseClass:       form
*
DEFINE CLASS multform AS form

    DoCreate = .T.
    Caption = "Form"
    Name = "multform"

    *-- The Instance Number of this form
    ninstancenumber = .F.

    PROCEDURE Init
        *-- This code will determine what instance number
        *-- this form is and set the header accordingly.

        LOCAL lnNumInstances, lnThisInstance, lcInstance

        lnNumInstances = AInstance(laInstances, this.class)
        lnThisInstance = 1
        FOR lnCounter = 1 TO lnNumInstances
```

```
            lcInstance = laInstances[lnCounter]
            lnThisInstance = MAX(lnThisInstance,&lcInstance..nInstanceNumber + 1)
        ENDFOR

        this.nInstanceNumber = lnThisInstance

        IF lnThisInstance > 1
            this.caption = ALLTRIM(this.caption) + ": " +
ALLT(STR(lnThisInstance))
        ENDIF
    ENDPROC

ENDDEFINE
*
*-- EndDefine: multform
**************************************************
```

ACLASS

If you have an involved class hierarchy, it can be difficult to remember what classes precede the instantiated class in the hierarchy. Take, for example, the following class hierarchy:

```
DEFINE CLASS myBaseForm AS FORM
ENDDEFINE

DEFINE CLASS myModalBaseForm AS MyBaseForm
ENDDEFINE

DEFINE CLASS ModalDialog AS myModalBaseForm
ENDDEFINE
```

When an object is instantiated from ModalDialog, you might wonder what the class hierarchy looks like. ACLASS answers that question. Assume this:

```
loModalDialog = CREATEOBJECT("ModalDialog")
lnNumClasses = ACLASS(laClasses, loModalDialog)
```

If you assume as much, laClasses will have this:

```
LACLASSES Pub                    A
    ( 1) C        "MODALDIALOG"
    ( 2) C        "MYMODALBASEFORM"
    ( 3) C        "MYBASEFORM"
    ( 4) C        "FORM"
```

AMembers

AMembers is another very useful function. This function populates an array with the members of an instance. It comes in two flavors:

```
lnNumMembers = AMembers(<ArrayName>, <InstanceVar>)

lnNumMembers = AMembers(<ArrayName>, <InstanceVar>, 1)
```

The first version of this function creates an array with the properties of an instance. The array is unidimensional. For example, you would state the following to see the properties of the _Screen object:

```
lnNumMembers = AMembers(laMembers, _screen)
```

This function returns an array with the following information. For brevity, only the first few elements are shown here:

```
LAMEMBERS   Pub                         A
          (    1)  C          "ACTIVECONTROL"
          (    2)  C          "ACTIVEFORM"
          (    3)  C          "ALWAYSONTOP"
          (    4)  C          "AUTOCENTER"
          (    5)  C          "BACKCOLOR"
          (    6)  C          "BASECLASS"
          (    7)  C          "BORDERSTYLE"
          (    8)  C          "BUFFERMODE"
          (    9)  C          "CAPTION"
          (  10)  C          "CLASS"
```

The second version creates a two-dimensional array. The first column is the name of the member and the second column is the type of the member (event, method, object, or property). The following example inspects _Screen:

```
lnNumMembers = AMembers(laMembers, _screen, 1)
```

The laMember array element values are shown in Listing 14.3.

Listing 14.3 14CODE03—**Array Elements That Contain the Members of Screen Object**

```
LAMEMBERS   Pub        A
  (   1,  1)  C      "ACTIVATE"
  (   1,  2)  C      "Event"
  (   2,  1)  C      "ACTIVECONTROL"
  (   2,  2)  C      "Property"
  (   3,  1)  C      "ACTIVEFORM"
  (   3,  2)  C      "Property"
  (   4,  1)  C      "ADDOBJECT"
  (   4,  2)  C      "Method"
  (   5,  1)  C      "ALWAYSONTOP"
  (   5,  2)  C      "Property"
  (   6,  1)  C      "AUTOCENTER"
  (   6,  2)  C      "Property"
  (   7,  1)  C      "BACKCOLOR"
  (   7,  2)  C      "Property"
  (   8,  1)  C      "BASECLASS"
  (   8,  2)  C      "Property"
  (   9,  1)  C      "BORDERSTYLE"
  (   9,  2)  C      "Property"
  (  10,  1)  C      "BOX"
  (  10,  2)  C      "Method"
```

Note that the second version of AMembers returns a two-dimensional array and shows more members of the object than the first version. Without the additional ,1 parameter, only properties of the object are returned. The ,1 parameter adds methods, objects, and events to the list. Each version of this function has its uses. To look at an object when you are concerned only with its properties, you would use the first version of this function. To get more information, you would use the second version.

Inspecting Objects with AMembers

One of the more difficult aspects of working with object-oriented code is that a single memory variable can have a great deal of data and code attached to it. Take _Screen, for example. _Screen is a system memory variable that is an object based on the class Form. Changes made to _Screen are reflected in the main Visual FoxPro window. Thus, you could reset the main Visual FoxPro window's title with this line of code:

_Screen.Caption = "Visual FoxPro UNLEASHED With Object Orientation!"

In order to properly use this nifty little object, it is necessary to learn what is attached to the memory variable. AMembers is a useful way to get this information, as you saw in the previous example. The basic problem with this approach, though, is that there is so much information returned by AMembers that it is very difficult to make sense of it all. Clearly it would be beneficial to have some manner of presenting the information in a more useful format.

There are several ways to accomplish this goal. One simple method is to create the array with AMembers and to read the resultant array into a cursor. Listing 14.4 illustrates the use of the AMembers() function to create a cursor of the members of an object.

Listing 14.4 14CODE04

```
*   Program..........: CURSMEMB.PRG
*   Author...........: Menachem Bazian, CPA
*)  Description.......: Creates a cursor of the members of an object
*   Calling Samples...: =CURSMEMB(oObject)
*   Parameter List....: toObject - The Object to View
*   Major change list.:

LPARAMETERS toObject

IF TYPE("toObject") # "O"
    =MessageBox("Parameter must be an object!", 16)
    RETURN
ENDIF

*-- If we get this far, we can read the object...

LOCAL laMembers[1]
=AMEMBERS(laMembers, toObject, 1)
```

continues

Listing 14.4   Continued

```
CREATE CURSOR _members (cMembName C(25), ;
                        cMembtype C(25))

INSERT INTO _members FROM ARRAY laMembers

*-- And that's it
RETURN
```

This procedure is called with one parameter: the object to inspect. To see the members of the object, simply browse the _members cursor.

Taking the Inspector One Step Further

The Cursmemb.prg program, presented in Listing 14.4, provides a simple view of an object, but it still does not go far enough. Cursmemb.prg replaces an array view with the capability to browse and index a cursor. Although this is certainly an advance in how you can look at an object, it would be useful to see property values where possible and maybe even to get a prettier interface behind the information.

ObjectInspectorForm is a class that accomplishes this. This form-based class gives you a clean and easily readable form that you can use to view the contents of an object. The next section gives you a look at the interface; I show you how to call the object as well as explain the code behind it.

The User Interface

The interface has three controls. The first is the Order option group object, which enables you to switch between two display orders in the list: alphabetical and grouped. The Alphabetical option button shows all the members of the object in alphabetical order without regard to the members type. The Grouped option button shows all the members of a particular type together in alphabetical order. Events show first, then methods, objects, and properties. Figures 14.7 and 14.8 show an example of each display order.

FIGURE 14.7
The Object Inspector showing members in alphabetical order.

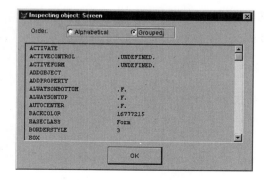

FIGURE 14.8

Object Inspector showing members in grouped order.

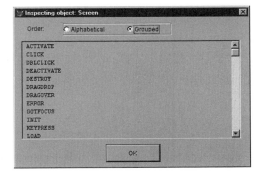

The second control is a `ListBox`, which lists all the members of the object.

Finally, the third control is the OK `CommandButton`, which releases the form.

All the properties in the list are shown with their values, as best as they can be determined, within the screen. Here is how this is accomplished—first, the class's code is presented in Listing 14.5.

Listing 14.5 14CODE05—Object Inspector Form Class Code Was Exported from the Class Browser

```
* Program: ObjInspector.prg
* Description: Test Program that creates ObjectInspectorForm objects
*              object to display the Form showing the_Screen object
*              properties.
oObjInspect = CREATE("Objectinspector",_Screen)
oObjInspect.Show()
RETURN
*  Class.............: Objectinspectorform
*  Author............: Menachem Bazian, CPA
*  Project...........: Visual FoxPro Unleashed!
*  Copyright.........: (c) Flash Creative Management, Inc. 1998
*) Description.......:
*  Notes.............: Exported code from Class Browser.

****************************************************
*-- Class:        objectinspectorform (d:\data\docs\books\vfu\code\oop2.vcx)
*-- ParentClass:  form
*-- BaseClass:    form
*
DEFINE CLASS objectinspectorform AS form

      DataSession = 2
      Height = 309
      Width = 466
      DoCreate = .T.
      AutoCenter = .T.
```

continues

Listing 14.5   Continued

```
BackColor = RGB(192,192,192)
BorderStyle = 3
Caption = ""
MaxButton = .F.
MinButton = .F.
ClipControls = .F.
WindowType = 1
PROTECTED cobjectbmpfile
cobjectbmpfile = (home()+"SAMPLES\GRAPHICS\BMPS\FOX\APPS.BMP")
PROTECTED cmethodbmpfile
cmethodbmpfile = (home()+"SAMPLES\GRAPHICS\BMPS\FOX\CLASSES.BMP")
PROTECTED cpropertybmpfile
cpropertybmpfile = (home()+"SAMPLES\GRAPHICS\BMPS\FOX\INDEXES.BMP")
PROTECTED ceventbmpfile
ceventbmpfile = (home()+"SAMPLES\GRAPHICS\BMPS\FOX\AUTOFORM.BMP")
Name = "objectinspectorform"

ADD OBJECT lstmembers AS listbox WITH ;
    FontName = "Courier New", ;
    Height = 205, ;
    Left = 12, ;
    Top = 48, ;
    Width = 438, ;
    ItemBackColor = RGB(192,192,192), ;
    Name = "lstMembers"

ADD OBJECT cmdok AS commandbutton WITH ;
    Top = 264, ;
    Left = 180, ;
    Height = 37, ;
    Width = 109, ;
    Cancel = .T., ;
    Caption = "OK", ;
    Default = .T., ;
    Name = "cmdOK"

ADD OBJECT label1 AS label WITH ;
    AutoSize = .F., ;
    BackStyle = 0, ;
    Caption = "Order:", ;
    Height = 18, ;
    Left = 24, ;
    Top = 15, ;
    Width = 40, ;
    Name = "Label1"

ADD OBJECT opgorder AS optiongroup WITH ;
    ButtonCount = 2, ;
    BackStyle = 0, ;
    Value = 1, ;
    Height = 25, ;
    Left = 96, ;
    Top = 12, ;
    Width = 217, ;
```

```
                    Name = "opgOrder", ;
                    Option1.BackStyle = 0, ;
                    Option1.Caption = "Alphabetical", ;
                    Option1.Value = 1, ;
                    Option1.Height = 18, ;
                    Option1.Left = 0, ;
                    Option1.Top = 4, ;
                    Option1.Width = 109, ;
                    Option1.Name = "optAlphabetical", ;
                    Option2.BackStyle = 0, ;
                    Option2.Caption = "Grouped", ;
                    Option2.Value = 0, ;
                    Option2.Height = 18, ;
                    Option2.Left = 127, ;
                    Option2.Top = 4, ;
                    Option2.Width = 73, ;
                    Option2.Name = "optGrouped"
PROCEDURE buildlist
        LPARAMETERS toObject

        #DEFINE COLUMNLENGTH 25

        WAIT WINDOW NOWAIT "Building members list. Please stand by..."

        this.lockscreen = .t.
        this.lstMembers.clear()

        SELECT _members

        IF this.opgOrder.value = 1
            SET ORDER TO TAG Alpha
        ELSE
            SET ORDER TO TAG Grouped
        ENDIF

        GO TOP

        lnCounter = 0

        SCAN
            lnCounter = lnCounter + 1
            lcText = PADR(_members.cMembName, COLUMNLENGTH)

            IF _members.cMembType = "Prop"
                *-- Now we need to get the value of the property
                lcText = lcText + ALLTRIM(_members.cMembVal)
            ENDIF

            thisform.lstMembers.additem(" " + lcText)

            lcBmpVar = "this.c" + alltrim(_members.cMembType)+"bmpfile"
            thisform.lstMembers.picture(lnCounter) = EVAL(lcBmpVar)
        ENDSCAN
```

Part

IV

Ch

14

continues

Listing 14.5 Continued

```
        this.lockscreen = .f.
        thisform.refresh()

    WAIT CLEAR
ENDPROC

PROCEDURE Resize
    this.lockscreen = .t.

    this.lstMembers.width = this.width - 24
    this.cmdOk.left = (this.width-this.cmdOk.width)/2
    this.cmdOK.top = (this.height - 8 - this.cmdOK.height)
    this.lstMembers.height = this.cmdOK.top - this.lstMembers.top - 11

    this.lockscreen = .F.
ENDPROC

PROCEDURE Init
    *   Class............: OBJECTINSPECTORFORM
    *   Author...........: Menachem Bazian, CPA
    *   Project..........: Visual FoxPro Unleashed
    *   Created..........: May 16, 1998 - 07:44:03
    *   Copyright........: (c) Flash Creative Management, Inc., 1998
    *)  Description......: When passed an object, it builds a list of the
    *)                   : members and displays them nicely.
    *   Calling Samples...: oForm = CREATEOBJECT("OBJECTINSPECTORFORM",
        ➡oObject)
    *   Parameter List....: toObject - Object to inspect
    *   Major change list.:

    LPARAMETERS toObject

    this.caption = "Inspecting object: " + ALLT(toObject.Name)

    IF TYPE("toObject") # 'O'
        =MessagebOx("You can only pass OBJECT type parameters!", 16)
        RETURN .F.
    ENDIF

    *-- If we get this far, we can inspect the object
    *-- Let's define some memory variables and do the AMembers()

    LOCAL laMembers[1], lcText, lcName
    =AMembers(laMembers,toObject,1)

    *-- In order to create the list in proper order, it is useful to have
    *-- a table to work off of (so we can INDEX). Hence:

    CREATE CURSOR _members (cMembName C(25), cMembtype C(25), cMembVal
    ➡C(40))
    INSERT INTO _members FROM ARRAY laMembers

    INDEX ON cMembName TAG Alpha
    INDEX ON cMembType + cMembName TAG Grouped
```

```
            SCAN FOR _members.cMembType = "Prop"

                *-- Determine the value of the property and place it in the
                *-- cMembVal field

                lcName = "toObject."+ALLTRIM(_members.cMembName)
                DO CASE
                    CASE TYPE(lcName) = 'U'
                        lcText = ".UNDEFINED."
                    CASE isnull(EVAL(lcName))
                        lcText = ".NULL."
                    CASE TYPE(lcName) = 'L'
                        lcText = IIF(EVAL(lcName), ".T.", ".F.")
                    OTHERWISE
                        lcText = ALLTRIM(PADR(EVALUATE(lcName),50))
                ENDCASE
                REPLACE _members.cMembVal WITH lcText
            ENDSCAN

            this.buildlist()
        ENDPROC

        PROCEDURE cmdok.Click
            release thisform
        ENDPROC

        PROCEDURE opgorder.Click
            thisform.buildlist()
        ENDPROC

    ENDDEFINE
    *
    *-- EndDefine: objectinspectorform
    ****************************************************
```

You can call the form as follows. (The example shows how you can call the InspectorForm to inspect the _Screen object.)

```
DO ObjInspector.prg
```

The key work in this class takes place in the form's Init method and in a custom method called BuildList.

The Init Method

The Init method has several responsibilities. It accepts the parameter toObject and makes sure that its data type is Object. If the parameter sent through is not an object, an error message is returned. Note that an error condition causes Init to return .F.. When .F. is returned from Init, the object is not instantiated.

The next step is to create a cursor, much like the one in the Cursmemb.prg program shown earlier in this chapter. The differences here are threefold. First of all, an additional field called cMembValue is added to the cursor. Second, cMembValue is populated with the actual value of the property. Third, the cursor is indexed. I use the indexes in BuildList later in this chapter.

You fill in the cMembValue field by creating a text string beginning with "toObject." (remember that toObject is the object passed through on the parameter line) and then adding the name of the object as recorded in the cMembName field. This gives you the name of the property you are trying to evaluate in a format you can use to query the value.

The next step is a little tricky. Sometimes an object might have a property that does not have a value. For example, if _Screen.ActiveForm is queried with no form open, Visual FoxPro returns an error. "U" for undefined is returned when you check the type of the property with the TYPE function (? TYPE("_Screen.ActiveForm"), for example)"". Therefore, a check has to be made of the data type of the property to avoid an error.

A property can also be NULL; you trap for that with the ISNULL function. Finally, a logical value is checked for and converted to a string. All other value types can be converted to a string with the PADR function, as done in the OTHERWISE clause of the CASE statement.

The BuildList Method

BuildList is responsible for building the contents of the list box based on the cursor. The method is very simple. It begins by clearing the list with the Clear method; then the value of the Order option group is queried and the index order is set accordingly. The next step is to loop through the cursor records and add the items from the cursor to the list. This is accomplished by using the AddItem method. Note that the value is added to the string passed through to AddItem for all the PROPERTY-type members. Finally, the picture property of each row is set based on the type of member stored in the row. The four picture filenames and locations are stored in the custom form properties cEventBMPFile, cMethodBMPFile, cObjectBMPFile, and cPropertyBMPFile.

One interesting tip that comes out of the BuildList method is the use of the LockScreen property of the form. When LockScreen is set to .T., it prevents the form's display from changing. This is very important in this case because a list box automatically refreshes itself every time AddItem is issued. This slows the process considerably. By setting LockScreen to .T. for the duration of the list building, you ensure maximum performance from Visual FoxPro during this process. A final call to the Refresh method after LockScreen is reset redraws everything nicely.

The Resize Method

The form's default size might not be large enough to display a property and its value if the value is a lengthy string. It would be nice to be able to resize the form and have the controls on the form automatically adjust to the new size of the form.

The `Resize` method responds to an event (when the user changes the size of the form, for example). The method is called when the user is done resizing the form. The `Resize` method in this case simply recalculates the height and width of the list box and makes sure that the command button is still situated at the bottom of the form. Setting `LockScreen` to `.T.` while the recalculation takes place prevents the controls from adjusting one at a time. It looks cleaner this way (and is more efficient, too). ●

Creating Classes with Visual FoxPro

An Overview of Classes

The previous two chapters covered the nuts and bolts of OOP in Visual FoxPro. You learned the applicable concepts behind object orientation in Visual FoxPro in Chapter 13, "Introduction to Object-Oriented Programming," and you learned how classes are created in Chapter 14, "OOP with Visual FoxPro."

In this chapter, you learn the typical types of classes you create with Visual FoxPro. Different categories of classes are investigated and explained, and examples of each type of class are presented as well.

Before I go further, I must say that there is no realistic limit to the types of classes you can create with Visual FoxPro (unless you think there are limits to your imagination). For the most part, the classifications presented in this chapter should be representative of what you can do. Don't let anyone tell you that a class you have dreamed up is invalid because it is not listed or does not fit into a category detailed in this or any book. You are the master of your system's destiny. Don't let anyone tell you otherwise.

The types of classes created in this chapter can be placed in two general categories: visual classes and nonvisual classes.

Visual Classes

A *visual class* is a class designed for display purposes. For example, a form is a visual class; so is a CommandButton and a CheckBox. The main purpose behind visual classes is for interface (usually called a Graphical User Interface or GUI) work.

Within this class category you can typically design classes in the following subcategories:

Single controls

Combination controls

Containers

Forms

Toolbars

A Terminology Issue

One of the base classes that comes built-in to Visual FoxPro is named control. In addition to this base class, all other classes used within a form (such as TextBox, CommandButton, and so on) are also given the generic name of *control*. Sound confusing? You're right, it is.

In order to bring some sense to this terminology, I have adopted the following conventions. When you learn how to create classes based on a form control, such as a CommandButton, you will see the term *single control*. For controls created from the control class, you will see the term *combination control*. These naming conventions work because the purpose of the control class is to combine multiple controls together so that they work as one control.

Showing Classes in Print

I want to take a moment to explain the code presented in this chapter. You develop classes in Visual FoxPro visually (using the Visual Class Designer). However, for the purpose of this chapter, code is the best way to present the contents of a class.

Fortunately, the Class Browser (which is discussed in Chapter 16, "Managing Classes with Visual FoxPro") includes a function that exports the code of a visual class. The code shown in this chapter (as well as in Chapters 16 and 17, "Advanced Object-Orientated Programming") is exported using the Class Browser.

Single Control Classes

A *single control* is a class designed to be used as a control on a form. This type of class is based on any FoxPro form control class that does not support the capability to add additional objects to itself. These classes include CommandButtons, TextBoxes, Labels, and so on.

There are two kinds of single control classes you typically create. The first kind is a single control class designed to set the default of the display characteristics for the control for future use. For example, if you were to decide on a standard font for all your controls (Windows 95 uses 9-point Arial as its standard), you could create single control classes with the proper settings and then subclass them. This ensures a common look throughout your applications.

The second type of single control classes are created after you are done with the standard look and feel. The classes you create from there on will in all likelihood be for functionality. I will illustrate this second type of class with a few examples.

The OK Command Button   A good example of a single control class is an OK button, which, when pressed, releases the form it is on. OkButton is a class that does this.

The following code shows a sample OK button:

```
*   Class.............: Okbutton
*   Author............: Menachem Bazian, CPA
*   Notes.............: Exported code from Class Browser.

**************************************************
*-- Class:        okbutton
*-- ParentClass:  CommandButton
*-- BaseClass:    CommandButton
*-- CommandButton that releases the form it's on.
*
DEFINE CLASS okbutton AS CommandButton

     AutoSize = .F.
     Height = 29
     Width = 41
     Caption = "OK"
     Default = .T.
     Name = "okbutton"

     PROCEDURE Click
```

```
        RELEASE thisform
    ENDPROC

ENDDEFINE
*
*-- EndDefine: okbutton
****************************************************
```

This button can be dropped on any form. When it is clicked, it will release the form. Figure 15.1 shows what the OK button looks like when you drop it on a form.

FIGURE 15.1
A form with an OK
button.

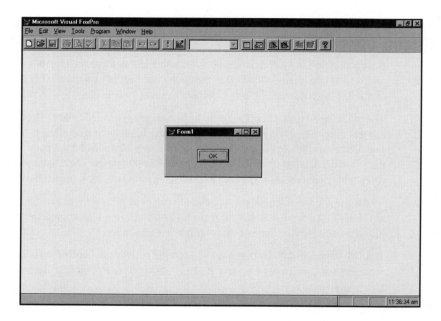

Notice that the method for releasing the form is to use RELEASE THISFORM in the Click event. The THISFORM keyword is mentioned in Chapter 14. This command releases the form the OK button is on.

By setting the Default property to .T., the command button's Click event is made to fire automatically when the user presses the Enter key when the cursor is not in an EditBox control. Conversely, if you want the button's Click event to fire when the user hits the Esc key, you should set the Cancel property of the button to .T..

Subclassing a Single Control Class   Technically, every class created in Visual FoxPro is a subclass of another class. Even the Custom-based classes are subclasses (Custom is the name of a FoxPro base class).

After you create a class, you can subclass it. How this works is detailed in Chapter 14, but here's a little example of it. Suppose you want a special version of the OK button that has tooltip text attached to it. (*Tooltip text* is the text that pops up when the mouse hovers over a control.) The following code, which creates a class called OkButtonWithToolTip, shows how to do this:

```
*   Class.............: okbuttonwithtooltip
*   Author............: Menachem Bazian, CPA
*   Notes.............: Exported code from Class Browser.

****************************************************
*-- Class:        okbuttonwithtooltip (d:\data\docs\books\vfu\code\oop2.vcx)
*-- ParentClass:  okbutton (d:\data\docs\books\vfu\code\oop2.vcx)
*-- BaseClass:    CommandButton
*-- Subclass of an OK button - adds a ToolTip.
*
DEFINE CLASS okbuttonwithtooltip AS okbutton

    Height = 29
    Width = 41
    ToolTipText = "Releases the form"
    Name = "okbuttonwithtooltip"

ENDDEFINE
*
*-- EndDefine: okbuttonwithtooltip
****************************************************
```

That's all there is to it. Notice that there is very little code attached to this button. The Click event is not represented here at all; it is inherited from the parent class. In fact, the only relevant code in this class is the value in the ToolTipText property.

For the record, most controls have a ToolTipText property. You might notice that although the property has been filled, the tooltip text does not show up when the mouse hovers over the control. If this happens, check out the ShowTips property on the form and make sure that it is set to .T.. Figure 15.2 shows an example of what you should expect to see.

To make sure that your tooltip shows up all the time, you can place code in the MouseMove event that checks the setting of the ShowTips property on the form and sets it to .T.. If you're wondering why the code does not go in the Init of the button, the answer has to do with the order in which controls are initialized with a container. You will learn about this in a little bit.

Why Subclass?   OkButtonWithToolTip seems to be a rather silly example of a subclass. After all, adding tooltip text is very simple. Why subclass the button at all? Why not make the change to the OK button itself? It's a judgment call, certainly. However, it is vital to bear in mind that changing a class will change every instance of that class as well as all the descendant subclasses. If you modify the base class, you will be making the assumption that all instances of the OK button will have this tooltip. This assumption might not be a valid one. Hence, you choose to subclass.

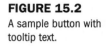

FIGURE 15.2

A sample button with tooltip text.

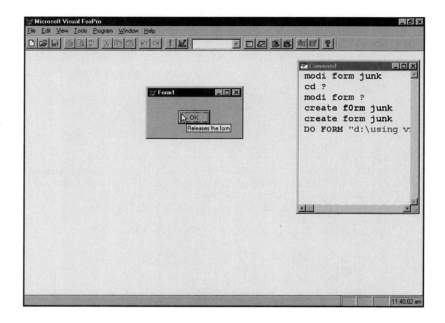

Another Single Control Example   Believe it or not, there are a series of published standards for Windows GUI interfaces. In fact, there is one standard for the Windows 3.1–based interface, which applies to Windows 3.1, Windows for Workgroups, and Windows NT 3.x, and another for Windows 95 and Windows NT 4.0. Windows 98 and Windows NT 5.0 have still other interface guidelines. One standard for Windows applications calls for error messages to be placed in a MessageBox()-type window. Visual FoxPro has the capability to automatically display an error message when the Valid method returns .F.. The error message is the character string returned from the ErrorMessage method. The problem is that the ErrorMessage method puts the error message in the form of a WAIT WINDOW instead of a MessageBox.

The ErrorMessage event fires automatically when the Valid method returns .F., that is, Valid fires when the control tries to lose focus. Therefore, the solution would seem to be to put a MessageBox()-type message in the ErrorMessage method and not return a value.

However, there is one little problem. If the ErrorMessage does not return a string, Visual FoxPro displays a default message of Invalid Input. The only way to turn this off is to set the SET NOTIFY command to OFF.

Not a big problem, right? Unfortunately, other classes might change this setting or might rely on the setting to be ON. In effect, you cannot rely on the SET NOTIFY setting unless you set it yourself. To do so, use SET NOTIFY OFF when the control gains focus and then set it back the way it was on the way out (that is, when the control loses focus).

NoNotifyTextBox is a sample of this type of control. A protected property called cNotifySetting has been added to hold the setting of SET NOTIFY before the class changes it. Here's the code:

```
*   Class.............: NoNotifyTextBox
*   Author............: Menachem Bazian, CPA
*   Notes.............: Exported code from Class Browser.

****************************************************
*-- Class:       nonotifyTextBox
*-- ParentClass: TextBox
*-- BaseClass:   TextBox
*-- Text box that sets NOTIFY off for error messaging.
*
DEFINE CLASS nonotifyTextBox AS TextBox

    Height = 24
    Width = 113
    Name = "nonotifyTextBox"

    *-- The setting of SET NOTIFY when the control got focus.
    PROTECTED cnotifysetting

    PROCEDURE LostFocus
        LOCAL lcNotify
        lcNotify = this.cNotifySetting
        SET NOTIFY &lcNotify
    ENDPROC

    PROCEDURE GotFocus
        this.cNotifySetting = SET("notify")
        SET NOTIFY OFF
    ENDPROC

ENDDEFINE
*
*-- EndDefine: nonotifyTextBox
****************************************************
```

Notice that the property cNotifySetting is protected. This follows the guidelines discussed in the last chapter for protecting properties. Because this property has no use to the outside world and, in fact, could harm the system if changed by the outside world, you just hide it and forget about it.

After you create classes like NoNotifyTextBox, you can use them in forms or subclass them as you see fit and be sure that you will have the behavior you are looking for.

Combination Controls

Sometimes you might want to combine several controls together to operate as one. For example, take the task of specifying the name of an existing file on a form. This requires two controls interacting as one: a TextBox that enables the user to enter a filename to validate a file's existence and a CommandButton that displays a GetFile() box and places the results in the TextBox.

You could create each control separately and drop them individually on a form. However, because both controls are coming together to do one task, it makes sense to make one control out of the two and drop them on the form as one control. This achieves several goals. First, you can encapsulate all the behavior and information in one place. Second, it makes it easier to add this functionality to a form. Third, you can duplicate the look and functionality on other forms easily. Fourth, it avoids any code at the form level (code necessary to get the two controls to interact).

The base class for this is the control class. The *control class* is a class designed to create composite classes where several controls come together to act as one. Conceptually, the control class is not much of anything except a package into which controls can be placed. You will learn the specifics of the control class "package" in the following section, "The General Idea." First, Listing 15.1 shows a sample class called GetAFile, which illustrates what you try to accomplish with a combination control.

Listing 15.1 15CODE01—Illustrates a Combination Control

```
*  Class.............: Getafilecontrol
*  Author............: Menachem Bazian, CPA
*  Notes.............: Exported code from Class Browser.

***************************************************
*-- Class:         getafilecontrol
*-- ParentClass:   control
*-- BaseClass:     control
*-- A combination of controls that allow a user to select an existing file.
*
DEFINE CLASS getafilecontrol AS control

    Width = 358
    Height = 26
    BackStyle = 0
    BorderWidth = 0
    cvalue = ""
    *-- The caption to display on the GETFILE box.
    cdisplaycaption = "Please select a file."
    *-- Caption for the OPEN button. See GetFile() for more information on this.
    copenbuttoncaption = "Open"
    *-- File extensions to allow for. See GetFile()
    *-- for more information on this.
    cfileextensions = ""
    *-- The type of buttons on the GetFile() dialog.
    *-- See GetFile() for more information on this.
    nbuttontype = 0
    *-- Should the path shown be a minimum path or not?
    lminimumpath = .T.
    Name = "getafilecontrol"

    ADD OBJECT cmdgetfile AS CommandButton WITH ;
        Top = 0, ;
        Left = 330, ;
        Height = 24, ;
```

```
    Width = 24, ;
    Caption = "...", ;
    Name = "cmdGetFile"

ADD OBJECT cfilenameTextBox AS nonotifyTextBox WITH ;
    Value = "", ;
    Format = "!", ;
    Height = 24, ;
    Left = 0, ;
    Top = 0, ;
    Width = 325, ;
    Name = "cFileNameTextBox"

PROCEDURE Refresh
    this.cFileNameTextBox.Value = this.cValue
    this.cFileNameTextBox.SetFocus()
ENDPROC

*-- Accepts a string parameter and validates that it is an existing file.
PROCEDURE validatefilename
    LPARAMETERS tcFileName
    LOCAL llRetVal

    llRetVal = EMPTY(tcFileName) OR FILE(ALLTRIM(tcFileName))

    IF !llRetVal
        =MessageBox("File does not exist: " + ALLTRIM(tcFileName))
    ENDIF

    tcFileName = ALLTRIM(tcFileName)

    IF llRetVal
        this.cValue = tcFileName
    ENDIF

    RETURN llRetVal
ENDPROC

*-- Display the files for the user to select from with a GetFile() dialog.
PROCEDURE displayfiles
    LOCAL lcValue, lcDialogCaption, lcOpenButtonCaption, lnButtonType

    lcDialogCaption = this.cDisplayCaption
    lcOpenButtonCaption = this.cOpenButtonCaption
    lcFileExtensions = this.cFileExtensions
    lnButtonType = this.nButtonType

    lcValue =    GETFILE(lcFileExtensions, ;
                         lcDialogCaption, ;
                         lcOpenButtonCaption, ;
                         lnButtonType)

    IF !EMPTY(lcValue)
        IF this.lminimumpath
```

continues

Listing 15.1   Continued

```
                lcValue = SYS(2014, lcValue)
            ENDIF
            this.cValue = lcValue
        ENDIF

        this.refresh()
    ENDPROC

    PROCEDURE cmdgetfile.Click
        this.parent.DisplayFiles()
    ENDPROC

    PROCEDURE cfilenameTextBox.Valid
        RETURN this.parent.validatefilename(this.value)
    ENDPROC

ENDDEFINE
*
*-- EndDefine: getafilecontrol
*****************************************************
```

The General Idea   First, some general theory: The idea is for the `TextBox` and the `CommandButton` to work together to enable the user to select a file. The `TextBox` provides for manual, type-it-in functionality. The `CommandButton` brings up a `GetFile()` dialog box from which the user can select a file. If a file is selected, it is shown in the `TextBox`.

The job of the container around these controls (that's the *controls* referred to in the class names) is to give the interface to the controls. From the outside world, the two controls packaged together are one control. The fact that a `TextBox` and a `CommandButton` are working together is something the developer of the class needs to know, but not something the developer using the control in an application needs to know. The job of the interface is to communicate with the outside world in terms of the options the user wants to set when selecting a file. An interface also holds the name of the file selected. This brings me to my next point.

The Control Package's Custom Properties   The package around the controls has the following custom properties added to it:

```
cvalue = ""
cdisplaycaption = "Please select a file."
copenbuttoncaption = "Open"
cfileextensions = ""
nbuttontype = 0
lminimumpath = .T.
```

The `cValue` property is the name of the file selected by the user. I used the name `cValue` because it is equivalent to the `Value` property of most data controls: It holds the value returned by the control. By the way, if you're wondering about the `c` in `cValue`, it's a common naming convention for all custom properties: The first character of the name indicates the data type of the property (which in this case is `Character`).

The cDisplayCaption property is the message that displays on the GetFile() box, which is displayed by the command button. The property name is based on the name of the corresponding parameter discussed in the GetFile() help topic.

The cOpenButtonCaption property is the caption for the Open button. By default, the name of the button on the GetFile() dialog box is OK; however, this class sets the default to Open instead. Again, the name is a naming convention version of the parameter name in the help file.

The cFileExtensions property is a list of file extensions to show in the GetFile() box (you can still select any file you like, by the way). The list of file extensions is separated by semicolons or vertical bars (¦). Visual FoxPro automatically parses out the file extensions in the GetFile() box. Again, the name is a naming convention version of the parameter name in the help file.

The nButtonType property is a numeric property that is also used for the GetFile() box. The number defaults to 0, which shows an OK button (which is really named Open by default) and Cancel button. A value of 1 shows OK, New, and Cancel buttons. A value of 2 shows OK, None, and Cancel buttons. Once again, the name is a naming convention version of the parameter name in the help file.

The lMinimumPath property specifies whether a minimum or absolute path is used. A filename specified with a path can be shown in one of two ways. The path can be an *absolute* path, in other words, the specified path is the path you want to store. The other way is to store a *relative* path, which adjusts the path to show the minimum path designation to get to the file from a directory. An absolute path, which is the type of value returned from GetFile(), can be converted to a relative path with SYS(2014). If lMinimumPath is set to .T. (as it is by default), the filename returned by the GetFile() dialog box is adjusted with SYS(2014) against the current directory.

The purpose of naming properties in this manner is to give the developer using the class a clue as to the values allowed, that is, it makes the class a little easier to use and understand.

Custom and Overridden Methods   The Refresh method sets the text box's Value property to match the cValue property of the control package. The SetFocus call to the TextBox puts the cursor in the TextBox for editing.

ValidateFileName is a custom method that tests the validity of a filename entered in the text box and is called by the text box's Valid method.

DisplayFiles is the method that actually displays the GetFile() dialog box and uses the properties of the control package as part of the GetFile() call. After GetFile() is done and the user has made a selection, the selected value is placed in the control package's cValue property. A call to Refresh keeps everything in synch.

Object Members   The object members are CmdGetFile and cFileNameTextBox.

CmdGetFile   This is a command button. The Click method cmdGetFile calls DisplayFiles, which displays a GetFile() based on the settings in the control package. The returned value is then stored to the cValue property of the package, and the box's Refresh method is called. The Refresh method puts the text box in synch.

cFileNameTextBox   This control enables the user to enter the filename manually. It is based on the NoNotifyTextBox class created previously in this chapter. Basing cFileNameTextBox on NoNotifyTextBox is a good example of how classes are reused in other classes.

The Valid method in this control checks the entered filename to make sure it is valid. An empty filename is considered valid; if it weren't, the user would have no way of exiting the TextBox control to get to the CommandButton. If the text box's Valid method returns .F., the ErrorMessage event calls the ErrorMessage method, which in turn displays an error message telling the user that file was not found.

If the entered filename is valid, the filename is stored in the cValue property of the control package.

Using the Combination Control in a Form   As far as the outside world is concerned (the outside world is anything outside GetAFileControl), the operative property is the cValue property. In order to get the name of the file entered or selected by the user, the outside world just queries the cValue property. In order to set up the control, the outside world sets the properties discussed previously. Figure 15.3 shows a form with GetAFileControl on it.

FIGURE 15.3
A form with
GetAFileControl.

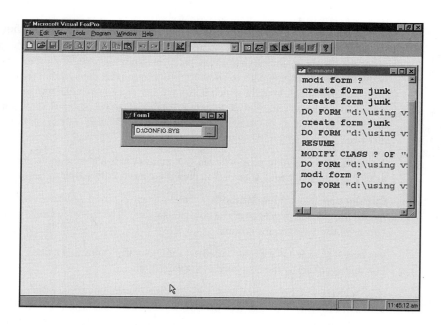

As far as the outside world is concerned, the only control that exists is GetAFileControl. The embedded TextBox and CommandButton controls do not exist. In other words, if this combination control were dropped on a form with the name GetAFileControl1, attempting to query GetAFileControl1.cFileNameTextBox.Value from the outside world would generate an error.

Why is this so? To understand why, you need to take a little closer look under the hood of the control class.

The Control Class

Now that you have seen an example of a combination control, take a step back and learn the technical issues related to working with this class.

First of all, although a control-based class is a composite class with additional member objects, the control class automatically makes all its member objects private. This means that anything using the class cannot see those member objects.

To illustrate this, take a look at Figure 15.4, which shows the property window of a form with `GetAFileControl` placed on it. I've expanded the list of objects to make the point. Notice that only the control package is on the list. The individual objects inside the control package do not exist as far as the form is concerned. You access the individual objects within the combination control class.

FIGURE 15.4
Objects shown for the `GetAFileControl` instance.

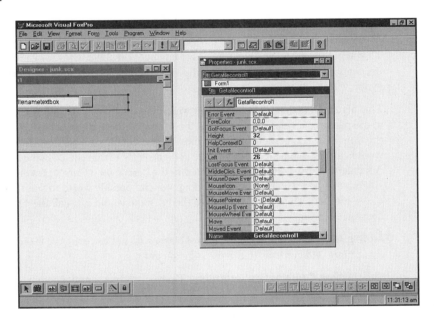

This behavior makes perfect sense. Because you're creating a *control* as far as the outside world is concerned, all the components of the control are one object. This does introduce some interesting issues, which are discussed next one at a time.

Communicating with Combination Controls By definition, the outside world can only communicate with a combination control through the package. This means that any information passing first goes to the package; the package must then transmit the information to the individual members.

A good example of this is the cValue property added to the GetAFileControl class. cValue can be set from the outside world but will be shown in the TextBox only when the Refresh method is called—it is the Refresh method's responsibility to transmit the value to the TextBox. Likewise, TextBox and CommandButton have the responsibility of telling the package about changes to cValue that happen as a result of actions taken within their control.

You can take advantage of a new feature in Visual FoxPro 6 by using the assign and access methods for the cValue property. By adding a method named cValue_access, you are creating an access method. An access method is like an event method that fires whenever the property it is associated with is accessed. In the GetAFileControl class, you might add a cValue_access method like the one shown in the following:

```
PROCEDURE cValue_access
IF THIS.cValue <> THIS.cFileNameTextBox.Value
   THIS.cValue = THIS.cFileNameTextBox.Value
ENDIF
RETURN THIS.cValue
```

This access method will run whenever any outside object tries to read the value of the cValue property, and its code ensures that the value of the TextBox and the cValue property are in synch with each other.

This also means that any methods to which the outside world needs access must be contained at the package level. For example, if the Click method of the CommandButton were applicable to the outside world, a method would have to be added to the package that the CommandButton would call (as opposed to placing the code directly within the CommandButton's Click method). Alternatively, the code could be placed in the CommandButton's Click method, but you would still have to add a method to the package for the outside world to run the CommandButton's Click method. The method added to the package would just call the Click method of the CommandButton.

Adding Objects at Runtime   Control classes do not have an AddObject() method; therefore, you cannot add controls to the package at runtime.

Subclassing Combination Controls   There are a few ramifications regarding subclassing combination controls.

Adding Controls to a Subclass   You cannot add controls to the package in a subclass (just as you cannot add a control to a subclass of the CommandButton class).

Accessing Package Contents in a Subclass   The objects contained in the combination control's package are not visible when you subclass it. This means that any methods or properties you might want to modify in a subclass must be hooked to the package as opposed to one of the member objects. This requires some care in designing the class hierarchy.

You can provide for this situation if you first fully define all the control classes that you will use in the package as classes, with all the necessary code, before you put them in the package.

For example, you could define a TextBox class as a subclass of the NoNotifyTextbox and name it GetAFileTextbox. Then, in the GetAFileTextbox class, you write the code for the Valid event and then use that class in the ADDOBJECT command of the GetAFileControl class.

This process, fully defining a class before you use it a package, is called *late composition*. It is called late because the package is not assembled until late in the class definitions.

If you look at GetAFileControl, you'll notice that all the methods for the TextBox and the CommandButton call methods on the package. In effect, this hedges your bets. You should do a little more work up front to preserve flexibility down the road.

A Final Word   As container-type classes go, the control class does have limitations, but the limitations of the control class are its strength. It gives you the opportunity to create tightly controlled classes to use on your forms. However, many developers find control classes limiting because of the lack of capability to add controls at runtime, to add controls to a subclass, or to access the controls within the package can present a restrictive working environment.

The container class, on the other hand, gives you the ability to create composite classes with more flexibility. This is the next topic.

The Container Class

A container class is similar to the control class with one major exception: The controls in a container class's package are visible to the outside world (unless specifically protected in the class).

By the way, there are many classes that support containership. For example, a form is a type of container class (only more specialized). Page frames and grids are also examples of classes that support containership. This discussion focuses on the container class, but many of the discussions are applicable to the other container-type classes as well.

Container classes are wonderful for a whole host of different jobs. In fact, any time multiple objects need to be brought together, a container can do the job. (I usually prefer to combine controls in a container to accomplish a task.)

To illustrate the difference between a control class and a container class, I'll redefine the GetAFileControl class to work off the container class instead of the control class. First, Listing 15.2 shows the exported code.

Listing 15.2 15CODE02—The GetAFileControl **Class Defined as a Container**

```
*   Class............: Getafilecontainer
*   Author...........: Menachem Bazian, CPA
*   Notes............: Exported code from Class Browser.


**************************************************
*-- Class:        getafilecontainer
*-- ParentClass:  container
*-- BaseClass:    container
*-- A combination of controls that allow a user to select an existing file.
*
DEFINE CLASS getafilecontainer AS container

    Width = 358
    Height = 26
    BackStyle = 0
    BorderWidth = 0
    cvalue = ""
    *-- The caption to display on the GETFILE box.
    cdisplaycaption = "Please select a file."
    *-- Caption for the OPEN button. See GetFile() for more information on this.
    copenbuttoncaption = "Open"
    *-- File extensions to allow for. See GetFile() for more information on
this.
    cfileextensions = ""
    *-- The type of buttons on the GetFile() dialog. See GetFile() for more
information on this.
    nbuttontype = 0
    *-- Should the path shown be a minimum path or not?
    lminimumpath = .T.
    Name = "getafilecontainer"

    ADD OBJECT cmdgetfile AS cmdGetfile WITH ;
        Top = 0, ;
        Left = 330, ;
        Height = 24, ;
        Width = 24, ;
        Caption = "...", ;
        Name = "cmdGetFile"

    ADD OBJECT cfilenameTextBox AS cFileNameTextBox WITH ;
        Value = "", ;
        Format = "!", ;
        Height = 24, ;
        Left = 0, ;
        Top = 0, ;
        Width = 325, ;
        Name = "cFileNameTextBox"

    *-- Accepts a string parameter and validates that it is an existing file.
    PROCEDURE validatefilename
        LPARAMETERS tcFileName
        LOCAL llRetVal

        llRetVal = EMPTY(tcFileName) OR FILE(ALLTRIM(tcFileName))
```

```
        IF !llRetVal
            =MessageBox("File does not exist: " + ALLTRIM(tcFileName))
        ENDIF

        tcFileName = ALLTRIM(tcFileName)

        IF llRetVal
            this.cValue = tcFileName
        ENDIF

        RETURN llRetVal
    ENDPROC

    *-- Display the files for the user to select from with a GetFile() dialog.
    PROCEDURE displayfiles
        LOCAL lcValue, lcDialogCaption, lcOpenButtonCaption, lnButtonType

        lcDialogCaption = this.cDisplayCaption
        lcOpenButtonCaption = this.cOpenButtonCaption
        lcFileExtensions = this.cFileExtensions
        lnButtonType = this.nButtonType

        lcValue =    GETFILE(lcFileExtensions, ;
                             lcDialogCaption, ;
                             lcOpenButtonCaption, ;
                             lnButtonType)

        IF !EMPTY(lcValue)
            IF this.lminimumpath
                lcValue = SYS(2014, lcValue)
            ENDIF
            this.cValue = lcValue
        ENDIF

        this.refresh()
    ENDPROC

    PROCEDURE Refresh
        this.cFileNameTextBox.Value = this.cValue
        this.cFileNameTextBox.SetFocus()
    ENDPROC


ENDDEFINE


DEFINE CLASS cmdGetFile AS CommandButton
    PROCEDURE Click
        This.parent.DisplayFiles
    ENDPROC
ENDDEFINE

DEFINE CLASS cFileNameTextBox AS NoNotifyTextBox
    PROCEDURE Valid
        RETURN This.parent.validatefilename(this.value)
```

continues

Listing 15.2   Continued

```
      ENDPROC
ENDDEFINE

DEFINE CLASS nonotifyTextBox AS TextBox

    Height = 24
    Width = 113
    Name = "nonotifyTextBox"

    *-- The setting of SET NOTIFY when the control got focus.
    PROTECTED cnotifysetting

    PROCEDURE LostFocus
        LOCAL lcNotify
        lcNotify = this.cNotifySetting
        SET NOTIFY &lcNotify
    ENDPROC

    PROCEDURE GotFocus
        this.cNotifySetting = SET("notify")
        SET NOTIFY OFF
    ENDPROC

ENDDEFINE
*
*-- EndDefine: getafilecontainer
***************************************************
```

At first glance, the code in Listing 15.2 does not seem very different than the GetAFileControl class from the previous section. In fact, it isn't. One thing that I changed was to define each of the controls as a class before I put them in the container. Another difference is how the two classes (GetAFileControl and GetaFileContainer) operate within the form.

Figures 15.5 and 15.6 show a key difference between when you are working with control-based classes as opposed to container-based classes. Notice the value of _screen.activeform.activecontrol.name, which is tracked in the Debug window, and how it differs from the top control (an instance of GetAFileControl) and the lower container (an instance of GetaFileContainer).

To the naked eye, the two controls seem the same. Behind the scenes, however, they are very different—the control version shows no ActiveControl for the form regardless of whether the TextBox has the focus or the CommandButton has the focus. The container version, on the other hand, shows the name of the TextBox as the name of the active control.

By the way, this is a good example of the use of _screen to assist in debugging. You might not always know the name of the variable behind a form, but you can usually count on _screen.activeform to give you a reference to the active form.

FIGURE 15.5

A form with
`GetAFileControl`
active.

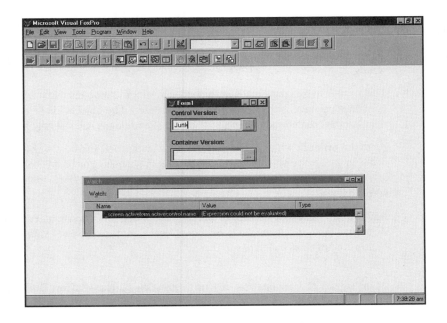

FIGURE 15.6

A form with
`GetaFileContainer`
active.

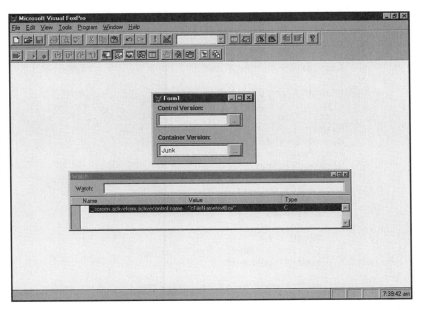

TIP In Visual FoxPro 6, you can use _VFP and _SCREEN interchangeably.

Order of `Inits` So, you have a package with multiple objects in it. You put code in one object's `Init` that references the container. But when you try to instantiate the package, you get an error message in the `Init` code and the package refuses to instantiate. What did you do wrong?

The answer to this puzzle lies in the order in which the objects are created. As it turns out, the container package is the last object to get created. The objects inside are created first, and the container is created only after all the objects inside have successfully been created.

As to the order in which the internal objects instantiate, the best way to find out is to look at the order in which the objects appear in the property sheet. For best results, try not to put code in any of the `Init` events that depends on the order in which objects instantiate. You'll be a lot safer that way.

`Navigator`—Another Container Class A container of `CommandButtons` used for navigating through a table in a form is a good example of a container class. Listing 15.3 shows an example of this kind of class called `Navigator`.

Listing 15.3   15CODE03—A Container-Based Navigation Button Set

```
*   Class............: Navigator
*   Author...........: Menachem Bazian, CPA
*   Notes............: Exported code from Class Browser.


***************************************************
*-- Class:        navigator
*-- ParentClass:  container
*-- BaseClass:    container
*
DEFINE CLASS navigator AS container

    Width = 350
    Height = 32
    BackStyle = 0
    BorderWidth = 0
    Name = "navigator"

    ADD OBJECT cmdnext AS cmdNext WITH ;
        Top = 0, ;
        Left = 0, ;
        Height = 31, ;
        Width = 60, ;
        Caption = "Next", ;
        Name = "cmdNext"

    ADD OBJECT cmdprev AS cmdPrev WITH ;
        Top = 0, ;
        Left = 72, ;
        Height = 31, ;
```

```
            Width = 60, ;
            Caption = "Prev", ;
            Name = "cmdPrev"

    ADD OBJECT cmdtop AS cmdTop WITH ;
        Top = 0, ;
        Left = 144, ;
        Height = 31, ;
        Width = 60, ;
        Caption = "Top", ;
        Name = "cmdTop"

    ADD OBJECT cmdbottom AS cmdBottom WITH ;
        Top = 0, ;
        Left = 216, ;
        Height = 31, ;
        Width = 60, ;
        Caption = "Bottom", ;
        Name = "cmdBottom"

    ADD OBJECT cmdok AS okbuttonwithtooltip WITH ;
        Top = 0, ;
        Left = 288, ;
        Height = 31, ;
        Width = 60, ;
        Name = "cmdOK"




ENDDEFINE

DEFINE cmdNext AS CommandButton
    PROCEDURE Click
        SKIP 1
        IF EOF()
            =Messagebox("At end of file!", 16)
            GO BOTTOM
        ENDIF

        thisform.refresh()
    ENDPROC
ENDDEFINE

DEFINE CLASS cmdPrev AS CommandButton
    PROCEDURE Click
        SKIP -1
        IF BOF()
            =Messagebox("At beginning of file!", 16)
            GO TOP
        ENDIF
```

continues

Listing 15.3 Continued

```
            thisform.refresh()
      ENDPROC
ENDDEFINE

DEFINE CLASS cmdTop AS CommandButton
      PROCEDURE Click
            GO TOP
            thisform.refresh()
      ENDPROC
ENDEFINE

DEFINE CLASS cmdBottom AS CommandButton
      PROCEDURE Click
            GO BOTTOM
            thisform.refresh()
      ENDPROC
ENDDEFINE

DEFINE CLASS okbuttonwithtooltip AS okbutton

      Height = 29
      Width = 41
      ToolTipText = "Releases the form"
      Name = "okbuttonwithtooltip"

ENDDEFINE

*
*-- EndDefine: navigator
****************************************************
```

Each button on the container executes the necessary navigation instructions and then executes a call to the host form's Refresh method. It might seem strange to put code to work with a form on a class that is not yet physically part of a form, but that's OK. When you document the class, just make sure to specify how it is meant to be used.

In order to use the Navigator class, all you need to do is drop it on a data entry form and you have the ability—without coding one line—to move within the file. Figure 15.7 shows a sample data entry form with this class dropped on it.

When this class is dropped on a form, as shown in Figure 15.8, a view of a form's property window and all the controls are available for editing and on-the-fly subclassing. You can even extend the container and add another control to it in the form. The additional control, of course, is not added to the class in the VCX file; it's a special version for that form only.

FIGURE 15.7
A form with a
Navigator container.

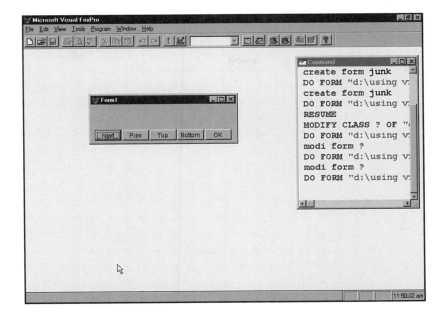

FIGURE 15.8
The property window of
a container.

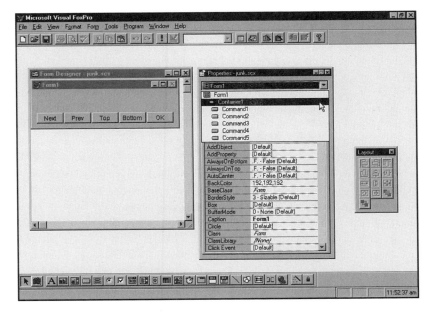

The next bit of code is a representation of a form that adds a New button to the container (it's available as MoreBtns.SCX).

```
*  Form.............: Form1
*  Author...........: Menachem Bazian, CPA
*  Notes............: Exported code from Class Browser.

****************************************************
*-- Form:          form1 (morebtns.scx)
*-- ParentClass:   form
*-- BaseClass:     form
*
DEFINE CLASS form1 AS form

    Top = 0
    Left = 0
    Height = 182
    Width = 463
    DoCreate = .T.
    BackColor = RGB(192,192,192)
    BorderStyle = 2
    Caption = "Form1"
    Name = "Form1"

    ADD OBJECT text1 AS textbox WITH ;
        BackColor = RGB(192,192,192), ;
        ControlSource = "test.cmembname", ;
        Height = 24, ;
        Left = 48, ;
        Top = 24, ;
        Width = 113, ;
        Name = "Text1"

    ADD OBJECT text2 AS textbox WITH ;
        BackColor = RGB(192,192,192), ;
        ControlSource = "test.cmembtype", ;
        Height = 24, ;
        Left = 48, ;
        Top = 60, ;
        Width = 113, ;
        Name = "Text2"

    ADD OBJECT navigator1 AS navigator WITH ;
        Top = 120, ;
        Left = 12, ;
        Width = 421, ;
        Height = 32, ;
        Name = "Navigator1", ;
        cmdNext.Name = "cmdNext", ;
        cmdPrev.Name = "cmdPrev", ;
        cmdTop.Name = "cmdTop", ;
        cmdBottom.Name = "cmdBottom", ;
        cmdOK.Top = 0, ;
        cmdOK.Left = 360, ;
        cmdOK.Height = 31, ;
```

```
        cmdOK.Width = 61, ;
        cmdOK.Name = "cmdOK"

    ADD OBJECT form1.navigator1.cmdnew AS commandbutton WITH ;
        Top = 0, ;
        Left = 288, ;
        Height = 31, ;
        Width = 61, ;
        Caption = "New", ;
        Name = "cmdNew"

    PROCEDURE cmdnew.Click
        APPEND BLANK
        thisform.refresh()
    ENDPROC

ENDDEFINE
*
*-- EndDefine: form1
******************************************************
```

Notice how the additional command button (cmdNew) is added within the code. An ADD OBJECT command adds the CommandButton to the container. This is just one of the powerful capabilities of the container class: You can add objects to it on-the-fly.

Figure 15.9 shows what the form looks like. As you can see, there is no visible indication that the additional CommandButton was not part of the original class.

FIGURE 15.9
A form with an additional CommandButton.

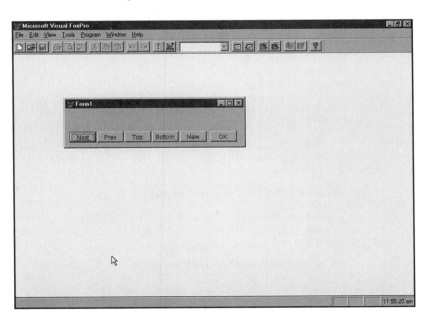

The Flexibility of the Container Class The container class is a very versatile class. It has little display baggage and yet has the full capabilities one would expect from a container. You can add controls to it on-the-fly with ADD OBJECT and AddObject(), and you can combine virtually any controls to create combinations that are limited only by your imagination.

Think about two simple controls: a TextBox and a Timer control. Individually, they each have specific duties. Combine them in a container and you can create something totally different: a clock.

A *Clock* Class A clock, as a class, is simply a combination of a Timer and a TextBox, as shown in Listing 15.4.

Listing 15.4 15CODE04—A Clock Built Using a Timer and Some Text Boxes in a Container

```
*   Class.............: Clock
*   Author............: Menachem Bazian, CPA
*   Notes.............: Exported code from Class Browser.


****************************************************
*-- Class:        clock
*-- ParentClass:  container
*-- BaseClass:    container
*
DEFINE CLASS clock AS container

    Width = 367
    Height = 27
    BorderWidth = 0
    SpecialEffect = 2
    ntimeformat = 0
    Name = "clock"

    ADD OBJECT txtdate AS txtDate WITH ;
Height = 22, ;
        Left = 5, ;
        Top = 3, ;
        Width = 250, ;
Name = "txtDate"

    ADD OBJECT txttime AS textbox WITH ;
Height = 22, ;
        Left = 268, ;
        Top = 3, ;
        Width = 77, ;

    ADD OBJECT tmrtimer AS trmTimer WITH ;
        Top = 0, ;
        Left = 120, ;
        Height = 24, ;
        Width = 25, ;
Name = "tmrTimer"
```

```
ENDDEFINE

DEFINE CLASS txtDate AS TextBox
    Alignment = 0
    BackColor = RGB(255,255,0)
    BorderStyle = 0
    Value = (CDOW(date())+" "+CMONTH(date())+" "+  ;
            ALLT(STR(DAY(date())))+", "+ALLT(STR(YEAR(date()))))
    Enabled = .F.
    DisabledForeColor = RGB(0,0,0)
    DisabledBackColor = RGB(255,255,255)
ENDEFINE

DEFINE CLASS txtTime AS TextBox
    Alignment = 0
    BorderStyle = 0
    Value = (IIF(THIS.PARENT.TimeFormat = 0, ;
            IIF(VAL(SUBSTR(time(),1,2))>12,;
            ALLT(STR((VAL(SUBSTR(time(),1,2))-12)))+SUBSTR(time(),3,6),;
            time()),time()))
    Enabled = .F.
    DisabledForeColor = RGB(0,0,0)
    DisabledBackColor = RGB(255,255,255)
ENDDEFINE

DEFINE CLASS tmrTimer AS Timer
    Interval = 1000

    PROCEDURE Timer
        this.Parent.txtDate.Value = CDOW(date()) + " " + ;
                                    CMONTH(date())+" "+ ;
                                    ALLT(STR(DAY(date()))) + ;
                                    ", "+ALLT(STR(YEAR(date())))

        IF this.Parent.nTimeFormat = 0
            this.Parent.txtTime.Value = ;
                    IIF(VAL(SUBSTR(time(),1,2))>12, ;
                    ALLT(STR((VAL(SUBSTR(time(),1,2))-12))) + ;
                    SUBSTR(time(),3,6),time())
        ELSE
            this.Parent.txtTime.Value = time()
        ENDIF
    ENDPROC
ENDDEFINE
*
*-- EndDefine: clock
****************************************************
```

The Timer control enables you to run a command or series of commands at timed intervals.
When the Interval property is set to a value greater than zero, it controls the amount of time
between executions of the timer's Timer event in milliseconds (1/1000 of a second units).
When you combine this capability with the display characteristics of the TextBox control to
display the time calculated by the timer, you have a clock.

Attached to the container is a custom property, `nTimeFormat`, that governs whether the time is shown in 12- or 24-hour format. Setting the property to `0` shows the time in AM/PM format, whereas setting the property to `1` shows the time in military format. Figure 15.10 shows what the clock looks like when you drop it on a form (it's on the Web site as a class called `ClockForm` in `CHAP15.VCX`).

FIGURE 15.10

The `Clock` form.

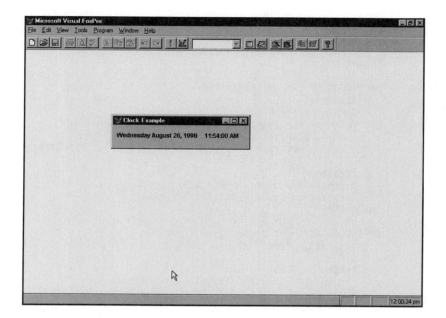

Once a second the `Timer` event fires and recalculates the time. The results of the calculation are placed in the `Value` property of the `txtTime` text box.

> **CAUTION**
>
> Remember always that a timer's interval is specified in milliseconds and not seconds. If you want a timer to fire once every second, give it an interval of 1000. Using an interval of 1 will cause your system to appear locked up because the timer is firing 1,000 times each second.

Providing a Consistent Interface   Notice the placement of the `nTimeFormat` property in the `Clock` class: It is placed on the container. Why put it there? You could have just as easily put the property on the `Timer` or even the `TextBox`.

Whenever you work with a composite class, it is very important to provide a consistent interface for the user of the control. It is crucial not to force the users of your classes to drill down into the member controls in order to accomplish what they need to do, especially when you are working with a container that can have many controls.

You should use the container to communicate with the outside world. Controls within the container can communicate with each other, but users should not have to communicate with the controls inside the container in order to use your classes. Chapter 16 shows some more examples of container-based controls.

The Form

There is not much to talk about regarding form-based classes that you have not already come across in the discussions of the Form Designer or other classes. Rather than discuss how to create form classes, I will show you how form classes are different from SCX-based forms.

Bringing Up the Form   You are familiar with the DO FORM syntax; however, this syntax is no longer used to work with forms stored as classes in a VCX file. Instead, the familiar CreateObject() syntax, the means by which all objects are instantiated from their classes, is used. Notice that after a form is instantiated with CreateObject(), you must call the Show method to display it.

 T I P   In Visual FoxPro 6, you can use the NewObject() function to create objects from classes. This includes form classes as well as any other class.

Making a Form Modal   There are two ways to make a form modal. One is to set the WindowType property to 1 (0 is modeless). The other is to call the Show method with a parameter of 1. Here is an example:

```
oForm = CreateObject("Form")
oForm.Show(1)
```

or

```
oForm = NewObject("Form")
oForm.Show(1)
```

Modeless forms raise two issues when dealing with VCX-based forms: reading systems events and variable scoping.

Reading System Events   Consider the following procedure:

```
*-- ShowForm.Prg

SET CLASS TO junkme
oForm = CreateObject("Form")
oForm.Show()
```

If you run this program from the command window, you will see the form flash and then disappear. This happens because of the scoping of oForm. Because oForm is a memory variable, the procedure ends and oForm loses scope when the Show method finishes and the form appears. Because the variable is released, the form it references is released, too, and disappears. The main problem is that the program never stops. There is no wait state to tell Visual FoxPro to stop and read system events. This is not an issue with the DO FORM command, though, because it contains its own inherent wait state in which the form operates.

The answer to this problem is to issue a READ EVENTS command, which, in effect, is a replacement for the old foundation read. It tells Visual FoxPro to stop and read system events. Without it, the program does not stop and eventually terminates.

Variable Scoping Revisited The READ EVENTS command does not completely eliminate the issue of variable scoping. The READ EVENTS command stops the program so that it can read system events. You can still instantiate a form in a procedure and have it flash if the variable loses focus.

You need to be careful with the scoping of your form instance variables. Just issuing a Show method does not stop processing. When the Show method completes, control is returned to the calling program. A typical example is a form called from the Click event of a CommandButton. Unless something is done to keep the variable around, the variable loses scope and the form flashes. There are several strategies to deal with this problem, and all the strategies deal with the same issue: keeping the instance variable in scope.

Attaching the Variable to Another Object One way to keep the variable in scope is to attach the instance variable to the object calling the form. For example, consider the class shown in Listing 15.5.

Listing 15.5 15CODE05—A Command Button Class That Launches Forms

```
*   Class............: Launchform
*   Author...........: Menachem Bazian, CPA
*   Notes............: Exported code from Class Browser.

**************************************************
*-- Class:        launchform
*-- ParentClass:  CommandButton
*-- BaseClass:    CommandButton
*
DEFINE CLASS launchform AS CommandButton

    Height = 29
    Width = 94
    Caption = "LaunchForm"
    *-- The form to Launch
    oform = .NULL.
    Name = "launchform"

    PROCEDURE Click
        this.oForm = CreateObject("Form")
        this.oForm.Show()
    ENDPROC

ENDDEFINE
*
*-- EndDefine: launchform
**************************************************
```

This `CommandButton` maintains scope as long as the form it is attached to maintains scope; therefore, any properties of the `CommandButton` retain scope, too. In this example, the form launched from within the `Click` event of the `CommandButton` would stick around.

A similar strategy is to attach the form instance variable to a public object. For example, it could be added to `_screen`. There is an example of this in Chapter 17.

Making the Variable Global   Another way to keep the variable in scope is to make the variable holding the form reference global. This is not the most elegant of solutions, but it does work. Perhaps a more elegant method is to declare an array in the start up program for the application and use the array as the repository for forms you want to keep around.

Global variables are not necessarily `PUBLIC` variables. A variable can be of three scopes, `PUBLIC`, `PRIVATE`, or `LOCAL`. `PUBLIC` variables exist from the moment they are created until they are either released with the `RELEASE` command or Visual FoxPro closes. `PRIVATE` variables exist from the moment they are created until the routine that created them ends (or they are released by the `RELEASE` command). `LOCAL` variables have the same scope as `PRIVATE` variables except that they are not visible to the routine called from the one that created them.

So, to create a global variable in an application, all that is needed is to create a `PRIVATE` variable in the highest level program of the application. This `PRIVATE` variable would be available to all other routines in the system.

The *only* reason to ever create a `PUBLIC` variable is so that the variable can be referenced by some routine higher in the calling stack than the one creating the variable. Having a routine reference a variable that will be created by some subroutine is a poor design choice, though, because it creates a situation of strong external coupling of the subroutine to the routine that calls it.

The problem with the global approach is managing the public variables. Having many public variables in a system that can be used and modified in many programs can be a little hairy at times. It's really the same issue with using public variables in a system in general. Conventional wisdom seems to shy away from this type of solution, but it will work if you need it.

Data Environments   One of the more significant differences between forms in an SCX file and form classes is in the area of data environments. You use a *data environment* to specify what tables, views, and relations are used in the form. When a form class is created, you cannot save a data environment with it. If you save a form as a class that had a data environment attached to it, the data environment is lost.

This might look terribly negative, but it really isn't. Although you lose the graphically created data environment capabilities, you can still create data environment classes in code (this is discussed in greater detail in Chapter 17). Also, there might be many cases in which the data environment for the form is not determined by the form but rather by another class on the form (for example, a business object, which is also discussed in Chapter 17).

If you don't want to get involved with data environment classes, you can still do what you want with relative ease. All you need to do is place code in the `Load` event to open the tables.

Take the example shown in Listing 15.6, which opens the Customer table in the TESTDATA database and then presents some of the fields for editing (the form is shown in Figure 15.11).

Listing 15.6   15CODE06—A Form Class That Opens Data Tables for Editing

```
*  Class.............: Customerdataform
*  Author............: Menachem Bazian, CPA
*  Notes.............: Exported code from Class Browser.

****************************************************
*-- Class:       customerdataform
*-- ParentClass: form
*-- BaseClass:   form
*
DEFINE CLASS customerdataform AS form

    DataSession = 2
    Height = 238
    Width = 356
    DoCreate = .T.
    AutoCenter = .T.
    BackColor = RGB(192,192,192)
    Caption = "Sample Customer Data"
    Name = "dataform"

    ADD OBJECT txtcust_id AS TextBox WITH ;
        ControlSource = "customer.cust_id", ;
        Enabled = .F., ;
        Height = 24, ;
        Left = 120, ;
        Top = 24, ;
        Width = 205, ;
        Name = "txtCust_Id"

    ADD OBJECT txtcompany AS TextBox WITH ;
        ControlSource = "customer.company", ;
        Height = 24, ;
        Left = 120, ;
        Top = 72, ;
        Width = 205, ;
        Name = "txtCompany"

    ADD OBJECT txtcontact AS TextBox WITH ;
        ControlSource = "customer.contact", ;
        Height = 24, ;
        Left = 120, ;
        Top = 120, ;
        Width = 205, ;
        Name = "txtContact"

    ADD OBJECT txttitle AS TextBox WITH ;
        ControlSource = "customer.title", ;
        Height = 24, ;
```

```
            Left = 120, ;
            Top = 168, ;
            Width = 205, ;
            Name = "txtTitle"

        ADD OBJECT label1 AS label WITH ;
            AutoSize = .T., ;
            BackStyle = 0, ;
            Caption = "Customer Id:", ;
            Height = 18, ;
            Left = 12, ;
            Top = 24, ;
            Width = 80, ;
            Name = "Label1"

        ADD OBJECT label2 AS label WITH ;
            AutoSize = .T., ;
            BackStyle = 0, ;
            Caption = "Company:", ;
            Height = 18, ;
            Left = 12, ;
            Top = 72, ;
            Width = 64, ;
            Name = "Label2"

        ADD OBJECT label3 AS label WITH ;
            AutoSize = .T., ;
            BackStyle = 0, ;
            Caption = "Contact:", ;
            Height = 18, ;
            Left = 12, ;
            Top = 120, ;
            Width = 52, ;
            Name = "Label3"

        ADD OBJECT label4 AS label WITH ;
            AutoSize = .T., ;
            BackStyle = 0, ;
            Caption = "Title:", ;
            Height = 18, ;
            Left = 12, ;
            Top = 168, ;
            Width = 32, ;
            Name = "Label4"

        PROCEDURE Load
            OPEN DATA _SAMPLES+" \data\testdata.dbc"
            USE customer
        ENDPROC

ENDDEFINE
*
*-- EndDefine: customerdataform
****************************************************
```

FIGURE 15.11
The Customer data
form.

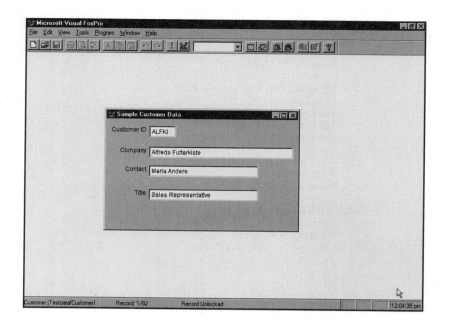

Visual FoxPro 6 has a new system memory variable named _SAMPLES. This variable holds the path to
the Visual FoxPro sample files. This is a big help because with Visual Studio 6, the samples for all of
the Visual Studio products are stored in a common directory structure. Visual FoxPro 6 does not put its
sample files in the familiar Sample directory under the Visual FoxPro home directory.

In Listing 15.6, you can see the _SAMPLES variable used to locate the TESTDATA database.

If you combine this form with the Navigator container you saw earlier, you have a complete
data entry package. Listing 15.7 shows what it looks like in code; a visual representation is
shown in Figure 15.12.

**Listing 15.7   15CODE07—The Preceding Data Form with the Navigation
Buttons Added to It**

```
*   Class.............: Custformwithnavcontainer
*   Author............: Menachem Bazian, CPA
*   Notes.............: Exported code from Class Browser.

**************************************************
*-- Class:          custformwithnavcontainer
*-- ParentClass:    customerdataform (d:\data\docs\books\vfu\code\oop2.vcx)
*-- BaseClass:      form
*
DEFINE CLASS custformwithnavcontainer AS customerdataform

    Height = 283
    Width = 370
```

```
            DoCreate = .T.
            Name = "custformwithnavcontainer"
            txtCust_Id.Name = "txtCust_Id"
            txtCompany.Name = "txtCompany"
            txtContact.Name = "txtContact"
            txtTitle.Name = "txtTitle"
            Label1.Name = "Label1"
            Label2.Name = "Label2"
            Label3.Name = "Label3"
            Label4.Name = "Label4"

            ADD OBJECT navigator1 AS navigator WITH ;
                Top = 240, ;
                Left = 12, ;
                Width = 350, ;
                Height = 32, ;
                Name = "Navigator1", ;
                cmdNext.Name = "cmdNext", ;
                cmdPrev.Name = "cmdPrev", ;
                cmdTop.Name = "cmdTop", ;
                cmdBottom.Name = "cmdBottom", ;
                cmdOK.Name = "cmdOK"

        ENDDEFINE
        *
        *-- EndDefine: custformwithnavcontainer
        ******************************************************
```

FIGURE 15.12

The Customer data form with the Navigator container.

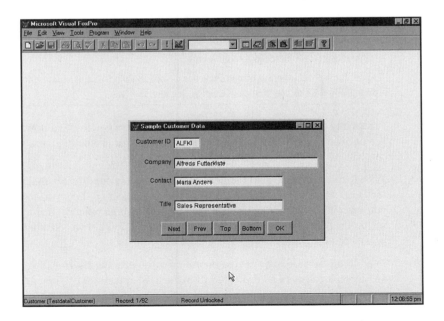

As it turns out, even without the native data environment capabilities, creating forms as classes is a very viable way to create and display forms in Visual FoxPro.

CREATEOBJECT("form") Versus DO FORM   Why should you create a form as a class instead of using an SCX file and calling it with DO FORM? This question brings up a few issues you should consider.

The first issue is subclassing. You can subclass forms only if they are stored as classes.

Form classes are also more flexible to use than the DO FORM syntax. I like being able to instantiate a form object with CreateObject() and then play with it a little before issuing a call to the Show() method. Finally, the CreateObject() syntax does provide uniformity among the components of an application. I like the simple elegance of having a similar syntax for all my objects as opposed to using CreateObject() most of the time and DO FORM some of the time.

Having said this, you can handle the situation in any way you feel comfortable. To a degree, it does come down to programmer preference.

Build Forms as Classes or Use the Form Designer?

Using the Form Designer versus forms as classes is a question that might never have an answer. Both methods work fine in many applications. The key point about the whole issue is that you should use one methodology so that your applications are consistent in how they work.

Mixing and matching different methods will only cause your applications to be more difficult to maintain over time. Neither method really has any particular advantages over the other. You can use subclasses as complete forms if the forms are defined as classes, however, you can use form classes to create forms with the Form Designer also, so the form class issue has no influence over whether or not you can use subclassing as a specialization technique.

The Form Designer can be used to create Formsets, which contain more than one form. But you can programmatically control which forms in the set are visible, so the issue of multiple forms being defined in a single meta file is moot as well

Again, the key point here is consistency: If you want to build forms as classes, do it that way all the time. If you want to use the Form Designer, use it all the time.

Protecting Members on Forms   In earlier chapters you learned how to protect members from the outside world. If you recall, the rule of thumb for protecting members is to protect them if the outside world has no use for them.

With forms, the rules are changed on this issue. It is conceivable that you might want to protect something (a method, property, or even an object on the form) from the outside world but you want it accessible to objects within the form. Unfortunately, if you protect something within the form, it is private throughout the form. In other words, if it is private, it is considered private to everything.

In addition, beware of protected members on objects themselves. If you protect a member on an object, it can even be protected from itself. Sound strange? Then get a load of this. Remember the NoNotifyTextBox text box created earlier in this chapter? It had a protected member called cNotifySetting, which held the setting of SET NOTIFY when the control got focus. Now, suppose I dropped it on a form, as shown in Listing 15.8.

Listing 15.8 15CODE08—A Form with the NoNotifyTextBox Class on It as an Object

```
*   Author...........: Menachem Bazian, CPA
*   Notes............: Exported code from Class Browser.

PUBLIC oform1


oform1=CREATEOBJECT("form1")
oform1.Show()
RETURN

****************************************************
*-- Form:        form1 (d:\data\docs\books\vfu\code\protect.scx)
*-- ParentClass: form
*-- BaseClass:   form
*
DEFINE CLASS form1 AS form

     Top = 0
     Left = 0
     Height = 57
     Width = 301
     DoCreate = .T.
     Caption = "Form1"
     Name = "Form1"

     ADD OBJECT nonotifytextbox1 AS nonotifytextbox WITH ;
         Left = 84, ;
         Top = 12, ;
         Name = "Nonotifytextbox1"

     PROCEDURE nonotifytextbox1.MouseMove
         LPARAMETERS nButton, nShift, nXCoord, nYCoord
         WAIT WINDOW this.cNotifySetting
     ENDPROC

ENDDEFINE
*
*-- EndDefine: form1
****************************************************
```

This is an .SCX-type form with a NoNotifyTextBox text box in it. Notice the MouseMove event for NoNotifyTextBox. The code has been entered into the property at the form level (that is, the control was not subclassed in a VCX file and the code added in the subclass).

If you run this form and move the mouse over the TextBox, you will get an error stating that cNotifySetting does not exist (see Figure 15.13). This is because the code was not put in the class itself or in a subclass—it was entered at the form.

FIGURE 15.13

A form with an error message.

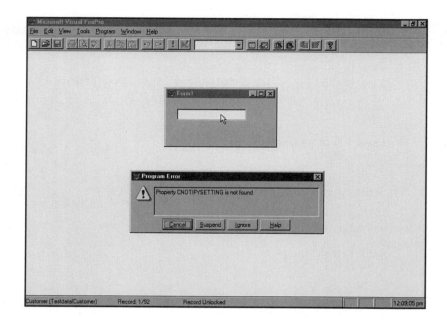

That's the way it works. Keep an eye out for this one.

N O T E   The property `cNotifySetting` cannot be seen by the code written in the `NoNotifyTextBox` instance on the form because the code added in the Form Designer is added to the form and not the text box. Look at the code above and you will notice that the method name for the new code is part of the form's class definition. This means that the reference to the `cNoNofitySetting` property is being made by the form. Because the form is not the text box, the protected property of the text box is hidden from the form. ■

Toolbars

The final type of visual class covered in this chapter is the `Toolbar`. You can think of toolbars as a special type of form. You create them by dropping objects on them (usually `CommandButtons` but other objects can be added as well). The toolbar always stays on top, docks itself automatically (by default) when dragged to the top, bottom, right, or left borders of the FoxPro desktop, and resizes just like any other toolbar in Visual FoxPro. I will illustrate this with a simple navigation toolbar.

Listing 15.9   15CODE09—A Navigation Toolbar

```
*    Class.............: Simplenavbar
*    Author............: Menachem Bazian, CPA
*    Notes.............: Exported code from Class Browser.
```

```
**************************************************
*-- Class:       simplenavbar
*-- ParentClass: toolbar
*-- BaseClass:   toolbar
*
DEFINE CLASS simplenavbar AS toolbar

    Caption = "Navigator Buttons"
    Height = 31
    Left = 0
    Top = 0
    Width = 177
    Name = "simplenavbar"

    ADD OBJECT cmdnext AS CommandButton WITH ;
        Top = 4, ;
        Left = 6, ;
        Height = 25, ;
        Width = 33, ;
        FontBold = .F., ;
        FontSize = 8, ;
        Caption = "Next", ;
        Default = .F., ;
        ToolTipText = "Next record", ;
        Name = "cmdNext"

    ADD OBJECT cmdprev AS CommandButton WITH ;
        Top = 4, ;
        Left = 38, ;
        Height = 25, ;
        Width = 33, ;
        FontBold = .F., ;
        FontSize = 8, ;
        Caption = "Prev", ;
        Default = .F., ;
        ToolTipText = "Previous record", ;
        Name = "cmdPrev"

    ADD OBJECT cmdtop AS CommandButton WITH ;
        Top = 4, ;
        Left = 70, ;
        Height = 25, ;
        Width = 33, ;
        FontBold = .F., ;
        FontSize = 8, ;
        Caption = "Top", ;
        Default = .F., ;
        ToolTipText = "First record", ;
        Name = "cmdTop"

    ADD OBJECT cmdbottom AS CommandButton WITH ;
        Top = 4, ;
        Left = 102, ;
        Height = 25, ;
        Width = 33, ;
```

continues

Listing 15.9 Continued

```
        FontBold = .F., ;
        FontSize = 8, ;
        Caption = "Bott", ;
        Default = .F., ;
        ToolTipText = "Last record", ;
        Name = "cmdBottom"

ADD OBJECT separator1 AS separator WITH ;
        Top = 4, ;
        Left = 140, ;
        Height = 0, ;
        Width = 0, ;
        Name = "Separator1"

ADD OBJECT cmdok AS okbuttonwithtooltip WITH ;
        Top = 4, ;
        Left = 140, ;
        Height = 25, ;
        Width = 33, ;
        FontBold = .F., ;
        FontSize = 8, ;
        Default = .F., ;
        Name = "cmdOK"

PROCEDURE cmdnext.Click
     IF TYPE("_screen.activeform") # 'O' ;
        OR isNull(_screen.activeform)

          WAIT WINDOW "No form active!"
          RETURN
     ENDIF

     SET DATASESSION TO _screen.activeform.datasessionid

     SKIP 1
     IF EOF()
        =Messagebox("At end of file!", 16)
        GO BOTTOM
     ENDIF

     _screen.activeform.refresh()
ENDPROC

PROCEDURE cmdprev.Click
     IF TYPE("_screen.activeform") # 'O' ;
        OR isNull(_screen.activeform)

          WAIT WINDOW "No form active!"
          RETURN
     ENDIF

     SET DATASESSION TO _screen.activeform.datasessionid
```

```
            SKIP -1
            IF BOF()
                =Messagebox("At beginning of file!", 16)
                GO TOP
            ENDIF

            _screen.activeform.refresh()
        ENDPROC

        PROCEDURE cmdtop.Click
            IF TYPE("_screen.activeform") # 'O' ;
                OR isNull(_screen.activeform)

                WAIT WINDOW "No form active!"
                RETURN
            ENDIF

            SET DATASESSION TO _screen.activeform.datasessionid

            GO TOP
            _screen.activeform.refresh()
        ENDPROC

        PROCEDURE cmdbottom.Click
            IF TYPE("_screen.activeform") # 'O' ;
                OR isNull(_screen.activeform)

                WAIT WINDOW "No form active!"
                RETURN
            ENDIF

            SET DATASESSION TO _screen.activeform.datasessionid

            GO BOTTOM
            _screen.activeform.refresh()
        ENDPROC

        PROCEDURE cmdok.Click
            IF TYPE("_screen.activeform") # 'O' ;
                OR isNull(_screen.activeform)

                WAIT WINDOW "No form active!"
                RETURN
            ENDIF

            SET DATASESSION TO _screen.activeform.datasessionid

            _screen.activeform.release()
        ENDPROC

    ENDDEFINE
    *
    *-- EndDefine: simplenavbar
    ****************************************************
```

Notice the differences between this version of the Navigator buttons and the container version previously shown. In the container-based version, each button had the code to move within the current table. The code was simple and straightforward. The code for the Toolbar version is a bit more obtuse. Instead of working directly with the form, I use _screen.activeform, and there is a SET DATASESSION command thrown in. The OK button does not issue RELEASE thisform but rather calls the Release method. Why the additional work?

The container version is designed to work with a single form; each form that uses the container version has an instance of the container on it. The toolbar, on the other hand, is designed to work generically with many forms.

Because the Toolbar exists independently of any individual form, you have to deal with the issue of data sessions. A form might work in its own data session or in the default one. There is no way at design time to know the one with which you will be dealing (unless you set rules one way or the other).

The solution to this issue is to specifically set the current data session with the SET DATASESSION command to the current form's data session (which is stored in the form's DataSessionId property). One way to get to the current form is to use _screen.activeform. The problem is that _screen.activeform might be null even if a form is visible—hence the check on _screen.activeform in the CommandButton's Click methods.

Furthermore, notice how the form is released. The Release method (which is a built-in method in the Form base class) takes care of this action quite nicely. The reason for not using something like RELEASE thisform is because the CommandButton is not sitting on a form at all; in addition, it has no clue as to the name of the instance variable to release. _screen.activeform.Release handles these issues for you.

One final note: When objects are added to the toolbar they are placed flush against each other. Unlike other classes that support containership, you cannot dictate the placement of the objects in the toolbar—the class handles that for you. All you can dictate is the order in which they are placed.

In order to achieve a separation between objects, you need to add a separator control. The control doesn't really do much of anything, it just adds a space between controls on the toolbar. Figure 15.14 shows an example of a data form with the toolbar. In this case, the data form is the simple Customer form with the SimpleNavBar class; both are instantiated separately.

Internal Characteristics of a Toolbar   Toolbars to do not behave like other forms. They have some specific characteristics, including the following:

- Toolbars are always on top.
- Toolbars automatically dock when they are moved to any of the main Visual FoxPro window borders.
- When toolbars aren't docked, they have a half-height title bar.
- When the size of a toolbar is changed, the controls are arranged to fit.
- You can move a toolbar by clicking and dragging in any area of the toolbar that isn't a control.

FIGURE 15.14

A form with
`SimpleNavBar`.

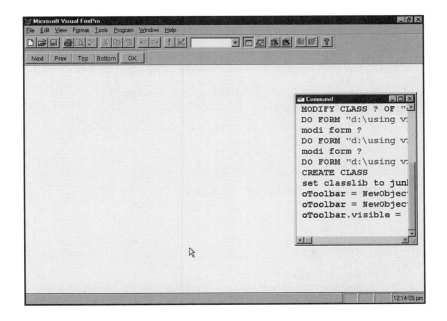

- Many controls placed on the toolbar do not receive the focus when they're chosen.
- Access keys in controls placed on a toolbar are disabled.
- Toolbars never get focus.
- Timer controls do not work on a toolbar.

In addition to these built-in behaviors, there are some additional characteristics that good toolbars should have. Here's a list of them:

- All objects on a toolbar should have tooltips.
- Pictures are very effective on a toolbar.
- Buttons should all be the same size.
- Avoid large objects (such as a list box) on docked toolbars.

Large Objects on a Toolbar   If you need to put a lot of data on a toolbar, it is a good idea not to force a large object to exist on the toolbar when it is docked. For the most part, large objects (such as a list box) can be mimicked with other objects that take up less space (a drop-down list object, for example). The idea here is to create a toolbar with both the large versions and small versions of the objects on it and to show or hide the objects based on whether the toolbar is docked.

Consider the following scenario. You have a toolbar that displays a list of customers in the table. (The specific functionality isn't important, only that you need to have a toolbar with a list.) You prefer to use the list box because it is larger, but you cannot afford the space on the desktop when the toolbar is docked.

Listing 15.10 demonstrates how you could handle the situation.

Listing 15.10   15CODE10—A Morphing Toolbar

```
*   Class.............: Morphbar
*   Author............: Menachem Bazian, CPA
*   Notes.............: Exported code from Class Browser.

***************************************************
*-- Class:        morphbar
*-- ParentClass:  toolbar
*-- BaseClass:    toolbar
*
DEFINE CLASS morphbar AS toolbar

    Caption = "Toolbar1"
    DataSession = 1
    Height = 121
    Left = 0
    Top = 0
    Width = 332
    Name = "morphbar"

    ADD OBJECT list1 AS listbox WITH ;
        RowSourceType = 6, ;
        RowSource = "customer.company", ;
        Height = 115, ;
        Left = 6, ;
        Top = 4, ;
        Width = 170, ;
        Name = "List1"

    ADD OBJECT combo1 AS combobox WITH ;
        RowSourceType = 6, ;
        RowSource = "customer.company", ;
        Height = 21, ;
        Left = 175, ;
        Style = 2, ;
        Top = 4, ;
        Width = 153, ;
        Name = "Combo1"

    PROCEDURE AfterDock
        IF this.DockPosition = 1 or this.DockPosition = 2
            *-- Note, you cannot use the Dock() method to undock
            *-- a toolbar... you have to use the Move() method.
            *-- Using the Dock() method with the -1 parameter results
            *-- in a totally bogus error message.

            this.move(1,1)
        ENDIF
    ENDPROC

    PROCEDURE Init
```

```
        IF this.docked
            this.list1.visible = .F.
            this.combo1.visible = .T.
        ELSE
            this.list1.visible = .T.
            this.combo1.visible = .F.
        ENDIF
    ENDPROC

    PROCEDURE BeforeDock
        *-- nLocation shows where the toolbar will be after
        *-- is complete. -1 means it will be undocked. 0,1,2,3
        *-- mean top, left, right and bottom respectively.

        LPARAMETERS nLocation

        DO CASE
            CASE nLocation = -1  && Not DOcked
                this.List1.Visible = .T.
                this.list1.Enabled = .T.
                this.Combo1.visible = .F.

            CASE nLocation = 0 OR nLocation = 3  && Top or bottom
                this.List1.Visible = .F.
                this.Combo1.visible = .T.
                this.Combo1.Enabled = .T.
        ENDCASE
    ENDPROC

ENDDEFINE
*
*-- EndDefine: morphbar
****************************************************
```

Notice that there are two objects on this toolbar. The list box is kept visible whenever the toolbar is not docked. The combo box is made visible whenever the toolbar is not docked. The toolbar automatically adjusts its size based on the visible controls on it. Cool stuff, no?

Neither a combo box nor a list box work well when docked to the side because they just take up too much real estate on the desktop. The solution taken in this example is not to let the user dock the toolbar to the left or right sides.

The BeforeDock event fires when an attempt is made to dock or undock the toolbar. The nLocation parameter tells the event where the toolbar is going. Based on where the toolbar is being docked, the visible properties of the lists are adjusted appropriately.

A few notes are in order here about the data behind the lists. In order to use this class, the TESTDATA database, which is located in the Sample files \DATA directory (_SAMPLES will give you the path to the Visual FoxPro sample files), has to be open and the Customer table has to be in use. Here are the commands to do this:

```
OPEN DATABASE _SAMPLES+" \data\testdata.dbc"
USE customer
```

You can't really open the data in this class. Unlike its cousin, the `Form` class, the `Toolbar` class does not have a `LOAD` method. The `RecordSource` properties of both lists look to the `Customer` file. As a result, when Visual FoxPro tries to instantiate the class, it looks at the properties of the contained objects and validates them. If the `Customer` table is not open, the object does not instantiate. Even opening the table in the `Init` method of the lists won't work.

Coordinating Forms with Toolbars   Another issue to consider is that of coordinating forms with toolbars. You have already learned how to coordinate data sessions with a form; however, there are many other issues to consider. Here are just a few:

- Dealing with forms that do not "do" data
- Releasing the toolbar when the last data form is released
- Making sure the toolbar is up when a form that needs it is instantiated

Coordination is merely a matter of sending the appropriate messages back and forth. By placing a custom property on data forms, you can determine whether a form is a data form by the existence of the custom property. When a data form is instantiated, it looks for a global variable (goNavToolBar). If the variable exists, the toolbar is assumed to exist (you make the toolbar nonclosable). Each new instance of a data form also sends a message to goNavToolBar telling it that there is a new data form in town (in the following example the toolbar maintains a count variable and the new instances increase it by one). When an instantiated form is released, it tells the toolbar that there is one less data form. If this is the last data form visible on the desktop, the toolbar releases itself. Listing 15.11 shows the code for the example, Figure 15.15 shows you what it looks like.

Listing 15.11   15CODE11—A Navigator Toolbar That Is Aware of the Forms That Are Visible

```
*    Class.............: Navigatortoolbar
*    Author............: Menachem Bazian, CPA
*    Notes.............: Exported code from Class Browser.

****************************************************
*-- Class:        navigatortoolbar
*-- ParentClass:  simplenavbar
*-- BaseClass:    toolbar
*
DEFINE CLASS navigatortoolbar AS simplenavbar

    Height = 31
    Left = 0
    Top = 0
    Width = 171
    *-- The number of forms active that use this toolbar.
    *-- When this property reaches 0, the toolbar will release.
    PROTECTED nnumforms
    nnumforms = 0
    Name = "navigatortoolbar"
    cmdNext.Top = 4
    cmdNext.Left = 6
```

```
      cmdNext.Default = .F.
      cmdNext.Name = "cmdNext"
      cmdPrev.Top = 4
      cmdPrev.Left = 38
      cmdPrev.Default = .F.
      cmdPrev.Name = "cmdPrev"
      cmdTop.Top = 4
      cmdTop.Left = 70
      cmdTop.Default = .F.
      cmdTop.Name = "cmdTop"
      cmdBottom.Top = 4
      cmdBottom.Left = 102
      cmdBottom.Default = .F.
      cmdBottom.Name = "cmdBottom"
      cmdOK.Top = 4
      cmdOK.Left = 134
      cmdOK.Default = .F.
      cmdOK.Name = "cmdOK"

  *-- Add a form to the toolbar form count.
  PROCEDURE addform
      *-- This method should be called by form.init()

      this.nNumForms = this.nNumForms + 1
  ENDPROC

  *-- Remove a form from the toolbar form count.
  PROCEDURE removeform
      *-- This method should be called by form.destroy()

      this.nNumForms = this.nNumForms - 1

      IF this.nNumForms = 0
          this.release()
      ENDIF
  ENDPROC

  *-- Release the toolbar. Mimics a form's RELEASE method.
  PROCEDURE release
      RELEASE thisform
  ENDPROC

  PROCEDURE Refresh
      IF TYPE("_screen.activeform.lIsDataForm") = 'L'
          this.cmdNext.Enabled = .T.
          this.cmdPrev.Enabled = .T.
          this.cmdTop.Enabled = .T.
          this.cmdBottom.Enabled = .T.
      ELSE
          this.cmdNext.Enabled = .F.
          this.cmdPrev.Enabled = .F.
          this.cmdTop.Enabled = .F.
          this.cmdBottom.Enabled = .F.
      ENDIF
  ENDPROC
```

continues

Listing 15.11 Continued

```
      PROCEDURE Destroy
          this.visible = .f.
      ENDPROC

ENDDEFINE
*
*-- EndDefine: navigatortoolbar
**************************************************

*   Class.............: Custformlinkedtotoolbar
*   Author............: Menachem Bazian, CPA
*   Notes.............: Exported code from Class Browser.

**************************************************
*-- Class:        custformlinkedtotoolbar
*-- ParentClass:  customerdataform
*-- BaseClass:    form
*
DEFINE CLASS custformlinkedtotoolbar AS customerdataform

    DoCreate = .T.
    Name = "custformlinkedtotoolbar"
    txtCust_Id.Name = "txtCust_Id"
    txtCompany.Name = "txtCompany"
    txtContact.Name = "txtContact"
    txtTitle.Name = "txtTitle"
    Label1.Name = "Label1"
    Label2.Name = "Label2"
    Label3.Name = "Label3"
    Label4.Name = "Label4"
    lisdataform = .F.

    PROCEDURE Init
        IF TYPE ("goNavToolBar") # 'O' OR isnull(goNavToolBar)
            RELEASE goNavToolBar
            PUBLIC goNavToolBar
            goNavToolBar = CreateObject("NavigatorToolBar")
            goNavToolBar.Dock(0,1,0)
            goNavToolBar.Show()
        ENDIF

        goNavToolBar.AddForm()
        goNavToolBar.Refresh()
    ENDPROC

    PROCEDURE Activate
        goNavToolBar.Refresh()
    ENDPROC

    PROCEDURE Deactivate
        goNavToolBar.Refresh()
    ENDPROC
```

```
        PROCEDURE Destroy
            goNavToolBar.RemoveForm()
        ENDPROC

    ENDDEFINE
    *
    *-- EndDefine: custformlinkedtotoolbar
    ********************************************************
```

FIGURE 15.15
The Customer data
form with
`NavigationToolBar`.

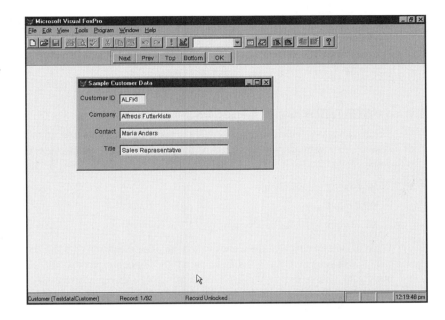

A Final Word on Visual Classes

When you create classes in Visual FoxPro, it is not uncommon to think only in terms of visual classes. Visual classes certainly are fun to create—working with GUI elements has an element of art to it. Creating a form that is both functional and pleasing to the eye is something of an achievement.

However, OOP does not stop with visual classes. Unlike some languages that only support GUI classes, Visual FoxPro supports nonvisual classes. What you can do with nonvisual classes is no less remarkable.

Nonvisual Classes

A *nonvisual class* is any class that is not designed primarily to be displayed. For example, `CommandButton` is a class that is specifically designed to display on a form. The `Timer` class, on the other hand, does not show on a form at all.

Nonvisual classes in Visual FoxPro are typically descendants of the Custom or Timer class and often have no display component attached to them at all. However, a nonvisual class can have a visual component attached to it. And to make matters more confusing, classes typically thought of as *visual* classes can be the basis for nonvisual classes, too.

 TIP Because nonvisual classes have no display component, that is, they are invisible, you can use any base class in Visual FoxPro as the basis for a nonvisual class. I often use the Label base class for the basis of my nonvisual classes for two reasons. One, it takes up less memory than most of the other classes. Two, I can give it a caption that is seen clearly in the form or Class Designer and still set its visible property to .F. so that the user never sees it.

I can add properties and methods to the Label class as needed for it to perform the functionality it is required to.

Why Create Nonvisual Classes?

There are many reasons why you would create a nonvisual class. In fact, there are as many reasons to create nonvisual classes as there are to create visual ones. Here are the main reasons:

- Code maintenance
- Code reuse
- Functionality enhancement

What's the difference between nonvisual and visual classes? The basic difference lies in the type of classes you create. Visual classes typically center around the user interface, whereas nonvisual classes play key roles in management functions. Nonvisual classes also incorporate the type of class that is most often neglected when people discuss object orientation in systems development: business classes.

Types of Nonvisual Classes

Here are some of the more common types of nonvisual classes that you will typically create and use in your applications.

Wrapper Classes When you create classes written for management roles, you want to consider the many different aspects of management for which you can create a class. One aspect is to manage the interface between one program and another. A good example of this would be the management of the interface between Visual FoxPro code and DLLs, FLLs, or other function libraries. These classes are created for several reasons:

- To make it easier to use these sources of functions
- To enhance their capabilities
- To encapsulate the definition, loading, and error trapping required when working with the function library

This process is known as *wrapping a class* around some existing functionality. Appropriately, these classes are called *wrapper classes*.

Manager Classes   Another typical nonvisual class is a class that manages other classes. A good example is a class that handles multiple instances of forms. Such a class enables you to create functions such as Tile All Windows. These classes are known as *manager classes*.

Business Classes   A *business class* is a class designed to model an entity in a business environment. A good example is the Customer class. These classes are a combination of information and actions designed to do what a business entity needs to do within the context of the problem domain (that is, the environment being modeled and automated).

The responsibilities of a business class are determined after careful analysis and design. Business class responsibilities can be very abstract in nature and require careful modeling before implementation. Some common responsibilities might be the following:

- Can retrieve its information from the database
- Can print itself
- Can save itself to the database

Business classes are a little more difficult to classify as visual or nonvisual. Business classes can, and often do, have visual components. A business class can be based on a visual class (a Form class, for example) with the appropriate properties and methods added to the form. In which category does a business class belong? It depends on how the object is created. In reality, it's all semantics anyway; you can call it what you want.

Wrapper Classes

The purpose of a wrapper class is to create a class that manages and perhaps even enhances the functionality of some other code. Any code can be wrapped into a class. If you have an old procedure library written in earlier versions of FoxPro, you could wrap a class around it if you like. The tough part is deciding when it is appropriate to wrap a class around something.

The best reason to wrap a class around something is to make it easier and better to use. A perfect example of a candidate for a wrapper class is a DLL or FLL. These function libraries can be obscure, their parameters can be difficult to determine, and their error-handling requirements can be rather extensive. For example, if you are using an FLL library (for example, FOXTOOLS), what do you do if someone else's code unloads it accidentally with SET LIBRARY TO? Can you rely on the fact that the library is there all the time? Take the example of calling some of the Windows API functions (the functions to write and read from INI files, for example). These can be difficult to learn to use.

When a class is wrapped around some other piece of code, the class developer has the ability to control which portions of the DLL or FLL are available to the outside world, how they are called, and even what values are returned.

Wrapper classes carry a myriad of benefits with them. First of all, if a DLL or FLL is used with a wrapper class, the developers who use that class do not have to know anything about the DLL or FLL that serves as the basis for the class. They also do not have to be concerned with issues of loading the DLL or FLL or registering its functions. In effect, the result is a much reduced learning curve and coding time for all concerned.

Listing 15.12 shows an example of a wrapper class. This class is a wrapper around a library of functions called FOXTOOLS.FLL that ships with Visual FoxPro.

N O T E   Although in Visual FoxPro 6 most of the functions contained in FOXTOOLS.FLL are now part of the VFP language, this example of a wrapper class is still a good exercise for seeing how wrapper classes are built. ■

Listing 15.12   15CODE12—A Wrapper Class for FOXTOOLS.FLL

```
*   Class............: Foxtools
*   Author...........: Menachem Bazian, CPA
*   Notes............: Exported code from Class Browser.

**************************************************
*-- Class:       foxtools
*-- ParentClass: custom
*-- BaseClass:   custom
*
*
DEFINE CLASS foxtools AS custom

    Name = "foxtools"
    PROTECTED lloaded

    PROCEDURE loadlib
        IF !"FOXTOOLS" $ SET("library")
            SET LIBRARY TO (SYS(2004)+"FOXTOOLS")
            this.lLoaded = .T.
        ENDIF
    ENDPROC

    PROCEDURE drivetype
        LPARAMETERS tcDrive
        LOCAL lnRetVal
        lnRetVal = (drivetype(tcDrive))
        RETURN lnRetVal
    ENDPROC

    PROCEDURE justfname
        LPARAMETERS tcString
        LOCAL lcRetVal
        lcRetVal = (justfname(tcString))
        RETURN lcRetVal
    ENDPROC

    PROCEDURE juststem
        LPARAMETERS tcString
        LOCAL lcRetVal
        lcRetVal = (juststem(tcString))
        RETURN lcRetVal
    ENDPROC
```

```
PROCEDURE justpath
    LPARAMETERS tcString
    LOCAL lcRetVal
    lcRetVal = (this.addbs(justpath(tcString)))
    RETURN lcRetVal
ENDPROC

PROCEDURE justdrive
    LPARAMETERS tcString
    LOCAL lcRetVal
    lcRetVal = (this.addbs(justpath(tcString)))
    RETURN lcRetVal
ENDPROC

PROCEDURE justpathnodrive
    LPARAMETERS tcString
    LOCAL    lcRetval, ;
             lnAtPos

    lcRetVal = this.justpath(tcString)
    lnAtPos  = AT(':', lcRetVal)
    IF lnAtPos > 0
        IF lnAtPos < LEN(lcRetVal)
            lcRetVal = this.addbs(SUBST(lcRetVal,lnAtPos+1))
        ELSE
            lcRetVal = ""
        ENDIF
    ENDIF

    RETURN (lcRetVal)
ENDPROC

PROCEDURE addbs
    LPARAMETERS tcString
    LOCAL lcRetVal
    lcRetVal = (addbs(tcString))
    RETURN lcRetVal
ENDPROC

PROCEDURE isdir
    LPARAMETERS tcString
    LOCAL llRetVal, lcTestString, laFiles[1]

    lcTestString = ALLTRIM(this.addbs(tcString)) - "*.*"
    IF ADIR(laFiles, lcTestString, "DSH") > 0
        llRetVal = .t.
    ELSE
        llRetVal = .F.
    ENDIF

    RETURN (llRetVal)
ENDPROC
```

continues

Listing 15.12   Continued

```
    PROCEDURE cleandir
        LPARAMETERS tcString
        RETURN(UPPER(sys(2027, tcString)))
    ENDPROC

    PROCEDURE cut
        =_edcut(_wontop())
    ENDPROC

    PROCEDURE copy
        =_edcopy(_wontop())
    ENDPROC

    PROCEDURE paste
        =_edpaste(_wontop())
    ENDPROC

    PROCEDURE Error
        LPARAMETERS tnError, tcMethod, tnLine
        LOCAL lcMessage

        tcMethod = UPPER(tcMethod)

        DO CASE
            CASE tnError = 1  && File not found -- Cause by the library not
loaded
                this.loadlib()
                RETRY

            OTHERWISE
                ?? CHR(7)
                lcMessage = "An error has occurred:" + CHR(13) + ;
                            "Error Number: " + PADL(tnError,5) + CHR(13) + ;
                            "      Method: " + tcMethod + CHR(13) + ;
                            " Line Number: " + PADL(tnLine,5)

                =MESSAGEBOX(lcMessage, 48, "Foxtools Error")
        ENDCASE
    ENDPROC

    PROCEDURE Destroy
        IF this.lLoaded
            RELEASE LIBRARY (SYS(2004)+"foxtools.fll")
        ENDIF
    ENDPROC

    PROCEDURE Init
        this.lLoaded = .F.
        this.loadlib()
    ENDPROC
```

```
ENDDEFINE
*
*-- EndDefine: foxtools
*****************************************************
```

Before you go into the theory behind the class, learn all the methods and properties that make up this wrapper class. Table 15.1 presents the methods and properties for Foxtools.

Table 15.1 The Methods and Properties for Foxtools

Property/Method	Description
lLoaded	The lLoaded property is a protected property that keeps track of whether the FOXTOOLS library was loaded by this class or from the outside world. If Foxtools loaded the library, it releases the library when the instance is cleared.
addbs([tcPath])	This function is the equivalent of the AddBs() function in FOXTOOLS. It accepts a path string as a parameter and adds a backslash to it if there isn't one already.
cleandir([tcPath])	This function really doesn't use FOXTOOLS.FLL at all but has related functionality. It accepts a filename with a path attached and cleans it up with SYS(2027). Cleaning up means interpreting back steps in path strings and redrawing them. Here is an example: `oFtools.CleanDir("D:\APPS\FOX\VFP\..\") && Returns "D:\APPS\FOX\"`
copy()	This method copies selected text to the Clipboard using the _edCopy() function.
cut()	This method copies selected text to the Clipboard and then deletes it using the _edCut() function.
Destroy()	This method is called when the object is released. The method releases FOXTOOLS.FLL if the object loaded it. drivetype([tcDriveLetter]) This method calls the DriveType() function to get the type of the drive specified.
Error()	This method is called when a program error occurs in the class. It takes precedence over ON ERROR. If the error is an error number 1 (that is, file not found), the method assumes it occurred because someone unloaded FOXTOOLS.FLL, in which case the Error() method just loads the library with LoadLib() and then retries the command. If the error is something other than a "File not found" error, an error dialog box is presented.

continues

Table 15.1 Continued	
Property/Method	**Description**
Init()	This method is called when the object is instantiated. It calls LoadLib() to load the library if needed.
isdir([tcPath])	This method accepts a path string as a parameter and tests it to make sure it's a directory. This method returns a logical value.
	IsDir() does not really use Foxtools, but it is related to the functionality of the library and is therefore included here.
justdrive([tcPath])	This method accepts a filename with path string and returns only the drive designation.
justfname([tcPath])	This method is the same as JustDrive(), but it returns the filename.
justpath([tcPath])	This method is the same as JustDrive() except that it returns the path. The drive designator is included in the return value.
justpathnodrive	This method is the same as JustPath except that the drive designator is removed from the string.
juststem([tcPath])	This method is the same as JustFName() except that this returns the filename minus the extension.
loadlib()	This method loads Foxtools if it is not already loaded. lLoaded is set to .T. if this method loads the library.
paste()	This method pastes the contents of the Clipboard at the insertion point.

This class shows the various purposes of a wrapper:

- *Ease of use—encapsulating error trapping*   When a library is loaded within Visual FoxPro, it can be unloaded by other objects by issuing one command. The Foxtools class automatically loads FOXTOOLS.FLL (if it is not already loaded) when the object is instantiated. If the library is released by another module or object and a FoxTools function is called, Visual FoxPro generates a "File Not Found" error message. In this case, the error method calls the LoadLib() method to reload the library. This gives developers a simple way to use Foxtools without having to worry about someone else's code unloading the library.

- *Enhancing existing functionality*   The JustPath() function in Foxtools calculates what portion of a filename string is the path designation and returns that path as a string. The string can have a backslash at the end. In order to promote consistency, the method that calls JustPath() also calls the AddBs() method to add a backslash at the end of the string if one does not already exist there. This is an example of enhancing functionality, which gives developers a simple, consistent return value.

■ *Adding functionality*   The `CleanDir()` method is designed to adjust a path string for back steps. For example, a path string of `C:\WINAPPS\VFP\SAMPLES\DATA\..\GRAPHICS\` adjusts to `C:\WINAPPS\VFP\SAMPLES\GRAPHICS\`. This function does not call `Foxtools` at all; however, its functionality is related to the other functions included in this class. By adding a method for this function, you are giving developers access to related functionality in one place without requiring them to load multiple classes.

The ability to create and use wrapper classes is a major benefit to software development. Because the complexity of working with something can be hidden within a class without compromising the class's functionality, developers who use the wrapper will immediately notice an increase in their productivity because they can have the wrapper in their arsenals without the cost of learning its intricacies.

Manager Classes

A second type of nonvisual class that is often created is a manager class. This class typically manages instances of another class. A good example of this is the management of multiple instances of a form to ensure that subsequent instances are properly placed on the screen with an identifiable header (for example, `Document1`, `Document2`, and so on).

The example shown in Listing 15.13 deals with this issue, showing a manager class that manages a simple form class.

Listing 15.13   15CODE13—A Form Manager Class

```
*   Program..........: MANAGER.PRG
*   Author...........: Menachem Bazian, CPA
*   Created..........: 05/03/95
*)  Description.......: Sample Manager Class with Managed Form Class
*   Major change list.:

*-- This class is designed to manage a particular form class and make
*-- sure that when the forms are run they are "tiled" properly.

DEFINE CLASS FormManager AS Custom
    DECLARE aForms[1]
    nInstance = 0

    PROCEDURE RunForm
        *-- This method runs the form. The instance of the form class
        *-- is created in the aForms[] member array.

        LOCAL lnFormLeft, llnFormTop, lcFormCaption
        nInstance = ALEN(THIS.aForms)

        *-- Set the Top and Left Properties to Cascade the new Form
        IF nInstance > 1 AND TYPE('THIS.aForms[nInstance -1]') = 'O' ;
                AND NOT ISNULL(THIS.aForms[nInstance -1])
            lnFormTop = THIS.aForms[nInstance -1].Top + 20
            lnFormLeft = THIS.aForms[nInstance -1].Left + 10
```

continues

Listing 15.13   Continued

```
            ELSE
                lnFormTop = 1
                lnFormLeft = 1
            ENDIF

            *-- Set the caption to reflect the instance number
            lcFormCaption = "Instance " + ALLTRIM(STR(nInstance))

            *-- Instantiate the form and assign the object variable
            *-- to the array element

            THIS.aForms[nInstance] = CreateObject("TestForm")
            THIS.aForms[nInstance].top = lnFormTop
            THIS.aForms[nInstance].left = lnFormLeft
            THIS.aForms[nInstance].caption = lcFormCaption
            THIS.aForms[nInstance].Show()

            *-- Redimension the array so that more instances of
            *-- the form can be launched
            DIMENSION THIS.aforms[nInstance + 1]
        ENDPROC
ENDDEFINE

*-- This class is a form class that is designed to work with
*-- the manager class.

DEFINE CLASS TestForm AS form
    Top = 0
    Left = 0
    Height = 87
    Width = 294
    DoCreate = .T.
    BackColor = RGB(192,192,192)
    BorderStyle = 2
    Caption = "Form1"
    Name = "Form1"

    ADD OBJECT label1 AS label WITH ;
        FontName = "Courier New", ;
        FontSize = 30, ;
        BackStyle = 0, ;
        Caption = (time()), ;
        Height = 61, ;
        Left = 48, ;
        Top = 12, ;
        Width = 205, ;
        Name = "Label1"
ENDDEFINE
```

Notice that forms are instantiated through the RUNFORM method rather than directly with a CreateObject() function. This enables the manager function to maintain control over the objects it instantiates.

By the way, this can be considered a downside to working with manager classes, too. If a developer is used to working with the familiar CreateObject() function to instantiate classes, working through a method like the RUNFORM method might be a bit confusing at first.

By the way, remember the discussion earlier in this chapter about instance variable scoping (see "Reading System Events" and "Variable Scoping Revisited")? FormManager is an example of how to manage instance variable scoping. The aForm[] property is an array property. Each row in the array holds an instance of the form.

Figure 15.16 shows what the forms look like when they are instantiated. Notice how they are properly tiled (with the exception of a few moved aside to show the contents of the form) and that each one has a different caption and time showing.

FIGURE 15.16
Managed forms.

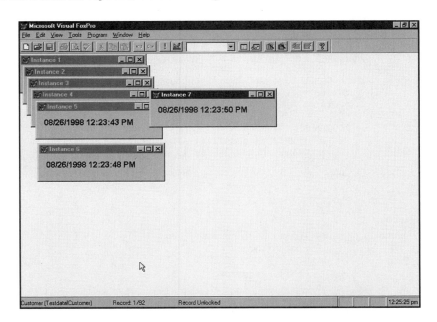

Manager functions are very useful. They provide a simple way to encapsulate code that would normally have to be duplicated every time an object is instantiated into one single place.

Business Classes

Business classes are object-oriented representations of business entities (for example, a customer). The responsibilities of these classes vary depending on the behavior of a particular object within the problem domain.

The purpose of a business class is multifold. At an abstract level, it is possible to determine the basic functionality of a business object and then to create a class around it. For example, the basic responsibilities of a business object might be the following:

- To retrieve its data from the database
- To move within the database tables (First, Last, Prev, or Next)
- To display itself
- To print itself

These functions could be abstracted in a class. *Abstracting* in this sense means that the functionality can be placed in its own class rather than repeating it in multiple classes. The abstract class is created as a basis for other classes, not to be used in instantiating objects (see Listing 15.14).

Listing 15.14   15CODE14—**A Business Class**

```
DEFINE CLASS BaseBusiness AS custom
    cAlias = ""
    oData = .NULL.

    PROCEDURE INIT
        IF !EMPTY(this.cAlias) AND !used(this.cAlias)
            =MessageBox("Alias is not open!", 16)
        ENDIF
    ENDPROC

    PROCEDURE next
        SELECT (this.cAlias)
        SKIP 1
        IF EOF()
            GO BOTTOM
        ELSE
            this.readrecord()
        ENDIF
    ENDPROC

    *-- Additional methods here for movement would mimic
    *-- procedure NEXT

    PROCEDURE readrecord
        *-- This procedure is initially empty
        SCATTER NAME this.oData
    ENDPROC

    *-- Additional methods for saving would follow mimicking
    *-- procedure readrecord.

ENDDEFINE
```

In order to create a `Customer` object, all you need to do is subclass it as follows:

```
DEFINE CLASS customer AS basebusiness
    cAlias = "Customer"
ENDDEFINE
```

The fields in the `Customer` alias are automatically added as members of `oData`. Thus, if an object called `oCust` were instantiated from the `Customer` class, the `cName` field would be held in `oCust.oData.cName`.

Of course, the beauty of this method of development is that there is little coding to do from one business class to another. In effect, all you do is code by exception.

This is one way to create business classes. You will learn more about business classes and a sample framework for working with business classes in Chapter 17.

Rounding Out the Story: Creating a Framework

The classes you create in Visual FoxPro, as in any object-oriented language, cover many different areas and serve many different purposes. Some classes will be created to serve a specific need in the software. For example, creating a `Customer` class might be an example of a class designed specifically to the needs of a software project. However, as you learned previously, classes can be created simply because the functionality represented in the class provides a good basis for further subclassing. For example, `NoNotifyTextBox` is a generic-type class you can create and reuse and from which you can subclass.

When you are starting out with an object-oriented language, the first step you probably take is to create a series of classes that will be the basis on which you create classes for your applications. These classes, taken together, are known as the *application framework*. Part of the framework will be generic; that is, they will be based on the FoxPro base classes to provide baseline functionality. For example, a subclass of the controls can be created with default font and size characteristics. A base form class can be created with a default background color, logo, and so on.

In addition, the framework might also call for a methodology for adding business classes to applications. Although working with a framework imposes some limitations, it is well worth it in terms of standardization among applications as well as speed in development. Chapter 17 shows a portion of a framework.

A good framework is the key to success in an object-oriented environment. Creating a solid framework (or purchasing one) saves you hours in the long run. However, if the framework is shoddy your application can suffer greatly. Be careful. ●

Managing Classes with Visual FoxPro

What's the big deal about managing classes? You have VCX files with classes in them. What can be so difficult? Well, as it turns out, managing class libraries is not something to take lightly. Without proper management, disaster can easily strike not only one application, but an entire department or even a company.

In Chapter 15, "Creating Classes with Visual FoxPro," you learned about application frameworks. An *application framework* can consist of hundreds of classes on which you can design other classes for your applications.

In order to properly keep track of the classes, you will probably want to keep them grouped in a logical manner in different files. For example, the *base classes* (such as NoNotifyTextBox, discussed in Chapter 15) in the framework might be stored in a .VCX file called CONTROLS.VCX. Another .VCX file might have a more specialized version of these controls (such as the OKButton and OKButtonWithToolTip classes discussed in Chapter 15). Yet a third .VCX file might have combination classes, such as the Navigator toolbar. There might be a UTILS.VCX file as well that has ObjectInspectorForm.

When you put all these disparate class libraries together, you have a basis for creating all your applications. Now, imagine what might happen if someone modified the TextBox base class and introduced a bug into it. Conceivably, every application in the company could up and die right there. Sound farfetched? Believe it.

Recently I was speaking to a user group in New York, and we got into the issue of managing class libraries. One of the attendees, who programmed in a mainframe environment (and you know how tightly a mainframe environment is controlled), told me that an application he had just modified and tested began dying shortly after he updated the production software. Immediately, the company reverted to the prior version of the software, but still the problems persisted. This set off two weeks of hectic work trying to track down the cause of the problem, but all efforts failed. Finally, as he was almost ready to give up, he bumped into a friend in the company cafeteria. After his friend remarked that he had not seen him for several weeks, the attendee explained that he had been going nuts trying to track down this problem. His friend turned red. It seems he had modified one line of code in a base routine and never told anyone—he had inadvertently introduced this bug.

The problem illustrated in this story can become even more acute in OOP. Objects, which are self-contained, are not meant to be reviewed and understood by everyone in depth. All a user needs to know is how to interact with them. If something high in the class hierarchy is accidentally broken, hundreds of classes can go south for the winter and no one will understand what happened. The key, therefore, is to ensure proper control over the class libraries.

Class Library Structure

In a typical organization, you might see as many as three levels of class libraries. The first level is a corporate-wide set of standard libraries. For example, the corporate framework and standard utilities might be part of these libraries. At the second level, a specific department or business unit within a company might have a more specialized set of classes used across their applications. For example, a set of base business classes could be created for each business unit. Finally, at the third level, each application has class libraries specifically for its own use. Figure 16.1 shows what the hierarchy would look like in terms of an organization chart.

FIGURE 16.1
The class library structure.

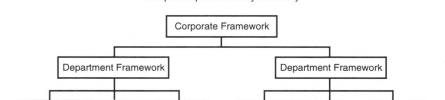

Sample Corporate Library Heirarchy

Each level of classes requires an individual responsible for managing the libraries. The generic term for such an individual is the *class librarian*.

The Class Librarian

The class librarian's job is to control what goes into the class libraries. At the corporate level, a corporate class librarian is responsible for the content and integrity of the corporate framework. Each department has similar responsibilities. The leader of each application project, or someone he or she designates, does the same for the application libraries.

Criteria for Inclusion in Class Libraries

It would be unfair to assume that the class libraries at any level should be static and not subject to change. First of all, as time goes by, enhancements can and should be introduced. Developers will work on applications and might have significant contributions to make to the frameworks, in terms of new and enhanced classes. No one is suggesting that this should not take place, but rather that it should be controlled.

Classes that are created for inclusion in the class libraries at any of the three levels are created by the developers and stored in temporary .VCX files. When the developer is done with the classes and is satisfied with their completion, the classes are submitted to the appropriate class librarian for consideration.

The class librarian should carefully review each class for the following items:

- *Completeness*—The class must accomplish the agreed-to responsibilities. It should also trap the appropriate errors, and so on.
- *Standards*—Many organizations have standards, such as naming conventions for variables, properties, and methods, commenting requirements, and so on. The class librarian, or someone designated by the class librarian, reviews the code to ensure that it

meets the organization's standards. Without strict adherence to standards, the class library will be almost impossible to maintain.

- *Documentation*—Any good class library is well-documented. The documentation should discuss the public interface (such as methods that are callable, what public properties do and mean and what their return values are, and so on). The documentation must be complete, so that someone totally unfamiliar with the class can use it in the course of developing applications by either directly instantiating or subclassing the class. The rule should be "No documentation, no acceptance."

- *Robustness*—The robustness of a class refers to how resistant the class is to errors. For example, if a bad parameter is sent to a method, will the method gracefully catch the errors or will it bomb?

- *Compatibility*—The class librarian must ascertain that the new class will not break any old code. It is probably a good idea to have a test case for every new class so that subsequent versions can be tested for compatibility. It should be axiomatic that any new or modified class must be properly and completely tested against existing code. This should be viewed as a primary responsibility of the class librarian.

Merging the New Classes

After the submitted classes have been reviewed and approved, the next step is to merge the classes into the class libraries. This should take place at regular intervals—once a week or once a month. A rapidly changing class library is difficult on developers because it removes the important element of stability. In addition, once merging is complete, the class librarian should inform all the class libraries' users about the changes and additions.

As a good rule of thumb, never make a change to the class libraries without telling everyone about it. That way, if something does accidentally break, the developer will have a good idea where to look.

Technical Aspects of Managing Class Libraries

On the technical side, there are three basic actions a librarian normally has to take regarding the management of classes in .vcx files:

- Moving or copying a class from one class library file to another
- Changing the name of a class
- Removing a class from a class library

Visual FoxPro has commands for each of these tasks.

Copying a Class

The ADD CLASS command is used to copy a class from one visual class library file to another. Here's the syntax:

```
ADD CLASS <ClassName>;
    [OF <ClassLibrary1>] ;
    TO <ClassLibrary2> ;
    [OVERWRITE]
```

ClassName is the name of an existing class. The class can be a class already accessible in a VCX file loaded with SET CLASSLIB, or it can be one you specifically reference from *<ClassLibrary1>* with the optional OF *<ClassLibrary1>* clause. The name of the VCX file in which to store the class is specified with the TO *<ClassLibrary2>* clause.

If the class already exists in *<ClassLibrary2>*, an error is generated by Visual FoxPro to prevent the accidental overwriting of a class in a class library. The OVERWRITE keyword overrides this message and automatically overwrites the existing class.

Removing a Class

The REMOVE CLASS command removes a class from a class library. Here is the syntax:

```
REMOVE CLASS <ClassName> OF <ClassLibrary>
```

ClassName is the name of the class to remove, and *ClassLibrary* is the name of the VCX file from which the class is removed.

> **CAUTION**
>
> Removing a class is very dangerous because it can break the chain in a class hierarchy. For example, if you have a class hierarchy and remove one of the classes in the middle of the hierarchy, you will invalidate everything from the class you deleted on down. You will not be able to even edit those classes. As far as native Visual FoxPro is concerned, the classes are toast. Period.
>
> So, what do you do if you accidentally remove a class? The simple answer is to open the .VCX file as a table and recall (using the RECALL command) the records you just deleted. Visual FoxPro does not have a command for deleting a level from a class hierarchy. You can do it with the Class Browser's redefine feature, which is covered later in this chapter.

Moving a Class Between Class Libraries

There is no MOVE CLASS command. In order to move a class, you need to copy it into the new class library and then remove it from the original one.

Renaming a Class

You can change a class in a visual class library file using the RENAME CLASS command. Here is the syntax:

```
RENAME CLASS <OldClassName> ;
    OF <ClassLibrary> ;
    TO <NewClassName>
```

OldClassName is the class name as it exists in the VCX file prior to the renaming. ClassLibrary is the name of the VCX file, and NewClassName is the new name for the class.

> **CAUTION**
>
> Be *very* careful with this command. If you rename a class, it only affects the classes open in the Class Browser. Therefore, any classes subclassed from this class that are *not* currently open in an open instance of the Class Browser will no longer be able to find it. Starting with Visual FoxPro 5.0, the Class Browser updates references to a renamed class in all associated subclasses that are open in Class Browser windows.

How would you successfully rename a class that has subclasses if the subclasses were not open in the Class Browser when the class was renamed? The easiest way is to open all subclasses in the Class Browser before you rename a class. If you forgot to do that when you renamed a file, you will have to modify the .VCX file. This may seem scary, but actually it is pretty easy. A .VCX file is a table and can be opened with the USE command. Open the .VCX file, look for instances of the old class name in the CLASS field, and manually change them to the new class name.

I know this sounds scary, but I have done this many times successfully. If you're worried, back up the old class library first. Actually, come to think of it, you should back up the old class library anyway. Paranoia is definitely your friend here.

If you missed a record in the .VCX, don't worry. When you try to edit a class based on the renamed class that has not had the parent class name changed, FoxPro will return an error. You can cancel at that point, find the offending name in the class field, and fix it before moving on.

Finally, if you use the class in a form or container, that container will be affected as well and will not be editable until the appropriate change is made.

If you don't like the idea of opening the .VCX file manually and doing batch updates, there is another alternative. Using the Class Browser's Redefine feature, you can manually redefine each class to work off the newly renamed class. You can only do it one class at a time, but it will work.

The other alternative is to create an add-in for the Class Browser so that it can go through the class tree and handle all the work for you. The Class Browser is covered after the next section. Look for an add-in to take care of this issue for you.

Managing Classes Visually

Visual FoxPro gives you the commands to perform the rudimentary functions associated with managing class libraries. Add, Remove, and Rename basically cover the bulk of what you want to do.

On the other hand, they aren't very pretty. After you've seen the fancy Form Designer and Visual Class Designer, you would probably be disappointed if you had to manage class libraries by hand. Fortunately, you don't. That's where the Class Browser comes in.

The Class Browser

The Class Browser is a Visual FoxPro application (written entirely in Visual FoxPro) that's designed to provide a user-friendly, visual way to work with and manage class libraries. Loading a class library into the Class Browser provides all the functionality you have learned (and much more) at the touch of a mouse button.

There is one interesting note about the Class Browser. When I think of the Class Browser, I think of it for managing classes. However, because the file structures of .scx and .vcx files are identical, the Class Browser also enables you to load .scx files. This is really nice because most (but not all) of the Class Browser's functionality works equally well with a .scx-based form as it does with a .vcx file. Figure 16.2 shows you what the Class Browser looks like.

FIGURE 16.2

The Class Browser with its Shortcut menu open.

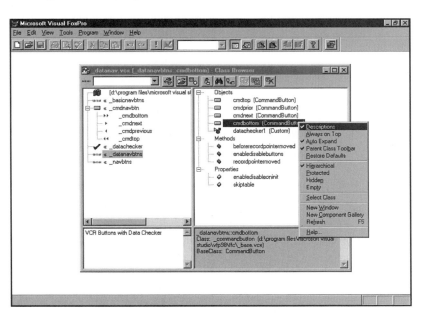

The interface is very clean. The following sections explain the features presented in the Class Browser.

Form Caption

The title of the Class Browser form shows the name of the currently selected class and the name of the .vcx or .scx file to which the selected class belongs.

Action Buttons

At the top of this modeless form is a series of command buttons that launch the bulk of the Class Browser's actions. Here is a list of them:

Button	Purpose
Component Gallery	Toggles between the Component Gallery and the Class Browser. The Component Gallery is described in Chapter 19, "The Visual FoxPro Component Gallery."
Open	Opens a class library. Any open class libraries are closed when the new one is opened.
View Additional File	Opens an additional class library and shows it with the current one. This is useful when the parent class of a class is stored in a different .vcx file.
View Class Code	Exports the code for the currently selected class and shows it in a window. If the currently selected class is the .vcx file itself, the entire class library is exported all at once.
Find	Finds text within a class in the open libraries.
New Class	Creates a new class based on the currently selected class. To create a new class in a .vcx file based on a Visual FoxPro base class, position the list on the .vcx file item and then click the New Class button.
Rename	Renames the currently selected class.
Redefine	Changes the parent class of the current class.
Remove	Deletes the currently highlighted class.
Clean Up Class Library	Packs the .vcx file associated with the currently selected class.
Add-Ins	Runs an installed add-in. Add-in buttons are placed at the right side of the toolbar. However, none are present in Figure 16.2.

As you can see, there is a lot here. The following sections explain the functions of the command buttons.

If you right-click on a member in the Member list (right panel), a shortcut menu opens, as shown in Figure 16.2. You can also right-click on a class in the Class list (left panel) or the Class Browser toolbar. The shortcut menu is context-sensitive, and the Class Browser displays only those menu items that are relevant to the object on which you've right-clicked. Here is a list of the shortcut menu items:

Button	Purpose
Descriptions	Toggles on (checked) and off the display of class library and class descriptions at the bottom of the screen. The Class and Members Description panels are displayed only if this option is checked.
Always on Top	When checked, the Class Browser stays on top all the time.
Auto Expand	When checked, the class list expands or collapses automatically when it refreshes.
Parent Class Toolbar	When checked, a button is placed on the Visual FoxPro Systems toolbar that you can click on to edit the ParentClass's method.

Restore Defaults	Restores Class Browser settings to their defaults, which are as follows:
	
	√ Descriptions
	  Always on Top
	√ Auto Expand
	√ Hierarchical
	  Protected
	  Hidden
	  Empty Filter

Hierarchical	When checked, classes are displayed in a hierarchy. Subclasses are displayed beneath parent classes. When not checked, classes are displayed in alphabetic order.
Protected	When checked, the Class Browser displays protected members in the Members list.
Hidden	When checked, the Class Browser displays hidden members in the Members list.
Empty	When checked, the Class Browser displays empty methods in the Members list.
Modify	Launches the Class Designer to modify the selected class or launch the Form Designer to modify a form.

continues

continued

Button	Purpose
Rename	Renames the selected class, property, or member. For classes, the Class Browser renames all references to a renamed class in all files open in all instances of the Class Browser.
Redefine	Selects a new `ParentClass` for the selected class.
Remove	Removes a selected class.
View	Views the current value for a selected property.
Font	Chooses a font attribute for all of the controls in the Class Browser.
Export	Saves to a file and displays the class definition, values of the properties, and method code for the selected class.
Container Icon	Selects an icon for the selected class.
Select ParentClass	Selects the parent class of the selected class. If the Class Browser does not already display the `ParentClass`, the visual class library containing the `ParentClass` is added to the Class Browser.
New Window	Creates a new incidence of the Class Browser Window.
New Component Gallery	Creates a new Component Gallery window.
Refresh (F5)	Refreshes the Class Browser display.
Add-ins	Selects an add-in to place on the toolbar from a menu of all registered add-in programs, classes, and applications.
Help	Launches Visual FoxPro Help for the Class Browser.

Open   This button opens a file; both .VCX and .SCX files can be opened. Visual FoxPro shows a GetFile() dialog box with the list of .VCX files in the current directory (actually, the last directory GetFile() looked to, but that's another story). From this dialog box, you select a file. To select a .SCX file, change the file filter at the bottom of the dialog box. Figure 16.3 shows the dialog box with .SCX files.

Selecting Cancel aborts the request to open a file. Also, when you open a new file, all files already opened in the Class Browser are closed.

View Additional File   This button enables you to show an additional file in the Class Browser. This is extremely useful when files are stored in more than one .VCX file.

View Class Code   This button generates code for the currently selected class and shows the code in a window. If a file is selected in the class list, all classes in the file are generated and shown.

FIGURE 16.3
The Class Browser
`GetFile()` dialog box,
showing `.SCX` files.

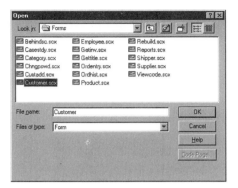

For the most part, the code generated will run if it is pasted into a `.PRG` file, but there are limitations to this. For example, if you have a container on a form (such as a page frame) with objects added to the class, the code presented in Listing 16.1 is generated by the Class Browser and will not run. Figure 16.4 shows what the form looks like in the designer.

FIGURE 16.4
The `WontRun` form.

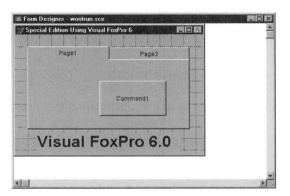

Listing 16.1 `16CODE01`—**Example of a Program Generated by the Class Browser Export Operation That Will Not Run**

```
*****************************************************
*-- Form:         frmwontrun (d:\seufpw6\chap16\wontrun.scx)
*-- ParentClass:  form
*-- BaseClass:    form
*-- Notes:        Exported code from Class Browser
DEFINE CLASS frmwontrun AS form
DoCreate = .T.
Caption = "Special Edition Using Visual FoxPro 6"
Name = "frmwontrun"
ADD OBJECT pageframe1 AS pageframe WITH ;
```

continues

Listing 16.1   Continued

```
ErasePage = .T., ;
        PageCount = 2, ;
        Top = 24, ;
        Left = 24, ;
        Width = 325, ;
        Height = 173, ;
        Name = "Pageframe1", ;
        Page1.Caption = "Page1", ;
        Page1.Name = "Page1", ;
        Page2.Caption = "Page2", ;
        Page2.Name = "Page2"


    ADD OBJECT frmwontrun.pageframe1.page1.command1 AS commandbutton WITH ;
        Top = 44, ;
        Left = 143, ;
        Height = 73, ;
        Width = 133, ;
        Caption = "Command1", ;
        Name = "Command1"


    ADD OBJECT label1 AS label WITH ;
        FontBold = .T., ;
        FontSize = 24, ;
        Caption = "Visual FoxPro 6.0", ;
        Height = 48, ;
        Left = 43, ;
        Top = 204, ;
        Width = 288, ;
        Name = "Label1"


  ENDDEFINE
  *
  *-- EndDefine: frmwontrun
  ****************************************************
```

Note that this form will run fine with a DO FORM command. Running it as a .PRG file doesn't work—it will bomb when it attempts to the add the command button to the page frame.

Find   This button presents a dialog box (see Figure 16.5) where you enter the text you want to find. The text is first searched for in the names of the classes, then in the class descriptions, and finally in the descriptions of the custom methods and properties.

New Class   This button creates a new class. If the currently selected class is actually a filename, the Class Browser assumes that the parent class is a base class and displays the New Class dialog box accordingly (see Figure 16.6). Notice how the name of the file where the new class is stored is automatically filled in. The Store In object on the dialog box defaults to the name of the .VCX where the currently selected class is stored.

FIGURE 16.5
The Find dialog box.

FIGURE 16.6
The New Class dialog box, based on a base class.

If a class is selected in the class list, the Class Browser assumes that the new class is a subclass of the currently selected class. Accordingly, all the fields in the dialog box are automatically filled in. All you have to supply is a class name (see Figure 16.7).

FIGURE 16.7
A new subclass.

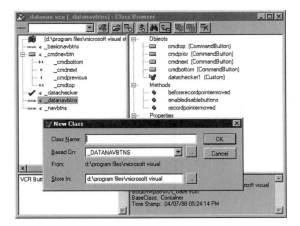

Rename This button enables you to rename a class in the dialog box that is displayed (see Figure 16.8).

> **CAUTION**
> Just a friendly reminder: The caution I gave you for the RENAME CLASS command in the section "Renaming a Class" applies here too.

Redefine This button or shortcut menu item enables you to change the parent class of the currently selected class. This function is available only in the Class Browser, by the way. Here's how it works.

FIGURE 16.8

The Rename dialog box.

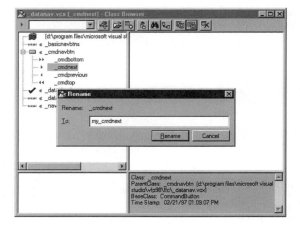

The Redefine dialog box is displayed (see Figure 16.9). In order to redefine a class as a sub-class of its Visual FoxPro base class, leave the fields blank and select Redefine. Otherwise, type in the name of the class to be the new parent class. Note that the dialog box automatically assumes that the new parent class is in the same class library as the class you are redefining. If it isn't, you will have to either type in the name of the class library or click on the command button with the ellipsis on it to get a GetFile() dialog box to select the .VCX file.

FIGURE 16.9

The Redefine dialog box.

There is one restriction on this function. The new parent class must have the same base class as the prior one. For example, you can't redefine a CommandButton-based class as a CheckBox-based class.

Remove   The Remove button or shortcut menu item deletes the currently selected class. The Class Browser gives you a warning before it deletes the class.

> **CAUTION**
>
> The caution I gave about REMOVE CLASS in the section "Removing a Class" applies here, too.

Clean Up Class Library   This option packs the .VCX file.

Add-Ins   This option displays a list of add-ins. See the section "Putting It All Together with Add-Ins" later in this chapter for more information.

Type Filter

If you have multiple .VCX files open or have a lot of classes in one file, it may be difficult to find classes in the list. The Type filter at the left of the toolbar enables you to set a filter on the type of class in the list. The dropdown list box shows the list of Visual FoxPro base classes (CommandButton, ToolBar, and so on). As an alternative, you can type in class names to filter the list. Figure 16.10 shows the Class Browser with a filter applied.

Part
IV

Ch

16

FIGURE 16.10
The Class Browser with a filter applied.

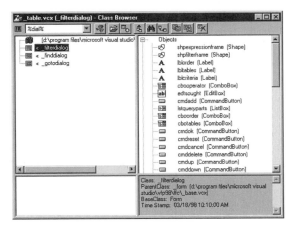

The Type filter fully supports wildcards. For example, to find every class with "Button" in the name, you could specify %Dial% (case doesn't matter). Button* shows all classes with names beginning with "Button". The question mark (?) is a single-character wildcard.

If you type in your own filters, they are automatically added to the filter list for that session.

Display Method

The Class Browser can show the classes in hierarchical order (the default order) or in alphabetical order. Hierarchical order shows the classes in tree form, with subclasses beneath parent classes. Alphabetical order ignores the class hierarchy and just shows all the listed classes in alphabetical order. Figure 16.11 shows the Class Browser in alphabetical order.

Protected Member

By default, the Class Browser will not list protected properties and methods when a class is displayed. If you select the Protected shortcut menu item, the protected members are displayed at the appropriate position in the member's list. If this menu option is selected, a check mark appears to the left of the Protected Member menu item. If a property or method is protected, it is shown in the Members list and is preceded with an asterisk (*), and a protected icon (a key) appears next to the member's icon. See Figure 16.11 for examples of protected members.

FIGURE 16.11
The class list in
alphabetical order.

Empty Method

By default, custom methods (methods not inherited from prior classes) that are attached to a class will be displayed only if there is code in them. If you select the Empty shortcut menu item, the empty methods are displayed at the appropriate place in the Members list. If this menu option is selected, a check mark appears to the left of the Empty Method menu item.

If an empty method is shown in the Members list, the method's name is preceded by a tilde (-).

Hidden Members

By default, the Class Browser does not display hidden properties or methods in the Members list. A hidden member can not be accessed or modified outside of its associated class. If you select the Hidden shortcut menu item, the hidden members are displayed at the appropriate place in the Members list. If this menu option is selected, a check mark appears to the left of the Empty Method menu item.

If an empty method is shown in the Members list, the member's name is preceded by a tilde and a hidden icon (a lock) is displayed beside the member's icon in the member list. You can see examples of hidden members in Figure 16.11.

Class Icon

The Class icon is the picture just above the left corner of the list of classes. It's a visual representation of the class currently selected in the list. You can set the icon in the Class Information screens by right-clicking on it. This is discussed in Chapter 15.

The icon is more than a picture, though. It is also the Drag/Drop button. Clicking and dragging this icon to a form in design mode will automatically add that class to the form. It is functionally equivalent to loading the class library into the Form Controls toolbar and dropping the class library on the form.

But there's more. By dropping the icon on the desktop, you attempt to instantiate and run the class right then and there. This can be a cool way to test your classes, especially for most form classes.

Finally, you can use drag-and-drop to move or copy classes from one .VCX file to another. Here's how you do it. Open the Class Browser twice (once for each .VCX file). To open a new Class Browser instance, choose the New Window menu item from the shortcut menu. Then open another visual class library. Grab the Class icon that you want to move and drag it to the other Class Browser instance, as shown in Figure 16.12. If you want to copy the class, press the Ctrl key while you drag the Copy icon. Be careful, and watch the drag icon to make sure that it changes to the Move or Copy icon before you drop the class. The Copy icon is like the Move icon, except it contains a plus sign (+). When you drop the class, it will be added to the second Class Browser instance.

FIGURE 16.12

The Class Browser with the Class icon.

Class icon ———

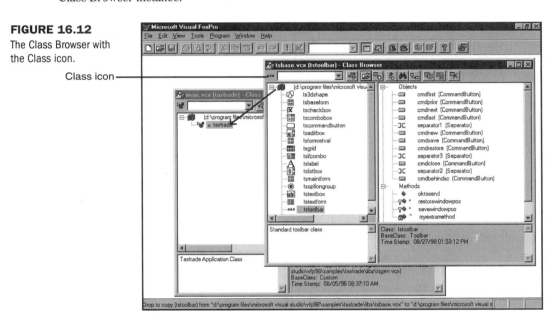

List of Classes

The Class list is in the left panel of the Class Browser. This list is based on the outline control that ships with Visual FoxPro. When the Class list is in hierarchical mode, you can expand or contract a branch of classes by clicking the + or - icons.

Double-clicking the class name loads the class into the Visual Class Designer for editing. Double-clicking the folder moves to the parent class for that class.

If a class is based on a class in another .VCX file that is not shown, a chevron (<<) appears between the folder and the class name. (See Figure 16.13.) If you choose the Show Parent Class item from the shortcut menu, the Class Browser automatically loads the .VCX file with the parent classes before moving to the parent class, as shown in Figure 16.14.

FIGURE 16.13
A class based on another .VCX class.

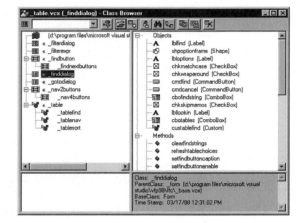

FIGURE 16.14
The Class Browser with a parent .VCX file loaded.

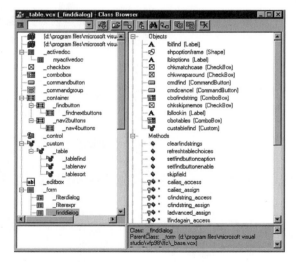

Members List

The right panel of the Class Browser shows the members of the currently selected class as a hierarchy, with a tree branch for Object Members, Methods, and Properties.

Class Description

This edit box enables you to view and edit the description for a class. The description entered in this box is automatically placed in the .VCX file and appears in the Description box of the Class Info dialog box. This is particularly nice because it is not uncommon to add some descriptions at the end of the process, and this saves having to go into the Visual Class Designer to do so.

Member Description

This edit box is the description of a selected member in the Member lists. For example, if an object member is selected, the edit box will show the class and base class names of the object member. For methods and properties, the edit box is read/write and has the description for the property or method entered in the New Property/Method or Edit Property/Method dialog box. Because this edit box is read/write, you can enter or edit the description in the Class Browser and have the description carry forward to the .VCX file. Finally, if an instance variable is selected, the edit box is read-only and shows information about the instance.

Starting the Class Browser

You can start the Class Browser in one of three ways. One way is to use the menu by selecting Tools, Class Browser. A dialog box appears and asks you for the name of the class library to load. If you type in the name of a class library that does not exist, the Class Browser creates it for you.

The second way to load the Class Browser is to use the _browser system variable. _browser is typically set to BROWSER.APP, which is located in the Visual FoxPro home directory. Issuing the command

```
DO (_browser)
```

is equivalent to using the menus. In addition, you can pass a parameter through with the name of the class library to load. The following example will load ABOUT.VCX for the TASTRADE sample application:

```
DO (_browser) WITH HOME()+"samples\mainsamp\libs\about"
```

Optionally, you can add a second parameter to the command that will automatically select a particular class from the list. The following example will load the About library and select the Aboutbox class:

```
DO (_browser) WITH HOME()+"samples\mainsamp\libs\about", ;
    "aboutbox"
```

The next example will start the Class Browser with the form Customer.SCX loaded:

```
DO (_browser) WITH HOME()+"samples\Tastrade\Forms\customer.scx"
```

The Class Browser and .SCX Files

 TIP One neat feature of the Class Browser shows an SCX file in the hierarchy with its parent class.

Visual FoxPro enables you to use the Tool, Options menu item on the Forms tab to specify what the form template class is (see Figure 16.15). The template form is the form used as the base class when a new form is created with CREATE FORM.

FIGURE 16.15
Specifying
DefaultForm.

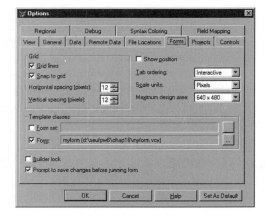

Suppose you have a form class called DefaultForm and you create a form with CREATE FORM. The form I created to illustrate this is called FromDef. Figure 16.16 shows the form in the Form Designer.

Now you can bring up the form in the Class Browser, as shown in Figure 16.17. For the record, I have also added the .VCX file with the DefaultForm class in it. Although FormDef is an .SCX-based form, it shows up in the proper place in the class hierarchy in the Class Browser class list.

There's more. Once you get a view like this one going, you can even change your form's parent class (that is, its super class) with the Redefine function. Cool stuff.

Under the Hood with the Class Browser

The next step in working with the Class Browser is to understand the methods, properties, and object members that make up the class. Why, you ask? One of the nicest features of the Class Browser is that, as an object, it is totally open and extensible. You can manually call methods from outside the Class Browser. Here is an example:

```
_obrowser.cmdexport.click()
```

This example runs the Click() method behind the Export item in the shortcut menu, and brings up the code for the currently selected class as if the button had been clicked.

FIGURE 16.16

`FromDef.SCX` in the Form Designer.

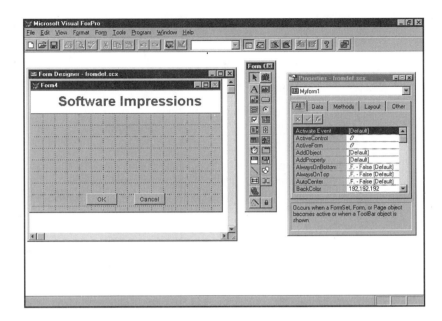

Part IV
Ch 16

FIGURE 16.17

Class Browser with `FormDef.SCX`.

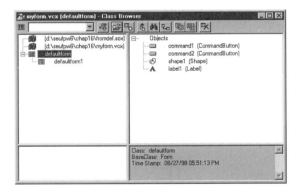

Being able to access the methods and properties of the Class Browser is important for two reasons. First of all, it enables you to create programs that can interact with the Class Browser in all kinds of ways. The public methods and properties of the Class Browser and all its members are open for you to work with at your pleasure. The second reason is that the Class Browser supports add-ins, which can be hooked to objects and methods in the Class Browser. You'll learn about add-ins later in this chapter in the section "Putting It All Together with Add-Ins."

The point here, however, is that in order to use these powerful capabilities, you have to know what goes on under the hood of the Class Browser.

By the way, _oBrowser is the name of a system memory variable that references the Class Browser when it is up (otherwise it is .NULL.). This is typically the way in which you would access the Class Browser's properties and methods (as opposed to using _screen.activeform). If you find the name lengthy, you can always assign it to another, shorter variable name.

The next step: the object members, methods, and properties of the Class Browser.

Object Members

The object members listed here are all named with standard naming conventions. For example, an object with a name starting with CMD is a command button.

Object Name	Class Browser Object
cmdOpen	Open command button
cmdAdd	Add command button
cmdExport	View Class Definition Code command button
cmdFind	Find command button
cmdSubclass	Add Subclass command button
cmdRename	Rename command button
cmdRedefine	Redefine command button
cmdRemove	Remove command button
cmdCleanup	Clean Up Library command button
opgDisplayMode	Display Mode option group
optHierarchical	Hierarchical option button
optAlphabetical	Alphabetical option button
chkProtected	Protected check box
chkEmpty	Empty check box
imgClassIcon	Class Icon image
cmdClassIcon	Class Icon command button
lblClassType	Type label for the Type combo box
cboClassType	Type combo box
txtClassList3D	Class List 3D effects control
oleClassList	Class List Outline OLE container
txtMembers3D	Members List 3D effects control
oleMembers	Members List Outline OLE container
lstMembers	Objects Member listbox
lstClassList	Methods list box
edtClassDesc	Class Description edit box
edtMemberDesc	Member Description edit box

The properties and methods of these objects are available for your use. As you saw earlier, you can call the methods with ease. You can also change the properties of these objects. For example, you could change the ToolTipText property of the cmdFind button as follows:

```
_oBrowser.cmdFind.ToolTipText = "Find that darn class!"
```

When this line of code executes, the Export Code ToolTip will be displayed when the mouse button hovers over the View Class Code button (as shown in Figure 16.18).

FIGURE 16.18
The Class Browser showing new tooltip text.

Find button

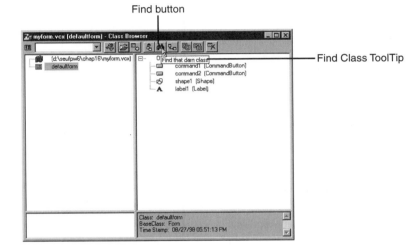

Find Class ToolTip

You can also hide an object by setting its visible property to .F.. This is a way to temporarily "remove" an object from the Class Browser form. Keep this one in mind, because I'll come back to it.

Methods

The Class Browser supports all the methods in the Form class (on which it is based). In addition, the following methods are supported.

AddClass()   This method copies a class from one class library (.VCX) file to another. AddClass() is used after a drag-and-drop operation between instances of the Class Browser. If the specified class does not exist, a class is created.

AddFile([<VCXFileName>])   This method adds a .VCX file to the Class Browser class list. It is used by the cmdAdd button to add a file to the Class Browser. If no parameters are passed, an AddFile dialog box appears by using the Class Browser GetFile method.

VCXFileName is the name of the file to add. It can be a .VCX file (which is the assumed extension) or an .SCX file (if you specify .SCX in the filename).

AddIn()   This method registers or removes an add-in in the Class Browser. See "Putting It All Together with Add-Ins" for a discussion of add-ins in the Class Browser, what they mean and how they can help you, and what methods the Class Browser has to support them.

AddInMenu()   This method displays the menu of installed add-ins. See the section on add-ins.

AddInMethod()   This method runs a method associated with an add-in. See the section on add-ins.

AutoRefresh()   This method determines whether the current class needs to be refreshed, and automatically refreshes the class if needed (that is, the list of members is automatically rebuilt).

BinToInt(cBinaryValue)   This method returns an integer value resulting from the conversion of a string containing a binary number. For example, a string containing "0101" would return 5.

CleanUpFile()   This method packs the .VCX file associated with the currently selected class.

ClearBrowser()   This method is for internal use only.

ClearClass(<lClearAll>)   This method releases the cache of classes from memory. It executes the Visual FoxPro CLEAR CLASS command for a designated class. Or, if the parameter, lClearAll, is true (.T.), it releases all of the classes from memory.

DisplayMenu(<tnMenuMode>)   This method displays shortcut memory based on the position of the mouse. The value of the tnMenuMode variable determines the shortcut menu that is displayed. Here are the allowable values:

TnMenuMode	Shortcut Menu
0	Class List shortcut menu
2	Member List shortcut menu

DeactivateMenu()   This method closes the menu of installed add-ins. See the section on add-ins.

DoAddIn([<cAddInName>])   This method executes either the current add-in or the add-in associated with specified record (cAddInName) from the table with the BROWSER alias. See the section on add-ins.

ExportClass([<tlShow>][,<cToFileName>])   This method generates the code for the currently selected class and then returns the text as a string. If the optional logical parameter is sent through as .T., a window will pop up with the code. If the path and filename of the output file is specified, the code is exported to the file.

FileMatch([cFileName][, cFileList])   This method searches the file list (cFileList) for a match on the specified file (cFileName) to find out if the file is associated with an add-in.

FindClass([<tcTextToFind>]) This method looks through the classes loaded in the Class Browser for the text passed. It first searches for the text as the name of a class in the list. If it does not find the text to match a name of a class, it then searches the class description. If it does not find the text in the class description, it then looks in the member names and descriptions for the text.

If the optional parameter *<tcTextToFind>* is not passed, a dialog box is displayed that enables you to type in the text to find.

FormAddObject(<Object Name> [, <X Coord>] [, <Y Coord>] [, <Activate Form?>] [, <Design Mode?>]) This method adds an instance of the selected class to an external form. Here is what the parameters mean:

Part
IV

Ch
16

Object Name	The name of the form to which you want to add the class. The form can be running or a form in design mode.
X Coord	This parameter is the horizontal position. It defaults to the current mouse position.
Y Coord	This parameter is the vertical position. It defaults to the current mouse position used.
Activate Form?	This is a logical parameter. If the parameter is true (.T.), the destination form is activated when the object is added to it. If the parameter is false (.F.), the Class Browser remains active.
Design Mode?	This is a logical parameter. If true (.T.), the object reference is an object currently in the Form Designer or Class Designer.

FormAddObject is a useful method that enables you to do some interesting things. For example, consider the form presented in Listing 16.2.

Listing 16.2 16CODE02—Example Form Class Code Exported from the Class Browser

```
*  Form.............: RUNFORM.SCX
*  Author...........: Menachem Bazian, CPA
*  Notes............: Exported code from Class Browser.

*****************************************************
*-- Form:          form1 (runform.scx)
*-- ParentClass:   form
*-- BaseClass:     form
*
DEFINE CLASS form1 AS form

    DoCreate = .T.
    Caption = "Form1"
    Name = "Form1"
```

continues

Listing 16.2 Continued

```
PROCEDURE DragDrop
    LPARAMETERS oSource, nXCoord, nYCoord

    oSource.Parent.FormAddObject(this)
ENDPROC

ENDDEFINE
*
*-- EndDefine: form1
****************************************************
```

The code in the DragDrop method accepts a parameter called oSource, which is the object dropped on the form.

With this code, run the form with the Class Browser running. Then take a class from the Class Browser, drag it over the running form, and drop it. The DragDrop event for the form is activated. In this case, oSource represents the oSource property of the Class Browser. Thus, oSource.Parent references the Class Browser itself. Calling FormAddObject and passing it the form as a parameter adds the currently selected class in the Class Browser (that is, the class you dropped onto the running form) to the form.

FormatMethods(<Method Text>) This method formats the text of generated methods in the display of the class definition code. The text of the methods is passed in the one parameter to the method. This method is designed for internal use, but could be useful if you want to create your own export utility.

FormatProperties(<Properties Text>, lAddObject) This method formats the text of generated properties in the display of the class definition code (that is, lines with ADD OBJECT and a list of properties set on that command line). The text of the ADD OBJECT command is passed through in the one parameter to the method. This method is designed for internal use, but could be useful if you want to create your own export utility.

GetFile(<File Extensions>) This method opens the Class Browser GetFile dialog box and is intended for internal use. The difference between the GetFile method and the GetFile function is that the GetFile method will automatically read the cFileExt property of the Class Browser for the list of file extensions to list in the file filter on the GetFile dialog box.

IndentText(<Code>) This method indents a block of text (passed in the Code parameter) by one tab.

ModifyClass() This method opens the Visual Class Designer for the currently highlighted class.

MsgBox(<Message> [, <Dialog box Type>] [, <Dialog box Title>]) Based on the MessageBox function, this method brings up a message dialog box. The differences between this method and the MessageBox function are that the icon defaults to the exclamation point, the title defaults to the caption of the Class Browser window, and the buttons are OK and Cancel by default.

NewClass() This method creates a subclass of the selected class in the class list. To create a new class in a .VCX file based on a Visual FoxPro base class, position the list on the .VCX file item and then run NewClass().

NewFile([<FileName>] [, <Open Automatically?>]) This method creates a new .VCX file. If no parameters are passed, the Open File dialog box is displayed. If the FileName parameter is passed and is a new class library (.VCX file), the .VCX is automatically created (without the dialog box). Specifying .T. to the second parameter will automatically add the new .VCX file to the class list in Class Browser.

OpenFile([<FileName>]) This method opens a file and is the equivalent of the Open button. Passing a filename will open the file. If no filename is passed, an Open dialog box is displayed.

ProperBaseClass(<Base Class Name>) This method accepts a class name and makes a "proper" name out of it. For example, commandbutton becomes CommandButton. If the class name passed through is not the name of a FoxPro base class, the method capitalizes it (for example, mycommandbutton becomes Mycommandbutton).

RedefineClass([<New Parent Class>] [, <VCX File>]) RedefineClass redefines the currently selected class to be a subclass of <New Parent Class>, which is contained in <VCX File>.

> **CAUTION**
> The same caution regarding the renaming classes discussed in the "Renaming a Class" section applies here.

RefreshButtons() This method refreshes the Class Browser command buttons based on the file type. Different command buttons are enabled and disabled based on the type of file loaded (.VCX or .SCX file). This method checks the buttons against the file type.

RefreshClassIcon() This method reloads the class icon from the icon file.

RefreshClassList([<Class to Select>][, <Ignore the table?>]) This method refreshes the class list. The first parameter dictates which class should be selected when the refresh is done. The second rebuilds the list based on the internal arrays and ignores the underlying .VCX file table.

RefreshClassListSubclass() This method is for internal use only.

RefreshFileAttrib() The Class Browser has a property called lReadOnly that signifies the read-only attribute of a Visual Class library. (A file can be flagged as read-only in FILER, for example.) This method checks the read-only attribute of the .VCX file and updates lReadOnly based on what it determines.

RefreshCaption() This method refreshes the caption of the Class Browser form.

RefreshDescriptions() This method is for internal use only.

RefreshMembers([tcDefaultMember])   This method refreshes the Members list to display the members associated with the selected class in the class list.

RefreshPrefRecNo()   This method refreshes the BROWSER.DBF preference record pointer for the class library (.VCX file) or form (.SCX file) being edited.

RefreshRecNo()   This method refreshes the current record pointer of the class library (.VCX file) or form table (.SCX file) for the file of the selected class.

RemoveClass([<Confirm Before Removal?>])   This method removes the selected class in the class list from its associated class library (.VCX) file. If .T. is passed, the Class Browser will present a warning before removing the class.

> **CAUTION**
>
> By default, this method removes the selected class without a warning. Beware of this. If you accidentally remove a class, it will be deleted from the .VCX file. To recover a class, you will have to open the .VCX file and recall the records manually.

RenameClass(<New Class Name>)   This method changes the class name of the selected class in the class list to the name specified in the parameter. If a name is not passed, a dialog box is presented that enables you to enter the new class name.

> **CAUTION**
>
> The same caution regarding the renaming classes discussed in the "Renaming a Class" section applies here.

SavePreferences()   This method saves current preference settings to the BROWSER.DBF registration table. BROWSER.DBF is a table similar to the FOXUSER file. It saves preferences for every .VCX file opened. The preferences saved include items such as form size, left and top coordinates, and so on. Add-in registrations are also saved in BROWSER.DBF.

ScaleResize()   When the Class Browser form is resized, the controls on it are automatically resized to fit the form. ScaleResize is the method that handles this process.

SeekClass(<Class> [, <VCX File>])   This method moves the list pointer to a specified class. The parameter can be either numeric (that is, the list pointer moves to the class n in the list, where n is the number passed through as the Class parameter) or the name of the class to find.

The VCX File parameter is useful if you have multiple class libraries open and the same class name is in several viewed .VCX files. Specifying the .VCX filename will limit the search to that .VCX file.

The parameters are not case sensitive. The class you search for must be visible in order for it to be found, and the method returns a logical value indicating whether SEEK() was successful.

SeekMember(<tcMember>)   This method repositions the member list pointer to the specified member. The parameter, tcMember, can be either numeric or the name of the member. If the parameter is numeric, the member position pointer is moved to member number tcMember in the list.

SeekParentClass()   This method displays the parent class for the selected class. If the parent class is in a different .VCX file not shown in the list, the associated .VCX file is automatically loaded. This method returns a logical value indicating the success of the search.

SetBusyState(<Is State Busy?>)   Sets the lBusyStatus property to true (.T.) or false (.F.) based on the logical parameter BusyState. If the Class Browser is set to busy (.T.), the mouse pointer is set to an hourglass shape. Otherwise it is set to an arrow. Other than this, SetBusyState does not really do much.

SetFont(<FontName>,<FontSize>)   This method sets the font and font size used by the Class Browser for its form, controls, and dialog boxes. Note that you do not have to pass the font name each time. You could use the following example:

```
_oBrowser.SetFont(,10)
```

This sets the Class Browser to a 10-point font size without changing the font itself.

ShowMenu(<Menu Array>[, <Command on Select>])   This method displays a menu based on an array. If a menu is a single-dimension array, this method displays a list of all items in the menu. When an item is selected, the command specified in *<command on select>* is executed. Here is an example:

```
DECLARE laMenu2[3]
laMenu2[1] = "IBM"
laMenu2[2] = "Intel"
laMenu2[3] = "Microsoft"
_oBrowser.ShowMenu(@laMenu2, "Wait Window Prompt()")
```

Wait Window Prompt() is the *<command on select>* and will execute if any of the items on the menu are selected. As shown in Figure 16.19, the menu is brought up at the location of the mouse pointer.

If the array is two-dimensional, the first column becomes the list of prompts on the array and the second column is assumed to be the command to execute when the associated menu item is selected. Here is an example:

```
declare laMenu[3,2]
laMenu[1,1] = "IBM"
laMenu[2,1] = "Intel"
laMenu[3,1] = "Microsoft"
laMenu[1,2] = "WAIT WINDOW 'International Business Machines'"
laMenu[2,2] = "WAIT WINDOW 'Intel Corporation'"
laMenu[3,2] = "WAIT WINDOW 'Microsoft Corporation'"
_oBrowser.ShowMenu(@laMenu2)
```

If an item is selected, the command in the second column in that array is executed. For example, selecting IBM will execute the WAIT WINDOW 'International Business Machines' command.

Part
IV

Ch
16

FIGURE 16.19

The Class Browser with a menu showing.

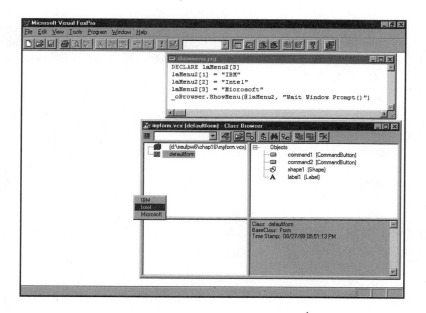

TrimExt(<FileName>) This method accepts a filename as a parameter and returns the name minus the extension. Here is an example:

```
? _oBrowser.TrimExt("BROWSE.DBF") && Returns "BROWSE"
```

TrimFile(<FileName with Path>) This method accepts a filename as a parameter and returns the path only (that is, it trims off the filename).

TrimPath(<FileName With Path>[,<Trim the extension?>]) This method accepts a filename as a parameter and returns the filename and extension only (the path is removed).

Here is an example:

```
? _oBrowser.TrimPath("D:\APPS\BROWSE.DBF")
* Returns "BROWSE.DBF"
```

VersionCheck(<Show Error Message?>) This method validates the open class library (.VCX file) or form (.SCX file) and returns .T. if the file is valid, .F. if it is not. If a parameter of .T. is passed, an invalid file will cause an error message to appear.

How does this method work? It checks the contents of the field Reserved1 for a proper version number. If you want to call this method on your own, make sure that the record pointer in the .VCX file is set to the top of the file (setting the list selection won't work—that works off an array). The .VCX file you are looking for is open in the Class Browser's data session with an alias of Metadata<n>, where n is the number of the .VCX file (the first .VCX file opened is given an alias of metadata1, the second is metadata2, and so on).

You can find which metadata file to work with by checking the DBF file underlying the metadata<n> alias with the DBF function. When DBF matches the name of the current .VCX file (you can get this from the Class Browser's cFileName property), simply issue GO TOP and then run the versioncheck method.

This method runs automatically when the .VCX file is loaded into the Class Browser. You shouldn't have to use this method too often, but it's good to know.

Part

IV

Ch

16

UpdateReference(<tcOldClassLoc>, <tcOldClass>, <tcNewClassLoc>, <tcNewClass> [,<lAllInstances>])   This is a powerful new method that was added to Visual FoxPro Version 6. It updates all class references when a class is renamed, or when a class is moved from one instance of a Class Browser to another. The tcOldClassLoc and tcNewClassLoc arguments refer to the ClassLoc field contents in the .VCX or .SCX file. The tcOldClass and tcNewClass arguments refer to the Class field in the .VCX or .SCX file. The UpdateReference() function changes all files in all Class Browser windows if the tlAllInstances argument is true (.T.). If it's false (.f.), the UpDateReference() function changes only the files in the current Class Browser.

ViewProperty(cProperty)   This method displays the value of the designated property for the selected class in a message box. For example, if you want to know what the caption is for a form class, click on the class and execute the following command from the Visual FoxPro Command window:

```
_oBrowser.ViewProperty("Caption")
```

The value of the Caption property is displayed in a message box, as shown in Figure 16.20. Notice that the message box title bar contains the name of the class and its visual class library.

FIGURE 16.20

ViewProperty() displays a message box showing the value of a property.

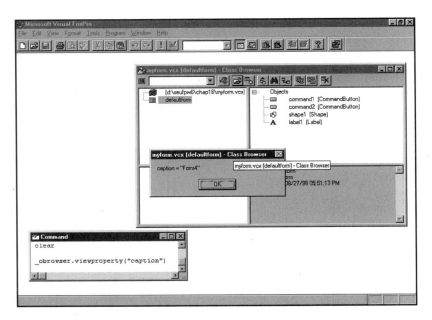

WildcardMatch(<Wild Card Expression List>, <Expression to Search>) This
method compares strings for a wildcard match with the filters specified in the Type box. Here
is an example:

```
? ox.Wildcardmatch("ox?", "OxyMoron")          && Returns .F.
? ox.Wildcardmatch("ox?, ox*", "OxyMoron")     && Returns .T.
```

Properties

Table 16.1 presents the properties of the Class Browser.

Note that some properties are marked as "No" in the "Can It Be Changed?" column. This does not
mean that these properties cannot be changed if you issue the commands to do so. These properties
are not protected. However, if you do change these properties, you could cause problem for the Class
Browser. It may abend, work improperly, or who knows what all.

Simple lesson: if the chart says "No," it means that you change the property at your own risk.

Table 16.1   Properties of the Class Browser

Property Name	Description	Can It Be Changed?
aClassList	An array with two dimensions that holds information about each class in the class list. Here's the structure of the array: [Row,1] The class name. [Row,2] The record number in the .VCX file. [Row,3] The number of levels indented in the list. [Row,4] The .VCX file with the parent class. [Row,5] The parent class name. [Row,6] The path of the parent class's .VCX file.	No
aFiles	An array listing the files open in the Class Browser.	No
aInstances	An array of instances for the selected class in the list.	No
BackColor	The background color of the form.	Yes

Property Name	Description	Can It Be Changed?
cAddInMethod	The name of the method that called the currently executing add-in. See the section on add-ins beginning with "Putting It All Together with Add-Ins."	No
cAlias	The alias of the .VCX file for the current class (for example, METADATA).	
Caption	The caption of the window.	Yes
cBaseClass	The name of the base class of the currently selected class in the Class Browser.	No
cBrowserTable	The name and full path to the Class Browser registration table (BROWSER.DBF).	No
cClass	The name of the currently selected class.	No
cClassLibrary	The name of the .VCX file where the parent of the current class is located. This is empty for classes based on a base class.	No
cClassType	The current Type filter.	No
cDefaultClass	The name of the initial class to select in the Class Browser (the third parameter on the DO (_browser) command line).	Yes
cDragIcon	The name of the icon file used as the picture for the drag icon.	Yes
cLastFindText	Internal use only.	No
cFileName	The .VCX filename of the currently selected class.	No
cFilter	The filter set on the .VCX file for the current class.	No
cGetFileExt	The extensions shown in the GETFILE() displayed by the Open button.	Yes

continues

Table 16.1 Continued

Property Name	Description	Can It Be Changed?
cLastSetComp	SET("compatible") before the Class Browser loaded.	No
cLastSetESC	SET("escape") before the Class Browser loaded.	No
cLastValue	For internal use only.	No
cLastSetUDFParms	For internal use only.	No
cParentClass	The parent class of the currently selected class.	No
cParentClassBrowserCaption	The ParentClass Browser Caption.	Yes
CparentClassSymbol	Symbol displayed (normally <<) to indicate that class is subclass of a class that is not displayed.	Yes
cPlatform	The current platform (Windows, for example).	No
cProgramName	Full path to BROWSER.APP.	No
cStartName	The name of the Class Browser before it was incremented by additional instances. (Showing more Class Browsers will increment the name to Classbrowser1, Classbrowser2, and so on.)	No
cTimeStamp	The timestamp of the currently selected class. For internal use only.	No
DataSession	The data session setting for this form. (The Class Browser runs in a private data session.)	No
DoCreate	For internal use only.	No
FontName	Default form font.	Yes
FontSize	Default form font size.	Yes
Height	Form height.	Yes
HelpContextID	The Help ID for the Class Browser.	No
Icon	The icon file for the form when minimized.	Yes

Property Name	Description	Can It Be Changed?
lActive	Specifies whether the Class Browser has focus. For internal use only.	No
lAddInMode	Is .T. when an add-in is running and .F. when it is complete.	No
lAddInTrace	If set to .T., the Class Browser lists each method to which an add-in can be hooked as it is executed. See the section on add-ins (beginning with "Putting It All Together with Add-Ins") for more information.	Yes
lAutoExpand	Determines whether class hierarchies are shown expanded or collapsed by default.	Yes
lBusyState	If .T., a refresh operation is in progress. For internal use only.	No
ldescriptions	If .T., class descriptions are displayed in Description Edit boxes.	Yes
lDisplayHierarchyError	If .T., Display error message if Class Browser attempts to load class with invalid ParentClass.	No
LDragDrop	For internal use only.	No
LEmptyFilter	If .T., Empty Class Browser displays methods with no code.	Yes
LError	Error checking status. If .T., an error occurred and Class Browser displays error box. Set to .F. if you want to check for errors.	Yes
lExpanded	For external use only.	No
lFileMode	If .T., the currently selected class is really a file.	No
lFormAddObject	For external use only.	No
lHiddenFilter	If .T., hidden members are displayed in the members list. Default is .F..	Yes
lIgnoreErrors	For internal use only.	No

continues

Part
IV

Ch
16

Table 16.1   Continued

Property Name	Description	Can It Be Changed?
lInitialized	For internal use only.	No
lModalDialog	If .T., Class list is refreshed when Class Browser regains focus after activating a modal dialog box. Default is .T..	Yes
lNoDefault	Determines whether default method behavior is executed after the add-ins are registered for that method.	Yes
lOutlineOCX	If .T., classes are displayed in a tree view.	No
lParentClassBrowser	If .T., the Edit ParentClass Method toolbar is displayed. Default is .T..	Yes
ProtectedFilter	If .T., protected members are displayed in the members list. Default is .F..	Yes
lReadOnly	The status of the read-only attribute for the .VCX file associated with the currently selected class.	No
lRefreshMode	For internal use only.	No
lRelease	For internal use only.	No
lResizeMode	For internal use only.	No
lSCXMode	If .T., the currently selected class is actually an .SCX file.	No
lvcxscxmode	If .T., the selected class or file selected is a .VCX or .SCX file or is contained by a .VCX or .SCX file.	No
Left	The left coordinate of the Class Browser form.	Yes
MinHeight	The smallest height the form can have.	No
MinWidth	The narrowest width the form can have.	No

Property Name	Description	Can It Be Changed?
Name	The name of the Class Browser instance.	No
nAtPos	For internal use only.	No
nClassCount	The number of classes in the list.	No
cClassTimeStamp	Returns timestamp field value of selected class in the class list.	Yes
nClassListIndex	The position of the selected class in the class list.	No
nDisplayMode	Display mode (hierarchical or alphabetical). 1 is hierarchical and 2 is alphabetical. The default value is 1.

Note that changing this property will not change the display mode. In order to do that, you need to change the value of opgDisplayMode. | No |
nFileCount	The number of files open.	No
nInstances	The number of instances of the currently selected class.	No
nLastHeight	The height of the Class Browser form before it was last changed.	No
nLastRecno	For internal use only.	No
nLastWidth	The width of the form before the last resize.	No
nPixelOffset	For internal use only.	No
nRecCount	The total number of records in the .VCX file.	No
nStrLen	For internal use only.	No
oSource	The reference for an object dropped on a form from the Class Browser.	No
ScaleMode	Specifies how numbers are translated into coordinates.	No

continues

Table 16.1 Continued

Property Name	Description	Can It Be Changed?
ShowTips	Specifies whether tooltips for the objects appear or not.	Yes
tcDefaultClass	The name of the class sent through as the second parameter to the Class Browser.	No
tcFileName	The name of the file to open, passed through on the command line calling the Class Browser.	No
tlListBox	If .T., the Class Browser displays classes and members in a list box instead of a tree view.	Yes
Top	The top coordinate of the form.	Yes
Width	The width of the form.	Yes

Working with the properties of the Class Browser provides a neat beginning to customizing it for your own use and tastes. For example, you could change the height of the form with this:

```
_obrowser.height = _obrowser.height + 10
```

If you try it, you'll also notice that the form controls will be resized automatically. This happens because changing the height property automatically fires the Resize() method.

Putting It All Together with Add-Ins

Now you know all about the Class Browser internals. You know what the objects, properties, and methods are. What can you do with this knowledge?

The Class Browser has a wonderful little feature called add-ins. Basically, an *add-in* is a program you write that you can register with the Class Browser. Once registered, you can call the add-in to perform just about anything you like.

An Add-In Program

I will start with a simple example of an add-in. This add-in just displays a wait window with the name of the currently selected class. Although it's not very useful, it does give a good and simple starting place for understanding add-ins. The code is presented in Listing 16.3.

> **Listing 16.3 16CODE03—Code for a Simple Add-in That Displays the Current Class Name**
>
> ```
> *    Program..........: CLSNAME.PRG
> *    Author...........: Menachem Bazian, CPA
> *) Description.......: Simple add in for the Class Browser that
> *)                   : displays the current class' name.
> *    Calling Samples...:
> *    Parameter List....:
> *    Major change list.:
>
> LPARAMETERS toSource
>
> WAIT WINDOW toSource.ProperBaseClass(toSource.cClass)
> RETURN
> ```

Note the parameter. When the Class Browser calls the add-in, it passes itself as a parameter to the add-in. This enables you to do all kinds of neat things. Before we get into those, let's look at the nuts and bolts of registering and running add-ins.

Registering the Add-In

Next, register the add-in with the Class Browser. Note that the Class Browser has to be running in order to do this.

```
_oBrowser.AddIn("Class Name", "ClsName")
```

The Addin method registers an add-in. The syntax shown here specifies a name for the add-in (Class Name) and the program to run (ClsName.Prg).

Running the Add-In

You can run the add-in in several ways. First of all, the add-in can be run with the DoAddIn method. Here's the syntax for this method:

```
_oBrowser.DoAddIn("Class Name")
```

Passing the name of a registered add-in to the DoAddIn method will run that add-in. Another way that it can be called is to right-click on the toolbar and select the Add-In item from the shortcut menu. Selecting the Add-In menu item activates a menu with the installed add-ins. Figure 16.21 shows the Class Browser with the Add-In menu activated from the Add-In button.

You can manually expand the same menu using the AddInMenu method as follows:

```
_oBrowser.AddInMenu
```

Running this method will expand the menu at the location of the mouse pointer. You can close the menu with _oBrowser.DeactivateMenu, although you shouldn't need to because the menu is automatically closed when a selection is made.

FIGURE 16.21

The Add-In button.

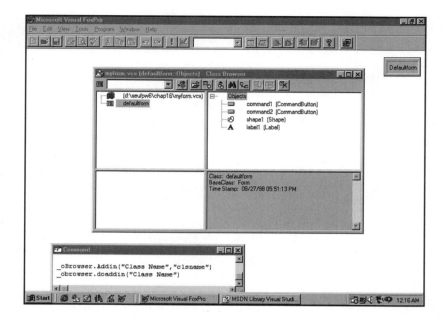

Unregistering an Add-In

You can remove an add-in from the Class Browser registration table with the `AddIn` method too. Here's how to do it:

```
_oBrowser.AddIn("Class Name",.NULL.)
```

If the program name is provided as a value of `.NULL.`, the add-in record in the Class Browser registration table is marked for deletion.

 TIP The help file says that the add-in is deleted if the second parameter (the name of the add-in program) is "empty." Don't you believe it. You have to pass through the parameter as a value of `.NULL.` for the add-in to be deleted.

Boosting Power with Add-Ins

Add-ins let you do all kinds of great things. The example you saw in the last section is a simple one. Basically, it displays the name of the currently selected class by accepting the object parameter (remember, the Class Browser is the parameter) and then accessing the `cClass` property in the `WAIT WINDOW` command.

Although this example is not particularly useful, it does illustrate a few key concepts. First, because the Class Browser sends itself as the parameter to the add-ins, every add-in has access to the full power of the Class Browser. That's why it is so important to take the time to learn about the properties and methods of the Class Browser. Another key point is that there is not much that an add-in cannot do for you. The remainder of this chapter talks about examples of this.

Here's another example of an add-in. You saw previously that all the class code shown in this chapter is exported with the Class Browser. For example, if you wanted to add some additional information at the top of the exported code (author name, copyright, and so on), you could do it with the add-in presented in Listing 16.4.

Listing 16.4 16CODE04—Code for an Add-in That Exports Code for a Class with Custom Headings

```
*     Program..........: DOCCLASS.PRG
*     Author...........: Menachem Bazian, CPA
*) Description.......: DocClass is an addin program for
*)                   : the Class Browser that exports
*)                   : the code for a class with a
*)                   : FlashStandard type heading at the top.
*     Calling Samples...:
*     Parameter List....:
*     Major change list.:

LPARAMETERS toObject
#DEFINE cr_lf chr(13)+chr(10)

_cliptext = toObject.ExportClass()

LOCAL laHdrLine[5], lcText, lnCounter

laHdrLine[1] = "*   Class.............: " + ;
        toObject.ProperBaseClass(toObject.cClass)
laHdrLine[2] = "*   Author...........: " + ;
        "<Your name>"
laHdrLine[3] = "*   Project..........: " + ;
        "<your project >nameSpecial Edition Using Visual FoxPro 6.0"
laHdrLine[4] = "*   Copyright.........: " + ;
        "(c)<your company name> "
laHdrLine[5] = "*   Notes............: " + ;
        "Exported code from Class Browser."

lcText = ""

FOR lnCounter = 1 TO ALEN(laHdrLine,1)
    lcText = lcText + ;
                laHdrLine[lnCounter] + cr_lf
ENDFOR

lcText = lcText + cr_lf

_cliptext = lcText + _cliptext
=MessageBox("Code exported to clipboard!", 32)
RETURN
```

In theory, this add-in is very simple. The ExportClass method is used to dump the code for the class into the Clipboard (you modify the Clipboard by modifying _cliptext). The array holds the additional header lines, which are then added with carriage returns and linefeeds to the output text. Once the add-in is run, all you have to do is paste the code into the word processor. This is a fairly good example of an add-in—it automates a procedure you need to do and reduces it to a few simple keystrokes.

Here's another add-in. This one attempts to provide a runtime preview of an object shown in the Class Browser by bringing up the ObjectInspectorForm shown in Chapter 15. The idea is fairly simple. You make sure that the class library for the class is in the SET CLASS list, instantiate it, and then send it off to the ObjectInspectorForm class (same as in Chapter 15). The code for the program (OBJINSP.PRG) is provided in Listing 16.5.

Listing 16.5 16CODE05—Code for Add-in to Inspect the Current Selected Class

```
*   Program...........: OBJINSP.PRG
*   Author............: Menachem Bazian, CPA
*   Description.......: Add-in to Inspect the current selected class
Procedure OBJINSP
LPARAMETERS toSource
*-- This Add-in instantiates an object based on
*-- the currently selected class and then passes
*-- it off to the ObjectInspectorForm
*-- class for display.

*-- First check to make sure we are not on the
*-- .VCX

IF '.' $ toSource.cClass
    =MessageBox("You must have a class currently selected!", 16)
    RETURN
ENDIF

*-- Step one, add the Class Library with the object
*-- we are instantiating to the SET CLASS list

LOCAL lcCLassLib
lcClassLibrary = toSource.cFileName
lcCurrentClassLibraries = SET("classlib")

IF !(UPPER(toSource.TrimPath(lcClassLibrary)) # SET("CLASSLIB"))
    SET CLASS TO (lcClassLibrary) ADDITIVE
ENDIF


*-- Instantiate the object
LOCAL loX, loObjInspect
loX = CREATEOBJECT(toSource.cClass)

*-- Send it off to the ObjectInspectorForm
loObjInspect = CREA("ObjectInspectorForm", loX)
```

```
*-- Show it as a modal form
loObjInspect.Show(1)

*-- Reset everything
SET CLASSLIB TO (lcCurrentClassLibraries)

*-- We're done
RETURN


* Description: Test Program that creates ObjectInspectorForm objects
*              object to display the Form showing the_Screen object
*              properties.  Example:
*   oObjInspect = CREATE("ObjectInspectorForm",_Screen)
*   oObjInspect.Show()
* Class............: Objectinspectorform
* Author...........: Menachem Bazian, CPA
* Project..........: Special Edition Using Visual FoxPro 6
* Copyright........: (c) Flash Creative Management, Inc. 19951998
*) Description......:
* Notes............: Exported code from Class Browser.

**************************************************
*-- Class:        objectinspectorform (d:\data\docs\books\vfu\code\oop2.vcx)
*-- ParentClass:  form
*-- BaseClass:    form
*
DEFINE CLASS objectinspectorform AS form

    DataSession = 2
    Height = 309
    Width = 466
    DoCreate = .T.
    AutoCenter = .T.
    BackColor = RGB(192,192,192)
    BorderStyle = 3
    Caption = ""
    MaxButton = .F.
    MinButton = .F.
    ClipControls = .F.
    WindowType = 1
    PROTECTED cobjectbmpfile
    cobjectbmpfile = (home()+"SAMPLES\GRAPHICS\BMPS\FOX\APPS.BMP")
    PROTECTED cmethodbmpfile
    cmethodbmpfile = (home()+"SAMPLES\GRAPHICS\BMPS\FOX\CLASSES.BMP")
    PROTECTED cpropertybmpfile
    cpropertybmpfile = (home()+"SAMPLES\GRAPHICS\BMPS\FOX\INDEXES.BMP")
    PROTECTED ceventbmpfile
    ceventbmpfile = (home()+"SAMPLES\GRAPHICS\BMPS\FOX\AUTOFORM.BMP")
    Name = "objectinspectorform"

    ADD OBJECT lstmembers AS listbox WITH ;
        FontName = "Courier New", ;
        Height = 205, ;
        Left = 12, ;
        Top = 48, ;
```

continues

Listing 16.5   Continued

```
            Width = 438, ;
            ItemBackColor = RGB(192,192,192), ;
            Name = "lstMembers"

    ADD OBJECT cmdok AS commandbutton WITH ;
        Top = 264, ;
        Left = 180, ;
        Height = 37, ;
        Width = 109, ;
        Cancel = .T., ;
        Caption = "OK", ;
        Default = .T., ;
        Name = "cmdOK"

    ADD OBJECT label1 AS label WITH ;
        AutoSize = .F., ;
        BackStyle = 0, ;
        Caption = "Order:", ;
        Height = 18, ;
        Left = 24, ;
        Top = 15, ;
        Width = 40, ;
        Name = "Label1"

    ADD OBJECT opgorder AS optiongroup WITH ;
        ButtonCount = 2, ;
        BackStyle = 0, ;
        Value = 1, ;
        Height = 25, ;
        Left = 96, ;
        Top = 12, ;
        Width = 217, ;
        Name = "opgOrder", ;
        Option1.BackStyle = 0, ;
        Option1.Caption = "Alphabetical", ;
        Option1.Value = 1, ;
        Option1.Height = 18, ;
        Option1.Left = 0, ;
        Option1.Top = 4, ;
        Option1.Width = 109, ;
        Option1.Name = "optAlphabetical", ;
        Option2.BackStyle = 0, ;
        Option2.Caption = "Grouped", ;
        Option2.Value = 0, ;
        Option2.Height = 18, ;
        Option2.Left = 127, ;
        Option2.Top = 4, ;
        Option2.Width = 73, ;
        Option2.Name = "optGrouped"

PROCEDURE buildlist
    LPARAMETERS toObject

        #DEFINE COLUMNLENGTH 25
```

```
        WAIT WINDOW NOWAIT "Building members list. Please stand by..."
        this.lockscreen = .t.
        this.lstMembers.clear()
        SELECT _members
        IF this.opgOrder.value = 1
            SET ORDER TO TAG Alpha
        ELSE
            SET ORDER TO TAG Grouped
        ENDIF

        GO TOP
        lnCounter = 0
        SCAN
            lnCounter = lnCounter + 1
            lcText = PADR(_members.cMembName, COLUMNLENGTH)

            IF _members.cMembType = "Prop"
                *-- Now we need to get the value of the property
                lcText = lcText + ALLTRIM(_members.cMembVal)
            ENDIF

            thisform.lstMembers.additem(" " + lcText)
            lcBmpVar = "this.c" + alltrim(_members.cMembType)+"bmpfile"
            thisform.lstMembers.picture(lnCounter) = EVAL(lcBmpVar)
        ENDSCAN

        this.lockscreen = .f.
        thisform.refresh()
        WAIT CLEAR
ENDPROC

PROCEDURE Resize
        this.lockscreen = .t.

        this.lstMembers.width = this.width - 24
        this.cmdOk.left = (this.width-this.cmdOk.width)/2
        this.cmdOK.top = (this.height - 8 - this.cmdOK.height)
        this.lstMembers.height = this.cmdOK.top - this.lstMembers.top - 11

        this.lockscreen = .F.
ENDPROC

PROCEDURE Init
        *  Class...........: OBJECTINSPECTORFORM
        *  Author..........: Menachem Bazian, CPA
        *  Project.........: Visual FoxPro Unleashed
        *  Created.........: May 16, 19951998 - 07:44:03
        *  Copyright.......: (c) Flash Creative Management, Inc., 19951998
        *) Description.....: When passed an object, it builds a list of the
        *)                 : members and displays them nicely.
        *  Calling Samples.: oForm = CREATEOBJECT("OBJECTINSPECTORFORM",
        ➥oObject)
        *  Parameter List..: toObject - Object to inspect
        *  Major change list.:
```

continues

Listing 16.5 Continued

```
      LPARAMETERS toObject

      this.caption = "Inspecting object: " + ALLT(toObject.Name)

      IF TYPE("toObject") # 'O'
          =MessagebOx("You can only pass OBJECT type parameters!", 16)
          RETURN .F.
      ENDIF

      *-- If we get this far, we can inspect the object
      *-- Let's define some memory variables and do the AMembers()

      LOCAL laMembers[1], lcText, lcName
      =AMembers(laMembers,toObject,1)

      *-- In order to create the list in proper order, it is useful to have
      *-- a table to work off of (so we can INDEX). Hence:

      CREATE CURSOR _members (cMembName C(25), cMembtype C(25), cMembVal
      ➡C(40))
      INSERT INTO _members FROM ARRAY laMembers

      INDEX ON cMembName TAG Alpha
      INDEX ON cMembType + cMembName TAG Grouped

      SCAN FOR _members.cMembType = "Prop"

          *-- Determine the value of the property and place it in the
          *-- cMembVal field

          lcName = "toObject."+ALLTRIM(_members.cMembName)
          DO CASE
              CASE TYPE(lcName) = 'U'
                  lcText = ".UNDEFINED."
              CASE isnull(EVAL(lcName))
                  lcText = ".NULL."
              CASE TYPE(lcName) = 'L'
                  lcText = IIF(EVAL(lcName), ".T.", ".F.")
              OTHERWISE
                  lcText = ALLTRIM(PADR(EVALUATE(lcName),50))
          ENDCASE
          REPLACE _members.cMembVal WITH lcText
      ENDSCAN

      this.buildlist()
ENDPROC

PROCEDURE cmdok.Click
    release thisform
ENDPROC

PROCEDURE opgorder.Click
    thisform.buildlist()
```

```
        ENDPROC

    ENDDEFINE
    *
    *-- EndDefine: objectinspectorform
```

Again, note how the Class Browser as a parameter is so useful. The Class Browser's properties give the necessary information to check that the current class is a class and not the .VCX file itself, what the class library needed is, and so on.

Changing Class Browser Behavior with Add-Ins

By installing the sample add-in in the manner shown in the previous section, you can run it by selecting a class, clicking the Add-In command button, and selecting the appropriate menu item.

Go back to the ObjInsp add-in for a moment. This is a powerful add-in. However, when you think about it, it is a utility to see what a particular class is like. This seems to be analogous to the Export command button, which is designed to show the class code for a "quick view" of the class.

If a left-mouse-click on the View Class Code command button exports the code to a window, wouldn't it be nice to have a right-mouse-click on the command button run the ObjInsp add-in? In fact, you can do just that. To show how this is accomplished, take a closer look at the syntax of the AddIn() method:

```
AddIn(<AddIn Name>, ;<Program Name>, ;<Method Name>, ;<Active For Files>, ;
      <PlatForm>, ;<Comment>)
```

This method installs or removes a Class Browser add-in.

The *<AddIn Name>* parameter is the name of the add-in. The name of the add-in can be one or more words, and case is not important (except that it will be displayed on the menu in the same manner as it is specified here). The add-in will be displayed in the Add-In menu if the third parameter (Method Name) is not specified.

The *<Program Name>* parameter is the name of a program to run. The program can be a .PRG, .APP, .EXE, or .FXP. In addition, you can specify an .SCX file. The assumed extension is .PRG; you can specify other extensions as appropriate.

The *<Program Name>* parameter can also be the name of an object. The syntax for this is *<VCX FileName, Class Name>*. Here is an example:

```
_oBrowser.AddIn("MyAddIn", "MyVcxVCX, MyClass")
```

When the add-in is run, the class MyClass of MyVcx.VCX file is instantiated. Remember that an object parameter is sent through to the class.

It's not a bad idea to specify a full path to the program in this parameter. This ensures that the add-in runs properly wherever you are in your hard disk. If the Class Browser cannot find the program or .VCX file when it tries to call an add-in, an error is generated.

The *<Method Name>* parameter is the name of a method to automatically call the add-in. Any valid method, either a method of the Class Browser form or one of its objects, can be a hook for a method. For example, if you wanted to hook MyAddIn to the Export command button's Click method, you could state this:

```
_oBrowser.AddIn("MyAddIn", , "CmdExport.Click")
```

Notice, by the way, that I did not specify the second parameter in this command. Because I did not need to modify the parameter, I left it out. The AddIn() method is smart enough to handle that.

This parameter is the key to the task that was just set out. By specifying the cmdExport.RightClick method in the third parameter, you can hook the add-in to the RightClick() event on the Export command button. The call to the Class Browser AddIn() method consists of the following line of code:

```
_obrowser.Addin("View Object Members",
        "ObjInsp.prg","cmdExport.RightClick")
```

Once the add-in is installed, you can select a class, right-click on the View Class button, and the Inspecting Object dialog appears, as shown in Figure 16.22.

FIGURE 16.22

Right-click on the View Class Code button and the Inspecting Object dialog box appears.

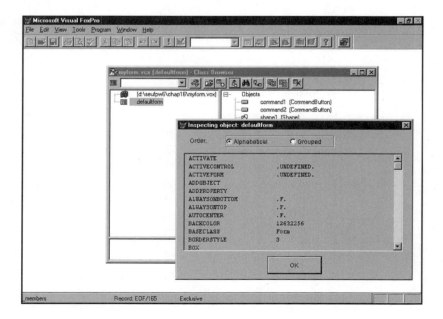

By the way, if you hook into a method that already has behavior (the Click method of cmdExport calls ExportClass, for example), the add-in runs first and then the original behavior runs. If you have multiple add-ins registered for a method, they will run in the order they were registered.

Finally, if you want to totally override the behavior of a method (you do not want cmdExport to call ExportClass, for example), the add-in must set the lNoDefault property on the Class Browser to .T.. If this property is set to .T., the Class Browser method will detect this and ignore the rest of the method.

The <Active For Files> parameter enables you to determine the files for which the add-in will work. By default, when an add-in is added to the Class Browser registration table, it is available for all the .VCX and .SCX files with which you might work. This parameter enables you to specify a file or list of files (separated by commas) for which this add-in is available. For other files loaded into the Class Browser, the add-in simply does not exist.

The <Platform> parameter specifies the platform (for example, Windows) in which the add-in will work. By default, it is available for all platforms.

The <Comment> parameter is an optional comment you can store with the add-in.

If you take a close look at the AddIn method, it gives a wealth of insight into the power and flexibility of the Class Browser. With add-ins, you can totally customize the Class Browser to run your code at almost any interval.

For example, assume you prefer to use Courier New as the font for the Class Browser. All you need to do is create an add-in like the one presented in Listing 16.6 (FONTSET.PRG) and register it for the Init method.

Listing 16.6 16CODE06—Code for an Add-in That Changes the Class Browser Font

```
*    Program..........: FONTSET.PRG
*    Author...........: Menachem Bazian, CPA
*)   Description.......:
*    Calling Samples...:
*    Parameter List....:
*    Major change list.:

LPARAMETERS toSource

toSource.SetFont("Courier New")
```

Here is how to register the add-in:

```
_oBrowser.AddIn("FontSet", "FontSet", "Init")
```

Advanced Object-Oriented Programming

Data Environment Classes

Back in Chapter 15, "Creating Classes with Visual FoxPro," I mention the concept of manually created data environment classes. You might already be familiar with data environments from working with forms. The following section is a quick review of data environments from that perspective.

Data Environments with Forms

When you create a form with Visual FoxPro's Form Designer, you can specify the tables that the form works with by creating a *data environment* for the form. As Figure 17.1 shows, a form's data environment is made up of cursors and relations. If you like, you can think of a data environment as a package (that is, a container) that holds the information necessary for setting up the data environment.

FIGURE 17.1

The data environment of a form.

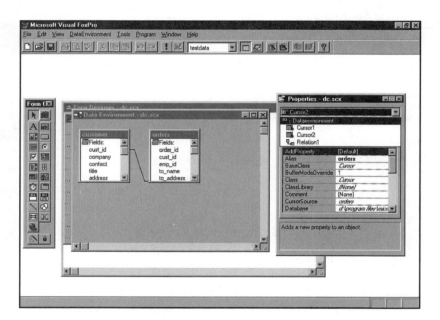

Data Environments and Form Classes

One of the limitations of a form class is that data environments cannot be saved with the class. However, as it turns out, data environments, cursors, and relations are classes in and of themselves. That means you can create data environment definitions by combining cursors and relations into one package.

There is one limitation on the data environment, cursor, and relation classes: They cannot be created visually. They can only be created in code.

The Cursor Class

The first class to examine is the Cursor class. A *Cursor class* defines the contents of a work area. The following sections provide a brief review of the properties, events, and methods of the Cursor class.

Properties   Table 17.1 describes the properties of the Cursor class. The Cursor class also supports the base properties discussed in Chapter 14, "OOP with Visual FoxPro."

Table 17.1   The Properties of the Cursor Class

Property	Description
Alias	This property is the alias to give the work area when opened.
BufferModeOverride	This property specifies the buffering mode for the cursor. Here are the values:

0	None (no buffering is done)
1	Use whatever is set at the form level
2	Pessimistic row buffering
3	Optimistic row buffering
4	Pessimistic table buffering
5	Optimistic table buffering

Property	Description
	If the data environment class is not used on a form, you should use a value other than 1.
CursorSource	This property is the source for the cursor's data. This could be a table from a database, a view (local or remote) from a database, or a free table. If CursorSource is a free table, you must specify the path to the DBF file.
Database	This property is the database that has the cursor source. If the cursor source comes from a database, this field must be completed with a fully valid path, including drive and directories.
Exclusive	This property specifies whether the cursor source is open in exclusive mode. It accepts a logical value.
Filter	This property is the Filter expression to place on the cursor source. The string placed here would be the string you would specify in a SET FILTER TO command.
NoDataOnLoad	This property, if set to .T., opens the cursor and creates a structure, but no data is downloaded for the cursor. Requery() will download the data.
Order	This property specifies the initial order in which to display the data. You must specify an index tag name.
ReadOnly	This property, if set to .T., opens the cursor as read-only; therefore, the data cannot be modified.

Events and Methods The Cursor class supports only the Init, Destroy, and Error events.

The Relation Class

The Relation class specifies the information needed to set up a relationship between two cursors in a data environment. The following sections cover the properties, events, and methods.

Properties To more easily explain the properties of the Relation class, consider the following situation. You have two tables in a cursor, one called Customer and the other named Invoice. Customer has a field called CID that holds the customer ID. Invoice has a field called cCustId that also holds the customer ID. Here is how you would normally set the relation:

```
SELECT Invoice
SET ORDER to cCustId
SELECT Customer
SET RELATION TO cId INTO Invoice
```

Table 17.2 presents the properties and their descriptions.

Table 17.2   The Properties of the Relation Class

Property	Description
ChildAlias	This property is the alias of the child table. In this example, it would be Invoice.
ChildOrder	This property specifies the order of the child table. In this example, it would be cCustId.
OneToMany	This property specifies whether the relationship is a one-to-many relationship.
ParentAlias	This property is the alias of the controlling alias. In this example, it would be Customer.
RelationalExpr	This property is the expression of the relationship. In this example, it would be CID.

Events and Methods The relation class supports only the Init, Destroy, and Error events.

The DataEnvironment Class

The DataEnvironment class is a container for cursors and relations, which, when taken together, make up an environment of data.

Properties Table 17.3 presents the properties of the DataEnvironment class.

Table 17.3 The Properties of the `DataEnvironment` Class

Property	Description
AutoCloseTables	This property specifies that tables should be closed automatically when the object is released. `AutoCloseTables` works in a form environment. In a coded `DataEnvironment` class, you would have to put code in the `Destroy` method for the tables to be closed. You would close the tables in the `Destroy` method by calling the `DataEnvironment`'s `OpenTables` method.
AutoOpenTables	This property specifies that tables should be opened automatically when the object is instantiated. `AutoOpenTables` works in a form environment. In a coded `DataEnvironment` class, you would have to put code in the `Init` method for the tables to be opened. You would open the tables in the `Init` method by calling the `DataEnvironment`'s `OpenTables` method.
InitialSelectedAlias	This property specifies which alias should be selected initially.

Methods Unlike the `Cursor` and `Relation` classes, the `DataEnvironment` class has two methods in addition to the base methods, as shown in Table 17.4.

Table 17.4 The Additional Methods of the `DataEnvironment` Class

Method	Description
CloseTables()	This method closes all the tables and cursors in the data environment class.
OpenTables()	This method opens all the tables and cursors in the data environment class.

Events Table 17.5 presents the events supported by the `DataEnvironment` class.

Table 17.5 The Events Supported by the `DataEnvironment` Class

Event	Description
BeforeOpenTables()	This event runs before tables are opened.
AfterCloseTables()	This event runs after tables are closed.

Building a Data Environment Class Now that you have seen all the elements that go into creating a data environment class, the next step is to build one. The examples I use here are based on the TESTDATA.DBC database located in Visual FoxPro's SAMPLES\DATA directory. The data environment class code, DE1.PRG, is presented in Listing 17.1.

Part

IV

Ch

17

Listing 17.1 `17CODE01.PRG`—Code for Sample Data Environment Class

```
* Program...........: DE1.PRG
* Author............: Menachem Bazian, CPA
* Description.......: A sample data environment class

DEFINE CLASS CUSTOMER AS cursor
    alias = "CUSTOMER"
    cursorsource = "CUSTOMER"
    database = HOME()+"SAMPLES\DATA\TESTDATA.DBC"
ENDDEFINE

DEFINE CLASS ORDERS AS cursor
    alias = "ORDERS"
    cursorsource = "ORDERS"
    database = HOME()+"SAMPLES\DATA\TESTDATA.DBC"
ENDDEFINE

DEFINE CLASS ORDITEMS AS cursor
    alias = "ORDITEMS"
    cursorsource = "ORDITEMS"
    database = HOME()+"SAMPLES\DATA\TESTDATA.DBC"
ENDDEFINE

DEFINE CLASS Cust_To_Orders AS relation
    childalias = "ORDERS"
    parentalias = "CUSTOMER"
    childorder = "CUST_ID"
    RelationalExpr = "CUST_ID"
ENDDEFINE

DEFINE CLASS Orders_To_OrdItems AS relation
    childalias = "ORDITEMS"
    parentalias = "ORDERS"
    childorder = "ORDER_ID"
    RelationalExpr = "ORDER_ID"
ENDDEFINE

DEFINE CLASS DE AS DataEnvironment
    ADD OBJECT oCUSTOMER                AS CUSTOMER
    ADD OBJECT oORDERS                  AS ORDERS
    ADD OBJECT oORDITEMS                AS ORDITEMS
    ADD OBJECT oCust_To_Orders          AS CUST_TO_ORDERS
    ADD OBJECT oOrders_To_OrdItems   AS ORDERS_TO_ORDITEMS

    PROCEDURE Init
        this.OpenTables()
    ENDPROC

    PROCEDURE Destroy
        this.CloseTables()
    ENDPROC
ENDDEFINE
```

Notice how all the first classes (that is, the Cursor and Relation classes) are manifestations based on the contents of the DBC file. The final class, DE, merely combines the cursor and relation classes under one roof. The Init method calls the OpenTables method so that all of the tables are automatically opened when the object is instantiated and the CloseTables() method is called when the object is released.

Notice also that the DE class shown in DE1.PRG uses all the cursor and relation classes in the program. You don't have to do this. Typically, when you work with data environment classes, you have one data environment class that opens all the tables (I call it a "default" data environment). You also have many other data environment classes that have only the cursor and relation objects that a particular function needs. For example, I could see the following data environment class added to DE1:

```
DEFINE CLASS SMALLDE AS DataEnvironment
    ADD OBJECT oCUSTOMER        AS CUSTOMER
    ADD OBJECT oORDERS          AS ORDERS
    ADD OBJECT oCust_To_Orders  AS CUST_TO_ORDERS

    PROCEDURE Init
        this.OpenTables()
    ENDPROC

    PROCEDURE Destroy
        this.CloseTables()
    ENDPROC
ENDDEFINE
```

This DataEnvironment class uses only the Customer and Orders cursors and the relation between them. It might be used, for example, for a list of order numbers belonging to a customer. This is not to say you *couldn't* use the default data environment class for everything. As a matter of course, however, I prefer to have only those cursors and relations referenced that I need.

One other item of interest in DE1.PRG is the settings for the Database property in all the classes. Using the Home function is perfectly reasonable: As long as the database name evaluates with a full path, the cursor will work fine.

Retrieving Definitions from a DBC File   There is one problem with retrieving definitions from a DBC file: It can be a major pain to type in all the cursor and relation classes you have in your DBC file. Furthermore, you might make changes to your DBC file during development and will then have to update the program with the data environment classes each time. This is not a pretty prospect.

Fortunately, it is relatively easy to get information from the database and generate your own program directly from the DBC file. Using functions such as ADBObjects, which retrieve information from the database, you can build a program automatically from the DBC file itself, thus saving yourself a lot of work. DumpDbc is a class that retrieves the information from a database and creates a program with the Cursor and Relation classes representing the contents of the database.

Class: DUMPDBC

DumpDbc a subclass of the Custom class. The following sections discuss its properties, events, and methods.

Properties   Table 17.6 presents DumpDbc's properties.

Table 17.6   The Properties of the DumpDbc Subclass

Property	Description
PROTECTED aRelations	This property is a list of relation objects in the DBC file.
PROTECTED aTables	This property is a list of table objects in the DBC file.
PROTECTED aViews	This property is a list of view objects in the DBC.
cDBCName	This property is the name of the DBC file you are exporting.
cPRGName	This property is the name of the PRG file to be created.
PROTECTED cPath	This property is the directory path to the database.
PROTECTED nRelations	This property is the number of relation objects in the DBC file.
PROTECTED nTables	This property is the number of table objects in the DBC file.
PROTECTED nViews	This property is the number of view objects in the DBC.

N O T E   Notice that all properties preceded by the keyword PROTECTED are protected members. ▦

Events and Methods   Now that you have seen the properties of DumpDbc, the next step is to learn the events and methods.

doit   This method initiates the action of writing the program. It is the only public method in the class, thus it ensures that the entire process is run properly from start to finish.

As part of getting the process going, this method checks to see whether a DBC file to generate and a program to create have been specified in the cDBCName and cPRGName properties, respectively. If either of these has not been specified, a Getfile() or Putfile() dialog box is displayed. Failure to select a file will terminate the operation.

cursorclasses   This PROTECTED method runs through all the tables and views in the DBC file (as listed in aTables and aViews) and generates cursor classes for them by calling the WriteCursorClass method.

readdbc   This PROTECTED method reads the relation, table, and view definitions from DBC using ADBObjects and places them in the aRelations, aTables, and aViews members' arrays.

relationclasses   This PROTECTED method generates all the relation classes for the DBC file and writes them to the output program file.

Unlike cursor classes, which can be given names based on the name of the table or view with which they are associated, relation classes are more difficult to name objectively. This class names them in consecutive order (Relation1, Relation2, and so on).

writeclasses()   This PROTECTED method launches the process of writing all the classes. It is called by the Doit method after the ReadDbc method completes it operation. The Writeclasses method calls the CursorClasses and RelationClasses methods to write the individual classes to the output file.

> **N O T E**   There are a few items to note. When developing applications, you might put the data in one place on the hard disk, but the data might live in a different place when installed at the user site. Because cursor classes require a full path to the database containing the cursor source, this could be a problem. ▪

Part
IV
Ch
17

The solution I have allowed for here is to use a declared constant called DATABASEPATH when generating the program. DATABASEPATH will have the path to the database when the program is generated. If you need to change paths somewhere along the line, you can modify this one defined constant. Otherwise, you could change this method in DumpDbc and have DATABASENAME refer to a table field, public variable, or property that has the data path. The advantage of this approach is that it does not require any code changes when moving the database.

The #DEFINE command is placed at the end of a header this method generates. The header enables you to keep track of how and when this generated program was created.

One of the last things that this method does is call the WriteDefaultClass method. This method writes a default data environment class that has all the cursors and relations in it.

writecursorclass(tcClassName)   This PROTECTED method writes a single cursor class to the program. The name of the class is always the same as the name of the view or cursor (which is passed through as tcClassName).

writedefaultclass   This PROTECTED method writes a data environment class called Default_de, which has all the cursor and relation classes from the DBC file.

The Code for the Dumpdbc Class   Listing 17.2 presents the code for the Dumpdbc class. This code was exported using the Class Browser from the Chap17a.VCX visual class library.

Listing 17.2   17CODE02.PRG—Code for Dumpdbc Class That Retrieves Information from a Database and Creates a Program

```
*   Class............: Dumpdbc.prg (D:\seuvfp6\Chap17\Chap17a.vcx)
*   Author...........: Menachem Bazian, CPA
*   Notes............: Exported code from Class Browser.
```

continues

Listing 17.2 Continued

```
******************************************************
*-- Class:         dumpdbc
*-- ParentClass:   custom
*-- BaseClass:     custom
*-- Create CURSOR and RELATION classes for a .DBC .
*
DEFINE CLASS dumpdbc AS custom

    *-- Number of relation objects in the .DBC
    PROTECTED nrelations
    nrelations = 0
    *-- Number of table objects in the .DBC
    PROTECTED ntables
    ntables = 0
    *-- Number of view objects in the .DBC
    PROTECTED nviews
    nviews = 0
    *-- Name of the .DBC to dump
    cdbcname = ""
    *-- Name of program file to create.
    cprgname = ""
    Name = "dumpdbc"

    *-- Path to the database
    PROTECTED cpath

    *-- List of relation objects in the .DBC
    PROTECTED arelations[1]

    *-- List of view objects in the .DBC
    PROTECTED aviews[1]

    *-- List of table objects in the .DBC
    PROTECTED atables[1]
    PROTECTED init

    *-- Reads the DBC into the arrays.
    PROTECTED PROCEDURE readdbc
        IF !dbused(this.cDbcName)
            OPEN DATABASE (this.cDbcName)
        ENDIF

        *-- I need FoxTools for some work here

        LOCAL loFtools
        loFtools = CREATEOBJECT("foxtools")
        this.cPath       = loFtools.JustPath(DBC())

        *-- And, just to make sure that there is no
        *-- path in the .DBC name...

        this.cDbcName    = loFtools.JustfName(DBC())

        *-- Now read the .DBC
```

```
        this.nTables    = aDBObjects(this.aTables, "Table")
        this.nViews     = aDBObjects(this.aViews, "View")
        this.nRelations = aDBObjects(this.aRelations, "Relation")
ENDPROC

*-- Writes all the classes.
PROTECTED PROCEDURE writeclasses
    SET TEXTMERGE TO (this.cPRGNAME) NOSHOW

    *-- Write the header first

    SET TEXTMERGE ON

    LOCAL lcOldCentury
    lcOldCentury = SET("century")
    SET CENTURY ON

    \*  Program...........: <<this.cPRGName>>
    \*  DBC...............: <<this.cDBCName>>
    \*  Generated.........: <<MDY(DATE()) + " - " + TIME()>>
    \
    \#DEFINE databasepath "<<this.cPath>>"

    SET TEXTMERGE OFF

    IF this.nTables > 0     OR this.nViews > 0
        this.CursorClasses()
    ENDIF

    IF this.nRelations > 0
        this.RelationClasses()
    ENDIF

    this.WriteDefaultClass()

    SET TEXTMERGE OFF
    SET TEXTMERGE TO
ENDPROC

*-- Processes all the cursor classes in the .DBC.
PROTECTED PROCEDURE cursorclasses
    LOCAL lnCounter
    SET TEXTMERGE ON
    FOR lnCounter = 1 TO this.nTables
        this.WriteCursorClass(this.aTables[lnCounter])
    ENDFOR

    FOR lnCounter = 1 TO this.nViews
        this.WriteCursorClass(this.aViews[lnCounter])
    ENDFOR
    SET TEXTMERGE OFF
ENDPROC

*-- Writes a cursor class to the output program file.
```

continues

Listing 17.2   Continued

```
PROTECTED PROCEDURE writecursorclass
    LPARAMETERS tcClassName

    \DEFINE CLASS <<STRTRAN(tcClassName, chr(32), "_")>> AS cursor
    \    alias = "<<tcClassName>>"
    \    cursorsource = "<<tcClassName>>"
    \    database = DATABASEPATH + "<<this.cDbcName>>"
    \ENDDEFINE
    \
ENDPROC

*-- Processes and writes all the relation classes.
PROTECTED PROCEDURE relationclasses
    LOCAL    lnCounter, ;
             lcClassName, ;
             lcChildAlias, ;
             lcParentAlias, ;
             lcChildOrder, ;
             lcRelationalExpr

    SET TEXTMERGE ON

    FOR lnCounter = 1 TO this.nRelations
        lcClassName = "RELATION"-Alltrim(Str(lnCounter))
        lcChildAlias = this.aRelations[lnCounter,1]
        lcParentAlias = this.aRelations[lnCounter,2]
        lcChildOrder = this.aRelations[lnCounter,3]
        lcRelationalExpr = this.aRelations[lnCounter,4]

        \DEFINE CLASS <<lcClassName>> AS relation
        \    childalias = "<<lcChildAlias>>"
        \    parentalias = "<<lcParentAlias>>"
        \    childorder = "<<lcChildOrder>>"
        \    RelationalExpr = "<<lcRelationalExpr>>"
        \ENDDEFINE
        \
    ENDFOR

    SET TEXTMERGE OFF
ENDPROC

*-- Writes the default DE class to the program
PROTECTED PROCEDURE writedefaultclass
    LOCAL laClasses[this.nTables + this.nViews + this.nRelations]

    FOR lnCounter = 1 TO this.nTables
        laClasses[lnCounter] = this.aTables[lnCounter]
    ENDFOR

    FOR lnCounter = 1 TO this.nViews
        laClasses[lnCounter+this.nTables] = this.aViews[lnCounter]
    ENDFOR
```

```
        FOR lnCounter = 1 TO this.nRelations
            laClasses[lnCounter+this.nTables+this.nViews] = ;
                "Relation" + ALLTRIM(STR(lnCounter))
        ENDFOR

        SET TEXTMERGE ON

        \DEFINE CLASS default_de AS DataEnvironment

        FOR lnCounter = 1 TO ALEN(laClasses,1)
            lcObjectName = 'o'+laClasses[lnCounter]
            lcClassName = laClasses[lnCounter]
        \    ADD OBJECT <<lcObjectName>> AS <<lcClassName>>
        ENDFOR
        \ENDDEFINE
        \

        SET TEXTMERGE OFF
ENDPROC

PROCEDURE doit
    *-- If no dbc name is specified, ask for one.

    IF EMPTY(this.cDBCName)
        this.cDBCName = GETFILE("DBC", "Please select DBC to dump:")
        IF !FILE(this.cDBCName)
            =MESSAGEBOX("No DBC selected! Aborted!",16)
            RETURN .F.
        ENDIF
    ENDIF

    *-- Same deal with a .PRG

    IF EMPTY(this.cPRGName)
        this.cPRGName = PUTFILE("PRG to create:","","PRG")

        IF EMPTY(this.cPRGName)
            =Messagebox("Operation cancelled!", 16)
            RETURN
        ENDIF
    ENDIF

    *-- As for overwrite permission here. I prefer to do this manually
    *-- (rather than let VFP handle it automatically) because it gives
    *-- me control.
    *--
    *-- Note how the SAFETY setting is queries first.

    IF SET("safety") = "ON" AND ;
        FILE(this.cPRGName) AND ;
        MessageBox("Overwrite existing " + ;
                    ALLTRIM(this.cPRGName) + "?", 36) # 6

        =Messagebox("Operation cancelled!", 16)
```

continues

Listing 17.2   Continued

```
            RETURN
        ENDIF

        *-- save the SAFETY setting

        LOCAL lcOldSafety
        lcOldSafety = SET("safety")
        SET SAFETY OFF

        this.readdbc()
        this.writeclasses()

        SET SAFETY &lcOldSafety
    ENDPROC

ENDDEFINE
*
*-- EndDefine: dumpdbc
***************************************************
```

N O T E   DumpDbc uses the Foxtools class created in Chapter 15. You will need to load the
Chap17a.VCX class library with the SET CLASSLIB TO CHAP17a command before
instantiating an object from the DumpDbc subclass. ▪

TESTDBC is a small test program that illustrates how this class can be used to generate a program for the TESTDATA.DBC database. The code is presented in Listing 17.3.

Listing 17.3   17CODE03.PRG—Program That Illustrates Usage of the Dumpdbc Class

```
*   Program..........: TESTDBC.PRG (D:\seuvfp6\Chap17\Chap17a.vcx)
*   Author...........: Menachem Bazian, CPA
*   Description.......: Illustrates usage of the DumpDbc class
*   Calling Samples...:
*   Parameter List....:
*   Major change list.:

*-- Note, FoxTool.VCX and Chap17a.VCX must be in the same
*-- Directory for this program to work.

Set ClassLib to Chap17
Set ClassLib to FoxTool ADDITIVE
oDbcGen = CREATEOBJECT("dumpdbc")
oDbcGen.cDBCName = "testdata" oDbcGen.cPRGName = "deleteme.prg"
oDbcGen.DoIt()
```

DELETEME.PRG is created by TESTDBC and is presented in Listing 17.4.

Listing 17.4   `17CODE04.PRG`—Code for `DELETEME.PRG` Program Output by the
`Dumpdbc` **Class**

```
*   Program...........: deleteme.prg
*   DBC...............: TESTDATA.DBC
*   Generated........: August 28, 1998 - 10:16:23

#DEFINE databasepath HOME()+"SAMPLES\DATA\"DEFINE CLASS CUSTOMER AS cursor
    alias = "CUSTOMER"
    cursorsource = "CUSTOMER"
    database = DATABASEPATH + "TESTDATA.DBC"
ENDDEFINE

DEFINE CLASS PRODUCTS AS cursor
    alias = "PRODUCTS"
    cursorsource = "PRODUCTS"
    database = DATABASEPATH + "TESTDATA.DBC"
ENDDEFINE

DEFINE CLASS ORDITEMS AS cursor
    alias = "ORDITEMS"
    cursorsource = "ORDITEMS"
    database = DATABASEPATH + "TESTDATA.DBC"
ENDDEFINE

DEFINE CLASS ORDERS AS cursor
    alias = "ORDERS"
    cursorsource = "ORDERS"
    database = DATABASEPATH + "TESTDATA.DBC"
ENDDEFINE

DEFINE CLASS EMPLOYEE AS cursor
    alias = "EMPLOYEE"
    cursorsource = "EMPLOYEE"
    database = DATABASEPATH + "TESTDATA.DBC"
ENDDEFINE

DEFINE CLASS RELATION1 AS relation
    childalias = "ORDERS"
    parentalias = "CUSTOMER"
    childorder = "CUST_ID"
    RelationalExpr = "CUST_ID"
ENDDEFINE

DEFINE CLASS RELATION2 AS relation
    childalias = "ORDERS"
    parentalias = "EMPLOYEE"
    childorder = "EMP_ID"
    RelationalExpr = "EMP_ID"
ENDDEFINE

DEFINE CLASS RELATION3 AS relation
    childalias = "ORDITEMS"
    parentalias = "ORDERS"
```

continues

Listing 17.4   Continued

```
        childorder = "ORDER_ID"
        RelationalExpr = "ORDER_ID"
ENDDEFINE

DEFINE CLASS RELATION4 AS relation
        childalias = "ORDITEMS"
        parentalias = "PRODUCTS"
        childorder = "PRODUCT_ID"
        RelationalExpr = "PRODUCT_ID"
ENDDEFINE

DEFINE CLASS default_de AS DataEnvironment
        ADD OBJECT oCUSTOMER AS CUSTOMER
        ADD OBJECT oPRODUCTS AS PRODUCTS
        ADD OBJECT oORDITEMS AS ORDITEMS
        ADD OBJECT oORDERS AS ORDERS
        ADD OBJECT oEMPLOYEE AS EMPLOYEE
        ADD OBJECT oRelation1 AS Relation1
        ADD OBJECT oRelation2 AS Relation2
        ADD OBJECT oRelation3 AS Relation3
        ADD OBJECT oRelation4 AS Relation4
ENDDEFINE
```

Notice that just instantiating `Default_De` in this case is not enough to get the tables open. In order to open the tables, you have to call the `OpenTables()` method. Furthermore, in order to close the tables, you need to run the `CloseTables()` method.

If you prefer to have these actions happen by default, you could create a subclass of the data environment class as follows:

```
DEFINE CLASS MyDeBase AS DataEnvironment
    PROCEDURE Init
        this.OpenTables()
    ENDPROC

    PROCEDURE Destroy
        this.CloseTables()
    ENDPROC
ENDDEFINE
```

Then, when generating classes, you could use the subclass as the parent of the data environment classes you create.

Increasing the Power of Data Environments with DataSessions

Data environments are powerful, no doubt about that. But wait a minute. Back in the old days of FoxPro 2.x, most developers opened all their tables and relations once at the beginning of their applications and left them open throughout the application session. If this were still the strategy in Visual FoxPro, data environments would seem to be a whole lot to do about nothing.

The truth is, however, that data environments are extraordinarily useful because the basic strategy of opening all tables and relations up front is no longer the way to do things. Why not open all the tables and relations at the beginning of an application? Because you can use multiple data sessions, which gives you a tremendous amount of additional flexibility. With data sessions, you can segregate the data manipulation in one function from the data manipulation of another.

However, there's a catch here: Only forms can create independent data sessions. This would be insurmountable except for one fact: No one ever said a form has to be able to display. In other words, just because a form is a visual class, there is no reason you can't use it as a nonvisual class.

Consider the form class presented in Listing 17.5.

Listing 17.5   `17CODE05.PRG`—Code for `Newdatasession` **Class**

```
*   Class............: Newdatasession.prg (D:\seuvfp6\Chap17\Chap17a.vcx)
*   Author...........: Menachem Bazian, CPA
*   Notes............: Exported code from Class Browser.

**************************************************
*-- Class:       newdatasession
*-- ParentClass: form
*-- BaseClass:   form
*
DEFINE CLASS newdatasession AS form

    DataSession = 2
    Top = 0
    Left = 0
    Height = 35
    Width = 162
    DoCreate = .T.
    Caption = "Form"
    Visible = .F.
    Name = "newdatasession"
    PROTECTED show
    PROTECTED visible

ENDDEFINE
*
*-- EndDefine: newdatasession
**************************************************
```

Notice that the `Visible` property has been set to `.F.` and has been protected, and that the `SHOW` method has been protected as well. In other words, I have just created a form that cannot be displayed.

This concept would be ludicrous except for the fact that the DataSession property has been set to 2, which indicates that this form has its own data session. When the object is instantiated, a new DataSession is created and can be referenced with the SET DATASESSION command (the ID of the form's data session is stored in its DataSessionId property).

This is a prime example of using a class that is normally thought of as a visual class as the basis for creating a nonvisual class.

> **CAUTION**
>
> In order to use the NewDataSession class, the instance must live as its own object and cannot be added to a container. If you want this object to be a property of another object, create the instance with CREATEOBJECT() and not with ADD OBJECT or ADDOBJECT(). If you use one of the two latter methods, you will not get a private data session because the data session is governed by the container package in a composite class. See Chapter 14 for more information.

Modeling Objects on the Real World

Objects are supposed to model the real world, right? Up until now, the classes I covered have been focused on functionality rather than modeling the real world. Now it's time to look at classes designed to model real-world objects.

The first object I present is a familiar one that provides a good opportunity to look at modeling functionality in objects: a stopwatch.

Defining the Stopwatch

The first step in any attempt to create an object is to define what the object is all about. This usually happens, when developing object-oriented software, in the analysis and design phase of the project. I briefly discussed this phase in Chapter 13, "Introduction to Object-Oriented Programming." In this case, it's a relatively simple exercise.

Consider a stopwatch. If you happen to have one, take it out and look at it. Notice that it has a display (usually showing the time elapsed in *HH:MM:SS.SS* format). The stopwatch has buttons that enable you to start it, stop it, pause it (lap time), and reset the display. Naturally, a stopwatch has the capability to track time from when it is started until it is stopped. This is a good list of the functions needed for a stopwatch class. When you have the required behavior of the object, you can then work on designing the implementation of the class.

Implementing the Stopwatch

Many factors can affect how a class is implemented, ranging from how the class is intended to be used to the personal preferences of the developer.

In this case, when designing the implementation of the stopwatch class, the functionality is divided into two parts. The first part is the engine (the portion of the stopwatch that has the functionality for calculating the time as well as starting, stopping, and pausing the stopwatch). The second class combines the engine with the display to create a full stopwatch.

Frequently, when working on a single class's implementation, opportunities present themselves for creating additional functionality at little cost. In this case, breaking the functionality of the stopwatch into an engine and a display portion gives you the ability either to subclass the engine into something different or to use the engine on its own without being burdened by the display component.

It's always a good idea to look at the implementation design of a class and ask the following question: Is there a way I can increase the reusability of the classes I create by abstracting (separating) functionality? The more you can make your classes reusable, the easier your life will be down the road.

The SwatchEngine Class

This class can be thought of as the mechanism behind the stopwatch. Based on the Timer class, the SwatchEngine class basically counts time from when it is started to when it is stopped. It does not enable for any display of the data. (A stopwatch with a display is added in class SWATCH). This class is useful for when you want to track the time elapsed between events. The SwatchEngine class code is presented in Listing 17.6.

Listing 17.6 17CODE06.PRG—Code for the SwatchEngine Class, Which Performs the Stopwatch Count-Down Operations

```
*   Class............: Swatchengine.prg  (D:\seuvfp6\Chap17\Chap17a.vcx)
*   Author...........: Menachem Bazian, CPA
*   Notes............: Exported code from Class Browser.

******************************************************
*-- Class:        swatchengine
*-- ParentClass:  timer
*-- BaseClass:    timer
*-- Engine behind the SWATCH class.
*
DEFINE CLASS swatchengine AS timer

    Height = 23
    Width = 26
    *-- Number of seconds on the clock
    nsecs = 0
    *-- Time the clock was last updated
    PROTECTED nlast
    nlast = 0
    *-- Time the clock was started
    nstart = 0
    Name = "swatchengine"

    *-- Start the clock
```

continues

Listing 17.6   Continued

```
        PROCEDURE start
            this.nstart   = SECONDS()
            this.nLast    = this.nStart
            this.nSecs    = 0
            this.Interval = 200
        ENDPROC

        *-- Stop the clock
        PROCEDURE stop
            this.timer()

            this.Interval = 0
            this.nLast    = 0
        ENDPROC

        *-- Pause the clock.
        PROCEDURE pause
            this.timer()
            this.interval = 0
        ENDPROC

        *-- Resume the clock
        PROCEDURE resume
            If this.nLast = 0 && Clock was stopped
                this.nLast = SECONDS() && Pick up from now
                this.interval = 200
            ELSE
                this.interval = 200
            ENDIF
        ENDPROC

        PROCEDURE Init
            this.nstart = 0
            this.Interval = 0
            this.nSecs = 0
            ·this.nLast = 0
        ENDPROC

        PROCEDURE Timer
            LOCAL lnSeconds

            lnSeconds    = SECONDS()
            this.nSecs   = this.nSecs + (lnSeconds - this.nLast)
            this.nLast   = lnSeconds
        ENDPROC

ENDDEFINE
*
*-- EndDefine: swatchengine
***************************************************
```

Properties   Table 17.7 presents the properties for SwatchEngine.

Table 17.7 The Properties for SwatchEngine

Properties	Description
Interval	The Interval property is not a new property—it is standard to the Timer class. If Interval is set to zero, the clock does not run; if Interval is set to a value greater than zero, the clock runs.
	In SwatchEngine, the clock runs at a "standard" interval of 200 milliseconds.
nsecs	This property is the number of seconds counted. It is carried out to three decimal places and is what the SECONDS function returns.
PROTECTED nlast	This property is the last time the Timer event fired. This is a protected property.
nstart	This property is the time the watch was started, measured in seconds since midnight.

N O T E For the record, the Timer's Interval property governs how often the Timer event fires. If set to 0, the Timer event does not run. A positive Interval determines how often the Timer event runs. The Interval is specified in milliseconds. ■

Events and Methods The following methods have a common theme: There is very little action happening. For the most part, all of these methods accomplish their actions by setting properties in the timer. For example, the clock can be started and stopped by setting the Interval property (a value of zero stops the clock, and anything greater than zero starts the clock). Table 17.8 presents the methods for SwatchEngine.

Table 17.8 The Methods for SwatchEngine

Method	Description
Init	This method initializes the nstart, Interval, nSecs, and nLast properties to zero.
Pause	This method calls the Timer() method to update the time counter and then stops the clock by setting the Interval property to 0.
Resume	This method restarts the clock by setting the Interval property to 200 (1/5 of a second). If nLast is not set to 0, the Resume() method knows that the clock was paused and picks up the count as if the clock were never stopped. Otherwise, all the time since the clock was stopped is ignored and the clock begins from that point.
Start	This method starts the clock and records when the clock was started.
Stop	This method stops the clock and sets nLast to 0.
Timer	This method updates the number of seconds (nSecs) property.

The Swatch Class

Now that the engine is done, you can combine the engine with a display component to create a stopwatch. The Swatch class is a container-based class that combines a label object (which is used to display the amount of time on the stopwatch) with a swatch engine object to complete the functional stopwatch.

Design Strategy The key to this class is SwatchEngine. The parent (that is, the container) has properties and methods to mirror SwatchEngine, such as nStart, Start(), Stop(), Pause(), and Resume(). This enables a form using the class to have a consistent interface to control the stopwatch. In other words, the form does not have to know there are separate objects within the container; all the form has to do is communicate with the container.

Figure 17.2 shows what the class looks like in the Visual Class Designer.

FIGURE 17.2

The Swatch class in the Visual Class Designer.

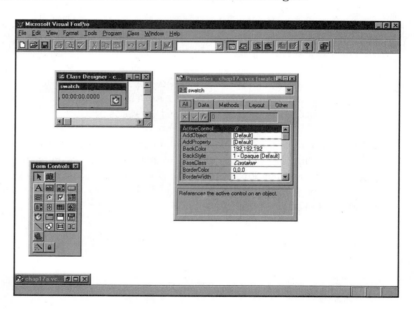

The code for the Swatch class is presented in Listing 17.7.

Listing 17.7 17CODE07.PRG—Code for the Swatch Class That Displays the Stopwatch Time

```
*  Class.............: Swatch.prg  (D:\seuvfp6\Chap17\Chap17a.vcx)
*  Author............: Menachem Bazian, CPA
*  Notes.............: Exported code from Class Browser.

****************************************************
*-- Class:        swatch
*-- ParentClass:  container
*-- BaseClass:    container
*
```

```
DEFINE CLASS swatch AS container

    Width = 141
    Height = 41
    nsecs = 0
    nstart = (seconds())
    Name = "swatch"

    ADD OBJECT lbltime AS label WITH ;
        Caption = "00:00:00.0000", ;
        Height = 25, ;
        Left = 7, ;
        Top = 8, ;
        Width = 97, ;
        Name = "lblTime"

    ADD OBJECT tmrswengine AS swatchengine WITH ;
        Top = 9, ;
        Left = 108, ;
        Height = 24, ;
        Width = 25, ;
        Name = "tmrSWEngine"

    PROCEDURE stop
        this.tmrSWEngine.Stop()
    ENDPROC

    PROCEDURE start
        this.tmrSWEngine.Start()
    ENDPROC

    PROCEDURE resume
        this.tmrSWEngine.Resume()
    ENDPROC

    PROCEDURE pause
        this.tmrSWEngine.Pause()
    ENDPROC

    *-- ,Property Description will appear here.
    PROCEDURE reset
        this.tmrSWEngine.nSecs = 0
        this.Refresh()
    ENDPROC

    PROCEDURE Refresh
        LOCAL lcTime, ;
              lnSecs, ;
              lnHours, ;
              lnMins, ;
              lcSecs, ;
              lnLen

        this.nSecs  = this.tmrSWEngine.nSecs
        this.nStart = this.tmrSWEngine.nStart
```

continues

Listing 17.7 Continued

```
                    *-- Take the number of seconds on the clock (nSecs property)
                    *-- and convert it to a string for display.

                    lcTime    = ""
                    lnSecs    = this.tmrSWEngine.nSecs

                    lnHours   = INT(lnSecs/3600)

                    lnSecs    = MOD(lnSecs,3600)
                    lnMins    = INT(lnSecs/60)

                    lnSecs    = MOD(lnSecs,60)

                    lcSecs    = STR(lnSecs,6,3)
                    lnLen     = LEN(ALLT(LEFT(lcSecs,AT('.', lcSecs)-1)))
                    lcSecs    = REPL('0', 2-lnLen) + LTRIM(lcSecs)

                    lnLen     = LEN(ALLT(SUBST(lcSecs,AT('.', lcSecs)+1)))
                    lcSecs    = RTRIM(lcSecs) + REPL('0', 3-lnLen)

                    lcTime    = PADL(lnHours,2,'0') + ":" + ;
                                PADL(lnMins,2,'0') + ":" + ;
                                lcSecs

               this.lblTime.Caption = lcTime
          ENDPROC

          PROCEDURE tmrswengine.Timer
               Swatchengine:Timer()
               this.Parent.refresh()
          ENDPROC

     ENDDEFINE
     *
     *-- EndDefine: swatch
     ***************************************************
```

Member Objects   The Swatch class has two member objects:

- lblTime (Label)
- tmrSWEngine (Swatch engine)

Custom Properties   Notice that the properties shown in Table 17.9 are properties of the container itself.

Table 17.9 The Custom Properties

Properties	Description
nStart	This property is the time the watch was started, measured in seconds since midnight.
nSecs	This property is the number of seconds counted. It is carried out to three decimal places and is what the SECONDS() function returns. The SwatchEngine properties in tmrSWEngine remain intact as inherited from the base class.

Events and Methods   Notice Table 17.10 presents the events and methods in the Swatch class.

Table 17.10 The Events and Methods in the Swatch Class

Event/Method	Description
Swatch.Start	This method calls tmrSWEngine.Start.
Swatch.Stop	This method calls tmrSWEngine.Stop.
Swatch.Pause	This method calls tmrSWEngine.Pause.
Swatch.Resume	This method calls tmrSWEngine.Resume.
Swatch.Reset	This method resets the nSecs counter to 0 and then calls the Refresh method. This is designed to enable the display portion of the stopwatch to be reset to 00:00:00.000.
Swatch.Refresh()	This method updates the container properties nStart and nSecs from the timer and converts the number of seconds counted to *HH:MM:SS.SS* format.
tmrSWEngine.Timer()	This method calls the SwatchEngine::Timer method, followed by the container's Refresh method.

Putting It Together on a Form

And now for the final step: putting all of this functionality together on a form. The form is shown in Figure 17.3. The code for the Swatchform form is presented in Listing 17.8.

FIGURE 17.3

The Stopwatch form.

Listing 17.8 `17CODE08.PRG`—Code for the `Swatchform` Form That Contains the Stopwatch

```
*   Class............: Swatchform.prg (D:\seuvfp6\Chap17\Chap17a.vcx)
*   Author...........: Menachem Bazian, CPA
*   Notes............: Exported code from Class Browser.

**************************************************
*-- Class:        swatchform
*-- ParentClass:  form
*-- BaseClass:    form
*
DEFINE CLASS swatchform AS form

     ScaleMode = 3
     Top = 0
     Left = 0
     Height = 233
     Width = 285
     DoCreate = .T.
     BackColor = RGB(192,192,192)
     BorderStyle = 2
     Caption = "Stop Watch Example"
     Name = "swatchform"

     ADD OBJECT swatch1 AS swatch WITH ;
          Top = 24, ;
          Left = 76, ;
          Width = 132, ;
          Height = 37, ;
          Name = "Swatch1", ;
          lbltime.Caption = "00:00:00.0000", ;
          lbltime.Left = 24, ;
          lbltime.Top = 12, ;
          lbltime.Name = "lbltime", ;
          tmrswengine.Top = 9, ;
          tmrswengine.Left = 108, ;
          tmrswengine.Name = "tmrswengine"

     ADD OBJECT cmdstart AS commandbutton WITH ;
          Top = 84, ;
          Left = 48, ;
          Height = 40, ;
```

```
        Width = 85, ;
        Caption = "\<Start", ;
        Name = "cmdStart"

ADD OBJECT cmdstop AS commandbutton WITH ;
        Top = 84, ;
        Left = 144, ;
        Height = 40, ;
        Width = 85, ;
        Caption = "S\<top", ;
        Enabled = .F., ;
        Name = "cmdStop"

ADD OBJECT cmdpause AS commandbutton WITH ;
        Top = 129, ;
        Left = 49, ;
        Height = 40, ;
        Width = 85, ;
        Caption = "\<Pause", ;
        Enabled = .F., ;
        Name = "cmdPause"

ADD OBJECT cmdresume AS commandbutton WITH ;
        Top = 129, ;
        Left = 145, ;
        Height = 40, ;
        Width = 85, ;
        Caption = "\<Resume", ;
        Name = "cmdResume"

ADD OBJECT cmdreset AS commandbutton WITH ;
        Top = 192, ;
        Left = 72, ;
        Height = 37, ;
        Width = 121, ;
        Caption = "Reset \<Display", ;
        Name = "cmdReset"

PROCEDURE cmdstart.Click
        this.enabled = .F.
        thisform.cmdStop.enabled = .T.
        thisform.cmdPause.enabled = .T.
        thisform.cmdResume.enabled = .F.
        thisform.cmdReset.enabled = .F.
        thisform.Swatch1.Start()
ENDPROC

PROCEDURE cmdstop.Click
        this.enabled = .F.
        thisform.cmdStart.enabled = .T.
        thisform.cmdPause.enabled = .F.
        thisform.cmdResume.enabled = .T.
        thisform.cmdReset.enabled = .T.
        thisform.swatch1.stop()
ENDPROC
```

Part

IV

Ch

17

continues

Listing 17.8 Continued

```
    PROCEDURE cmdpause.Click
        this.enabled = .F.
        thisform.cmdStop.enabled = .T.
        thisform.cmdStart.enabled = .F.
        thisform.cmdResume.enabled = .T.
        thisform.cmdReset.enabled = .F.
        ThisForm.Swatch1.Pause()
    ENDPROC

    PROCEDURE cmdresume.Click
        this.enabled = .F.
        thisform.cmdStart.enabled = .F.
        thisform.cmdPause.enabled = .T.
        thisform.cmdStop.enabled = .T.
        thisform.cmdResume.enabled = .F.
        thisform.cmdReset.enabled = .F.
        thisform.swatch1.resume()
    ENDPROC

    PROCEDURE cmdreset.Click
        thisform.swatch1.reset()
    ENDPROC

ENDDEFINE
*
*-- EndDefine: swatchform
****************************************************
```

The form, SwatchForm, is a form-based class with a Swatch object dropped on it. The command buttons on the form call the appropriate Swatch methods to manage the stopwatch (that is, start it, stop it, and so on).

There isn't much to this form, as the preceding code shows. All the real work has already been done in the Swatch class. All the objects on the form do is call methods from the Swatch class.

Member Objects   Table 17.11 presents the member objects of the Swatch class.

Table 17.11   The Member Objects of the Swatch Class

Member Object	Description
Swatch1	(Swatch Class) This object is an instance of the Swatch class.
cmdStart	(Command Button) This object is the Start button, which starts the clock and appropriately enables or disables the other buttons.
cmdStop	(Command Button) This object is the Stop button, which stops the clock and appropriately enables or disables the other buttons.
cmdPause	(Command Button) This object is the Pause button, which pauses the clock and appropriately enables or disables the other buttons.

Member Object	Description
cmdResume	(Command Button) This object is the Resume button. It resumes the clock and appropriately enables or disables the other buttons.
cmdReset	(Command Button) This object is the Reset button, which resets the clock display.

The Swatch Class: A Final Word

One of the keys to achieving reuse is to look for it when you design the functionality of your code. There is no magic to this process, but there are methodologies designed to assist in the process. The intent behind showing the Swatch class is to illustrate how a single class—when it is created—can evolve into more classes than one in order to support greater reusability. When you think of your design, think about reusability.

Working with Frameworks

In Chapter 15 I introduced the concept of a framework. A *framework*, put simply, is the collection of classes that, when taken together, represent the foundation on which you will base your applications. A framework represents two things. First, it represents the parent classes for your subclasses. Second, it represents a structure for implementing functionality within your applications.

Take the issue of creating business classes. A properly designed framework can make creating business objects easy. In the next section I show you why.

The Nature of Business Objects

At the simplest level, a business object (a customer, for example) has the functionality that would normally be associated with data entry and editing. For example, the responsibilities could include the following:

- Display for editing
- Moving between records (top, bottom, next, and previous)

You can add to this list of common responsibilities. Obviously, you need functions for adding new records, for deleting records, and so on. The five functions presented in this section serve as an example and are modeled in the framework.

In terms of creating the framework, the goal is to create a series of classes that interact with each other to provide the functionality you need. In order to make the framework usable, you want to keep the modifications needed for combining the classes into a business class as minimal as possible.

The framework I present breaks down the functionality as follows:

- *Navigation class* This is similar to the navigation classes covered in Chapter 15. This class will be a series of command buttons for navigation within a form containing a business class.

- *Form class*   This is a combination of a form and the navigation class and is designed to work with business objects.
- *Data environment loader class*   This is a class that handles loading the data environment for a business class.
- *Business class*   This class has the data and methods for the business class being modeled and has a data environment loader class in it.

The nice thing about this framework, as it will work out in the end, is that the only work necessary for implementing a business class will occur in the business class. All the other classes are designed generically and refer to the business class for specific functionality. I go through the classes one at a time in the following sections.

The Base_Navigation Class

The `Base_Navigation` class is a set of navigation buttons designed to be used with forms that display a business class. Figure 17.4 shows the `Base_Navigation` class in the Class Designer. The `Base_Navigation` class is also selected in the Class Browser. The code for the class ispresented in Listing 17.9.

> **N O T E**   The framework classes shown in this chapter can be found on the in the `FW.VCX` visual class library. The class listings were generated by the Class Browser View Class code function. ■

FIGURE 17.4

The Base Naviga-tion class.

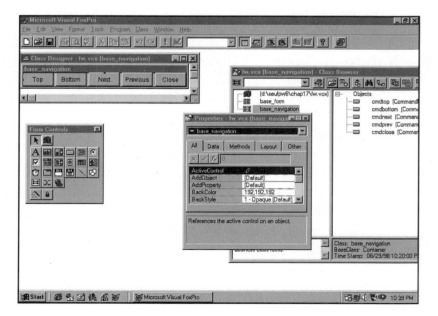

Listing 17.9 17CODE09.PRG—Code for Base_Navigation Class

```
*  Class.............: Base_navigation (D:\seuvfp6\Chap17\FW.vcx)
*  Author............: Menachem Bazian, CPA
*  Notes.............: Exported code from Class Browser.

**************************************************
*-- Class:        base_navigation
*-- ParentClass:  container
*-- BaseClass:    container
*-- Collection of nav buttons for business class forms.
*
DEFINE CLASS base_navigation AS container

    Width = 328
    Height = 30
    Name = "base_navigation"

    ADD OBJECT cmdtop AS commandbutton WITH ;
        Top = 0, ;
        Left = 0, ;
        Height = 29, ;
        Width = 62, ;
        Caption = "Top", ;
        Name = "cmdTop"

    ADD OBJECT cmdbottom AS commandbutton WITH ;
        Top = 0, ;
        Left = 66, ;
        Height = 29, ;
        Width = 62, ;
        Caption = "Bottom", ;
        Name = "cmdBottom"

    ADD OBJECT cmdnext AS commandbutton WITH ;
        Top = 0, ;
        Left = 132, ;
        Height = 29, ;
        Width = 62, ;
        Caption = "Next", ;
        Name = "cmdNext"

    ADD OBJECT cmdprev AS commandbutton WITH ;
        Top = 0, ;
        Left = 198, ;
        Height = 29, ;
        Width = 62, ;
        Caption = "Previous", ;
        Name = "cmdPrev"

    ADD OBJECT cmdclose AS commandbutton WITH ;
        Top = 0, ;
        Left = 265, ;
        Height = 29, ;
        Width = 62, ;
```

Part
IV

Ch
17

continues

Listing 17.9   Continued

```
           Caption = "Close", ;
           Name = "cmdClose"

     PROCEDURE cmdtop.Click
         LOCAL lcClassName

         lcClassName = thisform.cClass
         ThisForm.&lcClassName..Topit()
     ENDPROC

     PROCEDURE cmdbottom.Click
         LOCAL lcClassName

         lcClassName = thisform.cClass
         ThisForm.&lcClassName..Bottomit()
     ENDPROC

     PROCEDURE cmdnext.Click
         LOCAL lcClassName

         lcClassName = thisform.cClass
         ThisForm.&lcClassName..Nextit()
     ENDPROC

     PROCEDURE cmdprev.Click
         LOCAL lcClassName

         lcClassName = thisform.cClass
         ThisForm.&lcClassName..Previt()
     ENDPROC

     PROCEDURE cmdclose.Click
         Release ThisForm
     ENDPROC

ENDDEFINE
*
*-- EndDefine: base_navigation
****************************************************
```

There is nothing too exciting here. The class is almost a yawner—it doesn't seem to present anything new. However, there is one very important difference between this class and all the other navigation functionality you have seen so far. The Base_Navigation class looks for the custom property cClass on the form. This property has the name of the business class residing on the form. With that name, the navigation buttons can call the appropriate movement methods *in the business object*. The navigation class, in other words, has no clue how to move to the next record, for example. It delegates that responsibility to the business class.

The Base Form

The next step is to create a form that has the `cClass` property and has an instance of the `Base_Navigation` class on it. This form will be subclassed for all business object data entry forms (you'll see this later in the section "Using the Framework").

The class `Base_Form` is shown in Figure 17.5. The code for the `Base_Form` class is presented in Listing 17.10.

FIGURE 17.5

The base Business form.

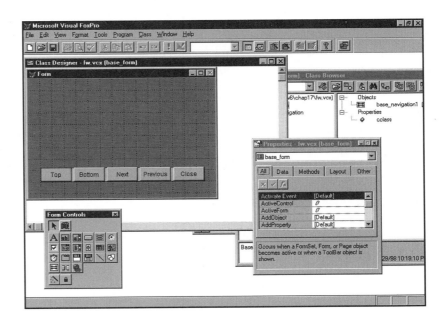

Listing 17.10   17CODE10.PRG—Code for the `Base_Form` Class

```
*   Class............: Base_form (D:\seuvfp6\Chap17\FW.vcx)
*   Author...........: Menachem Bazian, CPA
*   Notes............: Exported code from Class Browser.

*******************************************************
*-- Class:        base_form
*-- ParentClass:  form
*-- BaseClass:    form
*-- Base form for business classes
*
DEFINE CLASS base_form AS form

    DataSession = 2
    DoCreate = .T.
    BackColor = RGB(128,128,128)
    Caption = "Form"
```

continues

Listing 17.10 Continued

```
    Name = "base_form"

    *-- Name of business class on the form.
    cclass = .F.

    ADD OBJECT base_navigation1 AS base_navigation WITH ;
        Top = 187, ;
        Left = 25, ;
        Width = 328, ;
        Height = 30, ;
        Name = "base_navigation1", ;
        cmdTop.Name = "cmdTop", ;
        cmdBottom.Name = "cmdBottom", ;
        cmdNext.Name = "cmdNext", ;
        cmdPrev.Name = "cmdPrev", ;
        cmdClose.Name = "cmdClose"

ENDDEFINE
*
*-- EndDefine: base_form
****************************************************
```

There is nothing really exciting here, either. This form has a custom property called cclass that is designed to tell the navigation class onto which class to delegate the navigation method responsibilities. It also has an instance of the navigation class on it.

The Base Data Environment Class

Business classes use tables. Using tables typically calls for a data environment. The framework class for this is the Base_De class shown in Listing 17.11.

Listing 17.11 17CODE11.PRG—Code for the Base_De Class Used in Table Navigation

```
*  Class............: Base_de (D:\seuvfp6\Chap17\FW.vcx)
*  Author...........: Menachem Bazian, CPA
*  Notes............: Exported code from Class Browser.

****************************************************
*-- Class:        base_de
*-- ParentClass:  custom
*-- BaseClass:    custom
*-- DataEnvironment Loader
*
DEFINE CLASS base_de AS custom

    Height = 36
    Width = 36
    Name = "base_de"
```

```
*-- Name of the DE Class to load
cdeclassname = .F.

*-- The name of the program holding the DE class
cdeprgname = .F.

*-- Ensures that a dataenvironment class name has been specified
PROTECTED PROCEDURE chk4de
    IF TYPE("this.cDeClassName") # 'C' OR EMPTY(this.cDeClassName)
        =MessageBox("No Data Environment was specified. " + ;
                        "Cannot instantiate object.", ;
                    16, ;
                    "Instantiation Error")
        RETURN .F.
    ENDIF
ENDPROC

*-- Opens the Data Environment
PROCEDURE opende
    *-- Method OPENDE
    *-- This method will instantiate a DE class and run the
    *-- OpenTables() method.
    *--
    *-- Since the Container is not yet instantiated, I cannot do
    *--an AddObject() to it.
    *--
    *-- I'll do that in the container's Init.

    LOCAL loDe, lcClassName

    IF !EMPTY(this.cDEPrgName)
        SET PROCEDURE TO (this.cDEPrgName) ADDITIVE
    ENDIF

    lcClassName = this.cDeClassName
    loDe = CREATEOBJECT(lcClassName)

    IF TYPE("loDe") # "O"
        IF !EMPTY(this.cDEPrgName)
            RELEASE PROCEDURE (this.cDEPrgName)
        ENDIF
        RETURN .F.
    ENDIF

    *-- If we get this far, we can run the opentables method.

    loDe.OpenTables()

    IF !EMPTY(this.cDEPrgName)
        RELEASE PROCEDURE (this.cDEPrgName)
    ENDIF
ENDPROC
```

Part

IV

Ch

17

continues

Listing 17.11   Continued

```
PROCEDURE Init
    IF !this.Chk4dE()
        RETURN .f.
    ENDIF

    *-- Add code here to add the DE object at runtime and run the OPENTABLES
    *-- event. I will leave that out for now....

    RETURN this.openDE()
ENDPROC

ENDDEFINE
*
*-- EndDefine: base_de
****************************************************
```

Finally, here is something interesting to discuss. This class, based on Custom, is designed to load a data environment for the business class. It has two properties: the name of the data environment class to load and the name of the PRG file where the data environment class resides. Because data environment classes cannot be created visually, this class acts as a wrapper.

Why separate this class out? To be sure, the functionality for this class could have been rolled into the business class; however, when creating this framework, I could see the use of having this type of Loader class on many different kinds of forms and classes. By abstracting the functionality out into a different class, I can now use this class whenever and wherever I please.

Events and Methods   Table 17.12 presents the Base_De class's events and methods.

Table 17.12   The Base_De Class's Events and Methods

Event/Method	Description
Init	The Init method first calls the Chk4De method to make sure that a data environment class name has been specified. If not, the object's instantiation is aborted. It then calls OpenDe to open the tables and relations.
Chk4De	This method checks to make sure that a data environment was specified.
OpenDe	This method instantiates the data environment class and runs the OpenTables method.
	What about closing the tables? Well, the base form is set to run in its own data session. When the form instance is released, the data session is closed along with all of the tables in it. Don't you love it when a plan comes together?

The Base Business Class

The next class is the framework class for creating business classes. Figure 17.6 shows the
Base_Business class, and the code is presented in Listing 17.12.

FIGURE 17.6

The Base Business
class.

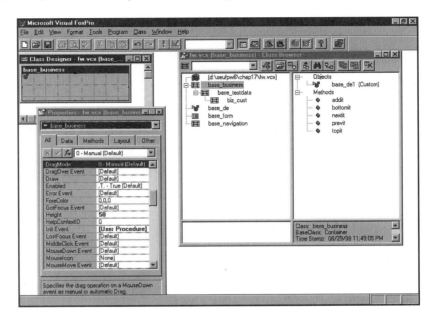

Listing 17.12 17CODE12.PRG—Code for the Base_Business Class That Creates
Business Classes

```
*    Class............: Base_business (D:\seuvfp6\Chap17\FW.vcx)
*    Author...........: Menachem Bazian, CPA
*    Notes............: Exported code from Class Browser.

******************************************************
*-- Class:         base_business
*-- ParentClass:   container
*-- BaseClass:     container
*-- Abstract business class.
*
DEFINE CLASS base_business AS container

     Width = 215
     Height = 58
     BackStyle = 0
     TabIndex = 1
     Name = "base_business"
```

continues

Listing 17.12   Continued

```
*-- Name of the table controlling the class
PROTECTED ctablename

ADD OBJECT base_de1 AS base_de WITH ;
    Top = 0, ;
    Left = 0, ;
    Height = 61, ;
    Width = 217, ;
    cdeclassname = "", ;
    Name = "base_de1"

*-- Add a record
PROCEDURE addit
    SELECT (this.cTableName)
    APPEND BLANK

    IF TYPE("thisform") = "O"
        Thisform.refresh()
    ENDIF
ENDPROC

*-- Go to the next record
PROCEDURE nextit
    SELECT (this.cTableName)

    SKIP 1
    IF EOF()
        ?? CHR(7)
        WAIT WINDOW NOWAIT "At end of file"
        GO BOTTOM
    ENDIF

    IF TYPE("thisform") = "O"
        Thisform.refresh()
    ENDIF
ENDPROC

*-- Move to prior record
PROCEDURE previt
    SELECT (this.cTableName)

    SKIP -1
    IF BOF()
        ?? CHR(7)
        WAIT WINDOW NOWAIT "At beginning of file"
        GO top
    ENDIF

    IF TYPE("thisform") = "O"
        Thisform.refresh()
    ENDIF
ENDPROC
```

```
        *-- Move to the first record
        PROCEDURE topit
            SELECT (this.cTableName)

            GO TOP
            IF TYPE("thisform") = "O"
                Thisform.refresh()
            ENDIF
        ENDPROC

        *-- Move to the last record
        PROCEDURE bottomit
            SELECT (this.cTableName)

            GO BOTTOM

            IF TYPE("thisform") = "O"
                Thisform.refresh()
            ENDIF
        ENDPROC

        PROCEDURE Init
            SELECT (this.cTableName)

            IF TYPE("thisform.cClass") # 'U'
                thisform.cClass = this.Name
            ENDIF
        ENDPROC


        PROCEDURE editit
        ENDPROC

        PROCEDURE getit
        ENDPROC

    ENDDEFINE
    *
    *-- EndDefine: base_business
    ******************************************************
```

This class is based on a container class. In Chapter 15, I discuss the flexibility of the container class, and here is a perfect example. The Base Business class is a container with methods attached to it that handle the functionality of the business class. The container also serves as a receptacle for a base data environment loader class. When subclassing the Base_Business class, you would add the GUI elements that make up the data for the business class. Because the data environment loader class is added as the first object on the container, it instantiates first. Thus, if you have controls in a business class that reference a table as the control source, the business class will work because the data environment loader will open the tables before those other objects get around to instantiating.

The Base Business class has one custom property, cTableName, which holds the alias of the table that controls navigation. For example, for an order business class, cTableName would most likely be the Orders table even though the Order Items table is used as well. The following section discusses the events and methods.

Events and Methods   Table 17.13 presents the events and methods for Base_Business.

Table 17.13	The Events and Methods for Base_Business
Event/Method	**Description**
Init	The Init method selects the controlling table. Remember, because the container will initialize last, by the time this method runs the data environment should already be set up.
	The next bit of code is interesting. The Init method checks to make sure that the cClass property exists on the form (it should—the check is a result of just a bit of paranoia at work) and then sets it to be the name of the business class. In other words, you do not have to play with the form when dropping a business class on it. The framework is designed to enable you to just drop a business class on the form and let it go from there.
Addit	This method adds a record to the controlling table. If the class resides on a form, the form's Refresh method is called.
Bottomit	This method moves to the last record of the controlling table. If the class resides on a form, the form's Refresh method is called.
Nextit	This method moves to the next record of the controlling table. If the class resides on a form, the form's Refresh method is called.
Previt	This method moves back one record in the controlling table. If the class resides on a form, the form's Refresh method is called.
Topit	This method moves to the top record of the controlling table. If the class resides on a form, the form's Refresh method is called.

Enhancing the Framework

Now that the framework is set up, the next step is to put it to use. In this case, a customer class is created to handle customer information in the TESTDATA.DBC database.

The first step in working with a corporate framework might be to customize it slightly for the use of a department or an application. In this case, I created a subclass of the Base_Business class for the business class I will show here. The subclass specifies the name of the data environment class to load as default_de (remember, default_de is automatically generated by

DumpDbc). You'll probably want to use different data environment classes for different business classes. In this case, to show how you might want to customize a framework (and to keep the business classes simple), I decided that I would always load the whole shebang. This being the case, it made sense to set it up once and subclass from there.

The subclass, called Base_TestData, also sets the name of the program to TD_DE.PRG, which is the name of a program I created with DumpDbc. Again, the point here is that you can enhance the framework for your use. In fact, you probably will to some degree. These modifications make up the department or application framework. In this case, Base_TestData would probably be part of the application framework. The code of this subclass is presented in Listing 17.13.

Listing 17.13 17CODE13.PRG—**Code for the** Base_TestData **Subclass of the** Base_Business **Class**

```
*   Class............: Base_testdata(D:\seuvfp6\Chap17\FW.vcx)
*   Author...........: Menachem Bazian, CPA
*   Notes............: Exported code from Class Browser.

*****************************************************
*-- Class:        base_testdata
*-- ParentClass:  base_business
*-- BaseClass:    container
*
DEFINE CLASS base_testdata AS base_business

    Width = 215
    Height = 58
    Name = "base_tastrade"
    base_de1.cdeprgname = "td_de.prg"
    base_de1.cdeclassname = "default_de"
    base_de1.Name = "base_de1"

ENDDEFINE
*
*-- EndDefine: base_testdata
*****************************************************
```

Using the Framework

Now that I have the framework just where I want it, I'll use it to create a business class for the Customer table and build a form for it. Just to illustrate how easy it is to use a framework (or at least how easy it should be), I will review the steps it takes from start to finish.

1. Subclass the base business class, Base_Business (see Figure 17.7).
2. Set the cTableName property to Customer (see Figure 17.8).

FIGURE 17.7
Step 1—The subclass
before modifications.

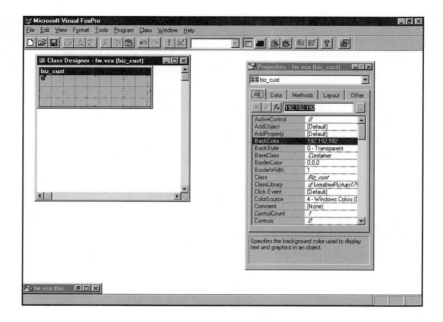

FIGURE 17.8
Step 2—Setting the
cTableName property.

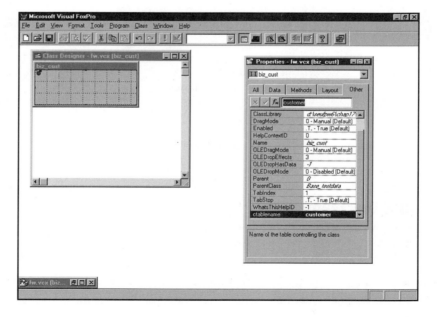

3. Add the GUI objects and save the class (see Figure 17.9).

FIGURE 17.9

Step 3—Adding GUI objects.

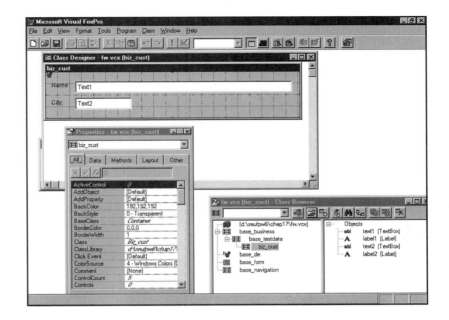

4. Drop the business class on a subclass of the base Business form, Base_Form (see Figure 17.10). An easy way to do this is to use the Class Browser. Select the Base_Form class and click on the New Class button. Enter a name for the new subclass class and the Class Designer opens. Click on the Base_Form class and drag the Copy icon to the new form class.

FIGURE 17.10

Step 4—Dropping the business class on the form.

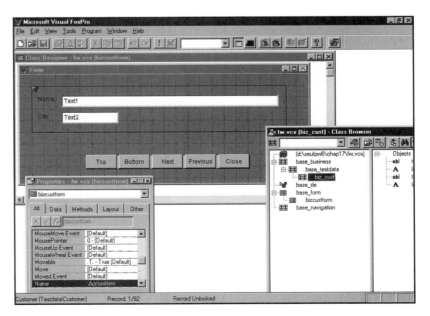

5. Instantiate the form by executing the following code:

```
SET CLASSLIB TO FW               && Establish the class library
oForm = CREATEOBJECT("bizcustform") && Create the form object
oForm.show()                     && Display the form
```

The instantiated form appears as shown in Figure 17.11.

FIGURE 17.11
Step 5—Running the form.

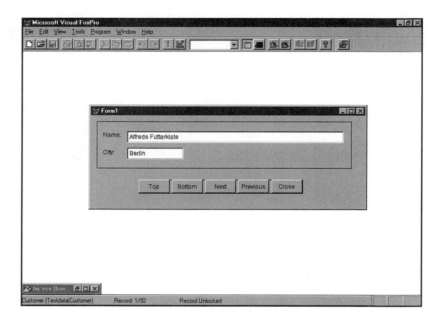

What you have here is two classes: the `Biz_Cust` class, which has the business class specifics, and the form class, `bizcustform`. The code for these two classes is presented in Listings 17.14 and 17.15, respectively.

Listing 17.14   17CODE14.PRG—Code for the `Biz_Cust` Subclass of the `Base_TestData` Class

```
*  Class.............: Biz_cust (D:\seuvfp6\Chap17\FW.vcx)
*  Author............: Menachem Bazian, CPA
*  Notes.............: Exported code from Class Browser.

***************************************************
*-- Class:       biz_cust
*-- ParentClass: base_testdata
*-- BaseClass:   container
*
DEFINE CLASS biz_cust AS base_testdata
```

```
            Width = 509
            Height = 97
            ctablename = "customer"
            Name = "biz_cust"
            base_de1.Top = 0
            base_de1.Left = 0
            base_de1.Height = 241
            base_de1.Width = 637
            base_de1.Name = "base_de1"

      ADD OBJECT text1 AS textbox WITH ;
            Value = "", ;
            ControlSource = "Customer.Company", ;
            Format = "", ;
            Height = 24, ;
            InputMask = "", ;
            Left = 60, ;
            Top = 20, ;
            Width = 433, ;
            Name = "Text1"

      ADD OBJECT label1 AS label WITH ;
            BackStyle = 0, ;
            Caption = "Name:", ;
            Height = 25, ;
            Left = 12, ;
            Top = 20, ;
            Width = 49, ;
            Name = "Label1"

      ADD OBJECT text2 AS textbox WITH ;
            Value = "", ;
            ControlSource = "Customer.City", ;
            Format = "", ;
            Height = 24, ;
            InputMask = "", ;
            Left = 60, ;
            Top = 54, ;
            Width = 113, ;
            Name = "Text2"

      ADD OBJECT label2 AS label WITH ;
            BackStyle = 0, ;
            Caption = "City:", ;
            Height = 18, ;
            Left = 12, ;
            Top = 56, ;
            Width = 43, ;
            Name = "Label2"

ENDDEFINE
*
*-- EndDefine: biz_cust
**************************************************
```

Listing 17.15 17CODE15.PRG—**Code for the** Bizcustform **Subclass of the**
Base_Form **Class**

```
*  Class............: Bizcustform (D:\seuvfp6\Chap17\FW.vcx)
*  Author...........: Menachem Bazian, CPA
*  Notes............: Exported code from Class Browser.

**************************************************
*-- Class:        bizcustform
*-- ParentClass:  base_form
*-- BaseClass:    form
*
DEFINE CLASS bizcustform AS base_form

    Top = 0
    Left = 0
    Height = 202
    Width = 549
    DoCreate = .T.
    Name = "bizcustform"
    base_navigation1.cmdTop.Name = "cmdTop"
    base_navigation1.cmdBottom.Name = "cmdBottom"
    base_navigation1.cmdNext.Name = "cmdNext"
    base_navigation1.cmdPrev.Name = "cmdPrev"
    base_navigation1.cmdClose.Name = "cmdClose"
    base_navigation1.Top = 156
    base_navigation1.Left = 108
    base_navigation1.Width = 328
    base_navigation1.Height = 30
    base_navigation1.Name = "base_navigation1"

    ADD OBJECT biz_cust2 AS biz_cust WITH ;
        Top = 36, ;
        Left = 24, ;
        Width = 509, ;
        Height = 97, ;
        Name = "Biz_cust2", ;
        base_de1.Name = "base_de1", ;
        Text1.Name = "Text1", ;
        Label1.Name = "Label1", ;
        Text2.Name = "Text2", ;
        Label2.Name = "Label2"

ENDDEFINE
*
*-- EndDefine: bizcustform
**************************************************
```

Consider the power of this approach. The developer concentrates his or her efforts in one
place: the functionality and information in the business class. As for the surrounding functionality (for example, the form, the navigation controls, and so on), that is handled by the framework.

Additional Notes on the `Business` Class

Creating the business class based on a container has an additional benefit. Whenever a program needs to work with customers, all you have to do is instantiate the business class and call the appropriate methods. Because all the functionality related to the business class is encapsulated within the confines of the container, no other function needs to worry about how to handle the data of the business class. If you're worried about the visual component to the class, you can stop worrying. There is no law that says you have to display the business class when you instantiate it (this also goes for the form I designed for creating new data sessions).

Finally, you can use the business class on forms other than a data entry form. For example, suppose you are working on an `Invoice` class and you need to provide the ability to edit customer information for an invoice. All you need to do is drop the business class on a modal form.

Frameworks: A Final Word

Creating a framework is not a small undertaking. In fact, it is quite a daunting prospect. Still, in the long run, having a framework that you understand and can work with and that provides the functionality and structure you need will prove absolutely essential.

As Visual FoxPro matures in the marketplace, there will be third-party vendors offering frameworks for development. As I write these words, there are several third-party frameworks in progress. The temptation will be strong to purchase an existing framework to jump-start yourself. It would be foolhardy to state that you can only work with a framework you create. Recreating the wheel is not usually a good idea. Besides, the popularity of frameworks, such as the FoxPro Codebook, proves my point.

Remember, though, that the framework you choose will color every aspect of your development. You will rely on it heavily. If it is robust, well documented, and standardized, you have a good chance of succeeding. Don't take this choice lightly. Subject the framework to rigorous testing and evaluation. Accept nothing on faith. If the choice you make is wrong, it can hurt you big time.

What should you look for in a framework? The criteria I discussed in Chapter 16, "Managing Classes with Visual FoxPro," relating to the class librarian's review of suggested classes will do nicely. To review, here are the criteria:

- Documentation
- Robustness
- Completeness
- Standards

By the way, if you're wondering what happened to *compatibility*, I left it out because the framework is the ground level by which compatibility will be measured.

Development Standards

It is critical to develop or adopt standards for coding when working with Visual FoxPro. There is a high degree of probability that the classes you create will be used by others (unless you work alone and never intend to bring other people into your projects). In order for others to be able to use your code, there has to be a degree of standardization that permeates the code. Without these standards, you will be left with a tower of Babel that will not withstand the test of time.

What kind of standards should you implement? The following sections provide some basic categories in which you should make decisions.

Variable Naming

I like to use a form of Hungarian notation. The first character denotes the scope of the variable and the second denotes the data type.

Scope Characters

L	Local
P	Private
G	Global (public)
T	ParameTer

Type Characters

C	Character
D	Date
L	Logical
N	Numeric, Float, Double, Integer
O	Object
T	DateTime
U	Undefined
Y	Currency

If you're wondering where these characters come from, they are the values returned by the Type function. The rest of the variable name should be descriptive. Remember that you can have *really* long names if you like; therefore, there is no need to skimp anymore.

Naming Methods and Properties

One of the nicest features of OOP lies in *polymorphism*, which means that you can have multiple methods and properties of the same name even though they might do different things. To use this feature effectively, it is important that naming standards are established that dictate the names of commonly used methods.

Imagine, for example, what life would be like if one class used the method name Show to display itself, another used the name Display, and another used the name Paint. It would be pretty confusing, wouldn't it?

Where possible, decide on naming conventions that make sense for you. I think it is a good idea to adopt the Microsoft naming conventions (use Show instead of something else, for example) when available. This maintains consistency not only within your classes but also with the FoxPro base classes. By the way, naming conventions apply to properties, too. A common way to name properties is to use as the first character the expected data type in the property (using the same character identifiers shown previously). This helps use the properties too. When standards are not applicable for methods and properties (that is, they are not expected to be commonly used), try to use a descriptive name.

The Effects of a Framework on Standards

The standards you adopt should be based on your framework if possible. If you are looking to purchase a framework and the framework does not have standards with it, I would be very leery of purchasing it. I personally consider well-documented standards the price of entry for a framework.

If you purchase a framework, take a look at the standards and make sure that you can live with them. Although I wouldn't recommend living and dying by standards (rules do have to be broken sometimes in order to get the job done), you will be working by those standards 98 percent of the time (or more). Let's face it, if you didn't work by the standards almost all the time, standards would be meaningless. Make sure that the standards dictated by a framework make sense to you. ●

The Visual FoxPro Foundation Classes

Familiarizing Yourself with the Visual FoxPro Foundation Classes

This chapter introduces you to a new feature of Visual FoxPro 6, the Visual FoxPro Foundation Classes. One major advantage of adopting object-oriented programming (OOP) technology is that OOP promotes object reusability to facilitate rapid application development (RAD). The only problem is determining where to get the class objects to reuse. In the past, you could reuse class objects that you developed for previous tasks, borrow them from your friends, or buy them from a third-party source. The new Visual FoxPro Foundation Classes that ship with Visual FoxPro contain over 100 reusable classes that you can add to your application to speed up and simplify your development effort while reducing the amount of code you have to write.

The Visual FoxPro Foundation Classes consist of a group of classes that provide a wide range of operations that most typical applications need. The classes that are provided support the following functionality:

- Database manipulation and management operations
- Database concurrency resolution
- Custom extendable components
- Web page development
- Windows API support
- Other varied application support

The Visual FoxPro Foundation Classes are stored as .vcx class libraries. You can add foundation classes to your applications to provide powerful functionality with little or no programming. Furthermore, you are free to distribute the foundation classes with your applications.

You can even load them in the Class Browser or Class Designer and examine all the structures and code. Not only do you find out how the classes operate, but you also can learn some advanced Visual FoxPro programming techniques.

Table 18.1 describes what each of the foundation classes does and identifies the associated visual class library file (.vcx). You will learn how to use these foundation classes in your applications later in this chapter.

Table 18.1 Visual FoxPro Foundation Classes

Class	Description	Class Library File
About Dialog	Adds an About dialog box to your project.	_dialogs.vcx
ActiveX Calendar	Adds a monthly calendar to your form to which you can bind date data fields.	_datetime.vcx

Class	Description	Class Library File
Application Registry	Provides a set of Registry functions that return application-related information.	registry.vcx
Array Handler	Provides methods that you can use to do certain array operations that are not performed by Visual FoxPro array functions, such as insertion and deletion of array elements and column scanning.	_utility.vcx
Cancel Button	Provides a button control that releases a form and discards any associated buffered data changes.	_miscbtns.vcx
Clock	Provides a control that displays the current time on a form.	_datetime.vcx
Conflict Catcher	Displays a dialog box that shows rows with conflicting values during an edit session using optimistic row or table buffering. The dialog box displays the original, current, and new values. You can choose the value to use.	_dataquery.vcx
Cookies Class	Used with MS Information server such as FoxISAPI to manipulate Internet cookies.	_internet.vcx
Cross Tab	Control generates cross-tab report.	_utility.vcx
Data Edit Buttons	Navigation bar component that includes Top, Previous, Next, Bottom, Find, Print, Add, Delete, Edit, and Save buttons.	Wizbtns.vcx
Data Navigation Buttons	A group of buttons including Top, Next, Prev, and Bottom. It also	_datanav.vcx

continues

Table 18.1   Continued

Class	Description	Class Library File
	contains the `DataChecker` class to check for conflicts during navigation between records.	
Data Session Manager	Manages and controls updates for current data sessions in all forms or form sets.	`_app.vcx`
Data Validation	Traps buffered data conflicts.	`_datanav.vcx`
Data Navigation Object	Nonvisual object used in conjunction with navigation controls to navigate records in a view or table. (When you use any form of navigation buttons, you must use this object.)	`_table.vcx`
_dbf2html	Visual FoxPro cursor (`.DBF`) to HTML. It contains hooks to control scope, visual layout, and HTML generation.	`_internet.vcx`
Distinct Values Combo	Fills a combo box with unique values in the `Controlsource` field.	`_dataquery.vcx`
Error Object	Generic error handler used with the Application Wizard-generated application framework.	`_app.vcx`
Field Mover	Displays a dialog box that lets you move fields from one list to another. One list box displays field values from the current data source.	`_app.vcx`
File Version	Fetches file version resource and stores it in an array.	`_utility.vcx`
Filter Dialog Box Button	Button control that displays the Filter dialog box.	`_table2.vcx`

Class	Description	Class Library File
Filter Dialog Box	Displays a dialog box that lets you create or modify a data filter for a designated field.	_table.vcx
Filter Expression Dialog Box	Displays a dialog box that lets you create or modify a complex data filter expression.	_table.vcx
Find Button	Displays a `Button` control that uses the `Find` object to locate a record based on designated criteria.	_table.vcx
Find Dialog Box	Displays a dialog box that searches for text in a table or view. Uses other find objects.	_table.vcx
Find Files/Text	Wraps the `FILER.DLL` COM object to search for files. This object is a stripped-down version of the `FILER` form.	_utility.vcx
Find Object	Creates a nonvisible object that locates a record based on specified criteria. The class also contains an optional `Find Next` method. It is used with the other `Find` controls to perform search operations.	_table.vcx
Find (FindNext) Buttons	Control containing Find and FindNext buttons. It uses the `Find` object to search for text in tables or views.	_utility.vcx
Font Combobox	Provides a combo box control that lists available fonts. The `tbrEditing` and `RTFControls` classes of `_format.scx` use this control.	_format.vcx

continues

Table 18.1   Continued

Class	Description	Class Library File
Font Size Combobox	Provides a combo box control that lists available font sizes. The tbrEditing and RTFControls classes of format.scx use this control.	_format.vcx
Format Toolbar	Provides a toolbar that you use to specify text font formatting in the active control	_format.vcx
FRX->HTML	Converts a Visual FoxPro report (.FRX) to HTML. Contains properties to control the scope and HTML layout.	_internet.vcx
GetFile and Directory	Provides a dialog box that you use to choose a folder and file.	_controls.vcx
GoTo Dialog Box Button	Provides a button that displays the GoTo dialog.	_table2.vcx
GoTo Dialog Box	Provides a dialog that prompts you for a record number to reposition the view or table.	_table.vcx
Graph By Record	Provides a container object that draws a graph at a record level. It also contains record navigation buttons.	_utility.vcx
Graph Object	Generates a chart by automating MS Graph. It uses the Graph Wizard engine.	autgraph.vcx
Help Button	Provides a button control that displays a Help topic. It searches for help associated with the specified HelpContextID property.	_miscbtns.vcx

Class	Description	Class Library File
Hyperlink Button	Provides a button control used to perform a Hyperlink object operation, which launches a Web browser.	_hyperlink.vcx
Hyperlink Image	Provides a Hyperlink object-type image control that you can click on to launch a Web browser.	_hyperlink.vcx
Hyperlink Label	Provides a Hyperlink object-type label control that you can click on to launch a Web browser.	_hyperlink.vcx
Item Locator	Provides a File Locator dialog box that lets you locate a file that your application needs but cannot find.	_dialogs.vcx
INI Access	Provides a set of Registry functions to let you access file settings from an .INI file.	Registry.vcx
Keywords Dialog Box	Provides a dialog box that displays a specified keyword list similar to the Gallery keyword dialog.	_dialogs.vcx
Launch Button	Provides a button control that you use to launch an application. It uses the RUN command.	_miscbtns.vcx
Locate Button	Provides a button that displays a dialog to locate a record based on the contents of a field. It operates like the LOCATE command.	_table2.vcx
Lookup Combobox	Provides a combo box control that is filled with field values. You use this control to let your users look up data values.	_dataquery.vcx

continues

Table 18.1   Continued

Class	Description	Class Library File
Mail Merge Object	Provides a Custom class that uses the Mail Merge Wizard engine to generate a Microsoft Word Mail Merge document.	Mailmerge.vcx
MessageBox Handler	Provides a wrapper around the MessageBox function to simplify custom message display operations.	_dialogs.vcx
Mover	Provides a simplified mover list box with Move and Remove buttons. See "Super Mover" later in this table.	_movers.vcx
MouseOver Effects	Provide the functionality to highlight a control when the mouse is dragged over it.	_ui.vcx
Navigation Shortcut Menu	Provides a shortcut menu that contains navigation, sorting, filtering, and finding options. This shortcut menu displays when the user right-clicks on a form.	_table2.vcx
Navigation Toolbar	Provides data navigation buttons and other controls in a toolbar.	_table2.vcx
Object State	Provides a control that determines the state of an object. You can use it to automatically or explicitly save, restore, or set the properties of an object.	_app.vcx
ODBC Registry	Provides a set of functions you can use to retrieve ODBC-specific Registry information. For	registry.vcx

Class	Description	Class Library File
	example, you can retrieve the driver names and data sources.	
Offline Switch	Provides a set of control buttons you can use with remote views to toggle between the use of online and offline data.	_dataquery.vcx
OK Button	Provides a button control used to release a form and update any modified buffered data.	_miscbtns.vcx
Output Object	A nonvisual object that provides report source and destination options from reports, labels, or a data source.	_reports.vcx
Output Control	Provides a control that prompts for a report output option. If you use it in conjunction with the Report object, you can also select which report to print.	_reports.vcx
Output Dialog Box	Provides a dialog box that prompts you for a reporting output option by using the Report object.	_reports.vcx
Password Dialog Box	Provides a dialog box that prompts the user for a password.	_dialogs.vcx
Pivot Table	Generates an Excel pivot table based on FoxPro data. It uses the PivotTable Wizard engine.	_Pivtable.vcx
Preview Report	Provides a button used to run a report preview using the Output dialog.	_miscbtns.vcx

Part

IV

Ch

18

continues

Table 18.1 Continued

Class	Description	Class Library File
QBF	Provides a button set used to perform a Query-By-Form.	_dataquery.vcx
Registry Access	Provides a nonvisible Custom class that you can use to retrieve information from the Windows Registry.	registry.vcx
Resize Object	Provides a nonvisible class that causes objects that you drag and drop in a form to resize and move with the Resize event of the form.	_controls.vcx
RTF Controls	Provide controls for applying font formatting to RTF text in an active control.	_format.vcx
Run Form Button	Provides a button that you use to launch a form.	_miscbtns.vcx
SCX->HTML	Converts a Visual FoxPro form (.scx) to HTML. Contains properties to control the scope, visual layout, and HTML layout.	_internet.vcx
SendMail Buttons	Provide a button that uses the MAPI ActiveX control to send mail messages from a form. You can use it to send the current record to your mail application.	_miscbtns.vcx
Shell Execute	Provides an object that you can use to launch an application or document from the current application.	_environ.vcx
Shortcut Menu Class	Provides an object that you can use to dynamically create a shortcut menu.	_menu.vcx

Class	Description	Class Library File
Simple Edit Buttons	Provide a set of Picture buttons consisting of the Add, Edit, Delete, Duplicate, Save, and Cancel buttons. You use these buttons to operate on a simple table or view. This is the same button set used on the Form Wizard.	Wizbtns.vcx
Simple Picture Navigation Buttons	Provide simple Next and Previous picture buttons used to navigate through a table or view.	_table.vcx
Simple Navigation Buttons	Provide Next and Previous navigation buttons.	_table.vcx
Sort Dialog Box Button	Provides a button that you use to display a Sort dialog box.	_table2.vcx
Sort Dialog Box	Provides a dialog box you can use to perform an ascending or descending data sort on a specified field.	_table2.vcx
Sort Object	Provides a nonvisible object you can use to sort a data source.	_table2.vcx
Sort Selector	Provides a set of buttons used to perform an ascending or descending sort.	_table2.vcx
Sort Mover	Provides an object that is a subclass of the mover list box class. You use it to automatically handle data sorting.	_movers.vcx
Sound Player	Provides the functionality to load and play a sound file using the Media Control Interface.	_multimedia.vcx

Part

IV

Ch

18

continues

Table 18.1   Continued

Class	Description	Class Library File
Splash Screen	Provides a simple splash screen for simple applications.	_dialogs.vcx
SQL Pass Through	Provides a method to execute a SQL Pass Through operation. You can also execute stored procedures on a remote database such as Microsoft SQL Server.	_dataquery.vcx
Stop Watch	Provides a stop watch-type control that displays time in the form *hh*:*mm*:*ss*.	_datetime.vcx
String Library	Provides a nonvisible control that removes carriage returns and line feeds from a character string. You just call the object's TrimCRLF method and pass it the string and indicators specifying whether to trim the left and right sides.	_utility.vcx
Super Mover	Provides a mover list box with Move, Remove, MoveAll, and Removal buttons.	_movers.vcx
System Toolbar	Provides a class that manages the placement of the system toolbars. You can use this class in your application to add and remove the Visual FoxPro system toolbars.	_app.vcx
Table Mover	Provides a list box class that automatically loads tables and fields from the current data source. It is a subclass of the Field Mover list box class.	_movers.vcx

Class	Description	Class Library File
Text Preview	Provides a simple text editor in a dialog box. It contains buttons to format text, save text, and close the dialog.	
Thermometer	Provides a standard thermometer control.	_controls.vcx
Trace Aware Timer	Provides a nonvisible control that controls the opening of the trace window and handles debugging timing as required.	_app.vcx
Type Library	Provides a class containing the FOXTLIB ActiveX control that retrieves type information from type libraries. It can create a text file with type library output.	_utility.vcx
URL Combo	Provides a combo box for entering an Internet Web URL. It launches Internet Explorer to navigate to the specified Web site.	_internet.vcx
URL Open Dialog Box	Displays a dialog box with a drop-down list that stores the URL history list.	_internet.vcx
VCR Buttons	Provides a set of record navigation buttons including Top, Next, Previous, and Bottom.	_table.vcx
VCR Picture Navigation Buttons	Provide a set of record navigation buttons including VCR-type picture buttons for Top, Next, Previous, and Bottom.	_table2.vcx

Part

IV

Ch

18

continues

Table 18.1   Continued

Class	Description	Class Library File
Video Player	Provides functionality to load and play a video file. It uses the Media Control Interface (MCI) to display the video file.	`_multimedia.vcx`
Web Browser Control	Provides a subclass of Microsoft Internet Explorer that is added to a Visual FoxPro form. This subclass also provides hooks to IE4 so that Visual FoxPro can have full control over the browser's operation.	`_webview.vcx`
Window Handler	Provides a nonvisible control that enables window management operations such as tiling and cascading.	`_ui.vcx`

How to Use the Visual FoxPro Foundation Classes

Most of the FoxPro Foundation Classes are added directly to a form and require little or no coding. Classes with a base class of `Form`, `Formset`, or `Toolbars` can be added only to a project and run programmatically.

The simplest way to add a foundation class to your application is to drag and drop it from the Component Gallery to your form or Project Manager. You can also drag and drop a class from the Class Browser, Project Manager, and the Forms Control toolbar to your form. Although the process is not described until Chapter 19, "The Visual FoxPro Component Gallery," using foundation classes is exceptionally easy. All you have to do to run them is to select Tools, Component, and the Component Gallery is displayed as shown in Figure 18.1. Notice that the foundation classes are grouped into 14 categories. When you click on one of the categories, the corresponding classes appear in the right panel. You can click on one of the classes and a brief description appears in the bottom panel. If you want more information about a class, right-click on the class and choose Help from the shortcut menu.

FIGURE 18.1

The Component Gallery showing the list of Foundation Classes categories in the left panel and the Button controls in the right panel.

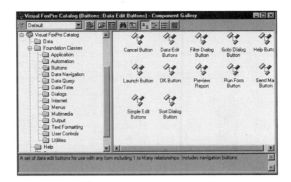

Another advantage of using the Component Gallery as a source of foundation classes for forms and projects is that it regulates which classes can be transferred to a form or project. For example, you do not have to be concerned if the base class for a foundation class is a Form class when you attempt to insert it in a form. In addition, the Component Gallery provides an option of creating a subclass when foundation classes are inserted in a project.

Adding Visual FoxPro Foundation Classes to a Form Using the Component Gallery

Now you can build an application that illustrates how you can use the Component Gallery to add a foundation class to a form. You will use the Data Edit Buttons foundation class that provides navigation and editing support for the application. This control appeared in the right panel of Figure 18.1. Follow these steps to build the application:

1. Create a project called `EmployeeList`.
2. Highlight the Form folder in Project Manager, and click on New to create a new form. Name it `Employee.scx`.
3. Choose View, Data Environment.
4. Right-click on the Data Environment dialog box, and choose a table. In this case, choose the `EMPLOYEE.DBF` table.
5. Add a grid to the form. Use the Grid Builder to define the fields and headings. To use the Builder, right-click on the form, and choose the Builder item from the shortcut menu.
6. Set the form's `Caption` property to `Employee List`.
7. Drag the Data Edit Buttons control to the form, as shown in Figure 18.2.

FIGURE 18.2

The Data Edit Buttons class is dragged from the Component Gallery and dropped on the form.

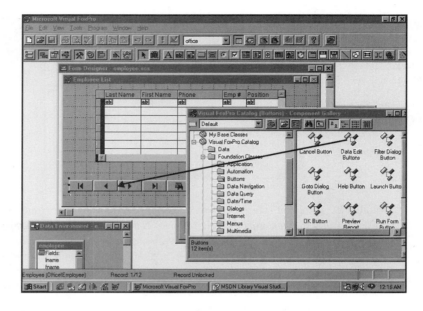

8. Add the following three lines of code to the Refresh event of the Data Edit Buttons control:

```
PICBTNS::Refresh
NODEFAULT
THISFORM.Grid1.SetFocus
```

9. Close the Form Designer, and name the form Employee.

10. Click the Project Manager Build button to compile and build the application.

Now you can execute the new Employee List application. The results are shown in Figure 18.3. The Data Edit Buttons object consists of 10 buttons: Top, Previous, Next, Bottom, Find, Print, Add, Delete, Edit, and Save. By adding a single control, you created a complete application that maintains the Employee table. You had to write three lines of code because the grid did not show the repositioned record pointer. The lines of code set the focus to the grid after the Data Edit Buttons object refreshes its display state. The NODEFAULT keyword suppresses the call to the default Refresh event because you already called it explicitly.

FIGURE 18.3

The Employee List form application using the Data Edit Buttons object from the Visual FoxPro Foundation Classes.

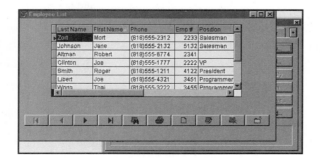

You can also add a class to a form or a project by right-clicking on the class in the Component Gallery and choosing the Add to Form option from the shortcut menu, as shown in Figure 18.4. In this example, the ActiveX calendar is added to the Employee List form.

FIGURE 18.4

The Component Gallery with its shortcut menu displayed.

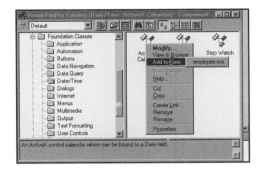

Follow these steps to add a calendar to the Employee List form:

1. Open the Form Designer to modify the Employee List form. Then open the Component Gallery.
2. Right-click on the ActiveX Calendar class in the Component Gallery. Next, choose the Add to Form shortcut menu item.
3. As soon as the calendar object is placed on the form, the _OLECalendar1 Builder appears. Enter DateHired in the Field Name to Bind Calendar edit box, as shown in Figure 18.5.
4. Rearrange and resize controls on the Employee List form as appropriate.
5. Add the following line of code to the Grid1.AfterRowColChange event:

```
THISFORM._OLECalendar.RefreshDisplay
```

Part IV Ch 18

FIGURE 18.5

The ActiveX Calendar Class Builder with the bound data field showing.

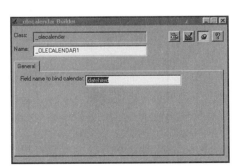

Each time the grid is moved to a new row or column, the Grid's AfterRowColChange event fires. At that time, the ActiveX Calendar's RefreshDisplay is called to update the calendar date and refresh the calendar display. The calendar date is updated from the bound DateHired field in the Employee table.

Now run the Employee List form and observe the results, as shown in Figure 18.6. Notice that when you move to a new row, the date in the calendar is the same as the grid's `Date Hired` field. This enhancement to the Employee List code took only one additional line of code. Imagine how many lines of code you would have to write to duplicate this example if you had to write it all from scratch.

FIGURE 18.6
Results of running
Employee List with a
calendar added.

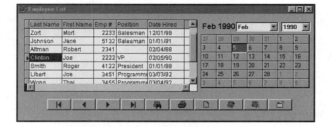

Adding Visual FoxPro Foundation Classes to a Form Using the Form Control Toolbar

You can add Visual FoxPro Foundation Classes from the Form Control toolbar, but first you have to add the visual class library file (.`VCX`) for your desired foundation class to your Form Control toolbar. The classes are all stored in the `\VFP98\ffc` directory. Table 18.2 lists the foundation categories and their associated visual class libraries.

Table 18.2   FoxPro Foundation Class Categories and Associated Visual Class Libraries

Category	Visual Class Library
Application	`_app.vcx`
Automation	`autgraph.vcx`
Buttons	`_miscbtns.vcx`
Data Navigation	`_datanav.vcx`
Data Query	`_dataquery.vcx`
Date/Time	`_datetime.vcx`
Dialogs	`_dialogs.vcx`
Internet	`_hyperlink.vcx`
Menus	`_table2.vcx`
Multimedia	`_multimedia.vcx`
Output	`_reports.vcx`

Category	Visual Class Library
Text Formatting	_format.vcx
User Controls	_ui.vcx
Utilities	registry.vcx

N O T E Notice that most of the names of the Visual FoxPro Foundation Classes begin with an underscore (_). It is added by convention to denote which foundation classes are derived from classes in the visual class library, _base.vcx. Specifically, foundation classes that begin with an underscore are subclassed from a _base.vcx class.

What is important is that you can make enhancements to the classes in _base.vcx. All other Visual FoxPro Foundation Classes that have their name preceded with an underscore can benefit from the enhancements because they are derived from _base.vcx classes. ▨

Follow these steps to add the classes to your Form Control toolbar from the options menu:

1. Choose Tools, Options. Then click on the Controls tab. Next, choose the Add option, and a File Open dialog box appears.
2. Choose one of the visual class libraries from Table 18.2 from the \VFP98\ffc directory.
3. Click the Save as Default button if you want the control to remain on the Form Control toolbar for subsequent Visual FoxPro sessions.
4. Click the OK button to exit the options menu.

If you want the foundation class to remain on the Form Control toolbar only for the current Visual FoxPro session, click on the View Classes icon on the Form Control toolbar, and choose the Add option. A File Open dialog box then appears. Then choose one of the visual class libraries in Table 18.2.

After you place the desired foundation classes on the Form Control toolbar, you can drag and drop a foundation class from the Form Control toolbar to your form. For example, I added the Date/Time category foundation classes to the Form Control toolbar, as shown in Figure 18.7. You can drag and drop the Clock class (_clock) to the form (see Figure 18.7).

If you run the enhanced Employee List form, it will appear as shown in Figure 18.8, complete with the date and time displayed, compliments of the clock object.

FIGURE 18.7
Adding the Clock foundation class to a form on the Form Control toolbar.

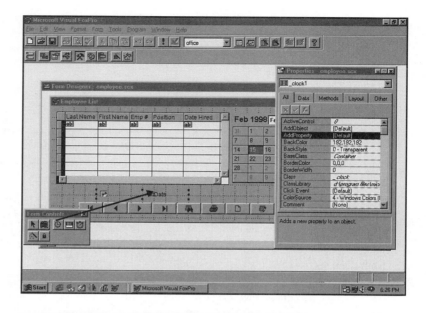

FIGURE 18.8
The Employee List form displaying the date and time, compliments of the clock object.

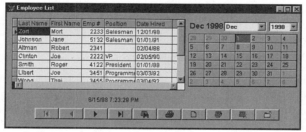

Adding Visual FoxPro Foundation Classes to a Project

Just as you can add foundation classes to a form, you can also add them to a project. Usually, you add foundation classes to a form. However, foundation classes with a base class of Form, FormSet, or Toolbar can be added only to a project. For example, the About dialog class or a Splash Screen class must be added to a project. Then you add code to activate them.

The easiest and best way to add a foundation class to a project is to drag a class from the Component Gallery to the project or choose the Component Gallery shortcut menu's Add to Project item. Of course, you can use other ways. You can drag the visual class library file (.vcx) from the Windows Explorer to the project. Another way is to choose the Project Manager Add button to add the visual class library file to the project.

When you add the foundation class to the project using the Component Gallery, the Add Class to Project dialog box is displayed, as shown in Figure 18.9.

FIGURE 18.9

The Add Class to Project dialog box is displayed when you add a foundation class to a project using the Component Gallery.

In this dialog box, you have three options. You can simply add the class to the project, create a new class derived from the selected class, or create a new form containing the class.

If you choose the Add Class to Project option, the visual class library file is added to the project. You should choose this option when you want to execute the foundation class programmatically, and you don't plan to enhance the functionality of the class.

If you want to change the foundation class's functionality, you can choose the Create New Class from Selected Class option. You are prompted to enter the name of the new class that is derived from the selected class. Then you can add code to modify the behavior of the class.

If you want to modify the appearance of the selected class's form, you can choose the Create New Form from Selected Class option. In this case, you are prompted to enter the name of the new form. Then you can modify the new form as you please.

Suppose you want to add an About box to the Employee List form. Here are the steps:

1. Open the `EmployeeList` project.
2. Drag the About box class from the Component Gallery to the `EmployeeList` project.
3. Choose the Create New Form from Selected Class option in the Add Class to Project dialog box.
4. When you are asked to name the new form, name it `About`.
5. After the Form Designer appears showing the new About form, change items on the form as appropriate. Figure 18.10 shows it with a Logo (`.GIF`) file added and some changes to labels and the `Caption` property.
6. Modify the Employee List form, and add a command button to the form with the `Caption` property set to `About`.
7. Add the following line of code to the `Click` event for the About button:
   ```
   DO FORM ABOUT
   ```
8. Build and run the application. Figure 18.11 shows the new About command button on the Employee List form and the new About dialog box that results when you click this button.

FIGURE 18.10

The Visual FoxPro Form Designer with the new About form open.

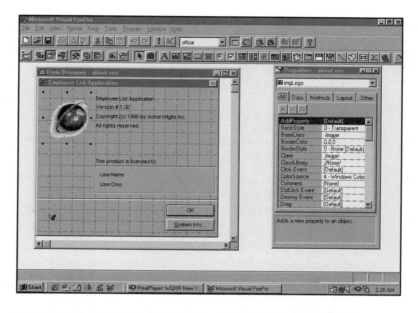

FIGURE 18.11

The Employee List and About forms at runtime.

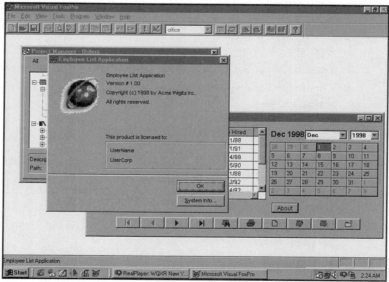

The next example illustrates how to add a splash screen to an application using the Splash Screen dialog class. The class will be executed programmatically to show the splash screen.

I added a program named EmployeeList.Prg to the EmployeeList project to display the splash screen before the Employee List dialog box activates. You don't need to add the Splash Screen class to the project because the `_dialogs.vcx` visual class library was added to the project when you added the About class. Follow these steps to create this example:

1. Open the `EmployeeList` project.
2. Click on the Programs folder, and click on the New button. A text edit window appears.
3. Enter the following code into the text window:

```
oSplash = NewObject("_splash","_dialogs")
IF VARTYPE(oSplash) = "O"
    oSplash.Picture = HOME()+"hlpglobe.gif"
    oSplash.nDuration= 5    && Set the duration to 5 seconds
    oSplash.Show()
ENDIF
DO FORM Employee
```

4. Save the program, and name it `EmployeeList.prg`.
5. Highlight the `EmployeeList.prg` program in the project, and choose Project, Set Main to make this program the main program instead of the Employee form.
6. Rebuild and run the application. The resulting splash screen is shown in Figure 18.12.

FIGURE 18.12

The `EmployeeList` application's splash screen.

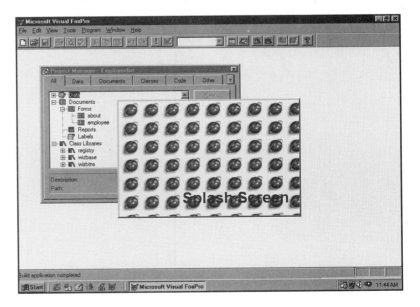

You use the `NewObject()` function in this application to open the Splash Screen class in the `_dialogs` visual class library and save the object variable `oSplash`. Next, you assign new values to the splash screen's `Picture` and `nDuration` properties. Finally, you launch the splash screen by using the `Show()` method.

More Examples of Using the FoxPro Foundation Classes

To help you learn how to use the FoxPro Foundation Classes and other aspects of Visual FoxPro, Microsoft has supplied the Solutions application in the `Samples` directory. When you execute the Solutions application, a dialog box appears, as shown in Figure 18.13. You can choose an application from the outline list and either run it or look at the code to find out how it works.

FIGURE 18.13

The Solutions sample application dialog box.

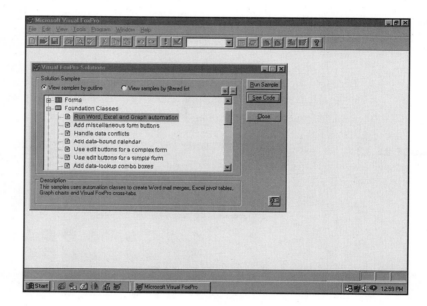

The Visual FoxPro Component Gallery

In this chapter

Using the Component Gallery

Visual FoxPro users have long benefited from the Project Manager. It gives them a way to easily organize and manage all the components for a project including programs, forms, reports, data, graphic files, and so forth. However, programming methodology has evolved. Now there exists a huge mass of reusable resources, which permits you to be much more productive. A new problem emerges: managing all these objects, resources, wizards, and tools. The Visual FoxPro Component Gallery is the solution to this problem.

The *Component Gallery,* shown in Figure 19.1, is a container that you can use to organize and maintain all your available Visual FoxPro resources. You can store visual class libraries, components, forms, programs, applications, graphics, tools, projects, and so forth. Furthermore, you can customize the Component Gallery any way you please. You can even create a visual representation of the same components in different logical groupings.

You can drag components from the Component Gallery and drop them on a form or project, as illustrated in Chapter 18, "The Visual FoxPro Foundation Classes." But then the Component Gallery supports all the functionality of the Project Manager and Class Browser, as you'll see later in this chapter.

FIGURE 19.1

The Visual FoxPro Component Gallery.

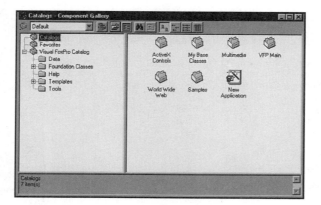

All you have to do to open the Component Gallery is to choose Tools, Component Gallery. You can open the Component Gallery from the Command Window by typing the following:

```
DO (_GALLERY)
```

In either event, the Component Gallery appears as shown in Figure 19.1. As you can see, the resources are organized in logical groupings similar to the Windows Explorer. The logical groupings are visually represented in the left pane as *folders,* or *catalogs.* A visual representation of the resources is associated with each folder or catalog in the right pane. The right pane is called the *Object Pane.* The left pane is referred to as the *Catalog Pane.*

The Default FoxPro Component Gallery Contents

By default, the Catalogs item in the left pane refers to the group of available catalogs. The set of catalogs shipped with the Visual FoxPro Component Gallery is presented in Table 19.1. When you highlight the Catalogs object in the Catalog Pane, all catalogs appear in the Object Pane. Then you can click on a catalog object to display its contents.

Table 19.1   Visual FoxPro Component Gallery Default Configuration

Catalog	Description
Catalogs	This catalog contains all the other catalogs.
VFP Main	This catalog contains components used by other catalogs in the gallery; it contains everything.
Favorites	This catalog is empty. You can put your favorite things here. When you create a program component from a wizard, it is placed in this folder. Note that the Favorites catalog is a *global* catalog. Global catalogs are always opened.
Visual FoxPro	This default catalog contains all the Visual FoxPro components, templates, and tools.
Data	This folder contains data-related tools and data sources.
Foundation Classes	This catalog contains all of the Visual FoxPro Foundation Classes. The classes are organized in categories with a folder for each class.
Help	This folder contains various readme files.
Templates	This catalog contains folders containing categories of wizard templates.
Tools	This folder contains tools and utilities that you might need while developing applications.
My Base Classes	This catalog contains subclassed Visual FoxPro base classes. They are for you to customize as you please.
ActiveX	This dynamic catalog contains either a list of all registered ActiveX Controls or a list of all Visual FoxPro ActiveX Controls.
World Wide Web	This catalog contains folders. Each folder contains useful Web site URLs. You can double-click one, and the Internet Explorer is launched to connect to the associated Web site. Most of the folders contain Microsoft Web site URLs. However, some folders contain URLs for Visual FoxPro user groups and other Visual FoxPro resources that you might find useful.

continues

Part

IV

Ch

19

Table 19.1 Continued	
Catalog	**Description**
Multimedia	This catalog contains folders with various images, sounds, and video files you can use in your applications.
Samples	This catalog contains folders with references to Visual FoxPro sample programs such as Tastrade, Solutions, and so forth.

Selecting Component Gallery Items

The Component Gallery is an extremely powerful context-sensitive system. It is pretty good at guessing what you normally want to do with an item when you select it based on the type of object you select. To perform an action on an item, you can do the following:

- Right-click on a selected item and choose an action from the Item Shortcut menu.
- Perform a drag-and-drop operation.
- Double-click on an item to perform an action.

You can drag an object from the Component Gallery and drop it on a form or project. The Component Gallery knows what kind of object you are dragging and won't let you drop it in the wrong place. And when the Component Gallery does drop the object, it knows what you want done with the object. Table 19.2 describes what happens when you drag and drop particular object types onto other particular object types.

 TIP You can use another unique drag-and-drop technique to perform an action on an object. It involves using the Move icon located at the far left of the toolbar. First, click an object in the Object Pane to select the object. Then drag the Move icon to the desired target and drop it. The selected object also is dropped. You'll learn more about the Move icon later in this chapter.

Table 19.2 Actions Performed When You Drag and Drop an Item from the Component Gallery Object Pane to a Target Object

Item Type	Target	Action
Class	Form	Adds a class to a form
	Project	Adds a visual class library to a project
Any item	Catalog	Adds an item to a catalog
	Folder	Adds an item to a folder
Data	Form	Creates a grid object containing the table or view
Form	Project	Adds a form to a visual class library or a project

Item Type	Target	Action
HTML Help File	Form	Adds an HTML button class to a form that launches the help
Image File	Form	Adds an Image class or sets the `Picture` property
	Control	Adds an Image class or sets the `Picture` property
	Screen	Sets the FoxPro wallpaper
Menu	Form	Adds a shortcut menu to a form
	Screen	Opens the Menu Designer to edit a menu
Program	Project	Adds a program to a project
	Screen	Opens designer to modify a program
Project	Screen	Opens the project
Sound File	Form	Adds a multimedia class to a form
Report	Form	Adds a button class to launch a report
Template	Project	Opens an appropriate wizard to create a program component and adds it to a project
Tool	Screen	Executes Tool
URL	Form	Opens a Web browser to connect to a Web site
Video File	Form	Adds a multimedia class to a form

In addition, you can double-click on an object, and some operation will be performed based on the type of object. Table 19.3 describes the actions performed when you double-click on an object.

Table 19.3 Actions Performed When You Double-Click on an Object in the Component Gallery Object Pane

Item Type	Action
Catalog	Opens that catalog in the Object Pane
Class	Opens the Class Designer
Form	Opens the Form Designer
HTML Help Files	Opens Help
Image File	Opens the Image Editor (MS Paint)
Menu	Opens the Menu Designer

continues

Table 19.3   Continued

Item Type	Action
Project	Opens the project
Program File	Opens a text editor
Sound or Video File	Opens the Media Player
Report	Opens the Report Designer
Template	Opens an appropriate wizard to create a program component and adds it to a project
Tool	Executes Tool
URL	Opens a Web browser to connect to a Web site

When you right-click on a selected item in the Object Pane, the Item Shortcut menu appears. The Component Gallery is so smart that it knows all the actions that you are allowed to perform on a given object. When you right-click on a specific object, the Item Shortcut menu that appears contains a list of allowable actions that can be performed on the selected object. Table 19.4 describes the various offerings in the Item Shortcut menu. A typical Item Shortcut menu is shown in Figure 19.2.

FIGURE 19.2
The Component Gallery item shortcut menu.

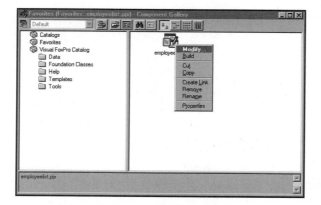

Table 19.4   Item Shortcut Menu Functions

Item	Action
Add to Project	If the Property Manager is open, and the selected object can be added to a project, this item appears in the list. This item is described in Chapter 18, "The Visual FoxPro Foundation Classes."

Item	Action
Add to Form	If the Form Designer is open, and the selected object can be added to a project, this item appears in the list. This item is discussed in Chapter 18, "The Visual FoxPro Foundation Classes."
Build	This item builds a project. If the selected object is a project, this menu item appears.
Modify	If a designer that can modify the selected object exists, this item appears in the menu. It opens the appropriate designer to edit the object. For example, if the selected object is a form, the Form Designer is opened.
View in Browser	If the selected object is a class-type object, this item opens the FoxPro Class Browser so that you can look at its properties and methods.
Cut	This item moves the selected object to the Gallery Clipboard, then dims the object. When a Paste operation is performed, the dimmed object is removed from the location of the cut.
Copy	This item copies the selected object to the Gallery Clipboard.
Create Link	This item creates a link to the selected object that can be inserted in a dynamic folder.
New Item	This item adds a new item to a folder or catalog. Highlight this menu item, and you can choose an object type from a submenu that appears. You can create a new folder or add an existing object to the Object Pane. The Item Shortcut menu contains this item if you right-click on an empty spot in the Object Pane.
Paste	This item adds the contents of the Gallery Clipboard to the selected folder.
Remove	This item deletes the selected object from the component gallery. A message box appears, in which you can confirm or reject the deletion operation.
Rename	This item enables you to rename the selected object.
Properties	This item displays the Properties dialog box so that you can review or modify the properties for the selected object.

Part
IV

Ch
19

The Component Gallery Toolbar

The Component Gallery Toolbar, shown in Figure 19.3, consists of a Move icon, a view type drop-down list, and some toolbar buttons. At the right side of the toolbar are four buttons that control the display of the components in the Object Pane. The options are also present on the Windows Explorer. In other words, you can display the components as large icons, small icons, a list, or a detailed list.

FIGURE 19.3

The Component Gallery toolbar.

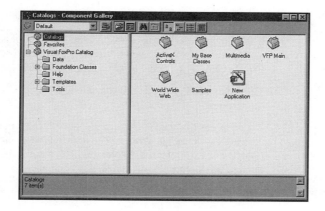

The Move icon is used as an alternative scheme for drag-and-drop operations. You can select an object in the Object Pane and then drag and drop the Move icon to a form or project. For example, you can select a class component and drag the Move icon to a form. You might consider the Move icon to be a strange interface operation. On the contrary, it is quite innovative. Suppose you want to drag a component from the Component Gallery to a large form; you might discover that the Component Gallery covers the drop spot. The solution is to select the component, move the Component Gallery so that only its upper-left corner is visible, and then drag the Move icon to the drop spot on the form.

You can use the View Items drop-down list to select the default and various user-defined views of the catalogs in the Component Gallery. You can define a view using the Find Component dialog box to search for components that match designated search criteria. You can activate the Find Component dialog box by doing the following:

- Clicking on the toolbar's Find Component button.
- Right-clicking on a folder and choosing the Find menu item in the Item Shortcut menu.
- Clicking on the toolbar's Option button and choosing the Dynamic View tab.

The Class Browser button is a toggle between the Component Gallery and the Class Browser. You use the Class Browser to examine and edit class methods, events, and properties.

The Open Catalog button displays the Open dialog box shown in Figure 19.4. You can specify a catalog to open by indicating either the name or filename of the catalog.

The Options button displays the Component Gallery Options dialog box, as shown in Figure 19.5. In it, you can alter the behavior of the Component Gallery.

FIGURE 19.4

The dialog box to open a catalog in the Component Gallery.

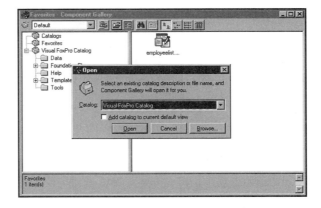

FIGURE 19.5

The Component Gallery Options dialog box with the Standard tab selected.

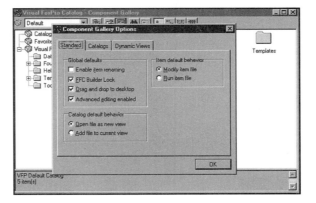

The Options dialog box has the following three tabs:

- Standard—You use the Standard tab to set global default values. Its options are described in Table 19.5.

- Catalogs—You use the Catalogs tab to add catalogs to the Component Gallery. You can specify whether a catalog is default or global. A *default* catalog is automatically opened when the Component Gallery starts up. A global catalog is always open, regardless of which catalog is open. For example, when you first install Visual FoxPro, the Favorites catalog is global. The ActiveX, My Base Classes, and Visual FoxPro catalogs are default catalogs.

- Dynamic Views—You use the Dynamic Views tab to add, edit, or remove views from the Component Gallery view list. Views are also created by the Find option on the toolbar.

Part
IV

Ch
19

Table 19.5   Standard Tab Option Dialog Box Items

Item	Action
Enable Item Renaming	If this check box is checked, you can rename a component in the Component Gallery by clicking on the component's label and typing a new name. The Item Shortcut menu renaming method is always available.
FFC Builder Lock	If this check box is checked, you can designate that a builder opens when you drop a FoxPro Foundation Class on a form.
Drag and Drop to Desktop	If this check box is checked, when you drop a visual class on the desktop, it appears as a sample on the desktop. For example, if you drop a control button on the desktop, a button will appear just as it would appear if it were dropped on a form. However, it has no functionality. You perform this test so that you can see what a class object looks like.
Advanced Editing Enabled	If this check box is checked, a more complex set of tabs is added to the Class Item Properties dialog box. If you want to make any advanced modifications to the Component Gallery, you should set this tab.
Catalog Default Behavior	
Open File as New View	If this option is selected, when you double-click on a Component Gallery item that can be either opened or added, the item will be opened. (default)
Add File to Current View	If If this option is selected, when you double-click on a Component Gallery item that can be either opened or added, the item will be added.
Items Default Behavior	
Modify Item File	If this option is selected, when you double-click on a Component Gallery item that can be either run or modified (such as a Form), the item will be run.
Run Item File	If this option is selected, when you double-click on a Component Gallery item that can be either run or modified (such as a Form), the item will be modified.

The Find Component button opens the Find Component dialog box, as shown in Figure 19.6. You can search the entire Component Gallery for a component or group of components and save the search results as a new Component Gallery view. You can specify search criteria for the components you want to include in the view.

FIGURE 19.6

The Component Gallery Find Component dialog box.

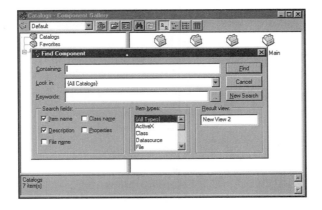

Now that you have looked at all facets of the Component Gallery, it is time to work with the Component Gallery. In the next section, you will create an application.

Creating an Application from the Component Gallery

You can easily create and maintain applications from the Component Gallery. Creating the application using the wizard templates is also easy. For this example, create a recipe book application. All you have to do is to open the Templates folder and click on the Recipes Template. The Enter Project Name dialog box then appears, as shown in Figure 19.7. Enter the name of the project for your new application, and adjust the directory if you want. Then click OK, and the application is created.

FIGURE 19.7

The Component Gallery and the Enter Project Name dialog box.

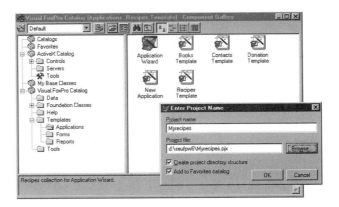

If you examine Figure 19.8, you will see that the template-driven Application Wizard automatically built the application complete with a project. The project was placed in the Component Gallery Favorites folder.

Part
IV

Ch
19

FIGURE 19.8

The MyRecipes project that was automatically created by the template-driven Application Wizard.

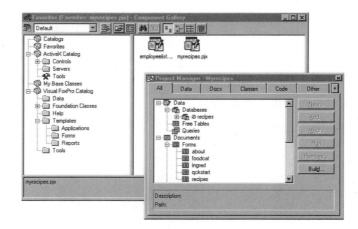

Now, click on Build with the Build and Run option set, and presto, you have an operational Recipe book application, as shown in Figure 19.9. Notice that it has multiple forms, and that Forms and Reports menus were added to the system menu.

FIGURE 19.9

Results from running the MyRecipes application showing the application forms and new menus.

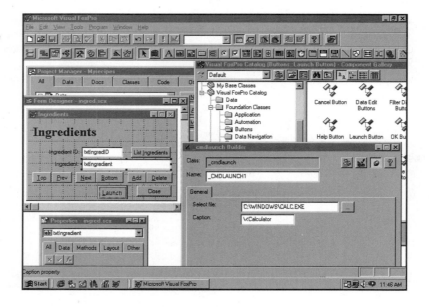

If this recipe book application is too simple for your needs, you can use the Component Gallery to enhance it. Perhaps you want to add a meal planner with an option to connect to the Internet grocery and order the ingredients automatically. Well, that might be a little ambitious. For now, use a simpler example. Let's use the Component Gallery to add a button that launches the Windows Calculator to the Ingredients form. Here are the steps:

1. Open the Favorites catalog in the Component Gallery.
2. Double-click on the MyRecipes project to open the Project Manager.
3. Double-click on the Ingredients form in the Project Manager, and the Form Designer opens.
4. From the Component Gallery, open the Foundation Classes folder. Then open the Buttons subfolder.
5. Drag the Launch Button class from the Object Pane to the Ingredients form, and drop it. The _cmdlaunch Builder dialog box appears (see Figure 19.10).
6. Enter the path and filename of the Windows calculator in the Select File text box (C:\WINDOWS\CALC.EXE). You can click on the button with the ellipsis (...) to the right of the text box to help you find the path.
7. Change the Caption for the launch button to \<Calculator. Now close the builder.
8. Reposition and resize the Calculator launch button, as you like.
9. Close the Form Designer.
10. Build and run the application.

N O T E   During the build process, you might have to supply the directory of the FoxPro Foundation Classes directory containing the Launch Button class. It is ...\VFP98\ffc. ▪

FIGURE 19.10
Using the Component Gallery to add a Calculator launch button to the MyRecipes project Ingredients form.

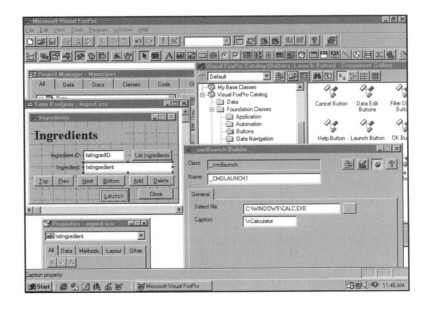

Part
IV

Ch
19

Now, when you click the Calculator button on the Ingredients form, the Windows Calculator appears.

Modifying the Behavior of a Component Gallery Catalog or Folder

As you become more familiar with the Component Gallery, you might want to revise it to conform to your lifestyle. You might want to create your own catalogs or folders, and rearrange the components and structure of the Component Gallery treeview.

Adding a Catalog or Folder

If you want to create a new catalog, just click on the Options button on the toolbar, and the Component Gallery Options dialog box appears. Click on the Catalogs tab, click the New button, and enter the name of the new catalog. Finally, click OK and exit from the Options dialog box. The catalog is added to the treeview.

Changing a Catalog to a Folder

With the exception of the Catalogs catalog, a catalog can contain only folders and items. Folders cannot be at the top level of the treeview. Therefore, if you want a catalog to be a folder, you can drag and drop your catalog into another catalog or folder. The former catalog becomes a folder, and its icon changes automatically from a catalog to a folder.

Changing the Behavior of a Catalog or Folder

If you want to change the configuration of a folder or catalog, right-click on the catalog or folder, and the Folder Properties dialog box appears. The dialog box contains the General, Node, Script, and Comments tabs. In the subsequent discussion, I will refer to a catalog, but the discussion relates to both catalogs and folders.

The General tab contains several text boxes, which are described in Table 19.6.

Table 19.6	Folder Properties Dialog Box General Tab Items
Item	**Description**
Name	Designates the catalog's text label.
Description	Displays text in the Description Pane when the catalog is selected. It is located at the bottom of the Gallery Window.
Picture	Contains the path and filename of the icon file used to visually represent the catalog in the Gallery Window. Typically, the only field you will change is the Description text box to provide a useful description of the catalog.
Item Picture	Specifies a default path and filename of the icon used to visually represent items in the catalog.
Item Desc.	Designates the default text for the Description Pane when the item is selected.

The Node tab establishes values that are global to all tables. In other words, the Node tab is used to maintain the treeview. Table 19.7 specifies the items displayed in Node tab.

Table 19.7   Folder Properties Dialog Box Node Tab Items

Item	Description
ID	Assigned when the catalog is created.
Link ID	Specifies the link to other catalogs in the treeview. It is set when you use drag-and-drop operations to reposition a catalog in the treeview.
Class name	Specifies the name of the class of the catalog.
Class Library	Specifies the path and filename of the visual class library for the catalog.
Item class	Specifies the class names of items in the catalog that have not yet been assigned classes.
Dynamic Catalog	Specifies the expression, filename, or URL that launches when you select this catalog.

For example, suppose you want to modify the behavior of a folder to act similarly to the Windows Explorer. All you have to do is to specify a directory name in the Dynamic Catalog field, for a specified folder. Here are the steps:

1. Click on the toolbar's Options button.
2. Click on the Catalog tab.
3. Click on the New button, and name the new catalog `Windows Directory`.
4. Drag the new catalog to the favorites catalog. (It becomes a folder.)
5. Right-click on the new folder, and choose Properties from the shortcut menu. The Folder Properties dialog box appears.
6. Change the Description field to `Display windows directory`.
7. Click on the Node tab, and change the Dynamic catalog field to `C:\Windows`.
8. Click OK.

When you select the Windows Directory folder, the appearance of the Component Gallery changes, as illustrated in Figure 19.11. Notice that even the folder icon changes.

The preceding example is an exception. Typically, the only Node tab field that you have to set is Item class to define default class items. For example, if a folder normally contains templates, specify `_templateItem` for the Class Name field. The interface and behaviors of the Component Gallery are maintained by classes in the Component Gallery class library (`VpfGallery.vcx`). Its path and filename are `...\VFP98\gallery\VpfGallery.vcx`.

The Class Name field in the Node tab for catalogs and items refers to classes in the Component Gallery class library. The types of classes are presented in Table 19.8.

FIGURE 19.11
Component Gallery
folder with the
characteristics of the
Windows Explorer.

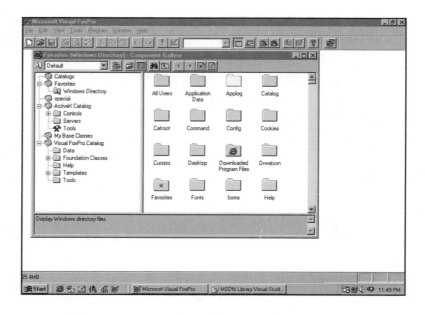

Table 19.8   Types of Classes in the Component Gallery Class Library

Item	Class Name	Object Types
ActiveX	_ActiveXItem	ActiveX control or server file (.ocx, .exe, .dll)
Catalog	_CatalogItem	Open Visual FoxPro catalogs
Class	_ClassItem	Any Visual FoxPro class from Visual class library file (.vcx) or from program file (.prg)
Data	_DataItem	Visual FoxPro data source (.dbc, .dbf, .qry, and so on)
Form	_FormItem	Visual FoxPro form file (.scx)
File	_FileItem	Any file with a valid associated application
Image	_ImageItem	Image files (.ani, .bmp, .cur, .dib, .gif, .ico, .jpg)
Menu	_MenuItem	Visual FoxPro menu (.mnx)
Program	_ProgramItem	Visual FoxPro program file (.prg)
Project	_ProjectItem	Visual FoxPro project file (.pjx)
Report	_ReportItem	Visual FoxPro report file (.frx)
Sample	_SampleItem	Visual FoxPro executable file (.app, .exe, .frx, .prg, .scx)
Sound	_SoundItem	Sound files (.wav, .rmi, .mid, .snd)

Item	Class Name	Object Types
Template	_TemplateItem	Script Item Type
URL	_UrlItem	Web Item Type: Web documents (URLs) Local document file (.htm) Active document file
Video	_VideoItem	Video file (.avi, .mov)

Typically, you do not have to specify any items in the Scripts tab for a catalog or folder. Occasionally, though, you do need to set properties for a Component Gallery class to modify its behavior.

The Comments tab lets you save comments related to a specific catalog. You might find it useful to place programming notes in the Comments tab fields.

Modifying the Behavior of a Component Gallery Item

You can modify the behavior of a Component Gallery item in the Class Item Properties dialog box. To display this dialog box, right-click on an item in the Object Pane, and choose Properties from the shortcut menu. Table 19.9 describes the contents of the Class Item Properties dialog box.

N O T E The Class Item Properties dialog box contains a group of advanced editing features that are not available by default because the item properties are usually handled automatically by the Component Gallery. If you need to access them, select the Advanced Editing Enabled check box in the Component Gallery Options dialog box. Then the Type, Scripts, Views, and Comments tabs appear.

Table 19.9 Class Item Properties Dialog Box

Item	Action
General Tab	
Name	Specifies the text value used as the component label.
Description	Specifies the text that displays in the Component Gallery Description Pane.
Picture	Specifies the path and filename of an icon, which provides visual representation of the item in the Component Gallery. Specifies

continues

Part IV
Ch 19

Table 19.9   Continued

Item	Action
Views Tab	
Views	Specifies Designates the view and folder that contains the selected item in the form: `viewName=folderName`
Keywords	Specifies keywords that can be used to locate the selected item using the Find Component command. The Find Component command generates a view; you execute it by clicking the toolbar's Find Component button.
Node Tab	
ID	Contains the item identification information.
Link	Contains the name of the source item if the selected object is a link.
Class Name	Specifies the Component Gallery class (refer to Table 19.8).
Class Library	Specifies the path and filename of the visual class library containing the specified class.
Scripts Tab	
Script	Specifies an event script associated with the selected item.
Properties	Specifies property assignments.
Comments Tab	
Comments	Specifies optional user comments.
User	Specifies optional usage-related comments.

An additional Item tab is specific to the type of object selected. For File, Form, Menu, Program, and Report type objects, the Item tab specifies the path and filename of the selected object.

If the object is a project, the Item tab contains the path and filename of the project plus some build options that designate what happens if you right-click on a project file and choose Build from the Items shortcut menu. The build actions include Rebuild All, Show Errors, and Run After Build. They are the same build options supported by the Project Manager.

The Item tab for a class object lets you specify the class name, its base class, and its visual class library path and filename. In addition, it specifies the path and filename of a file containing an example of the selected class item. ●

V

COM

Introduction to COM

What Is COM?

Microsoft has greatly enhanced support for COM in the latest version of Visual FoxPro (6). COM can greatly change the way you look at applications, but it is relatively simple to learn and use. This section of the book relates to the *Component Object Model* (*COM*), Microsoft's standard for inter-application communication.

This chapter introduces COM and discusses how you can use it to enhance Visual FoxPro applications. Chapters 21 and 22 will go into practical issues regarding using Visual FoxPro as a COM client and COM server, respectively.

COM is a standard for communicating between objects. The basic idea is to have a standard that says objects will accept and send messages in a particular way, thus enabling objects written in disparate languages to communicate with each other as if they were written in the same language.

The bottom line is that any COM object can communicate with any other COM object. So, in your Visual FoxPro applications, you can communicate with other objects written in Visual Basic, Visual C++, and so on.

Some COM objects are visual in nature. Any ActiveX control that ships with Visual FoxPro (such as the Calendar control) is a COM object. Although it was not written in Visual FoxPro, it has been designed to work with any application that complies with the COM standard for containing visual COM objects.

Other COM objects have no visual characteristics at all. For example, you can use a COM object designed to do highly specialized pricing calculations for a brokerage firm. The COM object can be written by a group responsible for creating pricing algorithms for the company (a highly specialized and sensitive field) and used by any application within the brokerage firm. This pricing object would have methods and properties that are used to store, retrieve, and process information, but no need to have a GUI at all.

Finally, some objects are parts of full applications in and of themselves, with portions "exposed" for the outside world to use. These applications have been designed not only for use by end users but also by developers. For example, a faxing application can have objects exposed for use so that a developer can automate faxing a document. Microsoft Office applications have portions exposed so that a developer can use the applications by "remote control."

A Little Background

Back in the "good ol' days" of DOS, applications had to have all their required functionality built in. Remember the old DOS printer drivers in FoxPro 2.x for DOS? This is a prime example. WordPerfect and Word also did the same kind of thing. Because DOS provided nothing in terms of operating system level support for such tasks as printing, the software had to provide all the functionality itself.

Needless to say, this led to a huge amount of duplication. All three applications just mentioned had printer drivers built in, but each had its own version of printer driver software. There was no commonality between the efforts and each company had to do the same effort on its own.

The advent of Windows changed that. Given some operating system support, standards were put in place for communicating with the operating system and enabling the operating system to do the rest. After Word, FoxPro, and WordPerfect migrated to Windows, their own versions of printer drivers went away.

However, Windows applications were still fairly *monolithic*. Monolithic applications are applications that have everything built in to them. With the advent of Windows, certain operating system level functions were standardized, but business functionality (such as word processor features that enabled you to write letters to clients) were still the realm of each application.

Then came *Dynamic Data Exchange (DDE),* which enabled one application to take control of another. In effect, you sent commands, instructions, and data from one application to another. The operating system had a built-in means of channeling the commands from the DDE client application to the DDE server application. In order for an application to be DDE-compliant, it had to conform to the rules for accepting and sending DDE instructions and information. Basically, if you followed the rules, you got to play with the other applications in the DDE sandbox.

The interaction afforded by DDE was rather kludgy to work with, but it did enable some flexibility. A developer no longer had to create a mini–word processor to generate letters, because the job could be passed on to some DDE-compliant word processor. All that was required from the developer was to learn how to control the DDE server application (no small task, by the way).

Then object orientation entered the picture and changed the way we look at software and business problems. As was discussed in Part IV, "Object-Oriented Programming," an object-oriented application is built based on discrete entities called *objects*. In their coded form, objects are called *classes*.

The nature of an object-oriented application is to build a group of distinct classes that interact as necessary to get the job done. If you think about it, this is not all that different from putting a team together to complete a project. Each member of the team has his or her own distinct set of responsibilities. However, in order to complete their work, the team members interact with each other. They pass information back and forth (for example, the GUI designer might work with the data designer to know what fields are used as control sources) and, in general, cooperate to complete the work. The same is true of an object-oriented application. Each class is a member of the team, and the classes collaborate to get the job done.

COM finally brings the whole issue of monolithic applications to closure. Gone is the kludgy means of inter-application communications represented by DDE. Now, you can use classes built into other applications directly. Instead of controlling an application by remote control, COM enables you direct access to the application. In effect, your applications get to run the same code as the COM server applications. In the rest of this chapter and throughout this section, you will see that the use of COM servers is practically transparent in the code.

Finally, disparate applications can use each other's functionality, thereby saving time, money, and resources.

What Does COM Represent?

COM, as an idea, is revolutionary in the realm of development strategies. Once upon a time, each application had to have all its functionality built into itself. That is no longer the case. We have entered an age of specialization, not only in terms of technology and development language but also in terms of business knowledge.

Accounting applications are a good example. For the most part, nuts and bolts accounting principles do not change. Yet, every time you write an application with accounting functionality, you have to either create it yourself or modify something else. If you're lucky, you get to write a module that runs "parallel" to the accounting software.

Now, let's face it. Writing accounting functionality is a bear. A ton of work goes into it. The minute you hear terms such as "General Ledger" and "Accounts Receivable," the time estimate to create an application jumps. I personally know of no people who look forward to writing a General Ledger module for their clients, especially when there are 50 gazillion packages out there that handle accounting.

So, what do you do? Many of us purchase an accounting package such as SBT and do either of the following things:

- Interface with it by writing directly to the tables (which means you have to re-create any accounting rules and controls in your code).

- Modify it (which usually means you have to live with the accounting software's way of doing things for the most part).

Neither means of accomplishing the task is necessarily the best.

Suppose one accounting software package was created to be COM compliant. The software package could give all the nuts and bolts accounting and expose the necessary functionality for interfacing with the various modules. Now all a programmer has to do is write his custom GUI and processing but leave the accounting up to the accounting software. And, because the accounting software is COM compliant, it can serve as the basis for thousands of applications without having to change one line of the accounting software's code.

Consider another example in which the pricing model mentioned earlier would be key. The pricing models created by the bank I used to work for on Wall Street were custom-designed by the bank. Pricing models are crucial to the success of the bank because they tell it what to charge customers for certain financial deals. However, although the pricing models might be used across many different business units, frequently the units use their own software, which might be written in different languages.

COM can play a huge part in this situation in two ways. First of all, for the bank, a department can create pricing model objects using COM. Business units can create software to their heart's content, with custom GUIs and data structures, and still use the bank's pricing model. Second, COM can play a huge role for the software vendors, too. A software vendor can write an application that is designed to use a COM object for pricing. It can then sell the application to the banks, saying, "Use our software and you can still use your own pricing models if you follow these standards."

The power and flexibility increase for an organization is potentially huge.

Scalability with COM/DCOM

Because COM objects are, in effect, applications themselves (or portions of applications), they exist as separate files (.EXE or .DLL) on the hard drive. One of the nicest things about COM is that you can place the .EXE or .DLL on another computer on the network and run the COM object on that other computer and still access the results on the client computer.

Let's take a moment to look at this.

In a conventional network situation, programs sit on the network but run on the local workstation. That's not what I am discussing here. I am looking at being able to execute a program, in the form of a COM object, on another computer, and have the program use the memory and processor resources of that other computer while it is being accessed from the local workstation that made the call.

This is called *Distributed COM (DCOM)*. Imagine the flexibility this introduces when scaling an application. If an application has grown in terms of the number of users, the COM components can be distributed around the network, thus enabling a fairer distribution of the processing load.

So, What Do I Need to Learn?

Not much. If you're used to using objects, methods, properties, events, and the like, you will fit right in with COM. The only difference here is that you do not create these objects, someone else does. If you think about the difficulties that arise from using someone else's code, the difficulties in using COM are not that different. The biggest difficulty lies in not knowing which methods and properties the COM server supports. If the COM server is well documented, though, you should be okay on that score.

How to Use a COM Object

You use a COM object just like any other object. You use CreateObject() to get an object reference. The only trick is to know the name of the class to instantiate. For Excel, the class is Excel.Application. For Word, use Word.Application.

When you issue a CreateObject(), Visual FoxPro does some checking to find the name of the class to instantiate. Here's the order in which Visual FoxPro looks for the name of the class:

- Visual FoxPro base classes
- User-defined class definitions in memory in the order they were loaded
- Classes in the current program
- Classes in .VCX class libraries opened with SET CLASSLIB
- Classes in procedure files opened with SET PROCEDURE
- Classes in the Visual FoxPro program execution chain
- The OLE Registry (if SET OLEOBJECT is ON)

After you have an object reference, you use the object as if you were dealing with a class created in Visual FoxPro.

By the way, note the difference in the name of the class to instantiate. You are probably used to one-word class names. With COM, you have two-word class names. The first word represents the application and the second represents the class within the application to access.

 TIP If all this seems to be very similar to a topic called *OLE automation*, you're right. OLE automation is part of COM. So, if you see OLE, think COM.

How Exactly Does COM Work?

When you install an application that is a COM server, it registers itself (and all its classes) in the Windows Registry. For example, look at the Windows Registry entries for Visual FoxPro (which is a COM server).

Under HKEY_CLASSES_ROOT there is a branch named Visual.FoxPro.Application.6. Within that branch are numerous sub-branches. The branch to take note of at this point is

```
HKEY_CLASSES_ROOT\Visual.FoxPro.Application.6\CLSID
```

A *CLSID (Class Identifier)* is a unique number (called a *GUID* or *Global Unique ID*) that identifies that class. Microsoft assigns the CLSIDs and guarantees uniqueness. There is a separate entry for Visual FoxPro's GUID (which is, by the way, {008B6020-1F3D-11D1-B0C8-00A0C9055D74}) in the Registry. The key for that is

```
HKEY_CLASSES_ROOT\CLSID\{008B6020-1F3D-11D1-B0C8-00A0C9055D74}
```

This tree in the Registry has all the information you need to get to the class you need. For example, the LocalServer32 branch has the path to Visual FoxPro.

When the client application issues a CreateObject() with the name of the COM class (in this case, Visual.FoxPro.Application.6), the client asks the operating system for an instance of the requested object. The operating system looks in the Registry to find the GUID of the COM object. The Registry has the location of the COM program file (either .EXE or .DLL). The OS then knows where to go to instantiate the object. After it instantiates the object, it returns a reference to the calling application and the process is complete.

Once instantiated, you can use methods and properties of COM objects as if they are native to your development environment.

 TIP If you're not sure what the COM class name is (and you do not have the application's COM documentation), look through the Registry and see what's there. For example, Excel has an .Application entry. You will typically find something useful there.

Understanding Type Libraries

A *type library* is basically documentation. It documents the collections, objects, methods (with their parameters), and properties (with their data types) that are exposed for use by COM client applications. All COM objects have type libraries.

Some development products, such as Visual Basic, use the type libraries to give online, in-line assistance. For example, when calling a method in a COM object, Visual Basic displays the expected parameters automatically.

Visual FoxPro does not use type libraries quite to that extent. You will learn more about type libraries and Visual FoxPro in Chapter 21, "Visual FoxPro as a COM Client."

A type library can be a part of an object file, in which case it will have an extension of .OLB. If a type library is a standalone file, it has an extension of .TLB.

Visual FoxPro COM Capabilities

At this point, you have learned the theory behind using COM with Visual FoxPro. Now, let's take a tour of Visual FoxPro's COM capabilities, commands, and functions.

CREATEOBJECT(ClassName)

As stated earlier, CreateObject() is the mechanism through which you create an instance of a COM object. One crucial point to note is that CreateObject() always creates a *new* instance of the COM server.

Try this. From the Command window, issue these commands:

```
ox=CreateObject("Word.Application")
oy=CreateObject("Word.Application")
```

Now, bring up the Close Program dialog in Windows 95/98 by pressing Ctrl+Alt+Del. In NT, you need the Task Manager: press Ctrl+Alt+Del and select Task Manager from the dialog. Look for WinWord and count how many times it's running. You'll see two (assuming you are not running WinWord someplace else).

Wait. It gets worse. Switch back to Visual FoxPro and release the variables. You can even quit Visual FoxPro. Check again to see how many instances of WinWord are running. You guessed it: both instances are still there. In order to get rid of an unwanted instance, you need to issue the Quit method for WinWord.

Part
V

Ch
20

You need to be careful with this because each instance of a COM server takes memory.

If you want to get a reference to an already running copy of a COM server, use GetObject().

GETOBJECT(FileName, ClassName)

GetObject() is similar to CreateObject(). It accepts two parameters. The first is the name of a file to open and the second is the class name to work with.

GetObject() has two uses:

- Referencing an existing file.
- Getting a reference to an already running server.

These uses are discussed in the following sections.

Referencing an Existing File   First of all, GetObject() can be used to open a file that the OLE Registry knows about.

Suppose, for example, you want to open BUDGET.XLS, which resides in the root directory of your C: drive. You have two options. Your first option is to create an instance of the Excel COM server using CreateObject() and then open the file manually with a call to a method of the Excel object.

GetObject() offers a one-step approach:

```
oExcel = GetObject("c:\budget.xls")
```

Here, you are simultaneously instantiating an Excel object, opening the file, and getting a reference to it.

Notice that you do not have to tell Visual FoxPro that the file is an Excel file. Windows knows that an .XLS file is an Excel spreadsheet and that's good enough.

 If you are dealing with an ambiguous situation (such as a file that is a particular type of document but the normal extension has been changed), you can specify the appropriate class name in the second parameter.

The cool part of all this is that GetObject() is smart enough to know if there is an instance of the server running. If the server is already running, it doesn't create a new instance; it uses the one already running.

Getting a Reference to an Already Running Server   If you just want to get a reference to an already running server, use GetObject() like this:

```
oExcel=GetObject(,"Excel.Application")
```

By only specifying the object, GetObject() shoots for getting a reference to the already running application. If the application is not running, an OLE error is displayed.

In Chapter 21, you'll see a generic means of getting a reference to an application that prevents an extra instance of applications.

SET OLEOBJECT

Visual FoxPro, by default, will look in the Windows Registry if it cannot find the class specified in a CreateObject() statement. This can be turned off with SET OLEOBJECT. In effect, SET OLEOBJECT turns off the capability to use COM objects.

Why would you do this? Well, the main reason is time. When Visual FoxPro looks in the Registry, it first has to load OLE support in case it is instantiating a COM object. This takes time and resources. The search through the Registry takes time, too. If you know that you are not using COM in your application, issuing SET OLEOBJECT OFF will save some time and resources.

If you're worried about ActiveX controls (or OLE objects you have in general fields), don't be. Because Visual FoxPro knows that these objects are, by definition, OLE objects, Visual FoxPro always loads OLE support before opening them.

For all intents and purposes, SET OLEOBJECT only affects behavior when you are trying to get an object reference in code.

One more point: GetObject() is designed to get a reference to an existing OLE object instantiated in Windows. Because SET OLEOBJECT OFF turns off OLE support, GetObject() returns an error when SET OLEOBJECT is OFF.

ComClassInfo(oObjec>,nInfoCode)

ComClassInfo() is designed to return some information from the Registry about an already instantiated COM object. oObject is the object reference, and nInfoCode is a numeric parameter indicating which information is requested, and has values described in Table 20.1.

Table 20.1 **Description of the Information Returned for Values of** nInfoCode

nInfoCode	Information Returned
1 (Default)	The object's "programmatic identifier" (ProgID). A ProgID is a Registry entry that can be associated with a CLSID; think of it as a name associated with the CLSID. Each version of the program has its own identifier. For example, Visual FoxPro has ProgIDs of Visual.FoxPro.Application.6 (for 6) and Visual.FoxPro.Application.5 (for 5.0). A ProgID is also a class name that can be used to instantiate the COM server. For example, you could issue CREATEOBJECT for either 5.0 or 6 using the ProgID as follows:

```
oVFP5 = CREATEOBJECT("Visual.FoxPro.Application.5")
oVFP6 = CREATEOBJECT("Visual.FoxPro.Application.6")
```

continues

Table 20.1   Continued

nInfoCode	Information Returned
	Typically, however, you don't want to be version-specific in a class name. You usually aren't interested in instantiating Visual FoxPro version 5 or 6, but rather want the latest version that's installed on the machine. You want to ask for a reference to `Visual.FoxPro.Application` and have the Registry determine what the latest version is and instantiate that class for you. That's the `VersionIndependentProgID`.
2	The object's `VersionIndependentProgID`. The `VersionIndependentProgID` associates a ProgID with a `CLSID`. It is used to determine the latest version of an object application, refers to the application's class, and does not change from version to version.
3	An English name for the object, referred to as the *friendly name*.
4	The object's class identifier (`CLSID`).

Here are the return values for a reference to Excel.Application for Excel 97:

1   `Excel.Application.8`

2   `Excel.Application`

3   Microsoft Excel 97 Application

4   `{00024500-0000-0000-C000-000000000046}`

CreateObjectEX(CLSID | ProgID, ComputerName)

As discussed earlier, DCOM means that the COM server application exists and runs from a different machine on the network. Normally, the client machine is configured and told where the COM server application is and a standard `CreateObject()` will do the trick. `CreateObjectEX()` removes the need for special configuration and enables you to specify the machine to use.

This can be useful if you want to distribute the load for an application among multiple machines on the network.

`CreateObjectEX()` requires Windows NT 4.0 or later, or Windows 95/98 with DCOM installed.

NOTE In case you're wondering, `CreateObjectEX()` can only be abbreviated to 13 characters, which gives you `CreateObjectE()`. If you want my opinion, don't bother. ■

ComArray(oObject [,nSetting])

As Visual FoxPro programmers, we are used to arrays whose first element is element 1. However, VFP is not necessarily standard in this regard; many languages expect arrays to start with element 0.

The ComArray() function enables you to designate the manner in which arrays are passed to a specified COM object. Basically, you are registering a behavior with Visual FoxPro to indicate how a particular instance of a COM server should be handled.

The function accepts two parameters as follows:

oObject   This is a reference to the COM object being queried or changed.

nSetting   This is an optional numeric setting to designate how you want arrays to be passed to the COM object. Table 20.2 describes the various possible settings. If nSetting is not provided, the function returns the current setting for the specified COM object.

Table 20.2   How Arrays Are Passed to the COM Object for Various Values of nSetting

nSetting	Description
0	The first element in the array is zero (0) and the array is passed by value to the COM object.
1 (Default)	The first element in the array is one (1) and the array is passed by value to the COM object. This setting is compatible with earlier versions of Visual FoxPro.
10	The first element in the array is zero (0) and the array is passed by reference to the COM object.
11	The first element in the array is one (1) and the array is passed by reference to the COM object.

Notice that ComArray() is only used when arrays are passed to COM objects using the following syntax:

```
oObject.Method(@laArray)
```

If the @ token is omitted, only the first element of the array is passed to the COM object and ComArray() has no effect.

Part
V
Ch
20

Visual FoxPro as a COM Server

So far, you have learned Visual FoxPro using other COM servers. But the power of Visual FoxPro and COM certainly doesn't stop there. You can create your own COM servers using Visual FoxPro. As you'll see in Chapter 22, you can do all kinds of wonderful things with Visual FoxPro COM servers. But first, Chapter 21 continues the discussion of working with Visual FoxPro as a COM client by looking at some practical issues and how you can enhance the functionality of your Visual FoxPro applications by using other applications such as those in the Microsoft Office suite. ●

Visual FoxPro as a COM Client

Application Interoperability and the Microsoft Strategy

In this chapter, you'll learn some practical examples of enhancing applications using COM servers, focusing primarily on Microsoft Office.

Whether you love it or hate it, you have to give Microsoft credit. It has set a vision and it goes for it full tilt. In this case, Microsoft has had a vision of developing applications using components (hence the term *Component Object Model*) and it bought into it bigtime. Microsoft Office has become a model for creating applications designed not only for end-user use but also for use by developers.

Office presents a huge array of functionality. From the WinWord document to the Excel spreadsheet to the Outlook cornucopia of functionality, Office offers developers a huge suite of ready-to-use functionality at no extra cost.

The one downside to using Microsoft Office applications as COM servers lies in learning their object models. *Object model*, in this context, refers to the objects that these applications expose as COM servers, what their contents are (object members, properties, and methods), and when to use what.

This chapter is not designed to teach you how to use applications such as Word and Excel as COM servers. Rather, it will show you some strategies for continuing the learning process and show you examples that you can use in your applications immediately.

Learning How to Use Word and Excel

If you're using something like Word or Excel as a COM server, it can be a little hairy to learn what the application does and how it's done. If you need to get something done in Word or Excel, and you are unsure how to do it, there is a simple trick that many people use to get themselves over the hump.

Basically, perform the operation you need to accomplish (such as printing a document) in the application (as any normal user would do it) while recording a macro for it. Then look at the generated macro. For the most part, you will be able to copy and paste that macro into Visual FoxPro with few modifications.

For example, suppose that you need to generate a report in Excel. When generating a report, you need to enter information, format cell contents, size columns, and so on. Here's a simple way to learn how to do this without a huge learning curve.

Start Excel and turn on the macro recorder by selecting Tools, Macro, Record New Macro. The dialog that pops up enables you to name the macro (see Figure 21.1).

FIGURE 21.1

The Excel Record Macro dialog appears when you initiate a new macro.

While you're recording the macro, the Macro Recording toolbar is visible (see Figure 21.2). Manually perform the operations that you want to automate, such as entering information, formatting the cells and columns, and so on. When you are done, and have accomplished at least one instance of every operation, stop the recorder.

FIGURE 21.2

The Macro Recording toolbar is visible while you record a macro in Excel.

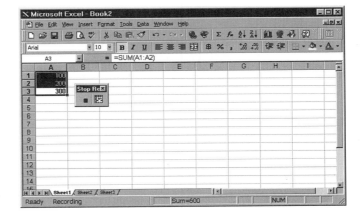

The next step is simple: Press Alt+F8 and you will see a list of all macros in the document, including the one you just created. Highlight the name of the macro you just created and click Edit. The code generated by the macro recorder appears in the Visual Basic Editor (see Figure 21.3). If you look at the code, you will see that it is remarkably similar to the code you would write in Visual FoxPro. In fact, it is so similar, you will not have to do much in the way of changes to get it to work in Visual FoxPro.

There is one problem, though. When Word and Excel record macros, the generated code uses a spate of defined constants without providing definitions for those constants. Fortunately, the constants have not been hidden from you. All constants used by these applications are documented in the application's type library. Some languages, such as Visual Basic, do not need anything other than the type library to understand these constants. Visual FoxPro cannot use the type library directly. Fear not, however, if you have the full Visual Studio, you can create an .H file for Visual FoxPro with a minimum of bother that will take care of the situation for you.

In the next section, I'll show the trick. For now, accept the fact that I have a header file called Excel.h that has all the constants in it.

Part

V

Ch

21

FIGURE 21.3
The Visual Basic Editor
shows the macro code
generated by the Record
Macro operation in
Excel.

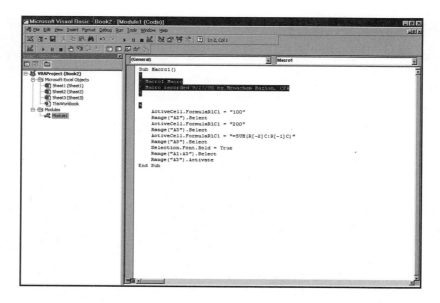

The code generated by the macro recorder is shown in Listing 21.1.

Listing 21.1   21CODE01—Macro Code That Was Recorded in Excel

```
Sub Macro1()
'
' Macro1 Macro
' Macro recorded 8/23/98 by Menachem Bazian, CPA
'
    ActiveCell.FormulaR1C1 = "Account Number"
    Range("B4").Select
    ActiveCell.FormulaR1C1 = "Description"
    Range("C4").Select
    ActiveCell.FormulaR1C1 = "Balance"
    Range("A5").Select
    ActiveCell.FormulaR1C1 = "'100"
    Range("A6").Select
    ActiveCell.FormulaR1C1 = "'200"
    Range("A7").Select
    ActiveCell.FormulaR1C1 = "'300"
    Range("B5").Select
    ActiveCell.FormulaR1C1 = "This is the account description"
    Range("B6").Select
    Columns("B:B").EntireColumn.AutoFit
    ActiveCell.FormulaR1C1 = "This is another account description."
    Range("B7").Select
    ActiveCell.FormulaR1C1 = "This is a third account description."
    Range("C5").Select
    ActiveCell.FormulaR1C1 = "100"
    Range("C6").Select
```

```
       ActiveCell.FormulaR1C1 = "200"
       Range("C7").Select
       ActiveCell.FormulaR1C1 = "300"
       Range("C8").Select
       Columns("B:B").EntireColumn.AutoFit
       Range("C5").Select
       ActiveCell.FormulaR1C1 = "1245.99"
       Range("C6").Select
       ActiveCell.FormulaR1C1 = "14290.26"
       Range("C7").Select
       ActiveCell.FormulaR1C1 = "-500.98"
       Range("B9").Select
       ActiveCell.FormulaR1C1 = "TOTAL"
       Range("C9").Select
       ActiveCell.FormulaR1C1 = "=SUM(R[-4]C:R[-1]C)"
       Columns("C:C").Select
       Selection.NumberFormat = "#,##0.00_);[Red](#,##0.00)"
       Columns("A:A").EntireColumn.AutoFit
       Rows("4:4").Select
       Selection.Font.Bold = True
       Range("B9:C9").Select
       Selection.Font.Bold = True
       Range("C7").Select
       Selection.Borders(xlDiagonalDown).LineStyle = xlNone
       Selection.Borders(xlDiagonalUp).LineStyle = xlNone
       Selection.Borders(xlEdgeLeft).LineStyle = xlNone
       Selection.Borders(xlEdgeTop).LineStyle = xlNone
       With Selection.Borders(xlEdgeBottom)
           .LineStyle = xlContinuous
           .Weight = xlThin
           .ColorIndex = xlAutomatic
       End With
       Selection.Borders(xlEdgeRight).LineStyle = xlNone
       Range("C9").Select
       Selection.Borders(xlDiagonalDown).LineStyle = xlNone
       Selection.Borders(xlDiagonalUp).LineStyle = xlNone
       Selection.Borders(xlEdgeLeft).LineStyle = xlNone
       Selection.Borders(xlEdgeTop).LineStyle = xlNone
       With Selection.Borders(xlEdgeBottom)
           .LineStyle = xlDouble
           .Weight = xlThick
           .ColorIndex = xlAutomatic
       End With
       Selection.Borders(xlEdgeRight).LineStyle = xlNone
       Range("A4").Select
       Columns("A:A").EntireColumn.AutoFit
   End Sub
```

The trick to getting this code to work in Visual FoxPro is simple. First, you have to include the header file. Also, you must define two constants for .T. and .F. (I like to define them separately; I'll explain why in the next section.)

Part

V

Ch

21

The next step is to work on the minor differences in syntax. Mainly, you need to add periods before each collection. For example,

```
With Selection.Borders(xlEdgeBottom)
```

becomes

```
With .Selection.Borders(xlEdgeBottom)
```

Another obvious difference is the End With command, which is two words in Visual Basic for Applications and one word in Visual FoxPro.

When you're done, the final code should appear as shown in Listing 21.2.

Listing 21.2 21CODE02—An Excel Macro Converted to Run in Visual FoxPro 6

```
* Program....: EXCEL1.PRG
* Version....: 1.0
* Author.....: Menachem Bazian, CPA
* Date.......: August 23, 1998
* Project....: Using Visual FoxPro 6 Special Edition
* Notice.....: Copyright (c) 1998 Menachem Bazian, CPA, All Rights Reserved.
* Compiler...: Visual FoxPro 06.00.8141.00 for Windows
* Abstract...:
* Changes....:

#INCLUDE excel.h
#DEFINE True .T.
#DEFINE False .F.

WITH oExcel

    .WorkBooks.Add
    .Sheets(1).Select
    .Range("A4").Select
    .ActiveCell.FormulaR1C1 = "Account Number"
    .Range("B4").Select
    .ActiveCell.FormulaR1C1 = "Description"
    .Range("C4").Select
    .ActiveCell.FormulaR1C1 = "Balance"
    .Range("A5").Select
    .ActiveCell.FormulaR1C1 = "'100"
    .Range("A6").Select
    .ActiveCell.FormulaR1C1 = "'200"
    .Range("A7").Select
    .ActiveCell.FormulaR1C1 = "'300"
    .Range("B5").Select
    .ActiveCell.FormulaR1C1 = "This is the account description"
    .Range("B6").Select
    .Columns("B:B").EntireColumn.AutoFit
    .ActiveCell.FormulaR1C1 = "This is another account description."
    .Range("B7").Select
```

```
.ActiveCell.FormulaR1C1 = "This is a third account description."
.Range("C5").Select
.ActiveCell.FormulaR1C1 = "100"
.Range("C6").Select
.ActiveCell.FormulaR1C1 = "200"
.Range("C7").Select
.ActiveCell.FormulaR1C1 = "300"
.Range("C8").Select
.Columns("B:B").EntireColumn.AutoFit
.Range("C5").Select
.ActiveCell.FormulaR1C1 = "1245.99"
.Range("C6").Select
.ActiveCell.FormulaR1C1 = "14290.26"
.Range("C7").Select
.ActiveCell.FormulaR1C1 = "-500.98"
.Range("B9").Select
.ActiveCell.FormulaR1C1 = "TOTAL"
.Range("C9").Select
.ActiveCell.FormulaR1C1 = "=SUM(R[-4]C:R[-1]C)"
.Columns("C:C").Select
.Selection.NumberFormat = "#,##0.00_);[Red](#,##0.00)"
.Columns("A:A").EntireColumn.AutoFit
.Rows("4:4").Select
.Selection.Font.Bold = True
.Range("B9:C9").Select
.Selection.Font.Bold = True
.Range("C7").Select
.Selection.Borders(xlDiagonalDown).LineStyle = xlNone
.Selection.Borders(xlDiagonalUp).LineStyle = xlNone
.Selection.Borders(xlEdgeLeft).LineStyle = xlNone
.Selection.Borders(xlEdgeTop).LineStyle = xlNone
WITH .Selection.Borders(xlEdgeBottom)
     .LineStyle = xlContinuous
     .Weight = xlThin
     .ColorIndex = xlAutomatic
ENDWITH
.Selection.Borders(xlEdgeRight).LineStyle = xlNone
.Range("C9").Select
.Selection.Borders(xlDiagonalDown).LineStyle = xlNone
.Selection.Borders(xlDiagonalUp).LineStyle = xlNone
.Selection.Borders(xlEdgeLeft).LineStyle = xlNone
.Selection.Borders(xlEdgeTop).LineStyle = xlNone
WITH .Selection.Borders(xlEdgeBottom)
     .LineStyle = xlDouble
     .Weight = xlThick
     .ColorIndex = xlAutomatic
ENDWITH
.Selection.Borders(xlEdgeRight).LineStyle = xlNone
.Range("A4").Select
.Columns("A:A").EntireColumn.AutoFit

    .Visible = .T.
ENDWITH
```

If you look closely at the code, the only modifications are:

- I added a header to the program.
- Instantiating the Excel COM server. Notice that the rest of the program is in a `With`/ `EndWith` construct.
- `End With` changed to `EndWith`.
- Periods before collection members (such as `.Selection.Borders`).
- Adding the `.H` file reference and the `#DEFINE` lines.
- Adding `.Visible = .T.` at the end.

To quantify the entire process, generating the macro and changing the code took a few short minutes. After I have the generated code, I can examine it to determine how certain things were done and then apply these methods to the entire report.

You'll see an example of a report I did in this manner in a little bit. Before I go into that, though, there is one open issue, which is addressed in the following section.

Dealing with Generated Constants in Macro Code

As said earlier, the constants in the generated code are not understandable to Visual FoxPro with a header file. The question is, how can I get that header file?

Before I go any further, let me state that the issue is one that can affect much more than Microsoft Office applications. Any application that you learn in this manner can have similar issues. So, the trick of generating an `.H` file for a COM server might prove useful beyond the Office suite.

The trick works like this: First you have to export the type library to a text file. You do this with Visual Studio's Object Viewer. After opening the Object Viewer (see Figure 21.4), use it to open the type library by choosing File, View TypeLib. Object Viewer requests the name of the file to open; for Excel, the file is named `Excel8.olb` and can be found in the `...Microsoft Office\Office\` folder.

After you select the file to view, the ITypeLib Viewer displays the type library (see Figure 21.5).

You see a text representation of the type library in the right pane of the viewer. Place your cursor in the viewer and select all the text with Ctrl+A and then press Ctrl+C to copy the selected text to the Clipboard. Open a text file using Visual FoxPro or Notepad and paste the text there. Save it. After you do this, run the program `MakeHFile` to parse it out and make a header file.

FIGURE 21.4

The Visual Studio Object Viewer is where you'll export the type library to a text file.

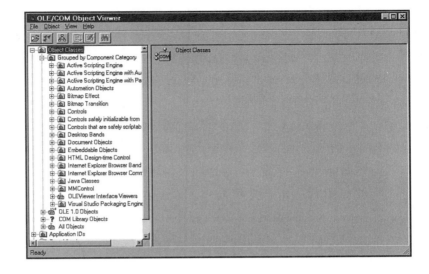

FIGURE 21.5

This viewer displays a type library.

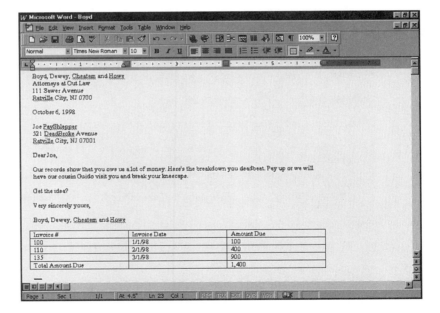

The code for MakeHFile is presented in Listing 21.3.

Listing 21.3 21CODE03—**Program That Creates a Header File from Type Library Constants**

```
*-- Program....: MAKEHFILE.PRG
*-- Version....: 1.0
*-- Author.....: Menachem Bazian, CPA
*-- Date.......: August 23, 1998
*-- Project....: Using Visual FoxPro 6 Special Edition
*-- Notice.....: Copyright (c) 1998 Menachem Bazian, CPA, All Rights Reserved.
*-- Compiler...: Visual FoxPro 06.00.8141.00 for Windows
*-- Abstract...:
*-- Changes....:

*-- Creates a header file for the constants in a type library.
*-- The type library contents have been
*-- exported with the OLE viewer prior to entering this program.
*--
*-- Parameters:
*--
*-- tcInFile - The name of the file to parse out.
*-- tcOutFile - The name of the .h file to create.
*--
*-- Note: Only the first parameter is required. If tcOutFile is not
*-- provided, the name of the input file is used as the name of
*-- the .h file. For example, Excel8.prh would output Excel8.h

LPARAMETERS tcInFile, tcOutFile

LOCAL lnInFile, lnOutFile, lcText, lcOutText, llOutput

*-- If the name of the file was not provided or it doesn't exist,
*-- error out.

IF PCOUNT() = 0 OR !FILE(tcInFile)
    MESSAGEBOX("Input file must be specified!", 16, "MakeHFile")
    RETURN
ENDIF

*-- If only the input file was provided, generate a .h file name

IF PCOUNT() = 1
    lnDotPos = RAT('.', tcInFile)
    tcOutFile = LEFT(tcInFile, lnDotPos - 1) + ".h"
ENDIF

CLOSE ALL
lnInFile = FOPEN(tcInFile)
lnOutFile = FCREATE(tcOutFile)

lcText = ""
lcOutText = ""
llOutPut = .F.
```

```
DO WHILE !fEof(lnInFile)
    lcText = FGETS(lnInFile)

    *-- At the close curly braces, the constants are done.

    IF "}" $ lcText
        llOutput = .F.
    ENDIF

    IF llOutPut
        lcOutText = ALLTRIM(lcText)
        lcOutText = STRTRAN(lcOuttext, '=', ' ')
        lcOutText = "#DEFINE " + ALLTRIM(lcOutText)

        IF RIGHT(lcOutText, 1) = ','
            lcOutText = SUBST(lcOutText, 1, LEN(lcOutText) - 1)
        ENDIF

        =FPUTS(lnOutFile, ALLTRIM(lcOutText))
    ENDIF

    *-- Look for Typedef Enum { in the file. That's the beginning
    *-- of the constants we need to export to the .h File

    IF "ENUM {" $ UPPER(lcText)
        llOutput = .T.
    ENDIF

ENDDO

CLOSE ALL
```

MakeHFile is called with one or two parameters. The first parameter, which is required, is the name of the file to parse. As a naming convention, I give the exported type libraries an extension of .PRH (for *pre-h file*), but you can name them whatever you like. The second parameter, which is optional, gives a name to the output file (the header file to be generated). If the second parameter is not provided, the name of the input file is used and a new extension, .H, is added.

The only thing that MakeHFile does not do is deal with the representation of True and False. Visual Basic represents the value "true" as True, and Visual FoxPro uses .T.. The same goes for False and .F.. As a general rule, you can create a second header file with general definitions like this (such as FoxPro.h) and include it there. In the example just shown, I specifically defined the constants in the code.

More on Excel

It would be very useful to take a quick look at the code generated by the macro recorded in Excel. Excel has a hierarchical object model. In this case, you start with a *workbook,* which is a collection of sheets. *Sheets* are a collection of cells. You can reference workbooks and sheets with an array. For example, Sheets(1) is the first sheet in the display order (that is, if you look at the tabs of the sheets in the workbook, it is the left-most tab).

You can add workbooks and sheets with the .ADD method each collection has. You can set properties of the sheets and workbooks. For example, to change the name of the sheet, just change its name property.

The good news about learning to use Excel, as well as Word and Outlook, is that syntax is rather consistent. Both the Workbooks and Sheets collections use the .ADD method to add a member to their collection. In Outlook, you add an appointment to the calendar collection with—you guessed it—.ADD.

The bad news about all this is that it can get a little hairy trying to work all this stuff out. The Help documentation that comes with Excel is fairly good, but it takes time to get used to working with the collections. Word is the same. However, I find it very useful to browse the objects I am using in the Visual Basic Object Viewer (see Figure 21.6).

FIGURE 21.6
The Visual Basic Object Browser provides an organized view.

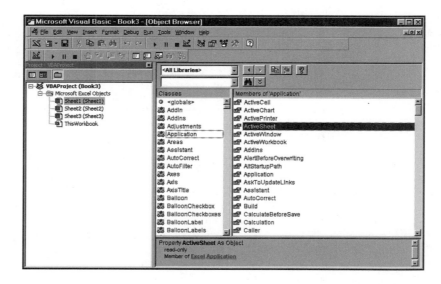

Notice that Excel starts with the application class. So, if I want to see what the members of the application class are, I scroll to Application in the list on the left and I can see all of its members, methods, and properties.

Using the Object Browser in conjunction with the generated code and the help files gives you a good way to learn how to use Excel and Word as COM servers.

Generating a Report with Excel

At this point you have seen some generated code, taken a brief look at the Excel object model, and have solved the problem of the constants. It's time to put your newfound skills to use and generate a report.

Excel is perfect for columnar reports. It especially shines when the report is one that the user might want to do ad-hoc analysis on (I did this for a client once and it saved them many hours of retyping information).

For the example here, I created a simple report based on the Customer table in the testdata sample database that ships with Visual FoxPro. The report lists the customer name and their total sales. The cells are formatted and the report is sorted by total sales (descending).

Take a look at the code for CustRpt.PRG as shown in Listing 21.4. Notice the comments in CustRpt.PRG, as they document the thoughts behind why certain things are done in a certain way.

Listing 21.4 21CODE04—Listing of Program That Dumps Customer Table Data into a Formatted Excel Report

```
*-- Program....: CUSTRPT.PRG
*-- Version....: 1.0
*-- Author.....: Menachem Bazian, CPA
*-- Date.......: August 23, 1998
*-- Project....: Using Visual FoxPro 6 Special Edition
*-- Notice.....: Copyright (c) 1998 Menachem Bazian, CPA, All Rights Reserved.
*-- Compiler...: Visual FoxPro 06.00.8141.00 for Windows
*-- Abstract...:
*-- Changes....:

*-- This program basically dumps all customers and their maximum order
*-- amount into a formatted Excel report.

*-- Include all the Excel stuff.

#INCLUDE Excel.h
#DEFINE False .F.
#DEFINE True .T.

*-- Default font and size I want. I #DEFINE it to make it
*-- easier to change later on.

#DEFINE RPT_FONTNAME "Comic Sans MS"
#DEFINE RPT_FONTSIZE 12

*-- First, open the database and table and run the report

CLOSE DATA ALL

*-- Note, this program uses the path from my development machine.
*-- yours may differ.

WAIT WINDOW NOWAIT "Selecting rows from Customer table..."

OPEN DATA ("D:\PROGRAM FILES\DEVSTUDIO\VFP\samples\data\testdata")
USE customer
```

Part
V

Ch
21

continues

Listing 21.4   Continued

```
SELECT * ;
    FROM customer ;
    ORDER BY MaxOrdAmt DESCENDING ;
    INTO CURSOR Output

*-- Now, get the instance for Excel.

LOCAL loExcel, lcOldError, lcRange, lnSheets, lnCounter

WAIT WINDOW NOWAIT "Starting Excel..."

lcOldError = ON("ERROR")
ON ERROR loExcel = .NULL.
loExcel = GetObject(, "Excel.Application")
ON ERROR &lcOldError

IF ISNULL(loExcel)
    loExcel = CreateObject( "Excel.Application" )
ENDIF

*-- At this point, I have an instance to Excel.
*-- I am *assuming* the existence of Excel. Not
*-- necessarily a valid assumption, but acceptable for
*-- the purposes of this sample program.

WITH loExcel

    *-- When you start Excel as a COM server, you have no workbooks.
    *-- So, I need to add one.

    .Workbooks.Add

    *-- One critical thing to do is make sure that the COM server
    *-- doesn't put up a dialog. DisplayAlerts is a property
    *-- roughly equivalent to Visual FoxPro's SET SAFETY. By setting
    *-- it to False, attempting to close the workbook without
    *-- saving it will not generate an error.

    .DisplayAlerts = False

    *-- By default, creating a workbook starts it with several
    *-- sheets. I want to be neat, so I am deleting all but the
    *-- one sheet I need.

    lnSheets = .Sheets.Count
    FOR lnCounter = 1 TO lnSheets - 1
        .Sheets(1).Delete
    ENDFOR

    *-- Next step is to rename the sheet. Again, for neatness sake.
    *-- The SELECT is probably not necessary but I like to be a bit
    *-- paranoid with this just in case.
```

```
WITH .Sheets(1)
     .Select
     .Name = "Testdata Customers"
ENDWITH

*-- And, get rid of the grid lines... I don't like them in a
*-- formatted report

.ActiveWindow.DisplayGridlines = False

*-- OK, now that we have the housekeeping stuff done, we can
*-- get down to business. First step is to build the header of
*-- the report. That includes the title of the report and
*-- and the date/time of the report.
*--
*-- Note that there are two ways to reference a cell in Excel.
*-- The Cells collection can be used in which case you specify
*-- the row and column of the cell as numbers. Cells(1,1) refers
*-- to A1. Cells(2,1) is A2.
*--
*-- The Range() collection does the same thing except I can reference
*-- a cell by its "English" name.
*--
*-- Of the Two, I prefer the Range() method when I am going for a
*-- particular cell because I think of the cells that way. Later on,
*-- I use the Cells() collection in the loop because the numeric
*-- parameters are perfect for that kind of cell populating exercise.
*--
*-- There is one other benefit to the Range() collection. You can
*-- work on a range of cells at the same time. For example,
*-- I can format a whole range of cells in one operation.
*-- I have an example of this later on in the program.

WAIT WINDOW NOWAIT "Building Header Rows"

WITH .Range("A1")
     .Value = "Testdata Customer Report"
     WITH .Font
          .Bold = .T.
          .Size = 14
          .Underline = xlUnderlineStyleSingle
     ENDWITH
ENDWITH

 *-- Center A1 over columns A and B
With .Range("A1:B1")
    .HorizontalAlignment = xlCenter
    .VerticalAlignment = xlBottom
    .WrapText = False
    .Orientation = 0
    .ShrinkToFit = False
    .MergeCells = False
    .Merge
EndWith
```

continues

Part

V

Ch

21

Listing 21.4 Continued

```
WITH .Range("A3")
    .Value = "=Now()"
    .NumberFormat = "m/d/yy h:mm AM/PM"
    .HorizontalAlignment = xlLeft
ENDWITH

*-- Now do the column headers
*--
*-- Just for fun, we'll color in the column headers.

.Range("A5").Value = "Customer Name"
.Range("B5").Value = "Maximum Order Amt"

lcRange = "A5:B5"

WITH .Range(lcRange)
    .Font.Bold = .T.
    .Font.Size = RPT_FONTSIZE
    .Font.Name = RPT_FONTNAME
    .HorizontalAlignment = xlCenter

    WITH .Borders(xlEdgeBottom)
        .Weight = xlMedium
        .LineStyle = xlContinuous
    ENDWITH

    WITH .Interior
        .ColorIndex = 42
        .Pattern = xlSolid
    ENDWITH
ENDWITH

*-- Now, scan through the XTAB table and put all
*-- the information in the spreadsheet

WAIT WINDOW NOWAIT "Populating cells:"

SELECT Output
GO TOP

*-- Populate the report
*--
*-- Note the use of Cells() in this case instead of Range().

lnRow = 7
SCAN
    WAIT WINDOW NOWAIT "Populating cells: Record " + ALLTRIM(STR(RECNO()))
    ➡+ ;
        " of " + ALLTRIM(STR(RECCOUNT()))
    *-- Read the record into the cells
    .Cells(lnRow, 1).Value = output.Company
    .Cells(lnRow, 2).Value = output.MaxOrdAmt
    lnRow = lnRow + 1
```

```
ENDSCAN

*-- OK, the body of the report is complete. Now, let's get the totals
*-- in there.

.Cells(lnRow + 2, 1).Value = "Totals"
WITH .Cells(lnRow + 2, 2)
    .Value = "=SUM(B7:B" + ALLT(STR(lnRow-1)) + ")"
    WITH .Borders(xlEdgeBottom)
        .Weight = xlMedium
        .LineStyle = xlDouble
    ENDWITH
ENDWITH

*-- Format the body of the report.

lcRange = "A7:B" + ALLTRIM(STR(lnRow+2))
WITH .Range(lcRange)
    .Font.Size = RPT_FONTSIZE
    .Font.Name = RPT_FONTNAME
ENDWITH

WITH .Range(ALLT(STR(lnRow+2)) + ":" + ALLT(STR(lnRow+2)))
    .Font.Bold = .T.
ENDWITH

WITH .Range("B7:B" + ALLT(STR(lnRow+2)))
    .NumberFormat = "$#,##0.00_);[Red]($#,##0.00)"
    .Font.Name = RPT_FONTNAME
    .Font.Size = RPT_FONTSIZE
ENDWITH

*-- Now some column formatting here. Note the use of the Columns()
*-- Collection.

*-- Here's another example of how wierd Excel can be. In order to
*-- have a column automatically size itself properly, you can:
.Columns("A:B").EntireColumn.AutoFit

*-- And that's it

ENDWITH

WAIT CLEAR

=MessageBox("Done")

*-- Setting the visible property to .T. will cause Excel to become
*-- visible and become the foremost application.

loExcel.Visible = .T.
Release loExcel
CLOSE DATA ALL

RETURN
```

Part

V

Ch

21

Managing Instances of a COM Application

Notice the code at the top of CustRpt.PRG where Excel is started. The whole reason for the rigmarole with first trying GetObject() and then CreateObject() (if GetObject() fails) is to prevent Excel from running multiple times on my machine.

In truth, you will probably want to try doing this with other servers as well. Therefore, it behooves us to abstract that code into a generic routine. GetCOMInstance.PRG is a program that does just that and is shown in Listing 21.5. Review the code and, once again, pay attention to the comments as they tell the story on how to use this handy little utility.

Listing 21.5   21CODE05—**Listing of UDF That Attempts to Retrieve an Instance of a COM Server**

```
*-- Program....: GETCOMINSTANCE.PRG
*-- Version....: 1.0
*-- Author.....: Menachem Bazian, CPA
*-- Date.......: August 23, 1998
*-- Project....: Using Visual FoxPro 6 Special Edition
*-- Notice.....: Copyright (c) 1998 Menachem Bazian, CPA, All Rights Reserved.
*-- Compiler...: Visual FoxPro 06.00.8141.00 for Windows
*-- Abstract...:
*-- Changes....:

*-- This UDF will try to get an instance of a COM server without
*-- running the application again.

LPARAMETERS tcCOMServerClass, tcDocumentFileName

*-- The parameter tcCOMServerClass is the name of the COM server class to
*-- instantiate. For example, "excel.application". This program
*-- specifically sets OLEOBJECT on (otherwise, why would we
*-- be calling this program?"
*--
*-- If the COM server cannot be instantiated, this program returns NULL.

*-- Step 1 - Make sure we got a parameter.

ASSERT TYPE("tcCOMServerClass") = "C" ;
     MESSAGE "You must provide a character parameter to GetCOMInstance."

IF PCOUNT() = 0 OR TYPE("tcCOMServerClass") # "C"
     RETURN .NULL.
ENDIF

*-- If we get this far, we can go ahead and attempt to instantiate the
*-- COM server with GetObject(). Trying to instantiate with GETObject
*-- will try to get an instance from an existing instance of the
*-- application.
*--
*-- Note also that this program will instantiate with GetObject on a file
*-- name. tcDocumentFileName has to be passed and the file has to exist.
```

```
    LOCAL loCOMInstance, lcOldError

    lcOldError = ON("ERROR")


    *-- See if the document file name has been passed through. If so, try
    *-- to create a reference to that file. If not, just create a regular
    *-- instance.
    *--
    *-- Note that only the GetObject and Createobject lines of code are
    *-- wrapped in the changes to ON ERROR. That's because the special
    *-- error handler is only applicable to those lines of code.

    IF PCOUNT() = 2 AND ;
        TYPE("tcDocumentFileName") = "C" AND ;
        FILE(tcDocumentFileName)

        ON ERROR loCOMInstance = .NULL.
        loCOMInstance = GetObject(tcDocumentFileName, tcCOMServerClass)
        ON ERROR &lcOldError
    ELSE
        *-- In this case, no documentfile name has been passed through.
        *-- Just create a standard COM instance

        ON ERROR loCOMInstance = .NULL.
        loCOMInstance = GetObject(, tcCOMServerClass)
        ON ERROR &lcOldError

        IF ISNULL(loCOMInstance)
            ON ERROR loCOMInstance = .NULL.
            loCOMInstance = CreateObject(tcCOMServerClass)
            ON ERROR &lcOldError
        ENDIF
    ENDIF

    RETURN loCOMInstance
```

Using Word

So much for Excel. You could write an entire book on Excel but time and space are limited here, so I will leave the rest up to you. Let's move on to an example of Word. You'll notice some marked differences here, but it should be similar enough that you can use the knowledge you have acquired in Excel to help you here.

By the way, I am a big fan of learning by example. In other words, I think the best way to learn how to work with a COM object is to make a task for yourself and work it through. By the time you have a task figured out, you will be well on your way to learning how to make the most out of the object.

In keeping with this philosophy, let's figure out something you can do with Word, dive right into it, and see where it leads you.

Part

V

Ch

21

A Hypothetical Problem

The law firm of Boyd, Dewey, Cheatem, and Howe has called you in as a Visual FoxPro and COM expert. They have an accounting system that was written in Visual FoxPro and they want you to write a report. Not any ordinary report, of course. BDCH wants to run a report of all the clients that owe them money and then have the system automatically generate letters to go to the customers. They provide you with a sample Word document named Boyd.doc and leave you to your own devices (see Figure 21.7).

FIGURE 21.7

The Boyd.doc document displayed in Microsoft Word.

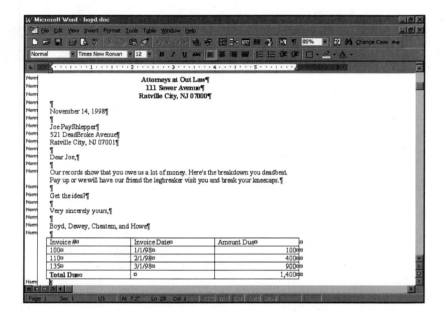

My Strategy

Not being too well informed about how to automatically generate these letters in Word, but having read *Using Visual FoxPro 6 Special Edition*, I have a perfect plan. I will type in the sample letter as a macro and see what is generated.

The macro that is generated is shown in Listing 21.6.

Listing 21.6   21CODE06—Macro That Was Recorded While Typing Document Boyd.doc into Word

```
Sub Macro3()
'
' Macro3 Macro
' Macro recorded 08/23/98 by Menachem Bazian, CPA
'
```

```
Documents.Add Template:="Normal", NewTemplate:=False
Windows.Arrange
Selection.TypeText Text:="Boyd, Dewey, Cheatem, and Howe"
Selection.HomeKey Unit:=wdLine, Extend:=wdExtend
Selection.Font.Bold = wdToggle
Selection.ParagraphFormat.Alignment = wdAlignParagraphCenter
Selection.EndKey Unit:=wdLine
Selection.TypeParagraph
Selection.TypeText Text:="Attorneys at Out Law"
Selection.TypeParagraph
Selection.TypeText Text:="111 Sewer Avenue"
Selection.TypeParagraph
Selection.TypeText Text:="Ratville City, NJ 0700"
Selection.TypeParagraph
Selection.Font.Bold = wdToggle
Selection.ParagraphFormat.Alignment = wdAlignParagraphLeft
Selection.TypeParagraph
Selection.InsertDateTime DateTimeFormat:="MMMM d, yyyy", InsertAsField:= _
    False
Windows("Boyd.doc").Activate
ActiveWindow.ActivePane.SmallScroll Down:=7
Windows("Document7").Activate
Selection.MoveDown Unit:=wdLine, Count:=1
Selection.TypeParagraph
Selection.TypeParagraph
Selection.TypeText Text:="Joe PayShlepper"
Selection.TypeParagraph
Selection.TypeText Text:="521 DeadBroke Avenue"
Selection.TypeParagraph
Selection.TypeText Text:="Ratville City, NJ 07001"
Selection.TypeParagraph
Selection.TypeParagraph
Selection.TypeText Text:="Dear Joe,"
Selection.TypeParagraph
Selection.TypeParagraph
Selection.TypeText Text:= _
    "Our records show that you owe us a lot of money. Here's the "
Selection.TypeText Text:= _
    "breakdown you deadbeat. Pay up or we will have our friendj G the "
Selection.TypeText Text:="legbreaker"
Selection.MoveLeft Unit:=wdCharacter, Count:=15
Selection.MoveLeft Unit:=wdCharacter, Count:=3, Extend:=wdExtend
Selection.Delete Unit:=wdCharacter, Count:=3
Selection.EndKey Unit:=wdLine
Selection.TypeText Text:=" visit you and break your kneecaps."
Selection.TypeParagraph
Selection.TypeParagraph
Windows("Boyd.doc").Activate
ActiveWindow.ActivePane.SmallScroll Down:=8
Windows("Document7").Activate
Selection.TypeText Text:="Get the idea?"
Selection.TypeParagraph
Selection.TypeParagraph
Selection.TypeText Text:="Very sincerely yours,"
Selection.TypeParagraph
```

continues

Listing 21.6   Continued

```
        Selection.TypeParagraph
        Selection.TypeText Text:="Boyd, Dewey, Cheatem, and Howe"
        Selection.TypeParagraph
        Selection.TypeParagraph
        ActiveDocument.Tables.Add Range:=Selection.Range, NumRows:=2, NumColumns:= _
            3
        Selection.TypeText Text:="Invoice #"
        Selection.MoveRight Unit:=wdCell
        Selection.TypeText Text:="Invoice Date"
        Selection.MoveRight Unit:=wdCell
        Selection.TypeText Text:="Amount Due"
        Selection.MoveRight Unit:=wdCell
        Windows("Boyd.doc").Activate
        ActiveWindow.ActivePane.SmallScroll Down:=6
        Windows("Document7").Activate
        Selection.TypeText Text:="100"
        Selection.MoveRight Unit:=wdCell
        Selection.TypeText Text:="1/1/98"
        Selection.MoveRight Unit:=wdCell
        Selection.TypeText Text:="100"
        Selection.MoveRight Unit:=wdCell
        Selection.TypeText Text:="110"
        Selection.MoveRight Unit:=wdCell
        Selection.TypeText Text:="2/1/98"
        Selection.MoveRight Unit:=wdCell
        Selection.TypeText Text:="400"
        Selection.MoveRight Unit:=wdCell
        Selection.TypeText Text:="135"
        Selection.MoveRight Unit:=wdCell
        Selection.TypeText Text:="3/1/98"
        Selection.MoveRight Unit:=wdCell
        Selection.TypeText Text:="900"
        Selection.MoveRight Unit:=wdCell
        Selection.Font.Bold = wdToggle
        Selection.TypeText Text:="Total Due"
        Selection.MoveRight Unit:=wdCell
        Selection.MoveRight Unit:=wdCell
        Selection.Paste
        Selection.MoveUp Unit:=wdLine, Count:=1
        Selection.HomeKey Unit:=wdLine
        Selection.MoveDown Unit:=wdLine, Count:=3, Extend:=wdExtend
        Selection.MoveLeft Unit:=wdCharacter, Count:=1, Extend:=wdExtend
        Selection.Delete Unit:=wdCharacter, Count:=1
        Selection.Font.Bold = wdToggle
        Selection.TypeText Text:="1,400"
        Selection.MoveUp Unit:=wdLine, Count:=3
        Selection.HomeKey Unit:=wdLine
        Selection.MoveDown Unit:=wdLine, Count:=3, Extend:=wdExtend
        Selection.ParagraphFormat.Alignment = wdAlignParagraphRight
End Sub
```

Syntactical Differences

One of the immediate problems in looking at this macro code is that it is in a different format than the Excel code. For instance, take the following line of code:

```
Selection.TypeText Text:="Total Due"
```

What in blazes is that? Well, here's where the help file comes in. A quick trip to the WordBasic help file shows that there are two syntaxes (in other words, you can call the same method or function in two different ways). In one, you can use named arguments as you see above. However, you can also specify the arguments as standard parameters. So, I could easily use the following syntax:

```
Selection.TypeText("Total Due")
```

What's the difference? Well, when you use named arguments, you do not have to worry about the order of parameters. It's no big deal, but it does mean that you have more work to do in getting this macro to work than you did in Excel.

> **N O T E** For the record, the commands I have used from generated code seem to include the names arguments in the order they need to appear as parameters. I don't count on that, though, and always check. ▨

Select What?

The next obvious thing that comes out is the `selection` object. In Excel, where it's easy to discern one piece of data from another, you have a cell object. Selection is more appropriate to a word processor and deals with the selected text. If you have no selected text, it deals with the location of the cursor.

A Final Look at the Macro

Now you can start taking the macro apart and turning it into COM instructions for WinWord.

Before you do that, though, I need to confess something to you. If you look at the generated code, you will see oddities. Take this code, for example:

```
Selection.TypeText Text:= _
        "breakdown you deadbeat. Pay up or we will have our friendj G the "
    Selection.TypeText Text:="legbreaker"
    Selection.MoveLeft Unit:=wdCharacter, Count:=15
    Selection.MoveLeft Unit:=wdCharacter, Count:=3, Extend:=wdExtend
    Selection.Delete Unit:=wdCharacter, Count:=3
    Selection.EndKey Unit:=wdLine
    Selection.TypeText Text:=" visit you and break your kneecaps."
```

This is a case of a typo being created and corrected. See the phrase `friendj G`? The original letter just said `friend`, so I had to go back and fix the accidental typing. I could have edited the macro prior to including it in this chapter, but I wanted you to see this. A secretary, I'm not. Although I type fast, I make a number of mistakes (this is one author who is grateful for spell check). If you're like me, plenty of this stuff happens when you're recording macros, and you'll need to correct it later, so you might as well get used to the idea up front.

The Fixed Macro

After working with the help file to get the alternative syntax and modifying the code in the macro to make it legible to Visual FoxPro, I came up with the code shown in Listing 21.7.

Listing 21.7   21CODE07—Visual FoxPro 6 Program Containing a Converted Word Macro

```
*-- Program....: WORD1.PRG
*-- Version....: 1.0
*-- Author.....: Menachem Bazian, CPA
*-- Date.......: August 23, 1998
*-- Project....: Using Visual FoxPro 6 Special Edition
*-- Notice.....: Copyright (c) 1998 Menachem Bazian, CPA, All Rights Reserved.
*-- Compiler...: Visual FoxPro 06.00.8141.00 for Windows
*-- Abstract...:
*-- Changes....:

*-- Word macro modified for Visual FoxPro
#INCLUDE msWord.h
#DEFINE True .T.
#DEFINE False .F.

*-- Step 1 -- get a reference to MS Word

LOCAL loWord, loTable, lnRow, lnColumn
loWord = GetCOMInstance("word.application")
loWord.Visible = .t.

*-- Now, build the letter

WITH loWord
     .Documents.Add("Normal", False)

     WITH .Selection

          .TypeText("Boyd, Dewey, Cheatem, and Howe")
          .HomeKey(wdLine,wdExtend)
          .Font.Bold = wdToggle
          .ParagraphFormat.Alignment = wdAlignParagraphCenter
          .EndKey(wdLine)
          .TypeParagraph
          .TypeText("Attorneys at Out Law")
          .TypeParagraph
          .TypeText("111 Sewer Avenue")
          .TypeParagraph
          .TypeText("Ratville City, NJ 0700")
          .TypeParagraph
          .Font.Bold = wdToggle
          .ParagraphFormat.Alignment = wdAlignParagraphLeft
```

```
        .TypeParagraph
        .InsertDateTime("MMMM d, yyyy", False)
*       .MoveDown(wdLine, 1)
        .TypeParagraph
        .TypeParagraph
        .TypeText("Joe PayShlepper")
        .TypeParagraph
        .TypeText("521 DeadBroke Avenue")
        .TypeParagraph
        .TypeText("Ratville City, NJ 07001")
        .TypeParagraph
        .TypeParagraph
        .TypeText("Dear Joe,")
        .TypeParagraph
        .TypeParagraph

*-- Up until this point, all I have really done is reformat the code
*-- from the macro (with deleting some extraneous commands that we
*-- didn't need,such as commands generated by my switching windows
*-- while originally generating the macro). Now, I have our first real
*-- modification to the macro code. Instead of many TypeText calls for
*-- the one paragraph,I changed it to one call.
*--
*-- As a general rule, the more calls you can eliminate and combine,
*-- the faster your execution speed will be.

lcText = "Our records show that you owe us a lot of money. Here's the
➡" + ;
        "breakdown you deadbeat. Pay up or we will have our friend the" +
        ➡;
        " legbreaker visit you and break your kneecaps."

        .TypeText(lcText)
        .TypeParagraph
        .TypeParagraph
        .TypeText("Get the idea?")
        .TypeParagraph
        .TypeParagraph
        .TypeText("Very sincerely yours,")
        .TypeParagraph
        .TypeParagraph
        .TypeText("Boyd, Dewey, Cheatem, and Howe")
        .TypeParagraph
        .TypeParagraph
ENDWITH

*-- Now to the next major modification. In the original macro, the table
*-- was created by inserting a 2 X 2 table and then "typing" the text.
*-- A table, however, is an object. Using the Table object, you can more
*-- directly populate and manipulate the table.
*--
*-- Why do I care about the table object? I did not, after all, bother to
*-- look for a more elegant way to do the body of the letter. Well, the
*-- is obvious when you look at the code. By using the table object, I can
```

Part
V

Ch
21

continues

Listing 21.7   Continued

```
*-- the code to populate the table generic. When this program is modified
*-- again to make it fully generic (and get the information from the
*-- firm's customer and transaction tables), the infrastructure exists.
*--
*-- Oh, by the way. Look at the code to work with the cells in the table.
*-- Doesn't it seem similar to Excel?

.ActiveDocument.Tables.Add(.Selection.Range, 5, 3)
loTable = .ActiveDocument.Tables(1)

DECLARE laTableData[5,3]
laTableData[1,1] = "Invoice #"
laTableData[1,2] = "Invoice Date"
laTableData[1,3] = "Amount Due"

laTableData[2,1] = "100"
laTableData[2,2] = "1/1/98"
laTableData[2,3] = "100"

laTableData[3,1] = "110"
laTableData[3,2] = "2/1/98"
laTableData[3,3] = "400"

laTableData[4,1] = "135"
laTableData[4,2] = "3/1/98"
laTableData[4,3] = "900"

laTableData[5,1] = "Total Amount Due"
laTableData[5,2] = ""
laTableData[5,3] = "1,400"

WITH loTable
    FOR lnRow = 1 TO ALEN(laTableData, 1)
        FOR lnColumn = 1 TO  ALEN(laTableData, 2)
            .Cell(lnRow,lnColumn).Range.InsertAfter(laTableData[lnRow,
            ➥lnColumn])
        ENDFOR
    ENDFOR

    *-- Our table is populated here. Now, all we have to do is autoformat
    *-- it. In case you were wondering.... I cheated... I autoformatted a
    *-- table, captured it in a macro, and then converted the macro code
    *-- here.

    loTable.AutoFormat(wdTableFormatClassic4, ;
                            True, ;
                            True, ;
                            True, ;
```

```
                                    True, ;
                                    True, ;
                                    True, ;
                                    False, ;
                                    False, ;
                                    True)

        ENDWITH

        *-- You need a page break between letters...

        .Selection.InsertBreak(wdPageBreak)
    ENDWITH

    *-- And that, as they say, is that.

    RETURN
```

A closer look at the code shows that only one section has been radically modified from the original code generated by WinWord. That's the section that generates the table. The changes, and the reasons for them, are documented in the code.

The Next Step

You're still not done, but the rest is the proverbial piece of cake. You now have a program that will generate one letter for a specific client, but you need to make it more generic. What can be so difficult about that? After you have this program working, the last step is a simple matter of pulling the information out of the company's tables, replacing the explicit text with fields or variables, and that should do it.

To illustrate this, look at word2.prg, which assumes that you have two tables, Customers and Invoices. These two tables are used to generate the letters for the clients.

The structures of Customers and Invoices and their contents are shown in Listing 21.8.

Listing 21.8 21CODE08—Structure and Contents of Sample Database Tables

```
Structure for table:                        CUSTOMERS.DBF
    Number of data records:     3
Date of last update:          08/24/98
    Code Page:                 1252
    Field    Field Name    Type         Width    Dec    Index    Collate    Nulls
        1    CCUSTNO       Character     10                                  No
        2    CORGNAME      Character     35                                  No
        3    CCONTACT      Character     35                                  No
        4    CSALUT        Character     10                                  No
        5    CADD1         Character     30                                  No
        6    CADD2         Character     30                                  No
```

continues

Listing 21.8   Continued

```
           7    CCITY        Character      15                          No
           8    CSTATE       Character       2                          No
           9    CZIP         Character      10                          No
** Total **                                178


Record #:            1

Ccustno  1
Corgname PayShlepper Enterprises
Ccontact Joe PayShlepper
Csalut   Joe
Cadd1    521 DeadBroke Avenue
Cadd2
Ccity    RatVille City
Cstate   NJ
Czip     07001

Ccustno  2
Corgname Owealot Industries
Ccontact G. I. Owealot
Csalut   G. I.
Cadd1    100 Owealot Way
Cadd2    Penthouse Suite
Ccity    New York
Cstate   NY
Czip     10111

Ccustno  3
Corgname PayNot Garments
Ccontact D. Ed Beat
Csalut   Ed
Cadd1    1022 WontPay Drive
Cadd2
Ccity    Moscow
Cstate   NY
Czip     10000

Structure for table:                       INVOICES.DBF
   Number of data records:      9
Date of last update:          08/24/98
   Code Page:                  1252
   Field    Field Name   Type       Width   Dec    Index Collate  Nulls
       1     CCUSTNO      Character     10           Asc   Machine   No
       2     CINVNO       Character     10                           No
       3     DINVDATE     Date          8                            No
       4     NAMOUNT      Numeric      10     2                      No
** Total **                            39
```

```
Record #:          1

Ccustno   1
Cinvno    100
Dinvdate  01/01/98
Namount     100.00

Ccustno   1
Cinvno    110
Dinvdate  02/01/98
Namount     400.00

Ccustno   1
Cinvno    135
Dinvdate  03/01/98
Namount     900.00

Ccustno   2
Cinvno    101
Dinvdate  01/01/98
Namount    1600.00

Ccustno   2
Cinvno    115
Dinvdate  02/15/98
Namount    2235.77

Ccustno   2
Cinvno    146
Dinvdate  03/01/98
Namount    2200.00

Ccustno   2
Cinvno    165
Dinvdate  04/01/98
Namount     500.00

Ccustno   2
Cinvno    199
Dinvdate  05/01/98
Namount    2722.00

Ccustno   3
Cinvno    111
Dinvdate  02/01/98
Namount    2233.98
```

Listing 21.9 contains the code for Word2.prg.

Listing 21.9   21CODE09.prg—Program That Generates a Letter for Each Customer Record

```
*-- Program....: WORD2.PRG
*-- Version....: 1.0
*-- Author.....: Menachem Bazian, CPA
*-- Date.......: August 24, 1998
*-- Project....: Using Visual FoxPro 6 Special Edition
*-- Notice.....: Copyright (c) 1998 Menachem Bazian, CPA, All Rights Reserved.
*-- Compiler...: Visual FoxPro 06.00.8141.00 for Windows
*-- Abstract...:
*-- Changes....:

*-- This is Word1.PRG modified to get the data from the firm's tables
*-- For all intents and purposes, the strategy of Word1.prg remains intact.
*-- However, some key modifications are present in this program:
*--
*-- 1. The functionality for building a paragraph has been moved into its
*--    own procedure.
*--
*-- 2. The mechanism for generating the letter has been moved into its own
*--    procedure.
*--
*-- 3. Certain additional functionality is required because we are dealing with
*--    data. The two key modifications is moving the addition of the page break
*--    to the beginning of the letter for a customer (if this is not the first
*--    customer letter) and passing the record number so we can get access to
*--    the right table object for a customer.
*--
*-- Finally, most of the comments from Word1.PRG that related to the upgrade of
*-- the code from VBA to VFP has been removed.

*-- Word macro modified for Visual FoxPro
#INCLUDE msWord.h
#DEFINE True .T.
#DEFINE False .F.

*-- Open the tables. We are assuming, for the purposes of this example,
*-- that the tables are the result of processing and represents the information
*-- be presented in the letters (i.e., I will not do any processing on the
*-- data other than what is needed to populate the Word letters).

*-- Step 1 -- get a reference to MS Word

LOCAL loWord, loTable, lnRow, lnColumn
loWord = GetCOMInstance("word.application")
loWord.Visible = .t.
loWord.Documents.Add
loWord.DisplayAlerts = .F.
```

```
*-- In order to make the code a little easier to modify and work with,
*-- I am moving the code that actually generates the letter to a procedure.
*--
*-- I will be sendind the procedure an object with the customer information
*-- and an array with the invoice information. As you will see, it will make
*-- some of the letter processing even easier.

CLOSE DATA ALL
USE customers
USE invoices IN 0

SELECT customers
SCAN
     SCATTER NAME oCust

     SELECT invoices.cInvNo, ;
         DTOC(invoices.dInvDate), ;
         invoices.nAmount ;
         FROM invoices ;
         WHERE invoices.cCustNo = oCust.cCustNo ;
         ORDER BY 1 ;
         INTO ARRAY laInvoices

     DO genletter WITH loWord, oCust, laInvoices, RECNO()
ENDSCAN


*------------------------------------------------------
* Procedure...: GenLetter
* Called by...: Word2
*
* Abstract....: Actually generates the word letter
*
* Parameters..: toWord - A reference to the word COM server.
*             : toCust - The customer information
*             : taInvoices - Array of open invoices for this customer
*             : tnRecno - Customer record number
*
* Notes.......:
*------------------------------------------------------
PROCEDURE genletter(toWord, toCust, taInvoices, tnRecno)

     *-- Now, build the letter

     WITH toWord

         WITH .Selection
             IF tnRecno > 1
                 *-- You need a page break between letters... Only add the
                 *-- page break starting with the second letter.

                 .InsertBreak(wdPageBreak)
             ENDIF
```

continues

Part

V

Ch

21

Listing 21.9 Continued

```
*-- Note that all text typing and paragraph mark functionality
*-- has been moved to AddParagraph. This saves on the code
*-- duplication.

.Font.Bold = .T.
.ParagraphFormat.Alignment = wdAlignParagraphCenter
AddParagraph(toWord, "Boyd, Dewey, Cheatem, and Howe")
AddParagraph(toWord, "Attorneys at Out Law")
AddParagraph(toWord, "111 Sewer Avenue")
AddParagraph(toWord, "Ratville City, NJ 0700")
.Font.Bold = .F.
.ParagraphFormat.Alignment = wdAlignParagraphLeft
AddParagraph(toWord)
.InsertDateTime("MMMM d, yyyy", False)
AddParagraph(toWord,"",2)

*-- Insert the customer information

IF !EMPTY(toCust.cContact)
    AddParagraph(toWord, ALLTRIM(toCust.cContact))
ENDIF

IF !EMPTY(toCust.cOrgName)
    AddParagraph(toWord, ALLTRIM(toCust.cOrgName))
ENDIF

IF !EMPTY(toCust.cAdd1)
    AddParagraph(toWord, ALLTRIM(toCust.cAdd1))
ENDIF

IF !EMPTY(toCust.cAdd2)
    AddParagraph(toWord, ALLTRIM(toCust.cAdd2))
ENDIF

LOCAL lcCSZ
lcCSZ = ALLTRIM(toCust.cCity) + ", " + ;
    toCust.cState + " " + ALLT(toCust.cZIP)

IF !EMPTY(lcCSZ)
    AddParagraph(toWord, ALLTRIM(lcCSZ))
ENDIF

AddParagraph(toWord)
AddParagraph(toWord, "Dear " + ALLTRIM(toCust.cSalut) + ",", 2)

lcText = "Our records show that you owe us a lot of money. Here's
➡the " + ;
    "breakdown you deadbeat. Pay up or we will have our friend
    ➡the" + ;
    " legbreaker visit you and break your kneecaps."

AddParagraph(toWord, lcText, 2)
AddParagraph(toWord, "Get the idea?", 2)
```

```
        AddParagraph(toWord, "Very sincerely yours,", 2)
        AddParagraph(toWord, "Boyd, Dewey, Cheatem, and Howe", 2)
ENDWITH

*-- Note how the table size is now based on the size of taInvoices...

LOCAL lnRows, lnCols, lnCounter, lnCount2, lnRow, loTable, lnTotal
lnRows = ALEN(taInvoices, 1)
lnCols = ALEN(taInvoices, 2)

.ActiveDocument.Tables.Add(.Selection.Range, lnRows + 2, lnCols)

*-- Each customer has one table... The record number of the customer
*-- will get us the right table in this case.

loTable = .ActiveDocument.Tables(tnRecno)

DECLARE laTableData[lnRows + 2, lnCols]
laTableData[1,1] = "Invoice #"
laTableData[1,2] = "Invoice Date"
laTableData[1,3] = "Amount Due"

FOR lnCounter = 1 TO lnRows
    FOR lnCount2 = 1 TO lnCols
            laTableData[lnCounter + 1, lnCount2] = taInvoices[lnCounter,
            ➥lnCOunt2]
    ENDFOR
ENDFOR

*-- Now the totals line

laTableData[lnRows + 2, 1] = "Total Amount Due"
laTableData[lnRows + 2, 2] = ""

*-- Do a quick sum here
lnTotal = 0
FOR lnCOunter = 1 TO ALEN(taInvoices, 1)
    lnTotal = taInvoices[lnCounter, 3] + lnTotal
ENDFOR

laTableData[lnRows + 2, 3] = lnTotal

WITH loTable
    FOR lnRow = 1 TO ALEN(laTableData, 1)
        FOR lnColumn = 1 TO  ALEN(laTableData, 2)

            *-- Processing is slightly different for the third
            *-- column. If we have a number, we want the number
            *-- formatted properly.
            *--
            *-- Also, we want it right aligned.
```

continues

Part

V

Ch

21

Listing 21.9   Continued

```
                IF lnColumn = 3
                    IF TYPE("laTableData[lnRow, lnColumn]") = "N"
                        .Cell(lnRow,lnColumn).Range.InsertAfter( ;
                            TRANSFORM(laTableData[lnRow, lnColumn],
                            ➥"999,999.99"))
                    ELSE
                        .Cell(lnRow,lnColumn).Range.InsertAfter( ;
                            laTableData[lnRow, lnColumn])
                    ENDIF

                    .Cell(lnRow,lnColumn).Range.ParagraphFormat.Alignment
                    ➥= ;
                        wdAlignParagraphRight
                ELSE
                    .Cell(lnRow,lnColumn).Range.InsertAfter( ;
                        laTableData[lnRow, lnColumn])
                ENDIF
            ENDFOR
        ENDFOR

        *-- Our table is populated here. Now, all we have to do is
        *-- autoformat it. In case you were wondering.... I cheated... I
        *-- autoformatted a table, captured it in a macro and then
        *-- converted the macro code here.

        .AutoFormat(wdTableFormatClassic4, ;
            True, ;
            True, ;
            True, ;
            True, ;
            True, ;
            True, ;
            False, ;
            False, ;
            True)

    ENDWITH


    *-- Move to the end of the document.

    .Selection.EndKey(wdStory)
ENDWITH

*-- And that, as they say, is that.


RETURN
ENDPROC &&* GenLetter
```

```
*-------------------------------------------------------------
* Procedure...: AddParagraph
* Called by...: GenLetter
*
* Abstract....: Adds a paragraph
*
* Parameters..:
*
* Notes.......:
*-------------------------------------------------------------
PROCEDURE AddParagraph(toWord, tcText, tnParagraphs)
    LOCAL lnCounter

    WITH toWord.Selection
        IF PCOUNT() >= 2
            .TypeText(tcText)
        ENDIF

        IF PCOUNT() < 3 OR TYPE("tnParagraphs") # "N"
            tnParagraphs = 1
        ENDIF

        FOR lnCounter = 1 TO tnParagraphs
            .TypeParagraph
        ENDFOR
    ENDWITH

    RETURN
ENDPROC &&* AddParagraph
```

A Final Word

I am sure that there are those who might look at the way in which these letters were generated and opine that there are better ways to do the task. Subjects like templates, running macros within Word, and more might come up.

The point behind this material was not to show you exactly how to use Word in your applications, but to take you through the learning process. The process whereby you learn how to use Word and Excel is more important than anything that can be documented within one chapter of a book. ●

Creating COM Servers with Visual FoxPro

What Do You Need COM Servers For?

Chapters 20 and 21 discussed working with COM servers within Visual FoxPro. However, Visual FoxPro as a COM client is only the beginning of the story. Visual FoxPro adds an incredible amount of power and flexibility to your application development arsenal by enabling you to easily create COM servers.

You're probably wondering why you need COM servers at all. Applications today are increasing in scope. Instead of applications being deployed on a single machine or even on a local area network (LAN), they are increasingly being deployed on an enterprisewide scale via the Internet or the corporate intranet. With applications now being accessed by larger numbers of users than ever before, a new strategy for deploying these applications is necessary.

Multi-tiered client/server applications are the means by which applications can be globally deployed with a minimum of fuss and bother.

A *multi-tiered application* is an application where the application is created in logical pieces. The user sees the front end, or the GUI. The data is stored on the back end. In the middle is a layer that is designed to enforce the business rules and handle the communications between the front and back ends.

The front end can be created in anything you want. Microsoft has been advocating the use of browser-based front ends for a few reasons. First of all, if your GUI is written using HTML, Dynamic HTML (DHTML), ASP, and the like, deploying the application is now a snap. In effect, all the client has to do is point to the right Web page and the application is deployed. What could be simpler? This makes it even easier to upgrade the application. In addition, using a browser-based front end has the benefit of reducing training time as more and more people are familiar with using browsers nowadays.

The back end can be anything you want. Visual FoxPro, SQL Server, you name it. It doesn't matter.

The mechanism used for the inter-layer communications is COM. The front end instantiates the middle tier, which passes data back and forth between the front end and the back end.

So, the idea is this: In a multi-tiered client/server application, the middle tier consists of COM servers. When push comes to shove, no one does data better than Visual FoxPro. Visual FoxPro is also a premier object-oriented development environment. When all is said and done, Visual FoxPro is the natural choice for creating the middle tier.

You'll see an example of Visual FoxPro as the middle tier in a three-tiered client/server application later in this chapter. In the meantime, focus on what it takes to create a COM server in Visual FoxPro. As you'll see, it is almost laughably simple.

A Simple COM Server Example

This chapter tackles a simple example of creating a COM server in Visual FoxPro. The following sections walk you through the task description, design plan, table creation, and initial code for this example.

The Task

Many organizations use timesheets, which are used to record time spent on projects so that clients can be billed.

Right now, the users enter their time using a custom Excel spreadsheet. Others have designed a special interface using Visual Basic. The task is to create a generic program that the users of these programs can use to populate the back-end tables (in this case, Visual FoxPro tables).

The Design

The first step is to design the solution to this task as if you were using Visual FoxPro in a single-tier application. In this case, the design is to create a single class with properties that match the fields in the timesheet transaction table. A method clears the properties (such as appending a blank record) and another method saves the data to the table.

Simple, right?

The Tables

First you'll need a timesheet transaction table. The structure of this table is presented in Listing 22.1.

Listing 22.1   22CODE01.DBF—Structure for Timesheet Transaction Table

```
Structure for table:        C:\CHAPTER22\TSTRANS.DBF
Number of data records:     0
Date of last update:        09/08/98
Memo file block size:       64
 Code Page:                 1252
   Field    Field Name    Type        Width  Dec    Index Collate   Nulls
      1      CEMPLOYEE     Character   10            Asc   Machine   No
      2      DDATE         Date         8            Asc   Machine   No
      3      CCLIENT       Character   45                            No
      4      CSERVICE      Character   10                            No
      5      MDESC         Memo         4                            No
      6      NHOURS        Numeric     10     2                      No
      7      NRATE         Numeric     10     2                      No
      8      NAMOUNT       Numeric     10     2                      No
 ** Total **                                                        108
```

- CEmployee holds the name or initials of the employee performing the service.
- CClient is the name of the client for whom the service is performed.
- CService is the title that identifies the type of service provided.
- DDate is the date of service.
- MDesc is the description of work performed.
- NHours is the number of hours worked.

- ■ NRate is the rate per hour charged for the service.
- ■ NAmount is the total bill for the line item.

Employees do not enter the rate charged for their services. In this mythical firm, a different rate is charged for each different service. So, you need a table for this. The Services rate table structure is shown in Listing 22.2.

Listing 22.2 22CODE02.DBF—**Structure for Services Rate Table**

```
Structure for table:            C:\CHAPTER22\SERVICES.DBF
Number of data records:         11
Date of last update:            09/08/98
 Code Page:                     1252
Field   Field Name     Type        Width  Dec    Index    Collate   Nulls
   1    CSERVICE       Character   10                                No
   2    NRATE          Numeric     10     2                          No
** Total **                                                          21
```

Before I go into the code model for this, here's the list of services and the rates charged:

Service	Rate
ADMIN	0.00
SALES	0.00
NEEDS	100.00
TECHSUPP	65.00
SPEC	100.00
PROGRAM	85.00
SYSTEST	85.00
USERDOC	80.00
TECHDOC	90.00
CODEREV	100.00
REPORT	75.00

The Code

The plan is to create a single class that models the table. The class would have one property for each field in the table. The idea is for the user to populate each property. After the properties have been filled, the data can be saved.

There are two issues that have not yet been addressed. First of all, there are some calculations that need to take place. Based on the service, a rate needs to be selected. After the rate has been selected, the billing amount is calculated by multiplying the number of hours entered by the rate.

This is accomplished by attaching assign methods to the service, rate, and hour properties. When a service is specified, the rate is looked up and placed in the `rate` property. When the rate is populated, the rate is multiplied by the number of hours. The `hours assign` method does the same thing as the `rate assign` (after all, the user could specify either the hours or the service first).

The code as exported from the class browser is shown in Listing 22.3.

Listing 22.3 `22CODE03.PRG`—**Source Code for the Timesheet Program That Was Exported from the Class Browser**

```
*-- Program....: TIMESHEET.PRG
*-- Version....: 1.0
*-- Author.....: Menachem Bazian, CPA
*-- Date.......: September 1, 1998
*-- Project....: Using Visual FoxPro 6 Special Edition
*-- Notice.....: Copyright (c) 1998 Menachem Bazian, CPA, All Rights Reserved.
*-- Compiler...: Visual FoxPro 06.00.8141.00 for Windows
*-- Abstract...:
*-- Changes....:

****************************************************
*-- Class:        timetrans (c:\Chapter22\timesheet.vcx)
*-- ParentClass:  line
*-- BaseClass:    line
*
DEFINE CLASS timetrans AS line


        Height = 17
        Width = 100
        cclient = ("")
        cdescription = ("")
        *-- Service Code
        cservice = ("")
        *-- Billing amount
        namount = 0.00
        nrate = 0.00
        *-- The employee who did the work
        cemployee = ("")
        *-- Date of service
        ddate = {}
        *-- Hours worked
        nhours = 0.00
        Name = "timetrans"


        PROTECTED PROCEDURE cdescription_assign
            LPARAMETERS vNewVal

            *-- Our billing program only prints up to 600 characters for the
            *-- description.
```

continues

Listing 22.3 Continued

```
        IF LEN(vNewVal) > 600
            vNewVal = LEFT(vNewVal, 600)
        ENDIF
        THIS.cDescription = m.vNewVal
ENDPROC


*-- Saves a transaction to the table
PROCEDURE save
        LOCAL lnSelect
        lnSelect = SELECT()

        IF !USED("tsTrans")
            USE tstrans
        ENDIF

        SELECT tstrans
        APPEND BLANK

        WITH this
            REPLACE ;
                cEmployee WITH .cEmployee, ;
                dDate with .dDate, ;
                cClient WITH .cClient, ;
                cService WITH .cService, ;
                mDesc WITH .cDescription, ;
                nHours with .nHours, ;
                nRate WITH .nRate, ;
                nAmount WITH .nAmount
        ENDWITH

        SELECT (lnSelect)
ENDPROC


*-- Clears out everything for a new record to be defined
PROCEDURE add
        WITH this
            .dDate = {}
            .cClient = ""
            .cService = ""
            .cDescription = ""
            .nHours = 0.00
            .nRate = 0
            .nAmount = 0
            .cEmployee = ""
        ENDWITH
ENDPROC


PROTECTED PROCEDURE cservice_assign
        LPARAMETERS vNewVal
```

```
*-- When we get a service in, we need to get the rate so we can
*-- do the math on it and then save it to the table.

LOCAL lnSelect, lcOldExact
lnSelect = SELECT()

this.cService = vNewVal

*-- Check that we got a character value.

IF TYPE("vNewVal") # "C"
    IF INLIST(_vfp.startmode, 1, 2, 3)
        this.cStatus = "cService Error"
    ELSE
        MessageBox("cService expects a CHARACTER type value.", 16)
    ENDIF
    RETURN
ENDIF

IF !USED("services")
    USE services
ENDIF

SELECT services
SET ORDER TO service

lcOldExact = SET("exact")
SET EXACT ON
SEEK UPPER(ALLTRIM(vNewVal))

IF !FOUND() OR EMPTY(vNewVal)
    this.nRate = 0.00
ELSE
    this.nRate = services.nRate
ENDIF

SET EXACT &lcOldExact
SELECT (lnSelect)
ENDPROC


PROTECTED PROCEDURE nrate_assign
    LPARAMETERS vNewVal

    *-- Calculate the billing amount for this number

    this.nRate = vNewVal

    IF TYPE("vNewVal") # "N"
        IF INLIST(_vfp.startmode, 1, 2, 3)
            this.cStatus = "Rate Error"
        ELSE
            MessageBox("nRate expects a NUMERIC type value.", 16)
        ENDIF
```

continues

Listing 22.3   Continued

```
            ELSE
                this.nAmount = this.nRate * this.nHours
            ENDIF
        ENDPROC


        PROTECTED PROCEDURE nhours_assign
            LPARAMETERS vNewVal

            *-- Calculate the billing amount for this number

            this.nHours = vNewVal

            IF TYPE("vNewVal") # "N"
                IF INLIST(_vfp.startmode, 1, 2, 3)
                    this.cStatus = "Hours Error"
                ELSE
                    MessageBox("nHours expects a NUMERIC type value.", 16)
                ENDIF
            ELSE
                this.nAmount = this.nRate * this.nHours
            ENDIF
        ENDPROC


    ENDDEFINE
    *
    *-- EndDefine: timetrans
    **************************************************
```

A Quick Status Report

At this point, you have a class that does what you want. To test it, you can write a simple program like the one shown in Listing 22.4 that will prove that the class indeed does work. If you run the program, you will see that the code does populate the tsTrans table with the information placed in the properties as well as the information gleaned from the services table and the amount calculation.

Listing 22.4   22CODE04.PRG—Structure for Timesheet Transaction Table

```
*-- Program....: TESTIT.PRG
*-- Version....: 1.0
*-- Author.....: Menachem Bazian, CPA
*-- Date.......: September 2, 1998
*-- Project....: Using Visual FoxPro 6 Special Edition
*-- Notice.....: Copyright (c) 1998 Menachem Bazian, CPA, All Rights Reserved.
*-- Compiler...: Visual FoxPro 06.00.8141.00 for Windows
*-- Abstract...:
*-- Changes....:
```

```
SET CLASSLIB TO TimeSheet
ox = CreateObject("TimeTrans")

ox.Add()
ox.cEmployee = "MB"
ox.dDate = {^1998-08-01}
ox.cClient = "SAMS"
ox.cService = "PROGRAM"
ox.cDEscription = "Work on the book"
ox.nHours = 8.25
ox.Save()

ox.Add()
ox.cEmployee = "MB"
ox.dDate = {^1998-08-02}
ox.cClient = "SAMS"
ox.cService = "USERDOC"
ox.cDEscription = "Write on the book"
ox.nHours = 8
ox.Save()
```

Creating the COM Server

Now that you have a working class, you are ready to make a COM server out of it. The process for this is very simple:

1. Modify the class.
2. Display the Class Info dialog (choose Class, Class Info) shown in Figure 22.1.
3. Check OLE Public.
4. Close the dialog.
5. Save the class.

FIGURE 22.1

The Class Info dialog enables you to expose a class.

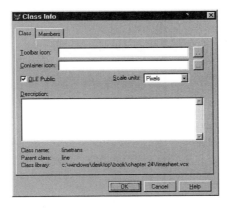

By checking the OLE Public check box, the class has been marked as exposed for OLE purposes.

The only thing left to do is to generate an executable or .DLL so that the server is registered. In order to create the .EXE or .DLL, you need a project. The project, which I have called TS.PJX, needs the class library and a "stub program," a .PRG that you can call the "main program" so that the executable or .DLL can be built.

In this case, the main program is called MAIN.PRG and has only one line of code:

```
*-- Program....: MAIN.PRG
*-- Version....: 1.0
*-- Author.....: Menachem Bazian, CPA
*-- Date.......: September 2, 1998
*-- Project....: Using Visual FoxPro 6 Special Edition
*-- Notice.....: Copyright (c) 1998 Menachem Bazian, CPA, All Rights Reserved.
*-- Compiler...: Visual FoxPro 06.00.8141.00 for Windows
*-- Abstract...:
*-- Changes....:

RETURN
```

You are now ready to build the .EXE or .DLL.

Build an .EXE or a .DLL?

What's the difference between building an .EXE or a .DLL? The basic difference lies in whether the OLE server will run as an InProc server or not. An *InProc server* is a server that runs within the same memory space as the application that calls it, and is implemented as a .DLL. An *OutProc server* runs in its own memory space and is implemented as an .EXE file.

I prefer to build my servers as .EXEs for a couple of reasons:

- If the server dies, the client program is still protected. Because the .EXE is in its own memory space, it cannot corrupt the memory of the client application.

- An .EXE can be deployed remotely, a .DLL cannot.

On the other hand, an .EXE can run a little slower than a DLL because the operating system has to open a pipe between the memory spaces. Chapter 12, "Organizing Components of an Application into a Project," describes how to use the Project Manager to build either an .EXE or a COM .DLL.

Back on Track

Okay, you have built the .EXE. The process of building the server generates the GUIDs and registers the server in the Registry. After the server is built, you will find the following entries in the Registry:

```
VB5SERVERINFO
VERSION=1.0.0

HKEY_CLASSES_ROOT\ts.timetrans = timetrans
HKEY_CLASSES_ROOT\ts.timetrans\NotInsertable
HKEY_CLASSES_ROOT\ts.timetrans\CLSID = {00F32181-47CC-11D2-B30B-F34CEA44F62D}
```

```
HKEY_CLASSES_ROOT\CLSID\{00F32181-47CC-11D2-B30B-F34CEA44F62D} = timetrans
HKEY_CLASSES_ROOT\CLSID\{00F32181-47CC-11D2-B30B-F34CEA44F62D}\ProgId =
ts.timetrans
HKEY_CLASSES_ROOT\CLSID\{00F32181-47CC-11D2-B30B-
F34CEA44F62D}\VersionIndependentProgId = ts.timetrans
HKEY_CLASSES_ROOT\CLSID\{00F32181-47CC-11D2-B30B-F34CEA44F62D}\LocalServer32 =
ts.exe /automation
HKEY_CLASSES_ROOT\CLSID\{00F32181-47CC-11D2-B30B-F34CEA44F62D}\TypeLib =
{00F32183-47CC-11D2-B30B-F34CEA44F62D}
HKEY_CLASSES_ROOT\CLSID\{00F32181-47CC-11D2-B30B-F34CEA44F62D}\Version = 1.0
HKEY_CLASSES_ROOT\INTERFACE\{00F32182-47CC-11D2-B30B-F34CEA44F62D} = timetrans
HKEY_CLASSES_ROOT\INTERFACE\{00F32182-47CC-11D2-B30B-F34CEA44F62D}\ProxyStubClsid
= {00020424-0000-0000-C000-000000000046}
HKEY_CLASSES_ROOT\INTERFACE\{00F32182-47CC-11D2-B30B-
F34CEA44F62D}\ProxyStubClsid32 = {00020424-0000-0000-C000-000000000046}
HKEY_CLASSES_ROOT\INTERFACE\{00F32182-47CC-11D2-B30B-F34CEA44F62D}\TypeLib =
{00F32183-47CC-11D2-B30B-F34CEA44F62D}
HKEY_CLASSES_ROOT\INTERFACE\{00F32182-47CC-11D2-B30B-
F34CEA44F62D}\TypeLib\"Version" = 1.0


; TypeLibrary registration
HKEY_CLASSES_ROOT\TypeLib\{00F32183-47CC-11D2-B30B-F34CEA44F62D}
HKEY_CLASSES_ROOT\TypeLib\{00F32183-47CC-11D2-B30B-F34CEA44F62D}\1.0 = ts Type
Library
HKEY_CLASSES_ROOT\TypeLib\{00F32183-47CC-11D2-B30B-F34CEA44F62D}\1.0\0\win32 =
ts.tlb
HKEY_CLASSES_ROOT\TypeLib\{00F32183-47CC-11D2-B30B-F34CEA44F62D}\1.0\FLAGS = 0
```

Notice that all this information is in a file called a *VBR file,* which is automatically generated when the .EXE is built.

Single Versus Multiple Instancing

After the EXE has been built and the server registered for the first time, you have one more thing to do: specify whether the server is single instancing only or multiple instancing.

This information is accessed from the Servers tab on the Project Information dialog box (see Figure 22.2).

FIGURE 22.2

You can specify how instancing of the server object will be handled.

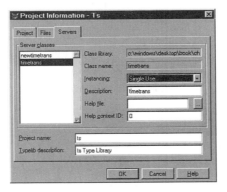

If you looked at this dialog before you built the .EXE, the servers in the project would not show up because they wouldn't yet have been registered.

The decision to be made now is how the instancing of the object will be handled. There are three options:

- *Multiple instancing* Several clients can use a single running instance of the server.
- *Single instancing* Each client gets its own copy of the server.
- *Not creatable* The server can only be used within Visual FoxPro.

> **CAUTION**
>
> Each server (an .EXE can have more than one) has to be set separately.

After you have all your servers set the way you want them, rebuild the .EXE or .DLL. Now you're ready to test it.

Testing the Server

The only thing left to do is test the new server. Because you are working in Visual FoxPro anyway, and Visual FoxPro is itself a wonderful COM client, there is little work necessary to create a test program. A simple modification to the test program you saw earlier will do (see Listing 22.5).

Listing 22.5 22CODE05.PRG—**Program That Tests the COM Server**

```
*-- Program....: TESTCOM.PRG
*-- Version....: 1.0
*-- Author.....: Menachem Bazian, CPA
*-- Date.......: September 2, 1998
*-- Project....: Using Visual FoxPro 6 Special Edition
*-- Notice.....: Copyright (c) 1998 Menachem Bazian, CPA, All Rights Reserved.
*-- Compiler...: Visual FoxPro 06.00.8141.00 for Windows
*-- Abstract...:
*-- Changes....:

*-- This test program tests the COM server.

ox = CreateObject("ts.TimeTrans")

ox.Add()
ox.cEmployee = "MB"
ox.dDate = {^1998-08-01}
ox.cClient = "SAMS"
ox.cService = "PROGRAM"
ox.cDEscription = "Work on the book"
ox.nHours = 8.25
ox.Save()
```

```
ox.Add()
ox.cEmployee = "MB"
ox.dDate = {^1998-08-02}
ox.cClient = "SAMS"
ox.cService = "USERDOC"
ox.cDEscription = "Write on the book"
ox.nHours = 8
ox.Save()
```

Part
V

Ch
22

Notice that the only change to this program is the `CreateObject()` call, which is clearly a call to a COM server (indeed, the one just built).

Testing the Server Outside Visual FoxPro

So far, things are going fantastically well. Nothing has gone wrong. The server, as promised, has been a breeze to put together. The Visual FoxPro class shown earlier has become a sophisticated OLE server with almost no work. You were even able to run it without any problems in Visual FoxPro. All you have left to do to put this to the real test is to test the server in another environment. For this, let's use Excel.

The Excel Development Environment

It's not my purpose to get deep into the Excel development environment. There are enough books out there to handle that. However, in order to understand what I am about to do, it will help to note a few quick things.

First, when creating an Excel macro or module that will use a COM server, you need to make sure that the VBA development environment knows about the COM server. You do this by telling it to reference the type library for the server you are using.

First, you obviously need to bring up the Visual Basic Editor. Then, after choosing Tools, References, make sure that `ts Type Library` is checked.

Second, in Visual Basic, unlike Visual FoxPro, you can specifically tell the language the data type of the memory variable you are using. This is known as *strong typing*. By telling the language the type of memory variable you are using, the compiler can do more error checking for you.

In addition, you can tell Visual Basic that the data type of a memory variable is a specific *type* of object. In this case, the *intellisense* feature kicks in and actually pops up a list of available properties and methods for you to choose from as you type.

The Excel Code

Now that you have covered a few details about Excel, the code for the Excel module is crystal clear. Here it is:

```
Sub TestComServer()
    '*-- Program....: TestComServer
```

```
'*-- Version....: 1.0
'*-- Author.....: Menachem Bazian, CPA
'*-- Date.......: September 2, 1998
'*-- Project....: Using Visual FoxPro 6 Special Edition
'*-- Notice.....: Copyright (c) 1998 Menachem Bazian, CPA, All Rights
'*-- Reserved.
'*-- Compiler...: Excel 97 SR-1
'*-- Abstract...:
'*-- Changes....:

'*-- This test program tests the COM server.

Dim ox As New ts.timetrans
Set ox = CreateObject("ts.TimeTrans")

ox.Add
ox.cemployee = "MB"
ox.ddate = #8/1/98#
ox.cclient = "SAMS"
ox.cservice = "PROGRAM"
ox.cdescription = "Work on the book - From Excel"
ox.nhours = 8.25
ox.Save

ox.Add
ox.cemployee = "MB"
ox.ddate = #8/2/98#
ox.cclient = "SAMS"
ox.cservice = "USERDOC"
ox.cdescription = "Write on the book - From Excel"
ox.nhours = 8
ox.Save
End Sub
```

A close look at the macro shows that there is an incredible correspondence between the Excel macro and the Visual FoxPro version. The only differences are extremely minor. A comment starts with a single quote ('). Dates are encased in pound signs (##). The DIM and CREATEOBJECT statements are slightly different. Beyond that, the code is straight from Visual FoxPro.

Close, But No Cigar

And the results? Well, the results in your case will depend, but in most cases, the macro will not run. In all probability, an Open dialog will appear on your Windows desktop asking you to locate SERVICES.DBF (in my case, it said C:\My Documents\Services.DBF Not found).

The reason for this is simple. When a Visual FoxPro COM server is loaded, the default directory is not the directory where the .EXE is. Sometimes, the default directory is the SYSTEM32 directory; other times, it is the default directory used by the COM client (as it is in this case with Excel). In any event, the lesson learned here is that you cannot be sure of the default directory, path, or anything like that. You need to set it yourself.

How do you set it? Well, the easiest way is to add a property to the class stating where the data files are hidden and tack that value onto the USE statements. This method, although kludgy, does work for simple COM servers where you are in total control of the environment. However, once you get into the question of network drives (which can be mapped differently from machine to machine), a more generic means is necessary.

Fortunately, the Windows API has the answer in the form of GetModuleFileName(), a function in the Win32 API.

Basically, GetModuleFileName() looks at the current running application and gives you the name of the file (.EXE) it is running. So, all you have to do is DECLARE the .DLL, send it the proper parameters, and you have your information. It's simple, and looks like this:

```
DECLARE INTEGER GetModuleFileName in win32api Integer,String @,Integer
```

GetModuleFileName() returns an integer, but what you want is the second parameter, which is the name of the .EXE that is running. Notice that the second parameter is passed by reference, and thus will get the value you want.

So, here's what you need to do in a program:

```
LOCAL lcFileName, lnRetVal
lcFileName = SPACE(400)
DECLARE INTEGER GetModuleFileName in win32api Integer,String @,Integer
lnRetVal = GetModuleFileName(0, @lcFileName, 400)
```

lcFileName is a placeholder of blanks. When passed to the function, the value of the variable is replaced with the name of the .EXE (with full path), padded out to 400 characters. The final parameter tells GetModuleFileName() how large the buffer is.

The return value tells how large the actual filename is. So, to get the full filename and path, all you need to do is

```
LcFileName = LEFT(lcFileName, lnretVal)
```

After you have the fully qualified filename, you can strip off the filename and are left with the directory where the .EXE is.

Now, all this is well and good if you are dealing with an .EXE. What about a .DLL? A .DLL is a little different because it runs in the same process space as the COM client. You first need to get a handle to the .DLL process and then you can call GetModuleFileName().

Here's how the whole mess works out in code. Keep in mind that this program (called simply TEST.PRG) would be placed into a class as a method:

```
*-- Program....: TEST.PRG
*-- Version....: 1.0
*-- Author.....: Menachem Bazian, CPA
*-- Date.......: September 3, 1998
*-- Project....: Using Visual FoxPro 6 Special Edition
*-- Notice.....: Copyright (c) 1998 Menachem Bazian, CPA, All Rights Reserved.
*-- Compiler...: Visual FoxPro 06.00.8141.00 for Windows
*-- Abstract...: Gets the location for a COM server
*-- Changes....:
```

```
*-- This code is meant to be placed in a method of a COM server. It
*-- assumes the presence of a property called cServerName which has the
*-- name of the .DLL (if this is a DLL)

LOCAL lcFileName, lnLength
lcFileName = space(400)
DECLARE INTEGER GetModuleFileName in win32api Integer,String @,Integer

*-- If we are starting up as a DLL, we need to first use GetModuleHandle to
*-- get a module handle for the DLL, otherwise we can use 0 as the module
*-- handle.

*-- It's important to understand that the first parameter in GetModuleFileName
*-- is the HANDLE (an integer) of the process we are trying to identify.
*-- The default value for this is the module that initiated the calling
*-- process. Now, if we are dealing with an out of proc server, then
*-- it is running in its own process. No problem. A DLL, on the other hand,
*-- runs in another process so we need the name of the DLL in order to get
*-- the module handle to call GetModuleFileName.
*--
*-- This.srvname is populated either by the developer or by some other process.

IF _vfp.startmode = 3 && Visual FoxPro started to service an In Process COM
Server
     DECLARE INTEGER GetModuleHandle in win32api String
     lnLength = Getmodulefilename( ;
                         GetModuleHandle(this.cSrverName + ".dll"), ;
                         @lcFileName, len(lcFileName))
ELSE
     lnLength = Getmodulefilename(0, @lcFileName, len(lcFileName))
ENDIF

lcFileName = LEFTC(lcFileName, lnLength)
RETURN LEFTC(lcFileName, RATC('\',lcFileName) -1)
```

Rebuilding the Server

You need to know one more thing before you can rebuild the server. The server program is not released from memory when it aborts (as it did when I ran the server from Excel). You need to manually end the task through the Task Manager (Windows NT) or the Close Program dialog (Windows 95/98).

If your process is not running and you still cannot rebuild the server, see whether Excel or any other application is open and referencing the type library. If the type library is referenced by an open application (for instance, a Visual Basic project), it cannot be overwritten.

Smoothing out a Few Wrinkles

There are a few specifics that should be noted that I did not do in the version of the class you have been testing. They are explained in the following sections.

Managing the Tables

First of all, it is not a good idea for the server to open a file and keep it open. Given the state-less nature of COM servers (they could be used by anyone at any time), it's a good idea to keep things extra clean. Open the tables only when you need them and close them soon after.

Deciding Which Class to Base It On

Which class should a COM server be based on? Well, in truth you could use just about any class. I use the Line class because it purports to have the lowest overhead.

Protecting Properties and Methods

You might have noticed that the assign methods in the TimeTrans class were all scoped as protected methods. A *protected method* is one that can only be used within the class and is not visible outside the class.

A general rule to follow is not to expose anything to the outside world that is not needed there. This means that all properties, methods, and events that are irrelevant to the COM client's interaction with the server should be protected or hidden.

With a Line class, there are a host of properties, methods, and events that are irrelevant. They should all be protected in a real-life COM server.

Dealing with Modals and Errors

A COM server should *never* stop. That's an axiom. In order to make sure that it doesn't, you need to make sure that you have a good ON ERROR routine (or Error method) that traps all errors and deals with them gracefully.

Sys(2335)

Visual FoxPro has a nifty little function called SYS(2335). This function toggles something called *Unattended Server Mode,* which tells Visual FoxPro that modal states—such as messagebox() calls—are strictly *verboten.* You turn it on using SYS(2335,0) and off using SYS(2335,1). When Unattended Server Mode is on, any attempt at a modal state in the application generates an error that can be trapped in your ON ERROR routine.

For the record, SYS(2335) is only applicable for .EXE COM servers. A .DLL is always in unat-tended mode. Issuing SYS(2335) without the second parameter returns the current setting.

The Final Version of the Server

After you correct your server for the issues mentioned above, here's what you come up with:

```
*-- Program....: TIMESHEET2.PRG
*-- Version....: 1.0
*-- Author.....: Menachem Bazian, CPA
*-- Date.......: September 3, 1998
```

```
*-- Project....: Using Visual FoxPro 6 Special Edition
*-- Notice.....: Copyright (c) 1998 Menachem Bazian, CPA, All Rights Reserved.
*-- Compiler...: Visual FoxPro 06.00.8141.00 for Windows
*-- Abstract...:
*-- Changes....:

*****************************************************
*-- Class:        newtimetrans (c:\chapter22\timesheet.vcx)
*-- ParentClass:  line
*-- BaseClass:    line
*
DEFINE CLASS newtimetrans AS line OLEPUBLIC


        Height = 17
        Width = 100
        cclient = ("")
        cdescription = ("")
        *-- Service Code
        cservice = ("")
        *-- Billing amount
        namount = 0.00
        nrate = 0.00
        *-- The employee who did the work
        cemployee = ("")
        *-- Date of service
        ddate = {}
        *-- Hours worked
        nhours = 0.00
        Name = "newtimetrans"
        PROTECTED csrvname
        PROTECTED cscriptdir

        *-- Returns the path to the data.
        PROTECTED cdatapath
        PROTECTED height
        PROTECTED width
        PROTECTED name
        PROTECTED baseclass
        PROTECTED bordercolor
        PROTECTED borderstyle
        PROTECTED borderwidth
        PROTECTED class
        PROTECTED click
        PROTECTED cloneobject
        PROTECTED colorsource
        PROTECTED comment
        PROTECTED dblclick
        PROTECTED destroy
        PROTECTED drag
        PROTECTED dragdrop
        PROTECTED dragicon
        PROTECTED dragmode
        PROTECTED dragover
        PROTECTED drawmode
```

```
PROTECTED enabled
PROTECTED error
PROTECTED helpcontextid
PROTECTED init
PROTECTED lineslant
PROTECTED middleclick
PROTECTED mousedown
PROTECTED mouseicon
PROTECTED mousemove
PROTECTED mousepointer
PROTECTED mouseup
PROTECTED mousewheel
PROTECTED move
PROTECTED parent
PROTECTED parentclass
PROTECTED readexpression
PROTECTED readmethod
PROTECTED resettodefault
PROTECTED rightclick
PROTECTED saveasclass
PROTECTED showwhatsthis
PROTECTED tag
PROTECTED uienable
PROTECTED visible
PROTECTED whatsthishelpid
PROTECTED writeexpression
PROTECTED writemethod
PROTECTED zorder
PROTECTED classlibrary
PROTECTED addproperty
PROTECTED olecompletedrag
PROTECTED oledrag
PROTECTED oledragdrop
PROTECTED oledragmode
PROTECTED oledragover
PROTECTED oledragpicture
PROTECTED oledropeffects
PROTECTED oledrophasdata
PROTECTED oledropmode
PROTECTED olegivefeedback
PROTECTED olesetdata
PROTECTED olestartdrag


PROTECTED PROCEDURE cdescription_assign
    LPARAMETERS vNewVal

    *-- Our billing program only prints up to 600 characters for the
    *-- description.

    IF LEN(vNewVal) > 600
        vNewVal = LEFT(vNewVal, 600)
    ENDIF
    THIS.cDescription = m.vNewVal
ENDPROC
```

```
*-- Saves a transaction to the table
PROCEDURE save
    LOCAL lnSelect
    lnSelect = SELECT()

    IF !USED("tsTrans")
        USE this.cDataPath + "tstrans"
    ENDIF

    SELECT tstrans
    APPEND BLANK

    WITH this
        REPLACE ;
            cEmployee WITH .cEmployee, ;
            dDate with .dDate, ;
            cClient WITH .cClient, ;
            cService WITH .cService, ;
            mDesc WITH .cDescription, ;
            nHours with .nHours, ;
            nRate WITH .nRate, ;
            nAmount WITH .nAmount
    ENDWITH

    SELECT (lnSelect)
    USE IN tsTrans
ENDPROC


*-- Clears out everything for a new record to be defined
PROCEDURE add
    WITH this
        .dDate = {}
        .cClient = ""
        .cService = ""
        .cDescription = ""
        .nHours = 0.00
        .nRate = 0
        .nAmount = 0
        .cEmployee = ""
    ENDWITH
ENDPROC
PROTECTED PROCEDURE cservice_assign
    LPARAMETERS vNewVal

    *-- When we get a service in, we need to get the rate so we can
    *-- do the math on it and then save it to the table.

    LOCAL lnSelect, lcOldExact
    lnSelect = SELECT()

    this.cService = vNewVal

    *-- Check that we got a character value.
```

```
    IF TYPE("vNewVal") # "C"
        IF INLIST(_vfp.startmode, 1, 2, 3)
            this.cStatus = "cService Error"
        ELSE
            MessageBox("cService expects a CHARACTER type value.", 16)
        ENDIF
        RETURN
    ENDIF

    IF !USED("services")
        USE (this.cDataPath + "services")
    ENDIF

    SELECT services
    SET ORDER TO service

    lcOldExact = SET("exact")
    SET EXACT ON
    SEEK UPPER(ALLTRIM(vNewVal))

    IF !FOUND() OR EMPTY(vNewVal)
        this.nRate = 0.00
    ELSE
        this.nRate = services.nRate
    ENDIF

    SET EXACT &lcOldExact

    USE IN services
    SELECT (lnSelect)
ENDPROC
PROTECTED PROCEDURE nrate_assign
    LPARAMETERS vNewVal

    *-- Calculate the billing amount for this number

    this.nRate = vNewVal

    IF TYPE("vNewVal") # "N"
        IF INLIST(_vfp.startmode, 1, 2, 3)
            this.cStatus = "Rate Error"
        ELSE
            MessageBox("nRate expects a NUMERIC type value.", 16)
        ENDIF
    ELSE
        this.nAmount = this.nRate * this.nHours
    ENDIF
ENDPROC
PROTECTED PROCEDURE nhours_assign
    LPARAMETERS vNewVal

    *-- Calculate the billing amount for this number

    this.nHours = vNewVal
```

```
        IF TYPE("vNewVal") # "N"
            IF INLIST(_vfp.startmode, 1, 2, 3)
                this.cStatus = "Hours Error"
            ELSE
                MessageBox("nHours expects a NUMERIC type value.", 16)
            ENDIF
        ELSE
            this.nAmount = this.nRate * this.nHours
        ENDIF
ENDPROC


*-- Gets the path to the EXE which also tells us the path to the data files.
PROTECTED PROCEDURE getpaths
        *-- Program....: GetPaths
        *-- Version....: 1.0
        *-- Author.....: Menachem Bazian, CPA
        *-- Date.......: September 3, 1998
        *-- Project....: Using Visual FoxPro 6 Special Edition
        *-- Notice.....: Copyright (c) 1998 Menachem Bazian, CPA, All Rights
        *-- Reserved.
        *-- Compiler...: Visual FoxPro 06.00.8141.00 for Windows
        *-- Abstract...: Gets the location for a COM server
        *-- Changes....:

        *-- This code is meant to be placed in a method of a COM server. It
        *-- assumes the presence of a property called cServerName which has the
        *-- name of the .DLL (if this is a DLL)

        LOCAL lcFileName, lnLength
        lcFileName = space(400)
        DECLARE INTEGER GetModuleFileName in win32api Integer,String @,Integer

        *-- If we are starting up as a DLL, we need to first use
        *-- GetModuleHandle to get a module handle for the DLL, otherwise we
        *-- can use 0 as the module handle.

        *-- It's important to understand that the first parameter in
        *-- GetModuleFileName is the HANDLE (an integer) of the process we are
        *-- trying to identify. The default value for this is the module that
        *-- initiated the calling process. Now, if we are dealing with an out
        *-- of proc server, then it is running in its own process. No problem.
        *-- A DLL, on the other hand, runs in another process so we need the
        *-- name of the DLL in order to get
        *-- the module handle to call GetModuleFileName.
        *--
        *-- This.srvname is populated either by the developer or some other
        *-- process.

        IF INLIST(_vfp.startmode, 0, 4)
            RETURN CURDIR()
        ENDIF
```

```
        IF _vfp.startmode = 3 && Visual FoxPro started to service an In Process
    ➥COM Server
            DECLARE INTEGER GetModuleHandle in win32api String
            lnLength = Getmodulefilename( ;
                            GetModuleHandle(this.cSrverName + ".dll"), ;
                            @lcFileName, len(lcFileName))
        ELSE
            lnLength = Getmodulefilename(0, @lcFileName, len(lcFileName))
        ENDIF

        lcFileName = LEFTC(lcFileName, lnLength)

        RETURN LEFTC(lcFileName, RATC('\',lcFileName))
ENDPROC
PROTECTED PROCEDURE cdatapath_access
        *To do: Modify this routine for the Access method
        *-- The idea here it to calculate the datapath if it has not yet
        *-- been calculated

        IF EMPTY(this.cDataPath)
            this.cDataPath = this.GetPaths()
        ENDIF

        RETURN THIS.cDataPath
ENDPROC


PROCEDURE Error
        LPARAMETERS nError, cMethod, nLine

        #DEFINE _TAB CHR(9)

        *-- Just write this to an error text file

        IF !FILE(this.cDataPath + "Errors.TXT")
            lnHandle = FCREATE(this.cDataPath + "Errors.TXT")
        ELSE
            lnHandle = FOPEN(this.cDataPath + "Error.TXT")
        ENDIF

        lcErrorStr = TTOC(DATETIME()) + _TAB + ;
                        TRANSFORM(nError, "9999") + _TAB + ;
                        cMethod + _TAB + ;
                        TRANSFORM(nError, "999999")

        FPUTS(lnHandle, lcErrorStr)

        =FCLOSE(lnHandle)
        RETURN
ENDPROC
```

```
ENDDEFINE
*
*-- EndDefine: newtimetrans
****************************************************
```

There are several important items to note, as explained in the following sections.

New Error Method

The error method is designed to keep the application running at all costs. In this case, it's a simple one and doesn't really do much. You'll need to come up with a more robust error method for your applications. For now, just bear in mind that you have to have one for a COM server.

 TIP Remember that if you don't like the Error method, you can always use an ON ERROR routine.

Protected Members

All members not specifically designed for use by a client program have been protected and are no longer visible.

New cDataPath Property

The new cDataPath property has the directory that holds the data. The Access method, which is called when the property is read, calls the new GetPaths() method, which uses the GetModuleFileName() API call discussed earlier.

COM in *N*-Tiered Client/Server Applications

This chapter has looked at the business of creating a COM server in Visual FoxPro. You've seen an example of a COM server and why one might be created. COM servers, however, really fit right into the world of *n*-tiered client/server applications.

The COM server just shown is, in effect, the middle tier of a three-tiered client/server application. In this case, Visual FoxPro fills the role of the back end as well. Excel fits nicely into place in the front end.

This is the way client/server development is going. With the proliferation of the Internet, applications are now being deployed over ever-greater geographical spans. Using a browser-based front end, with ASP, DHTML, XML, XSL, or any number of other technologies at your fingertips, you have a light client that can work really well as a front end. By placing Visual FoxPro COM servers in the middle tier, you have a mix that uses the best of the available technologies in their proper places. ●

VI

Other Visual FoxPro Topics

Error Detection and Handling

Getting Started When You Have a Problem

A program with errors in it cannot solve problems, save someone time, or make an organization more profitable. The bad news is that you will write few, if any, programs totally error-free right from the start. The good news is that you can learn how to detect and remove errors from code using a process called *debugging*.

The first case of debugging allegedly occurred many years ago when an insect caused some tubes to fail in one of the first computers. Thus, the term debugging came into use for getting the "bugs" out of a system. Whatever the origin, the purpose of debugging in the software development process is to locate problems that cause programs to fail or produce incorrect results. Often, this process resembles a detective's investigation. You run the program and collect clues such as the following:

- Which procedures execute and in what order?
- What tables does the program open?
- What was the last record processed? Were any skipped?
- Which index controls the table order?
- Why do certain variables contain the values they do?

In fact, the more clues you collect, the more likely you will solve "The Case of the Program-Killing Error."

Recognizing Common Coding Errors

There are hundreds of possible errors you can make when writing Visual FoxPro applications, at least if the number of error messages is any indication. (Visual FoxPro has more than 700 defined error messages.) Some errors are more common than others, and some are pretty esoteric. Many are syntax-related and often result from simple typing mistakes. Others result from under-developed programming practices such as failure to check for EOF() before reading or writing a record. With so many possible errors, your common errors might not be the same as mine or your fellow programmers. In fact, every developer has a slightly different set of common errors that they seem to be constantly correcting. You might find yourself encountering your own subset repeatedly, based on the types of errors you tend to make. You might also have to do a little digging into the reasons for a particular error. What can start out as syntax problem or a data type that is not what you intend might not be invalid as far as VFP is concerned. It will attempt to run with whatever you supply, and the condition that develops might result in an error that appears to make little sense when presented to you.

N O T E   There are various sources within the language and its help system for gathering information about errors. The Reference section under Visual FoxPro Documentation contains an entire section on the 700 or so possible error messages: an alphabetical listing of messages, a list of those same messages in numerical order by error code, and a list of messages that supply additional information (known as error message parameters) via the SYS(2108) function. ■

Unfortunately, in most cases, there is really nothing your program can do after the error has occurred. Most error conditions cannot be fixed in a live application. The best that you can hope for is to document what happened and then roll back transactions, close tables, and exit the program. The real challenge of error handling is to prevent the errors from occurring in the first place by writing proactive code that anticipates possible errors. You can also become more aware of common errors and thereby avoid them.

This section looks at a fairly representative set of common errors that I have seen while working with other developers. Maybe you will recognize a few of them in your own coding; don't worry if you do. Recognition is the first step in developing better habits that will eliminate common errors from your coding habits.

Syntax Errors

There are three major classes of errors in programming: logic, syntax, and exceptions. Of these, syntax errors are the easiest to find and correct. In fact, compiling your code is the fastest way to locate most of them, and the latest versions of Visual FoxPro have become even more stringent in their evaluation of syntax errors than earlier versions. Some errors that are syntax-related do not show up during compilation, however. Common syntax errors include

■ Forgetting an equal sign or other operator in an expression:

```
* Missing = sign after gnTotalDue
gnTotalDue pnNetDue * (1 + lnTaxRate)
```

■ Spelling a command or function name incorrectly:

```
* Missing second 'A' in DATABASE
OPEN DATBASE ptofsale
```

 T I P The VFP color-coded editor is quick to pick up spelling errors. As you type in the Command window or in your program, VFP shows reserved keywords in color. If you misspell a command, argument, or clause, it changes to normal black text. Make sure that you configure Tools, Options, Syntax Coloring to show Keywords in a color you will notice, and that you check Syntax Coloring in the Edit, Properties, Edit Properties dialog box. For more information on these settings, see Chapter 1, "Quick Review of the Visual FoxPro Interface."

■ Mispairing quotes around strings. This includes the common error of including the same type of quote inside a string as is used to delimit the string:

```
'This is Bill's statement' && Fails
"This is Bill's statement" && Succeeds
```

A variation on this error puts a single quote at one end of the string and a double quote on the other end.

 T I P Once again, the VFP color-coded editor can help you out. Setting up strings to appear in some jazzy way can help keep you from getting caught by mismatched quotes. I like to show strings highlighted by a background color, such as yellow or light green. This lets me know immediately if I fail to terminate a string properly.

Visual FoxPro recognizes 'single quotes,' "double quotes," and [brackets] as string delimiters. If you need to use any of these characters inside the string, pick a different delimiter.

■ Mispairing parentheses in complex expressions:

```
REPLACE pnboxno WITH PADL(VAL(pnboxno+1,'0',5)
```

 You can pick up some of these errors by clicking Verify in the Expression Builder dialog box, which is available through the design surfaces. The Expression Builder won't be able to evaluate UDFs or references to fields in unopened tables, however.

Although the language enables you to nest expressions to an impossibly complex level, your safest bet will always be to keep expressions as simple as possible. Identifying missing parentheses can become very frustrating, and logic can be hard to follow in this format. If necessary, you can break nested functions into multiple steps by using memory variables to hold intermediate results.

■ Using a reserved word for a memory variable or field name. Words Visual FoxPro uses for commands, functions, and keywords should not be used as variable names. This includes the use of four-character variable names that match the first four characters of a reserved word. When this happens, Visual FoxPro might try to interpret the variable or field name as the equivalent command. Usually, the command is out of context, resulting in an error. For example, the following statement generates the error Invalid use of a Visual FoxPro function as an array:

```
DIMENSION DATE[10]
```

■ Not matching CASE...ENDCASE, DO...ENDDO, FOR...ENDFOR, IF...ENDIF, or SCAN...ENDSCAN commands, or using the wrong terminator (ending a DO structure with ENDIF). Visual FoxPro calls this problem a *nesting error*:

```
IF gnTotalDue > 100
= MESSAGEBOX("Get a supervisor's signature")
ENDDO && ENDDO should be ENDIF
```

A common syntax error not found during compilation is the passing of variables of the wrong type to a procedure. Because Visual FoxPro is not a strong typed language, memory variables can assume any variable type during execution. Therefore, VFP has no way to determine during compilation that the calling program will pass a numeric value when the procedure is expecting a character string. In any case, the program fails with a syntax error when this procedure call is run.

N O T E Although most of the chapter refers to compilation occurring as a separate step, you can have VFP compile your program code (.PRG) every time you save it. This option can be set in the Edit Properties dialog box discussed in Chapter 1. Code stored as methods in forms, classes, and DBCs is compiled when these windows are closed or saved, regardless of any preference settings. ■

When you run a program, Visual FoxPro converts the source code to object code, if not previously compiled, and in the process detects references to other programs, procedures, and functions. It attempts to resolve these references within the current file or in other files included in the project. Suppose you attempt to call procedure SOMETHIN. If Visual FoxPro cannot resolve it, it interrupts the compilation to display the following message:

```
Unable to find Proc./Function SOMETHIN
```

VFP also displays four buttons labeled Locate, Ignore, Ignore All, and Cancel.

If you choose Locate, VFP displays an Open dialog box that enables you to find the missing file. Note, however, that this solves the problem only for the current compile. (Well, maybe. Suppose that you have a file with the same name in more than one directory or on more than one server drive on a network system. Can you be sure that you or your users will select the correct file? I think not!) If you recompile the program later without correcting this reference, either within the code or by adding the file to the Project Manager, you get another error.

Sometimes, you can ignore one or more errors during compilation if you know that the referenced procedure or function exists as a separate file or if it is an external reference. This often occurs when the compiler confuses an array reference with a function call. This problem can often be fixed by adding an EXTERNAL ARRAY *arrayname* in the program.

Part
VI

Ch

23

Resolving External References

EXTERNAL can be used to resolve references to classes, forms, labels, libraries, menus, procedures, queries, reports, screens, and tables. The most common reason for requiring EXTERNAL to resolve the reference is because the program code uses macro expansion to define the object. The following code shows an example of memory variables required to determine which of three queries and reports to open. The EXTERNAL command is used to resolve these references to the compiler.

```
EXTERNAL QUERY LATE
EXTERNAL QUERY PASTDUE30
EXTERNAL QUERY PASTDUE60
EXTERNAL REPORT LATE
EXTERNAL REPORT PASTDUE30
EXTERNAL REPORT PASTDUE60
DO CASE
   CASE DATE() < INVDATE+30
      lcQry = "LATE"
      lcRpt = "LATE"
   CASE DATE() < INVDATE+60
      lcQry = "PASTDUE30"
      lcRpt = "PASTDUE30"
   OTHERWISE
      lcRpt = "PASTDUE60"
      lcRpt = "PASTDUE60"
ENDCASE
DO (lcQry)
REPORT FORM (lcRpt) TO PRINTER
```

continues

continued

Another way to handle this situation is to reference the variable names in the calling program or any program in the project in such a way that they won't actually be used. You can accomplish this with an IF .F....ENDIF construct, as shown in the following code example. None of the code within the IF...ENDIF is executed, but all the references will be resolved by the Project Manager:

```
IF .F.
    DO Late.qpr
    DO PastDue30.qpr
    DO PastDue60.qpr
    REPORT FORM Late
    REPORT FORM PastDue30
    REPORT FORM PastDue60
ENDIF
```

You can also choose to note, but ignore, unresolved references to permit VFP to complete the compile and log syntax errors into an error file. To log errors, choose Tools, Options, and the General tab. Select the option Log Compilation Errors. (You can also use the command SET LOGERRORS ON.) Visual FoxPro then writes errors to a separate text file with the root name of the compiled file and an extension of .ERR. After compiling, you can open Project, Errors to see this error file (if you are compiling from the project). If you compile individual programs, you can view the error log by typing the following:

```
MODIFY FILE filename.ERR
```

If you do not log the errors, VFP merely shows the number of errors in the status bar at the end of the compile. This is not a very informative solution, especially because this message disappears after a few seconds. Information reported with each syntax error in the log includes the following:

- The program line that caused the error
- A line number where FoxPro determines that the error exists
- An error message

When you recompile the corrected program, Visual FoxPro automatically removes this file as the program compiles without error.

N O T E   An important point about the line number is that it does not always point to the line containing the error. For missing parentheses or operators, the line number points to the exact line of the error. For a missing or mismatched loop terminator (for example, ENDDO, ENDIF, ENDSCAN, or ENDFOR), the line number will probably be the end of the procedure. Visual FoxPro might not realize that an error exists until the procedure or program ends and the loop has not terminated properly.

In all likelihood, by the time VFP notices and reports an error condition, it's because something in your code has previously gone off track. The best place to start looking for *your* error is the line number that VFP identifies, and then work backward from there. ■

Always SET LOGERRORS ON

Closing a method-editing window in a form object also performs a syntax check. For syntax errors discovered during a compile, the alert box displays three options. You can Cancel the compile and return to the code to correct the problem. You can Ignore the error and check the balance of the code—until it finds another error or reaches the end of the code. Finally, you can Ignore All, which saves the code with all its errors. If you log errors, however, you can check the error log file to list the errors and resolve them one at a time.

If Visual FoxPro finds an error during execution that it does not find during compilation, it displays four options: Cancel, Suspend, Ignore, and Help. Cancel, of course, cancels the program. Suspend stops execution of the program and lets you enter the debugger to get more information about the error. You can also use the Command window to print values of memory variables or table fields to determine the problem. The Ignore button lets you ignore the problem; however, this is seldom a good choice. It might get you past this particular error, but chances are good that the application's memory has been compromised. Finally, the Help button opens VFP Help to give you more information about the error message.

There are some syntax errors that Visual FoxPro cannot detect until the program executes. These errors can result from mixing the order of parameters, passing the wrong number of parameters, or other similar problems. They are usually fairly easy to detect and fix. The following code lines show some runtime syntax errors:

- *Mixing the order of parameters passed to a function.* Visual FoxPro recognizes this error only if the switched parameters have a different type. It then responds with the Invalid function argument value, type, or count error. Mixing parameters of the same type generates logic errors at runtime.

  ```
  ? TRANSFORM('$$$,$$$.99', gnTotalDue) && Parameters are switched
  ```

- *Entering an incorrect parameter to a command that has a limited number of possible values.* For example, the ON KEY LABEL command expects specific key names. Anything else generates an error, but only at compile time, as would be the case with the following statement:

  ```
  ON KEY LABEL FJ9 ZOOM WINDOW PROPERTIES NORM FROM 0,0 ;
  TO 10,10
  ```

- *Using the wrong number of parameters or no parameters in FoxPro functions.* Passing too few parameters to a UDF is not automatically flagged as an error, but the procedure might fail if it attempts to use the missing parameters because VFP initializes them to .F.. This could result in a type error in subsequent statements. On the other hand, if you pass too many arguments to a procedure, you get the following error:

  ```
  Must specify additional parameters
  ```

  This might sound confusing, but look at it from the point of view of the procedure, which needs additional parameters to complete the request. The following code line attempts to use the LEFT() function to display a portion of a character string, but it does not pass the number of desired characters. This statement must fail because VFP will not know how long a string to return:

```
?LEFT(lcLastName)    && Number of characters to return is required
```

■ *Entering a comma instead of a period, or vice versa.* The difference between these two characters is hard to see on many monitors. For example, the following statement fails because a period rather than a comma separates two parameters:

```
LPARAMETERS lnErrNum. lcErrMessage
```

This problem is made worse by the fact that these two characters occur next to each other on the keyboard. But, they are not the only character pairs likely to cause problems. Another commonly confused pair includes the zero and uppercase O. Again, both characters occur close to each other on the keyboard and look almost identical on the screen. Another frequently confused pair is the number one and lowercase l.

This list represents some common syntax errors, but not all of them. As you develop programs, you might recognize other common syntax errors of your own.

Logic Errors

Logic errors are the second major category of errors. These errors are more difficult to detect and resolve. Compiling the program does not locate them. Sometimes, a serious logic error stops a program from executing, but not always; for example, referencing an array, or one of its elements, that does not exist results in a logic error. Perhaps the program defined the array in another procedure, but gave it a private scope rather than global. When VFP encounters any variable that does not exist, it stops the program's execution.

A similar type of logic error occurs when you overwrite existing variables when restoring variables from a memory variable file or a table. The RESTORE FROM command enables a program to use variables previously stored to a .MEM file. The following code line not only restores the .MEM file variables, it also erases all current memory variables. SCATTER MEMVAR performs a similar function when retrieving fields from a table and saving their values into memory variables. If a prior memory variable had the same name as a field in the table, its value will be replaced by a corresponding field in the current record.

```
RESTORE FROM Savevars.mem
```

or

```
USE CUSTOMER
SCATTER MEMVAR
```

If your program uses similar code and attempts to reference a previously defined variable, it could fail or at least generate incorrect results. The RESTORE FROM command actually causes more of a problem because it wipes out all prior memory variables before loading the ones from file. Fortunately, RESTORE FROM supports a clause to restore memory variable values without losing those already in memory. Simply include the ADDITIVE clause, as shown in the following snippet:

```
RESTORE FROM Savevars.mem ADDITIVE
```

You can still overwrite an existing variable that also exists in the `.MEM` file, but you won't lose the uniquely named ones.

Some logic errors create obviously wrong results. For example, you might see a string of asterisks in a field (`****`), which indicates a field overflow. In this case, either the field is too small or the value calculated is too large. Of course, errors do not have to be this dramatic. If a sales report calculates the total tax due as greater than the net cost of the items purchased, there is a problem. This error should be obvious to anyone who simply compares the sales totals before and after tax.

On the other hand, some errors are not obvious at all without an independent check of the calculations. Suppose that you use the following equation to calculate the number of acres in a square plot of land:

```
gnTotalAcres = (pnFront * pnSide) / 9 / 4480
```

This equation is valid and does not generate an error when executed. It multiplies the length of the front in feet by the length of the side in feet to get the area in square feet. It then divides by 9 feet per square yard. It divides the number of square yards by 4,480 rather than 4,840, however. Merely looking at the result might not reveal the fact that two digits were transposed. This type of error can go unnoticed for a long time.

Another difficult logic error to find occurs when using `REPLACE`. Suppose you try to change a field in a different table while the record pointer in the current table points to `EOF`. This error is subtle, as shown in the following code:

```
SELECT CUST
IF !SEEK(m.pcCustId)
  REPLACE ORDER.cCustId WITH 'NONE'
ENDIF
```

You might be surprised to find that this code fails. When FoxPro searches for the customer ID in table `CUST` and does not find it, it leaves the record pointer at the end of `CUST`. Even though the `REPLACE` statement clearly uses an alias to replace `cCustId` in table `ORDER`, the default scope of `NEXT 1` actually refers to the current work area, which is `CUST`, not `ORDER`. Because the record pointer in the current work area points to `EOF`, `REPLACE` fails. Obviously, the solution here is to precede `REPLACE` with a `SELECT Order` statement.

> **N O T E** This "feature" has haunted FoxPro developers since its earliest versions. Visual FoxPro now fixes the condition with a new `IN` clause to the `REPLACE` command, which scopes the command to that other work area. You must specifically name the other work area, not just use it as an alias. Change the above code to the following:
> ```
> REPLACE Order.cCustID WITH 'NONE' IN Order
> ```

Because VFP doesn't require that you qualify a field name with its alias, it's sometimes easy to forget that you are working with table fields instead of memory variables. You assign values to memory variables with an equal sign, but you put data into fields with `REPLACE`. Using names from the previous example, the following line will not fail, but it also won't give you the results you are looking for. VFP simply assumes you want to store the value into a variable:

```
cCustID = 'NONE'
```

Exception Errors

Exception errors, the third type of coding errors, occur due to circumstances outside of the program's direct control. For example, a program may fail because it cannot find a file it needs. Perhaps the file has been deleted or moved. Of course, if someone or some process deleted the file, there is no way for the program to continue. Even if someone has merely moved the file, you might not want to make the user responsible for finding it.

Said another way, you might not want users roaming around the file server looking for a "likely" table. First, they do not know where to look; second, they might open the wrong file, causing even more problems. Yet an expert user such as yourself might be very qualified and able to perform this search. Even experts, however, make mistakes. In any case, your program should use the FILE() function to determine whether a file exists before attempting to use it. Then, based on the user level (assigned elsewhere in your application), the code in Listing 23.1 shows one way to determine how to continue when the file does not exist. You might consider always calling a shutdown procedure when a file is not found by a program as protection against the ever-present possibility of accessing the wrong file. Alternatively, you might find some other suitable way of returning the user to the application without accessing the code that's looking for the missing file.

Listing 23.1   23CODE01.PRG—A Basic Way of Dealing with a File-Not-Found Exception

```
IF FILE('\VFP6BOOK\DATA\MYFILE.DBF)
* File found, open it
  USE \VFP6BOOK\DATA\MYFILE.DBF
ELSE
* File not found.
  WAIT WINDOW 'File: \VFP6BOOK\DATA\MYFILE.DBF NOT Found!' + ;
      CHR(13) + 'Press any key to continue'

* Can this user search for it?
  IF gnUserLevel > 1
    lcNewFile = GETFILE('DBF', 'Find MYFILE.DBF', 'SELECT')
    IF !EMPTY(lcNewFile)
      USE (lcNewFile)
    ELSE
      DO SHUTDOWN    && Or run another part of the application
    ENDIF
  ELSE
    DO SHUTDOWN    && Or run another part of the application
  ENDIF
ENDIF
```

The previous code can very easily be converted to a generalized form and made into a function that you can call from any program or procedure. Listing 23.2 shows one possible implementation.

Listing 23.2 `23CODE02.PRG`—A Generalized Function for Dealing with a File Not-Found Exception

```
IF FILE('\VFP6BOOK\DATA\MYFILE.DBF')
* File found, open it
  USE \VFP6BOOK\DATA\MYFILE.DBF
ELSE
* File not found.
  lcGetFile = FINDFILE('MYFILE.DBF')
ENDIF
*** REST OF PROGRAM CONTINUES

FUNCTION FINDFILE
LPARAMETER lcFileNam

* Tell user what is happening.
  WAIT WINDOW 'File: &lcFileNam. NOT Found!' + ;
       CHR(13) + CHR(10) + 'Press any key to continue'

* Can this user search for it?
  IF gnUserLevel > 1
    lcNewFile = GETFILE('DBF', 'Find '+lcFileNam, 'SELECT')
    IF !EMPTY(lcNewFile)
      USE (lcNewFile)
    ELSE
      DO SHUTDOWN    && Or continue in another part of the application
    ENDIF
  ELSE
    DO SHUTDOWN    && Or continue in another part of the application
  ENDIF
RETURN lcNewFile
```

Another type of exception occurs when an index does not exist. If the table is part of a database, the program could retrieve the definitions for that table's indexes from the .DBC file. It could then attempt to create the missing index. The potential problem here is that indexing requires an exclusive lock on the file. If the program cannot obtain that lock, the program should shut down gracefully.

Not all exception errors are as easy to deal with. In some cases, the best alternative might be to use an ON ERROR routine to document the system at the time of the error, roll back pending transactions, close all tables, and cancel the program.

N O T E ON ERROR executes a single command when Visual FoxPro encounters any error condition. That command typically uses DO to execute an error-handling procedure. ON ERROR still provides a global mechanism for handling errors in Visual FoxPro. ■

The rest of this chapter shows additional methods of avoiding errors when possible, and how to track down errors that inevitably sneak in anyway.

Modularizing Code to Minimize Errors

The number of errors in any program or procedure tends to increase as it grows in size. The reason is that it becomes increasingly difficult to remember all the details in the code. The demands on software grow daily as well. Very quickly, every programmer realizes that writing large single programs with hundreds or thousands of code lines causes more problems than several smaller programs that call one another. Obviously, the more errors, the greater the amount of time spent finding and removing them. On the other hand, dividing code into smaller functional units called procedures or functions reduces overall errors. It soon becomes obvious that each procedure or function should handle no more than one task. This process is known as *code modularization*.

Visual FoxPro facilitates code modularization. Any application can be thought of as a series of tasks. *Tasks* consist of data-entry screens, reports, or procedures that manipulate data. Menu choices provide access to each task. Each task often has two or more *subtasks*.

How do you go about breaking a task down into smaller units or subtasks? Think of a customer form as a single task. Within it, individual data fields represent subtasks. Individual pieces of information on that form might hold the customer's name, address, or telephone number. Visual FoxPro represents subtasks as control objects. Looking deeper into a control, you find individual methods that respond to various events. Object methods are used to accomplish the following:

- Set default values
- Determine a user's rights to a field
- Create pick lists
- Validate field entries
- Save or retrieve data
- Respond to mouse clicks or moves
- Display related forms
- Send messages to other objects instructing them to alter their own characteristics, or run some method they are responsible for

See the chapters in Part IV, "Object-Oriented Programming," for more information on interobject communication.

You have already seen how to generate forms, where each form represents a block of code functionally independent of the rest of the application. Within a form, methods further modularize the code needed to handle individual object events. You can create and store the code needed for a method in a variety of ways.

First, when you open a method in Visual FoxPro's form design mode, you can enter code directly. Although this approach works, it has some drawbacks. Mainly, it limits the use of that code to one method in one form. In order to use a similar routine in another form, you might resort to cut-and-paste. You could easily end up with the complicated task of maintaining many slightly different versions of the same routine in a variety of places. You could instead store the code in a separate file. The event method then simply references it with a user-defined function (UDF) call. That's the easy part. The hard part is deciding where to store this separate code. Again, several possibilities exist.

> **N O T E** In FoxPro 2.x, form generation produced real code that you could view and use. In VFP, the process is quite different, and there is no actual code. You can *pretend* that you are generating code as you did in FoxPro 2.x by directing the Class Browser to produce a listing for you. However, a VFP form is simply an .SCX file in either design mode or run mode. This difference, plus application of object-oriented principles, affects how you share coded routines among your application's objects. ◼

In FoxPro 2.x it was a commonly accepted practice to use a separate .PRG with the same name as the form to store the needed procedures and functions used by that form. This .PRG was also responsible for calling the form.

You could run this .PRG directly, or have the application's main menu call this form-launching program. Although not the recommended object-oriented approach, this methodology can be adapted to use with Visual FoxPro, which would then have no trouble finding the functions stored in the main program that calls the form.

This technique worked well in FoxPro 2.x because it enabled quicker editing of the code and did not require the form designer just to change the code for a method. However, it is not in the OOP spirit to code this way. It does not enable sharing of code between objects with similar methods in different forms. This is a big negative when you begin to develop class libraries. The UDF call will be inherited when you subclass from the base object, but the source UDF might not be available.

Another technique stores all procedure code in a single, separate file. This file establishes a library of procedures and functions. Then, any screen with a similar method, even a subclassed screen, can call a common function. This technique makes changing the code easier. If you need a new property or method, you add it in one place. Place the reference to the code in the appropriate method of the base class and place the code in the procedure library. If more than one form uses the same method code, it still appears in one place, not everywhere the object appears.

> **N O T E** A variation of this traditional concept is to turn a procedure library into a class, where each custom method is a commonly used routine. Simply drop this library object onto your application objects to make those methods available. There can be performance tradeoffs in referencing class methods versus functions in procedure files, so this technique might be better used to group more specialized routines related to a common activity. ◼

With VFP objects, you can build a subclass of the original class and include common method code in its definition. By encapsulating the method's code in the definition of the class itself, you don't have to worry about separate code libraries. By sharing the object through a class library, you still code it only once. This approach works best when many forms use the same object with the same methods. An example might be VCR buttons used to control movement through a table's records.

N O T E Before you store objects as custom classes in a class library, make sure to test them and all their associated code thoroughly. You can create a simple form and place the control on the form to test it. After you are satisfied with it, select the object and choose File, Save As Class. The resulting Save Class dialog box enables you to assign a class name and library file and save just the selected controls without the form. Debugging and modifying code after storing it in a class library requires more steps. ■

The point to this discussion is that object methods force you to divide code into individual tasks that are more easily comprehended and maintained. The theory is that if individual tasks work properly, the sum of the tasks works properly.

Of course, you can achieve many of these same benefits in standard code by using procedures and functions that accomplish a single task. If a procedure performs more than one task, it can probably be split into two or more procedures.

Code modularization at the task level leads to another benefit: reusability. This has been mentioned before in terms of objects and object libraries, but it applies just as strongly to other common code tasks. If you write a procedure to handle movement through a table's records using a set of VCR buttons, you can use that same procedure with every table. The code remains unchanged. Developing this concept further, consider developing a library of common procedures to use in any application. You benefit from time saved by not having to write and test the same code repeatedly. Your applications also exhibit a consistent look and feel.

TIP To learn more about using an object-oriented approach in your applications, see Part IV, "Object-Oriented Programming."

Using Proper Parameter Passing

Another common error occurs during planned and unplanned parameter passing. First you might wonder what unplanned parameter passing means. Remember that Visual FoxPro makes any variable defined as a public or private variable automatically available to routines it calls. This can unintentionally redefine a variable when calling a lower-level routine that uses a variable with the same name. Visual FoxPro will not flag this as an error. After all, it assumes that you intended to do it.

As a general rule, never use the same variables in programs that call one another or in different procedures in the same program. If you must use a variable in a called procedure, pass the parameter by value and assign it a local name in the called procedure. Accidentally redefining variables in lower routines results in errors that are extremely difficult to find.

TIP

If you are not sure whether a variable has been used in a higher procedure, define the scope of the variable as LOCAL or PRIVATE in the called procedure.

Pass parameter values into local variables by using the LPARAMETERS statement rather than PARAMETERS.

Another consideration is whether you pass parameters to procedures by value or by reference. When you pass a parameter by reference, the procedure uses the actual original variable. If the procedure changes the parameter value, the original variable's value changes also (see Listing 23.3).

Listing 23.3   23CODE03.PRG—An Example of Passing Parameters by Reference

```
* Default scope for these variables is PRIVATE
a = 5
b = 6
c = 7

DO NewVal WITH a

? 'a = ' + STR(a,1)    && After the subroutine, a contains 1
? 'b = ' + STR(b,1)    && … b has been protected, still contains 6
? 'c = ' + STR(c,1)    && … c has also been changed, value is now 8

PROCEDURE NewVal
PARAMETER b
b = 1
c = 8
RETURN
```

On the other hand, if you pass the parameter by value, the procedure creates a new variable to store the parameter value. It does not pass changes back to the original. The equivalent code is shown in Listing 23.4.

Listing 23.4   23CODE04.PRG—An Example of Passing Parameters by Value

```
a = 5
DO NewVal WITH (a)
? 'a = ' + STR(a,1)    && Original value of 5 has been preserved

PROCEDURE NewVal
PARAMETER b
b = 1
RETURN
```

Part
VI

Ch
23

When calling a procedure, Visual FoxPro's default method passes parameters by reference, except for any that you enclose in parentheses. However, when calling a function, the default method passes parameters by value (observe, functions enclose parameters in parentheses). To pass a parameter to a function by reference, you can do either of the following:

- Type SET UDFPARMS TO REFERENCE.
- Precede the parameter name with the @ character.

If you need to pass an array to a procedure or function, pass it by reference. If you attempt to pass it by value, it passes only the first element.

There is a limit of 27 passed parameters to procedures and functions.

Eliminating Multiple Exits and Returns

Not too many years ago, the "new" programming paradigm promoted the elimination of all GOTO statements. FoxPro developers have never had a problem with GOTOs because the language does not support a GOTO branch statement; the VFP GOTO command only navigates data files. Instead you use IF, CASE, and DO structures for conditional code processing and loops. As a result, few FoxPro developers today miss GOTO statements and the resulting tangled code they created.

Unfortunately, many FoxPro developers still use multiple exits from structured loops and multiple returns from procedures and functions. In almost all cases, there is no need for this practice. All that is usually required is a minor revision to the loop's logic. Examine the following code example:

```
PROCEDURE GetProdID
  IF EMPTY(m.lcProdId)
    RETURN
  ELSE
    < Code to test if lcProdId exists in PRODUCT.DBF >
    RETURN
  ENDIF
  USE
RETURN
```

This procedure has three exit points where only one is required. A restructured version of the same code follows:

```
PROCEDURE GetProdID
  IF !EMPTY(m.lcProdId)
    < Code to test if lcProdId exists in PRODUCT.DBF >
  ENDIF
  USE
RETURN
```

Why be concerned about multiple exit and return points? First, it adds a level of unnecessary complexity to the code that makes tracing its path more difficult. But more important, it sometimes causes the program to skip critical code segments that it should execute. For example, in the earlier code, should the procedure close the current table (the USE command)? The first code example never closes the current file and the second one always does.

This illustrates another danger with multiple EXIT or RETURN commands. It is easy to orphan code, isolating it so that it never executes. The first example ends each branch of the IF statement with a RETURN. As a result, the USE statement never executes.

The EXIT command exits a DO…ENDDO, FOR…ENDFOR, or SCAN…ENDSCAN loop prior to completing the loop based on the loop condition. For example, the following program segment loops through rental product records to find the serial number of a product still in stock. A simple SEEK finds a record that matches the product ID. Then, it must loop through all the records for that product until it finds the first one in stock.

```
USE RentProd ORDER ProdID
pcSerial = SPACE(4)
SEEK m.pcFindProdId
SCAN WHILE m.pcFindProdId = cProdId
  IF lInStock
    pcSerial = cSerial
    EXIT
  ENDIF
ENDSCAN
```

Observe that this code segment has two possible exits from the SCAN loop. If it finds at least one product in stock with a specific ID, it stores its serial number in variable pcSerial and exits. Otherwise, it continues to loop until the product ID changes.

A better way to write this code eliminates the extra exit. First, you need to recognize that you cannot simply eliminate the EXIT command. This would cause the loop to read through all records of the same product ID. The net effect would be to return the last available serial number rather than the first. The following code solves this problem by adding an extra conditional test to the SCAN:

```
USE RentProd ORDER ProdID
pcSerial = SPACE(4)
SEEK m.pcFindProdId
SCAN WHILE EMPTY(pcserial) AND m.pcFindProdId = cProdId
  IF lInStock
    pcSerial = cSerial
  ENDIF
ENDSCAN
```

Observe, in this case, that SCAN tests for an empty serial number memory variable first. If this field changes before the product ID does, an in-stock item has been found. This new condition also guarantees that the loop returns the first available serial number or a blank if there is no in-stock product.

N O T E   A case might be made that adding the extra condition test slows the loop and thus the extra EXIT actually improves the code performance. The programming world is loaded with tradeoffs. ▣

A similar case can be made for eliminating the use of EXIT in other loop structures. Thus, by careful use of IF blocks and additional conditional statements, you can eliminate most, if not all, multiple exits from programs. I hope that this will also eliminate another potential source of errors in your code.

Developing Libraries of Testing Routines and Objects

Using libraries, which are program files containing common procedures and functions, is one of the most effective methods of reducing the number of errors in code. Of course, you must first thoroughly test routines before adding them to a library. Once tested, however, new applications can use them with virtual assurance that they do not contain errors.

N O T E   This concept of building common libraries of functions has grown up in the object world in the form of class libraries. ▣

In fact, Visual FoxPro's builders and wizards provide the equivalent of a standard library of creation routines. They automate the building of forms, form controls, menus, queries, reports, data tables, and the like. You do not have to write the basic code for these objects. Visual FoxPro provides error-free objects for you; all you have to do is tweak them to fit your particular application's needs.

N O T E   VFP 6 comes with a greater selection than ever of new and enhanced wizards, and a complete set of source code to re-create them. See Chapter 27, "The Visual FoxPro Wizards," for more information about them. Completely new additions to this version are the Foundation Classes and the Component Gallery, which provide an expanded selection of pre-built tools you can use directly in your applications. You can count on these offerings being enhanced in future versions of VFP. For more information on these new features, see Chapter 18, "The Visual FoxPro Foundation Classes" and Chapter 19, "The Visual FoxPro Component Gallery." ▣

You can also build your own libraries of functions and procedures to call from any program or object method. To create a library, store the functions and procedures in a single file and save it. Then, in programs that use them, simply add a SET PROCEDURE statement before referencing them. The syntax for SET PROCEDURE is

```
SET PROCEDURE TO [FileName1 [,FileName2,...]] [ADDITIVE]
```

Visual FoxPro enables programs to reference more than one library. You can even reference additional libraries later in a program by including the ADDITIVE clause. Forgetting this clause closes any prior procedure libraries when opening the new one.

Procedure libraries provide an excellent way to store and use common routines. Create common routines to open files, create sorts, display messages, and perform other common functions.

In addition to procedure files, Visual FoxPro also lets you create object libraries of your own classes. To begin, subclass one of Visual FoxPro's base classes or an existing subclass in a .VCX file. Then add additional custom properties or methods to it. For example, you could create a class consisting of a group of buttons to navigate through a file. You can then use this custom class on any form that needs file navigation buttons.

N O T E It is important to distinguish between a *custom class* and a *customized class*. VFP provides a base class of type custom that comes with its own native properties, events, and methods. *Any* subclass, however, can be customized with the addition of user-defined properties and methods. ▨

To open and use a class library, use SET CLASSLIB. Its syntax is

```
SET CLASSLIB TO ClassLibraryName [ADDITIVE] [ALIAS AliasName]
```

As with SET PROCEDURE, you can have multiple class libraries open at the same time if you open each one with the ADDITIVE clause. Omitting this clause closes any previously opened class libraries.

Handling Corruption in Files

Data files can easily become corrupted. Because data files often are larger than the amount of RAM memory in a machine, Visual FoxPro constantly moves some of the files between memory and disk. Normally, everything works fine. If, however, the user turns off the computer without properly exiting the program, the file might be incompletely written. (This could be his frustrated reaction when your program fails without a proper error handling routine, and leaves tables open.) Unfortunately, the best protection against this sort of action and its resultant data corruption is a hardware UPS (uninterruptible power supply). You can take some precautions in your applications, though, primarily by tracking errors when they do occur.

In Chapter 1, "Quick Review of the Visual FoxPro Interface," an example code called a procedure, REALQUIT, to prevent the user from accidentally exiting FoxPro by clicking the wrong Close box. It proposed running a program called RealQuit when Visual FoxPro enters its ON SHUTDOWN event. Alternatively, you can add the ON SHUTDOWN command to any program to prevent the user from exiting Visual FoxPro or Windows prematurely. The procedure in Listing 23.5 should be called by ON SHUTDOWN. It includes some additional commands to properly close down Visual FoxPro. If called from an error handler, you could even build a procedure consisting of the core code inside the IF…ENDIF block.

Listing 23.5 `23CODE05.PRG`—A Procedure for Properly Closing Down VFP

```
PROCEDURE SHUTDOWN
* Include any commands in this routine needed to return the system
* to a default environment. Applications running interactively
* require more attention than compiled standalone applications.
* Standalone applications might merely need to close down all
* files safely.
IF MESSAGEBOX('Do you really want to exit Visual FoxPro?', 292) = 6
   * Reset common ON KEY definitions that the application may be using.
     ON KEY LABEL BACKSPACE
     ON KEY LABEL ENTER
     ON KEY LABEL SPACEBAR
     ON KEY LABEL ESCAPE

   * Turn printer and file redirection off
     SET ALTERNATE OFF
     SET ALTERNATE TO
     SET PRINT OFF
     SET CONSOLE ON

   * Close transaction - TRAP ERRORS
     IF TXNLEVEL() > 0
       ROLLBACK
       END TRANSACTION
     CLOSE ALL

   * Release all variables (and objects)
     RELEASE ALL

   * Deactivate windows
     DEACTIVATE WINDOWS ALL
     DEACTIVATE WINDOW DEBUG
     DEACTIVATE WINDOW TRACE
     ACTIVATE WINDOW COMMAND

   * Deactivate any application menus
     SET SYSMENU TO DEFAULT

   * Clear macros
     RESTORE MACROS

 ELSE
 * Let VFP terminate
 * QUIT
 ENDIF
 RETURN
```

Of course, the easiest way to fix a corrupted file is to restore a backup copy from tape or disk. If you perform daily backups, the most you lose is one day's worth of data. Even this minimal loss can be unacceptable, however. Whereas tools like dSalvage from Comtech and FoxFix from Hallogram (www.hallogram.com) worked well repairing individual tables from previous versions of FoxPro, the considerably more complex database structures in VFP require suitably sophisticated products to maintain their integrity. The best of these management and repair tools is Stonefield Database Toolkit from Stonefield Systems Group, Inc. (www.stonefield.com). Another excellent choice for database design and maintenance is xCase for Fox from RESolution Ltd. (available at www.f1tech.com). Because of the interrelated nature of database components, you need to supplement your data backup and restore procedures with some higher-level functionality that is provided by these database tools. The sorts of things you need to be able to do are as follows:

- Fix many errors in the file header.
- Recover lost memo field data.
- Reindex tables in the DBC without losing persistent relationships or referential integrity code.
- Manage the database container so that table header changes, such as table names, field names, and field properties, remain synchronized with the DBC.
- Rebuild entire databases or update individual structures at your own or client sites.

TIP A structural .CDX file is the easiest, safest—and therefore, most common—type of index to use and maintain. You should reserve the use of individual .IDX files for infrequently run, ad-hoc operations.

A corrupted index can occur when someone copies a backup .DBF to the current directory without copying its indexes. In this case, changes made to the original .DBF exist in the index, but not in the copied .DBF. Thus, the index might point to the wrong record, no record, or beyond the end of the table. This is further complicated by the fact that the database container itself (the DBC) tracks information about both the table and its index file.

You can fix simple index file problems by reindexing the table; however, even REINDEX doesn't help if the index file header is corrupted. Before Visual FoxPro, when life was simpler, you could save index definitions in a separate table, a database, a data dictionary, or simply on a piece of paper. You could then delete the corrupted index files, open the .DBF, and re-create them. This simplistic approach, however, creates new headaches in a VFP database, because you can lose other information about your files, such as persistent relationships with other files and referential integrity procedures.

The DBC, although containing a record to reference each tag name in the structural compound index of the table, does not store the index expression, nor does it store information about any other index (standalone or nonstructural). This means that copying backup tables into the current directory is a good way to get them out of synch with the DBC. You can find out more about this condition by issuing the VALIDATE DATABASE command in the Command window.

NOTE If your index file contains a primary key reference, it is not easy to simply delete an index file and re-create it. The problem is that the database container stores a reference to the primary key in two places, a tag record and in the properties of the table record itself. Removing the tag record from the DBC is easy. Removing the primary key reference from the table properties is not. See additional information about working with the database container in Chapter 4, "Advanced Database Management Concepts."

Corrupted form, label, and report files present an additional challenge. Visual FoxPro stores information for these objects in both a .DBF-type file and a memo file. Therefore, they are susceptible to the same types of damage and you can use the same tools and methods to fix them. Table 23.1 shows the corresponding file extensions for Visual FoxPro's key components.

Table 23.1   File Extensions of Common Visual FoxPro Files

File Contents	Data Extension	Memo Extension
Database	.DBC	.DCT
Menu	.MNX	.MNT
Classes	.VCX	.VCT
Project	.PJX	.PJT
Label	.LBX	.LBT
Report	.FRX	.FRT
Screen	.SCX	.SCT
Table	.DBF	.FPT

It might be possible to edit and remove some data corruption with programs. The safest solution, however, is to keep backup copies of all program and data files on cartridge, tape, or some other removable medium that can be stored offsite.

Designing a Test Plan

Testing your application should be considered a separate and very high priority planned task in its development. If you use a project planner such as Microsoft Project, identify testing as a separate task. There are many ways to design a test plan. Some developers test only after they completely write an application. The interactive nature of Visual FoxPro, however, makes concurrent testing during development easier and more productive. The problem is that it is harder for management to track the time spent on concurrent testing. This section looks at various testing techniques and analyzes their pros and cons.

Understanding Data-Driven Versus Logic-Driven Testing

Testing an application consists of two elements: validity and coverage. *Validity testing* checks to see whether the application generates the expected results for a specific set of inputs. *Coverage testing* checks to see whether all code statements have been executed by the tests. Any code not executed could harbor a hidden bug. I will talk more about coverage testing later. First, let's examine validity testing.

There are two basic approaches to validity testing. The first approach is data-driven. It does not assume a prior knowledge of the way the program works, rather, it focuses on selecting a variety of test data sets based on a random sampling of real-world or fabricated data. It then runs the program with the data to see whether it generates the expected results.

The second approach is logic-driven and requires extensive knowledge of the program's coding. It attempts to test every path the program can execute. It also tests how the program handles data limits by using data that pushes and exceeds known physical limitations.

Each method has advantages and disadvantages. The advantages to a data-driven approach include the fact that it does not consciously or subconsciously make assumptions about the program. Often a person "assumes" that a program never behaves a certain way and therefore fails to test it completely. Frequently, the parts of the program assumed to be correct are the very ones that fail. The primary disadvantage to a data-driven approach is that there is no guarantee that the test data sets cover all program paths and loops.

A logic-driven approach overcomes the weakness of data-driven testing. When properly designed, it tests every line of code in the entire system. The obvious disadvantage is that for a major application, fully testing every line of code requires multiple data tests. It takes time to develop the necessary data sets to ensure testing of each line of code. Further, logic-driven testing using an interactive interface can be hugely time-consuming.

Defining Testing Techniques

There are almost as many techniques for testing and debugging as there are programmers. Most approaches involve variations of just a few major techniques. The first several methods described here involve the design stage of a project. The more errors found and removed during the design phase, the less expensive the overall project becomes because it results in fewer false starts and less rework of code. This translates into reduced manhours and, thus, reduced cost.

Checking design documents involves a review of forms, reports, table layouts, and relations developed during the design phase. This occurs prior to any coding.

An *informal group design review* involves a group of programmers, users, and designers meeting to discuss various aspects of the project. It does not require a formalized step-through of the design specifications.

Formal design inspection analyzes the critical parts of the system design and attempts to determine whether it accounts for all possible situations. It often uses *decision-tree analysis* diagrams to ensure coverage. Decision-tree analysis traces each major path and operation in an application and graphically displays them on paper. Due to the usual branching of options, the resulting diagram resembles the limbs of a tree.

Personal desk-checking involves reviewing code listings and walking through the process on paper (or onscreen) without actually running the program. It often requires performing hand calculations using sample data in the actual code to check the results. Some developers refer to this technique as a *walkthrough*; however, the term walkthrough can also apply to other review types. This technique was more popular years ago when computer time was expensive and programmers were relatively cheap. Today, the reverse is true. Thus, this method might be called on mainly to find non-trivial errors such as complex logic errors.

Test often and test early. The longer an error exists, the more expensive it becomes to find and remove.

After coding begins, the focus shifts from paper and thought reviews to formal code reviews and actual physical testing. The following paragraphs describe a few of these techniques.

Formal code inspection involves careful scrutiny of critical code segments. It provides feedback about the code, standards, use of comments, variable naming, variable scoping issues, and so forth.

Modeling or *prototyping* uses available tools to quickly create an application shell. Its purpose is to show overall functionality of the system. With Visual FoxPro, this involves creating basic forms and reports linked together with a simple menu. Although the forms appear functional, they might not include processing of all the business rules. Similarly, reports might not include selection and sorting options. A common term for this technique today is *RAD (Rapid Application Development)*.

Syntax checking tests the basic correctness of the code. It checks the spelling of commands and text strings, the validity of expressions, and the basic structure of commands. FoxPro does most of this during compilation, although some syntax problems become evident only when you run the program.

 Visual FoxPro does not check spelling or syntax within strings, form captions, ToolTips, status bar text, or messages. Yet these are the most visible parts of the program to users and could reflect on the entire system.

One suggestion to assist in automating this cleanup is to write a program that collects all such strings into a table. For example, you can read through the various .VCX and .SCX files in the project, check the base class field to find objects with a caption property, and parse that caption out of the Properties field. These entries then can be printed out and checked visually, or subjected to a spell-checking program.

Unit testing exercises individual groups of statements. For example, when designing a new class definition, use unit testing to check the code associated with its methods. To perform unit testing, you must write a special program called a *driver*. The driver does not become part of the final code. Rather, you use it to set up the necessary program conditions, such as initializing variables, to test the code segment.

Even though you might test each procedure and function individually, their correct functioning does not guarantee that the program as a whole will work. However, it does narrow down the error possibilities. *System testing* specifically checks the interface connections between modules. Its purpose is to ensure that data and logic pass correctly to and from each module. This includes using proper parameter types and sizes. It can also look for unexpected changes to public or private variables redefined by a called procedure or function.

Functional testing checks that the major features of the program work as expected. When you select a report option from the menu, do you get the report you selected or another one, or perhaps even a form? If a form displays a message to press F2 for a list of possible values, it checks that the list really appears when you press F2. It does not necessarily include verification of the report results or that the list that appears when you press F2 contains the correct data.

Stress testing checks boundary conditions of the program, such as how the program responds to extreme data values. For example, if the program tracks weekly payroll, this form of testing might check what the program does if you enter 170 hours for the number of hours the employee worked this week (seven times 24 hours is only 168). Stress testing on a network concerns itself with how the program performs when multiple users run it. Can the program handle simultaneous updates to data? Do record and file locks perform correctly while minimizing the time when other users cannot access the data?

Part
VI
Ch
23

The speed of a program falls under *performance testing*. Visual FoxPro provides the flexibility to code most features in several ways, but all ways do not perform equally. In fact, some methods substantially outperform others. Performance testing looks for areas to improve program speed by identifying which portions of the program require the most time. Then you can try alternative programming methods to improve the speed.

N O T E Visual FoxPro itself is *extremely* fast. There are a lot of things built into the product to enhance performance (Rushmore Technology) and to diagnose bottleneck conditions (functions like SYS(3050) to adjust memory buffer size and SYS(3054) to analyze optimization in SQL SELECT statements). But most information about what to make of all this is shared anecdotally among developers: at conferences, in technical articles, and online. Among the best ongoing sources of help on that sort of issue are *FoxPro Advisor* magazine, *FoxTalk* newsletter from Pinnacle Publishing, CompuServe's VFOX and FoxUser forums, and www.universalthread.com. Annual large- and small-scale conferences are sponsored by Microsoft, Advisor Publications, various user groups, and companies around the world.

Finally, *compatibility testing* looks at how the program works in different environments. This can include different display monitor modes, different printers, and different directory structures. It can even involve the way the program displays regional or international fields such as time, dates, and money. Even the collating sequence of sorted data and the codepage of tables become important issues when internationalizing an application. Of course, the extent you need to concern yourself with these sorts of issues is determined by how widely your application will be distributed.

N O T E If yours is an international application, you might consider purchasing a third-party product to handle all the language, font, currency, and data type issues. The INTL Toolkit from Steven Black Consulting (www.stevenblack.com) is such a product that isolates the cross-cultural issues into a library. You simply include this library as an object, and then go on to address the business questions of your application.

Macros can be very handy in the testing process. They can be especially useful when you have a single set of commands that doesn't rely on decisions and optional logic branches. Select Tools, Macros from the system menu to bring up a dialog box for recording and managing user-defined macros. As you issue the keystrokes in your test, VFP interprets them into a code string, which you assign to a hotkey combination. In the future, typing the hotkey alone reruns the entire set of keystrokes.

Macros are limited to keystrokes. You can record typed entries and menu selections, but mouse movements aren't recognized.

Determining When Testing Is Complete

One might successfully argue that testing is never complete until the application becomes obsolete. There are always new combinations of data. Furthermore, most programs change over time, adding a feature here or a field there. With each new feature, you introduce the possibility of errors. Program paths might change, new variables might overwrite similar variables in other routines, and other side effects might affect existing code. For this reason, it is important to go back and retest working portions when you introduce new features. This is called *regression testing*.

Some developers use a bug rate factor to determine when to stop debugging. In other words, they measure the number of bugs found over time. Although this gives a nice, neat, numeric way to determine when to cut off testing, several variations exist. For example, you could monitor the cost of looking for bugs compared to the cost of leaving them in. For example, the cost of leaving a spelling error in a text label is very low. However, the cost of an error that subtracts sales tax from total due rather than adding it is higher. Another error at a higher cost level is one that returns the wrong product price when selecting products. Therefore, time is allocated for testing different parts of the program based on how serious an error would be in those parts.

No matter what method you use, it is nearly impossible to determine when all bugs have been found. Declaring testing complete just to meet a schedule, however, is dangerously short-sighted. Testing should continue until everyone involved feels confident in the application's performance.

The last section defined several techniques for testing software. The reason for so many different methods is that no one technique is perfect. In fact, a survey by Capers Jones, published in *Programming Productivity*, shows the effectiveness of the 10 most common techniques. Table 23.2 reproduces this table.

Table 23.2   Effectiveness of Software-Testing Techniques

Technique	Minimum	Average	Maximum
Checking of design documents	15%	35%	70%
Informal group design reviews	30%	40%	60%
Formal design inspection	35%	55%	75%

Technique	Minimum	Average	Maximum
Formal code inspection	30%	60%	70%
Modeling/prototyping	35%	65%	80%
Personal desk-checking of code	20%	40%	60%
Unit testing	10%	25%	50%
Functional testing	20%	35%	55%
Integration testing	25%	45%	60%
Field testing	35%	50%	65%
All of the above (used together)	93%	99%	99%

Part
VI
Ch
23

In this table, the three columns represent the minimum number of errors, as a percentage, found using each technique, the average number found, and the maximum number. These values assume one person is assigned to debug the code using one technique. The interesting point to the preceding table is that no one method guarantees error-free code. In fact, only a combination of methods finds close to all the errors.

Glenford J. Myers performed an interesting related study. He found that every programmer approaches debugging slightly differently. As a result, even the combination of as few as two programmers in the debugging process greatly improves the overall detection rate.

Creating a Test Environment

There are two important sets of issues concerned with creating a test environment: hardware issues and people issues. When testing an application, you should test it on the same hardware configuration that you plan to implement it on. If the application will run on a network, testing it on a standalone system can miss many of the potential problems related to record and file sharing.

N O T E You can simulate a multiuser environment even on standalone machines by opening multiple instances of VFP. Of course, having additional memory helps improve the performance of this technique. ▪

A similar problem occurs when the software must run in various display resolutions. The same "perfect" form on one display might have fields and labels that fall off the screen when run with different display options.

 Visual FoxPro gives some help in this regard. Choose Tools, Options from the system menu. On the Forms tab, use the Maximum design area combo box to select the resolution in which your application will run.

It is important to use real data to test the system when it nears completion. For that reason, a recommended mode of development creates and implements those modules needed to collect data first. Then users can begin using them to enter real data. This data can then serve as test data for subsequent development.

Of course, all development should occur physically separated from a live system and live data. If your new system is replacing an old one, you can continue the testing phase even after implementation by maintaining a parallel environment, including a duplicate set of live data files. This enables you to compare results from your new system against output as it is currently produced.

In spite of precautions, errors can occur during development that could destroy live data. For example, you could mistakenly enter the path of the live data rather than the test data and ZAP it. This also means that you should periodically back up even your test data and test programs.

Not everyone is good at testing. In fact, some people enjoy testing more than others. (These are often the same people who enjoy bureaucratic detail such as income tax forms.) Often the developers of an application make the worst testers. They know the program too well and tend to enter only correct data and keystrokes. They subconsciously don't want to make their own program fail, even if consciously they recognize the need for testing. They also don't necessarily approach the application the same way a user might. So, in order to improve an application's robustness, it is important to assign the task of testing to others besides those who created it.

On the other hand, other staff members might not have the emotional attachment to a program and therefore appear ruthless in their testing. Although "ruthless" testers might find more problems, they must exercise tact in discussing them with the developer. After all, a program is the product of someone's creativity, and you do not want to suppress that. Developers can assist the process by not taking it personally when testers uncover bugs. In order to succeed, testers and developers must maintain a mutual goal of making the application stronger.

Furthermore, Visual FoxPro provides many different ways to perform a task. Therefore, don't criticize a person's methods just because you might do it differently. If a better, more efficient way exists to perform a task, find a way to show the other developers how it is better. Help them to learn, don't force them to learn.

Defining Test Cases That Exercise All Program Paths

Test data can consist of *white box testing* or *black box testing*. White box testing thoroughly checks all program paths. Because it requires knowing the logic of the program, it is also called *logic-driven testing*. Black box testing requires no knowledge of the program logic. It just gathers test data and runs it. There is no inherent assumption that the test data actually tests all the program paths because the paths are not known.

A side benefit of creating white box test data is the need to review the program carefully to identify these paths. This process often uncovers problems even before testing begins. There are two goals with white box testing:

- Identify and test all defined paths required for the application.
- Ensure that no possible path is missing or unaccounted for by the application.

Defining Test Cases Using Copies of Real Data

Whenever programmers try to "generate" test data, they almost always, without fail, miss at least one special case. For that reason, a random sample of real data generally provides just as good a test of the real operating environment. Thus, you should try to collect real data as early in the project as possible.

The best way to do this in a completely new system is to develop data entry forms or other programs that collect data with minimal functionality as early as possible. The Form Designer makes this relatively painless. Forms should include at least minimal data validation but might not include all look-up tables, context-sensitive help, or other advanced features implemented through custom methods. Alternatively, if this is a rewrite, conversion, or extension of an existing application, you must find a way to convert existing data to the format your new modules will expect. This probably means writing a data export routine that will create new versions of files for you to work with while leaving the existing ones in place.

If the application involves several processes, the task of collecting real data becomes more complex. In a real system, the processing of data takes place continuously. Therefore, you really need to capture an instantaneous snapshot of the data. Any time delay that enables users to process data could cause the data to be unsynchronized. This causes false errors (errors due to bad data, not due to program logic) when testing the program. Significant time can be lost tracking down and resolving these "false" errors. If possible, collect a copy of live data from all tables when no one else is on the system, such as at 3:00 a.m.

Documenting Test Cases

If you just randomly run test cases, you really don't know how thoroughly they test the procedure or application. Not only do you need to know how thoroughly the cases cover all possible program paths, you need to know what each case tests. Documenting test cases provides historical case results to compare future changes to the application against.

> **N O T E** Although not specifically designed for Visual FoxPro, it is possible to create a series of scripts to test your application with Microsoft Test. ∎

Testing is so important that the IEEE (Institute of Electrical and Electronic Engineers) has developed standards for documenting tests. They are summarized in the following list:

- Identify the test case, its purpose, and what features it tests.
- Identify features not involved in the test.
- Identify any requirements for the test (such as data files, indexes, relations, drivers, and so on).
- Identify any additional hardware or software requirements. For example, OLE tests require other programs, such as Excel, Word, or Mail.
- Identify any assumptions made in the test (such as minimum memory, hard disk requirements, and available floppy drives).

- Identify the steps needed to run the test.

- Identify the criteria for what constitutes passing or failing the test.

- Identify where the tester might want to suspend execution to examine the program path or variable values.

- Identify any conditions that could cause the program to stop prematurely and detail what the tester should do at that point.

- Maintain a history of tests performed for each case, who performed it, the results, and any corrective action made to the code.

- Make an estimate of the amount of time needed to set up and perform the test. After running the test, document the actual times.

Using Additional Testing Guidelines

Following are some additional testing guidelines:

- Test early and test often. Basically, this means test code at the lowest level possible. If you use the Expression Builder, always click the Verify button to check the expression's syntax. If you are building custom classes, build a small driver program or form to test them before using them in an application. Test individual procedures and functions. Create macros to test interactive elements such as menu selections and form behavior.

- Create a flow chart to diagram the major program paths.

- Identify calculations that require special consideration to test more thoroughly. For example, a routine that calculates the number of workdays between any two dates has more complexity than a calculation of total days between two dates. This routine can be made even more complex if it considers the effect of holidays.

- Be able to verify test results by some other independent means. This requires either the capability to perform the calculation by hand or to compare it to other results.

- Use generalized routines and class libraries as much as possible. After these are developed and tested, you need not test them again unless you change them. This saves considerable time that you can invest in other parts of the program.

Also, examine each input field and determine whether it needs any of the following:

- A default

- A picture clause

- Special formatting

- A lookup option

- Special validation or range checking

 TIP   If you are going to require this same type of input field in more than one place in your application, consider making it a class.

Asking Questions During Testing

Although it might never be possible to absolutely guarantee that you have found all errors, by asking several questions about each module you write, you can minimize the number of errors. The following list provides just a few of the possible questions you might ask. Over time, you'll undoubtedly expand this list with your own questions.

- Examine the relations between fields. Do some fields require information from others, thus making the entry order important?
- Should the user be able to exit an incomplete form? If so, what happens to the data?
- What does the program do if a required program does not exist? If a required index does not exist? If a form or report does not exist?
- Where does the program expect to find data tables?

 TIP Remember that even if there is only one location for data, it's not a good idea to hard-code this path throughout the program. At the very least, you will want to maintain a separate location for test files. Devise a method to inform the program which path you expect it to use each time you run it.

- Must the user define the SET commands before running the program? If so, how? For example, do you know that in VFP, many of the SET commands are scoped to the current DATASESSION? This means that each form can support its own SET environment by simply setting its DataSession property to 2 (private data session).

Understanding Methods for Tracking Down Errors

Despite all the preceding preparation to avoid common errors and the development of test sets, errors still happen. Your first priority when an error occurs is to find it and fix it. You can later go back to your test cases to determine why they didn't discover it in the first place.

When an error occurs during program execution, Visual FoxPro displays an error box with a simple error message. Beneath the message, it has four buttons: Cancel, Suspend, Ignore, and Help. Most of the time, you do not want to ignore an error. If you write programs for other users, you never want them to ignore an error. In fact, you probably don't want them to see this default error message. Rather, you want to trap all errors with your own error handler, which documents the system at the time of the error and gracefully exits the application.

As is true of any rule, however, there might be a few exceptions. If the program fails because it cannot find a particular bitmap on the system where it's currently running, you might be willing to ignore that error. Most other errors you cannot ignore. If VFP cannot locate a table, ignoring the problem does not enable the program to run anyway. It needs that table for a reason. So just document the problem and quit the program.

As a developer, you will find that Suspend is a valuable option during testing. It stops program execution without removing current variables from memory. Any tables currently open remain open with their record pointers in place. Most important, you can then open the Trace window of the debugger. The Trace window displays the source code being executed, highlighting the current line. While suspended, time stops for the application, enabling you to examine details of the program and its variables. You can even use the Trace window to execute the program line-by-line.

Visual FoxPro includes several built-in functions to provide clues when errors occur. To use them, you must interrupt the default error handling of Visual FoxPro. Rather than display a sometimes cryptic message to the user, you want to pass control to an error-handling routine. Listing 23.6 shows a simple error routine that you should consider. It displays a little more information than the standard error window by using a multiline Wait window. You could use the same approach to log errors, along with some user identification, to a file instead of onscreen. That way you can review the entries to get a better picture of how frequently, and how universally, the errors occur. The user information enables you to track down who is having the problem so that you can get more information about what they were doing at the time.

Listing 23.6   23CODE06.PRG—A Routine to Move Beyond the Standard Error Window to a More Informative Approach

```
ON ERROR DO ErrLog WITH ;
    ERROR(), MESSAGE(), MESSAGE(1), LINENO(1), PROGRAM()
** Rest of the application **

PROCEDURE ErrLog
LPARAMETER lnErrorNo, lcMessage, lcErrorLine, ;
           lcErrLineNo, lcModule
  WAIT WINDOW ;
    'An error has occurred in: ' + lcModule + CHR(13) + ;
    'ERROR: ' + STR(lnErrorNo, 6) + ' ' + lcMessage + CHR(13) + ;
    'On Line: ' + STR(lcErrLineNo, 6) + ' ' + lcErrorLine
RETURN
```

The ERROR() function returns a number that represents the error. The appendix in the Developer's Guide lists all error numbers along with a brief description, as does the Error Messages section of VFP's online Help.

Perhaps more useful is the MESSAGE() function. When used without a parameter, MESSAGE returns an error message associated with the error. This message is usually the same one that appears in the Error dialog box displayed by Visual FoxPro. As a bonus, MESSAGE(1) returns the program line that caused the error.

The function LINENO() returns the program line number that suspended the program. By default, this line number is relative to the first line of the main program. Because a typical application calls many procedures and functions, this value has less importance than the one returned by LINENO(1). This function returns the line number from the beginning of the current program or procedure. Use this value when editing a program by opening the Edit pull-down menu and selecting Go to Line. After entering the line number at the prompt, the editor places the insert cursor at the beginning of the error line. The default Visual FoxPro text editor can display line numbers if you check Show Line/Column Position in the dialog that appears when you select Edit, Properties. If you want to see line numbers in the Trace window, select Tools, Options, Debug and choose the Trace option button.

PROGRAM(lnLevel) returns the name of the executing program if lnLevel is 0, and the main program if it equals 1. It reports deeper call levels as the value of lnLevel increases until it returns an empty string. Visual FoxPro supports nested program calls up to 128 levels deep. This function is similar to SYS(16) except that SYS(16) also includes the path. When the error occurs in a procedure or function, SYS(16) begins with its name. Then it displays the path and the parent program name.

SYS(16,lnLevel) also supports a second parameter that tells it to print the program names at a specific level in the calling sequence. If lnLevel is equal to zero, the function returns the name of the currently executing program. An lnLevel value of 1 begins with the main program. Sequential values step through the procedure calling sequence until reaching the procedure or function containing the error. At that point, subsequent values of the parameter return an empty string. The code that follows traces the calling sequence up to the error:

```
lnLevel = 1
DO WHILE !EMPTY(SYS(16, lnLevel))
  ? SYS(16, lnLevel)
  lnLevel = lnLevel + 1
ENDDO
```

Testing Errors While Suspended

The most obvious place to start tracking down reasons for an error is at the point where the program fails. You might not know exactly where that point is, but you probably have a good idea of which routine is giving you a problem. Maybe you see a hard crash every time you enter data into a particular field or click a certain button on the form. Or it might be more subtle than that. Maybe the crash occurs while you're closing the form, and parenthetically, saving data and cleaning up from previous tasks.

The first thing to do is run the program up to a point as close to the failure as you can get and then suspend execution. You accomplish suspension in any of a variety of ways. Many developers set up a hotkey that enables them a backdoor into debugging mode. A command such as the following enables you to suspend your program even at points that don't appear interruptible—for example, when you are in a "wait state" because the current command is READ EVENTS:

```
ON KEY LABEL F12 SUSPEND
```

If you are successful in getting to a point where things have not yet gone off track, you will have an environment with all memory variables and tables intact and open. You can then use the Command window, the View window, and the debugger to display all sorts of information to lead you to the error.

You can print things such as variable values to the screen, checking for undefined or unusual types. If you find an undefined variable, you at least know what to look for. You can examine the code preceding the current line for any clues as to why the variable has not been defined.

Remember to issue an `ACTIVATE SCREEN` command before displaying any values on the desktop. The default for commands such as `DISPLAY MEMORY`, `DISPLAY STATUS`, and `?lcVariable` is to use the currently active output window, which is probably one of your application's screens.

Prominent West Coast developer Ken Levy is credited with first coming up with this trick: Place an `ACTIVATE SCREEN` command in the `Deactivate()` method of the highest-level `Form` class. This enables all forms in your system to inherit the behavior. And the command keeps you from trashing your application forms while suspended.

If all the variables look correct, you can enter and test the line that failed. If the line contains a complex expression, test portions of it to determine where it fails. If you find a simple error, it might be possible to correct and test it while you are still in the Command window.

 Copying and pasting ensures that you don't add new syntax errors by retyping lines.

Suppose that the expression looks correct and all variables are defined, but the line still fails. You might have the wrong syntax for a function, be missing a parenthesis, or have some other syntax error. In this case, use FoxPro's online help to check the proper syntax for any command or function.

 To get fast help on a Visual FoxPro command or function, highlight it in the program edit or Command window and press the F1 key.

Bring Up the Data Session Window   There are a lot of things you can do while your program is suspended. You can bring up the Data Session window (known as the View window in FoxPro 2.x) and check out much of the data picture through it. You can browse files, check sort orders, inspect structure, and even open additional files.

 If the system menu has been replaced by an application menu, you might not have access to Window, Data Session. If that's the case, simply enter `SET` in the Command window.

You might be surprised to see unexpected files or even no files at all listed in the window when it first appears. Chances are you are looking at the environment for the default data session, but you have set up your form in a private data session. Check the entry in the drop-down list labeled Current Session. Pull down the list and select the one corresponding to your application form and you should see the expected files.

Tricks in the Command Window   VFP provides you with some extremely powerful new `SYS()` commands that you can use for debugging. In particular, `SYS(1270)` has become the darling of many developers of my acquaintance. To use it, position the mouse over something on the screen, and type the following in the Command window:

```
ox = SYS(1270)
```

The variable ox then contains an object reference to whatever was pointed to. That object can be a running form or a control on the form, depending on just what was under the mouse. Or, the object reference might be to a class or a form or a control in design mode. You can tell exactly what that reference is by typing **?ox.Name** in the Command window. If you're interested in something further up or down the containership hierarchy, reposition the mouse and reissue the SYS(1270) command.

So, why is this useful? After you have a reference to some object, you can find out anything you want about that object. You can check its ControlSource property, for example, to make sure you're getting data from the right place. Maybe you notice that the object just isn't behaving as you expect. Try displaying ox.ParentClass or ox.ClassLibrary to make sure you're working with the intended version. Better yet, you can change any enabled properties on the object, or fire events, simply by typing appropriate lines into the Command window, like this:

```
ox.AutoCenter = .T.
ox.Hide()
```

TIP   SYS(1270) is another command you might want to attach to a hotkey. Save yourself having to type it every time you want to change the object reference by instead typing the following line once:

ON KEY LABEL F11 ox = SYS(1270)

Break Down Complex Commands

Sometimes an error occurs in a section of code that you cannot test separately. BROWSE and SELECT statements often extend over many lines. When Visual FoxPro reports an error in these commands, it cannot tell you which line within the statement contains the error. For these long commands, it can be difficult to quickly spot the error. The SELECT statement that follows illustrates this situation with a complex SELECT that includes several tables as well as a union between two separate SELECTs:

```
SELECT A.cStoreId, A.cTicket, A.cItemId, A.nQuantity, ;
       A.nUnitPrice, A.nExtPrice, ;
       B.cEmplId, B.cCompanyId, B.cDeptNo, B.cBatch, ;
       B.dDate AS DATE, ;
       C.cCenterNo, D.cLastName, ;
       LEFT(E.cProdDesc,25) as ProdDesc, ;
       G.cCoName, H.cDeptName ;
   FROM TKTDETL A, TICKET B,  CENTERS C, CUSTOMER D, ;
       PRODUCT E, COMPANY G, DEPARTMT H ;
  WHERE A.cStoreId+A.cTicket = B.cStoreId+B.cTicket AND ;
       A.cStoreId+A.cTicket+A.cItemId = ;
       C.cStoreId+C.cTicket+C.cItemId AND ;
       &FiltStr1 ;
  UNION ALL ;
SELECT A.cStoreId, A.cTicket, A.cItemId, A.nQuantity, ;
       A.nUnitPrice, A.nExtPrice, ;
       B.cEmplId, B.cCompanyId, B.cDeptNo, B.cBatch, ;
       B.dDate AS DATE, ;
       SPACE(10) AS cCenterNo, D.cLastName, ;
       LEFT(E.cProdDesc,25) as ProdDesc, ;
       G.cCoName, H.cDeptName ;
```

```
   FROM TKTDETL A, TICKET B,  CUSTOMER D, ;
        PRODUCT E, COMPANY G, DEPARTMT H ;
  WHERE A.cStoreId+A.cTicket = B.cStoreId+B.cTicket AND ;
        A.cStoreId+A.cTicket NOT IN ;
           (SELECT F.cStoreId+F.cTicket from CENTERS F) AND ;
        &FiltStr2 ;
  INTO CURSOR MPA
```

Debugging a SELECT statement this complex is difficult without taking advantage of another technique called *code reduction* or *decomposition*. The purpose of code reduction is to reduce the amount of code used in a test. In this case, an obvious first attempt at reducing the test code is to split the individual SELECT statements and test each one separately. After you determine which SELECT statement causes the error, you can remove additional code from it until it finally works. With a SELECT, further reduction can mean removing one table at a time along with its related fields and relations. Or, you could begin by removing sorts or groupings. With any method you choose, at some point the SELECT statement begins to work. It is then a relatively simple matter to determine what is wrong with the code just removed.

After finding and correcting an error, you can proceed in several ways. You could take a pessimistic approach and incrementally rebuild the SELECT one table or feature at a time making sure it continues to work. Or you could take an optimistic approach and test the changes in the original complete SELECT statement. Of course, there are levels in between. In this case, you might want to test the individual SELECT statement with the correction before copying it back into the union.

You can apply this same approach to any code, not just single commands like SELECT. Take any program or procedure that does not work and comment out functionality until it does. Whatever you mark as comments probably contains the error.

Clues in the Code

A review of recent program changes provides another good clue to an error's cause. The most likely place to look when an error occurs in an existing program that ran fine previously is in any recent code changes. This is not a guarantee. After all, the error might reside in a code path that was not executed before. However, it is a good place to begin.

This brings up another point. When you make changes to your programs, it's a good idea to leave the old code in place for reference, at least until you're certain that the replacement code runs correctly. Of course, you don't want the program to run both the old and the new code. You should insert a comment identifying the nature of the change and comment out the old code.

N O T E   Although you can comment out individual program lines by adding an asterisk in front of each one, this can become tedious for blocks of code. As a shortcut, select the lines of code you want to comment by clicking the mouse at the beginning of the first line and dragging through the lines to highlight everything you want to skip. Then choose Format, Comment from the system menu or right-click and choose Comment.

Another way to handle this is to bracket the unwanted code with IF .F.…ENDIF. Because the expression .F. (False) is never true, the block of code will not be executed. ■

Adding Wait Windows or Other Printed Output

Not all errors point to obvious lines of code. Sometimes a logic error originates in an entirely different section of the code from where the program finally fails or displays erratic behavior. In these cases, you need to spot check the program's activity at various points.

One way to check a program's path is to embed WAIT statements throughout the code using the following format:

```
WAIT WINDOW 'Beginning of PROCEDURE COPYDATA' NOWAIT
```

Every time execution passes a statement like this, a Wait window appears in the upper-right corner. The NOWAIT option enables the program to continue without pausing. (If you want the program to pause, skip the NOWAIT option or use the MESSAGEBOX() function with only the first argument to display a message.) Adding WAIT statements has an additional advantage for programs that perform extensive background processing. Even when used in a production environment, they assure the user that the program is still executing. Users who think a program has stopped might reboot the computer, which can lead to data corruption.

Part

VI

Ch

23

You can also halt the program at any point with the SUSPEND command or add commands to print or list information about the program such as those shown in Listing 23.7.

Listing 23.7 23CODE07.PRG—Commands to Output Information About the Current Program State

```
lcMemFile  = 'MEM' + LEFT(CTOD(DATE()),2) + ;
             SUBSTR(CTOD(DATE()), 4, 2) + '.TXT'
lcStatFile = 'STAT' + LEFT(CTOD(DATE()),2) + ;
             SUBSTR(CTOD(DATE()), 4, 2) + '.TXT'
LIST MEMORY TO FILE &lcMemFile
LIST STATUS TO FILE &lcStatFile
```

Of course, you don't want these commands to execute every time a user runs the program. If you enter them as shown previously, there is a high risk that you will forget and leave them in the final user version. Because users do not need to see this output, you might want to bracket these commands with an IF…ENDIF such as the following:

```
IF glDebugMode
     << Place any debug command here >>
ENDIF
```

You could then initialize the variable glDebugMode at the beginning of the program to turn these commands on or off. By using a variable and defining it in the main program, you need to change and compile only one routine to turn these statements on. A better technique stores the value for glDebugMode outside the program, perhaps in a configuration table or memory variable file. Then you can activate the debug mode without having to recompile the system at all.

Even when these commands are inactive, they require memory, both for the additional program lines and the memory variable. An alternative uses the #DEFINE and #IF…#ENDIF directives to include or exclude the debug code at compile time.

```
#DEFINE glDebugMode .T.
#IF glDebugMode
   << Place any debug commands here >>
#ENDIF
```

Asserts

A variation on the idea of displaying information in windows throughout the application is to use a feature that was introduced in VFP 5. Instead of WAIT WINDOW or MESSAGEBOX() calls, code ASSERT commands at strategic points using this syntax:

```
ASSERT lExpression MESSAGE cMessageText
```

When the program encounters this command, it evaluates the expression you've coded. If the expression is True, execution continues. If it evaluates to False, VFP displays your message in a dialog box with the options Debug, Cancel, Ignore, and Ignore All. Your message is optional. If you omit it, VFP issues a default: Assertion failed on line *n* of procedure *cProcedureName*.

There's a catch. In order to get VFP to test your assertions, you must issue SET ASSERTS ON. Maybe you've tested the code extensively and you're pretty certain it's working as expected. You can leave the individual ASSERT commands in place and simply issue SET ASSERTS OFF to keep your program from having to continue running through the assertion tests each time.

 Put ASSERT commands in logic paths you believe will never be reached. This might be an OTHERWISE in a DO CASE...ENDDO where you believe all conditions are accounted for, like this:

```
DO CASE
   CASE eCondition1
      < Statements >
   CASE eCondition2
      < Statements >
   CASE eCondition3
      < Statements >
   OTHERWISE
      * I should never get here…
      ASSERT .F.     && But if I do, I'm covered!

ENDCASE
```

 When you have reason to believe that your code is straying into places it shouldn't be, simply use SET ASSERTS ON before running the program.

The Debugger

Visual FoxPro provides an excellent tool called the *debugger*, which actually consists of a series of tools. One of these is the familiar Trace window used in previous versions. This window is joined by the Watch, Locals, Call Stack, and Debug Output windows. The Watch window resembles the Debug window of previous versions, but it has a few significant enhancements.

See Chapter 1, "Quick Review of the Visual FoxPro Interface," for information on setting up the debugger. If you configure the new debugger to be housed in its own environment, the Debug Frame, you will see something like Figure 23.1 when you start the debugger.

FIGURE 23.1
The Visual FoxPro debugger in its own frame with `TasTrade` running. All the windows are docked, like toolbars, against each other.

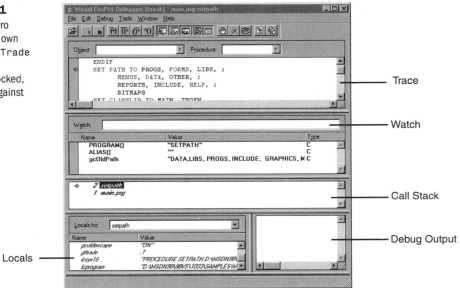

Of course, you are not limited to keeping the debugger in its own frame or to having the individual windows docked. You configure the first option in VFP itself via Tools, Options, Debug. Choose FoxPro Frame in the Environment drop-down list to keep all the debugging windows within the VFP desktop. In this case you are free to open any or all of its individual windows as you see fit.

N O T E You can only change your choice of debugging environment when the debugger is not active. ▪

 When you configure the debugger to be in its own frame, you are less likely to encounter situations in which VFP confuses the debugging windows with its open application windows. This problem was prevalent with the debugger in all releases of FoxPro prior to VFP 5. It caused actions in the Trace and Debug windows to be intermixed with application events.

 When the debugger is in its own frame, it can seem to disappear when your VFP application is active. It has not closed. The window that currently has focus might simply be covering it. You can switch between FoxPro and the debugger using any of the methods for switching among Windows applications, such as Alt+Tab.

If you right-click any of the five windows, you see a context-sensitive menu appropriate to that window. All five allow you to enable *docking view*. When checked, you should be able to position that window alongside any of the four walls of its frame, adjacent to any of the other debug windows, or docked to another toolbar.

Using the Trace Window   The debugger provides the Trace window, a powerful tool, to debug code. Trace opens a window that displays the program's commands as they execute. It also enables you to step through the program one command at a time so that you can see the exact path being followed. Figure 23.2 shows a typical Trace window.

FIGURE 23.2

The Trace window shows code from `TasTrade` and a breakpoint set on the highlighted line.

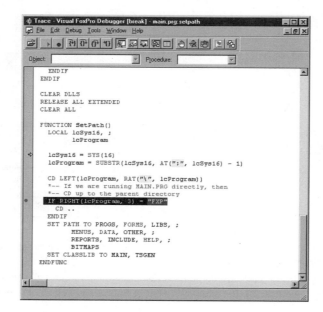

There are several ways to enter Trace mode. One way is to place the command

```
SET STEP ON
```

in the code, recompile the program, and run it. When the program executes this command, it stops and displays a Trace window. Early in the debug process, you might be tempted to put this command throughout the program. As with SUSPEND or hard-coded print statements, the danger is in forgetting to remove one or more of them.

Another way to open the Trace window is to select Debugger from the Tools menu, or simply enter **DEBUG** in the Command window before executing the program. This opens the debugger, from which you can open the Trace window. If it is not already open, open the Trace window by selecting Windows, Trace or by clicking the Trace button in the toolbar. Notice that the Trace window activates other options in the debugger's menu bar. Figure 23.3 defines the toolbar buttons.

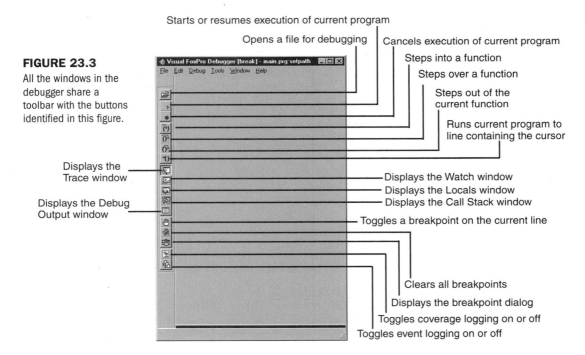

FIGURE 23.3

All the windows in the debugger share a toolbar with the buttons identified in this figure.

Starts or resumes execution of current program

Opens a file for debugging

Cancels execution of current program

Steps into a function

Steps over a function

Steps out of the current function

Runs current program to line containing the cursor

Displays the Trace window

Displays the Debug Output window

Displays the Watch window

Displays the Locals window

Displays the Call Stack window

Toggles a breakpoint on the current line

Clears all breakpoints

Displays the breakpoint dialog

Toggles coverage logging on or off

Toggles event logging on or off

To select an application or program, choose File, Open. This displays the Open dialog box. By default, it shows .PRG, .FXP, and .MPR files in the current directory. It also shows .APP and .EXE files. If you select an .APP file, a dialog box appears so that you can select a program from within the application. If only .FXP files can be found for the application, they are shown with dimmed text, because they cannot be used in the Trace window. You must have access to the source files.

Activating and Deactivating Debugger Windows

If the Visual FoxPro debugger window is open, you also can open the Trace window with the command

```
ACTIVATE WINDOW TRACE
```

and close it with

```
DEACTIVATE WINDOW TRACE
```

Similarly, you can open the other debugger windows with the commands

```
ACTIVATE WINDOW WATCH
ACTIVATE WINDOW LOCALS
ACTIVATE WINDOW "CALL STACK"    && or ACTIVATE WINDOW Call
ACTIVATE WINDOW "DEBUG OUTPUT"  && or ACTIVATE WINDOW Debug
```

and close them with

```
DEACTIVATE WINDOW WATCH
DEACTIVATE WINDOW LOCALS
DEACTIVATE WINDOW "CALL STACK"    && DEACTIVATE WINDOW Call
DEACTIVATE WINDOW "DEBUG OUTPUT" && DEACTIVATE WINDOW Debug
```

You can even deactivate the debugger window itself, as follows:

```
DEACTIVATE WINDOW "Visual FoxPro Debugger"
```

Because deactivating a window does not remove it from memory, you can reactivate it with the following:

```
ACTIVATE WINDOW "Visual FoxPro Debugger"
```

Or simply type:

```
DEBUG
```

If you select a program (.PRG) file, Visual FoxPro displays the source code in the Trace window. Notice that the Trace window also supports syntax coloring, just like the editor.

After selecting a program or application module, use the vertical scrollbar to display different lines of the module. If the line is wider than the width of the Trace window, you can scroll horizontally to see it all.

N O T E This capability to horizontally scroll the Trace window is great, but you should still try to limit the length of each line to the width of the editor window (assuming that the window is as wide as possible on your screen). Long lines are harder to read onscreen because of the need to keep switching from the vertical scrollbar to the horizontal one. Similarly, printed listings of the code with long lines are difficult to read. If you have a long command, split it across several lines by ending each line, except the last, with a semicolon. This punctuation tells Visual FoxPro that the command continues on the next line. ■

To mark a line with a *breakpoint*, double-click in the shaded margin bar next to the line or place the cursor anywhere in it and press the Spacebar. You can also use the Toggle breakpoint button in the toolbar after selecting the line. If the line is an executable line, Visual FoxPro places a red circle to the immediate left of the line in the shaded margin bar, which serves as a visual reminder of the breakpoint. If you click a comment line, Visual FoxPro marks the next executable line after the comment. If you click one of a command's continuation lines, VFP marks the current command with the breakpoint. The circle is always placed on the last line of continuation lines.

Mark as many breakpoints as you need. Each time the program reaches a breakpoint, it treats it like a SUSPEND statement in the program and interrupts execution. It does not cancel the program. If you mark the wrong line, simply double-click it again (or highlight it and press Enter) to remove the mark.

While the program is suspended during a breakpoint, you can do any of the following:

- Read forward or backward through the code using the scrollbar.
- Choose to view a different object or routine using list boxes in the Trace or Locals window headers or point to a different procedure in the Call Stack.
- Open the Data Session window to check the status of open files, their indexes, current record status, or even browse the data.
- Enter commands in the Command window.
- Select options from the main menu.
- Check or change the current value of any memory or table variable.
- View the contents of entire arrays and change individual cells if necessary.
- See the hierarchy of routines that has called the currently running procedure.
- Change statement execution order.

The one thing you cannot do is change the executing program's source code.

The new debugger is extremely powerful in what it enables you to change while your application is still active. Make changes with caution, however, because you can easily leave the environment in a compromised state from which it can't recover. If you move a record pointer or change the current work area, for example, you must return everything to its original state. Otherwise, attempts to resume stepping through the program could fail. If you change the contents of memory, you might inadvertently leave out other settings that your program expects to go along with that value.

If you want to trace an application, but do not want to set a breakpoint, just click the OK button when VFP displays the application module list. Visual FoxPro always begins execution of an application from the main module regardless of which module appears in the Trace window.

When you finish debugging your application, you need to remove all breakpoints. You can do this one breakpoint at a time in the Trace window. A more efficient method uses the Clear All Breakpoints toolbar button, which removes all breakpoints from the entire application. This saves you from the trouble of having to remember where you set breakpoints. After making a change to a module, Visual FoxPro recompiles it before running it. Recompilation removes breakpoints. Therefore, you might have to mark them again.

The Debug menu contains an option, Throttle, that controls the length of a pause between each executed line. The default of 0 means that there is no delay. This does not mean that programs executing with the Trace window active run at the same speed as a normal program. In fact, their speed is greatly reduced. The video drivers cannot keep up with the speed at which Visual FoxPro usually executes code. However, you still might not be able to follow even this reduced pace. Therefore, you can increase the delay between each command from 0 to 5 seconds. While the trace is running, you can cut the speed in half by pressing any of the following buttons:

Ctrl

Shift

A mouse button

To cut it in half again, press any two of these at the same time.

NOTE You can also set the throttle by changing the value of the system memory variable _THROTTLE, as in:

```
_Throttle = 1.0
```

The value again represents seconds and can range from 0 to 5, with 0 meaning no pause between executing lines. ■

If you click the Resume button in the toolbar, select Debug, Resume, or press F5, the program begins execution. Visual FoxPro highlights each code line in the Trace window as it executes. Of course, unless you can speed-read program code, you probably cannot keep up with it without increasing the Throttle value.

You can interrupt program execution while the Trace window is open by pressing the Esc key as long as SET ESCAPE is not OFF. You can set this feature by checking Cancel Programs on Escape in the General tab of Tools, Options. This feature is useful to stop Trace mode without running the entire program.

 TIP Strongly consider adding the command SET ESCAPE OFF before distributing the application. This prevents users from aborting a program prematurely by pressing Esc.

While you are tracing a program, the toolbar provides four ways to step through your code, each with a keyboard alternative:

Steps into a function (F8)

Steps over a function (F6)

Steps out of the current function (Shift+F7)

Runs current program to line containing the cursor (F7)

The most used toolbar button is the Step Into button. It tells Visual FoxPro to execute the next line of the code and then to pause again. Use it to step through a program one line at a time at your own pace. At any time, you can stop to check variables or tables. To continue, activate the Trace window and click this button again. If the next line happens to be a call to a procedure or function, Trace continues stepping through the code in that procedure or function.

If you want to step through code only in the current procedure and not trace a procedure or function call, click the Step Over button. This tells VFP to execute the procedure or function, but not to trace the code. If you accidentally step into a procedure or function, use the Step Out button to execute the rest of the code in the current procedure or function and then return to trace mode when it returns to the calling program.

Another way to execute a block of code without tracing through it is to place the cursor in the line where you want to begin tracing again and then click the Run to Cursor button to execute the code without tracing until it reaches the line with the cursor. Note that if you do not select carefully, you could select a line that is not executed due to program loops or conditional statements. Thus, the program will not suspend again.

If you decide to stop tracing the code but want to finish executing it, click the Resume button. It tells Visual FoxPro to continue executing the program until it encounters either another breakpoint or reaches the end of the program. Click this option after stepping through a suspected problem area to complete the program normally. You also can terminate the program by clicking the Cancel button or by selecting Cancel from the Debug menu.

A new feature is the capability to set the next executable line while in trace mode. Normally, FoxPro executes each line one after the other sequentially. Only conditional statements, loops, and function/procedure calls change this sequential execution of code. Suppose, however, that you are testing a program that suspends due to an error in a line. You might not be able to change the line to correct it (with the Debug Fix option) without canceling the program. Suppose that you can enter the correct command line through the Command window and then change the program line pointer to skip the problem line to continue execution without having to cancel the program. That is exactly how you can use the Set Next Statement option in the Debug menu. Just remember to go back and correct the program line later before running it again.

 Another use for the Set Next Statement feature is the capability to bypass unwanted settings. For example, some routines set THISFORM.LockScreen = .T. while they manipulate a lot of information on the current form. VFP continues its processing, without stopping to refresh the display, until it encounters a THISFORM.LockScreen = .F. command. This makes the screen display appear snappier, but it makes debugging more difficult because you don't see any of the changes as they are taking place. Use the debugger to change the execution path and go around the LockScreen = .T. setting.

Another new feature is the Breakpoints dialog box. Click the third toolbar button from the right or select Breakpoints from the Tools menu. This displays the dialog box shown in Figure 23.4.

FIGURE 23.4

The Breakpoints dialog box enables you to define four types of breakpoints: two based on a program line and two based on expression values.

This dialog box defines options for each breakpoint. Notice the list box at the bottom of the dialog box. It lists all the breakpoints in the current module. Initially, no breakpoints are selected. Click one to see information about it.

The Location text box begins with the name of the program or function that contains the breakpoint and the line number from the beginning of that program or function. The File text box displays the name of the file where the program, procedure, or function is found. This includes the full path.

If you added the breakpoint by double-clicking to the left of the line or by using the Breakpoint toolbar button, the default breakpoint type is Break at Location. This means that the program merely pauses execution when it encounters this line. You have other options, however.

Even with the default breakpoint type, you can specify the Pass Count at which trace begins. Suppose that you have an error inside of a loop. You know that the first 100 times through the loop, the calculation is valid; however, an error occurs shortly after that. You certainly don't want to step through the loop 100 times before reaching the error. An easier way is to set Pass count to 100. This tells the debugger to start trace mode only after it has reached the 100th pass through the loop.

You can change the breakpoint type by opening the Type drop-down list. The options include the following:

> Break at Location
>
> Break at Location if Expression Is True
>
> Break When Expression Is True
>
> Break When Expression Has Changed

The second option is similar to the first but relies on an expression value rather than a pass count. For example, you might know that the error occurs when a specific variable is set to a specific value, but you don't know in which pass. Suppose that the variable TOTAL is zero when the expression attempts to use it as the dividend in an equation. Dividing by zero is not allowed. Therefore, you might want to set a breakpoint on the equation but set the expression to

TOTAL = 0. Note that you can also use the Expression builder button to the right of the field to help build the necessary expression.

Perhaps you would rather know when the variable TOTAL is set to zero. In this case, change the breakpoint type to Break When Expression Is True. Enter the expression TOTAL = 0 again and then click the Add button along the bottom right of the dialog box. This adds a new breakpoint to the list, but one that is not represented by a specific line in a specific code module. This option is equivalent to the way breakpoints were set to debug expressions in previous versions of FoxPro and Visual FoxPro.

Similarly, you can use the type Break When Expression Has Changed to cause the program to enter trace mode when the value of the expression entered in the Expression text box changes. Again, this breakpoint type cannot be represented by a specific line in the code.

N O T E   If you set your breakpoint to fire when an expression has changed, it will also fire when it goes out of scope. It can be pretty annoying to have your program stop every time you enter another method when you are trying to track a local variable. ■

As you can see by the buttons in the bottom-right corner of the dialog box, you can also re-move individual breakpoints by selecting them and clicking the Remove button. A new feature is the capability to disable a breakpoint without removing it. Click the Disable button while a breakpoint is selected to toggle the disable feature. Notice that this adds and removes the check in the box before the breakpoint description in the list box. This makes it easy to add breakpoints and selectively turn them on and off. Finally, the Clear All button lets you remove all breakpoints. You can also clear breakpoints in the Watch window that you have set in that window.

> **CAUTION**
>
> Canceling a program while you are in trace mode can leave files and windows open, updates partially complete, and records and files locked. In addition, environment SET variables might have changed the environment and might not have been reset.

Using the Locals Window   The Locals window remains empty until you run the program. At that point, it displays all the variables as they are defined, along with their current value and type. This list is by procedure or function. So local, in this context, means all variables that are "seen" by the currently selected procedure or function. Figure 23.5 shows some of the local variables defined early in the execution of the Tastrade example.

As you can see in Figure 23.5, the Locals window also shows object variables. Notice also in the Trace window, at the top of the figure, that the cursor is on the variable luRetVal. Beneath the cursor is a ToolTip-like box with the current value of this variable. The Trace window lets you position the cursor over any variable in the code and display the value of that variable. Notice that this is the same variable and value that appears at the bottom of the Locals list. If your program is long and has dozens of defined variables, this ToolTip-type method of checking a variable value can be quite useful.

FIGURE 23.5

The Locals window
displays variables
currently in use by the
application, including
objects.

Back in the Locals window, the box with the + in it, before the variable name for an object,
indicates that you can open this object to look inside. In fact, if you click this box, you can open
the object to see the values for all its properties. If the object is a container object, you can see
the objects it contains. These, too, can be opened. In fact, you can drill down through as many
levels as you like to get to the base objects and their properties. Figure 23.6 shows three levels
open in one of the objects from Tastrade. If you examine this code further, you will find that
there are many more than three levels, and you can see them all.

The drop-down list at the top of the Locals window enables you to look at the variables available
in any of the procedures or functions that have executed. Just open the list and pick a different
procedure or function to see what variables it can "see." Global variables are seen in all procedures after they are defined. Private variables can be seen in the procedure in which they are
defined and any called procedures. Local variables can be seen only in the procedure in which
they are defined.

Using the Watch Window   Sometimes, you don't want to see all the variables. Rather, you
want to see only one or two to determine why they don't get the values you expect. Or maybe
you want to set an expression that is not in the Locals window variables list. In this case, it
makes more sense to use the Watch window. Simply enter the variable names in the Watch text
box, or if you prefer, you can drag variables or expressions directly from the Trace or Locals
windows to either part of the Watch window. When you enter each variable or expression, it
appears in the list below the text box. After VFP has enough information to calculate a value, it
is displayed in the second column, and its type appears in the third column. If the variable has
not yet been defined or it is out of scope, the message Expression could not be evaluated
appears in the Value column.

FIGURE 23.6

The Locals window lets you view the variables currently defined by the running application, including objects and their properties.

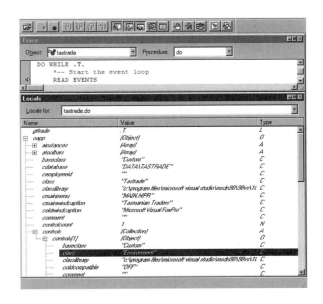

Figure 23.7 shows an example of this window using some of the fields from the Locals window. Notice that although the Locals window can look at any routine and what variables are defined there, the Watch window sees only the variables in the current procedure or function.

FIGURE 23.7

The Watch window makes it easier to monitor the values of a few selected variables and expressions.

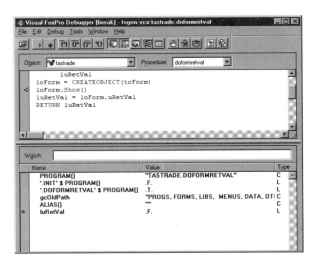

Note the circle in the left column next to the last watch variable. This shows another way to set a breakpoint on a variable. In this case, the program breaks whenever the value of `luRetVal` changes. To prove this, you can open the Breakpoints dialog box to see that the breakpoint appears in the list at the bottom of the dialog box.

The Watch window is also monitoring some expressions. You can set breakpoints on expressions as well as memory variables; for example, one that looks for a particular method name as part of the name of the current program.

Using the Call Stack Window   When you are executing an application, it is very easy to get lost in the number of procedure and function call levels. In fact, sometimes the problem is that the program is calling procedures or functions in a sequence different from what you expected. One way to determine exactly how the program got to the current line is to open the Call Stack window, as shown in Figure 23.8.

FIGURE 23.8

The Call Stack window shows the sequence of procedure and function calls from the start of the program (bottom) to the current one (top).

Just as the arrow in the Trace window shows the current line being executed, the arrow in the Call Stack window shows the currently executing procedure or function.

When you click any of the procedures or functions higher in the calling hierarchy, the debugger automatically changes the procedure looked at by the Locals window to show the variables known in that procedure. While you are looking at a procedure other than the current one, a black right-pointing arrow appears to the left of the procedure name. These changes do not affect which line is executed next.

Using the Debug Output Window   The Debug Output window displays character strings defined by the DEBUGOUT command. It also shows the names of system events that occur when event tracking is enabled.

The DEBUGOUT command has this syntax:

```
DEBUGOUT eExpression
```

This command can be placed in your program to print a string to the Debug Output window. Because output goes only to the Debug Output window, you can leave these commands in the code even when distributing the application to end users. Unless users have the full version of Visual FoxPro and have the Debug Output window of the debugger open, they will never know that these commands are there. Yet, any time you need to debug the application, you can simply open the Debug Output window to watch the values that print.

Typical uses of DEBUGOUT include:

■ Print the current value of any variable.

■ Print messages to indicate where the program is (at the beginning of procedures, object methods, and so on).

Using Event Tracking Sometimes, it helps to know in what order events are fired for different objects. The real secret to object-oriented programming is knowing what code to place in the methods of each event so that they execute in the correct order. Sometimes, when your program just isn't working right, the easiest way to determine whether you have code in the correct method is to turn on event tracking.

While in the debugger, select Tools, Event Tracking to display the Event Tracking dialog box, as shown in Figure 23.9.

FIGURE 23.9

The Event Tracking dialog box lets you determine which events should echo statements into the Debug Output window.

The top portion of this dialog box lets you select which events you want to track. By default, all events are preselected, but event tracking is not enabled. Remember to click the check box at the top of the dialog box to enable Event Tracking. To move an event from one list to the other, select it and then click one of the buttons between the two lists. You can also double-click an event to move it from one list to the other.

The bottom portion of the dialog box determines where VFP sends the output from event tracking. By default, the messages are sent to the Debug Output window of the debugger. For large programs, this list can get rather long, and you might want to send it to a file instead and use the FoxPro Editor to search for specific event occurrences. Figure 23.10 shows an example of the Debug Output window with several event tracking messages.

FIGURE 23.10

Use the Debug Output window along with Event Tracking to determine the order in which events fire and thus the optimal location to add custom code.

Using Coverage Profiler

VFP 6 comes with an all-new Coverage Profiler application. Making use of it is a multi-step process. First you have to turn Coverage Logging on by choosing Tools, Coverage Logging from the Debugger menu. You will be asked for a filename to store the raw data into, and whether you want to Append or Overwrite. Make your selections here, or with a SET COVERAGE TO command, and start up the application. When your application finishes, issue a SET COVER- AGE TO with no filename to stop sending raw data to the log file.

Next you have to start the Coverage Profiler application. Do this by selecting Tools, Coverage Profiler from the system menu or by typing the following command:

```
DO (_COVERAGE) WITH YourLogFileName
```

You should see a window split into three panes like the one shown in Figure 23.11.

In the upper-left pane are objects. In the upper-right pane you see the actual path to those objects. In the bottom pane is a listing of the method that fired for the highlighted object. The marks to the left of some of the lines of code indicate that those lines were not run. You can change the nature of the marks, and you can change whether they appear on lines that run or lines that are skipped. Make those option selections by clicking the Options toolbar button.

Instead of Coverage Mode, you could choose Profile Mode also by clicking a toolbar button. You would then see statistics about the number of hits alongside the program instructions, as shown in Figure 23.12.

VFP 5 had the beginnings of coverage analysis in it. You could turn coverage on and produce a stream of raw data about the runtime environment. It was up to you to parse and analyze those log files. VFP 6 has made many improvements to the process. It comes to you now as a fully realized, customizable application. But it also comes to you with all the components to modify, subclass, and re-create it, as shown in Table 23.3.

FIGURE 23.11
The Coverage Profiler application in Coverage Mode shows actual code from `TasTrade.app`, marking which instructions were and weren't run.

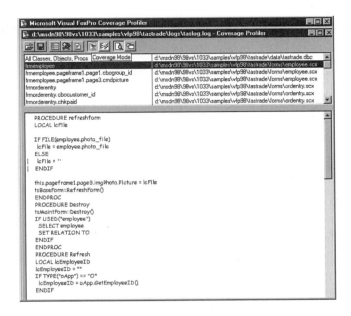

FIGURE 23.12
The new Coverage Profiler application in Profile Mode shows runtime statistics for `TasTrade.app`.

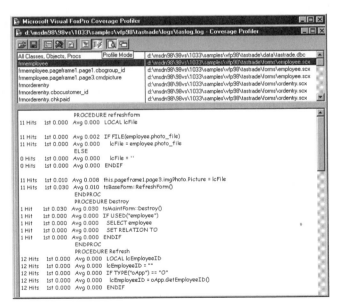

Table 23.3   Coverage Profiler Application Source Components

File	Description
Coverage.prg	A program to instantiate the object
Coverage.vcx/vct	Coverage Engine classes
Cov_Short.mnx/mnt	Shortcut menu
Cov_pjx.frx/frt	Default report
Coverage.h	Header file for all Coverage code
Graphics files	Various .ICO, .BMP, and .MSK files

Using Error Handlers

No amount of diligence in checking for common syntax, logic, or exception errors finds all errors. No amount of testing, even with the help of live data and the use of the debugger window, can guarantee an error-free program. Sometimes the application encounters a situation that you could not foresee and plan for. In many complex systems in use today, the number of combinations of possible data exceeds the national debt. Furthermore, no matter how foolproof you make a system, "fools" can be remarkably ingenious. It takes only one user to turn off the computer in the middle of a reindex to trash an entire file.

You have to accept the fact that at some point the program will fail. When it does, you do not want it to display a cryptic message to the user, who will probably just turn the machine off before calling you. At the very least, you want to direct the program to an error-handling routine using the ON ERROR trigger. The primary purpose of this error routine is to identify and probably record information about the error. This command redirects execution to the procedure ERRLOG:

```
ON ERROR DO errlog WITH ERROR(), MESSAGE(), MESSAGE(1), SYS(16), ;
    LINENO()
```

Once in the procedure, you can determine the error type by checking the error number.

There are three primary classes of errors from the user's standpoint. First are trivial errors. These include errors as simple as a printer or floppy drive that is not ready. In some cases, you can simply log the error and then skip the command causing the error and continue execution.

In other cases, a simple message to the user followed by a RETRY or RETURN command handles it. Examples of when to use this approach might be when the program attempts to read a file from a floppy drive and there is either no disk in the drive or the one the system is trying to write to is write-protected. A message to users telling them how to correct the situation along with a RETRY button makes sense here.

For another example, suppose that while using SKIP to move through records, you overshoot the end of file. Visual FoxPro reports this error as End of file encountered. More specifically, it is error number 4. There is no need to cancel the program for this type of error. To correct the problem, the program can simply reset the record pointer on the last record in the table. The version of procedure ErrLog shown in Listing 23.8 presents an outline of these techniques.

Listing 23.8 23CODE08.PRG—The ErrLog **Procedure to Handle End-of-File Situations**

```
****************
PROCEDURE ErrLog
LPARAMETERS lnErrorNo, lcMessage, lcErrorLine, ;
            lcmodule, lnErrorLineNo

* Check if beyond end of file, place on last record
  IF lnErrorNo = 4
    WAIT WINDOW 'AT LAST RECORD' TIMEOUT 2
    GOTO BOTTOM
  ELSE
    CANCEL
  ENDIF
RETURN
```

This example checks whether the error number equals 4. If so, it displays a window telling the user that it has moved the record pointer to the last record. It then exits the routine and re-turns to the line immediately after the one that caused the error. Presumably, this enables the program to continue executing. If any other error occurs, this routine cancels the program.

> **N O T E** When Visual FoxPro encounters RETURN in an error-handling routine, it attempts to continue execution from the line immediately after the one that caused the error. The RETRY command tells it to try to continue execution by reperforming the line that caused the error. You must determine which, if any, of these recovery methods apply to each error handled.

In addition to checking whether the record pointer is beyond the end of file, you can check other conditions. Listing 23.10, at the end of this chapter, shows a few more. However, it is not meant to be an all-inclusive example. Rather, it merely shows the types of ways you can handle selected errors.

A more serious error level is one that requires either more calculations or assistance from the user, but is still recoverable. It might involve files or indexes. Sometimes, files get deleted or moved, especially with systems on a network. In these cases, a program stops with an error as soon as it attempts to open a file but cannot find it. Listing 23.9 uses the GETFILE() command to prompt the user to locate the file. Because GETFILE() uses the Open dialog box, users can search any drive or directory they have access to in order to find it.

Listing 23.9   `23CODE09.PRG`—The `ErrLog` **Procedure to Enable the User to Locate a Missing File**

```
****************
PROCEDURE ErrLog
LPARAMETERS lnErrorNo, lcMessage, lcErrorLine, ;
            lcModule, lnErrorLineNo

* No table in use or table not found
  IF lnErrorNo = 1 OR lnErrorNo = 52
    LOCAL lcNewFile
    SELECT 0
    lcNewFile = GETFILE('DBF', 'Select a DBF:', 'SELECT')
    IF EMPTY(lcNewFile)
      CANCEL
    ELSE
      USE (lcNewFile) SHARED
      IF lnErrorNo = 1
        RETURN
      ELSE
        RETRY
      ENDIF
    ENDIF
  ELSE
    CANCEL
  ENDIF
RETURN
```

This example checks for two error values. Error number 1 indicates that the file does not exist. This means that the named file does not exist in the current directory or in the directory referenced by the program. The second error code, 52, says that no table is in use. This error occurs when the program attempts to perform any table related command while in an empty work area. In both cases, the program needs a file.

The preceding code prompts the user to select a file using `GETFILE()`. Of course, you might not want to do this for all users because they could easily load the wrong file; however, note that it is a possible solution. When the user selects a table, the program opens it. If the original error number is 1, the program probably is trying to open a file with the wrong name or directory. In this case, you want to continue execution on the line immediately *after* the error because the error handler has just allowed you to open a file manually. Otherwise, the program would continue to try to open the file in the wrong directory or with the wrong name.

On the other hand, if the program originally attempts an IO function in an empty work area, FoxPro generates error 52. In this case, once you've manually selected a file, you would want to continue execution on the same line that failed.

CAUTION

The authors do not recommend this technique as a general solution. It is too easy for the user to specify any file in any directory and potentially cause even greater damage. It is also possible that the filename could exist in more than one directory on the server and contain different data sets. In this case, they might continue executing, but with the wrong data and thus produce incorrect results. Generally, the best thing to do is to use the FILE() command to check for the existence of the file in the expected directory. If it is not found, display a message to the user, log the error, and exit the program.

Unfortunately, most errors are not recoverable from a user's standpoint. These errors range from coding errors to corrupted files. The best that you can do as a programmer is to document as much as possible about the system when the error occurs. Listing 23.10 shows one way to do this. Then, have the routine display a message to users telling them what has happened and terminate the program.

This listing shows a more complete version of an error-handling routine. Observe the code after the comment Unrecoverable Errors. This segment captures information about the system at the time of the error and saves it to a file. The filename is coded with the month, day, hour, and minute the error occurred. It handles even the possibility of multiple errors at the same time by changing the extension.

Listing 23.10 23CODE10.PRG—A More Complete Error-Handling Routine That Effectively Deals with Trivial, Recoverable, and Unrecoverable Errors

```
* Test driver for PROCEDURE ErrLog
CLOSE ALL
ON ERROR DO ErrLog WITH ERROR(), MESSAGE(), ;
                   MESSAGE(1), SYS(16), LINENO(1)

* Test reindex
  SET DEFAULT TO \VFP6Book\Data
  OPEN DATABASE PtOfSale
  USE Empl2
  SET ORDER TO TAG Empl2

* Create a cursor and attempt to pack it
  SET DEFAULT TO \VFP6Book\Data
  OPEN DATABASE PtOfSale
  USE Empl2
  SET ORDER TO TAG Empl2
  SELECT * FROM Empl2 INTO CURSOR mpa
  PACK

* Call for RESUME without a SUSPEND
  RESUME

* Use a file that does not exist
  USE Mickey
```

continues

Listing 23.10   Continued

```
RETURN

****************
PROCEDURE ErrLog
LPARAMETERS lnErrorNo, lcMessage, lcErrorLine, ;
            lcModule, lnErrorLineNo
**********************************************************
*                                                        *
* PROCEDURE ERRLOG                                       *
*                                                        *
* This routine demonstrates 3 ways to handle errors.    *
*                                                        *
* Parameters:                                            *
* lnErrorNo      - Error Number                          *
* lcMessage      - Error Message                         *
* lcErrorLine    - Line of code where error occurs       *
* lcModule       - Name of procedure where error occurs  *
* lnErrorLineNo  - Line number where error occurs        *
*                                                        *
**********************************************************
LOCAL lcError, lnExitMethod
lnExitMethod = 0
WAIT WINDOW 'Error: ' + STR(lnErrorNo) TIMEOUT 1

* Avoid recursive loop if errlog contains an error
  lcError = ON('ERROR')
  ON ERROR

* Each case in this structure represents one error type
* It handles trivial errors first, followed by recoverable
* errors. Finally, all other errors generate an ASCII text
* file with information about the system and error.
  DO CASE

*** Check for trivial errors
  * Check if beyond end of file, place on last record
    CASE lnErrorNo = 4
      GOTO BOTTOM

  * Check if before beginning of file, place on first record
    CASE lnErrorNo = 38
      GOTO TOP

  * Cannot pack a cursor
    CASE lnErrorNo = 1115

  * Check for Resume without Suspend
    CASE lnErrorNo = 1236

*** Check for recoverable errors
  * No table in use or table not found
    CASE lnErrorNo = 1 OR lnErrorNo = 52
      LOCAL lcNewFile
      SELECT 0
```

```
  lcNewFile = GETFILE('DBF', 'Select a DBF:', 'SELECT')
  IF EMPTY(lcNewFile)
    lnExitMethod = 2
  ELSE
    USE (lcNewFile) SHARED
  ENDIF

* Record is out of range
  CASE lnErrorNo = 5 OR lnErrorNo = 20
    LOCAL lcDBF, lcTagName, lcTagNo, lcTagExp, lcFilter, ;
          lcIndex, lcSafety, llExclusiveOn, lcUnique

  * Gather information about current DBF and index
    lcDBF     = DBF()                        && DBF name
    lcTagName = TAG()                        && Tag or IDX name
    lcTagNo   = SYS(21)                      && Index number
    lcUnique  = IIF(UNIQUE(), 'UNIQUE', '')  && Is index UNIQUE?
    IF VAL(lcTagNo) = 0
      WAIT WINDOW "No tag has been set. I don't know what to do"
      lnExitMethod = 2
    ELSE
      lcTagExp  = KEY()                       && Index expression
      lcFilter  = SYS(2021, VAL(lcTagNo))    && Index FOR condition
      lcIndex   = ORDER(1,1)                 && Full Index name

      IF LEFT(lcIndex, 3) = 'IDX'
      * Open table without index
        USE (lcDBF)

      * Turn safety off to allow reindex
        lcSafety = SET('SAFETY')
        SET SAFETY OFF
        IF EMPTY(lcFilter)
          INDEX ON &lcTagExp TO (lcIndex) &lcUnique ADDITIVE
        ELSE
          INDEX ON &lcTagExp FOR &lcFilter TO (lcIndex) ;
                  &lcUnique ADDITIVE
        ENDIF
        SET SAFETY (lcSafety)

      * Reopen table with new index
        USE (lcDBF) INDEX (lcIndex)
      ELSE
      * Open table exclusively to remove and recreate tag
        llExclusiveOn = ISEXCLUSIVE()
        IF !llExclusiveOn
          USE (lcDBF) EXCLUSIVE
        ENDIF

        DELETE TAG (lcTagName)
        IF EMPTY(lcFilter)
          INDEX ON &lcTagExp &lcUnique TAG (lcTagName)
        ELSE
          INDEX ON &lcTagExp FOR &lcFilter &lcUnique ;
                TAG (lcTagName)
```

continues

Listing 23.10 Continued

```
        ENDIF

      IF !llExclusiveOn
        USE (lcDBF) SHARED
        SET ORDER TO TAG (lcTagName)
      ENDIF
    ENDIF
    lnExitMethod = 0
  ENDIF

*** Unrecoverable Errors
  * Redirect output to a file
  OTHERWISE
    lnExitMethod = 2
    LOCAL lcChkDBC, lcCurDBC, lcErrorFile, lcSuffix, ;
          lnAnswer, lnCnt, lnWhichTrigger
  * Get a file name based on date and time
    lcErrorFile = SUBSTR(DTOC(DATE()), 1, 2) + ;
                  SUBSTR(DTOC(DATE()), 4, 2) + ;
                  SUBSTR(TIME(), 1, 2) + ;
                  SUBSTR(TIME(), 4, 2) + '.ERR'
  * Make sure the file name is unique by changing the extension
    lcSuffix = '0'
    DO WHILE FILE(lcErrorFile)
      lcErrorFile = STUFF(lcErrorFile, ;
                    LEN(lcErrorFile) - LEN(lcSuffix) + 1, ;
                    LEN(lcSuffix), lcSuffix)
      lcSuffix    = ALLTRIM(STR(VAL(lcSuffix)+1, 3))
    ENDDO
    SET CONSOLE OFF
    SET ALTERNATE TO (lcErrorFile)
    SET ALTERNATE ON

  * Identify error
    ? 'DATE:        ' + TTOC(DATETIME())
    ? 'VERSION:     ' + VERSION()
    ? 'FILE NAME:   ' + lcErrorFile
    ?

  * Next identify the error
    ? 'Error:'
    = AERROR(laErrorArray)
    ? '   Number: ' + STR(laErrorArray[1], 5)
    ? '   Message: ' + laErrorArray[2]

    IF !ISNULL(laErrorArray[5])
      ? ' Parameter: ' + laErrorArray[3]
    ENDIF

    IF !ISNULL(laErrorArray[5])
      ? ' Work Area: ' + laErrorArray[4]
    ENDIF
```

```
      IF !ISNULL(laErrorArray[5])
        lnwhichtrigger = laErrorArray[5]
        DO CASE
          CASE lnwhichtrigger = 1
            ? ' Insert Trigger Failed'
          CASE lnwhichtrigger = 2
            ? ' Update Trigger Failed'
          CASE lnwhichtrigger = 3
            ? ' Delete Trigger Failed'
        ENDCASE
      ENDIF

      IF laErrorArray[1] = lnErrorNo
        ? '     Module: ' + lcModule
        ? '       Line: ' + lcErrorLine
        ? '     Line #: ' + STR(lnErrorLineNo)
      ENDIF
      RELEASE laErrorArray, whichtrigger
      ?

* Next identify the basic operating environment
      ? 'OP. SYSTEM:      ' + OS()
      ? 'PROCESSOR:       ' + SYS(17)
      ? 'GRAPHICS:        ' + LEFT(SYS(2006), AT('/', SYS(2006)) - 1)
      ? 'MONITOR:         ' + SUBSTR(SYS(2006), AT('/', SYS(2006)) + 1)
      ? 'RESOURCE FILE:   ' + SYS(2005)
      ? 'LAUNCH DIR:      ' + SYS(2004)
      ? 'CONFIG.FP:       ' + SYS(2019)
      ? 'MEMORY:          ' + ALLTRIM(STR(MEMORY())), 'KB OR ' + ;
                             SYS(12) + 'BYTES'
      ? 'CONVENTIONAL:    ' + SYS(12)
      ? 'TOTAL MEMORY:    '
      ? 'EMS LIMIT:       ' + SYS(24)
      ? 'CTRLABLE MEM:    ' + SYS(1016)
      ? 'CURRENT CONSOLE:' + SYS(100)
      ? 'CURRENT DEVICE: ' + SYS(101)
      ? 'CURRENT PRINTER:' + SYS(102)
      ? 'CURRENT DIR:     ' + SYS(2003)
      ? 'LAST KEY:        ' + STR(LASTKEY(),5)
      ?

* Next identify the default disk drive and its properties
      ? '  DEFAULT DRIVE: ' + SYS(5)
      ? '     DRIVE SIZE: ' + TRANSFORM(VAL(SYS(2020)), '999,999,999')
      ? '     FREE SPACE: ' + TRANSFORM(DISKSPACE(), '999,999,999')
      ? '    DEFAULT DIR: ' + CURDIR()
      ? ' TEMP FILES DIR: ' + SYS(2023)
      ?

* Available Printers
      ? 'PRINTERS:'
      IF APRINTERS(laPrt) > 0
        FOR lncnt = 1 TO ALEN(laPrt, 1)
          ? PADR(laprt[lncnt,1], 50) + ' ON ' + ;
            PADR(laprt[lncnt,2], 25)
```

continues

Part VI
Ch 23

Listing 23.10 Continued

```
      ENDFOR
    ELSE
      ? 'No printers currently defined.'
    ENDIF
    ?

  * Define Workareas
    ? 'WORK AREAS:'
    IF AUSED(laWrkAreas) > 0
      = ASORT(laWrkAreas,2)
      LIST MEMORY LIKE laWrkAreas
      RELEASE laWrkAreas
      ? 'Current Database: ' + ALIAS()
    ELSE
      ? 'No tables currently open in any work areas.'
    ENDIF
    ?

  * Begin bulk information dump
  * Display memory variables
    ? REPLICATE('-', 78)
    ? 'ACTIVE MEMORY VARIABLES'
    LIST MEMORY
    ?

  * Display status
    ? REPLICATE('-', 78)
    ? 'CURRENT STATUS AND SET VARIABLES'
    LIST STATUS
    ?

  * Display Information related to databases
    IF ADATABASE(laDbList) > 0
      lcCurDBC = JUSTSTEM(DBC())
      FOR lncnt = 1 TO ALEN(laDbList, 1)
        lcChkDBC = laDbList[lncnt, 1]
        SET DATABASE TO (lcChkDBC)
        LIST CONNECTIONS
        ?
        LIST DATABASE
        ?
        LIST PROCEDURES
        ?
        LIST TABLES
        ?
        LIST VIEWS
        ?
      ENDFOR
      SET DATABASE TO (lcCurDBC)
    ENDIF

  * Close error file and reactivate the screen
    SET ALTERNATE TO
    SET ALTERNATE OFF
    SET CONSOLE ON
```

```
      ON KEY LABEL BACKSPACE
      ON KEY LABEL ENTER
      ON KEY LABEL ESCAPE
      ON KEY LABEL PGDN
      ON KEY LABEL PGUP
      ON KEY LABEL SPACEBAR

      SET SYSMENU TO DEFAULT

      WAIT WINDOW 'Check file: ' + SYS(2003) + '\' + lcErrorFile + ;
                CHR(13) + ' for error information'
      lnAnswer = MESSAGEBOX('View Error Log Now?', 292)
      IF lnAnswer = 6
        MODIFY FILE (lcErrorfile)
      ENDIF
    ENDCASE

  * Type of exit
    DO CASE
      CASE lnExitMethod = 0      && Retry the same line
        RETRY
      CASE lnExitMethod = 1      && Execute the next line of code
        RETURN
      CASE lnExitMethod = 2      && Cancel the program
        ON ERROR &lcError
        CANCEL        && SUSPEND during development
    ENDCASE
    ON ERROR &lcError
  RETURN
```

Using Error Events in Objects

The preceding example shows the typical way to handle errors using the ON ERROR statement. This method was available in all earlier versions of FoxPro. Although it still works, you have a few more options in Visual FoxPro. The most important one is that each object has its own error event. VFP first looks for an Error method in the current object when an error occurs. If you did not add code to this method, VFP then executes the global ON ERROR routine mentioned earlier. If you don't use a global ON ERROR routine, VFP uses its default error handler.

> **CAUTION**
>
> The default VFP error handler is about as useful to your users as sunscreen is to Eskimoes in the winter. It merely displays a message box containing the text of the error message and four buttons. The first says Cancel. Without other code, this could leave data transactions hanging uncommitted. If they are running inside VFP rather than in a standalone environment, they can Suspend the program (and do what?). The third button says Ignore. Very seldom do ignored errors just go away. The last says Help. How many users want to press Help just to get a more detailed error message, which does not generally tell them what to do next? The point is that you want to avoid letting the user ever see this default error handler.

The first thing you find is that an object's Error method receives three parameters from VFP:

- The error number
- The name of the method where the error occurred
- The line number in the method where the error occurred

At this point, you could design a small routine to examine the error that occurred and display the information passed as parameters, possibly also writing these to an error log. Note, however, that you must keep this code as simple as possible because if another error occurs while you're in your error-handling code, VFP throws you into its default error handler, even if you have an ON ERROR statement defined. I previously said that you never want to let the user see the default error handler with its limited and unfriendly button choices.

Another useful feature of Visual FoxPro is the AERROR() function. This returns an array with up to seven columns. The return value of the function identifies the number of rows in the array. This value is almost always 1, except possibly in the case of ODBC. Table 23.4 defines the columns returned by AERROR() when the error occurs in Visual FoxPro code.

Table 23.4   AERROR() Columns for Visual FoxPro Errors

Element	Description
1	A numeric value of the error number. Same as ERROR().
2	A string value of the error message. Same as MESSAGE().
3	Typically null unless the error has an additional error parameter such as those returned by SYS(2018).
4	Typically null, but sometimes contains the work area where the error occurred.
5	Typically null, but if the error is the result of a failed trigger (error 1539), it returns one of the following values: 1 - Insert trigger failed; 2 - Update trigger failed; 3 - Delete trigger failed
6	Null
7	Null

Although it is true that most of this information can be obtained without resorting to the AERROR() function, the resulting array is easier to work with. Furthermore, this function returns important information not otherwise available if the error is the result of an OLE or ODBC error. Table 23.5 documents the returned values for OLE errors.

Table 23.5 AERROR() Columns for OLE Errors

Element	Description
1	Error number
2	Character value with text of Visual FoxPro error message
3	Character value with text of OLE error message
4	Character value with name of OLE application
5	Null value typically—if a character value, holds the name of the application's help file
6	Null value typically—if a character value, holds the help context ID for an appropriate help topic in the application's help file
7	Numeric value with the OLE 2.0 exception number

Table 23.6 shows the column definitions for an ODBC error.

Table 23.6 AERROR() Columns for ODBC Errors

Element	Description
1	Error number
2	Character value with the Visual FoxPro error message
3	Character value with the ODBC error message
4	Character value with the ODBC SQL state
5	Numeric value with the ODBC data source error number
6	Numeric value with the ODBC connection handle
7	Null

Again, the point is not to fix the error, but to document it. Therefore, you will want to write formatted entries for each row in the array created by AERROR() to the error log.

When dealing with objects, you might not want to write error code in every method, of every instance, of the object you create and use. Rather, it is better to create your own class library from the base classes provided with VFP. In these classes, define your error-handler code (as well as any other unique changes you need in all instances of the object). Then build your forms and code from these base classes.

As you instantiate objects from your class library, each instance inherits the error method code from the parent class. Although it is okay to handle errors specific to an object in that instance, or in the subclass it is derived from, remember to include a line at the end of the method to reference the parent class code for those errors not specifically handled locally. To do this, simply add the following line to the end of the instance error method code:

```
DODEFAULT(nError, cMethod, nLine)
```

You can even add the following line to the classes in your class library to have them reference the error code from the containers in which you place them:

```
This.Parent.Error(nError, cMessage, nLineNo)
```

Ultimately, if the error gets passed up through the class structure and into the containers and still cannot be handled, the program should resort to a special error handler to document the error condition as much as possible before bailing out of the program.

N O T E   Author's note: Thanks to Malcolm C. Rubel for outlining the preceding approach. ■

The amount of time you spend testing code before putting it into use depends on several factors:

- How quickly the users need it.
- How critical code failure is (such as software written to control aircraft or medical equipment).
- How management views the life cycle of projects. Do they expect it right the first time, or do they accept a break-in period?

Debugging can and should go on throughout the life of the application, although you might call it something different, such as "maintenance," once the software is in production.

There is no one correct answer for ensuring software quality. Similarly, there is no one correct way to write an error handler, especially when it comes to the complexities of handling objects, OLE, and ODBC. But the more methods employed, the better the overall system performs, and when errors do occur, the easier it is to find them.

Other Resources

Many of the notes and cautions throughout this book relate to things you need to watch closely to avoid errors in your code. This chapter has focused on additional concepts related to debugging and error handling. Reference texts in this area are relatively few. As a serious developer, you might want to check the few following listed references to learn more about debugging and software quality assurance:

- Glass, Robert L. *Building Quality Software.* Englewood Cliffs, N.J.: Prentice Hall, 1992.
- McConnell, Steve. *Code Complete.* Redmond, Washington: Microsoft Press, 1993.
- McConnell, Steve. *Rapid Development: Taming Wild Software Schedules.* Redmond, Washington: Microsoft Press, 1996.
- Maguire, Steve. *Writing Solid Code.* Redmond, Washington: Microsoft Press, 1993.

- Maguire, Steve. *Debugging the Development Process.* Redmond, Washington: Microsoft Press, 1994.
- McCarthy, Jim. *Dynamics of Software Development.* Redmond, Washington: Microsoft Press, 1995.
- Schulmeyer, G. Gordon, ed. *Handbook of Software Quality Assurance (3rd Edition).* New York: Van Nostrand Reinhold, 1998.

The following sources of information about Visual FoxPro occasionally feature information about debugging and error handling:

- FoxPro Advisor magazine (Advisor Publications)
- FoxTalk newsletter (Pinnacle Publishing)
- VFOX and FoxUser forums on CompuServe

Finally, check out upcoming Visual FoxPro conferences in your region and look for any sessions they might have on error handling. ●

Visual FoxPro and Year 2000 (Y2K) Compliance

In this chapter

What Is the Y2K Problem?

Every day you read in the newspaper or a magazine some nightmarish projection of how un-
prepared the world's computer systems are for the coming of the year 2000. You hear news
such as over half of the nation's largest corporations have not even completed their assessment
of the *Year 2000 (Y2K) problem*. Only a third of these companies have started converting their
systems to be *Y2K compliant*. The U.S. government appears to be just as far from compliance.
You also occasionally hear dismissals of the entire problem as hyperbole or an imagined concern. Some people say that the problem is exaggerated by software vendors in an effort to sell
Y2K software and development services.

At the risk of sounding alarmist, folks, 1998 is almost over! There is just one year left to modify
billions of lines of legacy code and legacy hardware to Y2K compliance. Systems critical to our
civilization, such as air traffic control, power grid control computers, transportation systems,
traffic signals, financial computing systems, and so forth are far from being Y2K compliant. Of
course, the Internet is also vulnerable because it relies on millions of computers, some of
which might not be Y2K compliant. But that is the least of your worries, because you might
have no electricity, water, gas, or telephone service, and your ATM and credit cards may be
rejected. If any of that occurs, Internet problems drop rapidly down the priority list.

What is the Y2K issue? It all stems from the fact that software designers wanted to make it
easier for the user to enter a date, so they decided to design their software so that the user
would only have to enter two characters to input a year. This saved keystrokes as well as expensive memory resources. Users were happy and bought more "easy-to-use" software. None of us
ever anticipated that the same software and hardware systems would still be used 20 to 30
years later. The problem was exacerbated because the traditional two-digit year data entry
became a standard for all new systems developed. The use of a date with a two-digit year for
data entry, storage, and retrieval is the basis for the Y2K issue.

Y2K compliance is not just a mainframe computer problem. Many microcomputer software
packages use dates with a two-digit year. About 90 percent of the personal computers (PCs)
made before 1997, and about 50 percent of those made in 1997, are said not to be Y2K compliant. The most common problem with these PCs is with the BIOS (Basic Input/Output System)
chip that is part of the PC hardware system. The BIOS contains code that boots the PC. The
computer also contains a clock chip that supplies the time and date to the BIOS. When you set
the time and date from your operating system, the BIOS writes it to the clock chip. It even
writes a four-digit year to the clock chip memory. Therefore, there is no problem setting the
clock to the year 2000. However, the clock chip used in most PCs increments only the last two
digits of the year. If the PC is operating when the clock strikes midnight on New Year's Eve of
1999, there is no problem because the real-time clock in the computer handles the time correctly and the clock chip is set correctly. However, if you shut down your PC before midnight
on that date, the clock chip increments only the last two digits of the year and the date goes

from 1999 to 1900. On New Year's Day, 2000, when you boot up your computer, your PC's clock is set to January 4, 1980. Why is it set to January 4, 1980? When your computer boots up, MS-DOS does not recognize January 1, 1900. MS-DOS is programmed to change an unrecognizable date to January 4, 1980. You probably will not even encounter this problem because Microsoft has incorporated logic in Windows NT 4.0, Windows 98, and Windows NT 5.0 to automatically change a 1900 date to 2000 when the PC boots up. Microsoft also provides a patch to fix the BIOS problem for Windows NT 3.51 (sp5) and Windows 95. This resolves the Y2K issue for most PCs. However, there exist a few PCs that have BIOS that Microsoft's solution will not resolve. These PCs simply do not accept a 21st-Century year. Your Visual FoxPro application might be completely Y2K compliant, but unless your customer's PCs are Y2K compliant, your application might not work properly. And guess whose problem it becomes.

On September 9, 1998, a U.S. House of Representatives panel gave grades to various government agencies regarding their Y2K compliance prior to that date. Most agencies received a poor grade, as indicated in Table 24.1.

Table 24.1   Grades Given to U.S. Government Agencies for Their Y2K Compliance as of 9/9/98

Government Agency	Grade
Social Security Agency	A
National Science Foundation	A
Small Business Administration	A
Department of Defense	D
Transportation Department	D
Justice Department	F
Dept. of Health and Human Services	F
Department of Energy	F
State Department	F
Dept. of Education	F
Agency for International Development	F

You might think that the United States Government is not prepared for the next millennium. The United States, however, is better prepared than most other countries, as shown in Figure 24.1. This chart shows the percentage of organizations in various countries that are expected to be Y2K compliant by January 1, 2000.

FIGURE 24.1
Percentage of organizations in various countries that will be Y2K compliant by January 1, 2000.

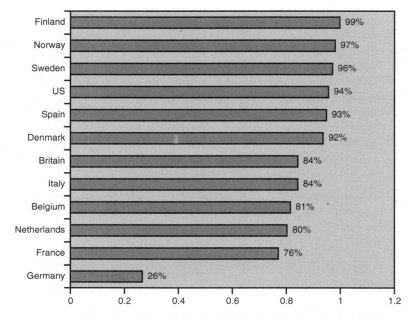

Percentage of Organizations That Will Be Y2K Compliant by Year 2000

Y2K Compliance of Previous Versions of Visual FoxPro

When dBASE III was designed, it was decided that the date stored in the tables (.DBF) and internally would contain a full four-digit year. The SET CENTURY ON/OFF command was also incorporated. Many systems such as Lotus 1-2-3, Access 95, and Excel 95 normally store a two-digit year. Because FoxPro is a clone of dBASE III, FoxPro also utilizes a four-digit year. As a result, FoxPro 2.6 is considered to be almost Y2K compliant.

All versions of FoxPro and Visual FoxPro treat a date as a numeric value representing the number of days since a fixed date. This number is stored in tables, variables, and is used to perform date calculations. The century is never lost. The only problem is that applications have been developed using a date with a two-digit year to simplify data entry. Visual FoxPro 5.0a treated dates with a two-digit year as 20th-century dates.

You should always use a four-digit date to achieve Y2K compliance by specifying the SET CENTURY ON command. However, the Visual FoxPro 5.0a SET CENTURY command had other features. The full Visual FoxPro 5.0a syntax for SET CENTURY was:

```
SET CENTURY ON ¦ OFF ¦ ROLLOVER
SET CENTURY ON ¦ OFF ¦ TO [nCentury [ROLLOVER nYear]]
```

The ON keyword specified that the date field would have a four-digit year (for example, 1/1/1999). The OFF keyword specified a date with a two-digit year and assumed the year to be in the 20th century (for example, 1/1/99). The optional TO [nCentury] clause specified a number from 1 to 99 designating the current century. The TO clause was only used with two-digit fields. If you omitted the nCentury number, the 20th Century was assumed. For example, if you specified SET CENTURY TO 21, the date {10/11/62} was assumed to be 10/11/2162. The ROLLOVER nYear clause specified a number from 0 to 99 designating a year. Dates with a year that was less than nYear were considered to be in the next century. Other dates were considered to be in the current century.

In the next section, you will be introduced to the enhancements to Visual FoxPro in version 6 that make it much easier to achieve Y2K compliance. But first, here are some recommendations to acquire Y2K compliance using Visual FoxPro 5.0a:

- Always use SET CENTURY ON.
- Always set the TextBox.Century to 1 to force a date to have a four-digit year for data entry.
- Never use the LUPDATE() function.

  You should not use the LUPDATE() function because the last update date stored in the .DBF file header is only two digits and the LUPDATE() function always assumes the 20th Century. For example, if you are working on a sunny June day in the year 2003, SET CENTURY is ON, and you use a file that was last updated on March 4, 2003, the LUPDATE() function returns 03/03/1903.

- Avoid using date constants of the form {mm/dd/yy}.

  This is a good rule of thumb even though a date like {12/18/08} is valid. In FoxPro 2.6 and 3.0, a date constant with a two-digit year is interpreted as a 20th-century date. However, in Visual FoxPro 5.0 and later, the SET CENTURY command causes the same date constant with a two-digit year to be evaluated according to the specific SET CENTURY TO value and ROLLOVER year. It is best to change all date constants to the form, {^yyyy/mm/dd}. The caret (^) character forces the constant into the YMD ordering.

- Avoid using the CTOD() and CTOT() functions to build a two-digit year.

You can see that Visual FoxPro 5.0a was rather well positioned for the next century. However, the Visual FoxPro developers at Microsoft made Visual FoxPro 6 even easier for developers to create applications that are Y2K compliant, as you will see in the next section.

Visual FoxPro 6 Y2K Compliance

Year 2000 will be here soon, and software developers are rushing around trying to ensure that their applications are ready for the year 2000. Visual FoxPro developers get some welcome assistance in their Y2K risk identification effort by utilizing the new strict date type and the optional type enforcement.

Part
VI

Ch
24

Strict Date Type

The current SET CENTURY and SET DATE settings are used when Date and DateTime constants are evaluated to determine how the data is to be interpreted. Their value can be different depending on when they were compiled and what date-related settings were active at compilation time.

Visual FoxPro 6 can detect and report any occurrences of ambiguous dates during compilation and execution. For example, which century are we talking about in the following assignment?

```
dBirthDate = {2/29/12 10:21}
```

I haven't a clue. Is it my mom's birthday or some date next century? The date is ambiguous. What were the settings for the SET DATE TO and SET CENTURY commands when this module was compiled? For example, what if the century changes, which it will soon? Suddenly, the date is for another century.

This is no longer a problem if you replace all the occurrences of ambiguous dates with dates conforming to *strict date* format. The format for a strict date is the following:

```
^yyyy-mm-dd[,][hh[:mm[:ss]][a¦p]]
```

where yyyy is a four-digit unambiguous year. The caret character (^) that precedes the year denotes the strict date format. The Date and DateTime values are interpreted in a consistent YMD format. Valid Date and DateTime separators for the date are hyphens (-), forward slashes (/), periods (.), and spaces. Empty Dates and DateTimes are considered always valid. Valid empty Date and DateTime formats include {}, {--}, and {--,:} {}.

Let us rewrite the assignment in a strict date format:

```
dBirthDate = {^1912.2.29 10:21}
dBirthDate = {^1912-2-29 10:21}
dBirthDate = {^1912/2/29 10:21}
```

Now that Visual FoxPro 6 enforces strict date formats, you can recompile your applications in Visual FoxPro 6. The compiler will find all of your Y2K non-compliant code. If the compiler encounters any Date or DateTime constants that are not in the strict format or that evaluate to invalid values, Visual FoxPro 6 will generate an error.

The largest valid date in Visual FoxPro 6 is December 31, 9999 AD, or {^9999/12/31}. The smallest date that you can specify is January 1, 1 AD or {^0001/1/1}.

The New SET STRICTDATE Command

The new SET STRICTDATE command controls Y2K compliance enforcement:

```
SET STRICTDATE TO nMode
```

The *nMode* value designates how format checking is performed, according to the following values:

nMode	Description
0	Strict date format checking is turned off. This mode is Visual FoxPro 5.0a–compatible and is the default mode for runtime and ODBC drivers. When STRICTDATE is set to 0, invalid Date and DateTime constants evaluate to an empty date.
1	All Date and DateTime constants are in the strict date format. Any Date or DateTime constant that is not in the strict format or evaluates to an invalid date generates an error, either during compilation, at runtime, or during an interactive session. For an interactive session, the default setting for nMode is 1.
2	This option is identical to setting STRICTDATE to 1. It reports a compilation error, 2033 - CTOD and CTOT can produce incorrect results, when either the CTOD() or CTOT() function is encountered in the code.

The CTOD() and CTOT() functions return a value that is based on the current SET DATE and SET CENTURY settings. As a result, the CTOD() and CTOT() functions are a Y2K non-compliance risk. You should use the DATE() and DATETIME() functions to create Date and DateTime constants and expressions.

Notice that the StrictDateEntry property is not controlled by the SET STRICTDATE command setting. The StrictDateEntry property remains unchanged in Visual FoxPro 6.

You can visually alter the default SET STRICTDATE setting. To do so, choose Tools, Options and click the General tab in the Options dialog (see Figure 24.2). Set the Strict Date Level using the list box in the Year 2000 Compliance group, which includes a Year 2000 Compliance drop-down list box. This list box specifies the SET STRICTDATE setting.

FIGURE 24.2
The General tab of the Options dialog is where you can change the STRICTDATE setting.

N O T E   Reminder: If you exit the Options dialog using the OK button, the value is set for the current
Visual FoxPro session. You must click on the Set As Default button to save the setting to the
Windows registry for the next Visual FoxPro session. ■

Enhanced DATE() and DATETIME() Functions

You can use the DATE() and DATETIME() functions to create Date or DateTime values. To support this functionality, numeric arguments have been added to the function syntax. These functions are a preferable method for creating Date and DateTime values. You do not need to use the CTOD() and CTOT() functions because they can increase the risk of Y2K non-compliance. In the following example, MyDate is assigned a Date value in both cases:

```
MyDate = CTOD(Date())    && Old form
MyDate = Date(1)         && preferred Y2K compliant form
```

Enhanced FDATE() Function

The FDATE() function has been modified to use an optional argument to determine the time a file was last modified. You no longer have to use the character manipulation functions. For example, in Visual FoxPro 5.0, you had to write code to determine when the file was last modified. Here is the code:

```
tLastModified = CTOT(DTOC(FDATE('MyTable.dbf')) + ' ' ;
                + FTIME('MyTable.dbf')
```

For Visual FoxPro 6 programs, the preceding code can be replaced with the following:

```
tLastModified = FDATE('MyTable.dbf', 1)
```

The Century Property and SET CENTURY Command

In Visual FoxPro 6, the default setting for the SET CENTURY command is ON and the Century property default is:

```
1 - On
```

In previous versions of Visual FoxPro, the default value for the SET CENTURY setting was ON and the default for the Century property was

```
2 - the SET CENTURY setting determines if the
    century portion of the date is displayed.
```

In Visual FoxPro 5.0, if SET CENTURY TO was used without any argument, it was set to 19 (the 20th century). In Visual FoxPro 6, the SET CENTURY TO command sets the century to the current century. Also, in new data sessions SET CENTURY TO is initialized to the current century.

In Visual FoxPro 5.0, the default value for *nYear* was 0. In Visual FoxPro 6, the default value for the ROLLOVER *nYear* clause for the SET CENTURY command is the last two digits of the current year plus 50 years. For example, if the current year is 1999, the default value for nYear is 49 (1999+50). ●

Internet Support

What's So Exciting About the Internet?

The Internet and the technologies that are driving it are hot these days! People are flocking to the Internet, and the World Wide Web in particular, by the millions, and new Web sites and other Internet-related businesses and institutions are keeping pace with the ever-increasing hook-up rates of new Web surfers. Building applications that are integrated with Internet technology and can connect databases to Web sites will likely become an important aspect in your software development, as companies like Microsoft integrate Web-based technology into every aspect of software from high-level applications down to the operating system.

Although traditionally the Internet has been made of mostly static content, there is a tremendous rush under way to make dynamic data available. Database connectivity is key to this concept, and Visual FoxPro is up to the task to provide the speed and flexibility to act as a database back end and integrate Internet functionality into existing applications.

There is a lot of hype about the Internet and, to be sure, some of the new technologies are not all that they are cracked up to be. The use of the Internet for business application development is still in its infancy, and there are quite a few limitations when compared to the application development facilities that you might be used to using.

Nevertheless, the Internet is bringing about a major shift in the way applications are deployed by making it much easier to build solutions that are open and widely distributed, even open to the public, over the World Wide Web. Over the last few years, you have probably heard a lot about *client/server* development. A *client* is normally a user application, such as an accounts payable program. A *server* is an active process, usually running on a separate computer, that provides a service for the client. In the case of database operations, a database server manages the databases and their indexes and keeps track of user resources. The Internet is providing the full promise of what client/server was always meant to be: a platform that enables you to build widely distributed applications that can be centrally maintained using a common front end provided by a Web browser.

The driving forces behind the popularity of the Internet and the World Wide Web in particular are

- Universal client interface
- Wide distribution with centralized management
- Open standards

The following sections look at these points in more detail.

The Universal Client Web Browsers as a Common Interface

The World Wide Web and the Web browsers used to cruise it are changing the way we look at applications today. Web browsers have brought a universal interface to applications in a way that no other software interface before it has ever achieved.

Web browsers are easy to use and provide a very simple interface to the user. The use of simple controls for navigation (back and forward buttons, a list of the last places visited, a "favorites" list, and so on) make the browser interface just about self-explanatory. It also provides a consistent interface across applications developed with a browser in mind. A typical example of a dynamically generated Web page is shown in Figure 25.1.

FIGURE 25.1
A Web page containing dynamically generated data. This order form shows items selected on a previous form, enabling the user to fill out order info for an online purchase using a secure transaction.

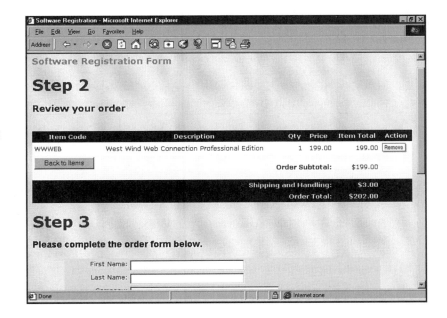

The hyperlink-based nature of Web pages, where you can simply click on a highlighted area and immediately be transported to the location of the relevant information, makes them an extremely powerful tool for integrating information from various sources, both internally from within a company and externally from the open Internet.

Ease of use is important, but even more compelling is the ubiquitous nature of Web browsers. Browsers exist for all the major computing platforms from Windows to Macintosh to UNIX. What this means is that an application interface developed for a Web browser will instantly run on all the platforms that support a Web browser. Cross-platform development has been an often-overlooked part of software development in the past because of its complexities, but with the Web browser interface, this feature is included for free in the one-time Web application development process.

Finally, Web browsers free developers from having to distribute huge application runtimes that need to be installed on each client system. Take a typical standalone Visual FoxPro application, for example. To distribute such an application across the company, you have to install the application runtimes on each of the machines. You distribute your .EXE, the runtime, and various system files that get installed on the client system. With a Web browser, none of this happens. There is a one-time installation for the browser after which all Web-based applications are

Part
VI

Ch

25

accessible. As long as the client system is equipped with a Web browser and access is available to the network that runs the application over either the public or company internal Web, the application can be run without any special installation procedures. Furthermore, the application can be run from anywhere, whether the user is at the office, on the road, or on vacation, as long as she has access to an Internet connection.

Distributed Applications Over the Web

The last point is extremely important! The Web has made distributed computing a reality for the first time by making it relatively easy to install applications that can be accessed publicly over the Internet or privately over an internal network (called an *intranet*). Prior to the Internet explosion, building a publicly accessible application was extremely difficult, inconvenient for end users, and very costly because proprietary communications and network protocols needed to be set up.

The promise of client/server has always been to create a distributed environment where there is a distinct line between the application interface and the database and business logic. The Web is providing this environment by clearly separating the client (the Web browser) and the server (the Web server and the back-end applications tied to it) as well as providing an open platform (a network running the TCP/IP protocol) to connect the two.

Web applications make it possible to distribute applications widely, including the capability to enable public access at reasonable cost. But at the same time, the application is maintained centrally at the server with no pieces of the application actually residing on the client side. This means that updates to an application don't require updating of any part of the client's system. All that's required is a code change on the back-end application, and all clients are automatically updated.

Open Standards

The Internet is based on *open standards*. Although there are quite a few struggles to extend standards and push them into company-specific directions, by and large, all the protocols and tools used are standards-based and supported by a wide variety of products and vendors. This is extremely important because it enables different companies to build tools that can interact with one another.

In addition, the open nature of the Internet is forcing companies to try to extend standards in non-proprietary ways. A good example is the struggle to extend HTML (Hypertext Markup Language), which is used to display output in Web browsers. The two leading browser vendors, Microsoft and Netscape, are the standard-bearers in this field, and both are trying to extend the standard beyond its current limitations. But unlike the past, when extensions were often proprietary, both of these companies are making the specifications widely available for developers to start using them immediately, thereby encouraging other browser vendors to pick up on the new extensions for use in their own products.

Many of the protocols used on the Internet are modular and relatively simple to implement. This means it's easy to integrate many of the connectivity features that the Internet provides with readily available protocols. Specifications are publicly maintained and accessible over the Internet. Because most of the protocols used are simple to implement, a wide variety of tools are available to use with these protocols; you can easily roll your own if you need specialized functionality.

All of this openness adds up to better interoperability of tools as well as immediate accessibility to the tools that are required to build advanced Internet applications.

Limitations of Building Web-Based Applications

Although the previous sections point out the glowing advantages of building Internet-based applications, it's important to keep in mind that this is a very young and still developing field. Most of the dedicated Web-only development tools that are available today are fairly limited. There are lots of solutions available to hook just about any kind of data to the Web, but the complexity or limits of the tools can often get in the way of building applications that provide the full breadth of functionality that a traditional standalone application can provide.

In this chapter, you will learn how to use Visual FoxPro as a database back end that gets around some of the Web application development limitations. Still, there are limitations in interface design that will require a change from the way you might be accustomed to building applications with visual tools like Visual FoxPro.

Part VI
Ch
25

For example, HTML and the distinct client/server interface that disallows direct access to the data from the Web browser requires building applications with the different mindset of server-based programming. HTML input forms are more reminiscent of the dBASE II days when you had to hand-code fields and had no immediate control over user input via field-level validation. All access to the data happens on the server end so that each request for a data update requires calling the Web server and requesting it to update the current HTML page with new data. In essence, this process requires reloading of the currently displayed page with the updated information. This is a somewhat slower process than what can be achieved with in-line field validation. However, it is a very sure process that is simple to develop and maintain.

Web-based form input is *transaction-based*, where you first capture all the information entered in the Web browser and then validate the input and return an error message relating to an entire input form on the Web server. Although new HTML extensions provide more control over input forms and active HTML display, the fact that the Web browser has no direct access to data makes it difficult to build truly interactive input forms that can immediately validate input against the database rules. To update the input form or even send back an error message, the original form has to be submitted, sent to the server, and then be redrawn from scratch with the updated information retrieved from the server.

Another limitation to consider is that Web applications cannot easily print reports. All you can do is display a page as HTML and then print the result; there's no full-fledged report writer to create banded and subtotaled reports. Instead of a report builder you have to hand-code.

Although these limitations are real and something you have to consider when building Web-based applications, Microsoft and Netscape are addressing these issues with extensions to

HTML that are starting to look more like the fully event-driven forms that you are used to with tools like Visual FoxPro. The not-too-distant future will bring tools to paint input forms with a form designer and enable attaching of validation code directly to fields. However, the lack of direct data access will likely continue to be a major difference between Web and desktop applications.

Limitations or not, the Web is hot, and those who have taken the first step toward building Web-based applications rarely look back as the advantages of the distributed environment and the easy scalability that goes with it often outweigh the disadvantages just mentioned.

Database Development on the Web

With the popularity of the World Wide Web, the need for database application development on the Web is exploding as more and more companies are realizing that to make maximum use of their Web sites, dynamic display of database information is essential to provide interesting and up-to-date content.

This section discusses the logistics of building database applications that run over the Web, how Web deployment affects the application development process, and what's required to make it happen.

Tools You Need to Develop Web Applications

To build applications to run over the World Wide Web, you need the following components:

- *The TCP/IP network protocol.* TCP/IP is available as an installable network protocol on Windows NT and Windows 95/98. Web servers require TCP/IP to receive requests. Although TCP/IP must be loaded on your machine, either bound to a network adapter or the dialup adapter (if you don't have a network adapter), you do not need a network to test a Web application. All components, Web server, Web browser, and your application, can run on the same machine if required.

- *A Web server, preferably running on Windows NT Server.* A *Web server* is a piece of software that is responsible for serving Web content as well as acting as an application server that handles routing requests to the appropriate helper applications. Although Windows NT Server is the preferred platform for best performance and stability of Web services, you can also use Windows 95/98 or NT Workstation with many Web servers (the big exception is Microsoft's Internet Information Server).

- *A Web Connection application.* The Web server calls a connector or script whenever it needs to generate dynamic output. A *script* is essentially an .EXE or .DLL application that runs in response to a Web request. A *connector* is a specialized script that passes the requested information to a separate back-end application such as Visual FoxPro.

- *A fast (120MHz or better) Pentium-based machine with 32M or more of RAM.* Although you can get by with less, this configuration is a suggested minimum when running a Web server and a back-end application. Web servers are resource-hungry services that suck up CPU cycles and memory. For optimal performance of high-volume online applications, multi-processor machines provide the best load distribution by enabling separate CPUs to handle the Web services and the database access.

- *A Web browser.* The Web browser is your interface to a Web-based application. Use either Internet Explorer (as all the examples here do) or Netscape, as these provide the most advanced features and carry 90+ percent of the browser market.

The preceding list provides a road map of tools you need to build Internet applications and test them on your local machine or over a local network. In addition, you must deal with the issue of connecting the application to the Internet. Several options are available:

- *Direct connection.* Your company or client might already have a direct connection to the Internet via a Frame Relay connection or full T1 or T3 access. This is the ideal setup when developing Internet applications, but also a very pricey one both in terms of the connection fees for Internet hookup as well as the network hardware requirements. A T1 runs from $2,500 to $5,000 monthly, depending on the type of connection. New alternatives to the T1/T3 connection are cable modems and DSL (digital subscriber lines). Both of these services are inexpensive and provide a dedicated connection that may be a cost-effective option in many circumstances.

Part VI Ch 25

- *Co-location.* Many Internet service providers (ISPs) enable you to stick a machine on their network and provide you direct Internet access. You can then run your own Web server or use the machine only as a database server. In order for this to work, you must make sure you get full remote-control access to your machine. Typical fees for this service run $300–$500 a month.

- *Low-speed connection.* Many When getting started, it might be sufficient to hook your site into an ISP's network via a low-speed connection via Frame Relay, ISDN, or even modem hookup. You need to get a permanent connection from your site to one of the ISP's modems. You're usually responsible for the cost of your own hardware, the extra hardware required on the ISP's end (such as an extra modem or router), plus the telco's monthly line charges. In addition, there's usually a small surcharge on the ISP's monthly access charge over a standard dialup account.

Running Applications Over the Web

Database connectivity over the Internet is essentially a specialized form of client/server: You have a front end (the Web browser) that accesses a back end (the Web server), which, in turn, is connected to the application that provides the database access. The front end and the back end are connected via an Internet connection, which in most cases will be the World Wide Web and HTTP (Hypertext Transfer Protocol). Figure 25.2 shows the relationship between the Web browser and Web server.

FIGURE 25.2

The Web server is responsible for data access using server extensions, and the browser is responsible for display of output.

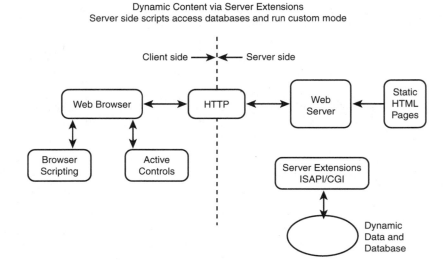

When you look at the diagram, keep in mind the clear distinction between the client and server sides—note the distinct line between the two. The Web browser has no direct access to the data, and the Web server on the other end has no direct access to the interface presented to the user. Think of the Web browser as the interface and the Web server as the database/application server. All interaction between the two is accomplished via a predefined protocol and transaction-based requests. Database

Web Browsers Get Smart: Scripting and Active Controls   On the browser side of Figure 25.2, you can see the browser scripting and active controls options. *Browser scripts* are client-side browser extensions, such as JavaScript for Netscape and VBScript for Internet Explorer, that provide programmable control over the browser's interface. These scripting languages provide additional control over the user interface used for input as well as provide programmable features for generating the HTML output; in essence, browser-side scripting provides logic smarts to the browser. Remember, though, there's no access to data from the browser.

Active controls refers to external controls that can be called by HTML pages and controlled by browser scripts. These controls can be automatically downloaded over the Web. In this context, active controls include *Java applets* and *ActiveX custom controls* (special-purpose, lightweight OLE controls that contain the logic to download and install themselves over the Internet) that can be executed or called by the scripting engines provided in the Web browser. Scripting languages provide the basic interface programmability and the active controls provide high-performance, optimized, and operating system-specific features to a Web browser. Many multi-media-related tools and controls are implemented as active controls, and, in the future, you will likely see controls that match common GUI interface controls, such as pop-up calendars for date validations, shipping rate calculators, and so on.

Database But even these high-powered controls do not have direct access to the data that resides on the server.

The Web Server: Providing the Link to Application and Database Connectivity   On the other end of the Internet sits the Web server. When dealing with applications running over the Internet, the Web server acts as the intermediary that negotiates access to the application and database. The Web server on its own knows nothing about applications, but instead calls helper applications known as *server scripts* to perform this task for it.

The flow goes something like this: The Web browser requests access to data by sending a request to execute a script on the server side. A *script* is essentially a program that runs on the Web server machine in response to a hyperlink hit or the click on an HTML form button. Scripts can either be .EXE files following the CGI (Common Gateway Interface) protocol, or a server-side API interface such as ISAPI (Internet Server API), which is available with Microsoft's Internet Information Server (IIS). The API-level .DLLs that are called in response to script links provide much better performance than the .EXE-based CGI scripts because they are loaded in memory as in-process .DLLs that don't need to be reloaded on each hit.

Keep the server-side script concept in mind, as all dynamic Web access is accomplished by calling scripts. Don't confuse *server-side scripts* with scripting languages such as JavaScript or VBScript either on the client or server side. Scripts in this context are external applications called by the Web server. These scripts can either be fully self-contained or can be used as connectors to call other applications such as Visual FoxPro to handle the database access, application logic, and the output display.

With each Web request, the browser makes available some information about itself—the browser type, its Internet address, and any field values defined on an input form—and passes this information to the Web server. When calling a server-side script, this information is passed to the script along with additional information the Web server makes available about itself. The script is then responsible for running its processing task and generating Web server-compliant output. The processing task could be anything from running a database query, adding records to a table, or simply sending back a plain HTML response page that shows the time of day.

Whenever a server-side script executes, it runs its own custom processing, but it is always required to return a response to the Web server. In most cases, the response is an HTML document that displays the results of the request: The result of a query or a confirmation or error page stating the result status of the request that was just processed. Although HTML output is the most common, other responses can also be sent, such as a request to authenticate a user, a redirection to send a user to another location, or a trigger to display a standard Web server error message.

Typically, a server script provides the following three functions:

- Retrieves information from the Web browser, the Web server, and HTML form variables.
- Builds the actual request logic. Usually this means running a query, inserting records into a table, handling business rule validations, and so on.
- Generates the output. In most cases, this will be HTML output, but you can also generate requests for authentication, redirect the user to a different page, or generate an error page.

Keep these three points in mind because flexibility in handling each of these tasks is important when choosing a tool with which to build Web applications.

How Visual FoxPro Fits In

Visual FoxPro is an excellent platform for building back-end applications because of its extremely fast data retrieval speed against local data, its flexibility when accessing remote data, and its powerful object-oriented, database-oriented language, which is ideal for programming complex data access and business rule logic.

Please note that to standardize this text, the following examples all use IIS. Some of the tools described work with other Web servers; I will point out what servers are supported.

N O T E   The rest of this chapter will focus on connecting Visual FoxPro databases to IIS, which is part of the operating system in Windows NT Server. Although some of the tools that will be mentioned work with other Web servers, I chose to standardize this discussion on IIS because it is built into Windows NT Server, which provides the ideal platform for hosting Web servers. Version 4.0 of Windows NT Server ships with this Web server. ▪

Following are several mechanisms available for accessing Visual FoxPro data over the Web:

- Access data via ODBC and a Web server-based tool such as the Internet Database Connector or Allaire ColdFusion.
- Use a Visual FoxPro OLE server to respond to Web requests.
- Use a Visual FoxPro application as a data server to process Web server requests.

ODBC-based tools are easy to set up and get started and provide integrated solutions that are closely tied to the Web server. However, ODBC is comparatively slow when running against local data such as Visual FoxPro and does not scale well if your server load gets heavy.

Using Visual FoxPro on its own for serving Web requests has distinct advantages over ODBC, as you get a significant database speed improvement and much better flexibility when building Web back ends using the full functionality of the FoxPro language.

To run Visual FoxPro as a standalone back-end tool, Visual FoxPro must act as a *data server*, an application that is preloaded in memory waiting for requests. This is necessary to provide timely response to requests without having to incur the overhead of loading the entire Visual FoxPro runtime on each incoming hit. A data server can be implemented in a variety of ways, whether it's as a standalone application, an OLE server, or a DDE server. I will discuss several methods in the following sections.

Why You Should or Shouldn't Use Visual FoxPro

There are a couple of things to keep in mind when using Visual FoxPro as a database back end.

The following are advantages of using Visual FoxPro:

- Extremely fast data engine; ODBC does not even come close to matching Visual FoxPro's native speed.

- Flexible language to build complex business logic using a real database development tool rather than a general purpose scripting language.

- Object-oriented nature enables building an easily reusable framework for processing requests.

- Unlike ODBC with local data, Visual FoxPro applications can be scaled across the network.

The biggest advantage of using Visual FoxPro as the database back end is its flexibility. Visual FoxPro is a high-end database tool, and you can take advantage of all the language and database functionality provided in it to create your Web application logic. You won't be limited by a cryptic general purpose scripting language, and there's no learning curve for new syntax (well, okay, you'll have to learn a little about HTML no matter how you slice it).

On the other hand, keep in mind the following disadvantages of using Visual FoxPro as a Web back end:

- Visual FoxPro is single-threaded; requests require multiple Visual FoxPro sessions to process simultaneously.

- Visual FoxPro is essentially detached from the Web server and requires a separate maintenance scheme.

At first glance, these limitations seem major. However, they are easy to overcome with proper implementation of the data server. Visual FoxPro's single-threaded nature can be handled by running multiple simultaneous sessions of the data server, which essentially simulates a multithreaded environment. Although speed will decrease for simultaneous requests occurring in this fashion, the same applies to true multitasked tools. The CPU load is the real performance factor; and whether you're running one or 10 simultaneous sessions or threads, the actual load that a single server can handle depends on the number and power of the CPUs available to handle that load.

The latter problem of maintenance is one to carefully consider. Running Visual FoxPro as a data server means that the application can respond to requests only while it's up and running; crash the server and you won't process requests. It's extremely important to build bulletproof code that can recover from any error and continue running.

Running Visual FoxPro as its own server also means that a separate startup procedure is required. It's easy enough to stick a shortcut to the data server into the system startup folder to have it load automatically when the system is rebooted, but unless you have the system log in automatically, some manual intervention for logging in is required. Unlike Web servers, Visual FoxPro cannot easily be run as a system service. Running a Visual FoxPro OLE Server provides some automation of this process as the OLE server is treated as a system component that's accessible directly from the system.

Updating code or data also translates to shutting down the data server, and that means either physical access to the machine or accessing it via remote-control software such as pcAnywhere to make the changes online. With OLE servers, the Web server might need to be shut down to handle code updates.

For in-house Web installations, the latter points won't be much of a problem. However, these issues can be especially problematic if you plan to install your application on a third-party ISP's network, as this will in essence mean that you need extensive security rights to access your data server. ISPs can be very touchy about what goes on their network and who is given access to network resources.

The Internet Database Connector

The first and most straightforward method to access FoxPro data is one of the ODBC-based tools that is available with IIS. IIS ships with the Internet Database Connector (IDC), which is a simple script-based tool that enables accessing Visual FoxPro tables or any other ODBC-accessible data source. Output is accomplished via a simple HTML-like scripting language that can be used to display the results from a SQL statement (SELECT, INSERT, UPDATE, DELETE, and so on).

N O T E The IDC uses SQL syntax that follows the ODBC SQL guidelines, which vary slightly from the Visual FoxPro SQL implementations. For example, you cannot call FoxPro's built-in functions from the SQL command line; instead, you have to use the ODBC/Transact SQL equivalent syntax. ■

To set up the IDC for use with a FoxPro database or directory of data files, start by configuring an ODBC datasource using the Visual FoxPro ODBC driver:

1. Bring up the 32-bit ODBC manager from your taskbar menu.

2. Click System DSN (the button on the bottom of the list window of installed drivers). It's extremely important that you add the new ODBC datasource using the system datasource rather than a standard ODBC source, or else IIS will fail to find your datasource and exit with an error. Figure 25.3 shows the resulting dialog box.

FIGURE 25.3
Create a new System DSN using the Visual FoxPro ODBC driver and store it in the directory that contains your DBC or directory containing free tables.

3. Add a new datasource for the Visual FoxPro ODBC driver. For the demo, name the new data source **QueVFP** and point the driver at the directory with the sample data.

After the ODBC driver is installed, you're ready to create the scripts that enable you to access this data. Take a look at Figure 25.4 and see how the data travels from Web browser to Web server and back to the browser.

FIGURE 25.4
An HTML form link
accesses the `.IDC`
script containing the
query information.
Results are displayed in
the `.HTX` document.

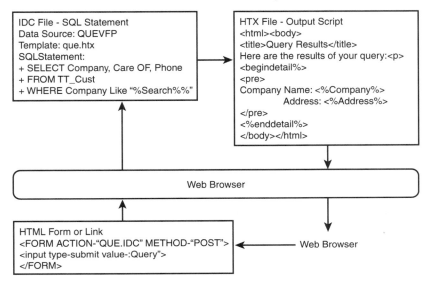

Internet Database Connector Components

All in all, a request generated via the IDC requires three files: an HTML file that contains the link or form that launches the script, the `.IDC` file responsible for defining the query parameters, and the `.HTX` HTML file template that is used to display the output. The example provided here is extremely simple but serves to illustrate the various pieces of the database connector.

The `.IDC` and `.HTX` files need to be placed into a directory that has been set up for execution rights in the IIS Service Manager application. By default, IIS assigns a `/scripts` directory for server scripts, but it's usually a good idea to create a separate directory for each of your applications. The example below uses a `/que` directory for this. To create this directory, follow these steps:

1. Bring up the IIS Service Manager.
2. Create a new Virtual Directory on the Directory tab of the Service Manager by clicking Add.
3. Set the directory to the physical DOS path of the script directory that you are creating.
4. Set the Alias to the name that you would like to use as part of your URL. For example, `/que` translates to a full URL of `http://servername.com/que/`.
5. Make sure you set the Execute check box to enable the server to execute a script in this directory.
6. Read access is optional. If you place HTML files in this directory as well, check the Read check box.

Part
VI

Ch
25

After you set up the script directory on the server, you can get to work and call the HTML page. The HTML form that captures input from the user looks like this:

```
<HTML><BODY>
<FORM ACTION="/cgi-win/QUE.IDC" METHOD="POST">
  Enter Name to Lookup: <input name=Search size=20><br>
  <input type=submit value="Retrieve Names"></FORM>
</BODY></HTML>
```

The script is fired off by the ACTION tag of the input HTML form. Here, you're retrieving input from the user and storing it to an HTML variable named Search.

Running Server Scripts

You can also run an IDC script from an HREF link:

```
<A HREF="QUE.IDC?">Run Query</a>
```

Notice the trailing question mark when running in this fashion. The ? is required to tell the browser that the link is a script. Without the question mark, some browsers might attempt to download the script and display it.

The question mark serves as a delimiter to signify the end of the executable and the beginning of the query string or the parameter list. You can pass additional parameters on the URL that can be evaluated inside of the script as if they were entered on a form:

```
<A HREF="QUE.IDC?UID=00001&Name=Rick">
```

These values can be retrieved in the .IDC file by using %UID% or %Name%.

When the user clicks the Retrieve Names button on this form, the QUE.IDC script is called. Behind the scenes, IIS calls an ISAPI DLL called httpodbc.dll that handles the routing, parameter translation, and evaluation of the .IDC and .HTX script files. The .IDC script file contains all the parameters that are related to the query to run:

```
Datasource: QUEVFP
Template: que.htx
SQLStatement:
+SELECT Company, Careof, Phone
+ FROM TT_Cust
+ WHERE Company Like "%Search%%"
+ ORDER BY COMPANY
```

You can specify a host of other parameters that enable you to limit the number of records returned from the query, specify the name of the user for database access, and provide default parameter values.

You can also run multiple SELECT statements by including multiple SQL statement clauses in the .IDC file (multiple queries work only with IIS 2.0, which ships with NT 4.0), but keep in mind that these run one after the other immediately without allowing you to tie logic to them. If you're using SQL server, you can also execute Transact SQL syntax here and execute stored procedures.

The most important options are used in the preceding .IDC file: datasource name, SQL statement, and name of the .HTX template file that is loaded when the query completes.

Output from this query is created with the .HTX template file, which is essentially an HTML document that contains embedded field values. Listing 25.1 shows what the .HTX file looks like.

Listing 25.1 25CODE01.HTX—The .HTX **Template File That Generates the HTML Output**

```
<html><body>
<title>Query Results</title>
<h2>Internet Database Connector Result</h2>
<HR>
Here are the results of your query for company search string:
<b><%idc.search%></B>
<p>

<TABLE CELLPADDING=5 BORDER=2 WIDTH=95% ALIGN=CENTER>
<TR>Company</TH>Contact</TH>Phone</TH>

<%begindetail%>
<TR><TD><%Company%></TD><TD><%CareOf%></TD><TD><%Phone%></TD></TR>
<%enddetail%>

</TABLE>
</body></html>
```

The <%BeginDetail%> and <%EndDetail%> tags provide a looping structure that runs through the result cursor. Any HTML between these two tags is repeatedly generated for each of the records in the result set. Field names can be embedded inside the page using the <%FieldName%> syntax that is used in the previous example. There are additional constructs available, such as a conditional <%IF%> (which can't be nested, though). For example:

```
<%if idc.company eq "West Wind Technologies"%>
    <H2>Special Message for West Wind Technologies</H2>
<%else%>
    <H2>Standard Message for <%idc.company%> </H2>
<%endif%>
```

For more detailed information on the .IDC and .HTX format options, you can look in the \IIS\IISADMIN\HTMLDOCS directory and search the index on the Database Connector (the actual page that contains this info is in \IIS\IISADMIN\HTMLDOCS\08_IIS.HTM).

The Internet database connector provides an easy mechanism for simple access to your Visual FoxPro data. When using this mechanism for accessing your data over the Web, keep the following advantages and disadvantages in mind:

Advantages:

- Easy to set up and use.
- Relatively good speed using the Visual FoxPro ODBC driver. Although not as fast as local Visual FoxPro data, it is still faster than any other desktop database ODBC driver.
- Ease of maintenance. The script files are fully self-contained and don't require any other application to run.

Part
VI

Ch
25

Disadvantages:

- Fairly limited in terms of functionality that can be implemented. The scripting language does not enable for complex logic, and you can't conditionally query the database from within a script.

- Single-transaction–based. Essentially, you can process only a single transaction at a time due to the inability to re-query the data from within the script.

- ODBC access does not scale well. You can't offload processing to another machine (at least not with FoxPro data; you can with SQL servers), and multiple simultaneous hits against data can easily overload both the Web server and the ODBC engine.

- No control over error handling. Database errors display cryptic ODBC message strings that are unsuitable for end users.

The central advantage of the IDC is that it is well-integrated with the Web server and provides an easy way to get started connecting databases to the Web. On the downside, the scripting mechanism is limited in the functionality that is provided when accessing data and creating dynamic HTML output. Furthermore, ODBC is slow compared to running Visual FoxPro natively. ODBC makes good sense when running against remote server data, but provides limited scalability against local data such as FoxPro tables.

Using Visual FoxPro as a Data Server

ODBC works well for small and simple Web applications, but for better performance and the ultimate in flexibility when creating applications based on FoxPro data, a Visual FoxPro data server is the ticket.

What exactly is a *data server*? The term implies that Visual FoxPro is used as a server that responds to requests rather than running as an interactive application. Although it's possible to run a FoxPro .EXE file directly in response to a Web server request, there are several problems with this approach. A Visual FoxPro .EXE file takes several seconds to load under the best of circumstances, and loading the .EXE directly in this manner causes the application to run invisibly on the desktop, which makes it next to impossible to debug your code should something go wrong. It's much more efficient for Visual FoxPro to be already loaded, waiting for incoming requests from the Web server and instantly springing to life when a request is received. This always-on state is a requirement for Web applications where fast response time is crucial. Using a data server, it is possible to return data-based page responses in sub-second times.

To provide the data server functionality, it's necessary to use an intermediary piece of software, called a *connector*, that passes requests from the Web server to Visual FoxPro. These connector applications are usually small library-type routines that are written in C to provide a messaging interface that communicates between the Web server and a Visual FoxPro server that is waiting for incoming requests. Following are descriptions of two different implementations of FoxPro data servers using ISAPI-based connector applications.

Using FoxISAPI and OLE Servers for Web Applications

N O T E   Using FoxISAPI with an OLE server for Web applications requires that the user have an ISAPI-based Web server, such as MS IIS, Commerce Builder, or Purveyor. ▓

Visual FoxPro's new capability to create OLE servers has brought about another slick option for implementing Visual FoxPro-based Web applications. What if you could use an OLE server to respond to a request placed from a Web page to handle the data processing and HTML page generation? With a tool called FoxISAPI that's provided with Visual FoxPro, you can do just that. You can find all the required files and an interesting example of an OLE server that makes use of FoxISAPI on your installation disk in the directory ..\SAMPLES\SERVER\FOXISAPI.

Before trying out this mechanism, be sure to read this entire section, especially the areas on setting up and creating the OLE server. Configuration is critical in getting FoxISAPI to work correctly.

How FoxISAPI Works   FoxISAPI consists of a small connector script .DLL that is called directly from an HTML page using a link similar to this:

```
<a HREF="/scripts/foxisapi.dll/
oleserver.myclass.mymethod?UID=1111&Company=Que+Publications">
```

Part
VI
Ch
25

The first thing that happens on a script call is that the FoxISAPI.dll is accessed. This .DLL is implemented as an Internet Server API (ISAPI) extension, which is an API that extends Internet Information Server via an in-process .DLL interface. Because ISAPI extensions run in the same address space as the Web server, are multithreaded, and are coded in a low-level compiled language such as C, these extension scripts are extremely fast.

The task of the ISAPI DLL is to provide an OLE Automation client that makes calls to your Visual FoxPro OLE server using the class ID (server, class, method) that is passed as part of the URL. The .DLL parses out the class string and makes an OLE Automation call to your OLE server accessing your class method directly. In response, your code should return a compliant result, which in most cases should be an HTML document. Figure 25.5 shows how a request travels from the Web server to your OLE server and back. Notice how FoxISAPI.dll is the mediator that receives both the outgoing script call and the incoming HTML output, sending the output to the Web server for display or processing.

FIGURE 25.5
FoxISAPI enables calling OLE server methods directly via an HTML script link or form submission.

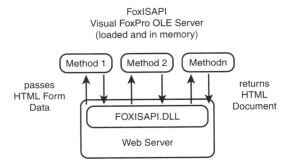

A Simple Example Server The FoxISAPI example provided by Microsoft in your \VFP\SAMPLES\SERVERS\FOXISAPI directory is a good way to check out some of the things you can do with a FoxPro-based data server. But a simpler example might be more adequate in showing how FoxISAPI works. Listing 25.2 demonstrates how FoxISAPI.dll calls a Visual FoxPro OLE server.

Listing 25.2   25CODE02.PRG—A Minimal Response OLE Server Using FoxISAPI

```
#DEFINE CR CHR(13)+CHR(10)

****************************************************************
DEFINE CLASS QueVFP AS FOXISAPI OLEPUBLIC
****************************************************************

***************************************************************************
* QueVFP : HelloWorld
*********************************
*   Function: Minimal response method for handling FoxISAPI call.
***************************************************************************
FUNCTION HelloWorld
LPARAMETER lcFormVars, lcIniFile, lnReleaseFlag
LOCAL lcOutput

* HTTP header - REQUIRED on each request!
lcOutput="HTTP/1.0 200 OK"+CR+;
         "Content-type: text/html"+;
         CR+CR

lcOutput=lcOutput+;
"<HTML><BODY>"+CR+;
"<H1>Hello World from Visual FoxPro</H1>"+CR+;
"<HR>The current time is: "+TIME()+CR+;
"This page was generated by Visual FoxPro...<HR>"+CR+;
"</HTML></BODY>"

RETURN lcOutput
ENDFUNC
* FoxISAPI

ENDDEFINE
* QueVFP
```

This example doesn't do much, but it demonstrates the basics of what's required of a method that responds to a call from the FoxISAPI.DLL. The idea is this: FoxISAPI calls your OLE server method with three input parameters (described in Table 25.1), so your method must always support these three parameters. The parameters provide all the information made available by the HTML input form as well as Web server and browser stats. You pull the appropriate information from these references in order to do your data processing. For example, you might retrieve a query parameter and, based on it, run a SQL SELECT statement. To complete the process, your code needs to then return an HTTP-compatible response to the Web server. In most cases, this response is an HTML document, as demonstrated by the preceding example code, which simply returns an HTML page along with the time, so you can assure yourself that the page is actually dynamically generated. Notice that the output must include an HTTP header that is created by the first assignment to lcOutput.

Just like the HelloWorld example method, every response method must have three parameters. If your code has fewer than three parameters, the OLE call will fail, generating a FoxISAPI-generated error.

Table 25.1   FoxISAPI Response Method Parameters

Parameter	Contents
cFormVars	This parameter contains all variable names and their contents in encoded form.
cIniFile	FoxISAPI creates an .INI file containing server/browser variables, which are stored in an .INI file; the name and path of this file is passed in this parameter.
nReleaseFlag	Passed by reference, this variable determines whether FoxISAPI.dll releases the reference to the OLE server. You can set this value in your code and it's returned to the .DLL. 0 is the default and means the server is not unloaded; 1 means it is unloaded.

Part
VI
Ch
25

The first parameter is probably the most important, as it contains the name and values of any fields that were filled out on an HTML form. All key/value pairs from an HTML form are returned; fields that are empty simply return an empty value. In typical CGI fashion, and because browsers do not support certain characters on the URL line, the string is MIME-encoded using various characters to signify "extended" characters and spaces. Before you can use the string, you typically have to decode it. Here's an example of a string passed in lcFormVars:

```
UserId=000111&BookTitle=Using+Visual+FoxPro
```

Each of the key/value pairs is separated by an ampersand (&) and spaces are converted to plus (+) signs. In addition, lower ASCII characters are converted into a hex code preceded by an ampersand. For example, a carriage return would be included as %0D (hex 0D or decimal 13).

Listing 25.2 doesn't use the parameters passed to it, so let's look at another example that does. Listing 25.3 demonstrates how to retrieve the information provided by the Web server using a simple FoxISAPI class provided in 25CODE02.prg. The code retrieves a couple of form variables passed on the URL of the request and then displays the entire .INI file in a browser window for you to examine.

Listing 25.3 `25CODE03.prg`—**How to Retrieve Information Provided by the Web Server**

```
*******************************************************************************
* QueVFP : TestMethod
**********************************
FUNCTION TestMethod
LPARAMETER lcFormVars, lcIniFile, lnReleaseFlag
LOCAL lcOutput

* Decode the Form Vars and assign INI file to class property
THIS.StartRequest(lcFormVars,lcIniFile)

* Must always add a content Type Header to output first
THIS.HTMLContentTypeHeader()

lcUserId=THIS.GetFormVar("UserId")
lcName=THIS.GetFormVar("UserName")

THIS.SendLn("<HTML><BODY>")
THIS.SendLn("<H1>Hello World from Visual FoxPro</H1><HR>")
THIS.SendLn("This page was generated by Visual FoxPro using FOXISAPI. ")
THIS.SendLn("The current time is: "+time()+"<p>")

THIS.SendLn("<b>Encoded Form/URL variables:</b> "+lcFormVars+"<BR>")
THIS.SendLn("<b>Decoded UserId:</b> "+ THIS.GetFormVar("UserId")+"<br>")
THIS.SendLn("<b>Decoded UserName:</b> " +lcName+"<P>")

* Show the content of the FOXISAPI INI server/browser vars
IF !EMPTY(lcIniFile) AND FILE(lcIniFile)
   CREATE CURSOR TMemo (TFile M )
   APPEND BLANK
   APPEND MEMO TFile from (lcIniFile)
   THIS.SendLn("Here's the content of: <i>"+lcIniFile+"</i>."+;
               "You can retrieve any of these with <i>"+;
               THIS.GetCGIVar(cVarname,cSection)+"</i>:<p>")
   THIS.SendLn([For example to retrieve the Browser use ]+;
               [THIS.GetCGIVar("HTTP_USER_AGENT","ALL_HTTP"): ]+;
               THIS.GetCGIVar("HTTP_USER_AGENT","ALL_HTTP") )

   THIS.SendLn("<PRE>")
   THIS.SendLn(Tmemo.Tfile)
   THIS.SendLn("</PRE>")
   USE in TMemo
ENDIF

THIS.SendLn("<HR></HTML></BODY>")

RETURN THIS.cOutput
```

The code makes heavy use of the FoxISAPI class' internal methods to simplify retrieving information and generating the output. Table 25.2 shows the public interface to the FoxISAPI class from which the QueVFP class in the examples is derived.

Table 25.2 FoxISAPI Class Methods

Method	Function
Send(cOutput, llNoOutput)	A low-level output routine that simplifies SendLn(cOutput, llNoOutput) creating HTML output by using a method call. This is also useful for abstracting the output interface in case you want to modify the way output is generated later on. SendLn is identical to Send, but adds a carriage return to the output.
StandardPage(cHeader, cBody)	A simplified routine that creates a full HTML page by passing a header and body. The page created includes minimal formatting and a title directive. Both header and body can contain embedded HTML codes that are expanded when the page is displayed.
ContentTypeHeader(llNoOutput)	Generates the HTTP header required by FoxISAPI. Generates a default header for HTML documents. *Required* for each output page.
StartRequest()	Call this method to automatically decode the FormVariable string and set up the internal handling for retrieving form and server variables using the following two methods. *Required* for each request that retrieves form or CGI variables using the internal methods.
GetFormVar(cVarName)	Returns the value for the form variable passed as the first parameter. Note that only single variables are returned; there's no support for multiselects.
GetCGIVar(cCGIVar,cSection)	Returns variables contained in the .INI file that is passed by FoxISAPI. Pass the name of the variable and the section that it is contained in. The default section is FoxISAPI.
ReleaseServer()	A full request method that takes the standard three request parameters and sets the lnReleaseFlag to 1, thus forcing the FoxISAPI .DLL to release the OLE server reference.

In the Testmethod code, notice the calls to THIS.StartRequest and THIS.ContentTypeHeader. StartRequest sets up the internal variable retrieval routines by assigning the input parameters to class properties so that they can be easily referenced by the internal methods such as GetCGIVar and GetFormVar. Both of these routines make it easy to retrieve information related to the current request from the Web server's provided information. ContentTypeHeader

Part VI Ch 25

creates the required header that must be sent back to the Web server in the result output. An HTTP header tells the server what type of content to expect and ContentTypeHeader obliges by providing the proper identification for an HTML document.

HTML output is accomplished by using the class Send method, which abstracts the output. Using this method is easier than concatenating strings manually and also provides the capability to build more complex output mechanisms that are required when your output gets longer than a few thousand characters. Behind the scenes, Send() does nothing more than add the text to a string property of the class. Notice that at the exit point, a RETURN THIS.cOutput is used to return the final result text to the FoxISAPI DLL.

The next snippet outputs the original lcFormVars encoded string and then uses GetFormVar() to print the decoded values of the actual values that were passed on the URL. GetFormVar() takes the name of the key as a parameter and returns the decoded value. If the key does not exist or the key is blank, a null string ("") is returned.

CGI variables returned by the server provide information about the server, browser, and the environment. FoxISAPI.dll captures most of the relevant information into an .INI file and the code wrapped in the IF statement outputs this file to the HTML page. All the keys are accessible with the GetCGIVar() method, which takes a keyname and section as parameters. For example, to retrieve the name of the Web server in use, you can use the following code:

```
THIS.GetCGIVar("Server Software ","FOXISAPI")
```

Let's take another look at the customer list example you used with the IDC and see how to implement it with FoxISAPI. Listing 25.4 shows the method code that accomplishes the task.

Listing 25.4   25CODE04—This Sample Method Generates a Customer List Based on a Name Provided on an HTML Form

```
*****************************************************************************
* QueVFP : CustomerLookup
*********************************
FUNCTION CustomerLookup
LPARAMETER lcFormVars, lcIniFile, lnReleaseFlag

* Decode the Form Vars and assign INI file to global var
THIS.StartRequest(lcFormVars,lcIniFile)

lcName=THIS.GetFormVar("Name")
lcCompany=THIS.GetFormVar("Company")
lcWhere=""
IF !EMPTY(lcName)
   lcWhere="UPPER(Careof)='"+UPPER(lcName)+"'"
ENDIF
IF !EMPTY(lcCompany)
   IF !EMPTY(lcWhere)
      lcWhere=lcWhere+" AND "
    ENDIF
    lcWhere=lcWhere+"UPPER(Client)='"+UPPER(lcCompany)+"'"
```

```
      ENDIF
      IF !EMPTY(lcWhere)
         lcWhere="WHERE "+lcWhere
      ENDIF

      SELECT Careof, Company, Address, Phone ;
         FROM (DATAPATH+"TT_CUST") ;
         &lcWhere ;
         INTO Cursor TQuery

      IF _Tally <1
         THIS.StandardPage("No matching records found",;
                           "Please enter another name or use a shorter search
                           ➥string...")
         USE IN Tquery
         USE IN TT_Cust
         RETURN THIS.cOutput
      ENDIF

      THIS.HTMLContentTypeHeader()

      THIS.SendLn([<HTML><BODY>])
      THIS.SendLn([<H1>Customer Lookup</H1><HR>])

      This.SendLn([Matching found: ]+STR(_Tally)+[<p>])

      THIS.Send([<TABLE BGCOLOR=#EEEEEE CELLPADDING=4 BORDER=1 WIDTH=100%>]+CR+;
               [<TR BGCOLOR=#FFFFCC>Name</TH>Company</TH>Address</TH>;
                          </ TR>]+CR)
      SCAN
         THIS.Send(;
               [<TR><TD>]+;
               TRIM(IIF(EMPTY(TQUery.Careof),"<BR>",Tquery.CareOf))+[</TD><TD>]+;
               TRIM(IIF(EMPTY(Tquery.Company),"<BR>",Tquery.Company))+[Company</
               ➥TD><TD>]+;
               TRIM(IIF(EMPTY(Tquery.Phone),"<BR>",TQuery.Phone))+[</TD></TR>]+CR)
      ENDSCAN

      THIS.SendLn([</TABLE><HR>])
      THIS.SendLn([</BODY></HTML>])

      USE IN Tquery
      USE IN TT_Cust

      RETURN THIS.cOutput
      * CustomerLookup
```

Setting Up for FoxISAPI   It's extremely important to correctly set up the Web server, the FoxISAPI.dll script connector, and your Visual FoxPro OLE server to get them to properly run under Windows NT. Windows NT 4.0 especially requires special attention to OLE server access rights and user configuration rights in order to run OLE servers driven by the Web server.

Here are the configuration steps for using FoxISAPI with Internet Information Server under NT 4.0:

- Start by creating your public OLE server. (See the following section for details on server creation.) Make sure you compile the server as OLEPUBLIC and that you create OLE ID for this server in the project's build options. If you run this server on an external machine, make sure you register the server on the Web server machine by using the /regserver command-line switch on an EXE server or by running regsvr32 yourdll.dll against a DLL server. Before going any further with configuration, make sure your OLE server works correctly by instantiating it from the Visual FoxPro Command window and testing the output.

- Download the latest version of FoxISAPI.DLL from http://www.microsoft.com/vfox to your \INETINFO\SCRIPTS directory. Double-check and make sure that the /scripts directory is set up as a virtual directory in the IIS service manager and that the directory has execute rights set on it.

- Make sure that your IUSR_XXXXX account is properly set up in the IIS service manager as the default for the anonymous user and that this user exists in your user manager as a guest account. This account is for every Web user that accesses your Web server.

- If you are building an .EXE-based OLE server, you have to run DCOMCNFG.EXE in your \WINNT40\SYSTEM32 directory. This utility sets the access rights for OLE servers in your system. Start by setting the selections on the Default Properties tab: Enable DCOM and set Default Authentication to Connect and Default Impersonation to Identify (both of these are the default). On the Default Security tab, add the IUSR_XXXX account to the Access and Launch permission button lists. If you compile your server on the same machine as the Web server, you have to run DCOMCONFG every time you recompile your program. A faster alternative is to build the server on another machine and simply copy it to the server as this does not update the server's CLSIDs on the server. This DCOM configuration step is extremely important!

- If you have created an EXE server and registered it, find it on the DCOMCNFG Applications tab. The name of the class should be found on this page. In the previous examples, the classname is QueVFP. Select it and click on Properties and then the Identity tab. Set the radio button to Interactive User and click Apply. This enables the server to access system libraries.

Deciding What OLE Server Instancing to Use   Whenever you build an OLE server, one of the important issues you need to deal with is server *instancing*. A server must provide a separate, identical process to handle each client request; each use of the process is an *instance*. In Web applications, instancing is even more critical as timing and freeing up of the server for quick handling of requests are crucial to provide adequate Web performance.

Visual FoxPro is a single-threaded application and as such can handle only one request at a time. OLE servers, even multiuse servers, are no different. If an OLE server is busy, it cannot handle another request until it finishes. Furthermore, although ISAPI DLLs are multithreaded, FoxISAPI blocks simultaneous OLE server access in its code to prevent Visual FoxPro from taking more than one request at a time.

Your instancing options are to use the following:

- *In-process DLL servers.* This is the fastest implementation of an OLE server as it runs in process of the Web server. Requests to the OLE server are queued. You can run only one DLL-based OLE server on a single machine. If you try to load a second DLL-based server, it will fail. DLL servers cannot be shut down unless the Web server is stopped. A crash in the OLE server DLL will likely bring down the Web server.

- *Multiuse EXE server.* This out-of-process OLE server creates a single, reusable instance of an OLE server, and is slightly slower than a DLL-based server because the server runs externally to the Web server. But because the instance stays loaded, there's no penalty for load time after it is loaded. Requests are queued, but you can run multiple different multiuse servers (would require separate `FoxISAPI.dll` files because each OLE server call blocks additional OLE calls).

- *Single use EXE server.* This is the slowest server that forces a full load for each instance of a server. Speed is noticeably slower than the DLL or multiuse servers, but multiple servers can load simultaneously. Although this option provides simultaneous access, keep in mind that FoxISAPI actually serializes requests, so you can't even take advantage of the multiple server feature. Because of this and the slow load time, this option is not recommended. If you do use this method, keep a session of the VFP runtime loaded with an idle application. After the runtime is in memory, startup speed can be reduced substantially.

The bottom line is that you should stick to DLL or multiuse servers. DLLs provide the best speed but they are volatile because a crash in the OLE server can crash the entire Web server and will require a server shutdown. Multiuse servers probably offer the best compromise between performance and flexibility. Speed for these multiuse servers is excellent and it is possible to shut them down without shutting down the Web server.

One major limitation of FoxISAPI to keep in mind is that you are limited in scalability. If you outgrow a single instance of your OLE server, FoxISAPI can't easily offload requests to another server. FoxISAPI can handle only one OLE Automation call at a time. It is possible to call different OLE servers simultaneously by making copies of `FoxISAPI.dll` and using a different name to call specific multiuse OLE servers, which are essentially one ISAPI DLL per OLE server. But even using this workaround, you can't call the same server simultaneously.

As long as a single machine and a single OLE server called serially can serve your needs, FoxISAPI provides a fast, efficient, and easily implemented interface to your FoxPro applications.

Part
VI

Ch
25

Using Web Connection for Web Applications

N O T E In order to use Web Connection, you must have ISAPI or a Windows CGI-based Web server (IIS, Commerce Builder, Website, Purveyor for NT).

FoxISAPI provides an easy, speedy interface for creating Web applications. But for maximum flexibility and scalability, a standalone Web application that runs as a data server can provide much better scalability, maintenance, and debugging functionality. FoxISAPI is limited to a single OLE server of the same type for handling like requests, which can be a serious limitation on busy sites. In contrast, when running a standalone Visual FoxPro application, it is possible to run multiple instances of Visual FoxPro to provide an imitation of multithreading for a Visual FoxPro-based Web application. Running only two sessions, others have tested up to 120,000 database requests per day on a single dual-processor Pentium Pro machine on a live site. With a tool like Web Connection, it's even possible to further scale the application to multiple machines across a network for even greater scalability by having remote nodes handle data processing over the network.

N O T E To provide working examples of how you can hook FoxPro code to process requests from a Web server, this section describes how to build Web applications using a third-party tool called Web Connection. A shareware version of the software can be found at `http://www.west-wind.com`. ■

Web Connection is a developer tool that provides a framework for connecting a Web server to Visual FoxPro. The framework provides many important features for developing industrial-strength Web applications: The capability to create external HTML pages with embedded FoxPro expressions to enable working with HTML designers, robust error handling and logging, automatic logging of Web hits, and an easy interface to retrieve information from and output HTML to the Web server.

Unlike FoxISAPI, which uses OLE as its messaging medium, Web Connection uses a file-based connector approach to communicate with the Web server. Figure 25.6 shows how data flows from the Web browser to the Web server to Visual FoxPro and your code.

FIGURE 25.6

With Web Connection, Visual FoxPro acts as an active server waiting for incoming requests from the Web server, responding by executing FoxPro code and generating an HTML page.

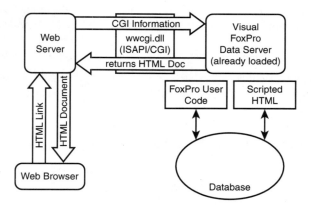

From Browser to Visual FoxPro

From Web Server to Visual FoxPro   A typical request starts off on the Web browser where the user clicks either a hyperlink or the submit button of an HTML input form:

```
<A HREF="/cgi-win/wwcgi.dll?Test_Page">Simple CGI Test</A>
```

The wwcgi.dll script captures the information that the Web server and Web browser make available. Like FoxISAPI, Web Connection captures the content information, including the HTML form variables, into an .INI file that can be easily accessed with the application framework provided.

Instead of using an OLE server as FoxISAPI does, Web Connection employs a Visual FoxPro application based on a set of framework classes that wait for an incoming message that is provided by the wwcgi.dll. The message comes in the form of a small file that contains the path to the content .INI file the .DLL creates for each request. Web Connection picks up the file, retrieves the .INI file path, and creates a CGI object that exposes all of the .INI file's content.

N O T E   If you would rather use OLE messaging similar to FoxISAPI's instead of Web Connection's standard file messaging, you can also use Web Connection's OLE connector, which uses all the Web Connection framework classes. You can access servers using the OLE object syntax and still use the CGI, HTML, and CGIProcess classes described here for generating your request code. ▨

Part
VI

Ch
25

The data server, which is responsible for picking up these requests, is implemented as a form class running with a timer and retrieves the filename and creates an object that facilitates access to the .INI file via a simplified class interface provided by the wwCGI class. After the Web Connection server has received the message file from the Web server, it takes the newly created CGI object and calls a user-defined function using the object as a parameter. This function is the hook that acts as an entry point for your own custom Visual FoxPro code.

Now it's your program's turn to take the information available via the CGI object and create HTML output. Your code can run any available FoxPro commands and functions, access class libraries, the data dictionary, and views to remote data—the entire language is available to you at this point. Web Connection facilitates creation of the HTML output by providing a CGIProcess class that contains both the CGI object passed to the Process function as well as an HTML object that is preconfigured to output the HTML (in most cases the response is HTML, but you can actually return any HTTP-compliant result) result to the proper output file.

After the HTML output has been generated, your custom code terminates and control returns to the wwCGIserver object, which, in turn, notifies the Web server that processing is complete. The Web server now takes the output file generated by your code and sends it over the Web for display by the Web browser.

A Look at the Components and the Setup Code   Before you dig in to the code, let's describe the components that make up Web Connection:

■   wwCGI.dll. wwCGI is the script connector that is called by the Web server. wwcgi.dll is a small Internet Server API Extension library that handles the interface with Visual FoxPro. Its task is to let Visual FoxPro know when a request is incoming and pass all the information the browser and the server are making available. Note that every Web request that accesses Visual FoxPro needs to call this script.

■ wwCGIServer class. The wwCGIServer class handles requests that are generated by the external wwCGI program. The wwCGIServer class is responsible for receiving incoming CGI requests, decoding them, and passing a CGI object to a user-defined procedure of your choice.

■ wwCGI class. This class encapsulates all the CGI information made available by the Web server. This includes the contents of form variables and status information about the Web server and the browser that called it. Your processing routine receives a wwCGI object as a parameter for you to use in generating an HTML document in response to the server's request.

■ wwHTML class. The HTML class provides an optional high-level interface to create HTML documents by providing a variety of methods that output HTML-formatted strings either directly to file or as string return values. The class supports single-method output of entire tables, display of pages from disk files or memo fields, and embedded FoxPro expressions or code in scripted HTML pages.

■ wwCGIProcess class. The wwCGIProcess class is a wrapper class that encapsulates the wwCGI and wwHTML objects into an easy-to-use framework that makes creating your own requests as easy as creating a new method in a subclassed version of this class.

In its simplest form, startup of the Web Connection CGI server requires only a handful of lines of code, as shown in Listing 25.5.

Listing 25.5   25CODE05.PRG—Simplified Web Connection Server Startup Code

```
***********************************************************************
FUNCTION CGITEST
*****************
*    Function: Web Connection server startup program.
***********************************************************************
#INCLUDE WCONNECT.H
SET PROCEDURE TO CGIServ ADDITIVE
SET PROCEDURE TO CGI ADDITIVE
SET PROCEDURE TO HTML ADDITIVE
SET PROCEDURE TO CGIPROC ADDITIVE
SET PROCEDURE TO WWUTILS ADDITIVE

* Starts up the server and gets it ready to poll
* for CGI requests. Call Process UDF() on a request
oCGIServer=CREATE("wwCGIServer","Process")
IF TYPE("oCGIServer")#"O"
   =MessageBox("Unable to load the CGI Request Server",;
     MB_ICONEXCLAMATION,"Web Connection Error")
   RETURN
ENDIF

oCGIServer.SetCGIFilePath("c:\temp\")

* This actually puts the server into polling mode - Modal Window
oCGIServer.show()
RETURN
```

The preceding code loads all the required code-based class libraries and simply creates a new wwCGIServer object. All the actual CGI request retrieval logic is handled transparently by this server class. The only crucial item in this piece of code is the second parameter in the CREATE command. The second parameter, Process, specifies a function of your choice that is called with a wwCGI object parameter each time a request is generated by the Web server. Notice the call to the SetCGIFilePath() method. The path specified here is inserted by the SETUP.APP installation program and should point to the location of the CGI temp files generated by each Web request.

When a request from the Web server hits, the code shown in Listing 25.6 is called.

Listing 25.6 25CODE06.PRG—The Process Procedure Is Called by Any Incoming Request

```
********************************************************************
FUNCTION Process
****************
*   Function: This is the program called by the CGI Server that
*             handles processing of a CGI request.
*
*             This example creates a process class, which
*             simplifies error handling and validation of
*             success. However, you can use procedural
*             code if you prefer.
*        Pass: loCGI -       Object containing CGI information
********************************************************************
LPARAMETERS loCGI

* Now create a process object. It's not necessary
* to use an object here, but it makes error handling
* document and CGI handling much easier!
loCGIProcess=CREATE("MyCGIProcess",loCGI)

* Call the Process Method that routes request types
* to methods in the loCGIProcess class
loCGIProcess.Process

* Debug: See what the input and output files look like
* RELEASE loCGIProcess  && Must release first or file isn't closed
* COPY FILE (lcIniFile) TO TEMP.INI
* COPY FILE (lcOutFile) TO TEMP.HTM
RETURN
```

This procedure is the entry point of the custom FoxPro code that can be executed in response to a Web server request. Notice that this function expects a wwcgi parameter when it is called from the Web server.

Although this routine creates another layer of abstraction by creating an instance of the CGIProcess class, this step is strictly optional (though highly recommended for ease of use). You could, at this point, use logic to retrieve the information passed by the Web server and start processing and generating HTML output right here. For maximum ease of use and maintainability, however, the CGIProcess class provides preconfigured settings that let you get to work immediately.

The Process Class: Putting Your Code to Work   For maximum ease of use and maintainability, the CGIProcess class created in Listing 25.6 exposes a framework that provides development and debug mode error handling, an easy mechanism for routing requests to your code and preconfigured CGI and HTML objects. With this class, adding your own code becomes as easy as adding a method to a subclassed version of the class.

Let's see how this works. First, here's a typical URL that generates a request in the running Web Connection server:

```
<A HREF="wwcgi.dll?MethodToCall~Parameter1~Parameter2">Que Test Request</a>
```

Notice the use of "parameters" on the URL to identify which method in the wwCGIProcess class to call.

When this request runs, the Web Connection server passes the request on to the Process function, which, in turn, creates a subclassed object of the wwCGIServer class as seen in Listing 25.6. After the object is created, its Process method is called.

Listing 25.7 contains a skeleton class definition.

Listing 25.7   25CODE07.PRG—A Skeleton Class Definition for Setting Up Your Own Request Handlers

```
****************************************************************
DEFINE CLASS webConnectDemo AS wwCGIProcess
****************************************************************
*  Function: This class handles the requests generated by
*            the wconnect.htm form and its results. The
*            class implementation makes error and output
*            doc handling much cleaner
*            Subclassed from a generic wwCGIProcess class
*            handler which provides error handling and
*            HTML and CGI object setup.
****************************************************************
* Properties defined by wwCGIProcess Parent Class
*  _ _ _ _ _ _ _ _ _ _ _ _ _ _ _ _ _ _ _ _ _ _
* oCGI=.NULL.
* oHTML=.NULL.
* Methods defined by wwCGIProcess Parent Class
*  _ _ _ _ _ _ _ _ _ _ _ _ _ _ _ _ _ _ _ _ _
* Init(oCGI) && Initializes and checks HTML and CGI objects
* Process    && Virtual Method always overridden, used to route requests
* Error      && Handles errors that occur in the Process code
* ErrorMsg(cErrorHeader,cMessage)  && Quick Message Display
********************************************************************************
* webConnectDemo : Process
***************************
*  Modified: 01/24/96
```

```
*   Function: This is the callback program file that handles
*             processing a CGI request
*       Pass: THIS.oCGI  Object containing CGI information
*     Return: .T. to erase Temp File .F. to keep it
***********************************************************************
FUNCTION Process
LOCAL lcParameter

* Retrieve first 'parameter' off the URL
lcParameter=UPPER(THIS.oCGI.GetCGIParameter(1))

DO CASE
   * Call the method if it exists
   CASE !EMPTY(lcParameter) AND PEMSTATUS(THIS,lcParameter,5)
      =EVALUATE("THIS."+lcParameter+"()")
   OTHERWISE
      * Generate Error Response Page
      THIS.ErrorMsg("The server was unable to respond "+;
          "to the CGI request.<br>"+;
          "Parameter Passed: '"+PROPER(lcParameter)+"'...",;
          "This error page is automatically called when a "+;
          "Visual FoxPro code error occurs while processing "+;
          "CGI requests.<p>It uses the wwHTML:HTMLError() method to "+;
          "output two error strings and generic server information, "+;
          "as well as overwriting existing HTML output for this request.")
ENDCASE
RETURN .T.

Function CustomMethod1
 ... Your code here
EndFunc

Function CustomMethod2
 ... Your code here
EndFunc

ENDDEFINE
```

You'll always create a Process method, which is used to route incoming CGI requests to the appropriate processing method within the wwCGIProcess subclass. This class can process requests generated by HTML tags with the following format:

```
/cgi-win/wwcgi.dll?Method~Optional+Parameter~Optional+Parm2
```

The method is an identifier that is used in the CASE statement to decide which method to call to process the request. The optional parameters are any additional parameters that you need to pass when processing a request. Note that the ~ is used as a parameter separator that is recognized by the wwCGI:GetCGIParameter(ParmNo) method to separate parameters passed on the URL following the ?.

Because of the way the class is designed, it consists almost entirely of your own custom code. The Process method is provided here more for reference than anything else; the code is actually defined in the base class. However, you often will want to override the Process method to use a more complex parameter scheme that enables you to call different classes for request processing (see the CGIMAIN example in the Web Connection samples to see how to call multiple projects from one session).

The main task of the Process method is to route the request by figuring out which method to call. This logic is handled by retrieving the first parameter on the URL, and then checking whether a method of that name exists with PEMSTATUS(). If the method exists, the EVALUATE() goes out and executes the method.

> **N O T E**   PEMSTATUS() is an extremely powerful function for writing generic code that checks for the existence of class properties and methods. The function provides a mechanism to query all aspects of properties or methods. You can determine Public/Protected status, whether the value was changed from the default, whether the property is read only, and what type a property is. ▪

What all of this does is provide you with an easy mechanism to hook your own code: All you have to do is add a method to your subclassed version of the CGIProcess class, and the code is practically called directly from a URL link.

Lights, Camera, Action   So what does the actual code you write to respond to requests look like? Let's take a look at a couple of examples.

For starters, let's use the same simple example you used with the Internet Database Connector:

```
<HTML><BODY>
<FORM ACTION="/cgi-win/wwcgi.dll?CustomerList" METHOD="POST">
  Enter Name to Lookup: <input name=Search size=20><br>
  <input type=submit value="Retrieve Names">
</FORM></BODY></HTML>
```

To respond to this request, add a new method to the wwConnectDemo class started previously (see Listing 25.8).

Listing 25.8   25CODE08.PRG—The Customer List Example Using Web Connection

```
***********************************************************************
* wwConnectDemo : CustomerList
*******************************
*   Function: Returns an HTML table customer list.
***********************************************************************
FUNCTION CustomerList
LOCAL loCGI, loHTML

* Easier reference
loCGI=THIS.oCGI
loHTML=THIS.oHTML

* Retrieve the name the user entered - could be blank
lcCustname=loCGI.GetFormVar("Search")
```

```
* Get all entries that have time entries (expense=.F.)
SELECT tt_cust.Company, tt_cust.careof, tt_cust.phone ;
   FROM TT_Cust ;
   WHERE tt_cust.company=lcCustname ;
   ORDER BY Company ;
   INTO CURSOR TQuery

IF _TALLY < 1
   * Return an HTML response page
   * You can subclass ErrorMsg to create a customized 'error page'
   THIS.ErrorMsg("No Matching Records Found",;
                 "Please pick another name or use fewer letters "+;
                 "to identify the name to look up")
   RETURN
ENDIF

* Create HTML document header
* - Document header, a Browser title, Background Image
loHTML.HTMLHeader("Customer List","Web Connection Customer List",;
                  "/wconnect/whitwav.jpg")

loHTML.SendLn("<b>Returned Records: "+STR(_TALLY)+"</b>")
loHTML.SendPar()
loHTML.SendLn("<CENTER>")

* Show entire result set as an HTML table
loHTML.ShowCursor()

* Center the table
loHTML.SendLn("</CENTER>")

loHTML.HTMLFooter(PAGEFOOT)

USE IN TQuery

ENDFUNC
* CustomerList
```

The logic of this snippet is straightforward. The code retrieves the value entered on the HTML form, runs a query, and then displays as an HTML table.

The important pieces in this code snippet are the uses of the CGI and HTML objects. As you can see, you don't need to create these objects because they are instantiated automatically when the CGIProcess object is created.

The loCGI.GetFormVar() method retrieves the single-input field from the HTML form. You can retrieve any field from an HTML form in this manner. Note that method always returns a string. If the form variable is not found, a null string ("") is returned, so it's safe in the preceding example to simply use the result in the query without further checks. The CGI class provides a ton of useful functionality. Here's a list of the most commonly used methods:

wwCGI **Method**	**Function**
GetFormVar(cFormVar)	Retrieves a field entered on an HTML form.
GetFormMultiple(aParams)	Retrieves multi-select field selections into an array.
GetBrowser()	Returns the Browser ID string.
IsHTML30()	Does the browser support HTML 3.0 extensions like tables?
IsSecure()	Does the browser support secure transactions?
GetPreviousURL()	Name of the page that generated this link.
GetRemoteAddress()	Returns the IP address of the user.
GetCGIVar(cKey,cSection)	Low-level CGI retrieval routine that enables retrieval of key values that don't have predefined methods. The section name defaults to the CGI section in the content .INI file.

The HTML class provides a simple output mechanism for generating HTML code. The class consists of both high-level and low-level methods that aid in creating your result output. At the low level are the Send() and SendLn() methods, which enable you to send string output to the HTML output file. It's entirely possible to generate your HTML output entirely using these two commands.

However, some of the higher-level functions can make life a lot easier. Here are a few of the functions available:

wwHTML **Method**	**Function**
Send()	Lowest-level function. All output must go through this method to enable for different output methods. All the methods in this class call this method for final output.
SendLn()	Identical to Send except it adds a carriage return/ linefeed at the end.
HTMLHeader()	Creates a standard HTML header with a title line, browser window title, and background image, as well as providing an easy mechanism to control HTTP headers passed back to the Web server.
HTMLFooter()	Adds <HTML><BODY> tags and enables for sending a standard HTML footer for pages.
ShowCursor()	Displays all fields of the currently open cursor/table as either an HTML table, or a <PRE> formatted list including headers and a title.
ShowMemoPage()	Displays HTML text from either disk file or a memo field contained in a system table (wwHTML.dbf). The file can contain embedded FoxPro character expressions. This function enables you to work with HTML designers for data-driven pages.

MergeText()	Merges text by translating embedded text expressions and returning the result. This function is more low level than ShowMemoPage and can be used for partial pages.
HRef()	Creates a hotlink.
List()	Creates various HTML list types.
HTMLError()	Creates an entire HTML page with a couple of text input parameters. Great for quick status displays or error messages.
SendMemoLn()	Formats large text fields.

The preceding example uses ShowCursor() to display the result table with a single line of code. This powerful method takes the currently selected table and parses out the headers and fields, creating an HTML table as output. ShowCursor() has the capability to display custom headers passed into the method as an array and the capability to sum numeric fields.

Another extremely powerful method of the wwHTML class is ShowMemoPage(). This method makes it possible to build external HTML pages stored on disk or in a memo field that can contain embedded FoxPro expressions and even entire code snippets to be evaluated by the Web Connection engine.

Now look at the more complex example in Listing 25.9, which provides an interactive guestbook browser. This example centers around a single page that shows a guestbook entry form, which is implemented as a standalone HTML document that contains embedded FoxPro fields.

Part VI
Ch
25

Listing 25.9 25CODE09.wc—The HTML Template Page for the Guestbook Application Contains Embedded FoxPro Expressions and Fields

```
<HTML>
<HEAD><TITLE>West Wind Guest Book Browser</TITLE></HEAD>
<BODY Background="/wconnect/whitwav.jpg">
<p>
<IMG src="/wconnect/toolbar.gif" USEMAP="#entry" border=0, ismap HSPACE=20>
<MAP NAME="entry">
  <!— Image Map Coordinates here —>
</MAP>
<FORM ACTION="wwcgi.dll?ShowGuest~Save~##pcCustId##" METHOD="POST">
<INPUT TYPE="SUBMIT" VALUE="##IIF(pcCustId="NEW_ID","Add Info to","Update")##
     ➥Guestbook" WIDTH=40>
<p>

##IIF(!EMPTY(pcErrorMsg),[<hr><font color="#800000"><h3>]+pcErrorMsg+[</h3>
     ➥</font><hr>],"")##

<PRE>
Entered on: ##IIF(EMPTY(guest.entered),DTOC(date()),DTOC(guest.entered))##
```

continues

Listing 25.9   Continued

```
Name: <INPUT TYPE="TEXT" NAME="txtName" VALUE="##guest. name##" SIZE="39">
Cust Id: ##pcCustId##
Company: <INPUT TYPE="TEXT" NAME="txtCompany" VALUE="##guest.company##" SIZE
    ="39">
Email: <INPUT TYPE="TEXT" NAME="txtEmail" VALUE="##guest.email##" SIZE="54">
Checking in from: <INPUT TYPE="TEXT" NAME="txtLocation" VALUE=
    "##guest.location##" SIZE="54">
</PRE>
<b>Leave a note for fellow visitors if you like:</b><br>
<TEXTAREA  NAME="txtMessage" ROWS=5 COLS=75>##guest.message##</TextAREA>
<BLOCKQUOTE>
    <b>Password:</b> <INPUT TYPE="TEXT" NAME="txtPassword" VALUE=
    "##pcPassword##" SIZE="8" MAXLENGTH="8"> (required to change entry)
</BLOCKQUOTE>
<CENTER>
<b>##STR(RecCount())## visitors have signed the guestbook.</b><p>
</CENTER>
</FORM>
<CENTER>
[<A HREF="/cgi-win/wwcgi.dll?ShowGuest-Top-##pcCustId##">First</A>]
[<A HREF="/cgi-win/wwcgi.dll?ShowGuest-Previous-##pcCustId##">Previous</A>]
[<A HREF="/cgi-win/wwcgi.dll?ShowGuest-Next-##pcCustId##">Next</A>]
[<A HREF="/cgi-win/wwcgi.dll?ShowGuest-Bottom-##pcCustId##">Last</A>]
[<A HREF="/cgi-win/wwcgi.dll?ShowGuest-Add-##pcCustid##">Add Entry</A>]
[<A HREF="/cgi-win/wwcgi.dll?BrowseGuests">Browse Guests</A>]
</CENTER>
<hr>

<IMG SRC="/wconnect/wcpower.gif" ALIGN="LEFT" HSPACE=5 ALT="Powered by
    Web Connection">
<FONT SIZE=-1><I>Query created by <A HREF="mailto:rstrahl@west-wind.com">
    Rick Strahl</A><br>
<A HREF="/wconnect/wconnect.htm">Web Connection demo page</A>
</BODY>
</HTML>
```

You'll notice the use of double pound signs (##) as delimiters to indicate embedded expressions in this HTML page. Between these delimiters you can find FoxPro character expressions that are evaluated by the ShowMemoPage() method. To use ShowMemoPage() in this manner, a Web Connection routine locates the record pointer(s) to the proper locations and then embeds the fields directly into the HTML form. When ShowMemoPage() is then called from code, it evaluates the character expressions and inserts the evaluated string in its place. Errors in expressions are automatically handled with an error string inserted instead.

The expressions can be database fields, variables, FoxPro expressions, even class method calls and user-defined functions. By storing this page in an externally edited file, it's possible to edit this page visually using an HTML editor such as FrontPage or WebEdit. As you might expect, this is easier and more maintainable than making changes inside of the actual FoxPro code. Furthermore, it enables you to design pages that can be edited by HTML designers who don't know anything about database programming.

Listing 25.10 contains the entire code for the Guestbook application shown in Figure 25.7. The code is wrapped into two methods that are part of the wwConnectDemo process class started above. This example is lengthy and a bit more complex than the previous one, but it demonstrates a full range of features in a realistic example of a Web application (you can find the code for this and the previous examples in the Web Connection examples).

FIGURE 25.7

The Guestbook browser demonstrates how you can build interactive Web pages that act a lot like standalone applications.

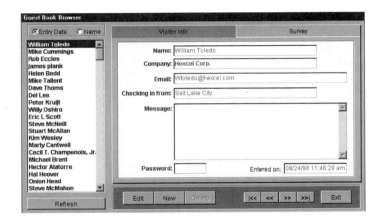

Part

VI

Ch

25

Listing 25.10 25CODE10.PRG—A Guestbook Application Implemented in Web Connection

```
*********************************************************************
* wwConnectDemo : ShowGuest
*********************************
*   Function: Guest Book Interactive Browser. Note that all this code
*             is not related to creating HTML at all, but rather
*             consists of setting up the logic for navigation and
*             adding editing entries.
*********************************************************************
FUNCTION ShowGuest
LOCAL lcCustId, lcMoveWhere, llError
PRIVATE pcErrorMsg, pcPassword

loHTML=THIS.oHTML
loCGI=THIS.oCGI

* Retrieve the Operation option (Next, Previous etc.)
lcMoveWhere=UPPER(loCGI.GetCgiParameter(2))

* Grab the commandline Customer Id
lcCustId=loCGI.GetCGIParameter(3)

pcPassword=""
pcErrorMsg=""
llError=.F.
```

continues

Listing 25.10   Continued

```
IF!USED("Guest")
  USE GUEST IN 0
ENDIF
SELE GUEST

IF EMPTY(lcCustId)
  lcMoveWhere="BOTTOM"
ELSE
  IF lcCustId#"NEW_ID"
     LOCATE FOR CustId=lcCustId
     IF !FOUND()
        pcErrorMsg="Invalid Record. Going to bottom of file..."
        lcMoveWhere="BOTTOM"
     ENDIF
  ENDIF
ENDIF

DO CASE
  CASE lcMoveWhere="GO"
     * Do nothing - just display
  CASE lcMoveWhere="NEXT"
     IF !EOF()
        SKIP
        IF EOF()
           pcErrorMsg="Last Record in table..."
        ENDIF
     ELSE
        GO BOTTOM
     ENDIF

     IF EOF()
        GO BOTTOM
        pcErrorMsg="Last Record in table..."
     ENDIF
  CASE lcMoveWhere="PREVIOUS" AND !llError
     IF !BOF()
        SKIP -1
     ENDIF
     IF BOF()
        pcErrorMsg="Beginning of File..."
     ENDIF

  CASE lcMoveWhere="TOP"
     GO TOP
     DO WHILE EMPTY(guest.name) AND !EOF()
        SKIP
     ENDDO

  CASE lcMoveWhere="BOTTOM"
     GO BOTTOM
     DO WHILE EMPTY(guest.name) AND !BOF() AND !EOF()
        SKIP -1
     ENDDO
```

```
  CASE lcMoveWhere="ADD"
     * Don't add record - move to 'ghost rec' to show blank record
     GO BOTTOM
     SKIP

     pcErrorMsg="Please fill out the form below and click the Save button..."

  CASE lcMoveWhere="SAVE"
     IF EMPTY(loCGI.GetFormVar("txtName")) AND ;
EMPTY(loCGI.GetFormVar("txtCompany"))
        THIS.ErrorMsg("Incomplete Input",;
"You have to enter at least a name or company.")
        USE IN GUEST
        RETURN
     ENDIF

     IF lcCustId="NEW_ID"
        APPEND BLANK
        REPLACE custid with sys(3), ;
                entered with datetime(), ;
                password with loCGI.GetFormVar("txtPassWord")
     ELSE
        * Check password
        pcPassWord=PADR(loCGI.GetFormVar("txtPassWord"),8)
        IF UPPER(guest.password) # UPPER(pcPassword)
           pcErrorMsg="The password you typed does not allow you to "+;
                      "change the selected entry..."
           pcCustId=guest.custid
           pcPassword=""
           loHTML.ShowMemoPage(HTMLPAGEPATH+"Guest.wc",.T.,"FORCE RELOAD")
           RETURN
        ENDIF
     ENDIF

     REPLACE name with loCGI.GetFormVar("txtName"), ;
             company with loCGI.GetFormVar("txtCompany"),;
             location with loCGI.GetFormVar("txtLocation"),;
             Email with loCGI.GetFormVar("txtEmail"),;
             Message with loCGI.GetFormVar("txtMessage")


     pcErrorMsg="Record saved..."
ENDCASE

* Prime pcCustId for all links
IF lcMoveWhere#"ADD"
   pcCustId=guest.custid
ELSE
   pcCustId="NEW_ID"
ENDIF
pcPassword=""

pcHomePath=HOMEPATH
```

continues

Listing 25.10 Continued

```
* Display GUEST.WC - This HTML form contains the fields and
* pcErrorMsg variable...
loHTML.ShowMemoPage(HTMLPAGEPATH+"Guest.wc",.T.,;
      IIF(ATC("MSIE",loCGI.GetBrowser())>0,"ForceReload","text/html"))

IF USED("Guest")
   USE IN Guest
ENDIF

ENDFUNC
* ShowGuest

******************************************************************************
* wwConnectDemo : BrowseGuests
*******************************
*   Function: Shows a list of Guests in table form for the Guest
*             Sample application.
*             This example manually creates the Browse page.
******************************************************************************
FUNCTION BrowseGuests
LOCAL loHTML, loCGI, lcOrder

loHTML=THIS.oHTML
loCGI=THIS.oCGI

* Retrieve the Order Radio Button Value - Name, Company, Location
lcOrderVal=TRIM(loCGI.GetFormVar("radOrder"))
IF EMPTY(lcOrderVal)
   lcOrderVal="Name"
ENDIF

* Build an Order By expression
lcOrder="UPPER("+lcOrderVal+")"

* Create Cursor of all Guests - Note the URL link is
* embedded in the SQL-SELECT
SELECT [<A HREF="wwcgi.dll?ShowGuest~Go~]+custid+[">]+Name+;
      [</a>] as Guest, ;
   company, location,;
   &lcOrder ;
   FROM Guest ;
   ORDER BY 4 ;
   INTO CURSOR TQuery

* Set up so we can use HTML tables
loHTML.SetAllowHTMLTables(loCGI.IsNetscape())

loHTML.HTMLHeader("Guest Book Browser",,BACKIMG,;
      IIF(ATC("MSIE",loCGI.GetBrowser())>0,"Force Reload","text/Âhtml"))
loHTML.SendLn([ <FORM ACTION="wwcgi.dll?BrowseGuests" METHOD="POST">])
loHTML.SendLn([ Sort by: <input type="radio" value="Name" name="radOrder" ;
]+IIF(lcOrderVal="Name","checked=true","")+[>Name ])
loHTML.SendLn([ <input type="radio" value="Company" name="radOrder" ;
```

```
]+IIF(lcOrderVal="Company","checked=true","")+[> Company  ])
loHTML.SendLn([ <input type="radio" value="Location" ;
name="radOrder"]+IIF(lcOrderVal="Location","checked=true","")+[> Location<br>])
loHTML.SendLn([ <input type="submit" value="Change Order">])
loHTML.SendLn([ </FORM> <p>])

* Explicitly set up headers so we only display first 3 cols
DIMENSION laHeaders[3]
laHeaders[1]="Name"
laHeaders[2]="Company"
laHeaders[3]="Location"

* Display the table
loHTML.ShowCursor(@laHeaders)

loHTML.HTMLFooter(PAGEFOOT)

IF USED("Guest")
   USE IN Guest
ENDIF

ENDFUNC
* BrowseGuests
```

Looking at this code, you can tell that the majority of the logic that takes place has to do with the navigation aspect of the application rather than the actual Web/HTML dynamics. Most of the display issues are wrapped up in the external HTML template page, which is displayed in Listing 25.9.

One difference from a typical Visual FoxPro application is the fact that the application is implemented as a transaction-based process: Every action is a request that is processed by a method call. There is no event-driven programming happening here, and all validation is happening at the FoxPro back end with error messages being sent back as a message on a regenerated HTML page. The actual error message is embedded on the HTML page with the following expression:

```
##IIF(!EMPTY(pcErrorMsg),[<hr><font
color="#800000"><h3>]+pcErrorMsg+[</h3></font><hr>],"")##
```

pcErrorMsg is a PRIVATE variable that is set in the code and then passed down to the evaluation engine in ShowMemoPage(). Because the variable is PRIVATE, ShowMemoPage() can still access the pcErrorMsg variable, as it is still in scope. Thus, any variables that are declared PRIVATE or PUBLIC in the processing method can be accessed in a subsequent call to evaluate an HTML page processed with ShowMemoPage(). ShowMemoPage() (and MergeText(), which is the actual workhorse routine that ShowMemoPage() calls) also makes available the CGI and HTML objects as poCGI and poHTML, respectively.   So, you could do something like this inside the HTML page:

```
##poCGI.GetBrowser()##
##poHTML.ShowCursor(,,,,.t.)##
```

The first expression displays the name of the browser used to access the current page. The latter expression displays a table of the currently selected cursor and embeds it inside the HTML page. Notice that all the HTML class methods can also be used to return a string rather than sending output directly to file so that HTML class methods can be nested inside of each other. All HTML class methods have a logical llNoOutput parameter, which, if set to .T., will return the output as string only.

Working with Web Browsers

Browsers are the interface to the user, and although there's no direct interaction from the Web server back-end application to the browser, the application does provide the interface in a non-interactive fashion by sending back an entire HTML page to display.

To give you an idea of just how important Web browsers are, Microsoft has integrated the Web browser interface directly into Windows 98. In Internet Explorer 4.0, there is no distinction between the Web browser and the other interface components for file browsing and even for the display of desktop applications. With your desktop using a browser interface that is fully customizable, any application on your local computer or on the Internet is only a click away at any time. The browser is fast becoming the all-encompassing application that provides the functionality required for navigating the Web, your local network, and even your own computer and its applications.

From the aspect of back-end Web applications, browsers are very frustrating beasts in that they are both intensely visual and seemingly interactive, yet at the same time have a mentality that is reminiscent of the dumb terminal of the mainframe days. I already discussed the issue of no direct data connectivity between the browser and the server, which makes for a purely transaction-based interface to the data.

Nevertheless, browsers are getting smarter; and although the data connectivity is an issue that will not likely get resolved for some time given the infrastructure of the Web, a lot of logic is moving to the browser.   New scripting languages such as Java, VBScript, and JavaScript enable extending the browser interface beyond its limited display-only capabilities. With these scripting languages, it is possible to build some validation logic into the client-side HTML pages. For example, you can validate input as long as no data lookup is required (that is, checking a phone number field for proper formatting, a credit card number to be valid, a proper state abbreviation). In addition, these scripting languages are extending the form control interface to be a lot more like a full GUI-based screen in that event code can be attached to input fields so that validation can be triggered automatically.

Although Java is getting all the attention these days, the simpler scripting languages such as VBScript and JavaScript make it easy to move some of the simpler validation-based and simple calculation-oriented functionality and implement it on the browser.

Because these scripting languages are implemented as HTML-embedded text that executes on the client side, you can use your Visual FoxPro back-end application to actually generate script code that runs when the page is displayed on the Web browser. It's sort of like getting a double execution punch.

One thing to be aware of is that not all browsers support all the features. Netscape and Microsoft are the market leaders with both of their browsers providing multitudes of extensions. Although the leading browsers from both companies are reasonably compatible and comprise 90 percent of the market, browsers from other companies do not support some of the more advanced features. If your site is public, hard choices have to be made whether to support only the most basic HTML features, or build state-of-the-art pages at the risk of turning away a small percentage of users with incompatible browsers.

Figure 25.8 shows an example of how taking advantage of browser-specific features can enhance the user interface. This page can be displayed in two modes: one using frames for IE 3.0 or Netscape 2.0 or later, and one using plain pages for browsers that do not yet support frames. The frames version is much more visually appealing and provides a more functional interface for navigating the site than a similar page that doesn't use frames. Notice the option on the frames page to go to no frames—important for laptop and low-resolution users. This site is providing a dual interface to serve both the latest HTML extensions and the low-end browsers, but a fair amount of extra design effort is required to provide this functionality.

FIGURE 25.8
Taking advantage of new HTML extensions can make your site easier to use.

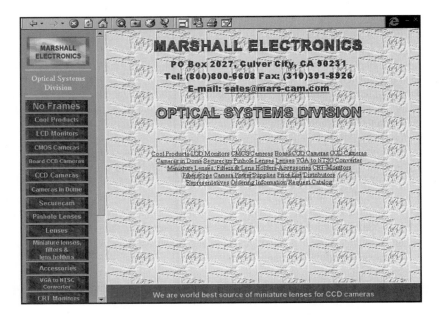

As a Web developer, you have to weigh carefully which features you want to implement. When building internal intranet applications, it's likely that you have control over the browser to use, so you can choose the one that provides the most functionality for the job at hand. For public applications, though, there is a tradeoff between using the newest, coolest features and leaving some users who haven't upgraded to the latest and greatest in the dust.

One strategy is to develop two sets of pages to satisfy both the hottest new developments and the older browsers. For example, the following function (implemented with Web Connection) checks for browser support and returns a letter that identifies the browser type: `"F"` for frames-based pages, `"M"` for IE 2.0, and `""` for all others:

```
*********************************************************************
* SurplusProcess : PageType
*********************************
*  Function: Returns the PageType based on the Browser name
*       Pass: llNoFrames    -  Override flag to use or not use frames
*     Return: "F"rames for Netscape 1.2/IE 3 or higher, "M" for MSIE 2
*             "" for all other Browsers
*********************************************************************
FUNCTION PageType
LPARAMETERS llNoFrames
LOCAL lcBrowser, lcType

lcBrowser=UPPER(THIS.oCGI.GetBrowser())
lcType=""        && Default to non-frames page
IF  INLIST(lcBrowser,"MOZILLA/2.","MOZILLA/3.") AND !llNoFrames
   lcType="F"
ENDIF

* Return "M" for MS Internet Explorer 2.0
* only on the Homepage
IF llHomePage AND ATC("MSIE 2.",lcBrowser)>0
   lcType="M"
ENDIF

RETURN lcType
* PageType
```

When a page is loaded for display, it is then loaded with the appropriate prefix:

```
loHTML.ShowMemoPage(HTMLPAGEPATH+THIS.PageType(THIS.lNoFrames)+
Â"ShowCats.wc",.T.)
```

If all pages are dynamically loaded, it's now possible to load the appropriate page for the specified browser by checking for specific browsers that support frames. All static pages reference the appropriate frames pages with the F prefix and the nonframe pages point at the nonframe, nonprefixed page names.

Web Development Issues in Working with Visual FoxPro

Web development feels a lot like two steps forward and one step back. When building FoxPro-based Web applications, here are several issues that you have to keep in mind:

- *Speed is extremely important on the Web.* Visual FoxPro's single-threaded nature makes it necessary to turn around requests as quickly as possible to free up the data server for the next request.

- *Bulletproof code is not an option, it's a requirement.* When running a data server, it's crucial that the code running on it does not crash. Crash the server and you bring the system to a stop. Good error-handling mechanisms are a must.

- *HTML is graphic art.* If you work on large-scale Web applications, be prepared to work with HTML designers. Don't code if you can build logic into external pages that can be loaded from within your VFP application—designers will expect this feature. It's also much easier to maintain a site this way, and you can leave page design to the graphic arts people.

- *Web apps are transaction-based.* It's not your typical GUI application, as database requests are sent from the browser to the Web server and your application in individual request chunks. Remember, the browser has no direct access to the data and your application has no direct access to the user interface. Get used to hand coding where before you might have used the screen builder or report writer.

Internet-Enabling Your Applications

Internet-enabling your applications doesn't have to be as complete a job as rebuilding them to run over the Web. Instead, you can use smaller and more easily integrated enhancements such as the capability to send email over the Internet, uploading or downloading files via FTP, or accessing a Web site through a Web browser controlled with Visual FoxPro.

The following examples for SMTP email and FTP functionality use third-party ActiveX controls from Mabry Software. Shareware versions of the Mabry controls are available at http://www.mabry.com.

NOTE The Web browser control example requires that you have Internet Explorer 3.0 or later installed on your system. ■

Downloading a File via FTP

The File Transfer Protocol (FTP) is the primary protocol used to transfer files between client and server machines. Although it's possible to download files directly over the World Wide Web simply by setting a link to point at a file, uploading files cannot easily be handled over the Web.

FTP is a widely used, relatively simple protocol. Using the Mabry FTP control, it's easy to build a class that enables sending and receiving of files via FTP. Figure 25.9 shows the class when running in visual mode, but the class also supports a programmatic interface that can run without displaying the form.

To create a form that contains the Mabry ActiveX FTP control, use the following steps:

1. Create a new form and grab two OLE container controls from the Form Controls toolbar. Insert the Mabry Internet GetAddress Control and the FTP Control from the Insert Control radio button selected list.

2. Assign `ocxGetAddress` and `ocxFTP` to the Name property of the controls in the property sheet.

FIGURE 25.9
The wwFTP class lets
you upload and
download files from an
FTP site. Uploads
require a username and
password, whereas
downloads can often be
anonymous.

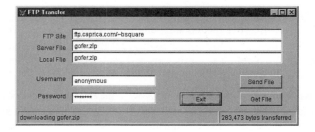

3. Add the following properties to the class: cFTPSite, cRemoteFile, cLocalFile,
   cUsername, and cPassword. These fields correspond to the input fields that are used on
   the form shown in Figure 25.9. Create input fields for each of these variables and point
   the datasource at the class properties you just created (that is, THISFORM.cFTPSite).

4. Add buttons for Sending and Receiving files. The Send button should call
   THISFORM.UploadFile(), and the Receive button should call THISFORM.GetFile().

5. Add the GetFile and Uploadfile class methods shown in Listing 25.11.

Listing 25.11 25CODE11.vcx—The Getfile Method of the wwFTP Class Is the
Workhorse That Sends and Receives Files

```
* Retrieves a file from an FTP site. All properties
* must be set prior to calling this method.
PROCEDURE GETFILE
LPARAMETER llSendFile
LOCAL lcSite

#DEFINE RETRIEVE_FILE  7
#DEFINE SEND_FILE  6

#DEFINE BINARY = 2

IF llSendFile
   lnMode=SEND_FILE
ELSE
   lnMode=RETRIEVE_FILE
ENDIF

lcSite=TRIM(THISFORM.cFTPSite)

THIS.statusmessage("Retrieving IP Address for "+lcSite)
THIS.cIPAddress=THISFORM.ocxGetAddress.GetHostAddress(lcSite)

IF EMPTY(THIS.cIPAddress)
   THIS.statusmessage("Couldn't connect to "+lcSite)
   RETURN
ENDIF

THIS.statusmessage("Connected to "+THIS.cIPAddress)
```

```
* Must Evaluate call to FTP Logon method since VFP balks at the Logon name
llResult=EVALUATE("THISFORM.ocxFTP.Logon( THIS.cIPAddress,TRIM(THIS.cUsername),;
                                          TRIM(THIS.cPassword) )")

IF !llResult
   THIS.statusmessage("Logon to "+lcSite+ " failed...")
   RETURN
ENDIF
THIS.statusmessage("Logged on to "+lcSite)

* Assign files to upload/download
THISFORM.ocxFTP.RemoteFileName = TRIM(THIS.cRemoteFile)
THISFORM.ocxFTP.LocalFileName = TRIM(THIS.cLocalFile)

IF llSendFile
   THIS.statusmessage("Uploading "+TRIM(THISFORM.cLocalFile) )
ELSE
   THIS.statusmessage("Downloading "+TRIM(THISFORM.cRemoteFile) )
ENDIF

THISFORM.ocxFTP.TransferMode = BINARY

* Send or Receive File
THISFORM.ocxFTP.Action=lnMode
ENDPROC

*— Uploads a file to the FTP site.
PROCEDURE uploadfile
THISFORM.GETFILE(.T.)  && .T. means send file
ENDPROC
```

Part
VI

Ch

25

The workhorse routine is the GetFile() method, which handles connecting to the FTP site, logging in, and then sending the file. The site connection is handled by the Mabry GetAddress Control, which resolves the domain name on the form (ftp.server.net, for example) to an IP address in the format of *000.000.000.000* that is required by the FTP control. A simple call to the control's GetHostAddress() method with the domain name returns the IP address. If the IP address cannot be resolved, a null string ("") is returned.

Once connected, the user must be logged in to the FTP site. When downloading files from public sites, it's often acceptable to access the site anonymously by specifying "anonymous" as both the username and password. For other sites and for uploads in general, a specific username and password might be required. The login operation is handled using the Login method of the ActiveX control, which takes an IP address and a username and password as a parameter. Due to a bug in Visual FoxPro, the Login method call is causing a compilation error, requiring the method to be called by embedding it inside of EVALUATE function call rather than calling the Login method directly:

```
llResult=EVALUATE(
"THISFORM.ocxFTP.Logon(THIS.cIPAddress,THIS.cUsername,THIS.cPassword)")
```

The actual file transfer operation is handled asynchronously: the `LocalFile` and `RemoteFile` properties are set with the filenames and the `Action` property is set to either `RETRIEVE_FILE` or `SEND_FILE`. As soon as a value is assigned to the `Action` flag, the transfer is started and control returns immediately to your program while the file transfer occurs in the background. You can use the following `IsBusy()` method of the `FTP` class to determine whether the current transfer is done:

```
*— Returns whether a file transfer is in progress.
PROCEDURE IsBusy
#DEFINE FTP_IDLE 5
RETURN (THISFORM.ocxFTP.CurrentState <> FTP_IDLE )
```

You should also check this method prior to starting another transfer. To receive a completion message of the last file transfer, call the `GetErrorMessage()` method of the class.

This class is implemented as a form, which can be activated with:

```
PUBLIC oFTP
SET CLASSLIB TO QueIP ADDITIVE
oFTP=CREATE("wwFTP")
oFTP.show
```

However, you can also control the class programmatically in code or from the Command window:

```
oFTP=CREATE("wwFTP")

oFTP.cFTPSite="ftp.gorge.net"
oFTP.cRemoteFile="/westwind/ww_web.zip"
oFTP.cLocalFile="C:\ww_web.zip"

oFTP.cUsername="anonymous"
oFTP.cPassword="anonymous"

*!* oFTP.Show()    && If you want to show the form and property settings

oFTP.GetFile()
```

Sending SMTP Mail

The Simple Mail Transfer Protocol (SMTP) provides a simple interface to sending mail over the Internet. The Mabry SMTP mail control enables you to take advantage of this protocol to send e-mail messages across the Internet with relative ease.

NOTE SMTP is an open protocol. When it originally was devised, it was designed to be accessible without any restrictions. This means a true SMTP mail server does not require a login and anybody on the Internet can use the server to send mail.

Newer versions of SMTP servers implement IP address restrictions and login requirements based on a username/password scheme. The SMTP control on its own does not support this functionality; you have to use the POP3 control to log in to the mail server and then use that connection to send SMTP mail.

The example described here works only with SMTP mail servers that do not require a login. ∎

To create a form that contains the ActiveX SMTP control, use the following steps:

1. Create a new form and grab a couple of OLE container controls from the Form Controls toolbar. Add a Mabry Internet GetAddress Control and the SMTP control to the form.

2. Assign ocxSMTP to the control in the property sheet.

3. Add the following properties to the class: cSendToAddress, cFromAddress, cSubject, cMessage, cMailServerName. These fields correspond to the input fields that are used on the form shown in Figure 25.10. Create input fields for each of these variables and set their Controlsource at the form property (that is, THISFORM.cSendToAddress). The form layout should look like Figure 25.10.

FIGURE 25.10

The wwSMTP class lets you send an email message over the Internet. With its public class interface, you can populate the form programmatically.

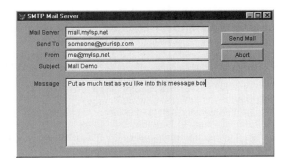

4. Add a Send button to the form. The Send button should call THISFORM.SendMail().

5. Create a new method named SendMail with the code shown in Listing 25.12.

Listing 25.12 25CODE12.vcx—The SMTP Class' Sendmail Method Is Responsible for Sending the Actual Message After the Message Properties Have Been Filled

```
*— Used to send a message. Mail properties must be set prior to calling this
method.
PROCEDURE Sendmail
LOCAL lcIPAddress

#DEFINE NORMAL_PRIORITY   3

IF EMPTY(THIS.cIPAddress)
    * Resolve Mail Server IP Address - you can speed this up by not
    * using this code and plugging the IP Address directly to the
    * mail control
    lcSite=TRIM(THISFORM.cMailServerName)

    * Clear out the IP Address first
    THIS.statusmessage("Retrieving IP Address for "+lcSite)

    lcIPAddress=THISFORM.ocxGetAddress.GetHostAddress(lcSite)
```

continues

Listing 25.12 Continued

```
   IF EMPTY(lcIPAddress)
      THIS.statusmessage("Couldn't connect to "+lcSite)
   ENDIF
ELSE
   lcIPAddress=TRIM(THIS.cIPAddress)
ENDIF

THIS.statusmessage("Connected to "+lcIPAddress)

THISFORM.ocxSMTP.OriginatingAddress = TRIM(THIS.cFromAddress)
THISFORM.ocxSMTP.OriginatingName = TRIM(THIS.cFromName)
THISFORM.ocxSMTP.HostAddress = lcIPAddress
THISFORM.ocxSMTP.DomainName = "west-wind.com"
THISFORM.ocxSMTP.MailApplication = "West Wind Web Connection"
THISFORM.ocxSMTP.MailPriority = NORMAL_PRIORITY

THISFORM.ocxSMTP.DestinationUserList=TRIM(THISFORM.cSendToAddress)
THISFORM.ocxSMTP.CCUserList=TRIM(THISFORM.cCCAddress)
THISFORM.ocxSMTP.MailSubject=TRIM(THISFORM.cSubject)
THISFORM.ocxSMTP.MailBody=TRIM(THISFORM.cMessage)
THISFORM.ocxSMTP.MailAttachment=TRIM(THISFORM.cAttachment)

THISFORM.statusmessage("Sending Message to "+TRIM(THISFORM.cSendToAddress))
THISFORM.ocxSMTP.Action=1
RETURN
```

As with the FTP class example, this SMTP example also uses the Mabry `GetAddress` control to resolve the mail server's domain name (`mail.server.net`, for example) to an IP address, which is required by the mail control. Because it's quicker to not resolve the address, there's also an option to pass an IP address in the class's `cIPAddress` property, which causes the name lookup to be skipped.

After the mail server is identified, the form properties are collected setting the mail control's internal properties. Finally, the mail control's `Action` property is set to 1, which causes the message to be sent and control is returned to your code immediately. As with the FTP class, an `IsBusy()` method tells whether a mail transfer is still in process:

```
*— Determines whether the Mail Server is busy sending a message.
*— While busy no other messages can be sent.
PROCEDURE isbusy
#DEFINE SMTP_IDLE 5
RETURN (THISFORM.ocxSMTP.CurrentState <> SMTP_IDLE )
```

In order to determine the final status of a sent message, the `Mail` control's `EndSendMail` event is used to update the `nErrorCode` custom property set up on the form class:

```
*— Fires when a message send is complete or failed
PROCEDURE ocxSMTP.EndSendMail
LPARAMETERS errornumber
```

```
THISFORM.nErrorCode=errornumber
THISFORM.statusmessage("Mail Transport done - Error Code: Â"+STR(errornumber),;
                        THISFORM.geterrormessage(errornumber) )
ENDPROC
```

This code basically traps the error code and updates the form's status window with the error information. After the error code is set, it stays set until the next message is sent.

The class is implemented as a form that can be run interactively with the following code:

```
SET CLASSLIB TO WwIPControls ADDITIVE

PUBLIC oSMTP
oSMTP=CREATE("wwSMTP")
oSMTP.show
```

However, you can also control the class under program control or from the Command window:

```
PUBLIC oSMTP
oSMTP=CREATE("wwSMTP")

oSMTP.cMailServerName="mail.server.net"

oSMTP.cFromAddress="rstrahl@west-wind.com"
oSMTP.cFromName="Rick Strahl"
oSMTP.cSendToAddress="rstrahl@gorge.net"  && Use Commas to separate more
                                          && than one recipient
* oSMTP.cCCAddress="rstrahl@west-wind.com,rstrahl@gorge.net"

oSMTP.cSubject="Test Message from QUE's Using Visual FoxPro!"
oSMTP.cMessage="This is a test message generated by the SMTP example..."

* oSMTP.cAttachment="c:\autoexec.bat"
* oSMTP.Show()    && If you want to display the form

oSMTP.SendMail()
```

You can then use oSMTP.IsBusy() to determine whether the control is still busy and oSMTP.GetErrorMessage() to determine the last result message of the mail message.

Activating a Web Browser from Visual FoxPro

The following is a little routine that is handy for support features or cross-linking a FoxPro application to the Web. Windows 95/98 and Windows NT 4.0 support the capability to execute URLs directly via the OLE extension mappings supplied in the Registry. If you have a browser installed in your system, and it's the default browser, when you click on an HTML document in your browser, you can use the simple code in Listing 25.13 to activate the browser and go to the specified URL.

Part
VI

Ch
25

Listing 25.13   `25CODE13.prg`—**This Routine Fires Up the Registered Browser and Goes to the Specified URL**

```
* GoWeb: Test out the GoURL procedure with call
GoURL("www.inprise.com")
*
********************************************************
FUNCTION GoURL
******************
*   Function: Starts associated Web Browser
*             and goes to the specified URL.
*             If Browser is already open it
*             reloads the page.
*      Assume: Works only on Win 95/98 and NT 4.0
*        Pass: tcUrl  - The URL of the site or
*                       HTML page to bring up
*                       in the Browser
*      Return: 2 - Bad Association (invalid URL)
********************************************************
LPARAMETERS tcUrl

tcUrl=IIF(type("tcUrl")="C",tcUrl,;
          "http://microsoft.com/")

DECLARE INTEGER ShellExecute ;
    IN SHELL32.dll ;
    INTEGER nWinHandle,;
    STRING cOperation,;
    STRING cFileName,;
    STRING cParameters,;
    STRING cDirectory,;
    INTEGER nShowWindow

DECLARE INTEGER FindWindow ;
    IN WIN32API ;
    STRING cNull,STRING cWinName

RETURN ShellExecute(FindWindow(0,_SCREEN.caption),;
                    "Open",tcUrl,;
                    "","c:\temp\",0)
```

To activate a URL from code, you can then simply use the following code and the IE screen displays as shown in Figure 25.11:

```
GoURL("www.inprise.com")
```

This function can be extremely useful for product support. You could, for instance, stick a button containing a call to this function onto a form, thereby sending users directly to your Web site for support, upgrades, or other information.

If you need more sophisticated control of URL access, you can also place a browser directly onto a Visual FoxPro form. The Microsoft Web Browser ActiveX control enables you to embed all of IE's functionality directly into your Visual FoxPro forms. How's that for full-featured power?

FIGURE 25.11

This is an example of launching IE 4.0 from the code shown in Listing 25.13.

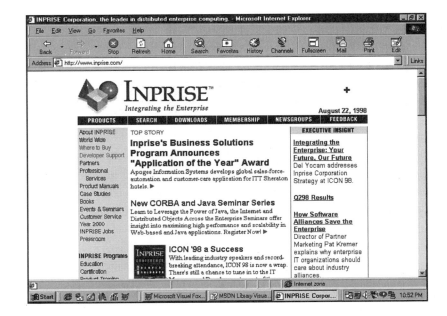

N O T E Unlike other ActiveX controls, the MS Web Browser is not fully self-contained and requires a full installation of IE 4.0 to run. This means you cannot use this control on computers that do not have a copy of IE installed. ▪

Visual FoxPro has added a Web browser control to its Visual FoxPro Foundation Classes. The *WEB Browser control* features a number of custom methods and events that enable you to control the Internet Explorer 4.0 operations. You can add the control on a form or a project from the Component Gallery. There is also a *URL ComboBox control* that manages history URLs in a FoxPro table. Both controls are in the in Foundation Class Internet folder in the Component Gallery Object pane. I have created the MyBrowser form to illustrate how easy it is to build your own custom Web Browser. Figure 25.12 shows the Component Gallery and the MyBrowser form in the Form Designer. Drag the Web Browser Control class and the URL Combo class to the form, and then add navigation buttons as shown.

I also added the Resize class to the form from the Foundation Class User Controls folder. It resizes all of the controls when you resize the form. Code was added to the form's Resize event that calls the Resize control's AdjustControls() method to perform control resize operations.

The buttons are used to navigate around the WWW. Each button calls one of the Web browser's methods. When you run the form, code exists in the form's Init event to initialize the Web browser and go to the user's home page. Note that a user-defined method, Navigate(), was added to the MyBrowser form. Form1.Navigate() calls the Web Browser class Navigate() method to navigate to a specified URL. The URL Combo class calls the THISFORM.Navigate() method and passes a user-entered URL. It calls Form1.Navigate() only when its `lFormNavigate` property is set to `.T.`. If `lFormNavigate` is set to `.F.`, the URL Combo actually launches the default browser.

FIGURE 25.12

This is an example of creating your own custom Web browser control, which enables inclusion of much of IE's advanced functionality in your own forms using drag-and-drop techniques.

Other than the button `Names` and the `Caption` properties of the various components, the only properties that needed to be set were for the URL Combo control and included the following:

```
_URLCOMBOBOX1.cURL = "www.microsoft.com"   && Initial WEB page.
_URLCOMBOBOX1.lFormNavigate   = .T.
_URLCOMBOBOX1.lrequestonenter = .T.
```

The user-defined code for the events in the `MyBrowser` form is presented in Listing 25.14.

Listing 25.14   25CODE14—The Methods of the `MyBrowser` Form Enable Control Over Browser URL Navigation and the `Resize` Control

```
* User-defined Navigate procedure called by _URLComboBox1
* class to navigate to current URL
PROCEDURE Form1.Navigate
LPARAMETERS tcURLTHIS._WEBBROWSER41.Navigate(tcURL)ENDPROC*
* Initialize form event goes to home URLPROCEDURE Form1.Init
THIS._WEBBROWSER41.GoHome()
ENDPROC
*
* Form Resize event calls Resize control to resize controlsPROCEDURE
Form1.ResizeTHIS._Resizable1.AdjustControls()ENDPROC*
* Refresh button click event refreshes current URL
PROCEDURE RefreshButton.Click
THISFORM._WEBBROWSER41.Refresh2()
```

```
ENDPROC
*
* Back button click event goes to previous URLPROCEDURE
BackButton.ClickTHISFORM._WEBBROWSER41.GoBack()ENDPROC*
* Foreword button click event goes to next URLPROCEDURE ForwardButton.Click
THISFORM._WEBBROWSER41.GoForward()
ENDPROC
*
* Stop button click event stops opening current URLPROCEDURE
StopButton.ClickTHISFORM._WEBBROWSER41.STOP()ENDPROC*
* Home button click event goes to home URLPROCEDURE
HomeButton.ClickTHISFORM._WEBBROWSER41.GoHome()
ENDPROC
```

Figure 25.13 shows the MyBrowser custom browser when it runs. Notice that you can view and select the URL history items by clicking on the arrow on the right of the URL Combo.

There are a number of additional events and methods that can be called. When you need them, you can look at the Help for the Foundation Class Web browser control.

FIGURE 25.13

This is an example of running your own custom Web browser control.

Part

VI

Ch

25

If you don't like the small form, just maximize it. The Resize control enlarges all the controls as shown in Figure 25.14.

Creating HTML Files from Forms, Reports, or Tables

There are FoxPro Foundation classes that convert a form, database, reports, labels, and menus to HTML. These classes provide controls to control the scope and layout. You can view these converted objects in a browser, send them as mail, or post them on a Web site. This capability is very useful for applications that need to periodically post Web pages containing data on the Internet or a company intranet.

You use one of these classes by placing one of the HTML classes (_spx2html, _dbf2html, or _frt2html) on a form. The builder appears and lets you specify the name of the source file (cSource property) and the name of the destination HTML file (cOutfile property). If you are displaying a Visual FoxPro table, you need to specify the cScope property, as in this example:

```
CScope = "Next 30"
```

FIGURE 25.14
This is an example of running your own custom Web browser control in its maximized state, which complements the FoxPro Foundation Class Resize control.

Also, you can set the properties at runtime. When you are ready to convert one of these objects to HTML, you call the object's GenHTML() method. Usually, you place the call to GenHTML() method in a Save As Menu item. You can set the nGenOutput property of the object to specify the type of output you want, which is defined as follows:

nGenOutput value	Description
0	Generates an output file.
1	Generates an output file and display file in the Visual FoxPro editor.
2	Generates an output file and display file in IE.
3	Displays a Save As dialog box and lets the user name the output file.
4	Generates an output file and creates a PUBLIC _oHTML object.
5	Creates a PUBLIC _oHTML object.

Here is an example that illustrates how to convert a .DBF table to an HTML file. The plan is to create a form with a button you press to convert a .DBF table to an HTML file. Here are the steps to create such a form:

1. Create a new form with the Screen Designer.
2. Add a button control and set its Caption property to **Save spx.dbf as HTML file**.
3. From the Foundation Classes Internet folder in the Component Gallery object pane, drag the DBF->HTML class to the form (see Figure 25.15).

4. Add the following code to the `Click` event of the button control:

```
THISFORM._DBF2HTML1.cScope = "ALL"      && Display all
recordsTHISFORM._DBF2HTML1.cSource= "SPX.DBF" && Convert this
fileTHISFORM._DBF2HTML1.cOutfile= "SPX"    && Name of HTML output
THISFORM._DBF2HTML1.nGenOutput = 2     && Create file; run IE4
THISFORM._DBF2HTML1.GenHTML()          && Do conversion
```

FIGURE 25.15

This is an example of creating a form that illustrates the conversion of a Visual FoxPro table to an HTML file. The DBF->HTML class is dragged from the Component Gallery to the form.

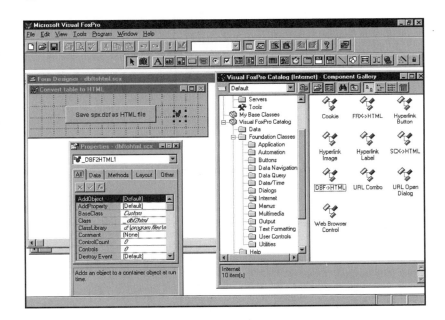

Figure 25.16 shows the appearance of the form when it runs. Press the button and the file `SPX.HTM` is created and displayed in the Internet Explorer as shown in Figure 25.17. There are other enhancements that can be made to the converted form. For example, the `cStyle` property defines numerous display styles that alter the behavior of the conversion.

FIGURE 25.16

This form converts a Visual FoxPro table (`SPX.DBF`) to an HTML file using the DBF->HTML class.

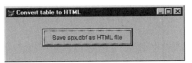

The Web Publishing Wizard will also convert a `.DBF` table to an HTML file. This wizard, which is accessed from the Tools menu, lets you select various styles, add headings, add images, and add other objects. All you have to do is to answer the questions and the Web Publishing Wizard converts contents of a `.DBF` table to an HTML file. The wizard was used to convert the `SPX.DBF` table used in the previous example to an HTML file. The results are shown in Figure 25.18.

Part
VI

Ch
25

FIGURE 25.17
IE displays the form
(SPX.HML) resulting
from the conversion.

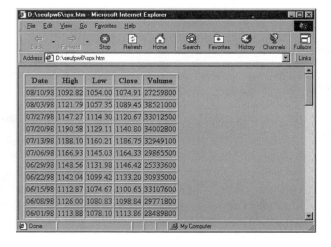

FIGURE 25.18
IE displays the form
(SPX.HML) that was
built using the Visual
FoxPro Web Publishing
Wizard.

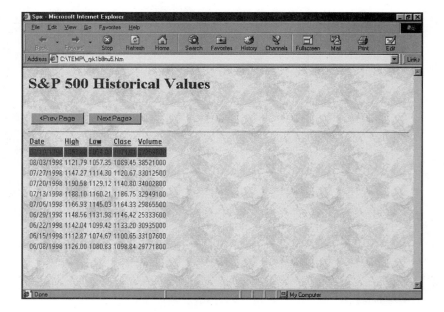

Active Documents

One of the innovative new features of Visual FoxPro 6 is its support for Active documents. An *Active document* is a special type of OLE embeddable document in which you can display different types of non-HTML documents from varied sources in the same Active document Web browser host. One example of a browser host is IE. One example of a source is Visual FoxPro 6.

An Active document takes over the entire client window of its browser host. Any menus associated with an Active document are automatically inserted into its host menu and toolbar system.

A key feature of Active documents is that they provide a seamless integration with other Web pages that are viewed on the Web. You cannot tell the difference. The menu and toolbar commands of an Active document can be routed to its host. For example, you can have a print command that links directly to the IE print command.

The most compelling feature of Active documents is that you can write a Visual FoxPro Active document client application that can run in an environment that uses an HTML-type client interface.

How Do I Create an Active Document?

A Visual FoxPro Active document is created just like any other Visual FoxPro application and can perform the same tasks. Most everything you can do in a Visual FoxPro application, you can do in a Visual FoxPro Active document. If you know how to create a Visual FoxPro project to create an application, you already know how to create an Active document, and I suspect that if you have followed all the material so far in this book, you are already an expert application builder.

The fact is that you can launch any application from HTML from within the Internet Explorer. But Visual FoxPro Active document applications support the hooks (properties, methods, and events) into the Active document host. The main difference between a regular Visual FoxPro application and a Visual FoxPro Active document is that Active documents are based on the ActiveDoc base class. The ActiveDoc base class provides all the properties, events, and methods required by an Active document application to interface with the Active document host.

The entry point, or *main file*, for a normal Visual Foxpro application is in either a program or a form. However, the main file for an Active document must be a class derived from the ActiveDoc base class. You must use the Class Designer to create your new class based on the ActiveDoc base class. Here are the steps to create a Visual FoxPro Active document application:

1. Create a new project named MyActiveDoc.pjx.
2. From the Component Gallery My Base Classes folder, drag the _activedoc base class to the new project as shown in Figure 25.19. The Add Class to Project dialog appears.
3. Indicate that you want to create a new class from the selected class and press OK. The New Class dialog appears, as shown in Figure 25.20.
4. Enter the new derived class name, MyActiveDoc, and press OK. This process adds the vfpgry.vcx visual class library that contains the _activedoc (ActiveDoc) class to the project.
5. Expand the vfpgry.vcx visual class library hierarchy by clicking on the plus (+) box at the left of the library name.
6. Select the class based on the ActiveDoc base class. Right-click on the class and choose Set Main from the shortcut menu to make MyActiveDoc the main file.

FIGURE 25.19

Drag the `_activedoc` base class from the Component Gallery to the `Myactivedoc` project to access the Add Class to Project dialog.

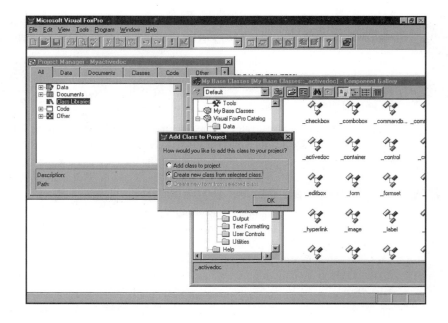

FIGURE 25.20

The New Class dialog prompts you to enter a new class name.

7. Now you need a form to display. From the Component Gallery My Base Classes folder, drag the `_form` base class to the Project Manager. The Add Class to Project dialog appears. Indicate that you want to create a new class from the selected class and press OK. The New Class dialog appears.

8. Name the New Class **MyForm** and press OK. The Class Designer displays, showing the new form.

9. Drag a `_commandbutton` class from the project to the MyForm form in the Class Designer. Change its Caption to **Panic** and add the following line of code to the `Click` event of the button:

   `MessageBox("Do not Panic")`

10. Add the following line of code to the `Destroy` event of the `MyForm` class:

    `CLEAR EVENTS`

11. Add any free table to the project (for the example, `SPX.DBF` was added).

12. Drag the free table from the project to the `MyForm` form in the Class Designer and a grid object is placed on the form (see Figure 25.21). Also add a label with its `Caption` property set to **This is an Active Document**.

FIGURE 25.21
The Class Designer is used to create the `MyForm` class that contains a button, a label, and a grid control.

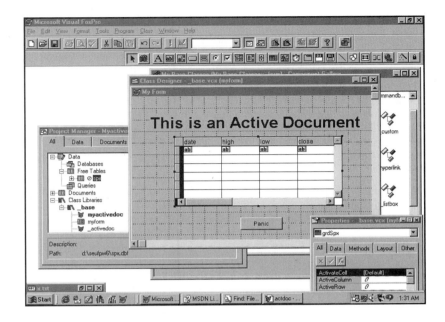

13. Close the `MyForm` class.

14. Double-click on the `MyActiveDoc` class in the project. The Class Designer opens, showing the `MyActiveDoc` class. Add the following code to the `Run` event for this class:

```
LOCAL odMyForm
oMyForm = NewObject('myform','_base.vcx')
oMyForm.SHOW()
READ EVENTS
```

15. Add the following code to the `MyActiveDoc` class:

```
CLEAR EVENTS
CLEAR ALL
```

16. Close the Class Designer and click on the Project Manager's Build button to create the `MyActiveDoc.app` application.

17. Choose Tools, Run Active Document and the Run Active Document dialog appears as shown in Figure 25.22. Enter the path and filename of the `MyActiveDoc.app` application and click OK.

FIGURE 25.22
The Run Active Document dialog prompts the user to enter the path and filename of the Active document.

IE is launched and runs the Active document. IE creates an Active document object from the MyActiveDoc class. The MyForm object is displayed as shown in Figure 25.23. The MyActiveDoc object responds to events and method calls. All components of the displayed form are active. You can press the Panic button and perform editing and navigation operations on the grid.

FIGURE 25.23

IE displays the Active document, MyActiveDoc. The MyForm form object is shown.

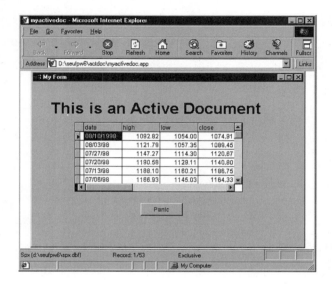

ActiveDoc Object Properties, Events, and Methods

The ActiveDoc class contains properties, events, and methods, which are defined in Tables 25.3, 25.4, and 25.5, respectively.

Table 25.3 ActiveDoc **Class Properties**

Property	Description
BaseClass	Contains the name of the Visual FoxPro base class on which the referenced object is based.
Caption	Specifies the text displayed in an object's caption.
Class	Contains the name of the class on which an object is based.
ClassLibrary	Contains the filename of the user-defined class library that contains the object's class.

Property	Description
Comment	Stores information about an object.
ContainerReleaseType	Specifies whether an Active document remains open and running when it is released by its host.
Name	Specifies the name used to reference an object in code.
Parent	References the container object of a control.
ParentClass	Specifies the name of the class on which the object's class is based.
Tag	Stores any extra data needed for your program.

Table 25.4 `ActiveDoc` **Class Events**

Event	Description
CommandTargetExec	This event is triggered when an Active document host notifies an Active document that a command is to be executed.
CommandTargetQuery	When an Active document host updates its user interface, this event is triggered.
ContainerRelease	When a host releases an Active document, this event is triggered.
Destroy	When the Active document is released, this event is triggered.
Error	When a runtime error in an Active document's method occurs, this event is triggered.
HideDoc	When the user navigates from an Active document, this event is triggered.
Init	This event is triggered when the Active document is created.
Run	This event is triggered when an Active document is prepared to run user-defined code. The Run command passes a URL to the Run event.
ShowDoc	This event is triggered when the user navigates to an Active document.

Part
VI

Ch
25

Table 25.5 ActiveDoc **Class Methods**

Method	Description
AddProperty (*cPropertyName* [, *eNewValue*])	This method adds a property to an object.
ReadExpression(*cPropertyName*)	This method returns the expression that the user enters in the Properties window for the specified property.
ReadMethod(*cMethod*)	This method returns the text associated with the specified method.
ResetToDefault(*cValue*)	This method restores a property, event, or method to its Visual FoxPro default setting. All of the user-defined code is removed if you are resetting a method or event. *cValue* is the name of the property, event, or method.
SaveAsClass (*ClassLibName*, *ClassName* [, *Description*])	This method saves an instance of a specified object as a class definition in the specified class library.
WriteExpression [*cPropertyName*, *cExpression*]	This method writes the specified expression to a property.

New Visual FoxPro Extensions That Support Active Documents

GETHOST() and ISHOSTED()were added to Visual FoxPro in version 6. These functions provide information relating to the host of an Active document. The GETHOST() function returns an object reference to the host of an Active document. The ISHOSTED() returns a true (.T.) value if the host of an Active Document exists. Otherwise, it returns a false (.F.) value.

In addition, various properties, events, and functions were added to form objects to support Active document applications.

Running Active Documents

Visual FoxPro Active documents require Vfp6.exe and Vfp6run.exe, or Vfp6run.exe, Vfp6r.dll, and Vfp6renu.dll (enu denotes the English version) to run. These files must be installed and registered on the computer on which IE is installed. When Visual FoxPro is installed, Vfp6.exe is installed in the Visual FoxPro directory, and the remaining files are installed in the Windows 95/98 Windows\System directory or the Windows NT WinNT\System32 directory.

The following options are available:

- In Browser (Default)—The Active document is run in IE using the Visual FoxPro runtime.
- Stand Alone—The Active document is run as a standalone application with the Visual FoxPro runtime.
- In Browser (Debugging)—The Active document is run in IE using the Visual FoxPro executable (Vfp6.exe). Debugging capabilities, the Command window, and all features of the Visual FoxPro development environment are available.
- Stand Alone (Debugging)—The Active document is run as a standalone application with the Visual FoxPro executable (Vfp6.exe), providing debugging capabilities, the Command window, and all features of the Visual FoxPro development environment. Choosing this option is identical to issuing DO *Active Doc Name* in the Command window.

You can also run an Active document by opening it from the Open File dialog box in IE, or by navigating to the Active document from another Web page with a hyperlink to the Active document.

The Visual FoxPro Runtime and Active Documents   From Visual FoxPro you can run an Active document by double-clicking the Active Document icon in the Windows Explorer. You can also run an Active document from a Visual FoxPro runtime application. The Visual FoxPro runtime consists of two files, Vfp6run.exe and Vfp6r.dll. Both must be installed and registered to run Active documents. The runtime can also be used to run other Visual FoxPro distributable files such as compiled Visual FoxPro programs (.fxp files).

Vfp6run.exe, once registered, can be used to run Active documents (and other Visual FoxPro distributable files) directly.

Here is the syntax for Vfp6run.exe:

```
VFP6RUN [/embedding] [/regserver] [/unregserver] [/security]
[/s] [/version] [FileName]
```

The arguments are described as follows:

/embedding	Loads Vfp6run.exe as an Active document server. In this mode, Vfp6run.exe is registered as a COM server capable of creating a Visual FoxPro Active document object. Without this argument, Vfp6run.exe doesn't act as a COM server.

 TIP   Chapter 22, "Creating COM Servers with Visual FoxPro," contains detailed information on Visual FoxPro's COM capabilities.

/regserver	Registers Vfp6run.exe.

/unregserver	Unregisters Vfp6run.exe.
/security	Displays the Application Security Settings dialog box, enabling you to specify the security settings for Active documents and other application (.APP) files.
/s	Silent. Specifies that an error is generated if Vfp6run.exe is unable to load the Vfp6r.dll runtime component.
/version	Displays Vfp6run.exe and the Vfp6r.dll version information.
FileName	Specifies the Visual FoxPro file to run.

Vfp6run.exe requires that the runtime support dynamic link library Vfp6r.dll be installed and registered. To register Vfp6r.dll, run Regsvr32 with the name of the runtime:

Regsvr32 Vfp6r.dll.

Creating Online Help

Getting to Know the HTML Help Workshop

You can use Microsoft's *HTML Help Workshop* to create really slick online help for your applications. The HTML Help Workshop is new as of Visual FoxPro 6 and replaces the very capable but more mundane Help Workshop 4.0. Each help page can resemble a Web page, complete with graphics, colors, and fancy formatting. You can easily link to other help pages, and even to Web sites. Your help system can have a much more polished look than you could easily achieve with Workshop 4.0. And, as an increasing number of applications migrate to the HTML Help Workshop, older help systems will begin to look dated.

If you have legacy applications, the Workshop includes a converter to transform earlier help files to the new standard. For brand-new applications, the Workshop includes a complete help authoring tool as well as an online tool for creating and editing images to make it easier to create attractive graphical help files.

The HTML Help Workshop provides you with all the tools you need to create help files that have some, or even all, of the following features:

- A contents page with a hierarchical view of your help topics.
- An index based on keywords that you provide.
- Text search capability to let users search for information using specific words and phrases.
- Text with multiple fonts, font sizes, and colors.
- Graphics, including bitmaps with multiple resolutions, Windows metafile format, and the standard HTML image formats (.JPG, .GIF, and .PNG).
- ActiveX, Java, and scripting capabilities with both JavaScript and Microsoft Visual Basic.
- HTML pages.
- The capability to jump from a help topic to an Internet site.
- Macros to automate the operation of the system.
- Hot spots, which are mouse-sensitive areas that you can use to link topics.
- Pop-up windows that display additional text.
- Segmented hypergraphics (graphics with one or more hot spots).
- Secondary windows.
- Customizable menus.
- DLLs.

The HTML Help Workshop is included with Visual Studio 6 and with Visual FoxPro 6. But, be sure to check for the very latest version at http://www.microsoft.com/workshop/author/htmlhelp.

Be sure to read the Readme file that comes with the HTML Help Workshop. There are still a few problems with Version 1.1 and these are thoroughly explained in the Readme. You can also find this information in the Workshop's Help Index under New Features.

How Does the Workshop Work?

The Microsoft HTML Help Workshop is a separate program from Visual FoxPro 6. It uses components of Microsoft Internet Explorer (IE) to display help content. You use the HTML Help Workshop to develop graphical help pages and menus to support the users of applications that you develop. After you develop your help pages and menus, use the Workshop to compile the elements that you've created into a Help file. The compiled help file has the file extension .CHM. The FoxPro command

```
SET HELP TO FILENAME.CHM
```

links your application to the help file that you've developed.

FoxPro with the HTML Help Workshop provides four ways to deliver help to the users of your applications:

- Help menu
- A Help button on a form
- Context-sensitive help
- What's This? help

These methods are described in the following sections.

Help Menu

You should have an item on the main menu bar of your application to give users access to your help system. By clicking this item, you should get an Index/Contents/Search screen like that shown in Figure 26.1, which contains Contents/Index/Search information that is pertinent to your application.

FIGURE 26.1
An Index/Contents/
Search screen. This
particular screen shows
the results of clicking
on the Help menu item
of the HTML Help
Workshop.

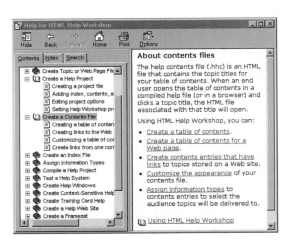

Part
VI

Ch
26

Help Button on a Form

One technique for delivering *context-sensitive help* is to put a Help command button on the form. This lets the user acquire help that is pertinent to the current form. Individual objects on the form can be described as subtopics on the help page. An example of this level of context-sensitive help is shown in Figure 26.2.

N O T E   Notice that the complete help system pops up, but with the context-sensitive help page already displayed. This makes it possible for the user to quickly move to another help topic in case the context-sensitive help that is displayed turns out to be incorrect or insufficient for her current needs. ■

Context-Sensitive Help via the F1 Key

Context-sensitive help with greater granularity is provided by linking the F1 key to a help page. This is the kind of help that pops up when an object that has an associated help topic has focus and the user presses the F1 key. This lets you have individual help pages for each object on a form that requires help. Among the objects that can have context-sensitive help tied to the F1 key are the following:

CheckBox	ComboBox
CommandButton	CommandGroup
EditBox	Form
Grid	Image
Label	Line
ListBox	OLE Bound Control
OLE Container Control	OptionButton
OptionGroup	Page
SCREEN	Server Object
Shape	Spinner
TextBox	ToolBar

What's This? Help

What's This? help is also context-sensitive help that a user can request about a particular object. This is similar to the What's This? help that was introduced with Windows 95. When a form has What's This? help, a question mark is displayed just to the left of the form's Close button. To activate the context-sensitive help for a screen object, the user clicks on the question mark. The cursor changes shape to indicate that it is ready. Subsequently clicking on any object that has an associated help topic produces a display similar to what you saw in Figure 26.2. A form designed to use What's This? help is shown in Figure 26.3.

FIGURE 26.2

A sample Context Help screen from the Visual FoxPro 6 sample project SOLUTION. This help screen is produced by either pressing F1 or clicking on the Help button for the main form of SOLUTION.

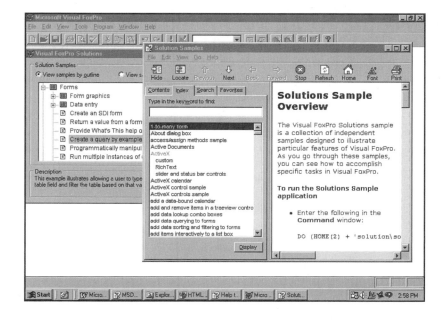

FIGURE 26.3

A simple Visual FoxPro form that can be used with What's This? help. Notice the question mark in the upper-right corner of the screen.

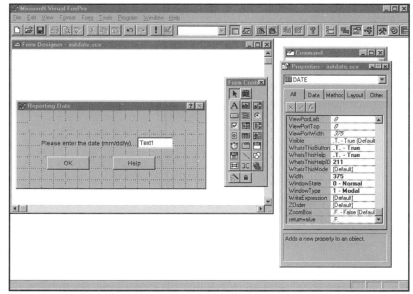

Using the HTML Help Workshop

It is not at all difficult to use the HTML Help Workshop to create custom help files for your FoxPro applications. The following sections step you through the basics of the Workshop. You'll find that the addition of HTML help to your applications will give the applications a more polished, professional appearance.

Installation

Your first step in using the HTML Help Workshop is to install it on your computer. The Workshop is not part of the standard FoxPro installation, so you'll need to install it separately. You'll find it on your Visual Studio CD #1 as a compressed executable named HTMLHELP.EXE. If, for some reason, you can't locate it on the CD, you can find it at http://www.microsoft.com/workshop/author/htmlhelp.

All you need to do to install the HTML Help Workshop is to double-click on HTMLHELP.EXE and follow the resulting wizard's instructions.

Creating a Help Project

The first step in developing your help system is to bring up the HTML Help Workshop and choose File, New. This activates a wizard that collects the necessary information to create new elements of your help system, and brings you to the screen shown in Figure 26.4.

FIGURE 26.4

This is the Help Workshop screen for creating new project elements.

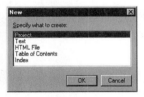

The help system essentially consists of a number of HTML files that provide the help information associated with an item in the table of contents, the index, or context-sensitive help. The *help project* is the wrapper that puts all of these elements together. Start by selecting Project from the New Items menu. This selection starts a wizard that collects the information for a new help project.

TIP

The Project Wizard is the vehicle for converting an existing WinHelp project to the new HTML help. It will convert .RTF files to HTML, convert the .CNT file to an .HHC file (a new table of contents), and transform the WinHelp project file into an HTML Help project file (.HHP).

The Project Wizard also determines the location of your new help project. It seems reasonable to place the project in the Help folder of your FoxPro project. FoxPro 6 automatically creates a Help folder for each new FoxPro project.

If you have already created a table of contents, an index, or HTML topic files, you can choose to have the Project Wizard incorporate these existing elements into the new project with the help of the Existing Files screen shown in Figure 26.5.

FIGURE 26.5

Use the Existing Files screen in the New Project Wizard to incorporate existing files into your project.

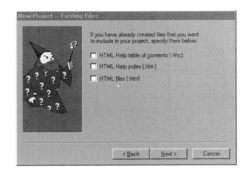

When you're finished with the Help Wizard, you have a new, empty project and your Help Workshop screen will look something like Figure 26.6.

FIGURE 26.6

Here's a screen for a new HTML Workshop project.

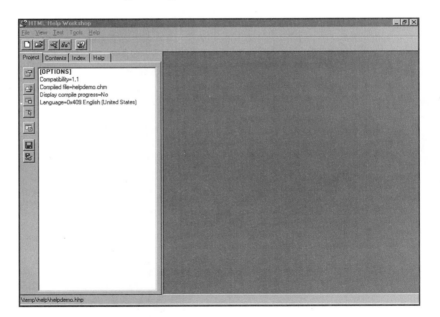

Notice that the Project window has four tabs: Project, Contents, Index, and Help.

CAUTION

Be cautious with the Help tab, because it can lock up the Workshop. In fact, you should be cautious about clicking on any Help tab except the one on the main menu.

Part

VI

Ch

26

Down the side of the window, you'll find seven speed buttons.

- Change project options
- Add/remove topic files
- Windows definitions
- API information
- View HTML source
- Save project files
- Save project files and compile

Table of Contents

The Project's table of contents is similar to that found in the help system of every Windows program, except that it contains only those items that you put there. It can contain as little or as much as you think necessary for your particular FoxPro project. To add a table of contents to your new project, either click on File, New and select Table of Contents from the menu (refer to Figure 26.4), or click on the Project's Contents tab (refer to Figure 26.6). You'll need to supply a name for the new contents file, and you can use whatever name you like, but stick with the file extension .HHC. A table of contents page in process will look like that shown in Figure 26.7.

FIGURE 26.7
Table of Contents under development.

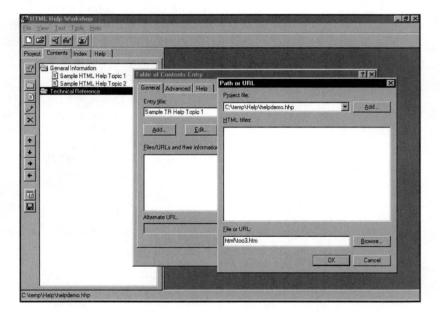

Notice that there are eleven speed buttons down the left side of the Contents window.

- Contents properties
- Insert a heading
- Insert a page
- Edit selection
- Delete selection
- Move selection up
- Move selection down
- Move selection right
- Move selection left
- View HTML source
- Save file

Inserting a heading adds a line that begins with an icon. The choice of icons (book or folder) is set by a check box in the Contents Properties form. The heading doesn't need to be associated with an HTML file or with a URL, although it can be. If you don't explicitly specify a link to the heading, the Workshop will automatically link the heading to the project's default topic. The default topic must be specified using the Add/Remove topic files button on the Project tab. If you forget to specify this default, the program will generate a runtime error when it is launched.

Inserting a page adds a line that begins with the icon that looks like a page. Page lines are normally offset from the left edge of the window. When you insert a page, as shown in Figure 26.7, you provide the Workshop with the Page title and then specify a help file or a Web URL. The file or URL that you specify doesn't have to exist at this time. However, if the file/URL doesn't exist when you run the compiled Help file, you'll get a cosmetic error when you click on the page title. The file can be either a text file or an HTML file.

Index

The project's index is also similar to that found in the help system of every Windows program, except that you must define the items for the index. As with the table of contents, the index can contain as little or as much as you think necessary for your particular FoxPro project. To add an index to your new project, either choose File, New and select Index from the menu (refer to Figure 26.4), or click on the Project's Index tab (refer to Figure 26.6). You'll need to supply a name for the new index file; you can use whatever name you like, but stick with the file extension .HHK. An index page in progress will look like that shown in Figure 26.8.

FIGURE 26.8

This is how an index under development looks.

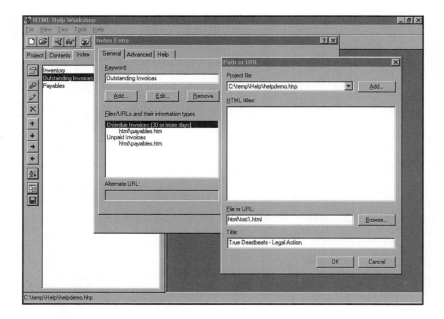

There are eleven speed buttons down the left side of the Index window:

- Index properties
- Insert a keyword
- Edit selection
- Delete selection
- Move selection up
- Move selection down
- Move selection right
- Move selection left
- Sort every keyword at same level as selection
- View HTML source
- Save file

Inserting a keyword adds a line in the Index window. The keyword itself is the text that appears in the Index window, but you also need to supply the file or URL that is to be linked to the keyword. You can also supply an optional title with each file/URL that is linked to the keyword. This optional title is used when you have multiple links for a particular keyword, as is shown in Figure 26.8 and the application (see Figure 26.9). As with the table of contents, the system won't complain if the linked file/URL doesn't exist. It will produce a cosmetic error when you run the compiled Help program, however.

FIGURE 26.9
This illustrates a keyword with multiple linkages.

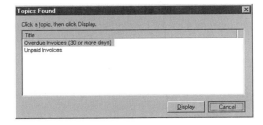

Adding HTML Topic Files

You need to create one HTML file for every help page that can be displayed for items in the table of contents, keywords in the index, and as context-sensitive help. To add HTML files, choose File, New and select HTML from the list of options. The HTML Help Workshop has a simple text editor that you can use to edit the files created with this option. However, you'll be better served to create and edit these files using a good HTML editor for your HTML files. When the Workshop creates a new HTML file, it provides some of the HTML structure as shown in Figure 26.10.

FIGURE 26.10
This is a basic HTML file created by the HTML Help Workshop.

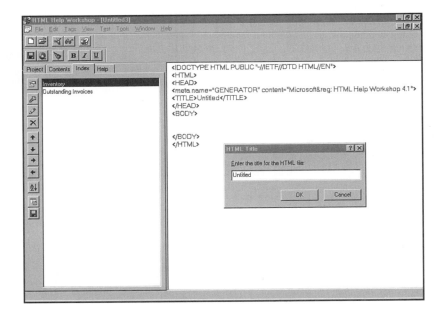

Part
VI

Ch
26

Another option that you shouldn't overlook is to use the Save As HTML feature in Microsoft Word. That way, you can use MS Word to develop all the HTML topic files that you need. In addition, there are quite a number of free—or almost free—design tools that you can make good use of in your page design. Finally, there are several commercial authoring tools that work with the HTML Help Workshop to produce stunning output with far less work on your part.

If you're going to need a substantial number of HTML topic files, you might consider putting these files into an HTML subdirectory of your Help folder. This will keep them separated from the other files used by your help project.

Links to Topic Files and URLs   You can create links between HTML topic files and between a topic file and URLs on the World Wide Web. To create a link between one HTML file and another, use the following syntax:

```
<a href="relative pathname">topic string </a>
```

where `relative pathname` is the name of the file that you want to link to, and `topic string` is the character sequence that will be displayed and underlined. For example:

```
<a href="html\payables.htm">See Also </a>
```

To create a link to a URL on the World Wide Web, use an HTML statement like the following:

```
<a href="http://www.microsoft.com">See Web Site</a>
```

Adding and Removing Topic Files   After you create an HTML topic file, you must add it to the project. This is accomplished with the Add/Remove topic files speed button on the Project tab, which produces a screen similar to that shown in Figure 26.11.

FIGURE 26.11

This screen is used for adding and removing HTML topic files.

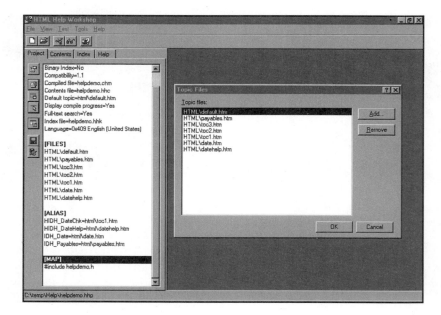

This is the list of HTML files that will be compiled into the project. Clicking on the Remove button will remove the reference to the selected file. It does not delete the file from the disk. Click on Add to bring up the Open dialog and select one or more of the displayed files to be added to the project, as shown in Figure 26.12. Click on Open to add the selected files.

FIGURE 26.12
Use the Open dialog box to add HTML topic files.

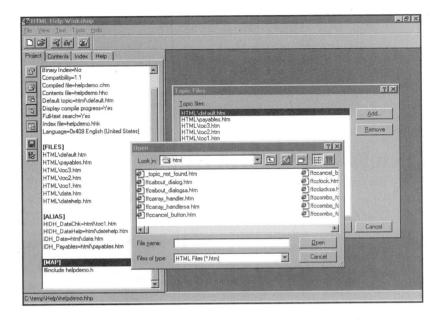

You should have a default topic file that says something to the effect of No matching topic was found. Be sure to add this default file to the list of topic files. You must also identify this file as the official default file. Click on Change Project Options to access the screen shown in Figure 26.13. Fill in the name of the default HTML Topic File and click OK.

FIGURE 26.13
Use this dialog box to specify the default HTML topic file.

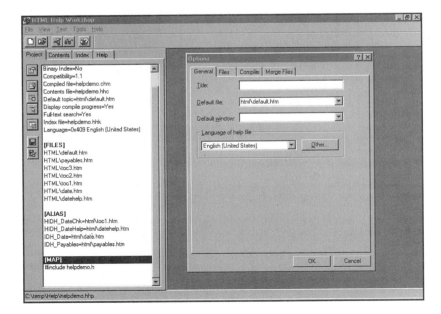

Compiling Your Basic Help System

At this point in the process, you have everything you need to provide the basic system level help when the user clicks on the Help selection of your application's main menu. To get the optional working model, select File, Compile. If you've done everything correctly, you will have a compiled help file that has the file extension .CHM. To connect this help file to your Visual FoxPro application, add this statement:

```
SET HELP TO filename.CHM
```

Context-Specific Help Topics

The next step in developing your help system is to add context-specific help. The first step is to add an optional Help command button to a form as seen in Figure 26.14. This button provides context-sensitive help at the form level, and the F1 function key will provide the same help.

FIGURE 26.14

Here's the setup for a Help command button on a form in Visual FoxPro 6.

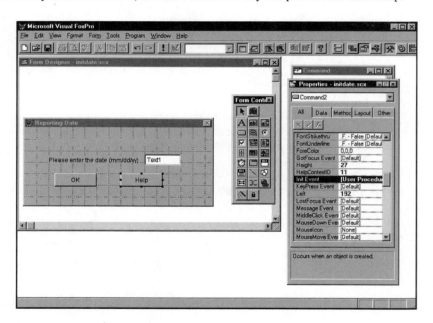

Next, complete these steps:

1. Set the form's HelpContextID to a value that is not used by any other HelpContextID in your Visual FoxPro project. In this example, HelpContexID is set to 11.

2. In the Init event for this form, set the HelpContextID property for all of the form's objects to this same value, as in the following line:

```
This.SetAll("HelpContextID",11)
```

3. Add the following line to the Click event for the Help command button:

```
Help ID This.HelpContextID
```

At this point, you've set up the Visual FoxPro end. Now you need to tell your help project how to handle this Help event.

Using the MAP File as a Connecting Link You need to create a new file that's going to provide the connecting link between your FoxPro application and the HTML help project. This link comes from the *MAP file*. You can call this file HelpDemo.h. The filename doesn't matter, but the extension must be .h. This is just a standard C header file. Add the following line to the MAP file:

```
#define IDH_DateButton 11 //this is the date help button
```

IDH_DateButton is the symbolic name for HelpContextID 11. You'll need additional lines like this in your MAP file, one for each HelpContextID in your Visual FoxPro application. You can add additional lines at any time, as long as you recompile the help project after each new set of lines.

Adding the Map to the Help Project In the HTML Help Workshop, click on the Project tab and then click on the HtmlHelp API information button. This will give you the screen shown in Figure 26.15. Use the Header File button to add the Map file to the project.

FIGURE 26.15

Use this dialog box to add map information to the help project.

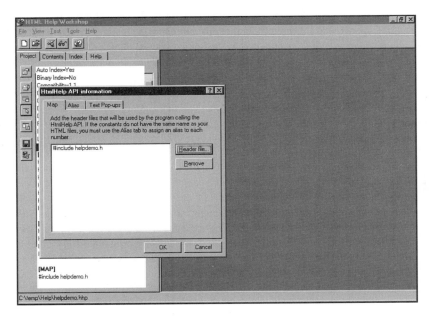

Part VI
Ch 26

Linking the HelpContextID to an HTML Topic File Your next step is to tell the project which HTML topic file is to be used for this HelpContextID. This is accomplished with the Alias tab in the HtmlHelp API Information dialog. Click on the HtmlHelp API information button to access a list of existing aliases. Click on the Add button to move to the dialog box shown in Figure 26.16.

FIGURE 26.16
Use this dialog box to add alias information to the help project.

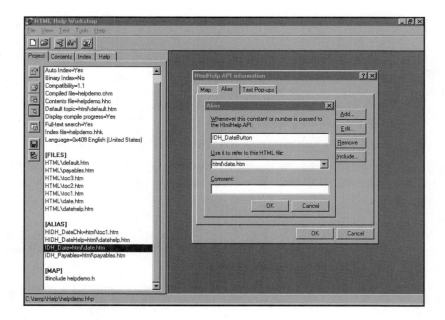

In the top line of the Alias dialog, enter the symbolic name that you assigned the `HelpContextID`. On the second line, enter the name of the HTML topic file that you want this `HelpContextID` to call. The Comment line is just for your future reference; it doesn't get compiled into the `.CHM` file.

You can now compile your help project. It will produce context-sensitive help in your FoxPro application. The specified HTML topic file will be displayed when users click on the Help button or press the F1 key.

What's This? Help Topics

What's This? help was first introduced with Windows 95. This is the help that's available when you a see a question mark displayed just to the left of a form's Close button. What's This? help is activated by clicking on the question mark and then clicking on the form itself, on a control, or on a toolbar. What's This? help is not available when a form has either Minimize or Maximize buttons on the form's title bar.

To have your form use What's This? help, you need to set certain properties of the form as follows:

■ `WhatsThisHelp = True`

■ `WhatsThisButton = True`

■ `WhatsThisHelpID = `*`unique value within project`*

■ `MinButton = False`

■ `MaxButton = False`

A Visual FoxPro 6 form that has been set up to make use of What's This? help is shown in Figure 26.17.

FIGURE 26.17
This Visual FoxPro 6 form has been set up to use What's This? help.

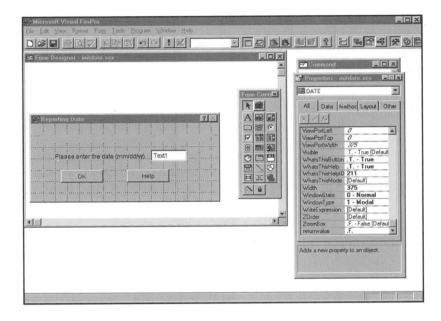

Setting up the Header File   Add lines like those shown below to your project's MAP file (this is the C header file that was introduced in the discussion on context-sensitive help):

```
#define HIDH_DateForm 211 //this is the date form
#define HIDH_DateField 212 // this is the date field
```

If your project doesn't yet have a MAP file, see the section "Using the MAP File as a Connecting Link" earlier in this chapter.

Incidentally, you can have multiple header files to map names to HelpContextID and WhatsThisHelpID values. You might find it more convenient to manage the assignment of unique names and numbers by using multiple header files, particularly if you have a large number of help topics. However, don't use the same value for a HelpContextID and a WhatsThisHelpID, even if the duplicates will be in different header files.

Setting the Aliases   Your next step is to tell the project which HTML topic file is to be used for this WhatsThisHelpID. This is accomplished with the Alias tab in the HtmlHelp API Information dialog box just as it was with context-sensitive help. Click on the HtmlHelp API information button to access a list of existing aliases. Click on the Add button to move to the dialog you saw in Figure 26.16.

In the top line of this dialog, enter the symbolic name that you assigned the WhatsThisHelpID. On the second line, enter the name of the HTML topic file that you want this value to call. The Comment line is just for your future reference; it doesn't get compiled into the .CHM file.

You can now compile your help project. It produces What's This? help in your Visual FoxPro application. The specified HTML topic file is displayed whenever users click on the question mark and then click on a control or field that has an associated WhatsThisHelpID.

Distributing Your Compiled Help System

You can distribute your compiled help system along with your FoxPro application. The HTML Help Workshop includes a setup program named HHUPD.EXE that you can redistribute. This program installs and registers the HTML help runtime components. Internet Explorer must be installed on the user's machine. And, don't forget to include your compiled help file.

The following components are installed by the setup program:

Component Name	Description
Hhctrl.ocx	HTML help ActiveX control
Itss.dll	Dynamic link library for compiled HTML
Itircl.dll	Full-text search dynamic link library
Hh.exe	HTML help viewer

The setup program can be called from other setup programs and will run in the quiet mode so that it doesn't interfere with existing setup programs. To obtain a list of the program's command line options, run **HHUPD.EXE/?**. ●

The Visual FoxPro Wizards

What Are the Wizards?

Magic wands and cauldrons of boiling liquid are the images I see when I think of wizards. Bearded men with long flowing robes and pointy hats come to mind. The Visual FoxPro Wizards don't fall into this category, though.

A *wizard* in Visual FoxPro is an interface that makes the creation of various components easier to accomplish. There are 22 Wizards available in Visual FoxPro:

Application	One to Many Report
Cross-Tab	Oracle Upsizing
Database	PivotTable
Documenting	Query
Form	Remote View
Graph	Report
Import	SQL Server Upsizing
Label	Setup
Local View	Table
Mail Merge	WWW Search Page
One to Many Form	Web Publishing

In this chapter, you will learn about five of the 22 Wizards: the Application, Documenting, Setup, WWW Search Page, and Web Publishing Wizards.

In the discussion of these wizards, you will see that they all have a consistent user interface, which will make it easy during your future development work to use a new wizard that you have not seen before.

Application Wizard and Builder

The *Application Wizard* creates a project and a project directory structure for an application. When the wizard finishes, the *Application Builder* is automatically run to enable you to add data, forms, reports, and other components to the application. Figure 27.1 shows the first screen of the Application Wizard.

You have three actions to take in this screen. First you enter the name of your application in the top text box labeled Project Name. The Project File text box is used to enter the name and path of the .PJX project file to be created. The final option is the check box labeled Create Project Directory Structure; checking this box will cause the Application Wizard to create a directory structure for your project.

FIGURE 27.1

The Visual FoxPro
Application Wizard.

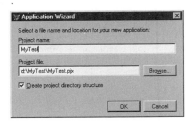

After you choose OK, the Application Wizard will create the project directory structure and the project file. The wizard will put the application components into the project file, open the Project Manager for this new project, and show you the help file entry for the Developing Applications Using the Application Framework. The directory structure created by the Application Wizard is shown in Figure 27.2.

FIGURE 27.2

The directory structure
that was created by the
Application Wizard.

The Application Wizard directory structure is used to organize the pieces of an application. The data files go in the Data directory, forms go in the Forms directory, and the other components go in their respective directories. This directory structure will make it easy for you to keep track of the components of your application.

The Project

After showing you the help file entry for Developing Applications Using the Application Framework, the Application Wizard runs the Application Builder. I will discuss the Application Builder in a moment, but first let's see what the Application Wizard has built. Figure 27.3 shows the project built by the wizard.

Notice that the Application Wizard has created a free table named mytest_app. This table is used by the application framework to manage the forms and reports that are part of the application (see Chapter 18, "The Visual FoxPro Foundation Classes," for more information about this table). This table is in the root of the project directory structure and not in the Data directory.

Figure 27.4 shows the Classes tab of the project manager with the class libraries that were added by the Application Wizard.

FIGURE 27.3

The Data tab of the project created by the Application Wizard.

FIGURE 27.4

The Classes tab of the Project Manager.

There are seven class libraries in the project. The only one that is stored in the Libs directory is the project-specific library named *ProjectName*_app. The other libraries are part of the foundation classes in Visual FoxPro 6 and are stored in the FFC and Wizards directories under the Visual FoxPro home directory.

The project-specific class library has subclassed some of the classes from the _framewrk class library for this project.

Figure 27.5 shows the Code tab of the Project Manager.

The two program files shown in Figure 27.5 are the application's startup program (MyTest_app.prg) and a utility program for creating objects (SetObjRf.prg).

Figure 27.6 shows the Other tab of the Project Manager.

FIGURE 27.5

The Code tab of the
Project Manager.

FIGURE 27.6

The Other tab of the
Project Manager for the
project created by the
Application Wizard.

You can see that the Application Wizard has added quite a few files to the Other tab. There are two menus: `MyTest_main` is the main system menu for the application and `MyTest_go` is an added pad to the main system menu.

The text files listed in Figure 27.6 include a `Config.fpw` file for configuring the Visual FoxPro runtime environment for the application. Also, there are a number of header files for defining manifest constants for the application components.

Notice that there are two files named after the project. The first is a header file (`.H`) with manifest constants defined in it. The second is a text file for use with the project hook object that the Application Wizard has added to the project.

Under the Other files section, bitmap images (`.BMP`) and their respective mask (`.MSK`) files have been added. These bitmap and mask files are the images used for command buttons and other items have images on them.

This is the complete work of the Application Wizard. The wizard creates a project and populates it with the basic elements needed for a project, including a complete application framework.

The Application Builder

After the Application Wizard has created the directory structure and project for a new application, the Application Builder is automatically run. Figure 27.7 shows the Application Builder form.

FIGURE 27.7
The Application Builder in Visual FoxPro.

The Application Builder is a tabbed form with a `PageFrame` in it. The tabs of the `PageFrame` are labeled General, Credits, Data, Forms, Reports, and Advanced.

You will be shown these tabs in the order they appear in the form.

The General tab is used to enter general information about your application. The project Name is entered automatically by the Application Builder. You can enter an Image filename, or browse for one by pressing the ellipsis button beside the Image text box. Press the ellipsis button in the Icon box in the lower-right corner of the form to browse for an image file to serve as the application icon (it's okay if this is the same file you specified as the Image file).

The balance of the options in this tab are described in Table 27.1.

Table 27.1   The Application Builder's General Tab Options

Option Category	Option	Description
Common Dialogs	Splash Screen	When checked, will create a splash screen that is displayed during the application's loading process, unchecked suppresses the splash screen.
	About dialog	Checked includes an About dialog on the help menu, unchecked excludes the About dialog.

Option Category	Option	Description
	Quick Start	The Quick Start screen is a menu form that enables the user to access the forms and reports without using the menu system. Checking this box includes a quick start form and unchecking the box excludes the quick start form.
	User Logins	Checking this box requires that users log into the application using a user name and password. Unchecking the box excludes this feature from the application.
Application type	Normal	The application will run in the Visual FoxPro desktop. The main Visual FoxPro screen will contain the forms for the application.
	Module	The application will be a module that is called from some other application.
	Top-Level	The application runs outside of the Visual FoxPro screen as a top-level application under Windows.

Figure 27.8 shows the Credits tab of the Application Builder.

FIGURE 27.8
The Credits tab for your application.

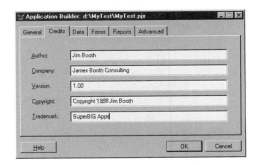

On the Credits tab, there are only five items to be entered: Author, Company, Version, Copyright, and Trademark. You enter the text exactly as you want to see it in the About dialog.

The next tab is the Data tab, which is shown in Figure 27.9.

FIGURE 27.9

The Data tab of the Application Builder.

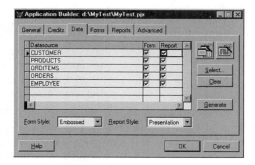

The options on this tab are described in Table 27.2.

Table 27.2 The Application Builder's Data Tab Options

Option Category	Option	Description
Datasource	Datasource	The names of the tables that hold the data for this application. This example used the Select button and chose the Testdata.dbc database that is included with the Visual FoxPro samples. When you select a database, all the tables in that database are included.
	Form	By checking the box beside each table name, the Application Builder will use the Form Wizard to create a form for that table.
	Report	This column is the same as the Form column, except it creates a report.
	Form Style	This combo box offers nine form styles: Standard, Chiseled, Shadowed, Boxed, Embossed, Fancy, Stone, Flax, and Colorful. These styles affect the coloring and style of the forms created by the Form Wizard for the tables.
	Report Style	Similar to the Form Style, this combo box offers five styles for reports: Presentation, Ledger, Executive, Banded, and Casual.
	Select	Produces the File Open dialog to enable you to search for tables or databases on the disk drive and include them in the list of tables.
	Clear	Clears out the list of tables to enable you to start over should you find you need to.
	Generate	Generates a form or report for the selected table in the grid using the Form Style and/or Report Style selected with the combo boxes.

The two buttons with the magic wands on them in the upper-right corner of the Data tab are used to run the Database Wizard and the Table Wizard, respectively. The second button (with only one browse window on it) runs the Table Wizard; the first runs the Database Wizard.

Figure 27.10 shows the Forms tab that is used to add forms that already exist to the application.

FIGURE 27.10

The Forms tab of the
Application Builder.

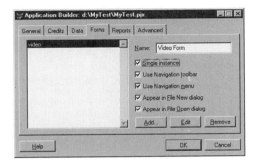

The first thing to do is to select the Add button and add the form named Video.scx, which is included with the Visual FoxPro samples. The Add button brings up the File Open dialog to enable you to navigate your disk drive and find the form you want to include in the application.

The Remove button can be used to remove the highlighted form from the application.

The Edit button is used to open the highlighted form in the Form Designer. If you choose to edit a form, you see the dialog box shown in Figure 27.11.

FIGURE 27.11

This dialog appears
when you choose to
edit a form in the
Application Builder.

This dialog asks you if you want the Application Builder to add a mediator object to the form so that the form will function properly within the framework of the application. You typically answer Yes to this dialog so that the forms added to the application will make use of the features of the application framework. If you answer No to this dialog, you will see the dialog every time you edit the form within the Application Builder until you answer Yes.

The five check boxes on the right side of the Forms tab are described in Table 27.3.

Part

VI

Ch

27

Table 27.3   The Application Builder's Forms Tab Options

Option	Description
Single Instance	Checked enables only one instance of the form to be open at a time, unchecked enables multiple instances of the form to be open.
Use Navigation Toolbar	Checked will include a navigation toolbar for the high-lighted form, unchecked omits the navigation toolbar.
Use Navigation Menu	Checked includes a navigation menu for the highlighted form, unchecked omits the navigation menu.
Appear in File New Dialog	Causes the form's name to appear in the application's New dialog.
Appear in File Open Dialog	Causes the form's name to appear in the application's Open dialog.

The next tab is the Reports tab, which is shown in Figure 27.12.

FIGURE 27.12

The Reports tab of the Application Builder.

The Reports tab is similar to the Forms tab except that it deals with reports rather than forms. It is used to include existing reports in the application. The Add, Edit, and Remove buttons function the same way they do on the Forms tab.

The only option on the Reports tab is named Appear in Print Reports Dialog. Checking this box causes the highlighted report in the list to be included in the application's Print Reports dialog.

Figure 27.13 shows the last tab, Advanced, in the Application Builder.

The options that you can set using the Advanced tab include a Help File Name that will be included in the application. The ellipsis button to the right enables you to browse for the help file you want.

FIGURE 27.13

The Advanced tab of the Application Builder.

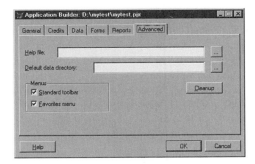

The Default Data Directory text box enables you to provide a path to the data that the application will use. The ellipsis button to the right enables you to browse for the directory you want.

The Menus box has two options in it, Standard Toolbar and Favorites Menu. Checking these options includes their respective components in the application.

The Cleanup button runs a routine to reconcile any changes you have made in the Application Builder with the project file.

Click the OK button to complete the Application Builder. This might bring up the dialog shown in Figure 27.14.

FIGURE 27.14

The Outstanding Items dialog of the Application Builder.

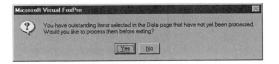

You get this dialog if you have never selected the Generate button on the Data tab of the Application Builder, which means that your forms and reports were not created. Answering Yes to this dialog causes the Application Builder to generate those files for you now.

The Application

After you're finished with the Application Builder, you should build the application and mark the Recompile All Files option. In the ongoing example, the application is named the same as the project, `MyTest.app`. After the application is built, you can run it from the command window by typing **DO MyTest.app**.

Figure 27.15 is the first screen you see in this application.

I chose to run the `Customer` form that the Application Builder created for me. Figure 27.16 shows the `Customer` form.

FIGURE 27.15

The Quick Start form of the Application Builder.

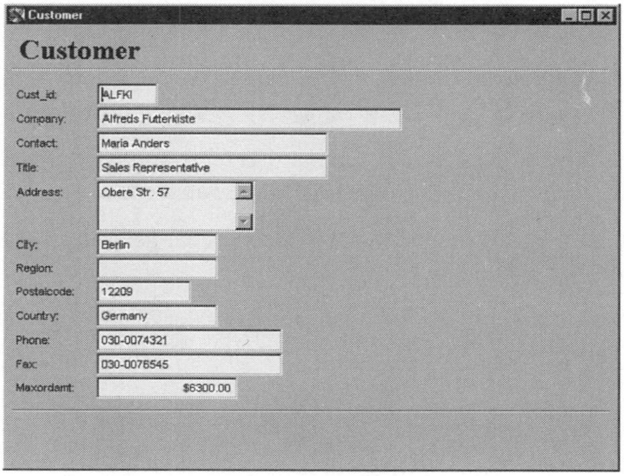

FIGURE 27.16

The `Customer` form created by the Application Builder.

Notice that there is a navigation toolbar in the toolbar area of the screen; this toolbar is there because I told the Application Builder that I wanted one for this form. The toolbar buttons can be used to navigate in the `Customer` form.

Explore the application that the builder created to find out more about the features of the resulting application. You can also refer to Chapter 18 to learn more about the way this application functions.

Documenting Wizard

The *Documenting Wizard* is used to create system documentation for a Visual FoxPro project. The documentation produced optionally includes formatted source code listings, action diagrams, cross-referencing of variables, fields, and properties, a listing of all files that compose the project, and tree diagrams showing the calling order.

Figure 27.17 shows the first step in the Documenting Wizard.

In the first step, you identify the project file for which you want to produce documentation. I used the project that I just built in the Application Wizard and Builder. After you identify the project, press the Next button to proceed to step 2. Figure 27.18 shows the form for step 2.

FIGURE 27.17

The first step in the Visual FoxPro Documenting Wizard.

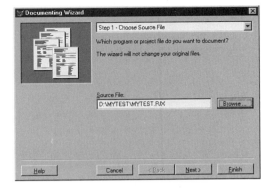

FIGURE 27.18

Step 2 of the Documenting Wizard.

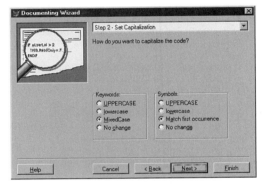

The Help button gives you a help screen specific to the step you are on and the Cancel button cancels the documenting of the project. In step 2 you determine how the capitalization will be applied to the source code listings and other diagrams produced later. The choices are listed in Table 27.4.

Table 27.4 Options for Capitalization of Keywords in Step 2 of the Documenting Wizard

Option	Description
UPPERCASE	All keywords will be in uppercase letters in the source code listings.
lowercase	All keywords will be in lowercase letters in the source code listings.
MixedCase	All keywords will be in mixed case letters in the source code listings.
No Change	Keywords will not be altered from the way they appear in the actual code in the source code listings.

Part

VI

Ch

27

Table 27.5 describes the capitalization options for the symbols in the source code listings.

Table 27.5   Options for Capitalization of Symbols in Step 2 of the Documenting Wizard

Option	Description
UPPERCASE	All symbols will be in uppercase letters in the source code listings.
lowercase	All symbols will be in lowercase letters in the source code listings.
Match First Occurrence	The capitalization of the symbols will be determined by the first occurrence of each symbol in the project code.
No Change	Symbols will not be altered from the way they appear in the actual code in the source code listings.

Figure 27.19 shows step 3 of the Documenting Wizard, which controls the indentation of the source code listings.

FIGURE 27.19
Step 3 of the Documenting Wizard.

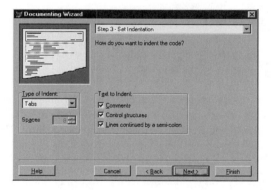

In step 3 you set the type of indentation that will be used to format the source code listings. The Type of Indent box enables you to choose Tabs or Spaces. If you choose Spaces, you will need to set the number of spaces to use for one level of indentation.

The other box, Text to Indent, provides check boxes to determine what text will be indented. The options you have are Comments, Control Structures, and Lines Continued by a Semicolon. The Comments option is self-explanatory. The Control Structures option controls the indentation of IF...ENDIF, DO CASE...ENDCASE, DO WHILE...ENDDO, FOR...ENDFOR, SCAN...ENDSCAN, and PROCEDURE/FUNCTION...ENDPROC/ENDFUNC constructs. Checking the Control Structures check box will indent the code inside of these program constructs.

The Lines Continued by a Semicolon check box determines whether the continuation lines using a semicolon will be indented under the first line of the command statement.

Figure 27.20 shows step 4 of the Documenting Wizard.

FIGURE 27.20

Step 4 of the
Documenting Wizard.

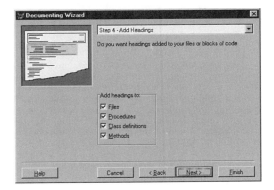

Step 4 is used to set the files for which you want headings added. The headings that will be added are comment blocks about the code that follows the heading. Using headings in your formatted source code listings can make the source code easier to read and understand.

The choices of files to add headings to are Files, Procedures, Class Definitions, and Methods. Files refers to all files that are not Visual FoxPro program files, such as .H header files or .TXT text files. Procedures includes all .PRG files and the PROCEDURE or FUNCTION declarations inside those .PRG files. Class Definitions includes those classes created with the DEFINE CLASS command and those in visual class libraries. Selecting Methods will put a comment header into each method code.

Figure 27.21 shows step 5 of the Documenting Wizard.

FIGURE 27.21

Step 5 of the
Documenting Wizard.

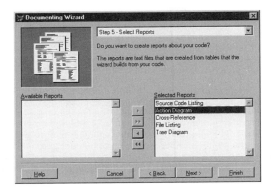

Step 5 is where you determine what documentation will be produced by the wizard. You have five pieces of documentation that you can select. In Figure 27.21 I selected all five. These pieces of documentation will be described in detail later in this section; for now, select them all and select Next to move on to step 6. Figure 27.22 shows the step 6 form.

FIGURE 27.22

The last step in the Documenting Wizard.

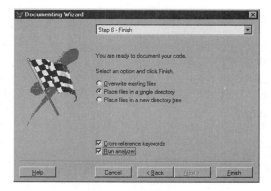

In step 6, you determine where the documentation files will be created and whether you want a Cross-Reference of Keywords produced and/or want to Run Analyzer. I elected to put all the documentation in a single directory and to produce the Cross-Reference Keywords and to Run Analyzer.

When you click the Finish button, the Documenting Wizard begins to produce the documentation you requested. The process of producing the documentation can take a few minutes depending on the size of your project.

When the Documenting Wizard has finished producing the documentation, the Visual FoxPro Code Analyzer is run (if you requested it). Figure 27.23 shows the Code Analyzer on the Symbols page.

FIGURE 27.23

The Symbols page of the Code Analyzer.

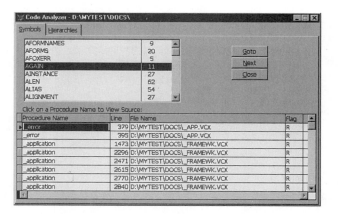

The list in the upper-left corner shows all the symbols found in the code. Highlighting an item in this list causes the grid below it to show all the places that the highlighted symbol is referenced. Clicking on one of the reference locations in the grid opens the editor for that item and highlights the occurrences of the symbol. Figure 27.24 shows what I saw when I selected AGAIN as the symbol and then clicked on _error in the locations grid.

FIGURE 27.24

The editor with the _error routine displayed and the AGAIN symbol highlighted.

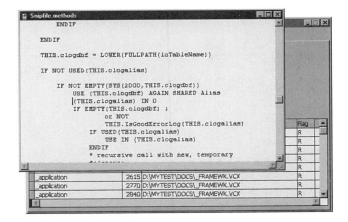

```
            ENDIF

        ENDIF

        THIS.clogdbf = LOWER(FULLPATH(lcTableName))

        IF NOT USED(THIS.clogalias)

            IF NOT EMPTY(SYS(2000,THIS.clogdbf))
                USE (THIS.clogdbf) AGAIN SHARED Alias
            |(THIS.clogalias) IN 0
                IF EMPTY(THIS.clogdbf) ;
                    or NOT
                        THIS.IsGoodErrorLog(THIS.clogalias)
                    IF USED(THIS.clogalias)
                        USE IN (THIS.clogalias)
                    ENDIF
                    * recursive call with new, temporary
```

			Flag
			R
			R
			R
			R
			R
_application	2615	D:\MYTEST\DOCS_FRAMEWK.VCX	R
_application	2770	D:\MYTEST\DOCS_FRAMEWK.VCX	R
_application	2840	D:\MYTEST\DOCS_FRAMEWK.VCX	R

Notice in Figure 27.23 that there is a Line column in the grid. This column shows you the line number that the selected symbol appears on in the procedure. The File Name column of the grid shows you the name of the file that the procedure is found in. The Flag column shows a single character value that represents the Type filed in the project's file. Table 27.6 lists the possible values for the flag column.

Table 27.6 Values Found in the Flag Column of the Grid in the Code Analyzer

Flag	Meaning
H	Header
K	Form
V	Visual Class Library
P	Program
M	Menu (.MNX)
m	Menu (.MPR)
Q	Query
R	Report
B	Label
L	Library
F	Format
d	Database
t	Associated Table

Part VI
Ch
27

continues

Table 27.6 Continued

Flag	Meaning
I	Index
x	File
T	Text File
Z	Application
i	Icon

The Hierarchies tab enables you to see the program Calling tree or the class diagram for the application. The calling tree shows what procedures call what other procedures and the class diagram shows the parent class to subclass relationships. Selecting the Close button closes the Code Analyzer.

Figure 27.25 shows a sample of a formatted source code listing with the header comments that were inserted by the Documenting Wizard.

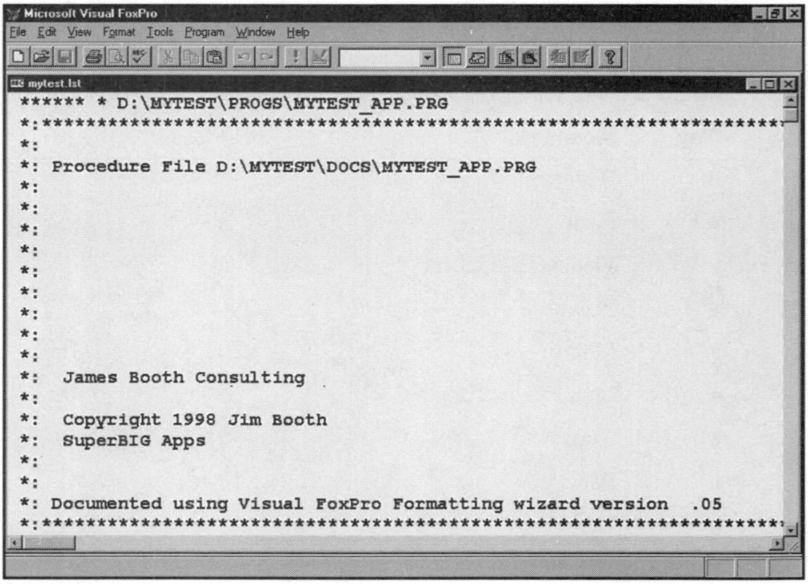

FIGURE 27.25

A formatted program listing produced by the Documenting Wizard.

```
****** * D:\MYTEST\PROGS\MYTEST_APP.PRG
*:*****************************************************************
*:
*: Procedure File D:\MYTEST\DOCS\MYTEST_APP.PRG
*:
*:
*:
*:
*:
*:
*:
*:
*: James Booth Consulting
*:
*: Copyright 1998 Jim Booth
*: SuperBIG Apps
*:
*:
*: Documented using Visual FoxPro Formatting wizard version   .05
*:*****************************************************************
```

Figure 27.26 shows a sample of an action diagram produced by the Documenting Wizard.

 TIP

To see the lines that mark out the logical constructs in the code, I had to change the font for the edit window to FoxFont 9 point. With any other font, the lines don't show correctly.

FIGURE 27.26

An action diagram produced by the Documenting Wizard.

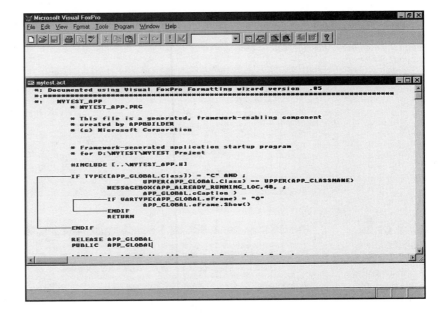

Figure 27.27 shows the symbol cross-reference listing produced by the Documenting Wizard.

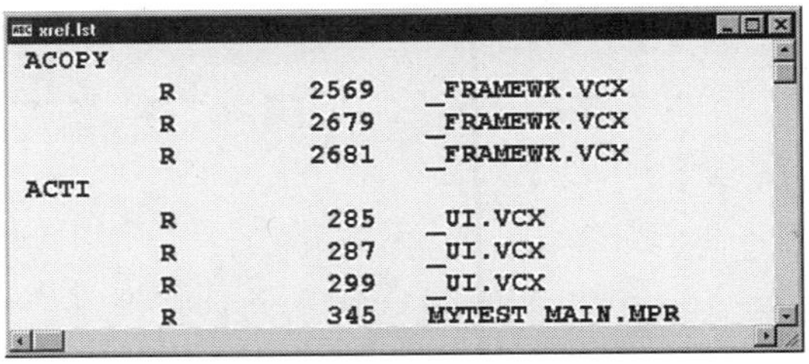

FIGURE 27.27

The symbol cross-reference produced by the Documenting Wizard.

The columns in the cross-reference are the symbol name, the flag used by the cross-reference program to produce this listing, the line number that the symbol appears on, and the filename that the symbol appears in.

Figure 27.28 is a sample of the `tree.1st` file produced by the Documenting Wizard to hold the tree diagram.

The section of the tree diagram shown in Figure 27.28 is the class hierarchy. The other section is a program calling stack listing.

Figure 27.29 shows the files list produced.

FIGURE 27.28

The tree diagram (tree.lst) from the Documenting Wizard.

FIGURE 27.29

The files list (files.lst) produced by the Documenting Wizard.

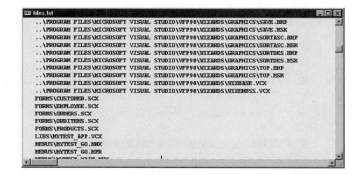

Setup Wizard

The process of installing a distributed Visual FoxPro application can be a complex one. There is the Visual FoxPro runtime library to be installed and there are several supporting files to be installed and registered on the target machine.

Thankfully, Visual FoxPro provides the *Setup Wizard* to create installation disks. Figure 27.30 shows the first dialog in the Setup Wizard.

FIGURE 27.30

The first dialog in the Setup Wizard.

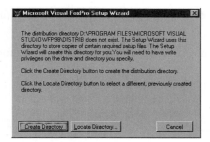

This dialog is only seen if the distribution directory does not exist. The dialog is informing you that the directory for storing the distribution files for the Visual FoxPro runtime library does not exist. The dialog offers you three choices:

- Create Directory—Creates a directory named Distrib under your Visual FoxPro home directory.
- Locate Directory—Enables you to locate the directory that you want the Setup Wizard to use.
- Cancel—Cancels this run of the Setup Wizard.

After the Distrib directory is created, the Setup Wizard moves on to step 1 of the process, as shown in Figure 27.31.

FIGURE 27.31
Step 1 of the Setup Wizard.

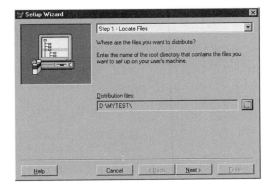

I selected the directory for the project I created earlier with the Application Wizard and Builder. In order to use the Setup Wizard for a project, you must create a directory structure on your machine that exactly represents the directory structure that the target machine will require. Then you must move all your application files to their appropriate directories within that structure. The Setup Wizard will create setup disks that mirror the directory structure you create. In step 1 of the Setup Wizard, you enter the path to the directory structure for the application.

Figure 27.32 shows step 2 of the Setup Wizard.

In step 2 you specify what components should be included in the setup process. The six options are described in Table 27.7.

Part
VI

Ch
27

FIGURE 27.32
Step 2 of the Setup
Wizard.

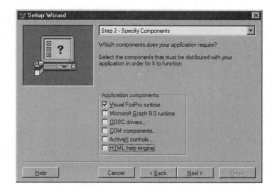

Table 27.7   Components Available in Step 2 of the Setup Wizard

Component	Size	Description
Visual FoxPro Runtime	4MB	VFP6r.DLL, the Visual FoxPro runtime library. This file is required if your application will be run on machines that do not have the full version of Visual FoxPro installed on them.
Microsoft Graph 8.0 Runtime	2.2MB	Required if your application has forms that use the Microsoft Graph 8.0 control for graphing data.
ODBC Drivers	4.3MB	Required if Visual FoxPro is accessing data through ODBC drivers. Checking this box will produce the ODBC Driver dialog so that you can select the particular ODBC drivers you need.
COM Components	Varies	Adds COM components in .EXE or .DLL files. You need to use this option to select any COM components that your application uses. Selecting this box brings up a dialog in which you can choose the COM components that you need.
ActiveX Controls	Varies	Required if your application makes use of any ActiveX controls. Selecting this box brings up the ActiveX Control dialog in which you can select any ActiveX controls that your application requires.
HTML Help Engine	700K	Includes the Microsoft HTML help engine for use with any help files your application might use.

After you identify the components required by your particular application, you can select Next to move on to step 3 (see Figure 27.33).

FIGURE 27.33
Step 3 of the Setup Wizard, Create Disk Image Directories.

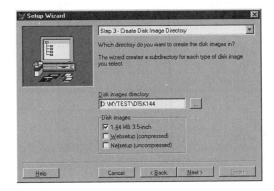

In step 3 you create the directories to hold the setup files for your application. The directory that you specify in the Disk Images Directory text box will have a number of subdirectories in it that depend on which setup types you select with the check boxes below that text box.

The three types of setups that you can choose from are 1.44 MB 3.5-inch, Websetup (compressed), and Netsetup (uncompressed).

The first setup type, 1.44 MB 3.5-inch, will create a set of subdirectories under the main setup directory named Disk1, Disk2, and so on. These directories will contain disk images for the disks in the setup set. After the directories have been created, you can copy Disk1 to the first disk, Disk2 to the second disk, and so on for all the disks required by the setup.

The Websetup (compressed) option will create one directory under the setup directory named Websetup. The Setup Wizard will put a compressed copy of all the setup files in this directory. These files can be used by executing the Setup.exe file that will reside in the directory. The files for this type of setup will be compressed so that they are more quickly downloaded from the World Wide Web with an Internet browser program.

The last setup type is Netsetup (uncompressed). This type will create a subdirectory named Netsetup under the setup directory and will put all of the files required to run the Setup.exe program in an uncompressed format. This option is designed for installations across a LAN. You can also use this type of setup to create CD-based installations: just copy the Netsetup directory to your writable CD drive. The user would insert the CD and run the Setup.exe file from the CD.

Figure 27.34 shows step 4 of the Setup Wizard.

Step 4 enables you to specify the title text that will appear in the setup program's window during installation, copyright information to appear during the setup process, and an executable file to be run at the end of the installation. After you specify this information, select Next to move to step 5.

Part
VI

Ch
27

FIGURE 27.34
Step 4 of the Setup
Wizard, Specify Setup
Options.

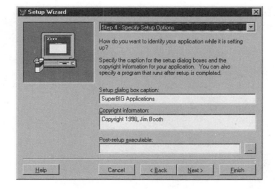

Figure 27.35 shows step 5 of the Setup Wizard.

FIGURE 27.35
Step 5 of the Setup
Wizard, Specify Default
Destination.

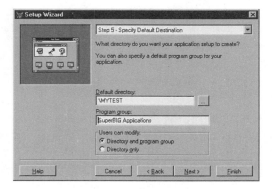

In step 5 you designate the Default Directory that should be used for installing the application on the target machine. You also designate the Program Group to which the application should be added.

The option buttons near the bottom of this screen enable you to control whether the user is allowed to alter the Target Directory and Program Group or the Directory Only.

Selecting Next moves you to step 6 (see Figure 27.36).

In step 6 you can alter the target directory for any particular file or files included in the setup process. You can also add certain files to the program group as icons so that they can be executed separately from the application. The last option is to designate the ActiveX components in your application so that they will be properly registered on the target machine.

You use the grid on this dialog to accomplish all the desired operations. Click on the file you want to alter, and then use the Target Dir column to establish the directory in which the file should be installed. Use the PM Item check box column to add the file to the program group. Finally, use the ActiveX check box column to identify the ActiveX components that must be registered on the target machine.

FIGURE 27.36
Step 6 of the Setup Wizard, Change File Settings.

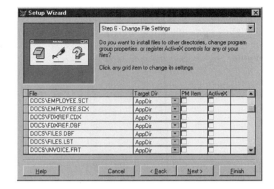

Select Next to move to the final step (see Figure 27.37).

FIGURE 27.37
The final step of the Setup Wizard.

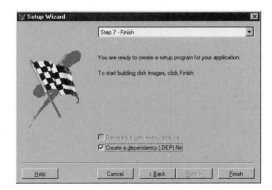

You have two options in the finish step of the Setup Wizard: Generate a Web Executable File and Create a Dependency (.DEP) File.

N O T E The option for creating a Web executable file is only enabled if there is an ActiveDoc component in your application. ▪

Figure 27.38 shows the progress dialog you see after clicking Finish in step 7.

FIGURE 27.38
The progress dialog of the Setup Wizard.

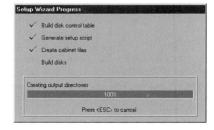

This dialog informs you of the progress made in creating the setup disk images you requested. When the Setup Wizard finishes creating the disk images, you see the dialog in Figure 27.39.

FIGURE 27.39

The Setup Wizard statistics dialog.

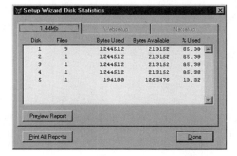

In this dialog you can see how many disk images were created. For each disk, you can see how many files are on it, the size of the files, the bytes left available, and the percent of the disk used by the files.

The report that is available with the Preview Report and/or Print All Reports buttons is shown in Figure 27.40.

FIGURE 27.40

A preview of the Setup Wizard report.

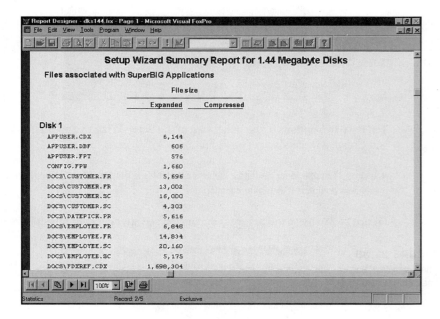

This report lists all the installation images created through the Setup Wizard. It shows every file that is on every disk and the expanded and compressed size for each file, and can be stored as documentation of the Setup Wizard's finished product.

T I P The Visual FoxPro Setup Wizard will create a directory in which to store the Visual FoxPro runtime files for distribution. In the preceding example, the directory was designated to be named `Distrib` and to reside under the Visual FoxPro home directory.

The files stored to this directory do not change from one distribution set to another. Therefore, it is a good idea to keep the directory intact for future runs of the Setup Wizard. The Setup Wizard will not create this directory if it already exists and has the Visual FoxPro runtime files in it.

CAUTION

If you ever upgrade your version of Visual FoxPro, you will need to clear out the `Distrib` directory so that the Setup Wizard will re-create it with newer runtime files for the newer version of Visual FoxPro.

WWW Search Page Wizard

The World Wide Web is the buzzword of the day. The question of whether a particular development language can have its applications deployed on the Web is ever present. The next two Wizards you will examine both have to do with the Internet. The first is the WWW Search Page Wizard, which enables you to create a Visual FoxPro–based search page for the Web. The second is the Web Publishing Wizard, which enables you to publish data in an HTML document for the Web.

Both of these wizards require that you use a Web browser to view their products.

The WWW Search Page Wizard also requires that you have an Internet server set up to use the search page that is created. The setup of an Internet server is beyond the scope of this chapter. This example will use the Microsoft Internet Information Server software running on Windows NT Server 4.0.

N O T E You can use Microsoft's Personal Web Server to build and test your Web search pages. This enables you to work with the WWW Search Page Wizard without having the full IIS installed. ■

When setting up an Internet server, one of the things you need to do is identify the root directory for the WWW server. In this installation, the directory is `D:\InetPub\WWWRoot`. You need to know the WWW root directory on your Internet server because you will need to copy some files into it for the Visual FoxPro Internet server application to run properly.

The WWW Search Page Wizard will create three files for you. These files are named *YourName*`.HTM`, *YourName*`.HTX`, and *YourName*`.IDC`. You will need to copy these three files into the WWW root directory for your Internet server application.

One other file must be placed in the WWW root directory: the `VFPCGI.EXE` file is found in the `Tools\Inetwiz\Server` directory under your Visual FoxPro home directory.

Part **VI**

Ch **27**

You start the WWW Search Page Wizard by choosing Tools, Wizards, All. Figure 27.41 shows the dialog you see with the WWW Search Page Wizard selected.

FIGURE 27.41

The Visual FoxPro Wizard Selection dialog.

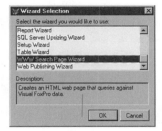

Click the OK button to continue with the WWW Search Page Wizard. Figure 27.42 shows the first screen of the wizard.

FIGURE 27.42

The first screen of the WWW Search Page Wizard.

There is nothing to do on the first screen; it is just a welcome page. Select Next to move on to step 1 of the Wizard (see Figure 27.43).

FIGURE 27.43

Step 1 of the WWW Search Page Wizard, Select Table.

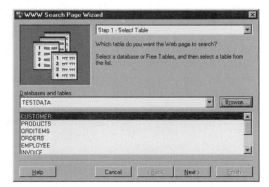

This figure shows the selection of the `Customer` file in the Visual FoxPro `samples` directory.

T I P Visual FoxPro 6 installs its samples in a different place than Visual FoxPro 5.0 did. The samples for all of the Visual Studio products are installed together. The new _SAMPLES system memory variable holds the path to the Visual FoxPro 6 sample files. You can display this path by typing **? _SAMPLES** in the command window and reading the output on the screen.

The Browse button enables you to navigate the disk drives to find the table you want.

The table you select will be used by the Search Page to retrieve data. After you select the table, select Next to go on to step 2 (see Figure 27.44).

FIGURE 27.44

Step 2 of the WWW Search Page Wizard, Choose Search Field.

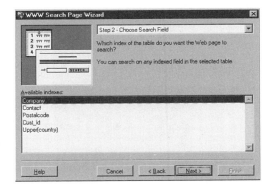

In this step you identify the index for your table that you want the search to use. The indexes shown are those that exist for the selected table. If you want to use some other index, you must create that index before you run the WWW Search Page Wizard.

I chose the `Company` index on the `Customer` table and then selected Next to go to step 3, which is shown in Figure 27.45.

FIGURE 27.45

Step 3 of the WWW Search Page Wizard, Set Search Page Options.

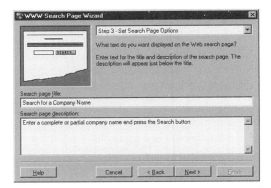

Part
VI

Ch
27

The first option in this step is the Search Page Title. The title will appear in the browser's title bar and will also appear centered on the page below the title bar.

The second option is the Search Page Description that will appear centered on the page below the title. This description can be used to describe how to use the search page. Although the title should be short and to the point, the description can be longer and more informative.

When you have entered your title and description, select Next to proceed to step 4 (see Figure 27.46).

FIGURE 27.46

Step 4 of the WWW Search page Wizard, Set Up Search Page.

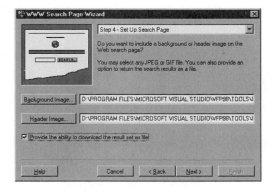

In this step you specify the graphics elements you want on your search page. The Background Image button can be used to navigate the disk drives to locate the image you want. The background image will tile the background of the search page.

The Header Image button lets you locate a .GIF or .JPG file to be used in the header of the search page.

The Provide the Ability to Download the Result Set as File check box presents the option for downloading the results to a file to the user of the search page.

You don't need to use any images on your search page, but images sure make the page more interesting. After you are finished with the search page options, select Next to move on to step 5, which is shown in Figure 27.47.

In this step you identify the fields that you want to send back on the results page of the search. You are limited to five fields using the WWW Search Page Wizard. After you select the fields you want, select Next to move on to step 6 (see Figure 27.48).

This page is similar to step 4 where you set the options for the search page, with the key difference that here you are setting up the page for the results of the search. The options for images are the same as they were for the search page in step 4.

FIGURE 27.47
Step 5 of the WWW
Search Page Wizard,
Select Result Fields.

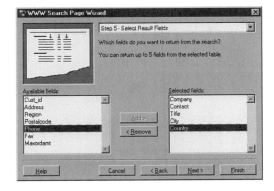

FIGURE 27.48
Step 6 of the WWW
Search Page Wizard,
Set Up Result Page.

In step 6 there are two more options to set:

- Maximum Records—Controls the number of records to be returned on the results page.
- ODBC Data Source—The datasource you are using for the search. It does not need to be specified if you are using local Visual FoxPro data.

When this step is completed, select Next to go to step 7, which is shown in Figure 27.49.

FIGURE 27.49
The final step of the
WWW Search Page
Wizard.

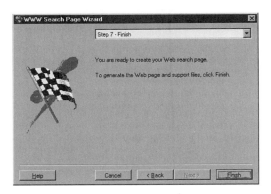

Part

VI

Ch

27

This This is the last step in the WWW Search Page Wizard. Clicking the Finish button creates your search page files. You see a dialog asking what name to save your search page files under (see Figure 27.50).

FIGURE 27.50

The Save As dialog seen when finishing the WWW Search Page Wizard.

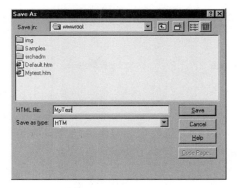

Use the dialog to navigate to your WWW root directory and enter the name you want your search page to be saved as in the HTML File text box. After you enter the name, click Save.

That completes the WWW Search Page Wizard. Now all you have to do is get the search page working.

The search page created with this wizard uses a technology known as *Common Gateway Interface (CGI)* to enable the search page to cause a Visual FoxPro data server to run a query and produce a results page. The VFPCGI.EXE file is the CGI engine for the Visual FoxPro server application.

Before you can use your search page, you must run the Visual FoxPro Server.app file found in the Tools\Inetwzi\Server directory under your Visual FoxPro home directory.

Figure 27.51 shows the dialog you see the first time you run Server.app.

FIGURE 27.51

The Server.app Default Directories dialog.

In this dialog, you must specify the path to the WWW root directory in the HTTP Server text box. The Scripts text box is used to enter the path to the WWW server's scripts directory. In the Path edit box, you must enter the path to the data table that your search page uses. After you set these items and click OK, you see the form shown in Figure 27.52.

FIGURE 27.52

The WWW Data Server Log form.

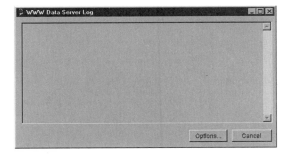

Although this form looks barren right now, it will get busier as you use your search page.

To use your search page, you must have an Internet server running. You can then use your favorite Internet browser to navigate to *//YourServerName/YourSearchPageName*.HTM. Figure 27.53 shows an example search page in IE.

FIGURE 27.53

The search page is pulled up in Internet Explorer.

Entering the letter **A** and clicking Search results in the page shown in Figure 27.54.

The results page shows you the customers with a company name that begins with the letter A. Figure 27.55 shows the WWW Data Server Log after a couple of searches have been done.

FIGURE 27.54
Internet Explorer with the results of a simple search.

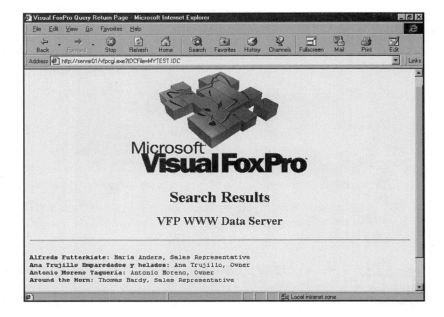

FIGURE 27.55
The WWW Data Server Log form showing the history of searches that have been executed.

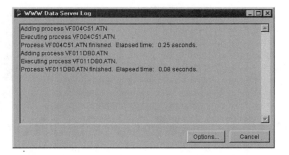

The three files created by the WWW Search Page Wizard—MyTest.HTM, MyTest.IDC, and MyTest.HTX—are, respectively, the search page HTML document, the query template for the WWW Data Server application, and the template for the HTML results document that the server will create.

Web Publishing Wizard

The Web Publishing Wizard enables you to publish data on the World Wide Web. Unlike the WWW Search Page Wizard, it does not create a search page for selecting data; rather, it simply publishes the data in an HTML file.

Figure 27.56 shows the first step in the Web Publishing Wizard.

FIGURE 27.56

Step 1 of the Web Publishing Wizard, Select Fields.

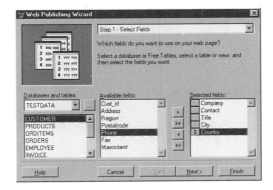

In this step you identify the table and the fields from that table that you want to publish. The ellipsis button can be used to locate the table on the disk drive. I chose the Customer table in the Testdata database, which is in the Visual FoxPro samples directory.

When you have chosen the table, you can use the mover lists to select the fields to be published. After the fields are selected, select Next to continue to step 2 (see Figure 27.57).

FIGURE 27.57

Step 2 of the Web Publishing Wizard, Sort Records.

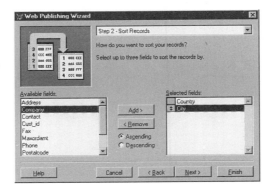

Use the mover lists to select the fields you want to use to order the data. Use the mover buttons in the list on the right to set the sort hierarchy. The Ascending and Descending option buttons will affect the currently highlighted field in the list on the right.

After the sorting is set up, select Next to go on to step 3, which is shown in Figure 27.58.

In this step you determine the style for your published data. The list titled Data Layouts is used to select a layout for the data. As you select different styles, the graphic in the upper-left corner reflects what each style will look like.

Part

VI

Ch

27

FIGURE 27.58
Step 3 of the Web
Publishing Wizard,
Choose Style.

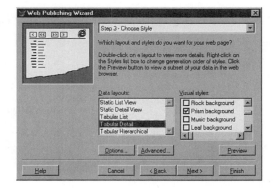

The list titled Visual Styles is used to select the background graphic to be used on the published page.

Clicking the Preview button shows your published page in the Internet browser installed on your computer. You can use Preview to try out different layouts and styles until you see the one you want.

Options and Advanced enable you to fine-tune the HTML settings if you are familiar with HTML.

Select Next to move on to step 4, as shown in Figure 27.59.

FIGURE 27.59
The final step of the
Web Publishing Wizard.

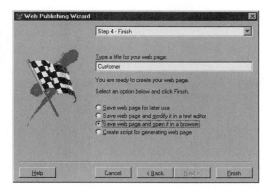

In this step you enter a title for the Web page, and then you have four choices:

Save Web Page for Later Use	Saves the .HTM file for you to use later.
Save Web Page and Modify It in a Text Editor	Saves the HTML document and immediately opens it for editing in a text editor.
Save Web Page and Open It in a Browser	Saves the HTML document and opens it in your Web browser for viewing.
Create Script for Generating Web Page	Creates a program that will dynamically create the HTML document.

For the example, I chose the last option to create the script and then clicked Finish.

The Save As dialog appears to name and place the file. I placed mine in the WWW root directory and named it **PubTest.prg**.

Figure 27.60 shows the program that was generated in the Visual FoxPro editor.

FIGURE 27.60

The program generated by the Web Publishing Wizard.

To use this program, you simply have to issue DO *programname* in the command window. Figure 27.61 shows the resulting HTML document viewed in IE.

FIGURE 27.61

The HTML page that
resulted from the Web
Publishing Wizard.

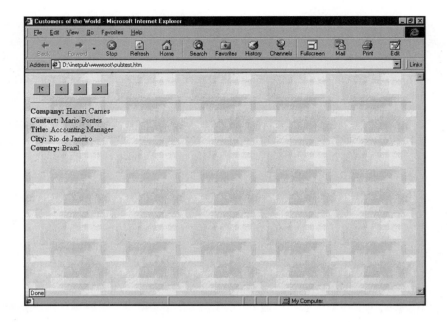

FIGURE 27.61

The HTML page that
resulted from the Web
Publishing Wizard.

Index

weak-typing, 81
see also error handling; error
  messages
**Esc key, terminating programs
  using, 56**
evaluators
  conditional evaluators, 88
  logical evaluators, 77, 87
  see also validating
**Event Tracking dialog box
  (Debug Output window), 799**
events
  base classes, 445
  coding with, 321–22
  cursor class, 584
  DataEnvironment class events,
    585
  error events, 812–13
  form objects, list of, 314–15
  Init() event, 318
  OOP (object-oriented
    programming), 423–24
  ProjectHook events list, 415–16
  relation class, 584
  SwatchEngine class events list,
    601
Excel (Microsoft)
  application structure and
    syntax, 697–98
  avoiding multiple server
    instances, 704–705
  macro code vs. Word macro
    code, 709
  modifying COM servers for,
    736–38
  testing COM servers in, 735–36
  using FoxPro tables in reports,
    698–703
  using in FoxPro, 688–94
**exception errors, identifying/
  handling, 758–60**
Exclude icon, 387
**Exclusive property (cursor
  class), 583**
.EXE (executable files), 39
  COM objects, 679
  creating COM servers with,
    732, 849
  creating using Project Manager,
    386, 397–98
  including/excluding files from,
    399
  read only files in, 399
  server-side scripts, 833
  in Web-based applications, 840
EXE servers, 849

**ExecuteOptions property (RDS
  object), 301**
executing programs
  identifying logic errors, 756–58
  identifying syntax errors,
    755–56
  subroutines, 91–92
  see also running
EXIT commands, 89
  problems with multiple, 764–66
Exit option (File menu), 18
**exiting programs, errors during,
  764–66**
**Export menu item (Class
  Browser), 540**
Export option (File menu), 18
**ExportClass() method (Class
  Browser), 554**
exporting files, 18
Expression Builder
  Expression Builder dialog box,
    752
  Report Designer, 351, 364
  Table Designer, 121–22, 133
expressions
  adding fields to, 121
  complex, 121–22
  compound expressions, 206
  conditional, definition order,
    169
  connection order, 169
  non-optimizable, 206
  optimizable, 204–207
**expressions, partially
  optimized, 266**
EXTERNAL command, 753

F

**Favorites catalog (Component
  Gallery), 657**
FDATE() function, 824
**Fetch Memo option (Options
  dialog box), 62**
**FetchOptions property (RDS
  object), 301**
**FFC Builder Lock function
  (Component Gallery), 664**
field comments, adding, 133
**Field Mapping page (Options
  dialog box), 49**

**Field Mover foundation class,
  634**
**field objects (Report Designer),
  350**
**Field Properties Validation Rule
  text box (Table Designer),
  133**
**Field Selection dialog box
  (Report Wizard), 368**
field types, setting defaults, 49
  see also data types
fields
  adding
    to existing tables, 114–15
    to expressions, 121
  caption values, 133
  changing
    data type, 114
    name length, 132
    names, 131
  comparing fields, avoiding
    errors, 247
  data types
    Character, 103
    Currency, 106
    Date/DateTime, 106
    Double, 106
    Float, 106
    General, 107
    Logical, 107
    Memo, 107–108
    Numeric, 103, 106–107
  default values, 133
  defining, 111–12
  deleting, 114–15
  key fields, nulls in, 144
  multiple
    as index expressions,
      120–24
    selecting, 332
  naming conventions, 102
    name sizes, 153–54
    prefixes, 152–53
    renaming, 114–16
  null data in, 113–14
  in queries, minimizing, 268
  redefining, 114, 116
  in reports, 351–53
  selecting
    for HTML files, 943
    in queries, 221–23
    in WWW search pages, 937
  size-related issues, 107
  sorting, 117
  unique fields, 111
  validation rules, adding to
    databases, 133
  in views, 274–80
  see also variables

X

Y

Z